Cultural Anthropology

FIFTH EDITION

Marvin Harris

University of Florida

Orna Johnson

University of California, Los Angeles

Allyn and Bacon

Boston • London • Toronto • Sydney • Tokyo • Singapore

Series Editor: Sarah L. Kelbaugh
Editor-in-Chief, Social Sciences: Karen Hanson
Developmental Editor: Susan Messer
Series Editorial Assistant: Jennifer DiDomenico
Composition and Prepress Buyer: Linda Cox
Manufacturing Buyer: Megan Cochran
Cover Administrator: Linda Knowles
Photo Researcher: Helane Manditch-Prottas
Production Administrator: Mary Beth Finch
Editorial-Production Service: The Book Company
Text Designer: Lisa Devenish
Electronic Composition: Omegatype Typography, Inc.

Library of Congress Cataloging-in-Publication Data

Harris, Marvin, 1927-
    Cultural anthropology / Marvin Harris, Orna Johnson.–5th ed.
      p.   cm.
    Includes bibliographical references and index.
    ISBN 0-321-03414-7
    1. Ethnology.   2. Anthropology.   I. Johnson, Orna.   II. Title.
GN316.H36 2000
306–dc21   99-046653

Printed in the United States of America

10 9 8 7 6 5 4 3 2 1   VHP   04 03 02 01 00 99

Photo and copyright credits appear on pages 371–374,
which constitute a continuation of this copyright page.

Contents

CHAPTER 1

Introduction / 1
The Five Fields of Anthropology / 2
What Is Distinctive about Cultural Anthropology? / 2
  Holism / 2
  Fieldwork and Participant Observation / 3
  Ethnography / 4
  Ethnology / 5
  Anthropology and Science / 5
Why Study Anthropology? / 5

CHAPTER 2

The Nature of Culture / 8
Definitions of Culture / 9
Society, Subculture, and Sociocultural System / 9
  Enculturation / 10
  Cultural Relativism / 11
Science and the Relativity of Truth / 12
  Limitations of the Enculturation Concept / 13
  Diffusion / 13
Fieldwork and the Mental and Behavioral Aspects of Culture / 16
  Emic and Etic Aspects of Culture / 17
  Emics, Etics, and Sacred Cows / 18
The Universal Pattern / 19
The Diversity of Anthropological Theories / 22
Cultural Materialism / 22

CHAPTER 3

The Evolution of the Capacity for Culture / 25
Genes and Natural Selection / 26
  Natural Selection and the "Struggle for Survival" / 26
  Natural Selection and Behavior / 27
Nonhuman Culture / 27
  Tools and Learning / 28
  Is It Culture? / 29
The Evolution of the Hominids / 31
  Cultural Takeoff / 32
Apes and Language / 33
Aggressive versus Cooperative Behaviors Among Apes / 35
AMERICA NOW: Attempts to Teach "Creation Science" in the Public Schools / 37

CHAPTER 4

Language and Culture / 38
Universal Features of Language / 39
  Semantic Universality / 39
Structural Linguistics: Elements of Language Analysis / 40
  Phonetics and Phones / 40
  Phonemics and Phonemes / 40
  Morphemes / 41
  Syntax / 41
Biological and Cultural Aspects of Language / 42
  Language and Symbolic Representation / 42
Language Issues and Theories / 43
  Innate Grammatical Knowledge / 43
  The Coevolution of Language and the Brain / 44
  Are There Superior and Inferior Languages? / 44
  Language, Thought, and Causality / 44
  Linguistic Naming Categories / 45

  Language and Consciousness / 46
Sociolinguistics / 46
  Language, Social Class, and Ethnicity / 46
  AAVE in the Public Domain / 47
  PROFILE: African-American Vernacular English (AAVE) / 48
  Code Switching / 48
  Obligatory Sexism / 49
  Linguistic Change / 50
AMERICA NOW: The Five Present Tenses of Ebonics / 52

CHAPTER 5

Production / 53
Evolution of Energy Production / 54
The Influence of the Environment and Ecology / 55
Carrying Capacity and the Law of Diminishing Returns / 55
  Sustainability / 56
  Law of the Minimum / 57
  PROFILE: Hunters and Gatherers—The !Kung San / 57
  Depletion and New Modes of Production / 58
Hunting and Gathering / 59
  PROFILE: Hunters and Gatherers—The Kwakiutl / 60
  Optimal Foraging Theory / 61
Agriculture / 61
  Slash-and-Burn Agriculture / 62
  PROFILE: Slash-and-Burn Horticulture with Hunting and Gathering—The Machiguenga / 63
  PROFILE: Slash-and-Burn Horticulture with Domesticated Animals—The Tsembaga / 64
  The Problem of Meat / 65
  Agropastoralism or Mixed Farming / 65
  Irrigation Agriculture / 66
  PROFILE: Irrigation Agriculture—Luts'un / 67
Pastoralism / 67
  PROFILE: Pastoralism—The Turkana / 68
Energy and the Evolution of Culture / 69
Industrial Food Energy Systems / 70
AMERICA NOW: Mode of Production / 72

CHAPTER 6

Reproduction / 75
The Relation between Production and Reproduction / 76
Population Pressure versus Population Growth / 77
Preindustrial Reproductive Practices / 77
  Treatment of Fetuses and Children / 78
  Treatment of Women / 78
  Lactation / 79
  Coital Frequency and Scheduling / 79
  The Influence of Disease and Other Natural Factors / 80
The Costs and Benefits of Rearing Children / 80
  Measuring the Costs and Benefits of Rearing Children / 82
  The Poverty Trap / 84
The Contraception, Abortion, and Infanticide Debate / 84
  PROFILE: Indirect Infanticide in Northeast Brazil / 85
Industrial Modes of Reproduction / 87
Women's Status, Education, and Fertility / 87
AMERICA NOW: Fertility and the World's Most Expensive Children / 90
  Reproductive Technologies, Embryos, and Designer Babies / 91

CHAPTER 7
Human Sexuality / 92
Sex versus Gender / 93
Human Sexuality / 93
  Sex in Mangaia / 95
  Sex in India / 95
  Sex in Inis Beag / 96
  Sex in America and Europe / 96
Heterosexuality / 96
Restrictive versus Permissive Cultures / 97
  PROFILE: The Mehinacu and Extramarital Affairs / 98
Male Homosexuality / 98
  PROFILE: Sambia Boy-Inseminating Rituals / 101
Female Homosexuality / 101
AMERICA NOW: New Gender Roles and Forms of Sexuality / 103

CHAPTER 8
Economic Organization / 105
Definition of Economy / 106
Exchange / 106
  Reciprocal Exchange / 106
  Reciprocity and the Freeloader / 107
  Reciprocity and Trade / 107
  Trade in the Kula Ring / 108
Redistributive Exchange / 110
Reciprocity versus Redistribution / 111
The Infrastructural Basis of Redistribution and
Reciprocity / 112
Stratified Redistribution / 115
Price Market Exchange: Buying and Selling / 115
  Money / 116
  Capitalism / 116
  PROFILE: Primitive Capitalism? The Kaupauku Case / 118
  Property Ownership / 118
Patterns of Work / 119
AMERICA NOW: Emergent Varieties of Capitalism / 123

CHAPTER 9
Domestic Life / 125
The Household and the Domestic Sphere of Culture / 126
Family Groups and the Mode of Production and
Reproduction / 127
  The Nuclear Family / 127
  Polygamous Families / 128
  PROFILE: The Nyinba—A Polyandrous Society / 130
  The Extended Family / 131
  PROFILE: Chinese Extended Families—Costs and Benefits / 132
  One-Parent Domestic Groups / 132
What Is Marriage? / 133
  Legitimacy / 135
Economic Aspects of Marriage / 136
  Bridewealth / 136
  Bride Service / 137
  Dowry / 137
Preferential Marriages / 138
Domestic Groups and the Avoidance of Incest / 139
  Social and Cultural Advantages of Exogamy / 140
  *Biological Risks of Inbreeding: The Observationalist
  Theory / 140*
  Motivations for Incest Avoidance / 140
  Sim Pua Marriage: "Adopt a Daughter, Marry a Sister" / 141
  Westermark in the Kibbutz / 141
  Avoidance within the Family / 142
AMERICA NOW: Matrifocal Families / 144

CHAPTER 10
Descent, Locality, and Kinship / 146
Kinship / 147
Descent / 147
Descent Rules: Cognatic and Unilineal Descent / 148
  Cognatic Bilateral Descent and Kindreds / 150

  Cognatic Ambilineal Descent and Cognatic Lineages / 151
  Unilineal Descent Groups / 151
Postmarital Locality Patterns / 152
  Determinants of Bilateral Descent Groups / 152
  Determinants of Cognatic Lineages and Clans / 153
  Determinants of Unilineal Lineages and Clans / 153
  Causes of Patrilocality / 154
  Causes of Matrilocality / 154
  Causes of Avunculocality / 155
Kinship Terminologies / 156
  Eskimo Terminology / 156
  Hawaiian Terminology / 156
  Iroquois Terminology / 157
Kin Terms Are Negotiated, Not Written in Stone / 158
AMERICA NOW: Changes in Family Structure / 159

CHAPTER 11
Law, Order, and War in Nonstate Societies / 162
Law and Order in Band and Village Societies / 163
  Primitive Communism? / 163
  Mobilizing Public Opinion / 164
  Shamans and Public Opinion / 165
Headmanship / 166
  PROFILE: The Mehinacu—Maintaining Peace / 168
The Leopard Skin Chief / 168
Nonkin Associations: Sodalities / 169
Warfare among Hunters and Gatherers / 170
Warfare among Sedentary Village Societies / 171
Why War? / 171
  PROFILE: The Yanomami—Warfare and Game Animals / 173
  Yanomani Warfare / 175
  Yanomami Trekking / 175
  Warfare and Female Infanticide / 176
  Warfare and Trade Goods / 176
Warfare, the Politics of Prestige, and the Big Man System / 177
  PROFILE: The Mae Enga—A Big Man Society / 177

CHAPTER 12
Origins and Anatomy of the State / 180
The Evolution of Big Man Systems into Chiefdoms / 181
  PROFILE: The Suiai—Big Men and Warfare / 181
Infrastructural and Structural Aspects of Political Control / 183
  PROFILE: The Trobriand Chiefdoms—Ranked Leadership / 182
The Origins of States / 185
  PROFILE: Hawaii—On the Threshold of the State 186
  PROFILE: Bunyoro—An African Kingdom / 188
  PROFILE: The Incas—A Native American Empire / 189
Ideology as a Source of Power / 190
The State and Physical Coercion / 192
AMERICA NOW: Law and Disorder / 193

CHAPTER 13
Class and Caste / 195
Class and Power / 196
  Emics, Etics, and Class Consciousness / 196
  Class and Lifestyle / 197
Peasant Classes / 198
The Image of Limited Good / 199
  A "Culture of Poverty"? / 201
  Poverty in Naples / 202
Castes in India / 203
  Caste from the Top Down and Bottom Up / 204
AMERICA NOW: Is There a Ruling Class in the United
States? / 206

CHAPTER 14
Ethnicity, Race, and Racism / 208
Ethnicity / 209
  PROFILE: Diversity among Hispanic Americans / 209
  Ethnic Empowerment / 211
  Confronting Ethnocentrism / 211

Biological Races versus Social Races versus Ethnic Groups / 212
  The One-Drop Rule / 214
  Biological Race and Culture / 215
The Competitive Dynamics of Ethnic and Racial Groups / 215
  Assimilation or Pluralism? / 215
  The Dynamics of Pluralism in the United States / 216
  Racial and Ethnic Chauvinism versus Class Consciousness / 217
  *PROFILE: Elmhurst-Corona—Joining Forces Across Ethnic and
  Racial Lines / 218*
Defining Racism / 218
  The Wages of Racism / 219
  Why Africa Lags / 219
  Social Race in the United States / 220
  Racism on the Campus / 220
  The Tragedy of Urban Black Youth / 222
AMERICA NOW: Race, Poverty, Crime, Drugs, and Welfare / 223

CHAPTER 15
Gender Hierarchies / 225
Gender Differences / 226
Gender Ideologies / 226
The Relativity of Gender Ideologies / 226
Are Women Equally Represented in Ethnographies? / 228
  *PROFILE: The Trobianders—Recognizing the Importance of
  Women / 229*
Gender Hierarchy / 230
Variations in Gender Hierarchies / 231
  Women among Hunter–Gatherers / 231
  Women among the Matrilineal Iroquois / 232
  Women in West Africa / 232
  Women in India / 233
Causes of Variation in Gender Hierarchies / 234
  Warfare and Gender Hierarchies / 234
  PROFILE: The Dahomey—Female Warriors / 236
Hoes, Plows, and Gender Hierarchies / 236
Gender and Exploitation / 238
Gender and Hyperindustrialism / 238
AMERICA NOW: A Theory of Gender Hierarchy Change / 241

CHAPTER 16
Psychological Anthropology / 244
Culture and Personality / 245
  Freud's Influence / 245
  Is the Oedipus Complex Universal? / 246
Cultural Patterns and Themes / 246
Basic Personality Structure / 249
  Modal Personality / 249
  National Character / 250
  PROFILE: Japanese National Character / 251
Childhood Training and Personality / 252
The Influence of Subsistence Patterns / 252
  Child Training and Male Initiation Rites / 253
  Six Cultures Study / 253
  The Effect of Social Environment on Children / 254
  Cultural Models of Child Care / 254
Subsistence and Adult Personality / 256
Schemas and Cognition / 257
Culture and Mental Illness / 258
  Depression / 258
  Schizophrenia / 258
  PROFILE: Schizophrenia in Rural Ireland / 259
  Culture-Specific Psychoses / 260

CHAPTER 17
Religion / 263
Animism / 264
Animatism and Mana / 264

Natural and Supernatural / 265
Magic and Religion / 266
The Organization of Religious Beliefs and Practices / 266
  Individualistic Beliefs and Rituals / 267
  Shamanistic Cults / 268
  Communal Cults / 270
  PROFILE: Ndembu Communal Rites of Circumcision / 272
  Ecclesiastical Cults / 273
  PROFILE: The Religion of the Aztecs / 274
Religion and Political Economy: High Gods / 276
Revitalization Movements / 276
  Native American Revitalizations / 277
  Melanesian Cargo Cults / 278
Taboo, Religion, and Ecology / 280
  Incest Taboo / 280
  Taboos Against Eating Pork / 281
  The Sacred Cow / 281
AMERICA NOW: The Electronic Church / 284

CHAPTER 18
Art / 287
What Is Art? / 288
Art as a Cultural Category / 288
  Art and Invention / 290
  Art and Cultural Patterning / 290
  Art and Religion / 291
  Art and Politics / 292
The Evolution of Music and Dance / 293
Verbal Arts / 295
  Myth and Binary Contrasts / 295
  *The Complexity of Primitive Art: Campa
  Rhetoric / 295*

CHAPTER 19
Applied Anthropology / 298
What Is Applied Anthropology? / 299
Research, Theory, and Action / 299
What Do Applied Anthropologists Have to
Offer? / 299
  Detecting and Controlling Ethnocentrism / 299
  A Holistic View / 300
  Etic and Emic Views of Organizations / 300
Applied Anthropology and Development / 301
  Without Holism: An Andean Fiasco / 302
  The Haitian Agroforestry Project / 302
  Archeology and Agricultural Development / 304
  Archaeology and Environmental Protection: Garbalogy / 304
  *Economic Development: Seaweed Farming in
  Zanzibar / 305*
  Preserving a Way of Life: Security for the Cree / 305
Medical Anthropology / 306
  AIDS (Acquired Immune Deficiency Syndrome) / 306
  Alzheimer's Disease / 307
Refugee Health Care / 307
Demographics: The U.S. Census Undercount / 308
Forensics / 308
Business and Anthropology / 308
Poverty and Health / 309
  Witnessing for the Hungry and Homeless / 310
Anthropological Advocacy / 311
  To Advocate or Not to Advocate: Is That the Question? / 311

APPENDIX: A History of Theories of Culture / 313
References / 320
Glossary / 344
Name Index / 354
Subject Index / 359

Preface

Goals of this Book: Past and Present

When *Cultural Anthropology* was first written, it had two major objectives: to present a holistic view of sociocultural systems that shows the interconnectedness of various aspects of culture, and to provide a unified theoretical framework for explaining sociocultural systems based on the premise that material constraints, such as technology and the environment, are a primary force in the evolution of sociocultural systems. Subsequent editions remain faithful to the belief that the work that anthropologists do has enduring relevance and is crucial to making informed decisions. The issues discussed in the text relate to the core of human biological and psychological health and well–being as well as the continued viability of the global environment.

The holistic approach used in the text provides a framework for explaining how the parts of sociocultural systems interrelate and change over time. This approach is based on attempts to draw rational connections among three core recurrent behavioral aspects of the sociocultural system, called the universal pattern:

- *INFRASTRUCTURE–production and reproduction* (how people obtain food and shelter, maintain a population base, and satisfy other basic biological and emotional needs and drives)
- *STRUCTURE–the domestic and political economy* (how people are organized to exchange and allocate goods and labor)
- *SUPERSTRUCTURE–the ideological and symbolic sectors of culture* (the religious, symbolic, intellectual, and artistic endeavors)

The current edition carries forward the effort to identify the many causal strands that explain the process of sociocultural change. The goal is to show how cultural materialism can make sense of the many seemingly irrational or arbitrary customs and institutions in small, technologically simple societies as well as in complex nation-states. Examples include how Hindu taboos against cattle slaughter have a positive effect on agricultural productivity in India, how religion and monumental architecture in early states sanctified the privileges of the ruling elite, and how the emergence of the feminist movement in the United States during the 1960s resulted from broad changes in the mode of production.

The text consistently draws the reader's attention to the basic premises of cultural materialism:

1. The importance of understanding the connections among the three realms universal pattern: *infrastructure, structure, and superstructure.*
2. The need to distinguish between people's thoughts and ideas and their actual behavior–because often people say one thing and do another.
3. The difference between *emic* (actor oriented) and *etic* (observer oriented) views and interpretations–because the world often looks different to the observer than it does to the participant.

What's New in the Fifth Edition

1. Each chapter includes **Key Concept statements** set in italics and called out with an icon to enable the student to focus in on main ideas described in the chapter. The Key Concepts are meant to provide a concise statement of the material that follows or to summarize the issues being discussed. We intend to have students use the "key concepts" as though they themselves highlighted them in yellow to pull out the most important ideas in each chapter.
2. The text includes new **ethnographic case studies.** These Profiles are designed to help the student understand the importance of ethnography in describing and explaining key issues. The Profiles also illustrate how societies use culture to adapt to local conditions of their environment.
3. Several chapters contain **new boxes** outlining the definitions of key concepts. These charts are intended to provide the students with summaries of terms such as emic and etic, egalitarian and stratified, bigman and chief, and the features of Yanomami warfare.
4. We provide a list of **Key Terms** and **Questions to Think About** at the end of each chapter. These are meant to help students review the most important ideas or understand the theoretical arguments described in the text.
5. The **America Now** features have been expanded and updated. These materials show the relevance of anthropology to the study of contemporary social issues. These examples are intended to help

students see that anthropological concepts can be applied to their daily lives.

6. The revisions attempt to clarify the role of symbolic-ideational features. We emphasize that not all structural and superstructural features can be explained in terms of material constraints, but we believe that cultural materialism provides the best available approach to explaining why customs and beliefs differ from one society to another and why, despite such differences, remarkable similarities exist in the way human beings live in even the most distant parts of the globe.

7. Eighteen chapters have been rewritten, updated, and expanded. The updates include new citations and references to research that is provocative and cause for thought and discussion. The goal of the updates is to keep the text theoretically current on the course of globally vital concerns.

Chapter Overview

- **Chapter 1, "Introduction,"** provides an overview of the branches of anthropology, the distinctive features of cultural anthropology, and how anthropology is used in academic and nonacademic settings.

- **Chapter 2, "The Nature of Culture,"** introduces the concept of culture and the ways anthropologists define it. Culture is discussed in terms of mental and behavioral patterns to show how anthropology uses scientific methods to carry out objective studies of cultural phenomena. Emic and etic ways of studying culture are outlined, and the cultural materialist viewpoint is introduced to explain how the universal pattern (infrastructure, structure, and superstructure) can be used to explain sociocultural differences and similarities.

- **Chapter 3, "The Evolution of the Capacity for Culture,"** lays the groundwork for understanding the human biological heritage and what makes people distinctly human. The chapter summarizes the principles of natural selection and adaptation, discusses learning and tool use among nonhuman primates, and shows how the capacity for language is closely linked to "Cultural Takeoff." The chapter also shows that the capacity for aggression as well as peacemaking is part of our human heritage and that there is a biological basis for peaceful coexistence.

- **Chapter 4, "Language and Culture,"** provides a revised and simplified overview of the universal features of language and structural linguistics. A new discussion of biological and cultural aspects of language leads into an overview of symbolic thought and how it may have sparked the emergence of language. An updated section on soci-olinguistics addresses the speech patterns of people in ethnically diverse communities and how speech can inform us about social relationships within cultures. An ethnographic profile of African American Vernacular English shows the internal consistency and logic of AAVE and its use in the public domain is discussed in the context of whether AAVE should be taught in school.

- **Chapter 5, "Production,"** brings infrastructure into focus by describing the major food-producing strategies (hunting and gathering, agriculture, and pastoralism), using seven ethnographic profiles (the !Kung, Kwakiutl, Machiguenga, Tsembaga, Lut-s'un and the Turkana) to illustrate how differences in technology and environment influence social life. Intensification of food production is discussed in terms of diminishing returns, possibilities for new productive technologies, and long-term implications of technological innovations.

- **Chapter 6, "Reproduction,"** continues to discuss infrastructure in terms of population growth and its implications for the mode of production. The costs and benefits of raising children under different modes of production are described as a key factor regulating reproduction. These factors also explain why people in poverty-stricken situations, such as the shantytowns of Brazil, continue to have large families and why high rates of infant mortality persist. Conversely, education and improved economic opportunities for women are directly associated with reduced fertility.

- **Chapter 7, "Human Sexuality,"** defines the difference between sex and gender in terms of biological versus culturally defined identities. A new section of female sexuality has been added and the discussion of sex in Mangaia has been revised to reflect more current research. Ethnographic profiles of the Mehinacu and Sambia provide examples of variation in sexual practices. The ecological and social conditions associated with sexual restrictiveness versus permissiveness and tolerance for homosexuality are discussed in terms of procreation and the control of property and social status.

- **Chapter 8. "Economic Organization,"** elaborates on how the !Kung, Trobriand Islanders, and the Kwakiutl manage exchange within their varied ecological contexts and how the infrastructure correlates with egalitarian versus stratified patterns of exchange. The chapter points out the important role of access to resources and how this access relates to differences in distribution, stratification, and reactions to capitalism. The ethnographic case of the Kaupauku illustrates that despite individual ownership of land, true capitalism is not possible without central political controls to defend the rich. Finally, new time-allocation data consistently show that people in more technologically complex economic systems work longer hours, despite the assumption that modern affluence brings greater leisure.

■ **Chapter 9, "Domestic Organization,"** clarifies the relationship between infrastructure (modes of production and reproduction) and domestic organization. We relate differences in family and household organization to labor patterns and access to resources. The chapter elaborates on the economic dynamics of polygamy, extended families, and single-parent families. An ethnographic profile of the Nyinba illustrates the economic and social dynamics of polyandry and profile of Chinese extended families discusses the costs and benefits of large families. The sections on marriage and incest avoidance have also been updated and expanded.

■ **Chapter 10, "Kinship,"** clarifies the definitions of the principal varieties of kinship groups and illustrates key kinship concepts with examples from specific cultures. We relate varieties of kinship to particular kinds of domestic groups and infratructural conditions. A new discussion of fictive kinship is added to show how kinship is extended to non-biological kin and examples of contemporary American families show how economic change affects family structure.

■ **Chapter 11, "Law, Order, and War in Nonstate Societies,"** describes the variation in political institutions and leadership roles in societies where law and order specialists do not exist. Emphasis is placed on how peaceful relations are maintained and on likely causes of warfare. Ethnographic profiles of the Mehinacu, Yanomami, and the Mae Enga are used to describe the conditions associated with peace and warfare.

■ **Chapter 12, "Origins and Anatomy of the State,"** outlines the infrastructural context in which political systems evolve from bigman systems to chiefdoms and states. As leaders gain control over food through staple finance, they increase their ability to support military and administrative specialists. They further expand their control over production through intensification, trade, and incorporation of new territories. Ethnographic examples of the Suiai, Trobriand Islands, Hawaii, Bonyoro and the Inca show the range of political complexity from a bigman system, simple and complex chiefdom, to state.

■ **Chapter 13, "Class and Caste,"** examines the varieties of stratified groups. Emic and etic aspects of class and caste are discussed. The cultural values and traditions of peasants and the urban poor are discussed in terms of lack of access to resources, economic opportunities and employment. Examples from the Indian caste system show that individuals from lower castes struggle for upward mobility and attempt to improve their position whenever possible.

■ **Chapter 14, "Ethnicity, Race, and Racism,"** outlines the difference between ethnicity, social race, and biological race to show the effects of linking race and culture. We discuss how race is culturally constructed in the United States and describe the social effects of this system of classification on assimilation, intermarriage, class-consciousness, and the social isolation of ethnic and racial minorities. An ethnographic profile of Hispanic Americans shows the diversity in the Latino population and a profile of a multi-ethnic community in Queens, New York shows how increased political activism aimed at improving neighborhood conditions can bring people from diverse backgrounds together to work for a common cause.

■ **Chapter 15, "Gender Hierarchies,"** has been revised to describe ideological aspects of gender and to show the ways men and women benefit differently in a variety of economic settings. Past systems of gender equality show that women have generally fared better in peaceful, noncompetitive environments, whereas female subordination developed in sociocultural contexts that included hand-to-hand combat against neighboring groups and animal-drawn plow agriculture. More recent research on Trobriand women reveals that important aspects of women's culture were previously overlooked and examples of female Dahomey warriors and American businesswomen show the conditions under which women have been able to achieve status.

■ **Chapter 16, "Psychological Anthropology,"** has been greatly expanded to include new material on the Oedipus complex and the influence of subsistence patterns on childcare and personality, cultural schemas, and mental illness. The difficulty of defining national character is shown in the ethnographic case of Japanese personality, and the cultural effects on schizophrenia are illustrated in an ethnographic profile of rural Ireland.

■ **Chapter 17, "Religion,"** outlines various definitions of religion and illustrates the principal varieties of beliefs and rituals that correlate with particular political and economic organization. An ethnographic profile of the Ndembu shows the process of communal rites of passage and a profile of the Aztecs discusses the role of ceremonial sacrifice in state religion. We also describe how religious beliefs and rituals exhibit adaptive relationships in

Reference Maps for Ethnographic Profiles

the form of sanctified messages and taboos, specifically in relation to the incest taboo, the taboo on eating pork, and the sacred cow in India.

■ **Chapter 18, "Art,"** describes the creative, innovative aspects of art as well as the formal continuity displayed in artistic traditions. We show how art is functionally related to technology, economy, politics, and religion and how it has undergone changes over time.

■ **Chapter 19, "Applied Anthropology,"** shows the practical applications of anthropology, including research, implementation, and advocacy. A number of applications are described, including economic development among Haitian peasants, the health care needs of Vietnamese refugees, business relations between Euroamerican managers and Hispanic workers, attempts to slow the spread of

AIDS in Africa and the United States, and how the bureaucratic machinery hinders poor people's ability to receive assistance.

■ **Appendix, "A History of Theories of Culture,"** provides a brief overview of theoretical orientations in anthropology.

Acknowledgments

Many people helped prepare this book. Sarah Kelbaugh, the series editor at Allyn and Bacon, guided the book through the production stage, and we are grateful for her help. We also want to thank Dusty Friedman of The Book Company for her support, guidance, and helpful suggestions during the production stages of the book. Susan Messer provided valuable

editorial insight, and we appreciate her advice on the incorporation of new material.

We would also like to thank the people at UCLA who made suggestions for this edition. Allen Johnson read the book in its entirety and provided critical insight and support throughout the two years of writing. Thanks are also due to Dan Fessler, Nancy Levine, Joseph Manson, Susan Perry, Joan Silk, Tom Weisner, and Diego Vigil for their comments on sections of the book, which prevented errors and greatly improved the content of the book. Thanks too to Susan Phillips for her help with photographs. Thanks are due to Tom Gregor of Vanderbilt University for his help with the Mehinacu profiles.

Thanks are also due to our research assistants Sandra Mitchell and Jennifer Kim and to B. J. Brown, who provided valuable help in updating the statistics.

Reviewers are appreciated for their suggestions and encouragement:

Peter R. Aschoff	University of Mississippi
Robert Dirks	Illinois State University
Stephen M. Childs	Valdosta State University
Richard H. Furlow	College of DuPage
Michael P. Freedman	Syracuse University
George L. Hicks	Brown University
Susan J. Rasmussen	University of Houston
Donald J. Metzger	The University of Akron
Dennis Gaffin	SUNY College Buffalo
Elizabeth Purdum	Florida State University
Mary Jo Schneider	University of Arkansas

CHAPTER 1

Introduction

Diversity in the U.S.A. Children wearing ethnic clothing.

The Five Fields of General Anthropology

**What Is Distinctive about
Cultural Anthropology?**
Holism
Fieldwork and Participant Observation

Ethnography
Ethnology
Anthropology and Science

Why Study Anthropology?

Summary

Anthropology is the study of humankind—of ancient and modern people and their ways of living. Different branches of anthropology focus on different aspects of the human experience. One branch focuses on how our species evolved from earlier species. Other branches focus on how we developed our facility for language, how languages evolved and diversified, and how modern languages serve the needs of human communication. Still others focus on the learned traditions of human thought and behavior, how ancient cultures evolved and diversified, and how and why modern cultures change or stay the same.

People from different continents who speak different languages and possess different values and religions find themselves living closer and closer together in a new global village. To all members of this new community, anthropology offers a unique invitation to examine, explain, and celebrate human diversity. At the same time, anthropology reminds us that, despite our different languages and cultures, we are all members of the same species and share a common nature and a common destiny.

The Five Fields of Anthropology

Departments of anthropology in the United States offer courses in five major fields of knowledge about humankind: cultural anthropology, archaeology, anthropological linguistics, physical anthropology, and applied anthropology.

- **Cultural anthropology** (sometimes called *social anthropology*) deals with the description and analysis of cultures—the socially learned traditions of past and present ages. It has a subdiscipline, ethnography, that describes and interprets present-day cultures. Comparing these interpretations and descriptions can generate hypotheses and theories about the causes of past and present cultural similarities and differences.
- **Archaeology** and cultural anthropology possess similar goals but differ in the methods they use and the cultures they study. Archaeology examines the material remains of past cultures left behind on or below the surface of the earth. Without the findings of archaeology, we would not be able to understand the human past, especially where people have not left any books or other written records.
- **Anthropological linguistics** is the study of the great variety of languages spoken by human beings. Anthropological linguists attempt to trace the history of all known families of languages. They are concerned with the way language influences and is influenced by other aspects of human life, and with the relationship between the evolution of language and the evolution of our species, whose

scientific name is *Homo sapiens*. Anthropological linguists also study the relationship between the evolution and change of languages and the evolution and change of cultures.

- **Physical anthropology** (also called *biological anthropology*) connects the other anthropological fields to the study of animal origins and the biologically determined nature of *Homo sapiens*. Physical anthropologists seek to reconstruct the course of human evolution by studying the fossil remains of ancient human and humanlike species. They also seek to describe the distribution of hereditary variations among contemporary human populations and to sort out and measure the relative contributions to human life made by heredity, the natural environment, and culture.
- **Applied anthropology** uses the findings of cultural, archaeological, linguistic, and biological studies to solve practical problems affecting the health, education, security, and prosperity of human beings in many cultural settings.

What Is Distinctive about Cultural Anthropology?

The common thread that ties the fields of anthropology together is the broad focus on humankind viewed across time and space. The purpose of anthropology is to understand all of humankind by studying all aspects of human behavior and ideas. Anthropologists recognize that immense differences lie between people—differences in physical traits, language, lifestyles, beliefs, values, and behavior. By studying these differences, we come to understand that ways of behaving and believing are intelligible in terms of the overall context in which they occur. By adopting this broad view of the human experience, perhaps we humans can tear off the blinders put on us by our local lifestyles. Thus anthropology is incompatible with the view that a particular group—and no one else—represents humanity, stands at the pinnacle of progress, or has been chosen by God or history to fashion the world in its own image.

Holism

The distinction of anthropology among the social sciences is that it is **holistic;** it tries to understand the processes that influence and explain all aspects of human thought and behavior.

Other disciplines in the social sciences are concerned with a particular segment of human experience or a particular time or phase of cultural processes. In contrast, anthropology uses a **holistic** approach that em-

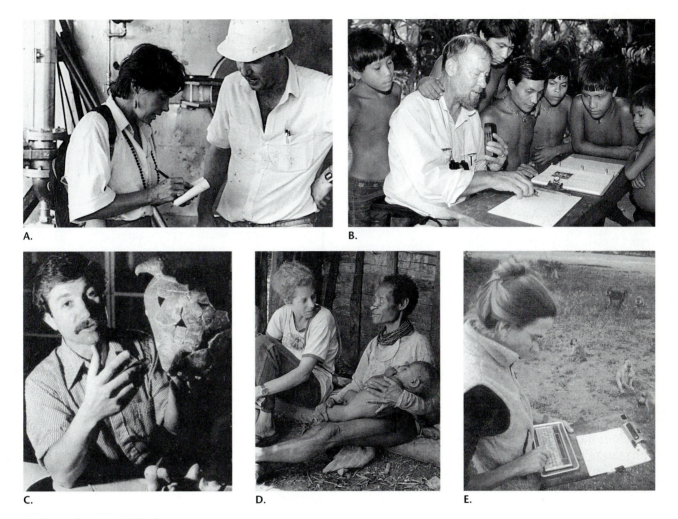

Anthropologists at Work
A. Ethnographer Nancy Scheper-Harris with the engineer of the Aguas Pretas Sugar Mill in Timbauka, Brazil.
B. Ethnographer Napoleon Chagnon charts kinship relationships among the Yanomami.   C. Jerald T. Milanich, archaeologist, Florida Museum of Natural History, with prehistoric (A.D. 200—900) Native American bird vessel.   D. Linguist Francesca Merlin with the speakers of a previously unknown language near Mt. Hagen, New Guinea.   E. Biological Anthropologist, Joan Silk records baboon behavior Amboseli, Kenya.

braces all the components and processes of social life; for example, the physical environment, methods of food production, family patterns, the political system, religious customs, and artistic endeavors. Because anthropologists study the interaction between biological and cultural differences, it is strategically equipped to address key issues concerning the origins of social inequality in the form of racism, sexism, exploitation, poverty, and international underdevelopment. Thus anthropology has much to contribute to our understanding of the major issues that divide contemporary society and threaten national and ethnic conflict.

Fieldwork and Participant Observation

In the early twentieth century, researchers studied cultures with the goal of describing them in as much de-

tail as possible. In recent decades, anthropologists have been focusing more on problem-oriented research. Some are committed to scientific and causal research to explain aspects of culture that sometimes seem "unexplainable" (Murphy and Margolis 1995), such as why some cultures prohibit eating certain foods for religious reasons. Other anthropologists favor more intuitive research that avoids hypothesis testing and favors evocative interpretationist descriptions in search of symbols, motivation, and meaning; for example, how apparently elusive conceptions of personhood are revealed in ceremonial conduct (Geertz 1973).*

Cultural anthropologists collect their primary data through **fieldwork**, an extended period of involvement

*See the first page of the References for an explanation of the system of citations used in this book.

that typically entails living in the community and immersion in the culture being studied. The fieldworker typically gathers information through **participant observation,** living close to the people and participating in their lives as much as possible. Just as children learn a great deal by observing family members, anthropologists learn about a culture by observing the behavior of others and participating in routine activities. However, coming from another culture, anthropological fieldworkers must keep an open mind and not let preconceptions get in the way of understanding the culture they are studying (DeWalt, DeWalt, and Wayland 1998).

Data collected by anthropologists are called *fieldnotes.* These include journals, daily logs, diaries, interviews, behavioral observations, and transcriptions of audiotapes. Some fieldnotes include everything the anthropologist writes down as she or he sees or hears it, as a source of background information, whereas others are devoted to more systematic records such as household census, life histories, gift exchange, or land tenure histories. The voluminous data collected in the field generally require many hours of analysis for each hour spent collecting them (Sanjek 1990).

During the beginning of new fieldwork research, anthropologists and other strangers to the culture commonly feel awkward and unsure. This feeling of anxiety and disorientation that develops in an unfamiliar situation when there is confusion about how to behave or what to expect is called **culture shock.** Once the initial period of adjustment passes, anthropologists often develop lifelong friendships with individual members of the community and may be adopted into local families through a relationship known as *fictive kinship* (see Chapter 10).

Anthropologists refer to the people who share information about their language and culture as **informants, participants,** or **respondents.** The process of working with informants is a painstaking effort to sort out information and knowledge. It is important to choose informants who are knowledgeable and articulate; moreover, no matter how reliable the source, anthropologists find it advisable to explore the same topics with several informants and to use a variety of interview techniques and methods appropriate to the goal of the study (Weller 1998).

Besides talking to informants, anthropologists commonly undertake **direct observations of behavior** as a traditional method of fieldwork. Although expensive in terms of field and analysis time, systematic observations are the only way to obtain accurate data on what people are doing and how much time they spend in various activities. Informant recall—or even the researcher's writeup of fieldnotes at the end of the day—will be shaped by selective remembering or forgetting that make descriptions based only on memory highly inaccurate (Johnson and Sackett 1998).

"Anthropologists! Anthropologists!"

Ethnography

Ethnography literally means "a portrait of a people." An **ethnography** is a written description of a particular culture—the customs, beliefs, and behavior—based on information collected through fieldwork. Anthropologists have tried to study small-scale societies before they had disruptive culture contact with modern societies. The resulting ethnographies often consisted of descriptions of traditional cultures as if they existed in the present. Ethnographies are still often written in the **ethnographic present,** and readers are cautioned that most cultures described may no longer exist.

Today anthropologists no longer restrict themselves to studying small traditional societies. Moreover, traditional anthropological approaches and methods are now used to study communities in complex nation-states. Today's research also tends to be more specialized and often focuses on more specific topics of interest. A few topics covered in this book are

- *Ecological anthropology,* which considers the interaction between environment and technology to study human adaptation and change
- *Economic anthropology,* which studies how goods and services are distributed through formal and informal institutions

- *Political anthropology,* which focuses on political integration, stratification, methods of conflict resolution, leadership, and social control

- *Medical anthropology,* which studies biological and sociocultural factors that affect health and illness

- *Psychological anthropology,* which is concerned with how culture affects personality, child rearing, emotions, attitudes, and social behavior

Nonetheless, the discipline tries to retain its holistic orientation. For example, people who identify themselves as political anthropologists are concerned with the effects of environments or economies on political behavior or on how people raise their children.

More recent social changes, resulting from increased globalization, have led ethnographers to describe local cultures as embedded in the regional and global economy. This movement has led to the concept of transnational research, which recognizes that the world is not a mosaic of isolated cultures, but a network of communities linked by immigration, tourism, media, and now cyberspace. This situation may require multisited field studies; for example, migrants must be studied both at home and abroad to understand the diverse cultural influences they experience (Hannerz 1998).

Ethnology

Anthropologists use the comparative method to understand patterns of thought or behavior that occur in a number of societies.

Anthropologists insist first and foremost that conclusions based on the study of a particular culture be checked against the evidence of other groups. In this way anthropologists hope to control biases and generalize their findings to specific kinds of societies.

Whereas ethnography presents the details and particulars of a single community or culture, **ethnology** is the comparative study of customs and beliefs that tries to formulate theories about the similarities and differences between cultures. Comparative research can provide answers to a number of theoretical questions. For example, certain customs and practices, such as writing systems, tool use, and folktale motifs, tend to recur in different societies. Sometimes this recurrence is the result of geographical proximity, but in other cases, where there has been no known contact, we find independent occurrences of certain traits due to similar governing conditions. Cross-cultural comparisons provide evidence for such patterns and help explain them.

Anthropology and Science

Anthropology is handled as a social science by some and as one of the humanities by others. The humanistic side of anthropology focuses on the rich, complex descriptions of human experience through life histories, personal narratives, and the contemplation of religious and aesthetic meanings. Science, in contrast, entails an explanatory framework and observational procedures for testing that framework.

Scientific theory is based on hypotheses that systematically explain phenomena.

A **hypothesis** is a proposition or tentative explanation of the relationship between certain phenomena. An explanation can be validated (or invalidated) by evidence collected according to explicit procedures. However, the social sciences do not yield precise and reliable long-range predictions. Scientific truth is not absolute, but what is considered to be most probable.

Science does not yield **certainties** or laws; it yields **probabilities.**

As our knowledge expands, some theories may prove better than others, and sometimes old truths are discarded as new theories become more probable.

Why Study Anthropology?

Most anthropologists make their living by teaching in universities, colleges, and community colleges, and by carrying out university-based research. But a substantial and increasing proportion of anthropologists find employment in nonacademic settings. Museums, for example—especially museums of natural history, archaeology, and art and folklore—have long relied on the expertise of anthropologists. In recent years, anthropologists have been welcome in a greater variety of public and private positions in government agencies concerned with welfare, drug abuse, mental health, environmental impact, housing, education, foreign aid, and agricultural development; in the private sector as personnel and ethnic relations consultants and as management consultants for multinational firms; and as staff members of hospitals and foundations (see Box 1.1 on page 6).

In recognition of the growing importance of these nonacademic roles as a source of employment for anthropologists, many university departments of anthropology have started or expanded programs in applied anthropology. These programs supplement traditional anthropological studies with training in

Box 1.1   An Anthropological Scorecard

Anthropologists frequently identify themselves with one or more specialized branches of the five major fields. The following is only a partial listing. Starred items have strong applied focus.

Cultural Anthropology

Ethnography. Description of contemporary cultures.

Medical anthropology. Study of biological and cultural factors in health, disease, and the treatment of the sick.

Urban anthropology. Study of city life, gangs, drug abuse.

Development anthropology. Study of the causes of underdevelopment and development among the less developed nations.

Archaeology

Historical archaeology. Study of cultures of the recent past, using both written records and archaeological excavations.

Industrial archaeology. Historical archaeology that focuses on industrial factories and facilities.

Contract archaeology. Conduct of archaeological surveys for environmental impact statements and protection of historic and prehistoric sites.

Physical (Biological) Anthropology

Primatology. Study of social life and biology of monkeys, great apes, and other primates.

Human paleontology. Search for and study of fossil remains of early human species and their ancestors.

Forensic anthropology. Identification of victims of murders and accidents; establishing identity of criminals.

Population genetics. Study of hereditary differences in human populations.

Linguistics

Historical linguistics. Reconstruction of the origins of specific languages and of families of languages.

Descriptive linguistics. Study of the grammar and syntax of languages.

Sociolinguistics. Study of the actual use of language in the communication behavior of daily life.

Applied Anthropology

---

statistics, computers, and other skills suitable for solving practical problems in human relationships under a variety of natural and cultural conditions.

Despite the expanding opportunities in applied fields, the study of anthropology remains valuable not so much for the opportunities it presents for employment as for its contribution to the basic understanding of human variations and relationships. Just as most students who study mathematics do not become mathematicians, so too most students who study anthropology do not become anthropologists. For human relations fields, such as law, medicine, nursing, education, government, psychology, economics, business administration, and communication media, anthropology has a role to play that is as basic as mathematics. Only by becoming sensitive to the cultural dimensions of human existence and learning to cope with them can one hope to become really effective in any of these fields.

Anthropology has much to contribute to the educational philosophy known as *multiculturalism,* which stresses the importance of viewing the world from the perspectives of all the cultures, races, and ethnic groups present in modern nations. As part of their attempt to broaden the cultural horizons of their students and combat ethnocentrism, many colleges have developed required "cultural diversity" courses. Cultural anthropology is the original multicultural approach to human social life, and it remains by far the most systematic and comprehensive alternative to traditional curriculums that view the world primarily in terms of "dead, White, European males." In anthropological perspective, multiculturalism consists not merely of the knowledge that cultures are different and worthy of respect, but also of a commitment to analyzing the causes of similarities as well as differences (Paredes and Pohl 1995).

Summary

1. Anthropology is the study of humankind. Its five major branches are cultural or social anthropology, anthropological linguistics, physical (or biological) anthropology, archaeology, and applied anthropology.

2. Anthropology is distinctive in its commitment to holism and to understanding all factors that influence human thought and behavior.

3. Through fieldwork, cultural anthropologists participate in social activities, directly observe behavior and conduct interviews to understand human thought and behavior.

4. An ethnography is a published account of a particular culture. Ethnology is the comparison of ethnographic information from two or more cultures.

5. Anthropology has much to contribute to understanding multiculturalism; it is committed to understanding the processes that underlie cultural similarities and differences.

KEY TERMS
anthropological linguistics
applied anthropology
archaeology
certainty
cultural anthropology
culture shock
direct observation of behavior
ethnographic present
ethnography
ethnology
fieldwork
holism
hypothesis
informants
participant observation
physical anthropology
probability
scientific theory

QUESTIONS TO THINK ABOUT
1. What does it mean to say that anthropology is holistic?
2. What are some goals of anthropological research?
3. How can anthropologists be useful outside of academic settings?

CHAPTER 2

The Nature of Culture

Navaho rug makers are made, not born.

Definitions of Culture

Society, Subculture, and Sociocultural System
Enculturation
Cultural Relativism

Science and the Relativity of Truth
Limitations of the Enculturation Concept
Diffusion

Fieldwork and the Mental and Behavioral Aspects of Culture
Emic and Etic Aspects of Culture
Emics, Etics, and Sacred Cows

The Universal Pattern

The Diversity of Anthropological Theories

Cultural Materialism

Summary

In this chapter, you will find alternative definitions of culture and of other key concepts such as society and enculturation. You will also encounter certain general processes that help explain why customs, traditions, and behavior are both similar and different around the world. Then we embark on the difficult but necessary task of identifying the principal parts of the system of behaviors and thoughts that constitute human social life. Finally, we will set forth the theoretical viewpoint of cultural materialism and the universal pattern of culture that guides the organization of this textbook.

Definitions of Culture

The term *culture* refers to the learned, socially acquired traditions of thought and behavior found in human societies.

When anthropologists speak of a human culture, they usually mean the total, socially acquired lifestyle of a group of people, including their patterned, repetitive ways of thinking, feeling, and acting.

Note that culture does not just mean the literary and artistic achievements and standards of "cultured" elites; because anthropologists, plumbers, and farmers are as "cultured" as art collectors and operagoers. And studying the lives of ordinary people is just as important as studying the lives of famous and influential people.

The definition of culture as consisting of patterns of acting (behavior) as well as patterns of thought and feeling follows the precedent set by Sir Edward Burnett Tylor, the founder of academic anthropology in the English-speaking world and author of the first general anthropology textbook:

> Culture . . . taken in its wide ethnographic sense is that complex whole which includes knowledge, belief, art, morals, law, custom, and any other capabilities and habits acquired by man as a member of society. The condition of culture among the various societies of mankind, in so far as it is capable of being investigated on general principles, is a subject apt for the study of laws of human thought and action. (Tylor 1871:1).

Some anthropologists prefer to view culture as a purely mental phenomenon consisting of the ideas that people share concerning how one should think and act.

The view that culture is "pure idea" has been compared to the notion of culture as a computer program—a kind of "software" that tells people what to do under various circumstances. According to Clifford Geertz (1973:44), "Culture is best seen . . . as a set of control mechanisms—plans, recipes, rules, instructions (what computer engineers call "programs")." This view implies that ideas (knowledge, rules, and meaning) guide and govern behavior. The drawback to this concept of culture as "pure idea" is that it excludes reference to repetitive patterns of behavior, which are part of culture, even when people are not conscious or fully aware of their existence.

Behavior can guide and cause ideas and behavioral events can affect the evolution of sociocultural systems even though people may not be fully cognizant of these events or actions.

The effect of behavior on cultural development can be seen in times when cultures change rapidly, as is happening today in most of the world. For example, before the 1970s many women who had husbands and school-age children in the United States believed that wives should depend on their husbands for family income. Pressured by rising prices and a desire to maintain or raise their standard of living, increasing numbers of married women with school-age children abandoned this "program" and joined the wage labor force, even though traditional family values still prevailed. Women left home to work because their earnings made the difference between getting by or falling into poverty. Today, the majority of married women with school-age children are in the labor force, and this change in behavior has brought forth a change in people's shared ideas and expectations about women's capabilities and their right to equal job opportunities. (See Chapter 15, America Now section, for a more detailed look at how and why the program governing marriage and the family in the United States changed.)

Another drawback of viewing culture as a mental program rather than as having both mental and behavioral aspects is that many of the most pressing social problems of our times are not programmed at all. The traffic jam, for example in Chapter 15, America Now describes a highly patterned cultural phenomenon that occurs despite the programming that drivers receive to keep moving.

Society, Subculture, and Sociocultural System

As used in this book, the term **society** means an organized group of people who share a homeland and who depend on each other for their survival and well-being. Each human society has an overall culture, but all societies contain groups of people who have lifestyles that are not shared by the rest of the society.

In referring to patterns of culture characteristics of such groups, anthropologists often use the term *subculture*.

Members of a **subculture** share certain cultural features that are significantly different from those of the rest of society.

Even small societies have subcultures associated with males and females, and children and adults. In larger and more complex societies, one encounters subcultures associated with, for example, groups based on ethnic, religious, and class distinctions. People may also change and renegotiate their affiliations and identities as they move from one social context to another.

Finally, the term *sociocultural* is a useful reminder that society and culture form a complex system of interacting parts (more about the components of sociocultural systems in a moment).

Enculturation

The culture of a society tends to be similar in many respects from one generation to the next. In part, cultural continuity is maintained by the process known as *enculturation*.

Enculturation is a partially conscious and partially unconscious learning experience whereby the older generation invites, induces, and compels the younger generation to adopt traditional ways of thinking and behaving.

Thus Chinese children use chopsticks instead of forks, speak a tonal ("sing-song") language, and worship their ancestors, because they have been enculturated into Chinese culture. Enculturation is achieved through the control that the adult generation exercises over the means of rewarding and punishing children. Each generation is programmed to reward thought and behavior that conforms to the patterns of its own enculturation experience and to punish, or at least not to reward, behavior that does not so conform.

The concept of enculturation (despite its limitations, as discussed later) occupies a central position in the distinctive outlook of modern anthropology. Failure to comprehend the role enculturation plays in maintaining each group's patterns of behavior and thought lies at the heart of the phenomenon known as *ethnocentrism*.

Ethnocentrism is the belief that one's own patterns of behavior are always natural, good, beautiful, or important, and that strangers, to the extent that they live differently, live by savage, inhuman, disgusting, or irrational standards.

A.

B.

C.

How, What, and When We Eat: Culture at Work
A. Midday meal, Rangoon, Myanmar. Food is good to touch as well as to eat.   B. Fast food, America's most notable contribution to world cuisine.   C. The correct way to eat in China.

People who are intolerant of cultural differences usually ignore the following fact: Had they been enculturated within another group, all those supposedly savage, inhuman, disgusting, and irrational lifestyles would now be their own. Recognizing the fallacy of

A.

B.

C.

Passing Culture On

A. In Bali, a man reads to his grandchildren from a script on narrow bamboo strips.   B. In India, a Sikh father teaches his daughter how to wrap a turban.   C. In Mission Viejo, California, young people learn the culturally approved manner of eating artichokes.

ethnocentrism leads to tolerance of cultural differences and a desire to learn more about them.

A certain degree of ethnocentrism is natural for people raised in a single culture; their values and ways of behaving appear desirable and superior to all others. Ethnocentrism however, is potentially dangerous when it leads to intolerance of other cultures and is used to justify the mistreatment of others. Taken to the extreme, it leads to the belief that people who are different from us are not worthy of basic human rights and therefore their mistreatment or annihilation is morally justified.

Cultural Relativism

Anthropologists place great emphasis on the viewpoint known as *cultural relativism.* This concept has several meanings. To some anthropologists, cultural relativism means not passing judgment on the moral worth of such cultural traits or institutions as cannibalism, first-cousin marriage, or eating insects. It means disavowing any absolute, universal moral standards that can be used to rank cultural beliefs and practices as good or evil, superior or inferior, right or wrong.

Probably the majority of anthropologists, however, would argue for a more provisional kind of relativism; namely, they would hold in abeyance any moral judgments until they have learned what the world looks like to people in different cultures (see Box 2.1 on page 12).

Cultural relativism stipulates that behavior in a particular culture should not be judged by the standards of another. Yet it is evident that not all human customs or institutions contribute to the society's overall health and well-being, nor should they be regarded as morally or ethically worthy of respect.

Box 2.1   Dog Meat and Culture Shock

To the Editor:

I read David M. Raddock's Sept. 2 letter on China with amusement. Yes, we are still eating dogs in China. What's wrong with that? I used to feel the same as May-Lee Chai (whose Aug. 26 letter Mr. Raddock replied to) whenever I read or heard Americans talk about this Dog Thing. I do not feel angry anymore. This is not a matter of who is more civilized or less civilized. It is simply a matter of different tastes.

Why is eating dog meat less dignified (at least that is how it is portrayed in the media here) than eating beef? Does one kind of an animal enjoy more rights than another? . . . I am not ashamed of eating dog. I have a different color of skin, I speak a different language and I come from a different cultural background, so I sometime eat different food (meat in this case). This is the beginning of my seventh year in the United States. America has been a perfect country for me except for one thing: I (miss) having dog meat back home.

I like Mr. Raddock's letter. It is factual and nonjudgmental. This kind of perspective is what we need when looking at different cultures. In today's world, linked by common interest, it is perhaps wise and beneficial not to impose our own values on others.

James Piao
New York

(*The New York Times,* September, 13, 1994)

Like everybody else, most anthropologists make ethical judgments about certain kinds of cultural patterns, but they seek to minimize the effect of these preferences and beliefs on the conduct of their research so they can understand why people think and act as they do. Ethical and moral decisions should be based on the best available knowledge of what is happening in the world. This knowledge is gained through reliable scientific methods that tell us who is doing what to whom and who is responsible for the suffering and injustice that needs to be remedied. If anthropologists want to tackle politically controversial issues such as the spread of AIDS in Africa, or the plight of landless peasants in Latin America, they need to understand social institutions and practices in objective scientific terms that will reveal possibilities for improving the moral outcome.

Science and the Relativity of Truth

It is important to distinguish clearly between the relativity of *values* and the relativity of *truth*. Values relativism says there are no universal moral values because values should be evaluated in terms of the cultural context; relativism of truth says objective truth about human thoughts and actions is unobtainable because all research is biased. Objective truth is unobtainable, according to some anthropologists, because all observers, even those who use scientific methods, are influenced by their own culture-bound experiences and their interpretations are affected by the values and perspectives associated with their nationality, ethnic group, class, and gender.

The position we adopt in this textbook is that anthropologists do not need to reject their values in order to carry out an objective study of cultural phenomena. They can disapprove of pollution, genocide, sexism, racism, poverty, child abuse, and nuclear war and still maintain scientific objectivity about these phenomena. Nor is there anything antiscientific in setting out to study certain cultural patterns because one wants to change them.

Scientific objectivity does not arise from having no biases—everyone is biased—but from taking care not to let one's biases influence the result of research.

Science is a system of knowledge; its most important feature is that it seeks to control the influence of various biases on the conduct of research.

Scientists seek to control bias by telling one another as clearly as possible what they have done to gather and analyze their data and by formulating coherent theories that can be tested and retested by other researchers. People who assert that scientific methods cannot be applied to sociocultural phenomena commit a basic error: They assume that objective truth means the absolute, final, unquestioned truth. Instead, science results in temporary and provisional objective truth.

Science involves a never-ending process of formulating and testing new and better theories.

This view of science derives from the positivist empiricist tradition that makes no claim to being "value free" but proposes to overcome inevitable biases of knowledge by using methodological rules that are open to public scrutiny. Just because the final, absolute, objective, certain truth can never be reached does not mean that all truths are equally arbitrary and biased (Collins

1989; D'Andrade 1995; Haraway 1989; Harris 1995; Holton 1994; Lett 1991; Watson 1990).

Limitations of the Enculturation Concept

It is easy to see that enculturation cannot account for a considerable portion of the lifestyles of existing social groups. Old patterns are not always faithfully repeated in successive generations, and new patterns are continually being added.

The replication of cultural patterns from one generation to the next is never complete.

In fact, the rate of innovation and nonreplication in the industrial societies has reached proportions alarming to each successive generation. Margaret Mead was among the first to call attention to the profound worldwide significance of the resulting "generation gap." Her description of the generation gap was written over two decades ago, but her words are as pertinent now as then:

> Today, nowhere in the world are there elders who know what the children know; no matter how remote and simple the societies are in which the children live. In the past there were always some elders who knew more than any children in terms of their experience of having grown up within a cultural system. Today there are none. It is not only that parents are no longer guides, but that there are no guides, whether one seeks them in one's own country or abroad. There are no elders who know what those who have been reared within the last twenty years know about the world into which they were born. (1970:77–78)

Enculturation can account for the continuity of culture, but it cannot account for the evolution of culture.

Even with respect to the continuity of culture, enculturation has important limitations. As indicated, not every replicated cultural pattern results from the programming that one generation experiences at the hands of another. Many patterns are replicated because successive generations adjust to similar conditions in social life in similar ways. Sometimes the programming received may even be at odds with the actual patterns; people may be enculturated to behave in one way but be obliged by conditions beyond their control to behave in another way. We have already mentioned traffic jams, which exist even though people try to avoid them. Poverty is another example. As we will see in Chapter 13, many poor people find

themselves living in houses, eating food, working at jobs, and raising families according to patterns that replicate their parents' subculture, not because their parents trained them to follow these patterns but because poor children confront educational, political, and economic conditions that perpetuate their poverty.

Diffusion

Whereas *enculturation* refers to the passing of cultural traits from one generation to the next, *diffusion* refers to the passing of cultural traits from one culture and society to another—for example, Americans eat sushi, the Japanese play baseball, and the whole world wears Levis.

Diffusion takes place when culture contact leads to borrowing and passing on of culture traits.

This process is so common that the majority of traits found in any society can be said to have originated in some other society. One can say, for example, that much of the government, religion, law, diet, and language of the United States was "borrowed" or diffused from other cultures. Thus the Judeo-Christian religions come from the Middle East; parliamentary democracy comes from Western Europe; the food grains in the American diet—rice, wheat, and maize—come from Asian, Middle Eastern, and Native American civilizations, respectively; and the English language comes from the amalgam of several different European tongues.

Early in this century (see Appendix), diffusion was regarded by many anthropologists as the most powerful explanation for sociocultural differences and similarities. The lingering effects of this approach can still be seen in popular attempts to explain the similarities among major civilizations as the result of their derivation from each other—Polynesia from Peru, or vice versa; lowland Mesoamerica from highland Mesoamerica (Mesoamerica is roughly Mexico plus Central America), or vice versa; China from Europe, or vice versa; the New World (the Americas) from the Old; and so forth.

In recent years, however, diffusion has lost ground as an explanatory principle because the adoption of new cultural traits requires that these traits be integrated into the recipient population. It is true that, in general, the closer two societies are to each other, the greater will be their cultural resemblance. But these resemblances cannot simply be attributed to some automatic tendency for traits to diffuse. Societies that live close together (in location) are also likely to occupy similar environments; hence the similarities between them may be caused by the effects of similar

A.

Culture, People, and the Sun

*The relationship between people and the sun is mediated by culture. Sunbathing **A.** is a modern invention.   On the beach at Villerville in 1908 **B.** only "mad dogs and Englishmen went out in the midday sun" without their parasols. As the rising incidence of skin cancer attests, sunbathing can indeed be hazardous to your health.*

B.

environmental conditions. Moreover, numerous societies that lived in close contact for hundreds of years retain radically different ways of life. For example, the Incas of Peru had an imperial government, whereas the nearby forest-dwelling societies lacked centralized leadership of any kind. Other well-known cases are the African Ituri forest hunters and their Bantu agriculturalist neighbors, and the "apartment house" Pueblos and their marauding, nomadic Apache neighbors in the southwest United States.

Resistance to diffusion is as common as acceptance.

If this resistance were absent, Catholics and Protestants in northern Ireland would not differ; Mexicans would speak English (or U.S. citizens, Spanish); and Jews would accept the divinity of Jesus Christ (or Christians would reject it). Furthermore, even if one accepts diffusion as an explanation, the question still remains of why the diffused item (say, monotheism or agriculture) originated in the first place.

Diffusion cannot account for many instances in which people who never had any contact with each other invented similar tools and techniques, and developed remarkably similar forms of marriage and religious beliefs.

Dramatic examples exist of such inventions and discoveries that occurred not only independently but also at approximately the same time (see Box 2.2, and Box 2.3).

Box 2.2   Old and New World Independent Inventions

All items listed were present in both Old and New Worlds prior to 1492.

Textiles

Purple dye
   Prepared from coastal mollusk
   Elite connotation of purple
Scarlet dye (cochineal/kermes)
Resist dyeing

Loom
Cotton
Clothing
Turban
"Nightcap"
Pointed-toe shoes
Long robes
Sash, mantle, sandals, loincloth

Weapons, armor

Kettle-shaped helmet
Sling
Thickened textile armor

Metallurgy

Lost-wax casting
Smelting, alloying, forging, hammering,
    gilding, etc.

Ceramics

Paper

Lime sizing of writing surface

Architecture

Colonnade, aqueduct, canal, cement-lined
    reservoir, highway
Corbeled arch
True arch
Walled city
Fired brick
Pyramids

Mathematics

Place value notation
Zero concept
Zero sign
Astrology and astronomy
Articulated lunar, solar, and stellar calendar counts
    360-day plus 5 extra days
Cycle of 7 days
Day measured sunset to sunset
Observatories
Eclipse records
Day names

Writing

Hieroglyph system
Ideographs, rebus

Social organization

Merchant class or caste
Organized trade, "caravans"
Corvée labor
Kingship complex
King concept
Divine mandate
Throne
Canopy

Umbrella or parasol as sign of dignity
    or rank
Sceptre
Crown or diadem
Tomb in elevated structure
Burial chamber with hidden entry
"Royal tombs" (conspicuous display)
Dedicatory sacrifice, subfoundation burial
of children
Gold necklace, sign of office
Heraldic devices
Litter
Deference of bowing, downcast eyes

Religion and ritual

Paradise concept
Underworld, "hell" concept
Dualism (good and evil)
Earth, air, fire, water as basic elements
Deluge motif
    Produced by rain
    A few persons saved in a vessel
    Bird sent forth to check drying
    Pyramid tower built for safety against deluge,
        destroyed by being blown down by wind

Sacrifice complex

Animals slain
Human sacrifice
Offerings burned on altar in
    ceremonial area
Communion in consumption of part of
    the sacrifice
Parched grain or meal as offering
Blood offered as sacrifice
Blood scattered over area and participants
Snake symbolism
    Signifying wisdom, knowledge
    Signifying healing
    Signifying fertility
Incense
    Incense mixed with cereal one type
        of offering
    Accompanying most rituals
    For purification
    For offering to gods—sweet, attractive
    Symbolizing prayer
    As route for ascent of soul

(Adapted from Riley et al. 1971)

Box 2.3   Simultaneous Independent Inventions

When the culture process has reached a point where an invention or discovery becomes possible, that invention or discovery becomes inevitable.

The discovery of sun spots was made independently by at least four men in a single year: by Galileo, Fabricius, Scheiner, and Harriott, in 1611. The parallax of a star was first measured by Bessel, Struve, and Henderson, working independently, in 1838. Oxygen was discovered independently by Scheele and Priestly in 1774. The invention of the self-exciting dynamo was claimed by Hjorth, Varley, Siemens, Wheatstone, and Ladd in 1866–1867, and by Wilde between 1863–1867. The solution of the problem of respiration was made independently by Priestley, Scheele, Lavoisier, Spallanzani, and Davy, in a single year, 1777. Invention of the telescope and the thermometer each is claimed by eight or nine persons independently and at approximately the same time. "Even the southpole, never before trodden by the foot of human beings, was at last reached twice in one summer." The great work of Mendel in genetics lay unnoticed for many years. But when it was eventually rediscovered, it was done not by one man but by three—de Vries, Correns, and Tschermak—and in a single year, 1900. One could go on indefinitely. When the growing, interactive culture process reaches a certain point, an invention or discovery takes place.

The simultaneity of multiple inventions or discoveries is sometimes striking and remarkable. Accusations of plagiarism are not infrequent; bitter rivalries are waged over priorities. "The right to the monopoly of the manufacture of the telephone was long in litigation; the ultimate decision rested on an interval of hours between the recording of concurrent descriptions by Alexander Bell and Elisha Gray."

(White 1949: 208–210)

In sum, diffusion is no more satisfactory than enculturation as a mode of explaining cultural similarities. If only diffusion and enculturation affected social life, then we should expect all cultures to be the same and to stay the same; this is clearly not the case.

It would not be accurate to conclude, however, that diffusion plays no role in sociocultural evolution. The nearness of one culture to another often does influence the rate and direction of change as well as the specific details of sociocultural life, even if it does not shape the general features of the two cultures. For example, tobacco smoking originated among the native peoples of the Western Hemisphere and after 1492 spread to the most remote regions of the globe. This diffusion could not have happened if the Americas had remained cut off from the other continents. (The tobacco plant did not grow outside the Americas.) Yet contact alone obviously does not tell the whole story. Hundreds of other Native American practices, such as living in wigwams or in matrilocal households (see Chapter 9) did not diffuse even to the colonists who lived next door to Native American peoples.

Fieldwork and the Mental and Behavioral Aspects of Culture

Cultural anthropologists employ many kinds of methods to learn about cultural patterns. These include survey questionnaires, censuses, life histories, genealogies, formal and informal interviews, filming, videotaping and audiotaping, and note taking (Bernard 1994; Sanjek 1990). The most distinctive anthropological method, however, is **participant observation.** This method involves living for extended periods among a people and participating as much and as closely as possible in their daily round of activities— talking, listening, and just plain looking. The aim of the fieldworker is to obtain knowledge of both the mental and behavioral aspects of a culture. The mental aspects consist of thoughts and feelings that exist at various levels of consciousness:

1. *Unconscious rules.* People may have a culturally prescribed "body language" and not be aware of it. For example, they may not be able to state the rules that govern the distance that they maintain between each other while holding a conversation, just as they are unaware of rules of grammar when they speak.

2. *Partially formalized rules.* Other culturally patterned ways of thought exist closer to consciousness; people may not routinely talk about certain cultural rules but can express them when questioned by the fieldworker. Thus they can usually state the values, norms, and proper codes of conduct for activities such as weaning babies, courting mates, choosing leaders, treating diseases, entertaining guests, categorizing kin, worshiping, and thousands of additional commonplace behaviors.

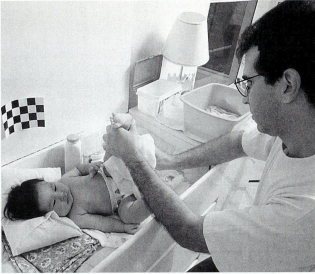

The Limits of Enculturation
A. Before the 1970's, fathers spent less than 3 minutes a day interacting with infants. **B.** *This cultural pattern was not passed on to today's generation.*

3. *Formal rules of conduct.* Cultures also have many fully conscious, explicit, and formal rules of conduct and statements of values, norms, and goals that people talk about during ordinary conversations, write down in law codes, or announce at public gatherings (rules about littering, making bank deposits, playing football, trespassing, and so on).

4. *Rules for breaking rules.* Finally, to make matters more complex, cultures have rules not only for behavior but also for breaking rules of behavior, such as when you park your car in front of a sign that says "No Parking" and gamble on not getting a ticket .

Knowledge of this inner world is not the only product of fieldwork. In addition, anthropologists observe, measure, film, and take notes about what people do during their daily, weekly, or annual rounds of activities. They watch births take place, attend funerals, go along on hunting expeditions, watch marriage ceremonies, and attend hundreds of other events and activities as they unfold. These events and activities constitute the behavioral aspect of culture.

Emic and Etic Aspects of Culture

The fieldworker can describe both mental aspects and behavioral events and still not offer a satisfactory description of culture. The problem is that both the thoughts and behavior of the participants can be viewed from two different perspectives: that of the participants themselves and that of the observers. In both instances, scientific and objective accounts of the mental and behavioral fields are possible.

When describing culture from the participants' viewpoint, the observer uses concepts and distinctions that are meaningful and appropriate to the participants **(emics)**.

When describing culture from the observer's perspective, the observer uses concepts and distinctions that are meaningful and appropriate to the observer (**etics**).

Traffic Jam in New York City
Despite clear traffic rules, traffic jams are a cultural pattern.

A.   B.   C.

Diffusion

Can you reconstruct the diffusionary history of the objects and activities shown in these scenes? **A.** *Sambura warrior in Kenya makes a call on a cellular phone.* **B.** *Mongolian metropolis.* **C.** *Brazilian woodsman with chainsaw.*

The first way of studying culture is called *emics* (pronounced *ee-miks*), and the second way is called *etics* (pronounced *et-iks*). (See Chapter 4 for the derivation of these terms from the linguistic concepts "phonemics" and "phonetics.")

The aim of emic descriptions is to produce a view of the world that the native participants accept as real, meaningful, or appropriate.

In carrying out emic research, anthropologists seek knowledge of the categories and rules one must know in order to think and act as a native. They attempt to learn, for example, what rule lies behind the use of the same kin term for mother and mother's sister among the Bathonga, or when it is appropriate to shame house guests among the Kwakiutl, or how to ask a boy or a girl out for a date among U.S. teenagers.

The aim of etic descriptions is to generate scientific theories about the causes of sociocultural differences and similarities.

Rather than employ concepts that are necessarily real, meaningful, and appropriate from the native point of view, the anthropologist interested in the etic aspects of a culture uses categories and rules derived from the vocabulary of science—categories and rules that are often unfamiliar to the native. Thus etic studies may involve the measurement and juxtaposition of activities and events that native informants find inappropriate or meaningless (Headland et al. 1990).

Emics, Etics, and Sacred Cows

The following example demonstrates the importance of distinguishing between emics and etics when trying to describe and explain cultural differences and similarities. In the Trivandrum district of the state of Kerala in southern India, farmers said that they obeyed the Hindu prohibition against the slaughter of cattle and that they never knowingly did anything to shorten the lives of their animals. Yet in Kerala the mortality rate of male calves is almost twice as high as the mortality rate of female calves. In fact, male cattle (oxen) 0 to 1 year of age are outnumbered by female cattle (cows) of the same cohort in a ratio of 67 to 100. The farmers themselves are aware that male calves are more likely to die than female calves, but they attribute the difference to the relative "weakness" of the males. "The males get sick more often," they said. When asked to explain why male calves get sick more often than females, some farmers suggested that the males eat less than the females. A few farmers even explained that the male calves eat less because they are not allowed to stay at the mother's teats for more than a few seconds. But no one said that male cattle were not as valuable in Kerala as they are in other regions of India, where

Box 2.4   Emics and Etics Represent Two Perspectives for Viewing Cultural Phenomena

Emics

Emics is derived from "phonemics"—sounds that native speakers recognize as being distinct and significant in distinguishing meaning (see Chapter 4).

Emic knowledge represents views of thoughts and behavior from the perspective of the participants.

Emic descriptions are regarded as meaningful and appropriate by members of the culture being studied.

Emic knowledge may not be applicable for generating scientific theories.

Emic knowledge achieves the status of "emic" by passing the test of native consensus.

Emic descriptions describe what is culturally meaningful rather than what is theoretically significant.

Etics

Etics is derived from "phonetics"—sounds that are distinguished by linguists but may or may not be meaningful to native speakers (see Chapter 4).

Etic knowledge represents views of thoughts and behavior from the perspective of the observer/researcher.

Etic accounts and descriptions are expressed in terms of categories that are regarded as meaningful and appropriate by the community of scientific observers.

Etic knowledge is obtained through direct observation or elicitation or through participants trained to be observers.

Etic knowledge must be applicable for generating theories of cross-cultural differences and similarities.

Etic descriptions do not have to be meaningful or appropriate to native informants to be deemed valid.

---

they are used for plowing dry fields. In Kerala, where rice, the principal crop, is grown in postage-stamp–size fields, oxen are at a disadvantage. They tend to get stuck in the mud and break their legs. Water buffalo have no such problems and are thus preferred over oxen to prepare the fields for planting. The emics of the situation are that every calf has the "right to live" regardless of its sex. But the etics of the situation are that cattle sex ratios are systematically adjusted to the needs of the local ecology and economy through preferential male "bovicide." Although the unwanted male calves are not slaughtered, many are more or less starved to death by selectively restricting their feed.

The comparison of etic and emic versions of culture gives rise to some of the most important and intriguing problems in anthropology. Of course, emic and etic descriptions need not always differ from each other. And even in this case, if one gets to know Indian farmers very well, some of them may reluctantly discuss the need they feel to cull animals of the unwanted sex. But only an etic perspective can lead one to understand why in northern India, where oxen are used to cultivate the soil, etic bovicide is practiced more against female than male cattle (resulting in some states in an adult cattle sex ratio of over 200 oxen for every 100 cows), whereas in the wet rice region of southern India, just the opposite takes place—bovicide is practiced against male cattle. Sex ratios are thus systematically adjusted to the needs of the local economy. (See Chapter 17 for more discussion on the emics and etics of cattle in India.)

Four viewpoints can be formulated from the data collected in southern India (Harris 1979b:38):

The farmers' emic mental view confirming the rule against the slaughter of cattle — "All calves have the right to life."

The farmers' emic view of their behavior — "No calves are ever starved to death."

The observer's etic inference of the farmers' mental beliefs based on the lopsided sex ratios. — "Let the male calves starve to death when feed is scarce."

The observer's etic view of the farmers' behavior based on the statistics of calf sex ratios. — "Male calves are starved to death."

The Universal Pattern

Anthropologists agree that every culture has patterns of behavior and thoughts related to making a living from the environment, raising children, organizing the exchange of goods and labor, living in domestic groups and larger communities, and expressing the creative, playful, aesthetic, moral, and intellectual aspects of human life. However, anthropologists do not agree on how many subdivisions of these categories should be recognized or what priority they should be given when it comes to doing research.

To compare one culture with another, the anthropologist must collect and organize cultural data in relation to cross-culturally recurrent aspects or parts of the sociocultural system. The total inventory

Body Language

People have unconscious cultural rules for maintaining space between them when greeting and conversing.

of these recurrent aspects or parts is called the **universal pattern.**

In this book, we will use a universal pattern consisting of three major divisions: infrastructure, structure, and superstructure (Box 2.5).

1. ***Infrastructure.*** Consists of the technologies and productive and reproductive activities that bear directly on the provision of food and shelter, protection against illness, and the satisfaction of sexual and other basic human needs and drives. Infrastruc-

---

Box 2.5   Components of the Universal Pattern*

Infrastructure

Mode of Production
The technology and the practices employed for expanding or limiting basic subsistence production, especially the production of food and other forms of energy, given the restrictions and opportunities provided by a specific technology interacting with a specific habitat.
  Technology of subsistence
  Technoenvironmental relationships
  Ecosystems
  Work patterns

Mode of Reproduction
The technology and the practices employed for expanding, limiting, and maintaining population size.
  Fertility, natality, mortality
  Nurturance of infants
  Medical control of demographic patterns
  Contraception, abortion, infanticide

Structure

Domestic Economy
The organization of reproduction and basic production, exchange, and consumption within camps, houses, apartments, or other domestic settings.
  Family structure
  Domestic division of labor

  Domestic socialization, enculturation, education
  Age and gender roles
  Domestic discipline, hierarchies, and sanctions

Political Economy
The organization of reproduction, production, exchange, and consumption within and between bands, villages, chiefdoms, states, and empires.
  Political organizations, factions, clubs, associations, and
    corporations
  Division of labor, taxation, tribute
  Political socialization, enculturation, education
  Law and order
  Class, caste, urban, and rural hierarchies
  Discipline, police and military control
  War

Superstructure

  Art, music, dance, literature, advertising
  Values
  Meaning
  Symbols
  Religious rituals, myths, and beliefs
  Sports, games, hobbies
  Science

*Remember, each of these components can be viewed from an emic, etic, behavioral, or mental perspective.

ture also embraces the limitations and opportunities placed on production and reproduction by a society's natural habitat, as well as the means employed to increase or decrease population growth. For example, a sketch of the infrastructure of modern-day Japan might include Japan's electronic computerized and robotized information and manufacturing economy, its dependence on imported raw materials, the effectiveness of its public health system, its reliance on abortions as a means of population regulation, and the extensive damage that has been done to the natural habitat by various forms of industrial pollution and economic growth.

2. **Structure.** Consists of the groups and organizations present in every society that allocate, regulate, and exchange goods, labor, and information. The primary focus of some groups is on kinship and family relations; others provide the political and economic organization for the whole society; still others provide the organization for religious rituals and various intellectual activities. To continue to use Japan as an example, structural features would

A.

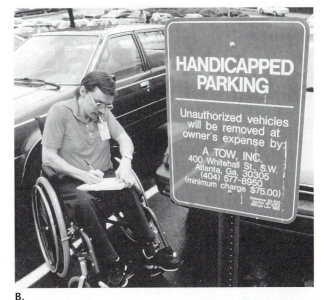

B.

C.

D.

Rules for Breaking Rules

*Cultural behavior cannot be predicted from knowledge of a simple set of rules. In **B.**, a handicapped driver is taking down the license number of a car that has parked against the rule. **A.**, **C.**, and **D.** tell their own sad stories.*

include a domestic economy based on small, male wage-earner, urban-dwelling nuclear families; a political economy that is characterized by global corporations regulated and assisted by the state; and a moderately democratic parliament. It would also include organizations such as universities, Buddhist temples, and art museums.

Obviously the focus of a given social group may overlap with the focus of another. Multinational corporations, for example, do more than produce and sell commodities; they also foster or create beliefs about free trade and consumerism. Governments may contribute to the regulation of every aspect of social life; established churches may regulate sexual and reproductive behavior as well as spread religious beliefs. To study these connections, we must begin with some preliminary map of a society's structure, based on the primary focus of its most important groups.

3. **Superstructure.** Consists of the behavior and thought devoted to symbolic, ideational, artistic, playful, religious, and intellectual endeavors as well as all the mental and emic aspects of a culture's infrastructure and structure. This would include, in the case of Japan, such features as the Shinto and Buddhist religions; distinctive forms of Japanese painting, theater, and poetry; a penchant for baseball and wrestling; and a belief in teamwork as a source of competitive advantage.

The Diversity of Anthropological Theories

The kinds of research that anthropologists carry out and the kinds of conclusions they stress are greatly influenced by the basic assumptions they make about the causes of cultural evolution. Basic assumptions made by anthropologists of different theoretical persuasions are called *research strategies,* or *paradigms.*

No textbook can conceivably be written so as to represent all the current research strategies with bias toward none and equal coverage for all. In this book, we have made a conscious effort to include alternative viewpoints on controversial issues. Inevitably, however, our own research strategy dominates the presentation.

Cultural Materialism

The point of view followed throughout is known as **cultural materialism.** This research strategy holds that the primary task of cultural anthropology is to give scientific causal explanations for the differences and similarities in thought and behavior found among human groups. The aim of scientific research is to formulate explanatory theories that are predictive, testable, and broad in scope. Scientific theories are accepted in accordance with their relative powers of predictability. Because science cannot guarantee absolute truth, free of error, we can only assert that our predictions are probable rather than certain. *Probabilistic determinism* seeks to make generalizations that are expected to be applicable more often than not.

Materialist theories aim to explain the probable causes of sociocultural differences and similarities by giving theoretical priority to infrastructure.

Cultural materialism makes the assumption that sociocultural explanations can best be carried out by studying the material constraints and opportunities to which human existence is exposed. Material constraints and opportunities arise from the need to produce food, shelter, tools, and machines and to reproduce human populations under conditions set by biology and the environment. They are called *material* constraints and opportunities in order to distinguish them from constraints or opportunities presented by ideas and other mental or spiritual aspects of a society's superstructure, such as values, religion, and art.

For cultural materialists, the most likely causes of variation in the mental or spiritual aspects of human life are the variations in a society's infrastructure.

Thus infrastructure, structure, and superstructure are not equally effective in determining the retention or extinction of sociocultural innovations.

- Innovations arising from the infrastructural level (industrial robots, for example), are likely to be preserved and passed on to future generations if they enhance the efficiency of productive and reproductive processes.

- Adaptive infrastructural innovations are likely to be selected, even if they do not conform with the preexisting structural and superstructural components (unionized, labor-intensive assembly lines; fear that robots will cause unemployment).

- In contrast, innovations originating in the structural or superstructural sectors (for example, new religions) are likely to cause substantial changes in other sectors but it is unlikely that they will be retained over time if they are not compatible with material constraints (that is, if they substantially impede the system's ability to satisfy basic human needs and drives).

This approach does not mean that the mental and spiritual aspects of cultures are somehow less significant or less important than production, reproduction, ecology, and other infrastructural aspects of sociocultural systems. Moral values, religious beliefs, and aesthetic standards are in one sense the most significant and most distinctly human of all our attributes. Their importance is clearly evident. The issue that cultural materialism addresses is why a particular human population has one set of values, beliefs, and aesthetic standards, whereas others have both similar and different sets of values, beliefs, and aesthetic standards. Cultural materialists hold that cultural differences and similarities in general arise from infrastructural similarities and differences (see the Appendix for a discussion of alternative theoretical approaches in anthropology).

Summary

1. Cultures as defined in this book consist of socially acquired ways, or traditions of thought, feeling, and behavior. *Enculturation*

2. Cultures maintain continuity by means of the process of enculturation. In studying cultural differences, one must guard against the habit of mind called *ethnocentrism,* which arises from a failure to appreciate the far-reaching effects of enculturation on human life. Enculturation, however, cannot explain how and why cultures change.

3. Not all cultural recurrences in different generations result from enculturation. Some result from reactions to similar conditions or situations.

4. Whereas enculturation denotes the process by which culture is transmitted from one generation to the next, diffusion denotes the process by which culture is transmitted from one society to another. Diffusion, like enculturation, is not automatic and cannot stand alone as an explanatory principle. Neighboring societies can have both highly similar as well as highly dissimilar cultures.

5. Anthropologists use many kinds of methods for studying cultures, but they are best known for participant observation. Unlike other social animals, which possess only rudimentary cultures, human beings can describe their thoughts and behavior from their own point of view.

6. In studying human cultures, therefore, one must make explicit whether it is the native partici-
emic → Native
etic → observer
pant's point of view or the observer's point of view that is being expressed. These are the emic and etic points of view, respectively.

7. Both mental and behavioral aspects of culture can be approached from either the emic or etic point of view. Emic and etic versions of reality sometimes differ markedly; but usually correspond to some degree.

8. All cultures share a universal pattern. The universal pattern as defined in this book consists of three main components: infrastructure, structure, and superstructure. These components in turn consist, respectively, of the modes of production and reproduction, the domestic and political economy, and the creative, expressive, aesthetic, and intellectual aspects of human life. Such categories are essential for the organization of research and differ according to the research strategy one adopts.

9. Anthropology encompasses many alternative research strategies; the one followed in this book is cultural materialism. The aim of this strategy is to discover the causes of the differences and similarities in thought and behavior that characterize particular human populations.

10. Cultural materialists regard infrastructure as the key to understanding the evolution of sociocultural systems. This does not mean, however, that structure and superstructure are less important or less essential for human social life.

infrastructure → tace

KEY TERMS

cultural materialism
cultural relativism
culture
diffusion
emics
enculturation
ethnocentrism
etics
infrastructure → *production & reproduction*
participant observation
science
society
structure
subculture
superstructure
universal pattern

QUESTIONS TO THINK ABOUT

1. Why is it important to distinguish between behavioral and ideological aspects of culture?

2. Why do anthropologists use the viewpoint of cultural relativism to understand cultures that are different from our own?

3. What does it mean to say that "all research is biased?" How can science try to overcome culture bound biases?

4. Why is it important to distinguish between emic and etic perspectives when describing cultural phenomena?

5. Why does cultural materialism attempt to explain the probable causes of sociocultural differences and similarities by giving causal priority to infrastructure (the mode of production and reproduction)?

6. Under what conditions are ideological innovations most likely to cause changes in other sectors that will be retained over time?

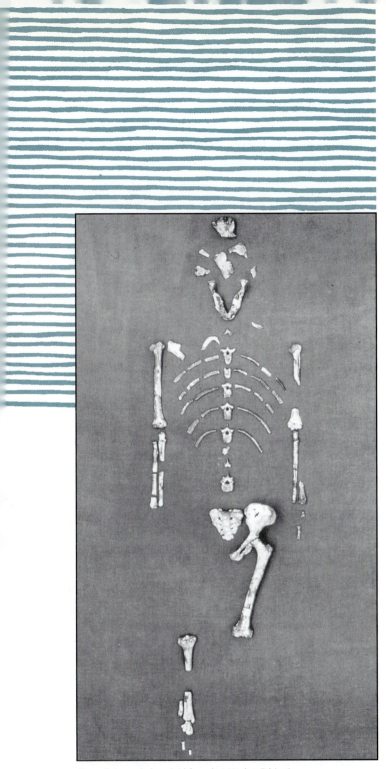

"Lucy." An early hominid found at Hadar, Ethiopia.

CHAPTER 3

The Evolution of the Capacity for Culture

Genes and Natural Selection
Natural Selection and the "Struggle for Survival"
Natural Selection and Behavior

Nonhuman Culture
Tools and Learning
Is It Culture?

The Evolution of the Hominids
Cultural Takeoff

Apes and Language

Aggressive versus Cooperative Behaviors Among Apes

Summary

America Now: Attempts to Teach "Creation Science" in the Public Schools

Human culture consists of the patterned, socially acquired traditions of thought and behavior found in human societies. In this chapter we will explore the capacity for culture as it evolved from rudimentary beginnings among our apelike ancestors. Once these ancestors passed certain biological thresholds under the influence of natural selection, cultural behavior underwent its own form of evolution, resulting in an increasingly complex social life and an increasing dependence of human beings on cultural practices for survival. This leads to the question, How much capacity for culture exists among nonhuman species: To answer this question, we shall examine evidence for the use of tools and language among chimpanzees and other primates—the species that most resemble humans. A point to be emphasized is that the biological processes that account for biological evolution and the learning-based processes that account for cultural evolution are quite distinct even though biological evolution shaped the learning processes that made cultural "takeoff" possible.

Genes and Natural Selection

The principal process responsible for biological evolution is known as natural selection. Natural selection takes place because individual organisms reproduce at different rates and because every species confronts limits on the space, energy, and resources that it needs for reproduction. Natural selection alters the frequency and type of *genes*—the fundamental units of heredity—present in successive generations of a particular species.

The term **natural selection** refers to changes in the frequencies of certain genetic traits in populations due to the differential reproductive success among individuals.

The theory of natural selection is based on three basic postulates:

1. All species are capable of producing offspring at a faster rate than they can increase the food supply and other necessities of life.
2. Variation among organisms affects their ability to survive and reproduce.
3. This variation is genetically transmitted from parents to offspring. Advantageous traits that are inherited by offspring will become more common in the population, whereas less favorable traits will be passed on less frequently and will eventually disappear.

Over time, those organisms that can better survive and reproduce in a given environment will increase their reproductive success and will replace organisms that are less well adapted.

The term **reproductive success** refers to the number of offspring an individual rears to reproductive age.

Reproductive success is correlated with many kinds of traits such as the organism's ability to resist disease, to gain or hold territory more securely, to obtain energy in larger or more dependable amounts, or to reproduce more efficiently and dependably. Natural selection can increase the frequency of the favored *genotypes* (types of genes) in a few tens of generations. Individuals who possess favorable traits will contribute more offspring to the next generation, so that over time these traits will become more common in the population. The power of natural selection to raise the frequency of even a rare gene variant can be seen in the evolution of penicillin-resistant strains of bacteria. The variants conferring resistance are present in normal populations of bacteria but in only a small percentage of individuals. As a result of the differential reproductive success of such individuals in the presence of the antibiotic, however, the rare resistant genotype soon multiplies and becomes the most common genotype. So far medical science has been able to develop new antibiotics to take the place of the ones that have lost their effectiveness. But the race between the effects of natural selection and the ingenuity of medical science is a close one and full of potential danger for humankind.

Natural Selection and the "Struggle for Survival"

Charles Darwin and Alfred Wallace formulated the basic principles of how **organic evolution** could result from natural selection. Under the influence of the prevailing philosophy of economic competition, however, both Darwin and Wallace accepted Thomas Malthus's concept of a "struggle for survival" as the main source of selection for reproductive success. Thus, in the nineteenth century natural selection was pictured incorrectly as the direct struggle among individuals for scarce resources and sexual partners. Even more erroneously, it was interpreted as consisting of aggressive behaviors such as organisms of the same species preying on and destroying one another. Nothing in Darwin's theory, however, holds that successful competition for resources must necessarily consist of aggressive encounters.

Today, biologists recognize that natural selection favors cooperation within species as much as it favors competition.

Although within-species killing and competition sometimes do play a role in biological evolution, the factors promoting differential reproductive success do not necessarily relate to an organism's ability to destroy other members of its own population or to prevent them from obtaining nutrients, space, and mates.

In social species, the perpetuation of an individual's genes often depends as much on the reproductive success of its close relatives as on its own survival and reproduction. Many social insects even have "altruistic" sterile "castes" that assure their own genetic success by rearing the progeny of their fertile siblings. As we will see, primates, although capable of murderous violence, also perform complex altruistic behaviors that are beneficial to both their own reproductive success as well as that of close relatives.

Natural Selection and Behavior

Natural selection shapes not only anatomy and physiology, but also behavior. Traits are adaptive when they present a selective advantage in relation to a particular set of environmental circumstances. An adaptive strategy leads to biological or behavioral adjustments that are selected for because they contribute to improving the health, well-being, and reproductive success of the innovators.

The term **adaptation** refers to biological and cultural traits that improve opportunities for individuals of a population to survive, and reproduce.

Science recognizes that in every organism behavior is the outcome of a highly complex combination of factors resulting from the interaction between genes and environment. An organism behaves in a particular way because of its genetic makeup and the characteristics of its environment. Nevertheless, we can say that behaviors range from extremely stereotyped, inflexible responses that are determined by genetic factors, to those that are highly flexible and dependent on learning. For example, when they try to avoid a hungry bird, some species of fruit flies fly upward and others downward. Some wasps lay their eggs in a particular species of caterpillar and in none other. Genes also largely determine the mating rituals of fish, the web building of spiders, the feeding of queen bees by workers, and countless other behavioral expressions of drives and instincts characteristic of different animal species. These behaviors evolve as a result of copying errors (mutations) in the replication of genotypes. The wasp's preference for one species of caterpillar, for example, was an error that was selected for because it increased the wasp's reproductive success. Thus a new

pattern of behavior, based on a new genotype, became part of the wasp's instinctual program.

Although it is very useful for organisms to be equipped with a program of detailed behavioral responses encoded in their genes, there is another type of behavior that is not programmed in the genes and that has many advantages. This is behavior that is learned and programmed in the organism's neural network and brain. For example, seagulls learn to recognize and to follow fishing boats; they learn the location of fast-food restaurants, town dumps, and other sources of garbage; and they learn all these behaviors without a single change in their genotype. Although the ability to learn to locate novel foods is genetically encoded, the behavior itself is not encoded in the genes or the genes of their offspring. Future generations of seagulls can acquire this knowledge only by learning on their own.

The ability to acquire new patterns of behavior through learning is a fundamental feature of all multicelled animals.

The capacity for learning has been widely selected for because it leads to a more flexible and opportunistic pattern of behavior than instinctual programs. Learning enables individuals to adjust to or take advantage of novel opportunities (such as feeding on french fries spilled in parking lots) without having to wait for the appearance and selection of mutations.

Nonhuman Culture

Selection for increased learning capacity set the stage for the emergence of culture.

The capacity for learning has depended on the evolution of larger and more complex brains and of more intelligent species. The great evolutionary novelty of culture is that capabilities and habits are acquired through *learning*, which is socially transmitted, rather than through the more ancient process of biological heredity. (It must be stressed, though, that actual cultural responses always depend in part on genetically predetermined capacities and predispositions.)

Many animals possess learned traditions that are passed on from one generation to the next and that can be thought of as rudimentary forms of culture. As we shall see in a moment, chimpanzees and other primates possess rudimentary learned traditions. However, only among the *hominids* (members of the human family) has culture become as important a source of adaptive behavior as biological evolution based on changes in gene frequencies. Able to stand and walk erect, their hands freed entirely from locomotor and support functions, the earliest hominids probably manufactured, transported, and made effective use of tools as a primary means of subsistence. Apes, in contrast, survive nicely with only the barest inventory of tools. Hominids, ancient or modern, have probably always depended on culture for their very existence.

Tools and Learning

Experimental approaches to behavior show that most birds and mammals and especially monkeys and apes are intelligent enough to learn to make and use simple tools under laboratory conditions. Under natural free-ranging conditions, however, the capacity to make and use tools is expressed less frequently. As a result of the process of natural selection, they have become adapted to their environment through such body parts as snouts, claws, teeth, hooves, and fangs.

Although primates are intelligent enough to make and use tools, their anatomy and normal mode of existence disincline them to develop extensive tool-using traditions.

Among monkeys and apes, the use of hands for tool use is inhibited by the importance of the forelimbs in walking, running, and climbing. That is probably why the most common tool-using behavior among many species of monkeys and apes is repelling intruders with a barrage of nuts, pine cones, branches, fruits, feces, or stones. Throwing such objects entails only a momentary loss of the ability to run or climb away if danger threatens.

Among free-ranging monkeys and apes, the most accomplished tool user is the chimpanzee. Over a pe-riod of many years, Jane Goodall and her associates have studied the behavior of a single population of free-ranging common chimpanzees in the Gombe National Park in Tanzania. They have discovered that the chimpanzees "fish" for ants and termites. Fishing for termites involves first breaking off a twig or a vine, stripping it of leaves and side branches, and then locating a suitable termite nest. Such a nest is as hard as concrete and impenetrable except for certain thinly covered tunnel entrances. The chimpanzee scratches away the thin covering and inserts the twig. The termites inside bite the end of the twig, and the chimpanzee pulls it out and licks off the termites clinging to it. Especially impressive is the fact that the chimpanzees will prepare the twig first and then carry it in their mouths from nest to nest while looking for a suitable tunnel entrance (Goodall 1986).

"Anting" provides an interesting variation on this theme. The Gombe chimps "fish" for a species of aggressive nomadic driver ant that can inflict a painful bite. On finding the temporary subterranean nest of these ants, the chimps make a tool out of a green twig and insert it into the nest entrance. Hundreds of fierce ants swarm up the twig to repel the invader. "The chimpanzee watches their progress and when the ants have almost reached its hand, the tool is quickly withdrawn. In a split second the opposite hand rapidly sweeps the length of the tool catching the ants in a jumbled mass between thumb and forefinger. These are then popped into the open, waiting mouth in one bite and chewed furiously" (McGrew et al. 1979:278)

In addition, chimpanzees can manufacture "sponges" for sopping up water from an inaccessible hollow in a tree. They strip a handful of leaves from a twig, put

Jane Goodall

Making friends with chimps Prof and Pax in Gombe National Park, Tanzania.

the leaves in their mouth, chew briefly, put the mass of leaves in the water, let them soak, put the leaves to their mouths, and suck the water off. A similar sponge is employed to dry their fur, to wipe off sticky substances, and to clean the bottoms of chimpanzee babies. Gombe chimpanzees also use sticks as levers and digging tools to pry ant nests off trees and to widen the entrance of subterranean beehives.

Observers in other parts of Africa report similar types of behavior—variants of fishing for ants, dipping for termites, and digging up insect nests or prying them loose. They have watched chimpanzees pound or hammer tough-skinned fruit, seeds, and nuts with sticks and stones. The chimps of the Tai forest of the Ivory Coast open the hard shells of the panda nut with rocks that serve as hammers. They search the forest floor for a suitable hammer stone, which may weigh anywhere from 1 to 40 pounds. Then they bring the stones back in the crook of their arm, hobbling on one arm and two legs, from as far as 600 feet. They place the nuts on thick tree roots or exposed rock that serve as anvils and skillfully pound away (Boesch and Boesch 1984, 1991; Whitesides 1985). In West Senegal, chimps use stone hammers to pound open the fruits of the baobab tree (Bermejo et al. 1989).

Inspired by these and other feats of chimpanzee ingenuity, Nicholas Toth and Kathy Schick of the University of Indiana have been teaching a chimpanzee named Kanzi how to make stone tools (Gibbons 1991; Savage-Rumbaugh and Levin 1994). Ultimately, Toth and Schick hope that Kanzi will teach his fellow chimps to do the same. (See section headed "Apes and Language" for more about Kanzi.)

Is It Culture?

There appears to be no specific genetic information that is responsible for chimpanzee termiting and anting. True, for this behavior to occur, genetically determined capacities for learning, for manipulating objects, and for omnivorous eating must be present in the young chimpanzee. But these general biological capacities and predispositions cannot explain termiting and anting. Given nothing but groups of young chimpanzees, twigs, and termite nests, termiting and anting are unlikely to occur on their own. Thus, although chimpanzees acquire complex skills such as anting and termiting, they have only a rudimentary form of culture.

Unlike humans, chimps and other social animals do not experience continuous cultural change. Their cultures remain rudimentary and do not evolve.

Extensive studies of nonhuman culture have been carried out with Japanese macaques. Primatologists of the Primate Research Institute of Kyoto University have found a variety of customs among macaques that are based on social learning. They have even observed the process by which behavioral innovations spread from individual to individual and become part of a monkey troop's culture independently of genetic transmission.

To attract monkeys near the shore for easier observation, Kyoto researchers set sweet potatoes on the beach. One day a young female began to wash the sand from the sweet potatoes by plunging them in a small brook that ran through the beach. This washing behavior spread throughout the group. Nine years later, 80 to 90 percent of the animals were washing their sweet potatoes, some in the brook, others in the sea (Itani 1961; Itani and Nishimura 1973; Miyadi 1967).

The limitation of primate learning is that it generally does not allow for the development of cumulative knowledge or complex culture. New behaviors such as potato washing are simple enough to be learned independently, through trial and error, by each macaque and it takes a long time for the behavior to spread through the group. It is unlikely that a macaque from one group could teach macaques from another group, where they have not been exposed to the same conditions, to wash potatoes. Primate learned behavior is individually acquired through a process of trial and error that leads to successful discovery (Tomasello 1994; Galef 1992).

Japanese Monkey Culture
A female monkey of Koshima troop washing a sweet potato.

Primates can be inspired by others to learn new behavior but they learn on their own, without **deliberate teaching** by others.

Jane Goodall (1971:161) describes young chimpanzees as they learn tool use techniques to "fish for termites." They learn through trial and error; each chimp invents the technique anew as his interest is drawn to the activity. At about 18 to 22 months they begin to termite on their own. At first their behavior is clumsy and inefficient. Novices often retrieve discarded sticks and attempt to use them on their own. They become proficient at termiting when they are about 3 years old. Fishing for ants, with the risk of being bitten, takes longer to learn; the youngest chimp to achieve proficiency was about 4 years old (McGrew 1977:282).

The conclusion that anting is a learned cultural trait is strengthened by the fact that chimps at other sites do not exploit driver ants even though the species is widely distributed throughout Africa. At the same time, other groups of chimps do exploit other species of ants and in ways that differ from the Gombe tradition. For example, chimps in the Mahale mountains 170 kilometers south of Gombe insert twigs and bark into the nests of tree-dwelling ants, which Gombe chimps ignore (Nishida 1987; McGrew 1992). Similarly, there is cultural variation in tool use. Throughout the area chimpanzees sometimes peel the bark from the twigs or vines they use for termiting; in some locations they then discard the bark, whereas at Gombe, after they peel the twigs or vines, they use the bark itself as a tool for termiting (McGrew et al. 1979).

Chimpanzee Termiting
A stick carefully stripped of leaves is inserted into the nest. The chimpanzee licks off the termites that cling to the stick when it is withdrawn.

People who are skeptical about the existence of nonhuman culture claim that "Culture is what humans do." Yet if we are willing to define culture more broadly as, "group behavior that is acquired, at least in part, from social influences," then we can say that culture is present in nonhuman species (McGrew 1998). There is little evidence for teaching in nonhuman primates. But much human learning also takes place without systematic instruction (see Box 3.1).

Box 3.1   Chimpanzee Culture

If we compare the British with Americans, we find differences in dialect, cuisine, and the way people drive. Similarly, chimpanzees display different behavior patterns that vary at different locations.

- Some chimpanzees fish for ants with short sticks, eating their prey off the stick one by one, whereas others use a more efficient technique of accumulating many ants on a long wand and then sweep the ants into their mouths with a single motion.

- Some chimps mop their brows with leaves; others raise their arms while companions groom them.

- In Tanzania, chimps at Gombe routinely use sticks to probe the ground for termites, but chimps 100 miles away in the Mahale mountains do not.

- Gombe chimps don't use stones to crack nuts, even though their terrain is strewn with rocks. But Tai rain forest chimps in the Ivory Coast use stone tools even though rocks are scarce.

- At Tai, grooming chimps wipe parasites on their forearms before mashing them with their forefingers. At Gombe, groomers mash parasites on a leaf.

- Courting styles also exhibit variation, just as they do among humans. In some places, the males knock on tree trunks to attract a female's attention; in other locales, they swing vegetation around.

In a synthesis of several researchers' observations (ranging over 8–38 years), primatologists report that our closest cousins display what was long thought to be a uniquely human attribute: cultural variation. These findings offer the most detailed evidence yet that nonhuman animals can pick up behaviors and then convey them to others. This means that chimpanzees learn from one another, in contrast to inheriting behaviors through genetics.

All in all, researchers have found 39 different behavior patterns, including tool usage, grooming, and courtship behaviors that are customary in some communities but not in others. Primatologist Frans de Waal says the evidence is overwhelming that chimpanzees have a remarkable ability to invent new customs and technologies, and they pass these on socially. So far, there is almost no evidence of chimpanzees teaching each other and only thin evidence of chimpanzees learning by imitation. Goodall has observed wild female chimps imitating their mothers by playing with their infants the same

way their mothers played with them. She has also seen young males imitating adult males in clanging empty fuel cans to make themselves seem more fierce. But in laboratory experiments chimps have failed to mimic precise procedures. For example, chimps have failed to imitate flipping a rake to make it a more efficient tool for raking bananas. It is therefore still unclear to what extent chimps learn by imitation or if they pick up behavior through ingenuity. If a young chimp sees his mother using a stick to fish out termites, he may then go find a stick and is likely to figure out how to use the tool on his own.

(Adapted from Whitten, Goodall, McGrew, Nishida, Renolds, Suguuuyama, Tutin, Wrangham and Boesch 1999, and de Waal 1999)

The Evolution of the Hominids

The ancestral line leading to the appearance of human beings separated from the line leading to chimpanzees, our closest (genetically similar) nonhuman relatives, more than 5 million years ago (mya). Fossils (mineralized bones) indicate that by 2.0 mya, there were at least two different kinds of **hominids** in Africa. Both of these hominids were bipedal (walked upright) and are associated with early tool use. One group, called the **australopithecines**, was the more ancient of the two. The other kind of hominid, known as early **Homo habilis**, includes a number of species such as *Homo habilis* and *Homo erectus* found in Africa and Eurasia with a substantially bigger brain size than australopithecines. This hominid group, was probably the one from which modern humans descended. Experts generally agree that the australopithecines including the well-known *Australopithecus afarensis* known as "Lucy" became extinct without contributing to the modern human genome (genetic pattern). But the experts do not agree on which of the brainier species should be included among the direct ancestors of modern human beings. This disagreement results from the number of new hominid fossils that are being discovered in Africa. The search for what used to be called "the missing link" has led to an unexpected proliferation of contenders for that role. A newly discovered species found in the Afar desert of Ethiopia has been named *Australopithecus garhi* ("garhi" means surprise in the Afar language). A. garhi is believed to be a possible link between the more apelike australopithecines and the more evolved Homo genus (see Figure 3.1 on page 32) (Asfaw et al. 1999). However, the presentation of any one family tree as a definitive rendition of human ancestry is still ill advised. But the abundance of early hominid fossils and their evolution toward modern human anatomical characteristics leaves no room for doubt that our species evolved from hominid ancestors during the past one or two million years.

The fossil record suggests that the first hominids were not initially selected for their braininess, but for the peculiar upright gait (**bipedalism**). In fact, we classify the australopithecines as hominids because

The Handy Chimp
This bonobo has been taught to make stone tools similar to those made by H. habilis.

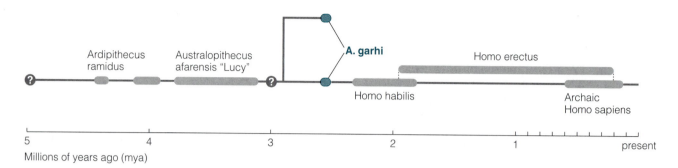

Figure 3.1   A Possible New Link in Human Ancestry

Australopithecus garhi found between 1996 and 1998 in Afar Ethiopia is a possible candidate for being a direct ancestor of humans.

their limbs were almost completely adapted to walking upright, and there are 3-million-year-old footprints that prove this.

Why bipedalism was selected for is still a matter of debate, but it is clear that once hands were no longer needed for walking or running, more use could be made of tools than was possible for monkeys and apes. Bipedal creatures could manufacture and carry tools such as clubs, digging sticks, stone hammers, and knives without lessening their ability to explore, move about, and flee from danger.

Much controversy also surrounds the question of where the final transition to fully modern types of **Homo sapiens** took place. One theory, called the "out of Africa" or single-origin theory, is that modern humans evolved from archaic humans between 200,000 and 150,000 years ago in Africa and from there spread out into the rest of the Old World, replacing the local archaic populations (Stringer 1992). The other theory, known as "the multiple-origins theory" (Frayer et al. 1993; Wolpoff and Caspari 1997) is that local archaic *Homo sapiens* evolved into modern *Homo sapiens* in parallel sequences that occurred at more or less the same time in several regions of the Old World, between 150,000 and 100,000 years ago.

Cultural Takeoff

At about 45,000 years ago, culture entered a period of "cultural takeoff." In the next 10,000 years the cultures of western Eurasia changed more than they had during the previous million years. Technological and artistic creativity greatly increased, signifying the emergence of the first culture that observers today would recognize as fully human, marked as they were by unceasing invention and variety (Bar-Yosef and Vandermeersch 1993:94).

Prior to this time, cultural and biological evolution seem to have occurred at comparable rates. There is little evidence of substantial technological or material innovation during the million years prior to 45,000 years ago, and cultural and biological changes seem to have been tied together. After cultural takeoff, the rate of **cultural evolution** increased dramatically without any concurrent increase in the rate of human biological evolution. The occurrence of cultural takeoff justifies the contention of most anthropologists that to understand the last 40,000 years of the evolution of culture, primary emphasis must be given to cultural rather than biological processes. Natural selection and biological evolution lie at the base of culture, but once the capacity for culture became fully developed, a vast number of cultural differences and similarities could arise and disappear entirely independently of changes in genotypes.

Closely linked with the capacity for cultural behavior is the uniquely human capacity for language

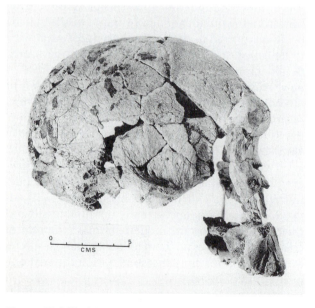

Homo Habilis (KNM-ER 1470)

This skull may be 2.0 million years old, and its volume is greater than that of the australopithecines living at the same time.

A.

B.

Japanese Monkeys Washing Wheat
A. Members of Koshima troop separating wheat from sand by placing mixture in water.
B. Central figure carrying the mixture in its left hand. Two monkeys in foreground are floating the wheat and picking it up.

and for language-assisted systems of thought. Although other primates use complex signal systems to facilitate social life, modern human languages are qualitatively different from all other animal communication systems. Most or all of our distinctly human traits, including our large brains, were probably established well before the development of language. The unique features of modern human languages (to be discussed in Chapter 4) undoubtedly arise from genetic adaptations related to both the development of the larynx and increasing dependence on social cooperation in culturally acquired modes of subsistence.

My Ambition in Life Is to Become Part of the Fossil Record.
Copyright © Patrick Kelly

The anatomy of the larynx makes "takeoff" possible by enabling humans to exert fine control over spoken sounds.

Scientists believe that modern human infants are born with the kind of neural circuitry that makes learning to talk as natural for them as learning to walk (Bickerton 1990; Pinker 1994). This circuitry in turn represents the kind of mental "wiring" useful for a species that needs to acquire and transmit large amounts of new information during its lifetime. Note, however, that no one knows for sure when fully modern forms of languages were acquired by our hominid ancestors, or what was the sequence of development.

One way to sum up the special characteristics of human language is to say that we have achieved "semantic universality" (Greenberg 1968). A communication system that has **semantic universality** can convey information about aspects, domains, properties, places, or events in the past, present, or future, whether actual or possible, real or imaginary, near or far.

Apes and Language

In recent years, a revolutionary series of studies has revealed that the gap between human and ape language capacities is not as great as had previously been supposed. Yet these same experiments have shown that innate species-specific factors prevent this gap from being closed.

Many futile attempts had been made to teach chimpanzees to speak in human fashion before it was found that the vocal tract of apes cannot make the sounds necessary for human speech.

Attention has shifted toward trying to teach apes to use sign languages and to read and write. Chimpanzees and gorillas trained in laboratory settings have acquired communication skills that far exceed those of animals in the wild. Experiments with a chimpanzee named Washoe soon demonstrated that apes could learn to communicate in Ameslan (American Sign Language). Washoe used sign language productively; that is, she combined the signs in novel ways to send many different messages. For example, she first learned how to sign the request "open" with a particular closed door and later spontaneously extended its use beyond the initial training context to all closed doors, then to closed containers such as the refrigerator, cupboards, drawers, briefcases, boxes, and jars. When Susan, a research assistant, stepped on Washoe's doll, Washoe had many ways to tell her what was on her mind: "Up Susan; Susan up; mine please up; gimme baby; please shoe; more mine; up please; please up; more up; baby down; shoe up; baby up; please move up" (Gardner and Gardner 1971, 1975).

Koko, a female gorilla trained by Francine Patterson, has acquired a vocabulary of 300 Ameslan words. Koko signed "finger bracelet" for ring, "white tiger" for zebra, and "eye hat" for mask. Koko also learned to talk about her inner feelings, signaling happiness, sadness, fear, and shame (Hill 1978:98–99).

A remarkable achievement of more recent studies is the demonstration that signing chimpanzees can pass on their signing skills as a cultural tradition to

Kanzi

nonsigning chimpanzees without human mediation. Loulis, a 10-month-old chimp whose mother had been incapacitated by a medical experiment, was presented to Washoe, whose baby had died. Washoe adopted the infant and promptly began to sign to him. By 36 months, Loulis was using twenty-eight signs that he had learned from Washoe. After about 5 years of learning to sign from Washoe and two other signing chimps, but not from humans, Loulis had acquired the use of fifty-five signs. Washoe, Loulis, and other signing chimps regularly used their sign language to communicate with each other even when humans were not present. These "conversations," as recorded on remote videotape, occurred from 118 to 659 times a month (Fouts and Fouts 1985, 1989:301).

But it is Kanzi, the pygmy chimpanzee genius who has learned to make stone tools (see section "Tools and Learning") who has captured everybody's attention. Without training, Kanzi has developed a true comprehension of 150 spoken English words. Like a human child, Kanzi acquired his comprehension of spoken words merely by listening to the conversations that surrounded him from infancy on (Savage-Rumbaugh and Levin 1994:247ff.). With the help of a keyboard and voice synthesizer, Kanzi can carry on extensive conversations in English. Every precaution has been taken in testing Kanzi's comprehension of symbols to make sure that no unconscious prompting or scoring bias has been introduced by his guardian teachers. (See Box 3.2.)

A vast gap still remains between the language performances of humans and apes.

Koko and Francine Patterson

Kanzi's comprehension of spoken English has led to a variety of tests of his understanding of vocabulary and syntax. In a vocabulary test, Kanzi listened to words presented over earphones and had to match them with one of three pictures presented to him. The person testing him could neither hear the word nor see the pictures that were presented. He responded correctly at 75 percent or better performance to 149 of the 194 words presented with natural speech and 103 of 150 words produced by a speech synthesizer that had no intonation. When 24 pairs of similarly sounding words were presented (orange–onion or shot–shirt), Kanzi correctly discriminated among 21 of the pairs. In a recent comprehension test, Kanzi was presented with more than 700 novel commands asking him to do things with objects or people in a way he had never done before. These novel sentences were presented by an experimenter who was out of sight, and the responses were evaluated by observers wearing headphones playing music so that they could not hear the commands. Kanzi responded correctly on more than 90 percent of these trials, indicating an ability to understand the symbolic referents of the words and the way in which the relationship between words was encoded by syntax. Because each sentence was novel, there is no possibility that rote learning accounts for the results. (Snowden, 1990:221–222.)

Despite all the effort being expended on teaching apes to communicate, none has acquired the linguistic skills we take for granted in 3-year-old children. Still, what all these experiments have shown is that natural selection could easily have given rise to the human capacity for semantic universality by selecting for intellectual skills already present in rudimentary form among our apelike hominid ancestors (Lieberman 1991; Parker 1985:622; Savage-Rumbaugh 1987; Snowdon 1990).

Aggressive versus Cooperative Behaviors Among Apes

Many researchers believe that chimpanzees display little aggression and conflict because they have stable dominance hierarchies. Such hierarchies result in predictable relationships that establish priority in gaining access to resources. More recent research, however, shows that violence and aggression may develop in chimpanzee communities despite dominance hierarchies. Jane Goodall and her colleagues witnessed several unprovoked and extremely violent attacks by groups of chimpanzees on lone neighboring chimpanzees. The killings occurred after members of an original group split off from the community and moved into another area of the Gombe National Park. Within a three-year period, the original group attacked and killed most of the members of the splinter group, who had denied them access to part of their former home range. Before the discovery of lethal, unprovoked aggression in chimpanzees, it was believed that only humans, among primates, were capable of killing over territory. Manson and Wrangham (1991) propose that these similarities between chimpanzees and humans indicate a common evolutionary background that is based on common socioecological conditions. While dominance hierarchies eliminate the need for escalated aggression, raiding and killing are common in a few primate species, but are rare in most. (See Boxes 3.3 and 3.4 on page 36.)

The capacities for aggression and peacemaking are both part of our biological heritage.

Chimpanzees also have the capacity for cooperation. They live in stable social groups and rely heavily on cooperative coalitions that define the status of members. Sociability is a costly arrangement, however, because animals who live in groups face greater competition for resources. Still, certain benefits com-

Rhesus monkeys sometimes react aggressively when they meet members of neighboring groups. Here mothers from two groups carrying babies attached to their bellies comfort each other.

Box 3.3   Chimpanzee Aggression

Chimpanzee social groups, called "communities," are composed of a number of semisolitary females with their dependent offspring along with adult males and subadult males. Lethal raiding occurs when a subgroup of males, sometimes accompanied by one or two females, carries out a "border patrol" into the overlap zone between two communities' ranges. If they encounter two or more adult males, the intruders retreat. But if they encounter a lone male, an estrous (in "heat") female, or a consorting male–female pair, the invaders may stalk the victim(s) and launch an attack. Five attacks observed by Jane Goodall all led to deaths. In each attack the animals coordinated their offensive behavior and the attack lasted for about ten minutes. The victims were held down, hit, dragged, bitten, and stamped on. The aggression was less severe toward females in estrous; sometimes they were forced to travel with their captors and transfer as potential mates to a new group (Manson and Wrangham, 1991:370–371; Goodall, 1986).

Box 3.4   Nonviolent Chimpanzees

Casting some doubt on an evolutionary predilection for violence and aggression is evidence from the bonobo, a species of chimpanzee that show remarkable suppression of personal violence. Bonobos are a peace-loving, love-making alternative to the violent chimpanzee. Bonobos have far fewer aggressive encounters over dominance, mating, and food sharing. In remarkable contrast to chimpanzee aggression, when members of different bonobo communities meet, they engage in communicative and "friendly" gestures. Bonobos also use sex to make friends, to calm someone who is tense, and as a way for community members to become reconciled after aggression (Wrangham and Peterson 1997:213). During an encounter in 1986 between members of different communities, females were the ones to initiate friendly gestures. At first it was a standoff, but gradually individuals sat down within a few yards of each other, separated by a sort of demilitarized zone. After 30 minutes of this strange truce, a female crossed the ground and had hoka–hoka (genital–genital rubbing, known as GG rubbing) with a female from the other community. For the next two hours, the two parties fed and rested together, almost as if they were members of a single community, with only the mature males keeping their social boundaries (Wrangham and Peterson 1997:214).

pensate for these costs. Two plausible theories about the benefits of sociability are

- Living in groups enables primates to defend their access to limited food resources.

- Grouping provides an effective means of reducing vulnerability to predators.

It appears that to minimize social disruption, monkeys and apes have developed methods for peaceful coexistence. Frans De Waal (1996) describes several tension-reducing behaviors that appear shortly after conflict has subsided. The most common gestures of reconciliation include reassuring and calming behavior that is remarkably similar to human gestures. These include extending an arm, a pat on the back, grinning, and mouth-to-mouth kissing. Among the highly sexual bonobos, reconciliation typically involves genital stimulation and invitations for sexual contact. Other conciliatory gestures include grooming, lipsmacking, embracing, and clasping of haunches. If two male rivals remain in the same proximity without physically reuniting, an adult female may initiate grooming contact with one of the two and subsequently try to bring the two former rivals together. These mechanisms regulate tension and contribute to the overall peacemaking behaviors of the group.

Summary

1. The human capacity for culture is a product of natural selection. Natural selection alters the frequencies of certain genotypes in a population through differential reproductive success but it is not synonymous with a struggle for survival between individuals. Fitness in humans results as often from cooperation and altruism as from struggle and competition.

2. Both anatomical and behavioral traits are shaped by natural selection and encoded in the genes. However, learning is a process of behavioral change that is entirely different from the behavioral change induced by natural selection. Learning permits organisms to adjust to or take advantage of novel contingencies and opportunities independently of genetic changes and is the basis of cultural traditions.

3. Although the capacity for acquiring traditions is shaped by natural selection and took off only with

the evolution of brainier species, culture is encoded in the brain, not in the genes.

4. Cultural behavior such as toolmaking and tool use occurs in many nonhuman species, especially monkeys and great apes. Yet even among monkeys and great apes, tool-using traditions remain rudimentary. One reason for this is that monkeys and apes use their forelimbs for walking and hence cannot readily carry tools.

5. Learning among monkeys and apes is based on social facilitation (not teaching or observation and imitation). This kind of learning is not cumulative but based on behaviors that individuals are able to learn on their own.

6. Early hominids such as the australopithecine and early *Homo sapiens* had ape-sized brains but upright posture. The evolution of bipedalism set the pattern for further evolution of the human brain and the unique degree of human dependence on tool use and culture.

7. The human capacity for culture accelerated dramatically about 45,000 years ago when culture "took off." Vast numbers of traditions began to evolve at a rapid rate without any significant changes in the size of the brain. A vital ingredient in this takeoff was the development of the human capacity for semantic universality.

8. As shown by numerous experiments, chimpanzees, and gorillas can be taught to use signs. Compared with 3-year-old children, however, apes have only rudimentary capabilities for language.

9. Both competition and cooperation are part of our evolutionary heritage. Lethal male raiding, as seen among the chimpanzees of Gombe, and tension reduction behaviors found among the bonobos and other species have biological origins that show the capacity for violence as well as peacemaking.

AMERICA NOW

Attempts to Teach "Creation Science" in the Public Schools

Some religious groups in the United States have challenged the way biology is taught. These groups claim that evolution is just a theory and that it should be presented along with the theory of "creation science" based on a literal interpretation of the Bible. Creationists believe that all biological species were divinely created a few thousand years ago and that all civilization can be traced to the Middle East.

Creationists have been active in state legislatures, demanding "equal time" for teaching creationism alongside evolution. Although they have lost several court cases, because of the First Amendment's separation of church and state, creationists are using a new approach; they are substituting euphemisms that sound less religious, such as "intelligent design theory" or "alternatives to evolution." The unfortunate consequence is that some teachers have elected to escape the political "controversy" by not teaching evolution at all (Jurmain et al. 1997:39–40).

It should be pointed out that labeling evolution as "theory, not fact," is partially correct. All scientific "facts," "theories," and "laws" are held provisionally and are subject to being overturned by new evidence, so it cannot be denied that evolutionism is theory, not fact. But the theories that scientists teach are those that have withstood rigorous testing and are supported by the greatest amount of evidence available. Creationist theory is not acceptable as science because it has not withstood rigorous testing and is contradicted by an enormous amount of evidence. No student should be prevented from reading about scientifically discredited theories, but no teacher should be compelled to teach every theory that has ever been proposed. There are still people who believe that the earth is flat (Berra 1990; Spuhler 1985; Numbers 1993).

KEY TERMS

adaptation
australopithecines
bipedalism
cultural evolution
cultural takeoff
deliberate teaching
hominids
Homo habilis
Homo sapiens
natural selection
organic evolution
reproductive success
semantic universality

QUESTIONS TO THINK ABOUT

1. What is the difference between biological and cultural adaptation? What role does each play in human evolution?

2. What is the basis for the claim that nonhuman primates have the capacity for culture? What are the limitations on primate acquisition of complex culture?

3. What is cultural takeoff, and how was it facilitated by semantic universality?

4. How is the capacity for aggression and peacemaking part of our biological heritage?

Linguistic diversity is common in many nations.

CHAPTER 4

Language and Culture

Universal Features of Language
Semantic Universality

Structural Linguistics: Elements of Language Analysis
Phonetics and Phones
Phonemics and Phonemes
Morphemes
Syntax

Biological and Cultural Aspects of Language
Language and Symbolic Representation

Language Issues and Theories
Innate Grammatical Knowledge
The Coevolution of Language and the Brain
Are There Superior and Inferior Languages?
Language, Thought, and Causality
Linguistic Naming Categories
Language and Consciousness

Sociolinguistics
Language, Social Class, and Ethnicity
AAVE in the Public Domain
PROFILE: African-American Vernacular English (AAVE)
Code Switching
Obligatory Sexism
Linguistic Change

Summary

America Now: The Five Present Tenses of Ebonics

Language serves an instrumental role in coordinating infrastructural, structural and superstructural activities and thus belongs to all three domains. Moreover, communication is the basis from which emic structure and superstructure are built. This chapter begins by describing the design features of language that make semantic universality possible. We then review the basic analytic concepts that are employed in formal linguistics (also called *structural linguistics*), which is the systematic study of language. We then move on to questions directly relevant to anthropological linguistics, such as the relative value and efficiency of different languages, the effect of language on culture, the relationship between language and gender, and the extent to which different languages are associated with different ways of seeing and understanding the world. Another issue to be discussed is the universal occurrence of change in a language's features. Ultimately, all languages are "corruptions" of parent languages, as we shall see from an examination of the processes responsible for linguistic change. A remarkable feature of languages is that they maintain their structural coherence through centuries of change without native speakers being aware of the changes taking place.

Universal Features of Language

In the last chapter we saw that although animals can communicate, there are fundamental differences between animal and human communication. Among humans, cultural takeoff coincided with linguistic takeoff.

The acquisition of language is an instrumental force in the creation of increasingly complex social activity.

Language is the medium by which ideas, inventions, and memories outlive individuals and generations. Linguistic competence makes it possible to formulate rules for appropriate behavior for situations that are remote in space and time. Language allows individuals within and across generations to replicate activities and maintain social traditions. Conversely, language also facilitates social change. And as people invent new patterns of social activity, they invent corresponding rules to fit the new practices. These rules are stored in the brain and passed on through language. With verbal-rule–governed behavior, humans easily surpass all other species in the complexity and diversity of social roles and in the formation of complex cooperative groups.

Semantic Universality

Semantic universality is a unique aspect of human communication. It refers to the communicative power of language—the fact that humans are able to convey information relevant to all aspects of experience and thought.

By carefully studying language, linguists have determined that all human languages have the same potential for effective communication because they share the same fundamental properties. Semantic universality is achieved through three distinctive features: productivity, displacement, and arbitrariness (Hockett and Ascher 1964).

- The term **productivity** refers to the infinite capacity of human language to create new messages—never before uttered—to convey information about an infinite number of subjects in greater and greater detail. Animals, in contrast, cannot efficiently increase the amount of detailed information they convey when they increase the length of their utterances. For example, with a characteristic call a gibbon can communicate "Danger." By screaming, or by repeating the message several times the gibbon can even emphasize the degree of danger, but this does not increase the information conveyed in the message. In contrast, the productivity of the human language makes it possible to convey specific and detailed information. We can say, "Be careful . . . there is movement over there . . . in the acacia tree . . . I think it is a leopard."

- The term **displacement** refers to the ability to send or receive a message without direct sensory contact with the conditions or events to which the message refers. Among animals, vocalizations or sounds are closely tied to specific types of stimuli. Thus a growl is made as a warning only when there is a direct perceived threat. Humans have no difficulty communicating information about displaced domains. We can talk about past events long after they have taken place, as well as future events and imaginary events. Displacement is the feature we have in mind when we refer to human language as having the capacity to convey "abstract information." Some of the greatest glories of human life—including poetry, literature, and science—depend on displacement, but so too do our most shameful achievements: lies and false promises.

- The term **arbitrariness** refers to the fact that there is seldom a connection between the abstract symbols employed by humans and the events and properties they signify. There is no inherent physical reason why "water" signifies clear liquid constituted of H_2O molecules. Human language is constructed out of sounds whose physical shape and meaning are not programmed in our genes. There are no genes that make English speakers say "water" and Spanish speakers say *"agua."* Animal communication, in contrast, consists of genetically stereotyped signals and decoding behavior, such as when dogs emit chemical signals as a sign of sexual receptivity or chimpanzees use facial expressions or hand gestures that are recognized by all members of their species. Among humans, sound units can be combined arbitrarily, so that people can refer to objects by different words. Because the assignment of meaning to sound is arbitrary, sounds are not tied to what they refer to, and therefore become flexible units of meaning (see discussion on language and symbolic thinking on p. 43).

Structural Linguistics: Elements of Language Analysis

As with other areas of scientific inquiry, linguists try to discover the underlying rules that govern language.

Linguists have discovered that although surface forms may differ, all human languages are composed of the same basic elements.

The following discussion gives a brief description of the components linguists have identified. These elements, taken as a whole are known as *grammar;* however, the "rules" of linguistic grammar differ from the prescriptive (do's and don'ts) of grammar taught in the classroom. An English teacher, for instance, would say the sentence "I are going to school" is incorrect grammatically, pointing out that standard English calls for a singular verb to match the singular subject "I." The structural linguist would only be interested in the facts that the sentence is understandable and that it contains a subject and verb. Linguistic grammar is therefore called descriptive, because it doesn't judge how a language should or should not be used; it describes how people talk.

Linguists describe how language is constructed, not proper usage.

Speaking and hearing language is an extraordinarily complex feat, but it is a largely unconscious process. We perceive language as a smooth, mostly continuous stream of sound and do not pay attention to the minute distinctions that make it comprehensible. The job of the linguist is to figure out the patterns

and rules that make the language work. As you will see, "unraveling" and segmenting language into individual units of analysis is a complex process. Like other scientific classification systems, structural linguistics breaks language down into hierarchical levels, which proceed from the smallest to broader, more inclusive categories. We begin here with the smallest unit, called a **phone**, and proceed to how sentences are formed and have meaning, which is called **syntax**.

Phonetics and Phones

Phonetics is the study of the phones or "individual" sounds that native speakers make.

The sounds used by languages differ from one another; phones that regularly occur in one language may not occur in another. For example, the "click" sounds that occur in several languages spoken in Africa and the sing-song tones of Chinese are not found in other languages. The smallest number of phones known in a natural language is 13 (Hawaiian), and English has between 35 and 40. No matter how many phones are used, human language can combine sounds to produce complex meanings. A repertory of only 10 phones, for example, can be combined to produce 10,000 words consisting of 4 phonemes (defined in the next section) each.

Linguists have identified all the phones in known languages. Because in most languages, pronunciation of the sound may differ depending on where it is positioned, linguists have developed an International Phonetic Alphabet (IPA), which consists of 81 symbols. For example, linguists would represent the "ph" of phone and the "f" in "farm" as [f] no matter what language they occur in. The IPA solves another problem in that it includes sounds not represented in most alphabets—such as the "click," which is shown by [!].

Phonetic sound patterns represent etic occurrences. They occur due to variations in the location of the tongue and lips and the stress, pitch and tone of the sound. They can be observed and identified in speech without having to question the speaker.

Phonemics and Phonemes

Phonemic differences are derived from patterns of sounds that are meaningful to native speakers.

Phonemes are units of sound (phones) that lack meaning in themselves, but they are the smallest sound *contrasts* that distinguish meaning. In English, the words "ban" and "van" mean different things. Yet the differences in sound between the two words are slight because the vocal mechanics involved in saying "b" and "v" are very similar. Because "b" and "v" make a difference in meaning, they are classified as phonemes in English. No two phones "naturally" contrast with each other. If we are able to distinguish one phone from another, it is only because as native speakers we have learned to accept and recognize certain phones and not others as being clearly distinguishable and contrastive. Although the phonemes /b/ and /v/ in the preceding example make a difference in meaning, for Spanish speakers this distinction does not exist and it is difficult for a native Spanish speaker to distinguish between the words "berry" and "very." Likewise, in Spanish there is a rolled "r," and a distinction is made between a short or long roll. Therefore, the words *pero* (the conjunction "but") and *perro* ("dog") are not readily detected by English speakers. Phonemes thus represent the fact that not all variations of a given sound result in differences of meaning. Another example makes this notion clearer: in English, the sound of "l" in "lake" is considered quite different from the sound of "r" in "rake"—the two sounds belong to different phonemes because they are *recognized as different* by English speakers. However, to Chinese the two sounds are not meaningful and do not appear to contrast with each other. English speakers laugh at "rots of ruck," yet do the same thing with "t" and "d" in the middle of a word when pronouncing the word "letter" as "ledder" instead using a crisply articulated [t].

The phonemic system—all the phonemes in a given language—thus consists of sets of phones that are arbitrarily but habitually perceived by the speakers as contrastive.

> It is native speakers who determine whether subtle contrastive differences between phones are phonemically significant or not.

Morphemes

The smallest part of an utterance that has a definite meaning is called a **morpheme**. A morpheme may consist of a single phoneme ("Oh?") or of strings of phonemes in different combinations and permutations. You may be asking yourself, "But isn't this the definition of a word?" and you would be partially correct. But if we examine words, we find that some are assembled from parts, each having meaning. For instance, the word "speaking" is really formed from two parts: the word "speak," and the suffix "-ing." Some morphemes can stand alone, whereas some can occur only in conjunction with other morphemes. "Hello," "stop," and "sheep" are called *free morphemes* because used by themselves, they can constitute the entirety of a well-formed (understandable) message. For example, to the question "Are those goats or sheep?" the answer "Sheep" constitutes a perfectly understandable message. In contrast, *bound morphemes* are embedded within words—such as the suffix /-ing/, the past-forming /-ed/ of "talked" or "looked" and the /-er/ of "speaker" or "singer." These and similar constructions are called *bound morphemes* because they can never constitute well-formed messages on their own. Words, then, are free morphemes or combinations of morphemes that can constitute well-formed messages. As a unit of analysis, morphemes are a useful comparative tool because languages vary widely in their reliance on free or bound morphemes. Chinese, for example, has many free morphemes, whereas Turkish has many bound morphemes.

The grammar of structural linguistics, as mentioned earlier, is not the same as the prescriptive rules for speaking English. Linguistic grammar has many facets: the rules for combining phonemes into morphemes (**morphology**) and the rules for combining morphemes into words and sentences (syntax), which will be discussed next. The existence of rules governing the formation of permitted sequences of phonemes is largely unconscious but can readily be seen in the reaction of speakers of English to common names in Polish such as "Zbigniew Brzezinski." English, unlike Polish, does not permit sound combinations such as "zb" and "brz." Similarly, speakers of English know by unconscious rule that the words "btop" and "ndak" cannot exist in English, because they involve prohibited sound combinations.

Syntax

Similar unconscious rules govern the combination of morphemes into sentences. This branch of grammar is called syntax. **Syntax** involves sentence structure and includes the construction of phrases and how words are ordered within the sentence. The unconscious rules of syntax arrange words into categories corresponding to basic features of the world—noun (things), verbs (actions, events), and adjectives (qualities), and govern the formation of sentences. They allow a listener to figure out what the speaker intended to report about the relationships among things, qualities, and actions. Native speakers can distinguish between grammatical and ungrammatical sentences even when they have never heard particular combinations before. Here is a classic example:

1. Colorless green ideas sleep furiously.
2. Furiously sleep ideas green colorless.

Most speakers of English will recognize sentence (1) as a grammatical utterance but reject (2) as ungrammatical even when both seem equally nonsensical. Still, native speakers can seldom state the rules governing the production of grammatical utterances. Even the difference between singular and plural nouns is hard to formulate as a conscious rule. Adding an "s" converts "cat" into "cats," and "slap" into "slaps," but something else happens in "house" when it turns into "houses" and yet another when "rose" changes to "roses" (try speaking these aloud to gain a sense of how the "s" varies in pronunciation). Three different variations of the same morpheme "s" has been used according to a complex rule that most native speakers of English cannot state, yet use with ease.

Biological and Cultural Aspects of Language

As we saw in Chapter 3, the capacity for language is the product of natural selection. We cannot reconstruct the detailed evolutionary history of language because there are no traces of human speech in the fossil record. Some scientists believe that language was fully developed several hundreds of thousands of years ago; others believe that it appeared as recently as 40,000 years ago. Scientists agree however, that language use resulted from and contributed to changes in the structure of the brain (see Pinker 1994:18).

Thus, although human language is part of culture, the capability that makes human language possible is the product of natural selection. The universal capacity for language is an evolved component of the human phenotype, similar to bipedalism and large molars. Language is a biological adaptation that allows speakers to modify the thoughts of their listeners. Boyd and Silk (1997) summarize the biologically adaptive properties of language in terms of universal cognitive capacities that allow people to communicate and compare them to writing, which is a cultural adaptation developed much later under conditions of greater technological and political complexity (see Box 4.1).

The invention of writing has had a profound impact on cultural development. Writing makes it possible for people to communicate across great distances in time and space. It enables people to accumulate knowledge far beyond what can be stored in the human brain, and it makes knowledge accessible without having to experience it directly. Jack Goody (1986) notes that written traditions have the capacity of articulating beliefs and interests in a semipermanent form that can expand their influence independently of political systems. Writing thus accentuates cultural differences, particularly class differences in stratified societies by contributing to the development of specialized knowledge that is not accessible to those who do not read or write. In terms of its impact on human cultural evolution, however, language has had by far the greater influence. No matter to which class a person belongs in a stratified society, whether they are literate or not, they will have the ability to speak a language.

Language and Symbolic Representation

Language is only one medium through which humans interpret, express, and transmit culture. The capacity for language is part of the more generalized human capacity for symbolically representing ob-

---

Box 4.1   Language and Writing

Language—A biological adaptation

- All societies have language.
- There is no correlation between grammatical complexity and social complexity (see p. 000). In fact, some societies with simple technology have highly complex and expressive languages.
- Most individuals within a society are fully competent language users.
- People do not have to be taught to speak. Particular spoken languages are cultural, but the capacity to learn to speak a language is not. Children learn without formal instruction, simply by being exposed to language.

Writing—A cultural adaptation

- Only a few societies developed written language.
- Technologically and politically sophisticated societies are more likely to have writing.
- Writing was invented in only a few places and then diffused to others. Until recently, only specialists such as teachers, priests, and scribes were literate.
- Unlike language acquisition, people have to be taught to read and write. Teaching children to read is difficult, whereas children learn to speak without help. (Adapted from Boyd and Silk 1997:502)

Symbols Communicate Complex Meaning

At the 1968 Olympics in Mexico City, gold medalist Tommie Smith and bronze medalist John Carlos give the Black Power salute during the playing of the National Anthem. They were barefoot, wore black gloves, and bowed their heads. They said that the clenched fists represented black strength and unity, the bare feet were reminders of black poverty, and the bowed heads showed that expressions of freedom in the National Anthem did not apply to African Americans.

jects, actions, and relationships. **Symbolic thought** occurs when a person simultaneously associates two or more complex ideas that evoke a reaction. The response to complex symbols is usually emotional and has meaning that most members of the culture understand. This is why people are intensely moved in the presence of culturally meaningful symbols, such as a war memorial or place of worship. Humans use complex symbols that represent associations not necessarily related to their referent (what the symbol stands for). For example, the clothes a person wears can symbolize class, occupation, sexual orientation, religion, or ethnicity.

- Several layers of symbolic meaning may be embedded in objects, words, or actions. A sports event, for example, can simultaneously represent several cultural ideals, such as team spirit, sportsmanship, courage, endurance, and defense of territory.

- The relationship between a symbol and its referent is arbitrary. Symbols are given meaning within their cultural context (for example, sacramental wine may be physically the same as table wine; it is considered sacred because it represents the blood of Christ).

- Symbols are capable of arousing passion and evoking thoughts and emotions that can lead to extreme behavioral responses, particularly when found within the context of political and religious structures.

The national flag is a common example of a symbol that has many associations such as unity, political loyalty, national pride, and a host of other emotionally provocative meanings. Its symbolic value has led to codified rules concerning how it should be placed and disposed of. Confrontations over its proper treatment have often resulted in violence and may even inspire people to sacrifice their lives. For many Americans, the famous statue of four soldiers struggling to raise the flag at Iwo Jima symbolizes this implicit understanding of what the flag symbolizes. Thus symbols are not mere substitutes for objects, but are vehicles for conceiving the meaning that the object has come to symbolize. As a public symbol, the flag is capable of evoking a response that can be mobilized into action; a protestor burning a flag may evoke an emotional response that can lead to aggressive and violent behavior of onlookers.

Language Issues and Theories

How is it possible for humans to create so many different messages and still be understood? No one is quite sure of the answer to this question.

Innate Grammatical Knowledge

One theory that explains how modern human beings acquired linguistic competency is proposed by Noam Chomsky. According to Chomsky (1973), human language is possible because of the existence of an **innate capacity for grammar.** Every utterance has a "surface" structure and a "deep" structure. Surface structures may be dissimilar—indeed, they often are—but the deep structure is the same. For example, "Meat and gravy are loved by lions" is superficially different from the sentence "Lions love meat and gravy," yet listeners understand their meaning to be the same. However, if we look at a third sentence, "Lions love meat and lions love gravy," we can see that the first two sentences are actually modeled from the information in it. Both are actually superficial transformations of the third sentence, which more closely reflects the deep, or underlying structure.

An essential feature of Chomsky's notion of grammar is that at the deepest levels, all human languages share an inborn species-specific structure that is "hard-wired" into neural circuitry.

According to Chomsky, the human brain contains a genetically transmitted blueprint for building words into sentences. It is the existence of this inborn structure that makes it possible for children to learn to speak at an early age and for adults to translate any human language into any other human language. Because of this hard-wired aspect, Chomsky's approach is called an *innatist,* or *rationalist,* explanation of the human capacity for language.

The Coevolution of Language and the Brain

Terrence Deacon challenges Chomsky's theory. He argues that language did not evolve as a result of "hard-wired," neural pathways responsible for a universal grammar; instead, language coevolved with an already developed brain structure for manipulating symbols. Deacon (1997) believes that the capacity to think symbolically preceded and then sparked the emergence of language. Symbolic communication was selected for because it was adaptive. "Somehow . . . our ancestors found a way to create and reproduce a simple system of symbols [which] quickly became indispensable'" (p. 45). The process of language evolution, like that of cultural evolution, was more rapid than biological evolutionary processes. Once humans surmounted the hurdle of complex symbolic thinking, language evolution took place, coevolving with other physical changes.

Deacon does not believe that the brain evolved specific neural circuitry for language, but that language processing evolved because the neural capacity for symbolic thinking was already in place.

Humans therefore were superb "hosts" for language because natural selection already laid the basis for increasingly efficient modes of concept formation and their linguistic expression.

Are There Superior and Inferior Languages?

Linguists of the nineteenth century were convinced that the languages of the world could be arranged in a hierarchical order. Europeans invariably awarded the prize for efficiency, elegance, and beauty to Latin, the mastery of whose grammar was long a precondition for scholarly success in the West. Linguists thought that languages spoken by contemporary "primitive" people were, in fact, intermediate between animal languages and modern civilized languages. They were forced to abandon this idea when they discovered that complexity of grammatical rules had no relationship to levels of technological and political development.

Simple human languages with limited vocabulary and grammar do not exist.

Although no language is logically superior to another, each speech community develops specific vocabulary that is equipped to express the ideas and experiences that are significant in its cultural context. For example, the Agta of the Philippines have thirty-one verbs meaning "to fish," each word referring to a particular type of fishing. Yet they lack a simple generic word meaning "to fish." In the Tupi languages spoken by Native Americans in Brazil, numerous words designate separate species of parrots, but no general word exists for parrot. Other languages lack words for specifics. They have separate words for numbers 1 through 5; thereafter, they simply rely on a word that means "many." Today linguists realize that the failure of a language to have a general or specific word has nothing to do with its evolutionary standing. It simply reflects culturally defined needs to be specific or general. The Agta, who depend on fish for much of their subsistence, never have any need to refer to fishing as a general activity; what is important to them are the specific ways fish can be obtained. Similarly, speakers of the language of preliterate societies need to know about the distinctive properties of plants. On average, they can name and identify 500 to 1,000 separate plant species, whereas the ordinary speakers of the languages of urban industrial societies can name only 50 to 100 such species. Not surprisingly, the urbanites do more lumping and get along with vague concepts such as *grass, tree, shrub, bush,* or *vine.* Speakers of languages that lack specific numbers beyond 5 also get along very well because they seldom have to be precise about large quantities. If an occasion arises when they have to be precise, they cope by repeating the largest term an appropriate number of times (Witowski and Brown 1978, 1985).

Language, Thought, and Causality

For many years, linguists have investigated to what extent languages influence how native speakers perceive and structure the world (Kay and Kempton 1984). At the center of this controversy are ideas set forth by Edward Sapir in 1929 and developed by Benjamin Whorf, known as the "linguistic relativity principle" or the **Sapir–Whorf hypothesis.** According to Whorf, when two language systems differ radically in their vocabularies and grammars, their speakers live in wholly different thought-worlds. The reasoning for this is that the experiences of native speakers of different languages are "filtered" through the grammars and categories of their respective languages. This "filter" has the effect of structuring the world in a particular way for its speakers. Thus, learning a new language causes a person to enter a new social reality based on the language habits of the group.

Box 4.2 ## There Are No "Primitive" Languages

Speakers in preliterate societies often lack specific words for colors. Lacking control over dyes and paints, they seldom need to be color conscious. But if the need arises, they can always adapt to the occasion by referring to "the color of the sky," or "the color of milk." Even parts of the body get named in conformity with the cultural need to refer to them. In the tropics, people don't wear much clothing, and they tend to speak languages that lump "hand" and "arm" under one term and "leg" and "foot" under another. People who live in colder climates and who wear special garments (gloves, boots, sleeves, pants, and so on) for different parts of the body more often have separate words for "hand" versus "arm" and for "foot" versus "leg." None of these differences therefore can be interpreted as evidence of a more primitive or intermediate phase of linguistic evolution. All of the three thousand or so languages spoken in the world today possess a common fundamental structure and need only minor changes in vocabulary to be equally efficient in storing, retrieving, and transmitting information and in organizing social behavior.

According to the Sapir–Whorf hypothesis, speakers of different languages will construct reality differently because language affects how individuals perceive reality.

Whorf believed that even such fundamental categories as space and time are experienced differently as a result of the linguistic "molds" that constrain thought. According to Whorf, English tense structures encourage English speakers to think of time as a divisible rod that starts in the past, passes through the present, and continues into the future—hence, the English language's past, present, and future tenses. Hopi grammar, however, does not locate events with reference to time; it has no equivalent of past, present, and future tenses. Does this mean that a Hopi cannot indicate that an event happened last month or that it is happening right now or that it will happen tomorrow? Of course not. But Whorf's point is that the English tense system makes it easier to measure time, and he postulated a causal connection between the tense system of Indo-European languages and the inclination of Euro-Americans to read timetables, make time payments, and punch time clocks.

Although language and thought are reflected in culture, it is incorrect to assume that language "causes" thought or that language "determines" culture.

Whorf's point of view implicitly distorts the fundamental causal relationships between language and culture. No one would deny that the absence of calendars, clocks, and timetables must have given preindustrial societies such as the Hopi an orientation to time very different from that of industrial-age societies. But we have no evidence to support the view that one kind of grammar rather than another facilitated industrialization or is responsible for the harried sense of time scarcity that comes with postindustrial existence and daily routines.

Linguistic Naming Categories

Whorf's idea that people who speak different languages see the world in fundamentally different ways has been tested in the domain of color categories. Some languages have separate terms only for brightness contrasts, such as those designated by black and white. Others have up to a dozen basic color terms. This difference would seem to indicate a highly relativistic or culture-specific form of color perception. Yet there is considerable evidence that even when their language contains only two or three basic terms, people actually tend to see the same parts of the color spectrum as those whose languages contain many color terms. When a language has only a few color words, distinctions can still be made by combining words (such as "pale red" for pink or "almost black" for gray) to describe colors that do not have separate color terms.

Berlin and Kay (1991) found definite regularities in the assignment of color terms in thirty different cultures. The number of basic color terms in a language increases with technological complexity—color terminology is most developed in languages where people have a history of using dyes and artificial coloring. Moreover, color terms tend to be added in a definite sequence. If a language is to have more than two basic categories, the third term will be red. If there is a fourth category, it will be either green or yellow; then yellow or green; then blue; then brown; and finally purple, pink, or orange (Berlin and Kay, 1991). Unfortunately we can find exceptions to this scheme, and the basic question of why different cultures have different color terms remains unresolved (Witowski and Brown 1978; Hewes 1992; MacLaury 1992; but see Agar 1994).

Is a language that has only two or three color terms at a disadvantage with respect to those that have a dozen or more? It seems unlikely, because one can always refer to additional colors by saying something is the color of some familiar object. In English, for example, orange was initially distinguished as that color found on the skin of oranges.

Language and Consciousness

Language and language change illustrate the remarkable forms that can emerge in human culture without the conscious design of the participants. As Alfred Kroeber pointed out,

> The unceasing processes of change in language are mainly unconscious or covert, or at least implicit. The results of the change may come to be recognized by speakers of the changing languages; the gradual act of change, and especially the causes, mostly happen without the speaker being aware of them. When a change has begun to creep in, it may be tacitly accepted or it may be observed and consciously resisted on the ground of being incorrect or vulgar or foreign. But the underlying motives of the objectors and the impulses of the innovator are likely to be equally unknown to themselves. (1948:245)

Sociolinguistics

As we have seen, structural linguistics concentrates on understanding the structure of language—the unconscious rules that predict how people in a society typically speak. Linguists have also taken a keen interest in the social context of language. Alessandro Duranti defines linguistic anthropology as "the study of language as a cultural resource and speaking as a cultural practice" (1997:2). Thus, anthropologists look at how language is used and what people do with it.

Sociolinguistics is concerned with how language is used in different social contexts and what it tells us about social relationships. Sociolinguistic data obtained in real-life social interactions provide important clues about structural and superstructural patterns such as status, class, and gender differences. Speakers may tailor their words for a particular audience. "Please lower your voice" and "Quiet down!" are linguistic options available for saying the same thing, in this case asking for less noise (Bonvillian 1997). Similarly, the way language is used in group activities such as storytelling reveals the dynamics of group membership; it displays patterns of deference and asymmetry, how gender is manifested, and how individuals are aligned within the group (Goodwin 1990).

Dialects may be used to create and maintain social boundaries between individuals in social groups. Groups maintain their identity through linguistic distinction. For example, the Native American Tewa of Arizona have had three centuries of contact with English, Spanish, and Hopi language speakers. Yet they continue to speak their ancient Tewa language, which marks their ethnic identity and maintains the social boundaries associated with Tewa traditions (Kroskrity, cited in Duranti 1997:76).

Sociolinguists who study gender differences have drawn attention to how men and women use language for different purposes; typically, women use language to establish closeness in private settings, whereas men use language competitively in public settings (Tannen 1990). Men and women not only have different conversational styles, but they also misinterpret each other's intentions. Daniel Maltz and Ruth Borker (1982) identify some of the ways American men and women come into conflict when they engage in casual conversation:

- Women use questions as a way to maintain a conversation, whereas men use them primarily as requests for information.

- Women explicitly acknowledge what has been said, whereas men do not refer to preceding comments and do pick up the conversation where they left off.

- Women discuss problems with one another to share experiences and offer assurances, whereas men hear women and other men who present them with problems as making explicit requests for solutions. Men respond by giving advice and act as experts.

Language, Social Class, and Ethnicity

It is not uncommon for certain linguistic styles and dialects to be considered inferior to others. Earlier we discussed language differences between cultures and saw that preliterate people with simple technologies do not have correspondingly simple languages. Here we will see that dialect differences within speech communities likewise do not reflect substandard or inferior language structure. Language superiority in complex stratified societies is associated with social and political motivations—specifically, maintaining the subordination of certain segments of society. Members of the elite strata often assert that the dialects of those in the lower strata are "substandard." This judgment has no basis in linguistic science. Labeling a dialect spoken by a segment of a larger speech

Gender Differences in Conversational Style
Men and women attach different meaning to what they say and are often frustrated in their conversations.

community substandard is a political rather than a linguistic phenomenon (Gal 1989). The demotion of dialects to inferior status can be understood only as part of the general process by which ruling groups attempt to maintain their dominant position (see Chapter 13). Linguistically, the phonology and grammar of the poor and uneducated classes are as efficient as those of the rich, educated, and powerful classes. This point should not be confused with the problem of functional vocabulary differences. Exploited and deprived groups often lack key specialized and technical words and concepts as a result of their limited educational experience. This lack constitutes a real handicap in competing for jobs but has nothing to do with the adequacy of the phonological and grammatical systems of working-class and ethnic dialects.

Well-intentioned educators often claim that poor inner-city children are reared in a "linguistically deprived" environment. In a classic study of the speech behavior of blacks in northern ghettos, William Labov (1972) showed that this belief reflects the ethnocentric prejudices of middle-class teachers and researchers rather than any deficit in the grammar or logical structure of the ghetto dialect.

The nonstandard English of the black ghetto, now called **African-American Vernacular English (AAVE**, also known as Ebonics, derived from "ebony" and

"phonics") contains certain features that are unacceptable in white, middle-class settings. Yet the use of these features in no way prevents or inhibits the expression of complex thoughts in concise and logically consistent patterns (see Profile 4.1 on page 48). The grammatical properties of AAVE are not haphazard and arbitrary variations of standard English. Nor is AAVE "bastardized English" or "fractured slang" as some have called it. On the contrary, it conforms to rules that produce regular differences with respect to the standard grammar and pronunciation. In fact, all languages, if they have enough speakers, have dialects—regional or social varieties that develop when people are separated by geographic or cultural boundaries. The language used by African Americans is not homogeneous but is characterized by heteroglossia (Box 4.3 on page 49). Many middle-class African Americans refuse to accept AAVE as representative of African-American culture, while others try to be "bicultural" by integrating AAVE with standard English (Morgan 1995). The use of AAVE is more common among the working class than the middle class, among adolescents than among the middle aged, and is generally used in informal contexts rather than formal ones (Rickford 1997). Nevertheless, linguists assert that AAVE is a systematic, rule-governed language and recognize its use as a marker of cultural identity.

AAVE in the Public Domain

Today many educators believe that using a child's "home" language in the classroom can speed the process of learning to read and write. There is widespread disagreement on the role that AAVE should have in the classroom. As AAVE has become recognized as an independent dialect, many teachers and parents have worried that any use of the children's home language in the classroom would interfere with their acquisition of Standard English.

In some cases educators have barred the "language experience" method of teaching reading, in which children learn to read stories they tell themselves. Other educators believe that children learn to read best when they start with their home language and make a gradual transition to standard English. On December 18, 1996, the school board of Oakland, California, initiated a national controversy through a resolution affirming that Americans of African descent spoke a distinct African language called Ebonics, which was not a dialect of English. (Shortly thereafter, this statement was modified to remove the implication that this language was a racial fact instead of a social fact.) The resolution provoked a

Profile 4.1   African-American Vernacular English (AAVE)

AAVE is an English dialect used by many African Americans in the United States, in familiar and informal settings. The term *vernacular* refers to the first form of language that a person learns to speak, one that is used among family and friends. Like other native languages and dialects, AAVE has a well-formed grammar that allows its speakers to express any logical statement or complex chain of reasoning.

Some linguists thought that African Americans in the southern states learned a nonstandard English from people who spoke other rural dialects, particularly Irish plantation workers. But as research progressed, scholars discovered that narratives told by former slaves lacked many features of contemporary AAVE, thus casting doubt on the theory that all these features originated among slaves. At the same time, linguists have found that many features of AAVE developed after rural blacks from the South moved to the large cities of the North from the 1930s onward.

AAVE has certain unique features:

- In indirect questions, AAVE preserves the order of a main question: "I asked him did he know."

- Modal auxiliaries such as *may, can,* and *might* often come in pairs, as they do in other southern dialects: "He might could do that."

- Double negatives occur more often in AAVE than in other dialects, often with inversion: "Can't nobody tell," "Don't nobody care."

- The absence of an *-s* on verbs in the third-person singular—as in "He walk home"—is a characteristic feature of AAVE, although speakers often pronounce the *-s* in formal speech.

Another typical features of AAVE is the grammatical use of *be* and *been* as a means of expressing a habitual action, as in "He be sayin' that" or "It don't be like that" (see p. 52). AAVE often lacks contracted forms of the verb *to be,* as in "He tired," but all speakers of AAVE occasionally use the full and contracted forms as well.

For example, the *be* in "He be doin' that" conveys the meaning that he habitually or usually does this, a meaning not present in "He doin' that." When *been* occurs before the verb, it indicates that the situation described has gone on for some time and still continues, as in "I been had that coat" or "It been busted." Similarly, *done* intensifies the verb it precedes, as in "You done done it now." Before the verb, *be done* can express the inevitability of a future result: "If you listen to them, you be done went batty."

Other features differentiate AAVE from mainstream English concern patterns of style and rhetoric, including

- Intricate patterns of ritual insults—known as *busting, woofing, sounding, chopping,* or *snapping*—which are not intended to be taken as true. For example, one person might put down another by saying, "Your mother plays dice with the midnight mice."

- Indirect ways of offering criticism called *signifying.* For example, a pregnant woman who swore she was not going to have more children, and now claimed to be just putting on a little weight, was told by her sister, "Now look here, we both be standing here soaking wet and you still trying to tell me it ain't raining."

- A form of mocking, sometimes called *marking,* which involves the precise imitation of another person's way of speaking.

The AAVE community has also developed elaborate patterns of excuse and pretense, known as *shucking* or *jiving.* For example, Eldridge Cleaver in his autobiography, describes how he dealt with a police officer after he ran a red light: Putting on a big smile, Cleaver explained that he thought he could make it but his old car was just too slow. Some observers have noted that when African Americans are most interested in what a speaker is saying, they frequently begin speaking themselves, rather than following the mainstream pattern of becoming silent. (Adapted from Labov 1972; 1973)

---

variety of reactions. Linguists agree that Ebonics is a dialect of English, although quite different from other dialects. But many linguists also agree that Ebonics serves a useful purpose in the classroom by calling attention to the importance of respecting a child's home language and of using that home language to speed the process of learning to read and write standard English.

Code Switching

Bilingual speakers often use another form of speech known as *code switching* (see Box 4.3), in which the speaker switches back and forth from one language to another during a conversation. Sometimes this is done mid-sentence, or sometimes when there is a change in subject. Code switching reflects a desire to retain an ethnic identity. As with AAVE, it is not haphazard

Box 4.3   Sociolinguistic Terms

Speech Community: Groups of people who speak the same language, and who share norms about the appropriate use of language.

Diglossia: Pattern of language use in a bilingual community, where two languages or dialects are used according to social circumstances.

Heteroglossia: The use of multiple "dialects" or language styles based on the social setting (such as formal, casual, professional) and social context (status and role relationships) of the speakers.

Code switching: The practice among multilingual speakers of selectively alternating between languages or dialects within a single conversational segment. For example, *Me voy* (I am going) *to the mall.*

Ethnography of speaking: The study of speech interaction in different cultures and of the interrelationships between language and other aspects of culture.

or "lazy" speech, but instead requires a thorough command of syntax in both languages and an ability to integrate them smoothly into a conversation. A unique example of code switching is found in New York among

Standard English Is Combined with AAVE to Establish Bicultural Identity.

The language features of African Americans are not homogeneous but vary according to class and social setting.

Puerto Rican Americans who speak "Nuyorican" (New York Puerto Rican), as they struggle to retain their identity while moving back and forth between Puerto Rico and the United States (Zentella 1990).

Obligatory Sexism

Languages differ in having certain obligatory categories built into their grammatical rules. English requires us to specify number. Speakers of the Romance languages must indicate the sex (gender) of all nouns. Certain Native American languages (for example, Kwakiutl) must indicate whether an object is near or far from the speaker and whether it is visible or invisible. These obligatory categories do not necessarily indicate any active psychological tendency to be obsessed with numbers, sex, or the location of people or objects. Still, grammatical conventions are not necessarily trivial either. Whorf's general hypothesis is correct when applied to some features of grammar. For example, certain obligatory categories in standard English seem to reflect a pervasive social bias in favor of male-centered viewpoints and activities. The traditional (although waning) use of the marriage announcement "I now pronounce you man and wife," which labels the man by his humanness and the woman by her relationship to him, is an example of such bias. Many nouns and pronouns that refer to human beings lack gender—*child, everybody, everyone, person, citizen, American.* However, teachers of standard English once prescribed masculine rather than feminine pronouns to refer to these words. Thus it was once considered "correct" to say, "Everyone must do his homework," even though the group being addressed consisted of both males and females. Newspaper columnists were fond of writing, "The average American is in love with his car." Obviously, a perfectly intelligible and sexually unbiased substitute is readily available in the plural possessive pronoun *their.* In fact, nowadays almost everybody uses the word *their* in their [sic] everyday conversation (Hill and Manheim 1992; Lakoff 1990).

Other male-centered conventions of the English language cannot be regarded as benign or trivial. The use of *him* and *he* as pronouns for God reflects the fact that men are the traditional priests of Judaism and Christianity. Feminists within the Catholic church regard the dominance of male gender categories in the Catholic liturgy as a major obstacle in their struggle to have women ordained as priests. It would be a mistake to blame gender hierarchy (to be discussed in Chapter 00) on obligatory linguistic categories; obligatory sexism in language is the consequence rather than the cause of male-biased religions.

Linguistic Change

Like all other parts of culture, language is constantly undergoing change. These changes result from slight phonological, morphemic, or grammatical variations. They are often identifiable at first as "dialect" differences, such as those that distinguish the speech of American Southerners from the speech of New Englanders. If New Englanders and Southerners were to move off to separate islands and lose all linguistic contact with each other and their homelands (no TV or radios), their speech would eventually cease to be mutually intelligible. The longer the separation, the less resemblances the languages would have.

Dialect formation and geographical isolation are responsible for much of the great diversity of languages. Many mutually unintelligible languages of today are "daughter" languages of a common "parent" language. This can be seen by the regular resemblances that languages display in their phonological features. For example, English *t* corresponds to German *z*, as in the following pairs of words:

tail	Zagel	tin	Zinn
tame	zahm	to	zu
tap	zapfen	toe	Zehe
ten	zehn	tooth	Zahn

These correspondences result from the fact that both English and German have a common parent language known as Proto-West Germanic.

In the 2,000 years that have elapsed since the Roman conquest of Western Europe, Latin has evolved into an entire family of languages, of which French, Italian, Portuguese, Rumanian, and Spanish are the principal representatives. If linguists did not know of the existence of Latin through the historical records, they would be obliged to postulate its existence on the basis of the sound correspondences among the Romance languages.

The anthropological linguist can see clearly that every contemporary spoken language is a transformed version of a dialect of an earlier language, and that even in the absence of written records, languages can be grouped together on the basis of their derivation from a common predecessor. Thus, in a more remote period, Proto-West Germanic was undifferentiated from a large number of languages, including the earliest forms of Latin, Hindi, Persian, Greek, Russian, and Gaelic, each of which is a member of the Indo-European family of languages. Inferences based on the similarities among the Indo-European languages have led linguists to reconstruct the sound system of the parent language from which they all ultimately derive. This language is called Proto–Indo-European (see Figure 4.1).

Many non–Indo-European languages spoken in Asia, Africa, and the Americas have also been shown to belong to linguistic superfamilies that originated in a single language thousands of years ago and were taken to their current territories by migrants (Renfrew 1994). The question that is now being debated among linguists is whether these protolanguages can

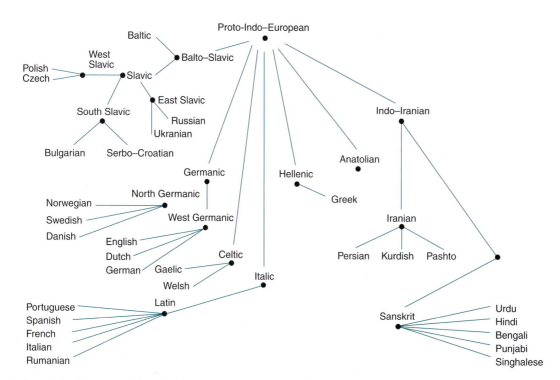

Figure 4.1   Indo-European Family of Languages

in turn be traced to a small number of still more ancient tongues—perhaps even to just one—the original language of the first anatomically modern humans (Ross 1991).

Languages may also change without any geographical separation of portions of a speech community. For example, within 1,000 years, English changed from Old English to its modern form as a result of shifts in pronunciation and the borrowing of words from other languages. The two languages today are mutually unintelligible. As these changes illustrate, Modern English can be regarded as a "corruption" of Old English. Indeed, all modern languages are corruptions of older ones. This does not prevent people from forming committees to save the "King's English" or to protect the "purity" of French.

Summary

1. The communicative power of language is due to semantic universality, which is enabled through three features: productivity, displacement, and arbitrariness.

2. Structural linguistics has identified universal patterns in language. Languages are based on etic sounds known as *phones*. The basic code elements, *phonemes,* consist of phones that are emically contrastive. Different languages have widely different repertories of phones and phonemes, neither of which conveys meaning in itself. The smallest units of meaningful sounds are called *morphemes*.

3. The ability to send and receive messages in a human language depends on the sharing of rules of grammar. There are two different aspects of grammar: morphology or rules for combining phonemes into morphemes and syntax or rules for combining morphemes into words and sentences. Knowledge of the rules of grammar makes it possible to produce completely novel utterances and yet be understood.

4. Human languages are part of cultures, but the capacity that makes human language possible is biological. All humans can speak language without being formally taught, whereas learning to write is not a universal human biological achievement.

5. Language ability, which consists of the ability to symbolize objects, actions, and relationships with words is an instrumental force in the transmission of culture but is not the only medium through which culture is transmitted. Humans also extend meaning to objects other than words. This is because language is part of a more general capacity for symbolic representation.

6. The capacity to manipulate complex symbols may have preceded language development. Humans endow virtually every aspect of the world with multiple layers of meaning. This is also a powerful means of communicating cultural practices, norms and beliefs.

7. Noam Chomsky, explaining how language speakers can produce and understand an infinite number of new sentences, states that all languages have a deep structure to which various superficially dissimilar utterances can be reduced. Novel sentences are transformations of these deep structures; at their core, all languages share an innate species-specific structure that is hard-wired in the brain. Terrence Deacon, in contrast, argues that language and the brain coevolved. The capacity for symbolic thinking was instrumental in the development of language.

8. All human languages are mutually translatable, and no one language has a more efficient grammar than the others. Grammars and vocabularies differ widely, but these differences do not indicate any inherent defect in a language or any intellectual inferiority of the speakers. General and specific categorizations as with numbers, plant classifications, and color terms, reflect the practical need for making general or specific distinctions under particular cultural and natural conditions. Moreover, the view that certain dialects of standard languages are "inferior" forms of speech reflects class and ethnic biases. Dialects such as African American Vernacular English do not in and of themselves inhibit clear and logical thought.

9. Attempts to show that linguistic differences determine how people think and behave in different cultures have not been successful. All humans, for example, probably have a similar set of perceptions of time and color differences despite the different ways in which their languages indicate time and color differences. Few, if any, correlations other than vocabulary can be shown between language and the major forms of demographic, technological, economic, ecological, domestic, political, and religious aspects of sociocultural systems.

10. Language is always found within a social and cultural context and studying language use can provide clues about structural and superstructural patterns within cultures. Sociolinguists study how language is used in different social situations, as well as the study of the other aspects of linguistics, that offer a glimpse into the unconscious processes that shape sociocultural systems.

11. Some dialects in complex speech communities are considered substandard. Such claims are based on political rather than linguistic grounds. Obligatory linguistic categories such as those concerned with gender may play a role in the maintenance of various forms of hierarchical relationships.

12. Languages, like all other aspects of culture, are constantly being changed as a result of both internal and external processes. Thus all languages are "corruptions" of earlier parent languages.

AMERICA NOW

The Five Present Tenses of Ebonics

Is Ebonics a different language from English or a different dialect of English? Linguists tend to sidestep such questions, noting that the answers can depend on historical and political considerations. For instance, spoken Cantonese and Mandarin are mutually unintelligible, but they are usually regarded as "dialects" of Chinese because their speakers use the same writing system and see themselves as part of a common Chinese tradition. By contrast, although Norwegian and Swedish are so similar that their speakers can generally understand each other, they are usually regarded as different languages because their speakers are citizens of different countries. As for Ebonics, most linguists agree that Ebonics is more of a dialect of English than a separate language, because it shares many words and other features with other informal varieties of American English. And its speakers can easily communicate with speakers of other American English dialects.

Yet Ebonics is one of the most distinctive varieties of American English, differing from standard English—the educated standard—in several ways. Consider, for instance, its verb tenses and aspects. ("Tense" refers to *when* an event occurs, "aspect" to *how* it occurs, whether habitual or ongoing.) When Toni Morrison referred to the "five present tenses" of Ebonics, she probably had usages such as these—each different from standard English—in mind:

1. He runnin. (He is running.)
2. He be runnin. (He is usually running.)
3. He be steady runnin. (He is usually running in an intensive, sustained manner.)
4. He bin runnin. (He has been running.)
5. He BIN runnin. (He has been running for a long time and still is.)

In standard English, the distinction between habitual or nonhabitual events can be expressed only with adverbs like "usually." Of course, there are also simple present tense forms, such as "he runs," for habitual events, but they do not carry the meaning of

an ongoing action, because they lack the *-ing* suffix. Note too that "bin" in example 4 is unstressed, whereas "BIN" in example 5 is stressed. The former can usually be understood by non-Ebonics speakers as equivalent to "has been" with the "has" deleted, but the stressed "BIN" form can be badly misunderstood. Years ago, I presented the Ebonics sentence "She BIN married" to 25 whites and 25 African Americans from various parts of the United States and asked them if they understood the speaker to be still married or not. While 23 of the African Americans said yes, only 8 of the whites gave the correct answer. (Adapted from John Rickford 1997)

KEY TERMS

African American Vernacular English (AAVE)
arbitrariness
code switching
diglossia
displacement
heteroglossia
innate capacity for grammar
morpheme
morphology
phone
phoneme
phonetics
productivity
Sapir-Whorf hypothesis
semantic universality
sociolinguistics
symbolic thought
syntax

QUESTIONS TO THINK ABOUT

1. Why do linguists describe how language is used in different social contexts?

2. In what ways is writing a cultural, not a biological, adaptation?

3. How does symbolic thinking affect human emotion and behavior?

4. What do linguists mean when they say, "There are no simple languages?"

5. How do new behavior patterns lead to the adoption of new vocabulary or speech patterns?

Production

Rice harvest in Bali, Indonesia.

Evolution of Energy Production

The Influence of the Environment and Ecology

Carrying Capacity and the Law of Diminishing Returns
Sustainability
Law of the Minimum
PROFILE: Hunters and Gatherers—The !Kung San
Depletion and New Modes of Production

Hunting and Gathering
PROFILE: Hunters and Gatherers—The Kwakiutl
Optimal Foraging Theory

Agriculture
Slash-and-Burn Agriculture
PROFILE: Slash-and-Burn Horticulture with Hunting and Gathering—The Machiguenga

PROFILE: Slash-and-Burn Horticulture with Domesticated Animals—The Tsembaga
The Problem of Meat
Agropastoralism or Mixed Farming
Irrigation Agriculture
PROFILE: Irrigation Agriculture—Luts'un

Pastoralism
PROFILE: Pastoralism—The Turkana

Energy and the Evolution of Culture

Industrial Food Energy Systems

Summary

America Now: Mode of Production

To provide a coherent framework for understanding the causes of sociocultural differences and similarities, we focus first on the principal varieties of infrastructures. In this chapter, we will be considering primarily the aspects of infrastructure that make up a society's mode of production. Moreover, the focus is on different modes of food production such as hunting and gathering, pastoralism, and preindustrial and industrial forms of agriculture. Cultures engage in many kinds of production besides food production (manufacturing tools, handicrafts, mining, and the like), but food production systems—the technology and practices used for expanding subsistence production—have been the main focus of productive effort throughout history and prehistory. We will use energy, measured in terms of caloric input and output, to look at how much energy is expended in producing food using different forms of technology under different environmental conditions. Although the intensification of production can lead to diminishing returns, diminishing returns can lead to new and more productive technologies. What, then, is the long-range result of technological innovation? The answer may surprise you.

Evolution of Energy Production

Human life and culture cannot exist unless societies capture and transform the energy available in the environment for the production of goods and services. The method of production and the amount of energy captured depend in turn on an interaction between the *energy-capturing technology* (how people apply human labor and technology to natural resources) and *the features of the environment* (such as sunlight, soils, forests, rainfall, or mineral deposits). Because neither technology nor the features of the environment can be changed limitlessly, a society's mode of energy production provides a powerful set of constraints and opportunities with regard to a people's entire way of life (Moran 1999; Price 1995).

During the time of the earliest hominids, all the energy that was used came from food. The first great step in the evolution of energy production was the use of fire. We do not know exactly when hominids began to use fire. Early hominids may have achieved partial control over fire, but full control may not have been achieved before the appearance of modern *Homo sapiens* (see Chapter 3, "Evolution of the Hominids"). Certainly by the time of cultural takeoff 40,000 years ago, fire was being used for cooking, warmth, protection against carnivores, driving game animals over cliffs or into ambushes, and possibly favoring the growth of desired plant species (Goudsblom 1992).

By 10,000 years ago, animals began to provide energy in the form of muscle power, harnessed first to sleds and then to plows and wheeled vehicles. At about the same time, humans began to use high-temperature charcoal fires, first for making ceramics and later for smelting and casting metals. We do not know with certainty when wind power was first used (probably to propel small canoes), but modern humans were sailing in large ships by the time the earliest states arose. Not until the medieval period in Europe was the energy in falling water tapped extensively. And only in the last 200 or 300 years have fossil fuels—coal, oil, and gas—come to dominate production.

New sources of energy have followed each other in a logical progression, with the mastery of later forms dependent on the mastery of earlier ones. In both the Old World and the New World, the sequence of inventions that led to metallurgy depended on the prior achievement of high-temperature wood fire ovens and furnaces for baking ceramics. In turn, the development of this technique depended on learning how to make and control wood fires in cooking and heating. Low-temperature metallurgical experience with copper and tin almost of necessity had to precede the use of high-temperature iron and steel. Mastery of iron and steel, in turn, had to precede the development of the mining machines that made feasible the large-scale use of coal, oil, and gas. Finally, the use of these fossil fuels spawned the Industrial Revolution, from which the technology for today's nuclear energy derives.

The dependence of later forms of technology on earlier forms acts as a powerful constraint on the evolution of sociocultural systems. This is not to say that all technological change has to occur in a single definite sequence throughout the world (Pfaffenberger 1992). The earliest known ceramics, for example, were figurines fired in special kilns 27,000 years ago in Czechoslovakia. Presumably, the artisans who made these small statues possessed sufficient knowledge to make pots. But ceramic pots are too heavy to be lugged from one campsite to another. Hence the full development of ceramic technology was put on hold until more sedentary villages developed toward the end of the last ice age. Similarly, the wheel was invented in pre-Columbian Mexico, but was used only as a toy, given the absence of appropriate domesticated traction animals and the prevalence of steep and rocky trails that were better managed by human bearers.

Throughout history, technological advances have steadily increased the average amount of energy available per person.

Infrastructure: Production

Nyinba Man with His Favorite Yak

Yaks are more rugged and better adapted to high altitude. They graze on mountain terrain and are used as pack animals.

Nyinba Man Milks a Cross Breed between a Cow and a Yak

Cross breeds provide better dairy products such as butter and cheese, and their hair is used to make tents. They are, however, sterile and do not reproduce.

Men Are Traders

Nyinba men travel over rough terrain to trade local salt for grain grown in the middle hills.

The Yanomami men of the village return from a five-day hunt to get meat for a village funeral-feast ceremony. On this occasion, thirty men hunting from morning to night for five days did not acquire enough game for the feast and had to go out again to a different locale. This is not uncommon.

Machiguenga women fishing with women's net. Women collect numerous sources of protein, including small fish and grubs.

A Yanomami man and his two young sons strip the peach palm fruit and store it in baskets to be boiled and distributed that day when a neighboring village arrives for a feast.

Machiguenga women preparing manioc beer. Boiled manioc is sifted through a trough and left to ferment for three days.

Yanomami women close in on drugged fish in a nearby stream. Bark from a tree has been stripped and put in the water, causing the fish to become stupefied and float to the surface. This is done only once or twice during the dry season, when the streams are quite shallow.

Chinese workers leaving terraced paddy fields in the evening.

Livestock provide energy-efficient traction for plowing fields in Indonesia.

A Vietnamese farmer irrigates his field with a foot-operated pump.

Nyinba women have several husbands but they do most of the agricultural work as exemplified by the woman on the left winnowing and this woman weeding.

Quechua women in Apurimac, Peru sorting atajo (a spinach-like vegetable) to be used as part of a ritual meal.

Quechua woman in Highland Peru sorting corn before storage.

The demand for increased investment in technology arises from the need to increase the range and quantity of food a population can produce in a given environment. As a population grows, it increases its need for production. To produce more food, a society must increase its per capita use of energy—by expending more per capita physical energy (working harder or longer hours) or harnessing energy from the natural environment (from draft animals, or **nonrenewable resources** such as irreplaceable fossil fuels). More technologically advanced cultures may harness more energy per capita but increased energy consumption does not mean a culture is better adapted, especially when the primary energy is based on **nonrenewable resources** or pollutes the environment.

Increased energy use does not necessarily bring a higher standard of living, nor does it mean that energy will be produced or used more efficiently.

Less "advanced" cultures may be better adapted to their environments than high-energy cultures, and social systems based on high energy consumption may seem more secure than they actually are. Many great civilizations have fallen in the midst of material plenty because they depended on a primary energy base that was not renewable.

The Influence of the Environment and Ecology

Humans learned to live in many different environments, ranging from deserts to tropical rain forests and arctic floes. People are able to live in these different environments through cultural adaptation; they select cultural patterns of behavior that best enable them to provide for their basic needs. For example, Inuit living in the Arctic where there is seasonal variation in game and fish, adapt to their environment by living in small nomadic groups linked by kinship and marriage, and by using technologies such as dogs and sleds for transportation. They schedule their movements, to adjust to the availability of resources in their environment. They have also developed extensive social ties that allow them to shift about in both short-term and long-term visits and to adjust the makeup of their groups according to the seasonal availability of resources.

Many strategies are used for coping with environmental problems. As we saw in Chapter 2, evolutionary theory emphasizes that individuals and groups adapt to their environments by making adjustments that increase their well being and the likelihood of

their survival. We would therefore expect individual acts and beliefs to respond to a broad range of environmental characteristics such as

- Fluctuations over time in the availability of resources
- Activities of other groups in competition for these resources
- Introduction of new technology that changes the way food is produced

Ecological anthropology sees the human population as an integral part of the ecosystem and focuses on human adaptation, including physiological, cultural, and behavioral relationships (Moran 1999; Wilson 1999).

Ecological anthropology is concerned with cultural and biological responses that affect or are affected by the survival, reproduction, and health and spatial distribution of human populations.

Ecosystems tend toward **homeostasis**—that is, they tend to resist change and remain in equilibrium (Odum 1971). Yet predictable patterns of change do take place. Change comes from a variety of sources that disrupt the ecosystem (Netting 1986). These include

- Climatic changes, such as those associated with drought or flooding, leading to migration, or internal conflict
- Technology that is transformed or replaced by more effective tools or by the diffusion of a new food crop
- Social organization that features new patterns of domestic organization or political institutions

Carrying Capacity and the Law of Diminishing Returns

The abundance of game, quality of soils, amounts of rainfall, and extent of forests, in combination with a particular form of technology, set an upper limit on the production of food and hence on the number of human beings who can live in a particular environment.

Carrying capacity is the upper limit on production and population in a given environment under a given technology, without degrading the resource base.

Note that for humans, carrying capacity must be defined relative to the given set of infrastructural and sociocultural conditions. If these conditions change—for example, as a result of deforestation or the introduction of new technologies—then carrying capacity will also change (J. Cohen 1995). Although carrying

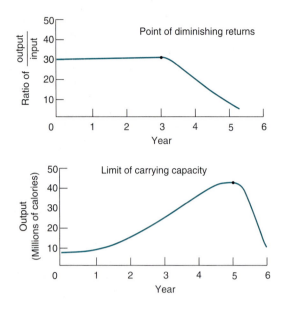

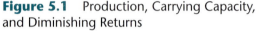

Figure 5.1 Production, Carrying Capacity, and Diminishing Returns

Point of diminishing return is reached in year 3, but limit of carrying capacity is reached in year 5. Production is intensified and continues to increase until year 5, then crashes.

capacity sets the upper limit to production and reproduction, most societies maintain their production and population below that limit.

To understand why this gap between carrying capacity and the actual level of food production and population occurs, we must identify another crucial feature of food production called the *point of diminishing returns* (Figure 5.1).

The **point of diminishing returns** is the point at which the amount of food produced per unit of effort begins to fall.

Slash-and-burn farmers, for example, bring on diminishing returns as they increase the number of years they consecutively plant in the same garden. They have to work harder in order to produce the same amount of food to maintain the same size population. The reason most food production systems maintain themselves below carrying capacity is that diminishing returns set in before carrying capacity is reached. No one willingly wants to work more for less. As a result, production and population will remain below carrying capacity.

However, unless population growth is also regulated, the temptation to maintain or even increase production will be very great. This can be done by in-

tensification, that is, by increasing the time and energy devoted to production.

Intensification refers to an increase in labor output (i.e., using more people, working longer hours or working faster), to produce greater yields without expanding the amount of land used.

Through intensification, a mode of production can be pushed far beyond the point of diminishing returns all the way to and beyond carrying capacity, thereby irreversibly damaging the resource base.

It is inevitable that intensification will lead to the depletion of nonrenewable resources.

The present condition of the ocean fisheries in many parts of the world illustrates what happens when production passes the point of diminishing returns. In general, the rate of return per unit of fishing effort has declined by almost half. And some local fisheries such as haddock in the Gulf of Maine have been completely destroyed (Brown et al. 1991; Royce 1987). Between 1950 and 1989, the annual world fish harvest increased from 22 to 100 million tons. This rise was made possible by intensifying fish production through the use of bigger boats, better electronic gear, bigger nets, spotter airplanes, and other technological advances. Since 1989, however, total production has leveled off, and production per capita has started to decline. Additional fisheries will soon collapse if these trends continue (Brown et al. 1994; Weber 1994).

Sustainability

In seeking to avoid depletions, environmentalists must consider the importance of maintaining production at a given level in order to feed and provide incomes for a particular population. This requirement has led to the concept of **maximum sustainable yield**, which may be defined as a level of production immediately prior to the point of diminishing return (Constanza 1991; National Research Council 1992). No one has yet demonstrated that **maximum sustainable yield** is a realistic goal for resource management. Indeed, some environmentalists flatly deny that scientists can reach a consensus on the maximum sustainable yield of any resource, and assert that resources throughout history and prehistory have often been overexploited (Ludwig et al. 1993:17; see Box 5.1).

Box 5.1   The Pristine Myth

The myth persists that in 1492 the Americas were a sparsely populated wilderness, "a world of barely perceptible human disturbance." There is substantial evidence, however, that the Native American landscape of the early sixteenth century was humanized landscape almost everywhere. Populations were large. Forest composition had been modified, grasslands had been created, wildlife disrupted, and erosion was severe in places. Earthworks, roads, fields, and settlements were ubiquitous (Denevan 1992:369).

Law of the Minimum

Environmental restraints on human food–energy systems are not always immediately apparent even to the expert. Extreme caution must be exercised before concluding that a particular culture could "easily" raise its total energy flow by increasing the size of its labor force or by increasing the amount of time put into food production. Allegations of untapped envi-

ronmental potential are especially dubious when based on short periods of observation. Many puzzling features of human ecosystems result from adaptations that are made to recurrent but infrequent ecological crises such as droughts, floods, frosts, hurricanes, and cyclical epidemics of animal and plant diseases.

A basic principle of ecological analysis states that communities of organisms adapt to the minimum life-sustaining conditions in their habitats rather than to the average conditions. One formulation of this principle is known as Liebig's *law of the minimum*: growth is limited by the minimum availability of any one necessary resource rather than by the abundance of all necessary resources. The short-term observer of human ecosystems is likely to see the average condition, not the extremes, and is likely to overlook the minimum factor when confronted with apparently unrestricted abundance. Liebig's law applies as well to seasonal minima such as the availability of water among the !Kung San (see Profile 5.1). As Richard W. Casteel (1975) has shown, the population of many subarctic North American hunters and gatherers was closely adjusted to the amount of fish available during the winter months rather than to land animals available throughout the year.

Profile 5.1   Hunters and Gatherers—The !Kung San

Location: The Kalahari desert of Botswana and Namibia in Africa

Production: Collecting mongongo nuts and plant foods and hunting wild game

Density: Less than 1 person per 10 square miles

Land Ownership: Communal; use rights acquired by belonging to the group

Time of Research: 1960s

The !Kung San (! designates a click sound; see Chapter 4, "Phonetics and Phones" section) are a hunter-gatherer people who live in the Kalahari Desert on both sides of the border between Botswana and Namibia in southern Africa. With at least two qualifications, they may be taken to represent the "simple" band-organized, mobile hunter-gatherers identified in Box 5.2. The first qualification is that the description that follows pertains to the way the !Kung lived in the 1960s. Since then, they have changed greatly and become involved in new commercial and political relationships. Although we will use the present tense, it should be understood as referring to

what anthropologists call the "ethnographic present"—how things were when the ethnographers did their fieldwork. The second qualification is that even before the 1960s, the !Kung had intermittently been more or less intensely involved with nearby groups of cattle-herding peoples with whom they traded and for whom they sometimes worked. Nonetheless, the !Kung of the 1960s practiced a way of life that was quite distinct from the cultures of their nearest neighbors in almost every respect (Lee 1993; Lee and Guenther 1991, 1995; Soloway and Lee 1990; Wilmsen and Denbow 1990).

Like most hunter-gatherers who inhabit sparse environments, the !Kung San move about a great deal from one camp to another in search of water, game, and wild plant foods. They build only temporary shelters and have few possessions, yet they are well nourished and moderately long-lived. As occurs almost universally among hunters and gatherers, !Kung San men specialize in hunting and !Kung San women specialize in gathering although, on occasion, women will bring small animals back to camp and men will help carry heavy loads of nuts.

(continued)

Profile 5.1   Hunters and Gatherers—The !Kung San *(continued)*

The number of people in a !Kung camp varies from 23 to 40, with an average camp size of 31 (20 adults and 11 children). During a four-week study period, Richard Lee (1979) calculated that 20 adults put in an average 2.4 days per week in hunting and gathering. On any particular day, the number of people hunting or gathering varied from zero to 16. About 71 percent of the calories consumed by a !Kung camp are provided by women's gathering activities. Women range widely throughout the countryside, walking about 2 to 12 miles a day round trip for a total of about 1500 miles a year each. On an average trip, each woman brings back from 15 to 33 pounds of nuts, berries, fruits, leafy greens, and roots, whose proportions vary from season to season.

Men hunt on the average only every 3 or 4 days and are successful only about 23 percent of the time they hunt. Hunting is therefore not an efficient source of energy for the !Kung. For every calorie (above basal metabolism) expended on hunting, only about 3 calories worth of meat was produced. Of the average total of about 2,355 calories consumed per person per day, meat provides about 29 percent, nuts and vegetables the rest. One nut in particular, the mongongo, alone accounts for about 58 percent of the !Kung caloric intake and a large share of protein as well.

Studies of the !Kung and similar band-organized hunter-gatherers have dispelled the notion that the hunting-gathering way of life, even in adverse environments, necessarily condemns people to a miserable hand-to-mouth existence, with starvation avoided only by dint of unremitting daily effort. About 10 percent of the !Kung are over 60 years of age (compared with 5 percent in countries such as Brazil and India), and medical examination shows them to be in good health. Judged by

!Kung Woman Gathers Mongango Nuts
The mongango is rich in protein and provides up to 58 percent of the calorie intake.

the relatively large quantity of meat and other sources of protein in their diet, their sound physical condition, and their abundant leisure, the !Kung San have a relatively high standard of living. The key to this situation is that their population is low in relation to the resources they exploit. They have fewer than one person per ten square miles on their land, and their production effort remains far below carrying capacity, with no appreciable intensification (except where they have become involved in raising livestock).

Depletion and New Modes of Production

What happens to a society when its modes of production are pushed beyond diminishing returns and into environmental collapse? Various scenarios may unfold: The people may migrate to a new habitat, or they may die off through hunger and disease.

In the past, environmental depletions have sometimes stimulated the adoption of new modes of production.

As suggested in the work of Ester Boserup (1965), when hunters and gatherers deplete their animals and plants, they are likely to begin to adopt a mode of production based on the domestication of animals and plants. When slash-and-burn agriculturalists deplete their forests, they may begin to cultivate permanent fields using animal fertilizer. And when rainfall agriculturalists using permanent fields deplete their soils, they may shift to irrigation agriculture. The shift from preindustrial to industrial and petrochemical forms of agriculture can also be seen as a response to depletions.

The depletion of ocean fish stocks illustrates this point. Aquaculture—the raising of fish in nets and ponds—is rapidly overtaking fishing in many parts of the world as a mode of fish production, just as agriculture and animal husbandry once replaced the hunting and gathering of terrestrial plants and animals. We have reason to believe, therefore, that if we deplete additional natural components of the industrial mode of production, new and still more productive infrastructures may yet arise. However, technology alone will never provide a long-term guarantee of high levels of production and consumption for the majority of human beings. No matter what the next mode of production may be, its increased efficiency will soon be strained to the limits if population growth is not checked. Ocean fisheries again provide an example of what we mean. Even though production increased from 22 to 100 million tons from 1950 to 1990, world population has been growing so fast that per capita production of fish has actually begun to decline (Brown et al. 1994:181).

Indeed, one might argue that the wisest course for humanity to follow in pursuit of affluence for all would be not only to prevent further growth of world population through family planning but also to promote gradual global population reduction by limiting each couple to one or two children. But how to impose so great a restriction on individual liberty without violating democratic principles remains an unsolved dilemma.

Hunting and Gathering

Hunting and gathering was the only mode of food production from the time of the first humans to about 12,000 years ago. Most of the living hunter-gatherers who have been studied by anthropologists or who are known through historical documents occupy regions that are unsuited for agriculture: the lands close to the Arctic Circle or deserts such as the interior of Aus-

tralia. Most of these hunter-gatherers are organized into small groups called *bands,* numbering from about 20 to 50 people. Bands consist of individual families who make camp together for periods ranging from a few days to several years before moving on to other campsites. Band life is essentially migratory; shelters are temporary and possessions are few. Yet hunters and gatherers are known for their relative "prosperity," leisure, and autonomy. When the !Kung San of Botswana were asked why they did not take up plant cultivation, they replied, "Why should we plant when there are so many mongongo nuts in the world?" (Lee 1968: 33). (See Profile 5.1).

One must be careful, however, not to overgeneralize about hunter-gatherers and their environments. Even in recent times, some hunter-gatherers lived in lush environments that provided the infrastructural basis for relatively complex sociocultural systems (Box 5.2). The hunter-gatherers who inhabited the coastal zones of the Pacific Northwest, an environment rich in fish, wild plants, and sea mammals, lived in permanent high-density villages during the winter months and then dispersed into small-family

!Kung Women Returning to Camp
They have been out gathering wild vegetables and are carrying digging sticks.

Box 5.2   Not All Hunter-Gatherers Are Alike

There are two main varieties of hunter-gatherer societies: simple and complex. The !Kung are an example of the simple variety, and the Kwakiutl are an example of the complex variety. Complex hunter-gatherers share many features in common with sedentary agricultural peoples. The major differences between the two varieties of hunter-gatherers are these:

Simple	Complex
Low-population density	High-population density
Not dependent on stored foods	Dependent on stored foods
Live in temporary camps	Live in villages most of the year
Weak distinctions of rank	Strong distinctions of rank
Sharing ethic	Sharing ethic weak
No ownership of resources	Family ownership of resources

(Hayden 1992; Keeley 1988; Testart 1982; Woodburn 1982a)

A.   B.

Hunters

A. Drawing a bow.   B. Returning from the hunt with a shotgun and a slain peccary. Animal protein is a major limiting factor in the Amazon. Today up to 80 percent of the game is killed by shotgun, further reducing the game population.

hunting and foraging groups during the early spring and summer (See Profile 5.2). Archaeological evidence from both Old and New Worlds indicates that in favorable environments, complex, sedentary vil- lagelike settlements long preceded the appearance of domesticated plants and animals. Thus anthropologists generally agree that recent band-organized hunter-gatherers cannot be regarded as typical of

Profile 5.2   Hunters and Gatherers—The Kwakiutl

Location: British Columbia, Canada
Subsistence: Nomadic fishing, hunting, gathering
Population Density: 2–4 persons per square mile
Time of Research: The late 1800s

The native societies of the Northwest Coast of North America possess an elaborate technology, an intensified mode of production and complex political organization that is considered atypical of hunter gatherer groups. A century ago, the Kwakiutl inhabited the dense forests along the western coast of Canada, abundant in large game animals and bird life, berry patches and a seacoast rich in a wide variety of marine life, most notably salmon and candlefish, which provide an abundant catch during their seasonal runs. Despite the high productivity of the natural ecosystem, the people expect and fear food scarcity. Although huge surpluses occur seasonably and in good years, there are unpredictable regional fluctuations in distribution. Food scarcity and even famines threaten survival during the winter months, when people live off the food they stored during the summer and fall.

The subsistence cycle is organized around the seasonal availability of resources. During the cold winter months, the Kwakiutl aggregate in large villages where they live mainly on the dried and smoked provisions accumulated during the summer and fall. This is a time for manufacturing and repairing canoes, tools, and clothing and for ceremonial feasting. In early spring, people move to the beaches for the great candlefish runs. Candlefish are rich in oil (it is said that if you stick a wick in a dried candlefish, it will burn like a candle) and they provide a valuable preservative and additive to dried foods. In late spring and summer people disperse into family groups, similar to those of the !Kung, to harvest wild food resources as they become available; to hunt, gather berries and collect shellfish. In August and September the salmon runs begin. This requires a heavy labor investment in catching and preserving the fish. In good years, large amounts of salmon are harvested without declining marginal productivity because for a short period there are more fish than can be harvested, as the salmon swim upriver to spawn. The fish then have to be processed—gutted, split lengthwise, and the backbone removed—then hung to dry or smoked. Households are able to store large quantities of oil, berries, and dried and smoked fish and game for the winter months. Storage, leads to differences in wealth, however, between individuals and communities—a precondition to social stratification, fierce warfare, and slavery (Johnson and Earle 1987; Kelly 1995; Donald 1997) hunter-gatherers of the remote past, when no agricul-turalists or pastoralists existed anywhere, and when every kind of habitat, dry or wet, cold or hot, bountiful or sparse, was available for occupation by hunter-gatherer peoples (Kelly 1995). (Not that hunter-gatherers were capable of sustaining themselves in every habitat. For example, the ability of human populations to subsist in tropical forests without planting food crops has been the subject of much recent debate; see Headland and Bailey 1991).

Optimal Foraging Theory

Despite their dependence on wild plants and animals, hunters and gatherers do not eat every edible species in their habitat. They pass up many edible plants and animals even when they encounter them while searching for food. Of some 262 species of animals known to the !Kung San, for example, only about 80 are eaten (Lee 1979:226). This pickiness also occurs among animals that, like human hunter-gatherers, must forage (search) for their food. To account for this selective behavior, ecologists have developed a set of principles known as *optimal foraging theory* (Box 5.3).

Optimal foraging theory predicts that hunters or collectors will pursue or harvest only those species that give them the maximum energy return for the time spent foraging.

At least one species will always be taken, namely, the one with the highest rate of energy return for each hour of "handling time"—time spent in pursuing, killing, collecting, carrying, preparing, and cooking the species after it is encountered. The foragers will take a second, third, or fourth species when they en-

Box 5.3   An Intuitive Explanation of Optimal Foraging

Imagine that you are in a forest in which some trees have a $1 bill and other trees have a $20 bill hanging from the topmost branches. Should you climb every money tree you come across, or should you climb only the $20 trees? The answer depends on how many $20 money trees there are. If there are a lot of them, it would be a mistake to climb $1 trees. On the other hand, no matter how scarce $20 trees might be, if you happened to find one, you would always stop to climb it.

counter it only if by doing so it raises the rate of caloric return for their total effort (Hawkes 1993; Hawkes et al. 1982; Smith and Winterhalder 1992). Of course, foragers do not actually measure how many calories they expend or obtain. But through repeated trial and error, they achieve a rather precise knowledge of whether it is worth their while to take a particular species. (If lions and wolves can develop this selective behavior, so can humans!)

Optimal foraging theory helps explain foraging strategies; foragers tend to maximize the time spent collecting food that has higher nutritional value. They will add items to their diets only as long as each new item increases (or does not diminish) the overall efficiency of their foraging activities.

This prediction is especially interesting with regard to the question of how the abundance of a food item, such as a food species, influences its position on or off the optimal diet list. Items that lower the overall rate of energy return will not be added to the list no matter how abundant they become. Only the abundance of the higher-ranked items influences the breadth of the list. As a high-ranking item becomes scarce, items previously too inefficient to be on the list get added. The reason for this is that the scarcity of the top-rated item means that more time must be spent before it is encountered. Therefore, the average rate of return for the whole list shifts downward so that it is no longer a waste of energy to stop for items that have a lower rate of caloric return (Hawkes et al. 1982). The theory helps explain why people on skimpy diets may pass up certain abundant food items, such as insects and earthworms, that have limited nutritional value; it is not the commonness or rarity of a food item that predicts whether it will be in the diet, but its contribution to the overall efficiency of food production.

A word of caution is needed here. Energetic efficiency is not the only factor determining the diet of human hunter-gatherers. Many other factors, such as the protein, fat, mineral, and vitamin composition of foods, may also determine which species are favored. But energetic efficiency is always an important consideration and is the factor that has thus far been measured most successfully by anthropologists.

Agriculture

Agriculture is the farming of domestic plants. Agricultural peoples tend to live in more permanent settlements than hunter-gatherers. But again, not all agricultural societies are alike. Many groups depend on a mixture of hunting and gathering and farming or stockraising. And, of course, many kinds of farming and stockraising exist, each with its own ecological and cultural implications. **Rainfall agriculture**, for example, utilizes naturally occurring showers as a source of moisture; **irrigation agriculture** depends on artificially constructed dams and ditches to bring water to the fields.

Several varieties of rainfall agriculture and irrigation agriculture, each with its own ecological and cultural implications, must also be distinguished. If rainfall agriculture is practiced, it is necessary to solve the problem of replenishing the nutrients washed away from the soil during successive planting of crops.

In irrigation agriculture, soil fertility is less problematic than in rainfall agriculture, because the irrigation water often contains silt and nutrients that are automatically deposited on the fields.

Irrigation agriculture varies greatly in type and scale (Hunt 1988; Price 1993). Some irrigation systems are confined to terraces on the walls of mountain valleys, as in the Philippines; others embrace the flood plains of great rivers such as the Nile and the Yellow.

Another form of irrigation involves mounding: Mud is scooped from shallow lakes and piled up to form ridges in which crops are planted, as in the misnamed "floating gardens" of Mexico. Throughout much of India, irrigation water is pulled up by oxen from deep brick-lined wells. More recently, India and other less industrialized nations have begun to rely on water that is pumped up by electric or gasoline-powered pumps through tube wells.

Slash-and-Burn Agriculture

Where rainfall agriculture is practiced, people face the perpetual problem of replenishing the nutrients taken from the soil by successive crops. One of the most ancient methods for solving this problem, still widely practiced to this day, is **slash-and-burn agriculture**—also known as shifting horticulture. With this method, a patch of forest is cut down and left to dry; then the vegetation is burned and crops are planted among the ashes, which contain a rich supply of nutrients.

Slash-and-burn farming requires large stretches of fallow land because long periods are necessary for the soil to be replenished.

Despite the lush vegetation of the tropics, the soil quality is poor because the heavy precipitation causes nutrients to filter deep into the soil (a process known as *leaching*), and it washes away the topsoil. In regions of heavy rainfall, a slash-and-burn garden cannot be

Planting in a Swidden (A Slash-and-Burn Garden)
This Machiguenga woman is planting tubers while nursing in a recently burned garden.

replanted for more than two or three seasons before the nutrients in the ashes become depleted. Slash-and-burn thus requires large amounts of land awaiting the regrowth of vegetation suitable for burning and planting.

Slash-and-burn agriculture produces high yields for relative low labor inputs.

The amount of labor input or energy expended per acre for slash and burn is much lower than for more intensive forms of farming, such as irrigation, hoe, or plow agriculture.

In the long run, slash-and-burn ecosystems use up a considerable amount of forest per capita, but in any particular year, only 5 percent of the total territory may actually be in production (Boserup 1965:31). Horticulturalists, such as the Machiguenga (Profile 5.3), who live in small hamlets of 15–30 people, remain in the same location for an average of 4 years until they have exhausted the best land. Then they build new houses within easy walking distance of new fields cut

Profile 5.3   Slash-and-Burn Horticulture with Hunting and Gathering—The Machiguenga

Location: Amazon headwaters of Peru

Subsistence: Slash-and-burn horticulture, hunting, gathering

Density: Less than 1 person per square mile

Time of Research: 1972–1973 and 1980

The Machiguenga (also known as Matsigenka) are tropical horticulturalists in southeastern Peru who live in small, scattered hamlets averaging 15–30 people. They live high in the rain forest, at a population density well below one person per square mile, where they practice slash-and-burn horticulture, hunt, and collect wild foods. Root crops such as manioc, yams and taro provide a surplus of starchy foods that are stored in the ground until needed. After being planted for one or two years, the fields are depleted of soil nutrients and become overgrown with weeds. Banana and papaya trees are left standing and the remaining manioc crop is left to lure wild game that is trapped or hunted on moonlit nights. After three years the entire garden is abandoned as it reverts to natural vegetation.

The Machiguenga are selective in choosing a location for a new garden. A central concern is to be near a good source of water, such as a stream that feeds into a river, and where the soil is soft and easy to cultivate. People are careful to avoid conflict over resources when new plots are staked out. They choose their sites well in advance to let their intentions be known. If no one objects and the land "clears title," then the process of cutting down forest begins. A general pattern is that the Machiguenga maintain "dual residence," moving back and forth while a new house is built and the garden starts producing (A. Johnson 2000).

About 10 percent of the diet consists of wild foods such as game, fish, and insects. Although only a small part of the diet, these represent foods rich in high-quality protein, fatty acids, and nutrients that are essential to nutritional well-being (A. Johnson 1989; Baksh 1984). The Machiguenga have adapted to the scarcity of wild game and fish by maintaining a dispersed population, with small widely scattered family groups that move to a new location about every three to five years.

Machiguenga households are capable of living alone for long periods. Husbands and wives are a complementary team that is self-sufficient in food production and manufacturing. The Machiguenga do not band together for defensive purposes or for hunting. In fact, individual families periodically leave their hamlets to camp out in "less crowded" areas where temporary shelters serve as "vacation homes" and wild food is more abundant. Or, when the river is low, families move down to the beach where fishing is easy. This pattern of dual residence also helps avoid disputes. People are afraid of confrontations and will disengage rather than risk violence. During the early 1900s the Machiguenga were able to survive the effects of Western diseases and forced labor capture on rubber plantations by escaping farther into the jungle, to live in isolated family households.

For slash-and-burn horticulturalists such as the Machiguenga, cooperation between households always has its costs as well as benefits. Sociability, sharing a windfall of wild food, and collaboration on fishing projects that require coordination in damming the river, all make cooperation attractive. But such activities do not last long, and when the specific event is over, people return to the autonomy of the family household (O. Johnson 1978, 1980). The exception is when a shaman, charismatic leader or, more recently, a schoolteacher, is able to attract several hamlets within an hour's walking distance. He brings people together by hosting feasts, after which the guests reciprocate by clearing a garden or planting crops. This provides the host with an abundant harvest to feed visitors and ample food for future feasts. Overall, however, the shortage of meat and fish limit population growth and keep people from aggregating in large village communities where fish and wild game are rapidly being depleted.

from virgin forest. In more densely settled societies, communities tend to remain in the same place for longer periods and people have to walk farther to their fields. The Tsembaga Maringa of New Guinea (Profile 5.4 on page 64), for example, plant only 42 acres in a given year. Nonetheless, over the years they have gardened a total of 864 acres. This is about the amount of forest that the Tsembaga need if their population remains at about 200 people and if they burn secondary-growth garden sites every 20 years. Rappaport (1984) estimates that the Tsembaga had at their disposal an amount of forest land sufficient to support another 84 people without permanently damaging the regenerative capacities of the environment.

Profile 5.4   Slash-and-Burn Horticulture with Domesticated Animals—The Tsembaga

Location: Highlands of Central Papua New Guinea

Density: 35 persons per square mile

Production: Slash and burn, domesticated pigs, gathering

Time of Study: 1960s

Roy Rappaport (1968, 1984) made a careful study of the food energy system of the Tsembaga Maring, a clan living in semipermanent villages on the northern slopes of the central highlands of New Guinea. The Tsembaga, who number about 204 persons, live in a crowded landscape, with a population density of about 35 people per square mile. They are surrounded by hostile warring neighbors; local clans assert rights to land, provide cooperative mutual defense, and organize ceremonies to create regional alliances. The Tsembaga plant taro, yams, sweet potatoes, manioc, sugar cane, and several other crops in small gardens cleared and fertilized by the slash-and-burn method. Slash-and-burn horticulture is an efficient method of meeting caloric needs, yielding 18 calories of output for every 1 calorie of input. Thus, the Tsembaga are able to satisfy their caloric needs with a remarkably small investment of working time: only 380 hours per year per food producer is spent on raising crops. At the same time, the Tsembaga manage to feed almost ten times as many people as the !Kung and to live in the same house for several years.

But tropical slash-and-burn modes of production are constrained by environmental limits. First, there is the problem of forest regeneration. Because of increased population density, agricultural land is badly depleted and overused. Leaching by heavy rains and the invasion of insects and weeds causes the productivity of slash-and-burn gardens to drop rapidly after two or three years of use, and additional land must be cleared to avoid diminishing returns (Johnson and Earle 1987:67ff). Optimum productivity is achieved when gardens are cleared from a substantial secondary growth of large trees. If gardens are cleared when the secondary growth is very immature, only a small amount of wood ash will be produced by burning to fertilize the soil. But if the trees revert to maximum size, they will be very difficult to cut down. Optimum regeneration may take anywhere from 10 to 20 years or more, depending on local soils and climates.

Pigs are an important domesticated animal for the Tsembaga, because most wild animals, such as wild pigs and marsupials, have been hunted out. Pigs account for less than 1 percent by weight of the Tsembaga diet, but are a major source of protein and fats. Pigs are primarily

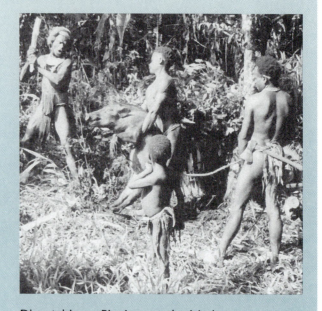

Dispatching a Pig Among the Maring

Pigs have a great ritual significance throughout New Guinea and Melanesia. The people in this scene are Fungai Maring, neighbors of the Tsembaga Maring.

a ceremonial food eaten at major intergroup slaughter ceremonies and during periods of health crisis. Pigs thus provide an important food storehouse that can be used in bad years. Yet pigs are costly to maintain because, as Rappaport (1967) has shown, pig maintenance requires about one calorie of human energy expenditure for each calorie returned. The pigs root for themselves during the day but come home to a meal of sweet potatoes and food scraps in the evening. An average Tsembaga pig weighs as much as an average person. Rappaport estimates that each pig consumes as much garden produce as each person.

When the Tsembaga pig herd is at its maximum, almost as much time and energy are devoted to feeding pigs as to feeding people. As in many New Guinea cultures, the Tsembaga allow their pig population to increase over a number of years, slaughtering them only on ceremonial occasions (Watson 1977). When the effort needed to care for pigs becomes excessive, a pig feast is held, resulting in a sharp decline in the pig population. This feast may be related to the cycle of reforestation in the Tsembaga's gardens and the regulation of war and peace between the Tsembaga and their neighbors (Morren 1984:173).

However, the bulk of this land lies above or below the optimum altitude levels for their major crops and thus would probably somewhat diminish efficiency if put into use. All slash-and-burn peoples confront the ultimate specter of "eating up their forest" (Condominas 1977) by shortening the fallow period to a point where grasses and weeds replace trees. In some parts of highland New Guinea permanent grasslands have replaced forests (Sorenson 1972; Sorenson and Kenmore 1974).

The Problem of Meat

Another problem with tropical slash-and-burn modes of production is the vulnerability to depletion of animal species. This problem is especially acute where the main staples are protein- and fat-deficient root crops such as sweet potatoes, plantains, yams, manioc, and taro.

The animals that inhabit tropical forests tend to be small, furtive, and arboreal. As human population density rises, these animals quickly become very scarce and hard to find. The total animal biomass—the weight of all the spiders, insects, worms, snakes, mammals, and so on—in a hectare of central Amazon rain forest is 45 kilograms. This compares with 304 kilograms in a dry East African thorn forest. In East African savanna grasslands, 627 kilograms of large herbivores are found per hectare, far outweighing all the large and small animals found per hectare in the Amazon (Fittkau and Klinge 1973:8).

Although plant foods can provide nutritionally adequate diets if eaten in variety and in large quantities, meat is a more efficient source of essential nutrients than plant food, kilo for kilo. Hence, one of the most important limiting factors in the growth of slash-and-burn energy systems is thought to be the availability of animal food (Good 1989; Gross 1975, 1981; M. Harris 1984; but see Collinvaux and Bush 1991).

Like virtually every other human group, the Tsembaga highly prize animal food, especially in the form of fatty meat. (Vegetarians who abstain from meat usually prize animal foods in the form of milk and yogurt.) But their population density is 67 people per square mile, compared with less than 1 per square mile among the !Kung San. It is not surprising, therefore, that they have depleted the wild animals in their territory. The meat eaten on most days ranges from nothing at all to less than 1 ounce.

Agropastoralism or Mixed Farming

A totally different solution to the problem of maintaining soil fertility is to raise animals as well as crops and to use the animal's manure as fertilizer. This system, known as **agropastoralism** or **mixed farming**, once characterized the European and American small-family farm. With the advent of the industrial era, soil fertility came to depend primarily on chemical fertilizers, eliminating the need for raising animals and crops on the same farm (but introducing a whole new set of problems associated with the toxic effects of the chemicals employed).

Subsistence plow farming turns and replenishes the soil and involves significantly shorter fallow periods than does slash-and-burn agriculture. Fields are left fallow for no more than a year; green manure and animal manure are used to add soil nutrients while the plow breaks up the soil so that oxygen can release the soil nutrients more quickly. This increases the productivity of the land and results in higher annual production per acre, which means that the land can support larger communities.

Plow agriculture is more labor intensive than slash-and-burn agriculture, but requires less farmland to support a given population.

Although domesticated animals, such as horses, oxen or water buffalo, provide heavy draft labor, more human labor is required to restore soil fertility under plow agriculture than with slash-and-burn systems. Moreover, as densities grow and regions become more populated, land must be kept under cultivation longer in order to extract increasingly larger quantities of food.

Two-thirds of the world's population raise both animals and plants. Although many environmentalists regard raising animals as an inefficient source of food, a distinction must be made between specialized industrial animal production for meat or milk, and generalized animal production that provides nonhuman sources of energy for farming and a variety of animal products. In the latter case, as with India's mixed farming system, meat is just one of the benefits and usually the least important. Animals provide traction for plows and for the transport of people and farm products. They provide dung for fertilizer, cooking fuel, and floor plaster; leather for baskets and thongs; and milk for cheese and other dairy products. In many cultures, animals also function as the only available "bank" in which savings can be held for future emergencies. Under preindustrial conditions, feeding root crops or grain to animals may be the only alternative to letting a harvest go to waste. In other words, writes Constance McCorkle (1994:4), the question is not whether people can afford to eat hamburgers. Rather, it is whether—without the incorporation of livestock into their farming systems—the majority of the world's agrarian producers and

A.   B.

Irrigation Agriculture

This form of agriculture occurs in many varieties, each with a special influence on social life.
A. Massive Chinese water works.   B. Terraces cover much of Javanese croplands.

the urbanite consumers would have anything to eat at all!

Irrigation Agriculture

Under favorable conditions, irrigation agriculture yields more food calories per calorie of effort than any other preindustrial mode of food production. And among irrigation farmers, the Chinese have excelled for thousands of years. The high population density in the irrigated parts of China is characteristic of societies that practice large-scale irrigation agriculture. It results from the fact that if the amount of water sent to the fields is increased, more labor can be applied to production without diminishing returns.

Under favorable conditions, irrigation agriculture yields more calories, per unit of land, than any other preindustrial mode of production.

Initially, the main impetus for irrigation was not to increase average yield, but to have water available in areas where rainfall was unpredictable. As irrigation systems spread, it was apparent that differences in productivity became greatly magnified—fields that used irrigation and drained well produced far more than those that were not suited to irrigation (Bates 1998:113). The wet rice fields of Asia are perhaps the most productive of all preindustrial agricultural systems. Plots of wet rice cultivation are capable of yielding a harvest year after year, with no fallow. Where water availability and drainage are especially good, the same plot can yield two or three harvests in a single year.

Whenever there is agricultural intensification, human societies grow in numbers and increase in technological and political complexity.

Managing a common water resource is critical to irrigation agriculture. Consequently, centralized decision making developed with respect to mobilizing labor to build and maintain waterways and rights of access. With increased production, segments of the population became full-time specialists, making crafts, tools, and other items that could be traded for food produced by others. Because of the efficiency of irrigation agriculture, villages such as Lut-s'un (Profile 5.5) produced five times more food than they consumed. What happened to the surplus? The villagers exchanged it through markets and money for nonfarm goods and services, they used it to pay taxes and rent, and they used it to raise large numbers of children and to sustain a high rate of population increase.

Profile 5.5   Irrigation Agriculture—Luts'un

Location: South China, Central Yunan Province

Production: Plow, fertilizer, irrigation—highly labor intensive

Density: 896 people per square mile

Time of Study: 1938–1943

Chinese villages provide a sharp contrast to the hunting, gathering, and horticultural people we have discussed so far. A detailed study of the labor inputs and weight yield of agricultural production in pre-Communist times was carried out by the anthropologists Fei Hsiao-t'ung and Chang Chih-I (1947) in the village of Luts'un, Yunnan Province. There the villagers obtained over 50 calories for each calorie of effort they expended in the fields.

The village is a typical Chinese farming community, located in a densely settled fertile plain, supported by intensive rice cultivation. Each household is an autonomous economic unit which holds property in common. Most village households owned their own land, but some landless tenant farmers are either forced to sell their land to pay off debts, or come from large families that did not have enough land to be subdivided for each son to inherit. In 1939–1940, the village had a population of about 700, living in 122 households—of these 38 did not own land.

Land parcels are less than an acre but the land is intensely cultivated so that each parcel yields a high return. The soil is fertilized using animal manure or human waste (known as night soil). The land is then plowed with the use of buffaloes. Irrigation is provided through the use of several large water wheels that draw water from the local river. As the river water flows over the dam, buckets attached to the wheel are filled—as the wheel turns, the water is emptied into a ditch that runs into the fields. The local irrigation council makes sure the water wheels and the ditches are kept in good condition.

The mild climate permits a perpetual growing season with double cropping. First rice is planted—the women take rice shoots from nursery beds and transplant them into the fields. Women also harvest the rice and the men are responsible for threshing and taking the rice to the storehouse. Then men immediately dig trenches so that two varieties of beans can be planted. Certain vegetables (legumes) improve the fertility by adding nitrogen to the soil.

Those without land, or little land, work as tenant farmers or hired workers for people who can afford to pay for their labor. People with sufficient skill or means become part-time craft specialists or merchants. According to Fei and Chang (1947), villagers need only 40% of the total yield of rice they produce, leaving 60% that can be sold to obtain other necessities and to pay taxes. These taxes cover the salaries of local administrators as well as government officials in distant cities.

Pastoralism

If one feeds grain (wheat, barley, or maize) to animals rather than to people and one then eats the meat, much of the energy available in the grains will be lost. Thus, for cattle in feedlots, it takes about 7 kilograms of grain to add 1 kilogram of live weight to each animal (Brown et al. 1994:192). The loss in efficiency associated with the processing of plant food through the gut of domesticated animals accounts for the relatively infrequent occurrence of cultures whose mode of food production is that called **pastoralism.**

Pastoralists are peoples who raise domesticated animals and who do not depend on hunting, gathering, or the planting of their own crops for a significant portion of their diets. Pastoralists typically occupy arid grasslands and steppes where precipitation is too sparse or irregular to support rainfall agriculture and where water for irrigation is not available.

There are two basic types of pastoralists. The first type consists of those who move their livestock in a regular seasonal pattern in relation to seasonal changes in the available pasture. This strategy is called **transhumance.** Transhumant groups move their camps and animals to higher and cooler mountain pastures during the heat of the summer and then reverse their steps to return to the lower elevations during winter. In some transhumant adaptations, as formerly practiced in the Swiss Alps, for example, only a small number of herders take the animals to the high pastures. In other cases, such as the Basseri of Iran (Barth 1961), people and animals stay close together during the entire migration.

The second major type of pastoralism does not involve movement back and forth along a traditional migration route. Instead, people and animals try to find the best pastures wherever they may be located. This strategy is called **nomadic pastoralism,** an adaptation that is often associated with migrations over vast distances of pastoral peoples such as the Mongols

Basseri of Iran on the Move

and Huns. Pastoralists seldom kill their animals for meat because they provide greater net return through the production of milk, blood, wool and traction. Pastoralists are not nutritionally self-sufficient. They need to supplement their animal foods with plant foods obtained through trade with their sedentary farming neighbors. In fact, a large portion of their food may come from trade with agricultural groups.

Successful pastoralists can increase their holdings at a faster rate than agriculturalists. Herding, however, is much more risky because animals are susceptible to disease, drought and theft and herds can be wiped out almost overnight. The advantage, however, is that pastoralists can exploit the vast areas that are unsuitable for agriculture and are able to move in response to changing economic and political conditions. People live together by choice rather than by coercion, and can simply move apart to minimize conflict (Bates 1996:95).

Pastoralists frequently attempt to improve their position by raiding the sedentary villagers and carrying off the grain harvest without paying for it. They can often do this with impunity because animals such as camels and horses make them highly mobile and militarily effective. Continued success in raiding may force the farming population to acknowledge the pastoralists as their overlords. Repeatedly in the history of the Old World, relatively small groups of pastoral nomads—the Mongols and the Arabs are the two most famous examples—have succeeded in gaining control of the large agricultural empires on their borders. The inevitable outcome of these conquests, however, was that the conquerors were absorbed by the agricultural system as they attempted to feed the huge popula-

Profile 5.6   Pastoralism—The Turkana

Location: Arid grasslands of Northern Kenya

Production: Nomadic herding of domestic livestock

Density: 3.3 persons per square mile

Times of Study: 1949, 1970s, early 1980s

The Turkana are nomadic, like the !Kung. But unlike the !Kung, the Turkana travel with their food supply—in the form of livestock; their movements depend as much on the needs of their animals as on their own. The advantage of owning domestic livestock in an arid climate is that animals convert otherwise inedible plant life into food for human consumption. This makes it possible for the Turkana to extract food value from animals in an environment that is too marginal for anything else.

The vegetation in the region consists of annual grasses and shrubs in the plains and perennial grasses and trees in the northern mountainous areas. The Turkana have adapted to the variability in the vegetation, terrain, and climate by herding five kinds of livestock and by moving quickly from one location to the next. According to Gul-

liver (1951), the frequent moves make it possible for the Turkana to make maximum use of the vegetation in the area by first utilizing areas that dry out early in the season and then moving on to better grazing where the vegetation lasts longer. The major livestock are cattle, sheep, goats, camels and donkeys, the latter used mainly for transport. In the dry season the Turkana divide up their herds; cattle and sheep require grass for grazing, whereas camels and goats can do well in drier bushy areas.

During most of the year the Turkana are deliberately scattered to avoid competing with each other for pasture. Kinship and friendship networks are used to exchange information, labor, and livestock and to ensure against herd loss in case a natural disaster decimates a family herd. Each homestead can turn to friends in another region for food and livestock to replenish their herd (Dyson-Hudson and McCabe 1985). In the past, these networks were also used to mobilize support in response to raiding and warfare with enemies from outside the group.

Table 5.1

Per Capita Energy Production

	Total Output in Calories (in thousands)	Population	Per Capita Output in Calories (in thousands)
!Kung	23,400	35	670
Tsembaga	150,000	204	735
Luts'un	3,790,000	700	5,411

tions that had fallen under their control (Barfield 1993; Galaty and Johnson 1990; Khazanov 994).

Energy and the Evolution of Culture

According to anthropologist Leslie White (1949:368–369), a basic law of energy governs the evolution of cultures: "Other factors remaining constant, culture evolves as the amount of energy harnessed per year is increased, or as the efficiency of the means of putting energy to work is increased." The first part of this law seems to be supported by comparing the per capita output of Chinese irrigation agriculture with the per capita output of the !Kung, and Tsembaga, as Table 5.1 shows. As can also be seen in Figure 5.2, enormous in-

creases in the per capita use of energy have occurred during the past century, as we have gone from draft animals, to steam engines, and on to internal combustion machinery.

The validity of the second part of White's law is not so clear. If one considers only human labor inputs, the ratio of output to input does go up in efficiency as technology increases in complexity. For example, the ratio of output to labor input measured in calories ranges from 11:1 for the !Kung to 18:1 for the Tsembaga to 54:1 for Luts'un. But these figures do not include the energy that the Tsembaga use in the combustion of trees to make their gardens, nor the considerable amount of energy they "waste" in converting vegetable foods to pork. Nor do the numbers for Luts'un include the considerable energetic cost of milling and cooking rice. As Timothy Bayliss-Smith (1977) has shown in an attempt to test White's law, South Sea communities drawn into participating in

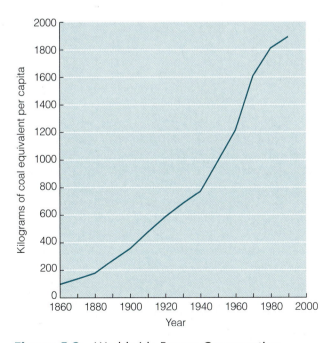

Figure 5.2 Worldwide Energy Consumption
There has been a sharp increase in the per capita consumption of coal during the last century.
Source: Price 1995:311.

Industrial Farming
Rice harvest near Yuba City, California. Consider the amount of energy it takes for food in industrialized societies to reach the dinner table.

aspects of modern industrial modes of production produce much more food energy per capita, but their efficiency in terms of energy output to input shows no clear upward trend.

If we consider the total energy inputs and outputs of food production in advanced industrial societies, the trend in efficiency of putting energy to work runs counter to White's prediction. When we include other sources of energy input, such as fossil fuels and machinery, we find that advances in technology have actually resulted in decreased efficiency of food production.

Industrial Food Energy Systems

Estimating the input–output ratio of industrial agriculture (see Barlett 1989) is difficult because the amount of indirect labor put into food production exceeds the amount of direct labor (Box 5.4). An Iowa corn farmer, for example, can produce 81 bushels of corn in 9 hours with an energy equivalent of 8 million calories (Pimentel et al. 1975). This gives a nominal ratio of 5000 calories of output for every calorie of input! But enormous amounts of indirect human labor are embodied in the tractors, trucks, combines, oil and gas, pesticides, herbicides, and fertilizers used by the Iowa corn farmer.

In the United States, 15 tons of machinery, 22 gallons of gasoline, 203 pounds of fertilizer, and 2 pounds of chemical insecticides and pesticides are invested per acre per year. This represents a cost of 2,890,000 calories of nonfood energy per acre per year (Pimentel et al. 1975), a cost that has increased steadily since the beginning of the century.

Before 1910, more calories were obtained from agriculture than were invested in it. By 1970, it took 8 calories in the form of fossil fuels to produce 1 calorie of food. Today, vast quantities of energy are used simply to process and package food.

In recent decades, scientists and technicians have altered their assessment of the ability of technology to dominate the environment. Increasingly, we have

Box 5.4   Energy Input in Packaging and Processing Industrial Food

Energy Required to Produce Various Food Packages

Package	kcal
Wooden berry basket	69
Styrofoam tray (size 6)	215
Molded paper tray (size 6)	384
Polyethylene pouch (16 oz)	559
Steel can, aluminum top (12 oz)	568
Small paper set-up box	722
Steel can, steel top (16 oz)	1,006
Glass jar (16 oz)	1,023
Coca-Cola bottle, returnable (16 oz)	1,471
Aluminum TV-dinner container	1,496
Aluminum can, pop-top (12 oz)	1,643
Plastic milk container, disposable (1–2 gal)	2,159
Coca-Cola bottle, nonreturnable (16 oz)	2,451
Polyethylene bottle (1 qt)	2,494
Polypropylene bottle (1 qt)	2,752
Glass milk container, returnable (1–2 gal)	4,455

Energy Required to Process Various Products

Product	kcal/kg
Instant coffee	18,948
Chocolate	18,591
Breakfast cereals	15,675
Beet sugar (assumes 17% sugar in beets)	5,660
Dehydrated foods (freeze-dried)	3,542
Cane sugar (assumes 20% sugar in cane)	3,380
Fruit and vegetables (frozen)	1,815
Fish (frozen)	1,815
Baked goods	1,485
Meat	1,206
Ice cream	880
Fruit and vegetables (canned)	575
Flour (includes blending of flour)	484
Milk	354

(Adapted from Pimentel and Pimentel 1985:38–39)

The Hidden Costs of the Industrial Mode of Production

A. Abandoned hazardous waste dump. Pit is 5 feet deep and covers 34,000 square feet. **B.** *Times Beach, Missouri. Floodwaters spread soil contaminated with dioxin, previously concentrated near highways, all over residential neighborhoods. Cleanup crews collect samples for analysis.*

seen that industrial modes of production have not liberated human social life from the constraints of nature. For example, we now realize that we have ignored or silently passed on many costs of industrial production to generations yet unborn. Specifically, we have depleted irreplaceable resources and polluted air and water in many parts of the world. Efforts are now under way in many industrial nations to reduce air and water pollution and to prevent the depletion and poisoning of the environment. The costs of these efforts testify to the continuing importance of the interaction between technology and environment. These costs will continue to mount, for this is only the very beginning of the industrial era. In the centuries to come, the inhabitants of specific regions may pay for industrialization in ways as yet uncalculated.

Summary

1. In the comparative study of modes of production, we consider the quantitative and qualitative aspects of energy production and of ecological relationships. Most of the energy flowing through preindustrial energy systems consists of food energy. Moreover, the technology of energy production cannot readily be altered. It has evolved through successive stages of technical competence, in which the mastery of one set of tools and machines has been built on the mastery of an earlier set.

2. Through technological advance, the energy available per capita has steadily increased. However, technology never exists in the abstract but only in the particular instances where it interacts with a specific environment.

3. Technology, interacting with environment, determines carrying capacity, which is the upper limit of production and consequently the upper limit of human population size and density as well. When a population exceeds its environment's carrying capacity, the resource base will deteriorate and production will decline precipitously.

4. The fact that a food energy system is operating below carrying capacity, however, does not mean that ecological restraints are absent. Production may be cut back after reaching the point of diminishing returns. But it may also be increased by intensifying the production inputs. Still, intensification if continued without technological change will result in irreversible damage to the habitat.

5. A common human cultural response to declining efficiency brought about by intensification is to alter technology and thereby adopt new modes of production.

6. Hunting and gathering was the universal mode of food production until the end of the Stone Age. Depending on the kind of technology and the environmental conditions, several types of hunter-gatherers can be distinguished.

7. The !Kung San are an example of the simple, band-organized, mobile variety found in less favored habitats. Their output-to-input efficiency is low, especially for the male-dominated activity of hunting. However, by maintaining low population densities and avoiding intensification, they enjoy a relatively high standard of living (good diets, unpolluted environments, and lots of leisure time). Energy efficiency plays an important role in the selection of the species that hunter-gatherers use for food.

8. The Kwakiutl are an example of hunters and gatherers who scatter during the summer months, collecting food that is processed and stored for the winter, and then gather in large, densely populated villages to live on dried and smoked provisions.

9. According to optimal foraging theory, foragers stop to take only those species whose handling time adds to or does not decrease the overall efficiency of their foraging effort.

10. Slash-and-burn agriculturalists such as the Machiguenga and Tsembaga Maring satisfy their caloric needs with greater efficiency than the !Kung San, but the Tsembaga have depleted the game animals in their habitat and must rely on costly domesticated pigs for their animal proteins and fats.

11. By using irrigation agriculture, the people of Luts'un produce a large surplus. Their output–input ratio for human effort is three times higher than the output input ratio of the Tsembaga.

12. Pastoralism, another preindustrial mode of food production, is practiced only in areas unsuitable for agriculture because feeding plant food to domesticated animals rather than consuming crops directly results in a 90 percent reduction in the efficiency of converting sunlight to human food.

13. As Leslie White predicted, the amount of energy harnessed per capita in the long run has steadily increased. Energy efficiency has also increased as measured by the return for human labor input.

But when other sources of energy are included in the calculation of efficiency, advances in technology have resulted in decreased efficiency of food production, as demonstrated by the enormous energy inputs that characterize industrial agricultural systems.

AMERICA NOW

Mode of Production

The mode of production in the United States is an advanced, increasingly high-tech form of industrialism. Industrialism denotes the mass production of goods, services, and information by means of a highly detailed division of labor in which workers use electronic and other kinds of petroleum driven machines in routinized, repetitive ways. Detailed division of labor is the separation of production tasks into many tiny steps carried out by different workers. The United States remains the top-ranking industrial manufacturing country in the world. Nonetheless, three-quarters of all employees produce information and services rather than tangible objects. Most employed adult Americans work in offices, stores, restaurants, schools, clinics, and moving vehicles rather than on factory assembly lines. They wait on customers; repair broken machines; keep accounts; write letters; transfer funds; and provide grooming, schooling, training, information, counseling, and therapy to students, clients, customers, and patients (Swasy and Hymowitz 1990). Farming, which once occupied the vast majority of American workers, now occupies only 3 percent of the workforce.

The rise of the service and information sectors has led to the characterization of the United States as a *postindustrial* society (Bell 1973). It would seem more appropriate, however, to call the United States and other advanced industrial societies, such as Germany and Japan, "hyperindustrial" (*hyper* means "extra strong") rather than postindustrial, because the shift to services and information processing has merely resulted in extending the detailed division of labor and the use of mass-production machines—office computers, word processors, duplicators, supermarket bar code scanners, electronic mail, automatic dialing machines—into additional kinds of production (D. Harris 1987; Sanderson 1991). Offices are factories whose product is information; this blurs the distinction between blue-collar and white-collar workers.

Here is a description of the work patterns of customer service operators in the "back office" of a large oil company:

Information Factory

Rows of Internal Revenue Service workers process information.

The pace is strenuous (an average of 160 calls per day) and automatically set by the computer's automatic call distributor; tasks are repetitive, and workers are isolated in carrels on duty, while their movement is restricted by their headsets and the necessary concentration on the VDT [video display terminal] screen. Machine-measured performance statistics are the basis for promotion: for each operator the computer measures the number of calls taken, the length of each call, the number of callers who "abandoned" before being answered, and the amount of time spent off the telephone or away from the work station. In order to monitor performance, supervisors listen in on 10% of each operator's daily call volume (approximately 16 calls) each month, using a telephone pickup that cannot be heard by the operator. More than three errors places the operator below the shop standard for "accuracy." One supervisor and former operator observed, "You can tell when they've been working the phones too long; their voices on the phone get louder and louder without their noticing it." (Nelson 1986:158)

These hyperindustrial factories have aptly been called "electronic sweatshops" (Belsham 1988; Garson 1988; Horowitz 1994).

KEY TERMS

agropastoralism

carrying capacity

ecological anthropology

homeostasis

hunting and gathering

intensification

irrigation agriculture

law of energy and the evolution of culture

law of the minimum

maximum sustainable yield

mixed farming

nomadic pastoralism

nonrenewable resources

optimal foraging theory

pastoralism

point of diminishing returns

rainfall agriculture

slash-and-burn

transhumance

QUESTIONS TO THINK ABOUT

1. What influence does environment and technology have on the mode of production?

2. What impact do intensification, carrying capacity, and the law of diminishing returns have on production? What is likely to happen just before carrying capacity is reached?

3. What does optimal foraging theory teach us about hunters and gatherers?

4. "Not all hunters and gatherers are alike." What key ecological differences set the !Kung and the Kwakiutl apart in terms of their mode of production and their domestic economy?

5. Tsembaga population density is over 60 times that of the Machiguenga. How does the Tsembaga mode of production support so many more people, per square mile of land, than the Machiguenga mode of production?

6. What are some of the differences between slash and burn and irrigation agriculture in terms of technology, population density, yields per calorie of effort, and resource management?

7. Pastoralists make a living by exploiting areas that are unsuitable for agriculture. What kind of special advantages do livestock offer pastoralists? How is herding a sustainable adaptation in arid environments?

CHAPTER 6

Reproduction

Parents and infant among the San of the Kalahari Desert.

The Relation between Production and Reproduction

Population Pressure versus Population Growth

Preindustrial Reproductive Practices
Treatment of Fetuses and Children
Treatment of Women
Lactation
Coital Frequency and Scheduling
The Influence of Disease and Other Natural Factors

The Costs and Benefits of Rearing Children
Measuring the Costs and Benefits of Rearing Children
The Poverty Trap

The Contraception, Abortion, and Infanticide Debate
PROFILE: Indirect Infanticide in Northeast Brazil

Industrial Modes of Reproduction

Women's Status, Education, and Fertility

Summary

America Now: Fertility and the World's Most Expensive Children
Reproductive Technologies, Embryos, and Designer Babies

We will now focus on the reproductive aspect of infrastructure. Given the potential that human beings have to increase population, how is population brought into balance with production and carrying capacity? We will see that preindustrial societies affect population growth through such means as sexual abstinence, prolonged nursing, abortion, and direct and indirect infanticide. Then why do people in poverty-stricken parts of the world persist in having large families, whereas people in rich industrial countries have fewer and fewer children? What explains rates of population growth is not the possession of contraceptives or abortifacients but the costs and benefits of raising children under different modes of production. What are the implications for the abortion debate if people have always regulated reproduction, both before and after birth?

The Relation between Production and Reproduction

Reproduction is a form of production—the "product" being new human beings. Under optimal conditions, women can have between 20 and 25 live births during their fertile years (which last roughly from age 15 to 45).

In all human societies, women on the average have far fewer children than they are capable of having.

Large Families Are Preferred in Developing Countries
High fertility rates improve peoples standard of living in the short term.

The record, 8.97 children per woman, is held by the Hutterites, a communitarian sect in western Canada (Lang and Gohlen 1985). If all children born live to reproduce, any number of births greater than two per woman would potentially result in population increase (holding death rates constant and without emigration). Even small rates of increase can result in enormous populations in a few generations. The !Kung, for example, have a growth rate of 0.5 percent per year. If the world had started 10,000 years ago with a population of 2, and if that population had grown at 0.5 percent per year, the world population would now be 604,436,000,000,000,000,000,000. No such growth has occurred because, through various combinations of cultural and natural factors, reproduction has been kept within limits imposed by systems of production (Box 6.1).

Much controversy surrounds the nature of the relationship between production and reproduction. Followers of Thomas Malthus, the founder of the science of demography (the science of population phenomena), have long held the view that the level of population is determined by the amount of food produced.

According to **Malthusian theory,** population would always increase more rapidly than the food supply; in fact, population growth would tend to rise faster than any conceivable rise in productivity, thereby dooming a large portion of humanity to perpetual poverty, hunger, and misery.

However, evidence from many nonindustrial societies shows that populations maintain their levels of production well below carrying capacity, as discussed next, and that Malthus was wrong in assuming that population growth would necessarily lead to scarcity and misery. Moreover, we could turn Malthus upside down and see the amount of food produced as being determined by the level of population growth.

Box 6.1   The Human Crop

The arithmetic of global population growth has become numbingly familiar: 1 billion in 1800, 2.5 billion in 1950, and 5.5 billion today. In the past four decades more people have been added to the globe than in all of history before the middle of this century. And growth continues unabated. The world's population is now expanding at the unprecedented rate of nearly one billion per decade. (Bongaarts 1994a, 1994b:771)

An alternative view has been advocated most forcefully by Ester Boserup. **Boserup's theory** holds that food production tends to rise to the level demanded by population growth. As population expands, and the point of diminishing returns is reached, people invent or adopt new and more efficient modes of food production.

In light of recent anthropological research, the position that seems most correct is that production and reproduction are equally important in shaping the course of sociocultural evolution, and that to an equal extent, each is the cause of the other. Reproduction generates population pressure (psychological and physiological costs such as malnutrition and illness), which prompts efforts to increase production through technological improvements.

Population pressure often leads to intensification, diminishing returns, and irreversible environmental depletions. Depletions often lead, in turn, to new technologies and to new modes of production.

Population Pressure versus Population Growth

Population pressure and population growth are not the same thing. **Population growth** is birthrate minus mortality, not counting migration in and out of a territory, whereas **population pressure** refers to pressure on resources that forces people to work harder to obtain the same amount of food. Under favorable environmental conditions, population size and density can increase, at least temporarily, without lowering a people's standard of living. During the nineteenth century, the settling of the American West was accompanied by high *fertility* rates, a rapidly rising population and, because the landscape was fertile, there was a rising standard of living among pioneer farm families.

Moreover, population pressures may exist even if a population is not increasing. For example, a stable population may deplete local resources if it is unable to expand into new territory. To prevent the erosion of their standard of living, people often employ physically and emotionally costly means of reproductive controls, such as **infanticide** and nonmedical abortion, to continue to keep their population growth at a low level. For example, Arctic hunter-gatherers live at very low population densities and virtually zero rates of population growth. They practice female infanticide as a means of keeping their population within the limits that can be sustained by their mode of production (Smith and Smith 1994).

The key to understanding population pressure is not population density but the numbers of people in an area relative to its resources.

Population pressure might even exist among people who are experiencing a population decline. Many Native American communities in the Amazon have declined in numbers because of epidemics, yet find it increasingly difficult to maintain their standard of living using their traditional mode of production because they have been forced, by more politically dominant groups, to occupy marginal environments, less capable of sustaining them, given their level of technology. Perhaps the best way to envision population pressure is to regard it as present with varying intensity among virtually all societies (the exception being societies that are expanding into uninhabited frontiers). Even in high-tech industrial countries where fertility rates have fallen below replacement levels (see America Now at the end of this chapter), largely by using modern methods of birth control, population pressure has a role to play in phenomena such as unemployment, crime, homelessness, child abuse, and pollution.

Given the finite nature of our capacity to produce energy, population growth can only drive up the price of energy and the goods and services energy makes possible. At best, population pressure is a destabilizing force. It interacts with natural sources of instability, such as changes in climate, to bring about both small- and large-scale shifts in modes of production. Thus, although production limits population growth, population pressure provides a perpetual motivation for overcoming such limits (Graber 1991, 1992; Johnson and Earle 1987; Keeley 1996).

Population and technology have a feedback relationship: Populations grow because new sources of food are discovered as new technology is used to increase production; technological change is invented or accepted because it enables people to intensify production and better adapt to their environment.

Preindustrial Reproductive Practices

Much evidence supports the view that preindustrial cultures reduced or controlled population pressure by keeping reproductive rates low. How did they do this in the absence of condoms, diaphragms, pills, spermicides, effective abortion drugs (Riddle and Estes 1992), or knowledge of the human ovulatory cycle? Four categories of practice have had the direct or indirect effect of regulating population growth:

- Care and treatment of fetuses, infants, and children
- Care and treatment of girls and women (and to a lesser extent of boys and men)
- Intensity and duration of lactation (the period of breastfeeding)
- Variations in the frequency of coital intercourse

Before describing these practices, we should point out that many anthropologists and demographers regard only conscious attempts to limit reproduction to a targeted number of children as evidence of population regulation (Wood 1990). Our view is that effective limits on population growth can be achieved both by direct, conscious efforts and by indirect and unconscious ones.

Treatment of Fetuses and Children

Maltreatment of fetuses, infants, and young children is a common means of lowering reproductivity.

Parental investment begins during pregnancy and includes a range of behaviors from full support to indifference, passive neglect, and active attempts to promote fetal death. Full support begins with caring for pregnant women, supplementing their diets, and reducing their workloads (MacCormack 1982:8). Indifference or neglect begin when heavy workloads and meager diets are imposed on pregnant women. Direct abortion involves trauma such as applying pressure to the mother's abdomen, jumping on her, or having her ingest toxic substances (Riddle and Estes 1992). In a study of 350 preindustrial societies, George Devereux (1967:98) found that direct abortion occurred in all 350. Modern medical abortions differ from more traditional methods that endanger the mother almost as much as the fetus. For example, medical abortion today is the principal form of fertility control in Japan (Jitsukawa and Djerassi 1994).

Infanticide is widely practiced in preindustrial societies because abortion is dangerous to the mother.

A subtle gradation leads from indirect to direct methods of infanticide. Full support of the life of a newborn infant requires that it be fed to gain weight rapidly and that it be protected against extremes of temperature and from falls, burns, and other accidents. *Indirect infanticide* begins with neglect and underinvestment—inadequate feeding, withholding emotional support, and careless and indifferent handling, especially when the infant is sick. *Direct infanticide* involves deliberate killing—starvation, dehydration, smothering, placing a child in a dangerous situation, or exces-

sive physical punishment (Scrimshaw 1983). Often no sharp emic distinction exists between abortion and infanticide. Where infanticide occurs, it usually happens early in life, before the child is regarded as a real person in the society. In this connection, it should be pointed out that many cultures do not consider children to be human until certain ceremonies, such as naming or hair cutting, are performed. Infanticide and the induced death of small children seldom take place after such ceremonies have been performed (Minturn and Stashak 1982). Hence, in emic perspective, such deaths are rarely seen as homicides.

Treatment of Women

The treatment of women can raise or lower the age at which women begin to be capable of bearing children and the age at which they can no longer conceive. It can also affect the total number of pregnancies women are capable of sustaining.

Women who are nutritionally deprived are not as fertile as women whose diets are adequate, although considerable controversy exists over how severe the deprivations must be before significant declines in fertility occur.

Still, periods of severe, famine-level nutritional deprivation can reduce fertility by 50 percent (Bongaarts 1980:568). Rose Frisch (1984:184), however, maintains that even a 10 to 15 percent weight loss is sufficient to delay menarche and to disrupt the menstrual cycle. Others assign less significance to the role of body fat in fertility (Wood 1990:234).

Other effects of malnutrition on mother, fetus, and infant are well established. Poor maternal nutrition increases the risk of premature births and of low birth weights, both of which increase fetal and infant mortality; poor maternal nutrition also diminishes the quantity if not the quality of breast milk, thus lowering the chances of infant survival still further (Frisancho et al. 1983; Hamilton et al. 1984:388). In turn, women who become pregnant and breastfeed from a nutritionally depleted body have elevated mortality rates (Adair and Popkin 1992; Kusin et al. 1993; Lunn 1988). These nutritional effects will all vary in interaction with the amount of psychological and physical stress imposed on pregnant and lactating women. In addition, life expectancy can be affected by exposure to toxic, body shock techniques of abortion, again in interaction with general nutritional status.

Extreme malnutrition and physical and mental stress can affect male **fecundity** (see Box 6.2) by reducing **libido** (sexual desire) and sperm count. The abundance of sperm, however, as compared with the small number of ova and a woman's limited capacity for birthing and nursing, mean that the treatment of women is far

Some Basic Demographic Concepts

Crude birth rate—The number of births per thousand people, in a given year.

Crude death rate—The number of deaths per thousand people, in a given year.

Fertility rate—The number of live births per thousand women ages 15 to 44, in a given year.

Completed fertility rate—The average number of children born to women who have completed their reproductive years.

Fecundity—The physiological capacity to produce a live child.

Mortality—Death as a factor in population stability or change.

Breastfeeding Older Children
San women breastfeed their children for 4 or 5 years per child.

more important than the treatment of men in regulating reproduction. High sickness and mortality rates among men are readily counterbalanced by the widespread practice of **polygyny** (one husband with several wives) and by the fact that one man can impregnate dozens of women.

Lactation

Lactation amenorrhea (disruption of the menstrual cycle) is a typical accompaniment of breast feeding and serves as another form of birth control.

The effect of lactation amenorrhea is associated with the production of prolactin, a hormone that regulates mammary activity. When an infant suckles at the breast, prolactin is activated, which in turn, inhibits the production of the hormones that regulate the ovulatory cycle. Lactating women therefore are less likely to ovulate and conceive.

Several biocultural factors appear to control the duration of lactation amenorrhea. To begin with, there is the state of the mother's health and her diet, which affect her ability to breastfeed. Additional variables include the intensity of suckling (more intense suckling produces more prolactin in the body), the age at which the infant is fed supplemental foods, the amount of time the infant spends at the breast, and how often suckling episodes take place.

Under favorable conditions, prolonged nursing itself can clearly result in birth-spacing intervals of three or more years, with a degree of reliability comparable to that of modern mechanical and chemical contra-

ceptives. But one must be on guard against the notion that any social group is free to adjust its fertility rate upward or downward merely by intensifying and prolonging lactation. Prolonged lactation cannot take place without suitably nourished mothers. Moreover, because human breast milk is deficient in iron, its use as the sole source of nourishment much beyond the age of 6 months will cause anemia in the infant.

Coital Frequency and Scheduling

Coital abstinence can be sustained long enough to reduce pregnancies, and delays in the onset of intercourse can shorten a woman's reproductive span (Nag 1983).

Various forms of nonreproductive sex can influence fertility rates.

Homosexuality, masturbation, coitus interruptus (withdrawal before ejaculation), and noncoital heterosexual techniques for achieving orgasm can all play a role in regulating fertility. Age of marriage is another important population-regulating variable, but its significance depends on the existence of taboos on extramarital sex and unwed motherhood.

Type of marriage is also relevant to fertility. Polygyny, for example, assures that almost all females will marry and engage in reproductive sex (in the absence of contraception). But because husbands rotate having sex with their wives, polygyny is effective in prolonging female sexual abstinence, reinforcing lactational amenorrhea. In addition, polygyny probably results in lower rates of coital intercourse per wife as husbands grow older (Bongaarts and Odile 1984:521–522; Hern 1992).

Some evidence shows that women whose husbands are polygynous tend to have a lower ratio of male to female children than those whose husbands are monogamous (Whiting 1993). However, evidence suggests that higher coital rates result in higher ratios of males to females at birth (Martin 1994). Although poorly understood, this effect seems to be related to the greater motility (speed) that Y-bearing sperm possess at insemination (they are lighter than the X-bearing sperm). This advantage fades rapidly after insemination as the lighter sperm quickly lose their energy. Frequent ejaculation of fresh sperm, however, maintains a high level of motile Y-bearing sperm that have an advantage in reaching the ovum during the brief fertile interval of the ovulatory cycle. Therefore, any circumstance that promotes a high rate of coital activity will raise the ratio of male to female births.

Clearly, preindustrial societies have never lacked means—conscious or unconscious—for regulating their reproductive rates in response to the limits and possibilities of their modes of production.

The Influence of Disease and Other Natural Factors

Most of the great lethal epidemic diseases—smallpox, typhoid fever, influenza, bubonic plague, and cholera—are primarily associated with dense urbanized populations rather than with dispersed hunter-gatherers or small village cultures. Even such diseases as malaria and yellow fever were probably less important among low-density populations that could avoid swampy mosquito breeding grounds. (Knowledge of the association between swamps and disease is very ancient even though mosquitoes were not recognized as disease carriers.) Other diseases such as dysentery, measles, tuberculosis, whooping cough, scarlet fever, and the common cold were also probably less significant among hunter-gatherers and early farmers (Armelagos 1990; Armelagos et al. 1991). Furthermore, the ability to recuperate from these infections is closely related to the general level of bodily health, which in turn is heavily influenced by the level of calorie and protein consumption.

Among many preindustrial societies, the role of disease as a long-term regulator of human population is to some extent a consequence of the success or failure of other population-regulating mechanisms.

Only if these other mechanisms are ineffective—resulting in a rise in population density, a drop in food production and deterioration of diet—will some diseases figure as an important check on preindustrial population growth (Post 1985).

Some evidence indicates that Stone Age hunter-gatherers were healthier than early farmers and the peasants of preindustrial state societies. Exactly when and where a deterioration occurred is the focus of continuing research (M. N. Cohen 1987, 1995; Cohen and Armelagos 1984). For much of the late Stone Age "artificial" population controls, such as those just outlined, rather than sickness were probably the principal factors governing rates of population growth (Handwerker 1983:20).

Obviously, a component in human birth and death rates reflects "natural" causes over which cultural practices have little influence. In addition to lethal diseases, natural catastrophes such as droughts, floods, and earthquakes may raise death rates and lower birthrates in a manner that leaves little room for cultural intervention. And of course, biology constrains the number of children a human female can have, as well as the length of human life.

The Costs and Benefits of Rearing Children

At the family level, parental perceptions of the costs and values of rearing children influence their reproductive decision making. The costs of rearing children include

- Extra food consumed during pregnancy
- Work not done by pregnant women
- Expenses involved in providing mother's milk and other foods during infancy and childhood
- Burden of carrying infants and children from one place to another
- In more complex societies, expenditures for clothing, housing, medical care, and education

In addition, the birth process itself is dangerous and often places the life of the mother at risk. The benefits that affect the demand for children include

- Emotional satisfaction children can bring
- Contributions that children make to food production and to family income in general
- Care and economic security children give their parents

- Role of children in marital exchanges and intergroup alliances
- Protection that large families may provide against outsiders

In many cultures, groups exchange sons and daughters in order to obtain husbands and wives. These exchanges are used to arrange alliances against aggressors. Hence, where chronic warfare exists, larger groups are safer than smaller ones; they have more alliances as well as greater military strength.

All this, of course, is not to deny that people have children for sentimental reasons as well (see Box 6.3). Humans may have a genetically controlled propensity, shared with other primates, to find infants emotionally appealing and to derive emotional satisfaction from holding and fondling them and from watching and helping them play and learn. As children grow older, their respect and love for their parents may also be highly valued. But this appreciation of infants and children, if it is innate, can be modified by culture so completely as to allow most people to have fewer chil-

A Javanese boy earning his keep.

Box 6.3   The Economy of Parental Love

Children fulfill a need for close, affectionate, emotional relationships with supportive, concerned, trustworthy, and approving beings. We need children because we need to be loved. In the support parents lavish on children, there is a culturally instructed expectation that a balance will be struck with the love and affection that children can be so good at giving in return. Even in their least giving mood, babies respond with warm, wet sucking and mouthing; they grasp your fingers and try to put their arms around you. Already you can anticipate the ardent hugs and kisses of early childhood, the tot who clings to your neck; the 4-year-old tucked in bed, whispering "I love you"; the 6-year-old breathless at the door or running down the path as you come home from work. And with a little more imagination, you can see all the way to a grateful son or daughter, dressed in cap and gown, saying, "Thanks, Mom and Dad. I owe it all to you." The fact that many of the sentimental rewards of parenthood are delayed does not mean that dreams rule the economy of love. As in every other kind of exchange, mere expectation of a return flow will not sustain the bonds indefinitely. The family sanctuary is a fragile temple. People will not forever marry and have children if the actual experience departs far from expectation. (Adapted from Harris 1989:230ff).

dren than they are biologically capable of producing and to enable others, such as monks, priests, nuns, and even some modern-day couples, to have none at all.

Much recent evidence suggests that the rate at which the parental generation has children is largely determined by the extent to which having each additional child results in a net gain of benefits over costs for the average couple (Caldwell 1982; Harris and Ross 1987; Nardi 1983). Among band-organized hunter-gatherers, the number of children is limited by the burden that infants present to mothers who must carry them hundreds of miles each year on their foraging expeditions. According to Richard Lee (1979, 1993), !Kung San mothers try to avoid having one child right after another in order to escape the burden of carrying two children at once. The benefits of additional children are further reduced among hunter-gatherers by the vulnerability of wild species of plants and animals to depletion. As band size increases, per capita food production tends to decline, because hunter-gatherers have no effective way of increasing the population of the wild plants and animals they use for food. Finally, the children of hunter-gatherers do not produce more food than they consume until relatively late in childhood. For these reasons, population densities among simple hunter-gatherers seldom rise above one person per square mile.

If contemporary hunter-gatherers are at all representative of prehistoric times, *Homo sapiens* must have been a very rare creature during the early Stone

Table 6.1

Rate of Growth of the Human Population

Period	World Population at End of Period	Percentage Annual Rate of Growth During Period
Paleolithic	5,000,000	0.0015
Mesolithic	8,500,000	0.0330
Neolithic	75,000,000	0.1000
Ancient empires	225,000,000	0.5000

Sources: Hassan 1978, 1981; Spengler 1974.

Age. Perhaps as few as 5–15 million people lived in the entire world in those times (Dumond 1975; Hassan 1978:78; Cohen 1977:54), compared with 5 billion today. For tens of thousands of years, the rate of growth of the human population was undoubtedly very slow (see Table 6.1).

Fertility is generally higher among sedentary complex hunter-gatherers (such as the Kwakiutl) and agriculturalists (Bentley et al. 1993; Roth 1985). Children no longer have to be carried about over long distances; they can perform many useful economic chores at an early age; and because the rate of reproduction of domesticated plants and animals can be controlled, a considerable amount of intensification and hence population growth can be achieved without a decline in per capita output. In many agricultural societies, older children rapidly begin to "pay for themselves." They contribute to the production of their own food, clothing, and housing, and, under favorable conditions, they may begin to produce surpluses above their own subsistence needs as early as 6 years of age. This transition is hastened with successive births, because older siblings and other children assume much of the cost of grooming and caring for their juniors.

Measuring the Costs and Benefits of Rearing Children

A number of attempts have been made to measure the economic value of children in contemporary peasant communities. For example, in village Java, boys of 12 to 14 years contribute 33 hours of economically valuable work per week, and girls 9 to 11 contribute about 38 hours a week of the same. Altogether, children contribute about half of all work performed by household members. Much household labor involves making handicrafts, working in petty trade, and processing various foods for sale. Similar findings are reported for Nepal (Nag et al. 1978; White 1982).

Costs are more difficult to measure, but Javanese children themselves do most of the work needed to rear

Nyinba Girl Carries Mud Home for Construction
Children perform a variety of tasks that make them useful to families in non-industrial societies.

and maintain their siblings, freeing mothers for income-producing tasks. In any event, larger households are more efficient income-producing units than smaller households in rural Java because in large households a smaller proportion of each individual's total labor time is required for non–income-producing household tasks (such as cooking and cleaning). Javanese women have about five births and four surviving children. This adds up to an alarming 2 percent per annum increase in population (White 1982:605). Meade Cain (1977:225) quantified both benefits and costs for male children in a rural Bangladesh village. Cain describes his findings:

> Male children become net producers at the latest by the age of 12. Furthermore, male children work long enough hours at high enough rates of productivity to compensate for consumption during their earlier periods of dependence by the age of 15. Therefore, in general parents realize a net economic return on male children for the period when they are subordinate members of the parental household.

Thus, the popular perception that people in less developed countries have large numbers of children simply because they do not know how to avoid conception does not hold up.

Much evidence tells us that in agricultural societies more children and larger households mean a higher, not a lower, standard of living in the short run.

In explaining why they did not wish to join any family-planning programs, the men of Manipur village in the Punjab explained, "Why pay 2,500 rupees for an extra hand? Why not have a son?" (Mamdani 1973:77). High fertility may simply mean that large families have a more favorable standard of living relative to that of smaller families in a situation where the farming sector is stagnant or even deteriorating (Weil 1986). As we see next, the opposite is true in communities where new income opportunities do not support child labor.

With the expansion of urban, industrial, technical, and white-collar employment opportunities, the net return from child rearing can be increased by investing in fewer but better-educated offspring.

In Rampur village, close to the Indian capital of New Delhi, the number of children per woman declined as wage opportunities increased outside the village (Das Gupta 1978). Tractors, tube wells, and pumps reduced the demand for child labor. In addition, parents wanted their children to get more education to prepare for higher-quality jobs in New Delhi. Furthermore, white-collar jobs are becoming available for which children are unsuited because they have not achieved the required levels of literacy and mathematical skills. Even families headed by manual workers desire to have children participate in white-collar, high-status jobs and to give them more schooling. Getting married to an educated and well-employed person has become the ideal, and this can be done only by postponing marriage, which in turn decreases the number of children per woman.

In Indian villages located near the city of Bangalore, three factors accounted for the trend against child labor:

- Land holdings had become fragmented and too small to absorb the labor of additional children in agriculture.

- New nonfarm employment opportunities requiring arithmetic skills and literacy had opened up.

- Educational facilities had been introduced or improved within the villages (Caldwell et al. 1983).

Similarly, on returning to the village of Manipur in the Punjab, Nag and Kak (1984) found a sharp increase in the number of couples practicing contraception and a sharp reduction in the number of sons regarded as desirable.

Manupur, Punjab, India
Collection of cow dung by children to make dung cakes for use as cooking fuel is becoming less important as families become more prosperous and the land is farmed more intensively.

Changes resulting from shifts in the mode of production, may lower the demand for child labor and lead to a reduction in family size.

Shortening or eliminating fallow periods, for example, has led to the disappearance of grazing land within the village so that young boys can no longer make themselves useful tending cattle. The loss of cattle and the increased reliance on petro chemical fuels and fertilizers have also done away with the childhood task of collecting cow dung to be used for fertilizer and fuel. With the introduction of industrial herbicides, children are no longer needed for weeding. Furthermore, the proportion of Manupur workers employed in industrial, commercial, and government sectors has risen substantially. Meanwhile, the mechanization of farm operations, the expanded use of credit, and the need to keep account books have made Manupur parents consciously eager to expand their children's educational horizons. Secondary school enrollment increased in a decade from 63 to 81 percent for boys and from 29 to 63 percent for girls. Parents now want at least one son to have a white-collar job so that the family will not be entirely dependent on agriculture; many parents want both sons and daughters to attend college.

The Poverty Trap

Analysis of the relationships that exist among population pressure, cost/benefits of children, and local environmental depletions helps to explain the persistence of poverty in many developing countries. As presented by the economist Partha Dasgupta (1995), these features form a vicious circle. In many poor countries, as resources are depleted, children must search for firewood and water over longer distances. This increases the demand for children, encourages parents to have additional babies, expands the population, and further exacerbates the depletion of resources. Finally, when they can find no more water or firewood, the families flee to the cities to join the homeless beggars and laborers who sleep on the sidewalks of Bombay and Calcutta. As Dasgupta (1995:44) notes, "No household on its own takes into account the harm it inflicts on others when bringing forth another child."

Fertility rates in developing countries are affected by whether individuals gain economically from increasing or restricting fertility.

John Caldwell (1982) proposes that changes in fertility rates can be accounted for by "wealth flows," which include labor services, goods, money and present and future securities. Higher rates of fertility are likely to be found where wealth flows upward, from younger to older members; where parents rely on children to actively contribute to the economic well-being of the family. This is characteristic of most "poor" subsistence-based societies where children's labor benefits the family. Stable market economies and education reverse this process; wealth begins to flow downward when parents become more economically secure and invest more in their children then they receive in return.

The Contraception, Abortion, and Infanticide Debate

If powerful cultural practices for raising or lowering fertility and mortality rates exist, that implies that human reproduction is much more than an act that takes place at a specific instant, such as the moment when an ovum and sperm unite. It implies that human reproduction is a social process that begins long before conception and that continues long after birth. For human reproduction to take place, prospective parents must have adequate material and psychological support; the pregnant woman and her fetus must be nourished and protected; the nursing mother and her infant must be fed and cared for; and a commitment must be made by the parents, relatives, and other supportive individuals and institutions to find the resources necessary to rear the newborn from infancy and childhood to adulthood.

The decision to make the social effort necessary to give birth to and rear children is heavily influenced by the balance of costs and benefits confronting prospective parents.

This means that when the balance is adverse, some form of birth or death control will be activated at some point in the reproductive process. When and how life or death control measures will be taken, vary from one culture to another. It may be shocking to Western sensibilities that many preindustrial societies employ reproduction-regulating measures that achieve their effect after children are born. That is, they practice some form of direct or indirect infanticide.

In many parts of the world, infanticide occurs when the mother is overburdened and cannot care for the child, the child is unlikely to survive, or the child's paternity is inappropriate.

We must keep in mind that the options for parents in traditional societies are very different from those in our own. !Kung women maximize reproductive success by wide birth spacing, achieved in part by infanticide; or poor and malnourished women may not be physically able to nurse nor have the resources to raise a child that is unlikely to survive (Scrimshaw 1984; Dickman 1984).

Moral issues raised by infanticide are obscured by the failure to distinguish between emic and etic viewpoints. Across cultures, infanticide is regarded as aberrant; yet there are differences in how terms such as "maltreatment," "abuse," and "neglect" are emically defined and the degree to which they are sanctioned by the culture. Yet it is possible to etically define the conditions under which child maltreatment is more or less likely to occur. These include high fertility rates, poverty, food scarcity, rapid socioeconomic change, social isolation, and alcoholism (Korbin 1981, 1987). Recognizing these patterns is essential to understanding the controversy concerning contraception and abortion. Much evidence exists that if reproduction is not limited before or during pregnancy, then it will be limited after pregnancy by direct or indirect infanticide or pedicide (the killing of young children). Attempts to discourage contraception, medical abortion, and other modern prepartum reproductive controls may inadvertently increase reliance on postpartum homicidal practices. With this possibility in mind, we present the case of indirect infanticide in northeast Brazil (Profile 6.1).

Profile 6.1   Indirect Infanticide in Northeast Brazil

Northeast Brazil is a region subjected to periodic droughts, chronic malnutrition, and widespread poverty. It is an area where people live in shantytowns and work as landless laborers on sugarcane plantations for insufficient wages. A large segment of the population suffers from chronic malnutrition that leaves them in a weakened state, prone to infection and disease. Life expectancy in the northeast is only forty years, and the rate of infant mortality is about 200 deaths per 1000 births in the first year of life (compared with a rate of less than 10 in developed countries). Nancy Scheper-Hughes has carried out a study of reproductive processes over a period of 25 years in a shantytown called Alto do Cruzeiro located in this region. Out of a total of 688 pregnancies (an average of 9.5 per woman!), there were 579 live births. Only 308 of these infants survived to age 5, an average of 3.6 infant and child deaths per woman (Scheper-Hughes 1992:307). From circumstantial evidence, it is clear that many of these deaths are best described as forms of indirect infanticide.

Scheper-Hughes found that Alto do Cruzeiro mothers often withdraw support from a particular infant whom they perceive as lacking in "readiness or fitness for life." Mothers express a preference for "quick, sharp, active, verbal, and developmentally precocious children." Children with the opposite traits are not given medical assistance when they became ill, and they are not fed as well as their sisters and brothers. Mothers spoke of children who "wanted to die," whose will and drive toward life are not "sufficiently strong or developed." These unwanted children tend to die during one of the crises of childhood: infections of the umbilical cord, infant diarrhea, or teething. The women regard some childhood diseases as incurable, but the diagnostic symptoms of these diseases are so broad that almost any childhood disorder can be interpreted as a sign that the child is doomed to die: fits and convulsions, lethargy and passivity, retarded verbal or motor function, or a "ghost-like" or "animal-like" appearance.

A.   B.

Doomed Infants, Northeast Brazil

A. Mother said that her 16-month-old son has an "aversion" to life and will not live much longer. The color of his hair and lack of teeth show that he is suffering from advanced protein-calorie malnutrition. But five years later Scheper-Hughes (1992: 389) found him still alive.   B. Baby has anemia and is listless and malnourished. The mother says she is conforming to God's will that the child will soon be an angel.

(continued)

Profile 6.1   Indirect Infanticide in Northeast Brazil *(continued)*

When a child marked with one of these fatal diseases dies, mothers do not display grief: They say there is no remedy, that even if you treat the disease, the child "will never be right," that it is "best to leave them to die," and that no one wants to take care of such a child. "It was a blessing that God decided to take them in their infancy" (Scheper-Hughes 1984:539). Scheper-Hughes (1992:365) estimates that 43 percent of child deaths are attributable to the withdrawal of support from infants and children. The implication for the abortion and contraception debate is this: If people are deprived of the means of preventing unwanted conceptions and births, that does not mean they will support the unwanted child after it is born. An important source of motivation for indirect infanticide is the belief that after babies and infants die, they become angels. The little corpses are placed in cardboard coffins and escorted to shallow graves by a smiling and laughing throng of children. Mothers do not weep when one of their babies becomes an angel (1992:429).

As Scheper-Hughes emphasizes, to the extent that mothers practice indirect (or direct) infanticide through neglect, they are reacting to life-threatening conditions that are not of their own making: shortage of food, contaminated water supplies, unchecked infectious diseases, lack of day care, absence of affordable medical care, and the other stigmas and penalties of extreme poverty. Although recognizing that mothers hasten the deaths of their unwanted children by rationing infant and child care, we must not fall into the trap of "blaming the victims." These women do not have access to modern forms of contraception or to medical abortion, and they are themselves too poorly nourished to limit their pregnancies by prolonging lactation. Moreover, sexual abstinence is difficult for them because of their need to attract male support and companionship. In Scheper-Hughes's words, because of the indignities and inhumanities forced on them, these women must at times "make choices and decisions that no woman and mother should have to make" (1984:541).

We must also guard against the impression that high rates of infanticide occur only in Brazil. Selective neglect of female infants accounts for the lopsided sex ratios found in many societies, including India and China (George et al. 1992). Both indirect and direct infanticide have been widely practiced in Europe in previous centuries (Kertzer 1993). In Japan, perhaps more than elsewhere, direct infanticide was used as a conscious means of family planning during the nineteenth century (Box 6.4).

Today in postindustrial societies women give birth to few children and invest heavily in each one, whereas in

Box 6.4   Infanticide in Nineteenth-Century Japan

Japan's country folk were at one time the world's most efficient managers of human reproduction. During the nineteenth century, Japanese farm couples precisely fitted the size and sexual composition of their broods to the size and fertility of their land holdings. The smallholder's ideal was two children, one boy and one girl; people with larger holdings aimed for two boys and one or two girls. But the Japanese did not stop there! As expressed in a still-popular saying, "first a girl, then a boy," they tried to rear a daughter first and a son second. According to G. William Skinner, this ideal reflected the practice of assigning much of the task of rearing firstborn

sons to an older sister. It also reflected the expectation that the firstborn son would replace his father as the farm's manager at an age when the father was ready to retire, and the son was not yet so old as to have grown surly while waiting to take over. A further complexity was the age at which couples got married. An older man would not dare to delay having a son, and so, if the firstborn was a male, he would count himself fortunate. Since the parents had no way of telling the sex of a child before birth, they were able to achieve these precise reproductive goals only by practicing systematic infanticide. (Skinner 1993)

some preindustrial societies women give birth to many children and invest selectively according to culturally favored characteristics.

Industrial Modes of Reproduction

Shifts in the costs and benefits of rearing children may explain the "demographic transition" that took place in Europe, the United States, and Japan during the nineteenth century. This transition involved a drop in both birthrates and death rates and a slowing of the rate of population growth (Figure 6.1).

With industrialization, the cost of rearing children rose rapidly, especially after the introduction of child labor laws and compulsory education statutes. The skills required to earn a living took longer to acquire; hence parents had to wait longer before they could receive any economic benefits from their children. At the same time, the whole pattern of how people earned their livings changed. Work ceased to be something done by family members on the family farm or in the family shop; rather, people earned wages as individuals in factories and offices. What the family did together was to consume; its only product was children. The return flow of benefits from rearing children came to hinge more and more on their willingness to help out in the medical and financial crises that beset older people. But longer life spans and spiraling medical costs make it increasingly unrealistic for parents to expect such help from their children. Thus, the industrial nations have been obliged to substitute old-age and medical insurance and old-age homes for the preindustrial system in which children took care of their aged parents. To meet the rise

in the cost of rearing children in industrial societies, wives as well as husbands must participate in the wage-earning labor force. As long as this situation continues, more and more men and women will decide to have only one child or none, and more and more individuals will find that the traditional forms of marriage, family, sex, and emotional togetherness are incompatible with the maintenance of middle-class status (Harris and Ross 1987; see also *America Now*).

Women's Status, Education, and Fertility

Demographers agree that a number of factors are responsible for fertility rates. Classic models of demographic change assume that in nation-states, high fertility will not decline until one of the following conditions exist:

■ **There is low infant mortality rate.** Couples will continue to have large numbers of children as long as they are not confident that children will survive and be there to care for them when they are old.

■ **Couples can benefit economically from restricting fertility.** Parents will weigh the costs and benefits of adding additional children to the household.

One of the highest fertility rates in the developing world—6.0 children per woman—occurs in sub-Saharan Africa. According to demographers John and Pat Caldwell (1993), mortality rates—more than half of which are caused by infectious and parasitic diseases—have begun to decline, but fertility rates are declining at a slower pace than in other developing regions. Poverty and rural conditions provide limited opportunities for women to work outside of agriculture. Women do not inherit land, even though they are the main contributors to agricultural production. Thus, land is passed from fathers to sons, leaving women dependent on male children to provide for them in old age. Without sons, a woman loses her right to use land after her husband's death. Women are encouraged to have children because it is an important way for them to gain status. Involuntary infertility is regarded with disdain and is considered punishment for transgressions (Goliber 1997).

There is a worldwide correlation between education and fertility decline. Women with no education have an average of two more children than women with a secondary education (Goliber 1997). Education empowers women to act in their own right.

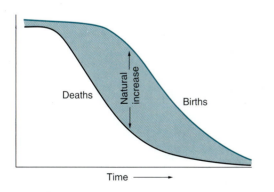

Deaths   Natural increase   Births

Time ⟶

Figure 6.1   Demographic Transition

Rapid fall in death rate followed by slower fall of birthrate cause a temporary increase in population growth until demographic transition is completed.

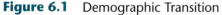

Box 6.5   Population Growth Is a Global Problem

The environmental and social impacts of population growth know no national boundaries and affect us all. Population growth anywhere in the world ultimately has an impact on the entire planet's environment. Many environmental problems, such as air and water pollution and global climate change, transcend national boundaries. As our population grows, demands for resources increase, adding to pollution and waste. More energy is used, escalating the problems of global warming, acid rain, oil spills, and nuclear waste. More land is required for agriculture, leading to deforestation and soil erosion. More homes, factories, and roads must be built, reducing agricultural land and the habitats of other species, leading increasingly to their extinction.

One example of the interconnectedness of our planet's environment is the depletion of tropical rainforests. Rain forest destruction is not only causing a loss of biodiversity, it is also upsetting the atmosphere's climate control capabilities. Sometimes called the "lungs of the Earth," rain forests are vital to all of us.

The world's current population is estimated to be 5.7 billion, with an annual growth rate of 1.5 percent. At this rate, 88 million people (more than the population of Germany) will be added to the population this year alone. That's nearly a quarter of a million additional people to feed every 24 hours!

Another way to see the impact of growth rates is to consider the doubling time of a population. In Kenya, for example, the population is growing at the rate of 3.3 percent and it will double in just 21 years. That isn't much time to build roads, houses, schools, and sanitation facilities to accommodate twice as many people. At the world's present growth rate of 1.5 percent, the Earth's population will double in just 47 years.

Although much of the world's hunger problem stems from uneven food distribution, to feed future populations, agricultural output levels must keep pace with the exponential population growth. Increased investment in agricultural research and technology may result in increased yields, but unless population growth is slowed, food production shortages and environmental degradation will persist. For just how long can we feed this many people? Too little is known about the long-term consequences of soil and water degradation and species extinction to be confident the earth's resources can be relied on to feed even today's population, indefinitely.

According to conservative projections by the U.S. Bureau of the Census, U.S. population could increase 50 percent to more than 390 million by the year 2050. Contrary to what many people believe, the population of the United States is expanding every day. Currently at 263 million, the U.S. population is growing by about 2.5 million people each year, making the United States one of the world's fastest-growing industrialized nations (Mc Falls 1998).

Moreover, women who are educated are more likely to be receptive to family planning (Caldwell 1982; Bradley 1997). Women opt for fewer children when they have opportunities other than child rearing. Finally, as we have seen, education makes children more expensive and less of a short-term benefit. By seeking higher education or jobs in the city, young families find they can no longer afford to raise as many children as their parents, especially if they plan on sending them all to school. (Bradley 1997).

Box 6.6   World Population Growth

In mid-1999, the world population totaled 6 billion, with 77 million people added each year. Since 1973, nearly 1 billion people are added to the world's population approximately every 12–14 years. According to the Population Division of the United Nations (1998), it took all of human history until the early 1800s for the world's population to reach the first billion. It then took

    123 years to reach the second billion
    33 years to add the third
    14 years to add the fourth

    13 years to add the fifth
    12 years to add the sixth.

The most commonly used projection indicates that the world's population will continue to increase rapidly for the greater part of the next century before starting to level off. Virtually all this growth is taking place in developing countries.

Large increases in absolute numbers continue even though the rate of population growth actually peaked in the late 1960s as a result of dramatic declines in birth

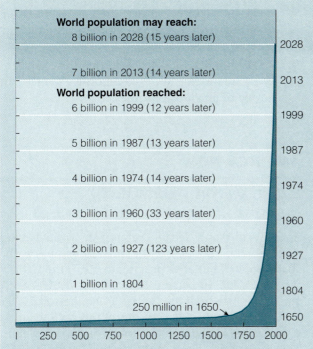

Figure 6.2 World Population Milestones

Source: United Nations 1998.

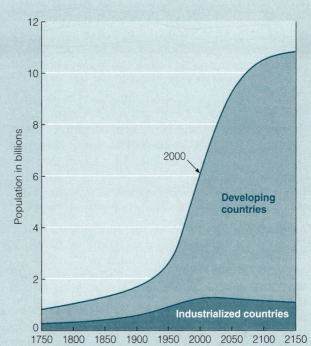

Figure 6.3 World Population Growth, 1750–2150

Source: Population Research Bureau 1997.

and death rates. Overall economic development and improvements in food production and distribution, and public health programs have led to dramatic declines in death rates. The absolute increases in population are the result of population momentum, which results from a high concentration of people in their childbearing years.

Women today are having fewer children than their mothers. However, because of high population growth rates in the past, there are more young men and women who are now beginning to have children; therefore, the total number of babies born continues to increase (Mc Falls 1998).

Summary

1. Production sets limits to reproduction. Contrary to the position advocated by Thomas Malthus, populations do not normally rise to the maximum limit of production, nor are they usually checked by starvation and other catastrophes.

2. Populations are usually maintained well below carrying capacity. Reproduction, however, leads to population pressure, which leads to intensification, depletions, and changes in the modes of production. This can be seen in the sequence leading from big-game hunting to agriculture.

3. Variations in reproductive rates cannot be explained by the universal desire to have children. Rather, reproductive rates reflect the variable costs and benefits of rearing children under different modes of production.

4. Band-organized hunter-gatherer reproduction rates are influenced by the need for women to avoid car-

rying more than one infant at a time over long distances, as well as by the limited intensifiability of the hunter-gatherer mode of production.

5. Sedentary agriculturalists rear more children because agriculture can be intensified, the burden of carrying infants and toddlers is reduced, children more rapidly "pay for themselves," and senior children can take care of juniors.

6. Findings from contemporary peasant societies lend support to the cost–benefit approach to reproductive rates. In Java, children contribute about half of all the wealth of household members. In Bangladesh, male children by age 12 produce more than they consume, and in three more years make up for all previous expenses incurred on their behalf. Moreover, contrary to the popular impression that the poorest peasant households have the most children, we often see a positive correlation between large numbers of children and wealthier families.

7. With the expansion of urban, industrial, technical, and white-collar employment, the benefits of raising fewer but "costlier" children outweigh the advantages of rearing many but "cheaper" children. In India and Sri Lanka, the number of children per woman has declined as children cease to have important roles in agriculture and as the offspring of peasants find advancement through white-collar jobs and business opportunities that require high levels of education. These shifts in the costs of rearing children in relation to new modes of production are similar to the shifts that brought about the demographic transition in nineteenth-century Europe and the United States.

8. Contrary to Malthusian theory, preindustrial cultures regulated the sizes of their families so as to minimize the costs and maximize the benefits of reproduction. Although they lacked a modern technology of contraception or abortion, they were nonetheless never at a loss for means of controlling birthrates and death rates.

9. Four principal categories of practices were used: care and treatment of fetuses, infants, and children; care and treatment of girls and women; intensity and duration of lactation; and variations in the frequency of heterosexual coitus. Subtle gradations exist from abortion to infanticide to induced child mortality. Family planning in nineteenth-century rural Japan is an example of how direct infanticide was used to maximize the benefits provided by children to farm households.

10. Much controversy surrounds the question of whether poor nutrition reduces the ability of women to conceive, but poor nutrition clearly jeopardizes the lives of mother, fetus, and child. The amenorrhea associated with lactation is a more benign form of fertility regulation widely practiced by preindustrial people. Finally, various forms of nonreproductive sex and the degree of sexual abstinence can raise or lower reproductive rates.

11. Although human death rates have a "natural" component, the influence of natural variables is always conditioned to some extent by cultural practices.

12. A vivid example of cultural response to extremely adverse conditions can be seen in Northeast Brazil: Impoverished mothers who lack access to modern contraception or medical abortion contribute to the extremely high rates of infant and child mortality through the selective neglect and indirect infanticide of their unwanted offspring.

13. These findings have important implications for the definition of the beginning of a new human life and the ban on medical abortions and modern contraception. Care must be taken not to blame the victims. Lacking the means of rearing all of their children, these mothers have no way to avoid a tragic choice.

14. It also should be remembered that direct and indirect infanticide were commonly practiced in Europe in previous centuries.

AMERICA NOW

Fertility and the World's Most Expensive Children

After World War II, fertility rates in the United States rose rapidly, producing the phenomenon of the "baby boom." But after peaking in 1957, the fertility rates fell a full 50 percent from 3.69 to 1.81 (Newitt 1985; U.S. Bureau of the Census 1994; Westoff 1989).

A common misunderstanding of this decline is that it was caused by the introduction of birth control pills. This is incorrect, because the decline began in 1957, and it was not until 1963 to 1964 that the pill was widely adopted. Beyond that, many contraceptive devices and practices were available in the 1930s, as demonstrated by the fact that the fertility rate in the 1930s was much lower than immediately after World War II. Moreover, as we have seen, even preindustrial populations have effective means of limiting family size.

The key to understanding the fall in fertility rates in America (and in other hyperindustrial societies) lies in the increased costs and lowered benefits of raising children. The U.S. Department of Agriculture's Family Economics Research Group projects that the cumulative cost of raising a child who will be 17 years old in 2007 will be $151,170 for low-income families, $210,070 for middle-income families, and $293,400 for high-income families (Exter 1991). Add between $50,000 and $100,000 for four years of college, and the cost of raising an upper-middle-class child to adulthood will easily reach half a million dollars. And the more the economy shifts toward services, information, and high-tech jobs, the greater the amount of schooling needed to achieve or maintain middle-class status. In other words, "higher-quality" children cost more.

The average U.S. family cannot rear more than one or two costly high-quality children without a second income, and wives are generally incapable of providing that second income if they have to raise more than one or two children (given the absence of adequate subsidized day care facilities). There are positive feedback effects among working in the labor force, staying in it, and paying the cost of rearing children. The more a woman puts into a job, the more she earns and the more it costs her in the form of "forgone income" to give it up. As forgone income increases, so does the cost of staying home to rear children—and the likelihood that fewer children will be born.

At the same time, children in hyperindustrial societies provide fewer benefits for parents. The counterflow of economic benefits from children to parents has steadily decreased. Children now work apart from parents, establish separate households, and are no longer capable of paying the medical and housing costs of their aged fathers and mothers.

Thus, the current balance of the costs and benefits of rearing children represents the climax of the long-term shift from agricultural to industrial modes of production and from rural to urban ways of life associated with the demographic transition.

Reproductive Technologies, Embryos, and Designer Babies

An increasing number of working couples in America are encountering difficulties conceiving a child. One factor in this increase is the postponement of child-bearing for the years it takes to establish a career and gain earning power. At age 40, women's chances of conceiving decline on an average of 30 percent, and drop off sharply in the following years. Many couples in this situation (sometimes labeled DINKS—"Double Income, No Kids") are able to pay for expensive reproductive procedures. With in vitro fertilization, conception is brought about by combining an egg and sperm in a petri dish. Once fertilization occurs, the resulting embryo can be implanted either inside the natural mother's womb, or a "host" womb to complete the pregnancy. These technologies, once considered radical and experimental, are now routine, and so successful that many reproductive medical specialists offer refunds if the procedure fails.

A woman who is infertile or unable to carry a child to term, must resort to a third party. Unlike male sperm donors, whose physical involvement is minimal, third parties brought in to carry a child for an infertile couple have long term involvement. This practice, known as *surrogacy,* or substitute birth mothering, remains controversial. A number of well-publicized legal cases over parental responsibilities and rights have resulted. As described by anthropologist Helena Ragone, surrogate motherhood consists of a contractual arrangement, usually brokered and supervised by a private agency specializing in surrogate mother programs. The prospective surrogate, who in some cases is married and has her own children, agrees to three or four months of attempted conception via artificial insemination, and nine months of pregnancy. When the child is born, custody is immediately given to the commissioning couple, who have paid for the service, for associated legal charges, and all the medical costs. On average, surrogate mothers receive $10,000–15,000. The cost to the couple is close to $45,000. The average family income of an unmarried surrogate is $16,000–24,000; married surrogates average about $38,700. The commissioning parents are usually educated professionals, with an average family income over $100,000 a year. Despite the etic implications of the disparity in their respective incomes, most surrogate mothers—while not dismissing the importance of the monetary benefits—say their primary motivation is to help the infertile couple. For surrogate mothers, "It's the ultimate gift of love" (Ragone 1994).

KEY TERMS

Boserup's theory
fecundity
infanticide
lactation amenorrhea
libido
Malthusian theory
polygyny
population growth
population pressure

QUESTIONS TO THINK ABOUT

1. What is the relationship between production and reproduction? How do you evaluate the views of Malthus and Boserup on population growth?

2. What are some conscious versus unconscious efforts to control population growth?

3. What are the costs and benefits of rearing children in preindustrial and industrial societies?

4. What is meant by "indirect infanticide?" What economic and health conditions explain child neglect in northeast Brazil?

5. Under what conditions are women in developing countries more likely to have fewer children?

6. What accounts for the decline in fertility rates in America? How would you explain the increasing use of in vitro fertilization and surrogate motherhood?

CHAPTER 7

Human Sexuality

Yam Harvest Dance, Losuia, Trobriand Islands.

Sex versus Gender

Human Sexuality

Sex in Mangaia
Sex in India
Sex in Inis Beag
Sex in America and Europe

Heterosexuality

Restrictive versus Permissive Cultures

PROFILE: The Mehinacu and Extramarital Affairs

Male Homosexuality
PROFILE: Sambia Boy-Inseminating Rituals

Female Homosexuality

Summary

America Now: New Gender Roles and Forms of Sexuality

There is no single pattern of human sexuality. As in all other domains of human life, the definition of what is normal or natural sex varies drastically from one culture to another. Categories such as "gay" and "straight," as defined in Western cultures, are not meaningful elsewhere. Homosexual behavior occurs to some extent in every society, but is as variegated as heterosexual behavior. This chapter is not intended either to change or to reinforce anyone's sexual preferences and practices. However, when we begin to see that our own preferences and activities seem strange to others, perhaps we will be more tolerant of those who seem strange to us.

Sex versus Gender

The etic sexual identity of human beings can be established by examining an individual's chromosomes, interior and exterior sex organs, and secondary sexual characteristics such as body build, size of breasts, and fat deposits (see Box 7.1). Although all societies recognize a distinction between male and female based on some of these features, the emic definition of being male or female, or some other gender, varies considerably from one society to another. The term **sex** refers to the anatomical and physiological attributes of the sexes, whereas **gender** refers to acquired cultural and psychological attributes. Anthropologists use the term *gender* to denote the variable emic meanings associated with culturally defined sex-based identities (Errington and Gewertz 1987; Gilmore 1990; Jacobs and Roberts 1989; Ortner and Whitehead 1981). Gender identity thus refers to a fundamental sense of maleness or femaleness that exists regardless of what one wears or does. In this chapter, we will be concerned with both the etic and emic views of sexual behavior and gender identity.

Human Sexuality

The quest for sexual pleasure motivates much of human behavior and should be seen as an aspect of infrastructure affecting the mode of reproduction. Needless to say, reproduction depends very much on the biological givens of human sexuality. The fact that it takes a male and a female to have sex that results in reproduction should not be taken lightly. Imagine the effects on social life that might occur if only one individual were needed. Or suppose it took three individuals instead of two to make babies. Surely the structural and organizational features of social life would differ vastly from anything that we know of here on earth.

Homo sapiens is capable of being the most sexually active species in the animal kingdom.

We are capable of spending more time in precopulatory courtship and in copulatory sessions than other primates. The capacity for female orgasm, although not unique to humans, as once thought, can be highly developed. So can the frequency of copulatory behavior. The peculiarly human nocturnal emissions from males—wet dreams—convey some notion of the strength of the human sex drive.

Rates of masturbation among both human males and females are matched only in primates kept in zoos or laboratories. Further, the human male seems psychologically preoccupied with sex. American youth

Box 7.1 How Many Biological Sexes Are There?

According to Anne Fausto-Sterling (1993:24), there are at least five biological sexes:

1. *Hermaphrodites:* Individuals born with one testis and one ovary and a mixture of male and female genitalia.

2. *Male pseudohermaphrodites:* Individuals who have two testes and a mixture of male and female genitalia but no ovaries.

3. *Female pseudohermaphrodites:* Individuals who have two ovaries and a mixture of male and female genitalia but no testes.

4. *Females:* Individuals born with two ovaries and female genitalia.

5. *Males:* Individuals born with two testes and male genitalia.

Some hermaphrodites have a large penis and a vagina and enjoy sex with either male or female partners. Fausto-Sterling questions the practice of using surgery and hormones to "correct" hermaphroditic conditions: "Why should we care if there are people whose biological equipment enables them to have sex "naturally" with both men and women? . . . Society mandates the control of intersexual bodies because they blur and bridge the great divide: they challenge traditional beliefs about sexual difference."

Kenyan Man with 40 Wives and 349 Children

Men and women have different reproductive strategies. Men try to win and inseminate as many females as possible so they can pass along more genes. Women in contrast, can bear only a limited number of offspring and attach themselves to men with resources and "good" genes.

ages 12 to 19 report thinking about sex on average every five minutes during their waking hours, and even at age 50, American males think about sex several times a day.

Humans, unlike other primates, have no innate breeding season; they can be ready for sex any hour of any day of any month.

In discussing the importance of biological strategies in human sexuality, one should not lose sight of the ability of culture to override such strategies. Despite the fact that of 186 cultures, 77 percent considered the male and female sex drives to be equally strong (Whyte 1978), female sexuality is often suppressed and denigrated. As we will see later, this suppression of female sexuality occurs most frequently in stratified societies where questions about inheritance

Box 7.2   Female Sexuality

Is there a distinctive pattern of female sexuality that is shared by women everywhere? This question is hard to answer, because the sexual behavior of women is shrouded by cultural taboos and a reluctance to discuss sexual matters. But certain differences between male and female sexual response and the sexuality of other primates provide important clues. Women have menstrual rather than estrous cycles. Unlike most nonhuman primates who mate with males during **estrus,** a restricted period when females are sexually receptive and capable of conceiving, human females mate at all phases of the hormonal cycle and ovulate regardless of whether they have intercourse or not. Women thus have the capacity to be continuously ready for sex and can use their readiness to their advantage. The absence of estrus and

concealed ovulation in females is seen as an adaptation that increases paternal investment—which enhances infant survival and reproductive success—and strengthens the bonds between males and females (Sillén-Tullberg and Møller 1993).

Bioevolutionary theory predicts that women are likely to be choosy in their sexual partners because women incur a heavy investment per child. They therefore choose to mate with men who are likely to contribute to the rearing of their children, but this does not preclude them from mating with other males with good genes if the opportunity arises. In contrast, the most likely **male reproductive strategy** is to mate with multiple partners (Small 1992).

of land and other forms of wealth reduce the freedom of women to mate as they wish.

Notice, however, that all interspecific comparisons of sexual performance can be expressed only as potentials. Because of the pervasive effects of culture, humans can be the least instead of the most sexy of primates.

While sexuality is part of our biological nature, all societies seek to regulate sexual behavior to some degree.

All aspects of sexual relationships, from infantile experiences through courtship and marriage, exhibit an immense amount of cultural variation (Frayser 1985; Gregersen 1986, 1994; Suggs and Miracle 1993). For example, consider the modes of sexuality found among the Mangaians of Polynesia as compared with those of Hindu India and the Irish of Inis Beag.

Sex in Mangaia

According to Donald Marshall (1971), the people of the Pacific Islands of Mangaia never hold hands or embrace in public. Mothers and daughters and fathers and sons do not discuss sexual matters with one another. And yet both sexes are enthusiastic participants in intercourse well before puberty. After puberty, both sexes enjoy an intense premarital sex life. Girls receive varied nightly suitors in the parents' house, and boys compete with their rivals to see how many orgasms they can achieve. The average girl will have three or four sexual partners between the ages 13 to 20, whereas boys may have an average of 10 or more sexual partners. Sexual intimacy is not achieved by first demonstrating personal affection; the reverse is true. For the Mangaian girl, demonstration of sexual virility and masculinity is the first test of her partner's desire for her and a reflection of her own desirability. Personal affection may or may not result from acts of sexual intimacy.

According to a consensus of Marshall's informants, young men expected to have as many as three or four orgasms per night. Sexual activities are described as a national pastime, in which both males and females participate enthusiastically. Marshall concludes there is no indication of anything like romantic love, only sexual attraction. How much confidence can we place in this account? Helen Harris (1995) has called Marshall's study into question on the grounds that his data were collected primarily from discussions with young men, who might have been prone to exaggerate their sexual prowess. She contends that Marshall was the victim of some "good-natured lying" (1995:108). Nonetheless, there are certain important points of agreement between the two accounts. As in many South Sea Polynesian societies, Mangaians have a rela-

tively permissive attitude toward sexual behavior. Romantic love was not absent but was deemphasized in comparison with contemporary patterns of courtship and marriage in other parts of the world. Thus Helen Harris (1995:123) writes of two distinct patterns of heterosexual interaction created by dissimilar emphasis placed on romantic love versus sexual attraction: "The Polynesian pattern emphasizes sexual expression to the point that researchers like Marshall actually overlook other (romantic) features of heterosexual relationships while the American pattern minimizes sex to such an extent that our own social scientists fail to consider it when discussing romantic love."

Sex in India

A very different attitude toward sexual activity appears to characterize Hindu India. There, Hindu men widely believe, as do men in other societies, that semen is a source of strength and that it should not be squandered.

Hindu Erotic Art: Temple of Kajuraho
Erotic themes are common in the sacred art of India.

In India it is commonly believed that semen is not readily available; it takes forty days and forty drops of blood to make one drop of semen. According to ancient belief, semen is ultimately stored in a reservoir in the head, whose capacity is 20 tolas (6.8 ounces). Celibacy was the first requirement of true fitness, because every sexual orgasm means the loss of a quantity of semen, laboriously formed (Carstairs 1967).

This attitude toward the loss of semen contradicts the stereotype of hypersexuality that is based on the prominence of erotic themes in Hindu temple art and architecture. Indeed some evidence indicates that coital frequency among Hindus is considerably less than among Anglo-Americans in the United States in comparable age groups (Nag 1972). India's high level of fertility and population growth are not the result of sexual overindulgence but of economic conditions that give large families a higher standard of living in the short term (see Chapter 6).

Sex in Inis Beag

The extreme opposite of sex in Mangaia, but still different from sex in Hindu India, is practiced in Inis Beag, an island off the coast of Ireland. Here sex is shrouded in guilt and sin; it is regarded as a duty women must perform for their husbands. Women remain entirely passive during coitus. They engage in a minimum of foreplay; there is rough fondling of the buttocks and some kissing. Husbands always initiate sex and reach orgasm as quickly as they can on the assumption that women have no interest in prolonging intercourse. Husband and wife keep their underwear on during intercourse and turn off the lights even though they are not visible to anyone but themselves (Messenger 1971).

Female orgasm is unheard of. Sex is never discussed among friends or family; parents are so embarrassed that they cannot bring themselves to discuss sex with their children. Instead, they believe that nature will take its course after marriage. Sex is also thought of as being injurious to one's health. Therefore, a man will refrain from having sex the night before he is to perform a strenuous activity.

Sex in America and Europe

Recent large-scale surveys provide new information on a wide range of sexual practices in the United States. Here are some of the more important findings (DeLamater 1995; Lauman 1994):

- The modal (most common) respondent engaged in sexual activity "a few times a month."

- Americans ages 18 to 59 fall into three groups: one-third have sex twice a week or more; one-third have sex just a few times a month; and the rest have sex just a few times a year or not at all.

- Vaginal intercourse is preferred by more men and women than any other sexual practice.

- Of those interviewed, 80 percent had had only one to zero sexual partners in the preceding year.

- Twenty-five percent of married men and 10 percent of married women engaged in extramarital sexual activity.

- Fifty percent of cohabiting relationships last less than one year.

- 4.9 percent of men and 4.1 percent of women report that they have had sexual activity with a same-gender partner since age 18.

Large-scale surveys carried out in the United Kingdom and France (Aldous 1992; Spira et al. 1992) do not support the stereotypes of the hypersexual Frenchman or the reluctant Britisher:

- Both United Kingdom and French men report an average of 1.2 sexual partners in a year.

- Both British and French women averaged about one partner per year.

- 3.6 percent of British men and 4.1 percent of French men report having had sex with a man.

Heterosexuality

Despite a high level of curiosity, very little is known about the actual forms of coitus in different societies. The major reason is that in virtually every society that has ever been studied, sex is performed in private. Anthropologists, therefore, have had to rely on accounts of sexual behavior elicited from informants rather than on actual observation. (Ethical issues inhibit discussion of participatory sexual observations, if any, by anthropologists during fieldwork.)

Bronislaw Malinowski's account (in the early 1900s) of lovemaking in the Trobriands, although told from the male perspective, remains one of the best descriptions of non-Western sexual performance. We find the young couple on their way to a secluded spot in the jungle. They spread their mat, and lie down side by side. When they are sure they are not being observed, pubic leaf and grass skirt are removed. They run their fingers through each other's hair and catch and eat each other's lice. They entwine their arms and legs and talk for a long time about their love for each other with endearing phrases. They rub noses, cheek against cheek, mouth against mouth. Their caresses become more passionate, tongue is rubbed against tongue, and they suck and bite the lower lip until blood comes; they bite each other's cheeks, noses, and especially their eyelashes. They scratch their backs with their fingernails, inflicting deep lacerations.

The woman lies on her back, the legs spread and raised, and the knees flexed. The man kneels against her buttocks, her legs resting on his hips. The more usual position, however, is for the man to squat in front of the woman and, with his hands resting on the ground, to move toward her, or, taking hold of her legs, to pull her toward him. When the sexual organs are close together, the insertion takes place. Again the woman may stretch her legs and place them directly on the man's hips, with his arms outside them, but the far more usual position is with her legs embracing the man's arms and resting on the elbows. As the act proceeds, the man . . . waits until the woman is ready for orgasm. Then he presses his face to the woman's, embraces her body and raises it toward him, she putting her arms around him at the same time and, as a rule, digging her nails into his skin. (1929:334ff)

According to Malinowski, the Trobrianders reject the "missionary position" (woman on back, legs spread with man on top facing her). Many other cultures also reject this position. But even making allowance for Western influence, it is probably the most common position worldwide. Rear entry is reported as the preferred position in a small number of cultures in South America and Africa. Intercourse performed standing is the most common position depicted in Hindu temple erotic art, but it was probably associated with temple prostitutes and was not otherwise in common use.

As for noncoital heterosexual practices, kissing is widespread among state-organized societies, but it is unknown among many other cultures. (Despite the importance of mouth-to-mouth contact among the Trobrianders, kissing is not part of their lovemaking.) Data on the frequency of heterosexual oral sex are scarce, but if cunnilingus is present, fellatio is also likely to occur. Masturbation occurs worldwide and is generally considered normal adolescent behavior, but when practiced by adults, it is almost universally condemned (Gregersen 1986:91, 1994).

This survey can claim to depict only a tiny portion of the immensely variegated forms of heterosexuality. For the most part, our information identifies only the statistically most frequent techniques found in a particular culture. A vast amount of individual variation in sexual preferences and avoidances remains. And on top of that, the picture is further complicated by the widespread occurrence of homosexual preferences and avoidances and various culturally constructed combinations of homosexuality and heterosexuality.

Restrictive versus Permissive Cultures

Why do some societies restrict heterosexual sex whereas others are more permissive? George Murdock notes that sexual behavior is more likely to be regulated where it serves the interests of society.

Greater restrictions on premarital sex occur in socially stratified societies.

Restrictions fall primarily on females and are largely a precaution against childbearing out of wedlock (Murdock 1949:265). Stratified societies with differential wealth are concerned with preventing their children from marrying beneath them. Premarital sexual restrictions thus ensure that daughters will be chaste and in a position to marry well.

Control over female sexuality is a way of controlling property and social status.

Widespread disapproval of adultery is based on the special sexual privilege associated with marriage. Yet some societies are more lax about extramarital affairs, as long as they are conducted discreetly (see Profile 7.1 on the Mehinacu on page 98). Adultery can be disruptive to social bonds and create uncertainty regarding paternity. Societies with patrilineal inheritance—particularly where there is land scarcity—are more likely to place restrictions on sexuality to ensure that a man's estate is passed on to his biological sons, and not those of a lineage rival.

In Naples, for example, religious ideology reinforces sexual control by making female purity sacred—virginity and chastity are essential to female purity. Motherhood is regarded with reverence, and a woman's identity is bound to her role as a caring mother. Women are expected to guard their sexuality to preserve their family honor. A woman who engages in sex outside marriage jeopardizes her position within her family and society (Goddard 1996).

Sexually permissive societies tend to be kin-based societies with corporate ownership of land, and minimal property inheritance. Here women increase their well-being by having sex with several men who assume possible paternity and provide food and protection for her and her offspring. Nisa, a !Kung woman, describes the rewards of multiple sex partners: "One man can

Profile 7.1   Mehinacu Extramarital Affairs

In the central Brazil village of the Mehinacu (see Profile 11.1), extramarital liaisons make up a large part of Mehinacu sexual activity. According to Thomas Gregor (1973, 1985), youngest men report having sex with other adulterous women four to five times more often than with their spouses. Sex with a mistress is said to be more pleasurable than with a spouse. Affairs are typically initiated by men. A man wants to be fairly certain he will not be rejected before approaching a woman outside the village, or he may use an intermediary to set up the relationship for him. Once the affair is established, the lovers arrange to meet in the forest in a secluded spot, invisible from the main path. When the couple meet, they may exchange small gifts and then have sex, often with minimum of foreplay, especially if they are concerned about being observed. Afterward they may talk for a while to assure one another that they enjoyed the experience. There is no word for a woman's sexual climax, and it appears that women do not have orgasms from intercourse (Gregor 1985:34). Women seem to take pleasure in sex, but their interest is lower than that of men. Men often begrudge the fact that women are "stingy with their genitals." Nonetheless, extramarital relationships are highly valued. When they are new they are often emotionally intense, and they may actually last a lifetime. Upon the death of a partner, the survivor may go through an attenuated and discreet mourning process, being sure that his or her spouse is not offended.

The Mehinacu do not believe that pregnancy results from a single sexual encounter. According to Gregor, "they believe that a newborn is literally composed of accumulated ejaculate from repeated instances of sexual intercourse" (1973:246). This theory of conception and paternity is incorporated into the kinship system so that if a woman has sexual relations with several lovers during pregnancy, they are all considered to have jointly produced the child along with the woman's husband. When her children mature, a woman identifies a lover who was close to her so that her children can recognize him as a kind of father, and honor the incest taboo in their relationships to his other children.

In a village of 37 adults, at the time of Gregor's initial study there were approximately 88 affairs (out of 150 theoretically possible pairings after eliminating incestuous relations). The average man engages in 4.4 affairs at a time, and most men are close to that average. Women, in contrast, have a much greater range: "The three most sexually active women in the village account for almost forty percent of the total number of liaisons, while the three least active women account for none of the community's extramarital relationships" (Gregor 1985:36).

The villagers' overt enthusiasm about sex is tempered with anxiety about the consequences of their sexuality. These anxieties are expressed in myth, dreams, and ritual. Men express a great deal of ambivalence toward women. The men claim, for example, that female sexuality, menstruation, and female genitalia are unattractive and can cause loss of strength, stunted growth and, in myth, even castration. Moreover, some men fear sexual dysfunction. Sexual function is a critical part of a masculine identity, and if a man's failure becomes common knowledge, his reputation as a lover is hurt by gossip. Also, because of the imbalance in male and female sexual interest, men's libido is always greater than the opportunity for sexual affairs. Thus, even in this permissive setting, sex is scarce relative to male demand, and the men experience sexual frustration and dissatisfaction.

---

give you very little. One man gives you only one kind of food to eat. But when you have lovers, one brings you something and another brings you something else. One comes at night with meat, another with money, another with beads. Your husband also does things and gives them to you." (Shostak 1981:271)

Male Homosexuality

Attitudes toward homosexuality range from horror to chauvinistic enthusiasm. Given the many ways in which humans separate sexual pleasure from unwanted reproduction, the widespread occurrence of homosexual behavior should come as no surprise. More surprising are the many people who masturbate themselves or their partners, take birth control pills, use condoms and spermicidal jellies, have abortions, and practice various gymnastic forms of noncoital heterosexuality but who condemn and ridicule homosexual behavior on the grounds that it is "unnatural." Were it not for medical advances, "good, clean, natural" heterosexual men and women would still be dying in vast numbers from syphilis. To say that homosexuality is as natural as heterosexuality is not to say that the majority of men and women find same-sex individuals to be as arousing and erotically satisfying as members of the opposite sex. But we have no evidence that people predisposed to prefer opposite-sex relationships are also predisposed to loathe and avoid same-sex relationships. The reverse is also true; that is, it is doubtful that the small numbers of humans who are genetically predisposed to prefer

Box 7.3   Is Homosexuality Genetic?

There is some evidence that at least one gene may be involved in predisposing men to develop homosexual preferences. It has long been known that in the United States brothers of gay men tend to be gay at a higher rate than men in the general population. (According to the latest studies, the frequency of male homosexuality in the United States is about 4 or 5 percent.) Because brothers tend to share the same environment, these data carry little weight. However, a study carried out by Dean Hamer and associates at the National Cancer Institute (Hamer 1993) further found more homosexual males on the mother's side than on the father's side, specifically among the maternal uncles and sons of maternal uncles. This indicates that if a gene for male homosexuality does exist, it is located on the X-chromosome, which is inherited exclusively through women. Hamer compared the X-chromosomes of the gay men in the study and found that most had the same set of genetic markers at the tip of the long arm of the X-chromosome, but as yet the gene or genes have not been found. Note that even if such genes actually exist, their presence will not be able to account for the very high rates of homosexuality found in societies like the Etoro, Sambia, and Azande, nor for the shift from homosexuality to heterosexuality as men in these societies grow up and get married. As with all human behavioral traits, sexual preference must be considered an outcome of both genetic tendencies and cultural conditioning.

same-sex relationships are born with phobic tendencies toward the opposite sex (see Box 7.3).

It takes a great deal of training and conditioning, parental disapproval, social ridicule, threats of fiery hell, and repressive legislation to convert our kind's bountiful sexual endowment into an aversion against the mere thought of homosexual attraction. Most societies—between 64 and 69 percent (Gregersen 1994:341), according to one survey—don't make the effort to create this aversion and either tolerate or actually encourage some degree of same-sex along with opposite-sex erotic behavior. If one includes clandestine and noninstitutionalized practices, then it is safe to say that homosexual behavior occurs to some extent in every human population.

Gay Couples
Not all gay men and lesbians live unconventional lives. Homosexual behavior is as diverse as heterosexual behavior.

Homosexual behavior in different cultural contexts is as variegated as heterosexual behavior (Weston 1993). For example, in many cultures there is a sharp contrast between male and female roles, which makes it difficult to accept effeminate males. Moreover, in many Latin countries there is a widely occurring distinction between active and passive homosexual roles. A man is never dishonored if he takes the active role, but the male partner who takes the passive role jeopardizes his masculinity. In Brazil, household surveys reveal that a high proportion of both heterosexual and homosexual men engage in anal sex to avoid unwanted pregnancies. Others do so for the pleasure and excitement associated with the nonconforming practice (Herdt 1997:143).

Several cultures studied by anthropologists incorporate male homosexuality into their systems for developing masculine male personalities, but do not have a concept for homosexual or gay. Thus, among Native Americans of the Great Plains, certain men donned a combination of male and female attire and dedicated themselves to providing sexual favors to great warriors. These individuals were regarded as a separate gender and were honored in turn. For a warrior to be served by one of them was proof of manliness (Callender and Kochems 1983; Fulton and Anderson 1992; Williams 1986). Similarly, among the Azande of the Sudan, also renowned for their prowess in warfare, the unmarried warrior-age males, who lived apart from women for several years, had homosexual relations with the boys of the age grade of warrior apprentices. After their experiences with "boy-wives," the warriors graduated to the next age status, got married, and had

Finds-Them-and-Kills-Them, a Crow male homosexual "man-woman" or "two-spirit."

Azande

Azande men were known for their prowess in warfare. Unmarried warrior males had homosexual relations with younger apprentices and then went on to marry and have many children.

children (Evans-Pritchard 1970). Although the Azande allow for age-structured relations between boys and men, they penalize any other form of homosexual relations that does not conform with the accepted pattern.

Male homosexuality was highly ritualized in many New Guinea and Melanesian societies. It was ideologically justified in a manner that has no equivalent in Western notions of sexuality.

Ritualized homosexuality was not viewed as a matter of individual preference but as a social obligation.

Men were not classifiable as homosexual, heterosexual, or bisexual. All men were obliged to partake in homoerotic acts as a matter of sacred duty and practical necessity. For example, among the Etoro, who live on the slopes of the central Papua, New Guinea, highlands, the emics of homosexuality revolve around the belief that semen is the source not only of babies but of manhood as well. Like the men of Hindu India, the Etoro believe that each man has only a limited supply of semen. When the supply is exhausted, a

man dies. Although coitus with their wives is necessary to prevent the population from becoming too small, husbands stay away from wives most of the time. Indeed, sex is taboo between husband and wife for over 200 days of the year. The Etoro males regard wives who want to break this taboo as witches. To complicate matters, the supply of semen is not something that a man is born with. Semen can be acquired only from another male. Etoro boys get their supplies by having oral intercourse with older men. But it is forbidden for young boys to have intercourse with each other and, like the oversexed wife, the oversexed adolescent boy is regarded as a witch and condemned for robbing his age-mates of their semen supply. Such wayward youths can be identified by the fact that they grow faster than ordinary boys (Kelly 1976).

Gilbert Herdt (1997:183) argues that the ancient Greeks, the Azande warrior, and the New Guinea villager are not homosexual, because they do not identify themselves as such. Same-gender relations have a different meaning in these cultures and should not be confused with what Americans call gay or lesbian (see the America Now section at the end of this chapter).

As Dennis Werner (1979) has shown, societies that experience population pressure on resources and that try to minimize population growth tend to accept or encourage homosexual and other nonreproductive forms of sex. Intolerance of homosexuality, in contrast, is associated with a desire for population growth

Profile 7.2   Sambia Boy-Inseminating Rituals

Among the Sambia of the southeastern highlands of New Guinea, boys are allowed to play with girls only until age 4 or 5. Thereafter, they are strictly regulated, and all heterosexual play is forcefully punished. Late in childhood, boys undergo a series of "inseminating rituals," which are not primarily intended to give pleasure but to help the younger males grow and become masculine. This gift of semen from their seniors is intended to prepare the young boys for warfare and to enhance their reproductive ability. Males must then continue to avoid any heterosexual contact until they are married (Herdt 1987).

"Boy-inseminating rituals" have several distinct features (Herdt 1997:84):

They are implemented through initiation or puberty rites that are collective rather than individualized.

The rites have religious sanctification in which the ancestral spirits bless the proceedings.

The erotic relations are associated with graded social roles that enable the boy to advance to a higher status.

These sexual relations do not preclude marriage and passion with women, which offers a different form of social achievement and sexual desire.

Ritualized insemination and semen beliefs in New Guinea and Melanesia are closely associated with a heightened level of male–female sexual antagonism, fear of menstrual blood, and exclusive male rituals and dwellings. Obligatory same-gender sexual relations and intense warfare in New Guinea are also strongly associated with each other. Warfare justified and rationalized an ethos of masculine prowess that placed men above women as desirable sexual partners (Herdt 1984a:169). Finally, as in other patrilocal warlike village societies (see Chapter 11, section on "Warfare and Female Infanticide") their juvenile sex ratios show a marked imbalance favoring males over females, attaining ratios as high as 140:100 (Herdt 1984b:57).

Today both warfare and boy-inseminating rituals have died out, yet a small number of men report voluntarily having had anal sex at the age of 16, without the support of traditional customs. Herdt suggests that within a generation same-gender relations may more closely resemble the kind of homosexual roles known elsewhere.

and opposition to abortion and infanticide. It is difficult to avoid the conclusion that ritual homosexuality in New Guinea and Melanesia is part of a population-regulating system. In addition, Melvin Ember (1982) has demonstrated that warfare in New Guinea is correlated with competition for scarce or depleted resources, which implies a high level of population pressure. However, there is some controversy among anthropologists regarding the relationship between ritual homosexuality and population control.

Whatever the explanation for obligatory male homosexuality may be, its existence should serve as a warning against equating one's own culturally determined expressions of sexuality with human nature.

Female Homosexuality

Less is known about female homosexuality than about male homosexuality because of the predominance of male-biased ethnographies (see Chapter 15). Unlike males, females seldom seem to be subjected to initiation rituals that entail homosexual relationships. It is reported, however, that among the Dahomey of

West Africa adolescent girls prepared for marriage by attending all-female initiation schools where they learned how to "thicken their genitalia" and engaged in sexual intercourse (Blackwood 1986).

With the exception of the Dahomey (see Profile 15.1), women seldom bear the brunt of military combat and thus have little opportunity to use same-sex erotic apprenticeships to form close-knit teams of warriors. Similarly, enforced absence from the classical Greek academies precluded women's participation in homosexual philosophical apprenticeships, and because men in most stratified societies controlled women's sexual behavior, the incidence of overt lesbian behavior between women of high rank and slave girls or other social inferiors was probably never very high.

More commonly, women do adopt socially sanctioned "not-man-not-woman" gender roles: dressing like men; performing manly duties such as hunting, trapping, and going to war; and using their in-between gender status to establish their credibility as shamans. Thirty-three Native American societies are reported to have accepted gender transformations in women (Albers 1989:135). Among several western Native American tribes, female not-men-not-women entered into

Lesbian Couple

Regardless of sexual orientation, everyone seeks love and sexual intimacy and pleasure.

enduring lesbian relationships with women, whom they formally "married" (Blackwood 1986).

Several reported cases of institutionalized lesbianism are related to the migration of males in search of work. On the Caribbean island of Carriacou, where migrant husbands stay away from home for most of the year, older married women bring younger single women into their households and share the absent husband's remittances in exchange for sexual favors and emotional support. A similar pattern exists in South Africa, where it is known as the "mummy baby game" (Gay 1986).

One of the most interesting forms of institutionalized lesbianism occurred in mid-nineteenth-century to early twentieth-century China in several of the silk-growing districts of the Pearl River delta region in southern Kwangtung. There, single women provided virtually all the labor for the silkworm factories. Although poorly paid, they were better off than their prospective husbands. Rather than accept the subordinate status that marriage imposed on Chinese women, the silk workers formed antimarriage sisterhoods that provided economic and emotional support. Although not all the 100,000 sisters formed lesbian relationships, enduring lesbian marriages involving two and sometimes three women were common (Sankar 1986).

Even when allowance is made for blind spots in the ethnographic reports of male observers, there ap-

pear to be fewer forms of institutionalized female than of male homosexuality. Does this mean that females engage in homosexual behavior less often than males? Probably not. More likely, most female homosexuality has simply been driven underground or has been expressed in noninstitutionalized contexts that escape observation. Although seldom reported, adolescence is probably an occasion for a considerable amount of female homosexual experimentation the world over. Only recently, for example, has it come to light that among the Kalahari !Kung, young girls engage in sexual play with other girls before they do so with boys (Shostak 1981:114). Polygynous marriage (see Chapter 9) is another context in which lesbian relationships probably flourish. The practice seems to have been common in West Africa among the Nupe, Hausa, and Dahomey, and among the Azande and Nyakyusa in East Africa. In Middle Eastern harems, where cowives seldom saw their husbands, many women entered into lesbian relationships despite the dire punishment such male-defying behavior could bring (Blackwood 1986; Lockard 1986).

Summary

1. Cross-cultural variations in sexual behavior prevent any single culture from serving as the model for what is natural in the realm of sex.

2. Mangaian heterosexual standards and practices contrast with those of Hindu India, Inis Beag, and contemporary industrial societies.

3. Restrictions on sexuality are related to increased stratification and the need to control property and social status.

4. Homosexuality also defies neat stereotyping, as can be seen in the examples of the Crow and the Azande. Ritual male homosexuality, as among the Etoro, Sambia, and other New Guinea and Melanesian societies, is an elaborate, compulsory form of sexuality that has no equivalent in Western societies. It was probably associated with the need to rear male warriors under conditions of environmental stress and intense intersocietal competition.

5. Although genes may contribute in a minimal sense to homosexual activities and preferences, it is clear from these examples and the worldwide variability of such activities and preferences that the way homosexuality is expressed is largely under the control of culture.

6. Female homosexuality is less frequently reported, possibly as a result of male bias among ethnogra-

phers and the suppression of female liberties by dominant males.

AMERICA NOW

New Gender Roles and Forms of Sexuality

A profound change has taken place in the United States regarding attitudes toward premarital and extramarital intercourse. The number of adults who in response to questionnaire surveys say that they sanction or accept premarital and extramarital intercourse rose from 20 percent to over 50 percent after World War II. During the same period, the number of unmarried couples who say they are living together increased almost as fast as the number of female-headed families (Herbers 1985). Considerable evidence points to an increase in premarital sexual activity among unwed juveniles and young adults. Planned Parenthood studies show that half of the teenagers graduating from high school have an active sex life.

Given the wide resistance to intensive, publicly supported contraceptive programs for teenagers (New York City is an exception), it is not surprising that the rate of teenage pregnancies has doubled since 1965 and that the United States now finds itself with the highest rate in the industrial world. This distinction is partially attributable to the very high rate of pregnancies among U.S. black teenagers, but the rate for white teenagers (93 per 1000) is double that of England and quadruple that of the Netherlands (Brozan 1985; Hacker 1992:77). Four out of ten American women will have become pregnant by the time they reach 20 years. With the spread of AIDS, condoms have become the first line of defense against teenagers giving birth to AIDS-infected infants.

The basic shift in U.S. attitudes toward sexuality can be described in terms of an ever-widening separation of the hedonistic from the reproductive aspects of sexual relations. One derivative of this trend is the increased production and consumption of pornographic materials, including "adult" books and magazines such as *Playboy, Hustler,* and *Penthouse.* Pornographic videocassettes make up a substantial percentage of the rental volume of stores that rent cassettes to home users, and pornography has quickly invaded the cyberspace of the Internet. "What would have been off-limits even in a red-light district a few years ago is now available for people to see in their living rooms" (Lindsey 1985:9).

The relaxation of U.S. laws against homosexuality can also be viewed as an expression of the same trend. As we have seen, societies that interdict homosexuality are strongly pronatalist and tend to condemn all forms of sex that do not lead to childbirth and parenting. Heterosexual couples committed to the separation of sex from reproduction do not differ from homosexual couples in this regard. The increase in the numbers of self-identified homosexuals testifies to the general liberalization of sexual rules of conduct since World War II. Today gay and lesbian teens are "coming out" in high school; the average age is 16—although awareness of same-gender attraction begins at about age 10. According to Herdt (1997:134), "A new kind of social and political activism has arisen. Lesbian and gay youths are challenging society in ways that are no less revolutionary than discriminations based on skin color, gender, or religion." At the same time, sexual promiscuity among both homosexuals and heterosexuals appears to be declining (Laumann 1994). There has been enthusiasm among gay activists for domestic partnership legislation and efforts to formally legitimize the domestic arrangements by expanding the legal definitions of "family." Gay couples are raising children who are turning out healthy and well adjusted (Herman 1996), and they insist on public recognition of their relationships (Lewin 1996).

Porn

Making money out of sex is a big industry in the United States.

Out of the Closet
A gay rights march in New York City.

KEY TERMS

cultural regulation of sexuality
estrus
gender
male and female reproductive strategies
male-inseminating rituals
sex

QUESTIONS TO THINK ABOUT

1. What are the differences in male and female mate selection?

2. Under what conditions is female sexuality most likely to be suppressed by society?

3. Under what conditions do husbands "allow" female infidelity? What do they gain in the arrangement?

4. Why are male-inseminating rituals not considered homosexual behavior?

5. Under what circumstances might women adopt homosexual social roles?

CHAPTER 8

Economic Organization

Market day in Columbia.

Definition of Economy

Exchange
Reciprocal Exchange
Reciprocity and the Freeloader
Reciprocity and Trade
Trade in the Kula Ring

Redistributive Exchange

Reciprocity versus Redistribution

The Infrastructural Basis of Redistribution and Reciprocity

Stratified Redistribution

Price Market Exchange: Buying and Selling
Money
Capitalism
PROFILE: Primitive Capitalism? The Kapauku Case
Property Ownership

Patterns of Work

Summary

America Now: Emergent Varieties of Capitalism

In this chapter, our concern is not with types of production processes, such as hunting and gathering, pastoralism, or industrial manufacturing, but with the way in which people organize labor and how they regulate or control access to resources, goods, and services. At this point, in other words, our focus will shift from the infrastructural to the structural aspects of society and culture. This will enable us to study the extent to which the organizational features of production can be explained by the evolution of particular kinds of infrastructures.

Economies differ according to their characteristic modes of control over production and exchange. We will identify the principal kinds of exchange and explore their relationship to infrastructural conditions. We will see that many societies organize their economic activities without the use of money and that money itself comes in many specialized forms in addition to the all-purpose money with which we are familiar. The subject of money leads to the question of whether capitalist economies can be found among nonstate societies. The chapter also takes up the question of whether people work harder in industrial than in hunter-gatherer societies.

sources, human labor, and technology to acquire, produce, and distribute material goods and specialist services in a structured, repetitive fashion"(Dalton 1969: 97).

These two definitions of economy are not incompatible. Anthropologists stress the fact that cultural traditions shape the specific motivations for producing, exchanging, and consuming goods and services. Different cultures value different goods and services and tolerate or prohibit different kinds of relationships among the people who produce, exchange, and consume. Some cultures emphasize economic cooperation; others emphasize competition. Some emphasize increased consumption as a means of increasing social status, whereas others value generosity and giving away goods as a means of achieving prestige.

To understand the economies of different cultures, anthropologists must consider the goals and motivations behind the decision-making process as well as the institutionalized activities and relationships that result from production and distribution.

Definition of Economy

In one sense, the term *economy* refers to the kinds of decisions people make when they have only limited resources or wealth and there are unlimited goods and services they would like to acquire or use. Most professional economists hold that in making such decisions, people tend to **economize**, to make choices they believe provide the greatest benefit to them. This approach views people as active strategists, as "economizing" actors who select the opportunities that yield the maximal good (or maximize benefits while minimizing costs; Plattner 1989:8). Unlike Western economic systems, which emphasize profit motivation, many people around the world place other goals above material wealth acquisition. People may define maximal good in terms of prestige, risk aversion or increased leisure time, depending on how a culture defines "self-interest." For most anthropologists, however, an economy refers to the activities people engage in to produce and obtain goods and services (setting aside the question of whether they are "economizing"). Economics is embedded in the social process; production is carried out in families and communities, and distribution, exchange and consumption have primary social and political functions. In this second sense, an "economy is a set of institutionalized activities which combine natural re-

Exchange

For the most part, humans either directly consume the products of their labor, or they distribute it by means of exchange. **Exchange** is the practice of giving and receiving valued objects and services. This practice is more highly developed in our species than in any other. Human beings could not survive infancy without receiving basic resources and services from their parents. However, patterns of exchange differ markedly from one culture to another. Following the work of the economist Karl Polanyi, anthropologists have come to distinguish three main types of exchange: reciprocal, redistributive, and market.

Reciprocal Exchange

One of the most striking features of the economic life of simple hunter-gatherers and small-scale agricultural societies is the prominence of exchanges conducted according to the principle known as *reciprocity*.

Reciprocal exchanges involve mutual giving and receiving among people of equal status in which there is (1) no need for immediate return, (2) no systematic calculation of the value of the services and products exchanged, and (3) an overt denial that a balance is being calculated or that the balance must come out even.

Reciprocity

Hunter-gatherers of the Kalahari exchange the day's catch.

Richard Lee has written a succinct description of reciprocity as it occurs among the !Kung: In the morning, anywhere from one to sixteen of the twenty adults in the !Kung band leave camp to spend the day collecting or hunting. They return in the evening with whatever food they have managed to find. Everything brought back to camp is shared equally, regardless of whether the recipients have spent the day sleeping or hunting. Eventually all the adults will have gathered or hunted and given as well as received food. But wide discrepancies in the balance of giving and receiving may exist among individuals over a long period without becoming the subject of any special talk or action.

Some form of reciprocal exchange occurs in all cultures, especially among relatives and friends. In many parts of the world, for example, husbands and wives, friends, and sisters and brothers, and other kin maintain informal, uncalculated, give-and-take transactions that are economic in nature. Teenagers do not pay cash for their meals at home or the use of the family car. Wives do not bill their husbands for cooking a meal. Friends give each other birthday gifts and Christmas presents. These exchanges, however, constitute only a small portion of the total acts of exchange. The great majority of exchanges in modern cultures involve rigidly defined counterflows that must take place by a certain time (as anyone who has forgotten to pay their credit card bill can tell you).

Reciprocity and the Freeloader

As we know from the experience of taking from parents or from giving a birthday or holiday gift and not receiving one in return, the failure of an individual to reciprocate in some degree will eventually lead to bad feelings, even between close relatives and friends or spouses. No one likes a **"freeloader"** ("moocher" or "sponge"). In economies dominated by reciprocity, a grossly asymmetrical exchange does not go unnoticed. Some individuals will come to enjoy reputations as diligent gatherers or outstanding hunters, whereas others acquire reputations as shirkers or malingerers. No specific mechanisms exist for obliging the debtors to even up the score, yet subtle sanctions discourage one from becoming a complete freeloader. Such behavior generates a steady undercurrent of disapproval. Eventually freeloaders may meet with violence because they are suspected of being bewitched or of bewitching others through the practice of sorcery (see Chapter 11, in the "Shamans and Public Opinion" section). Reciprocal exchange, therefore, does not mean that products and services are simply given away without any thought or expectation of return. No culture can rely exclusively on purely altruistic sentiments to get its goods and services produced and distributed. But in simple band and prestate village societies, people produce and reciprocally exchange goods in such a way as to avoid the notion of material balance, debt, or obligation. This system works because reciprocal exchanges are expressed as kinship obligations. These kinship obligations establish reciprocal expectations with respect to food, clothing, shelter, and other goods.

Kinship-embedded reciprocal exchanges constitute only a small portion of modern exchange systems, whereas among hunter-gatherers and small-scale agriculturalists almost all exchanges take place among kin, for whom the giving, taking, and using of goods have sentimental and personal meaning.

Reciprocity and Trade

Even hunters and gatherers, however, want valuables such as salt, flint, obsidian, red ochre, reeds, and honey that are produced or controlled by groups with whom they have no kinship ties. Economic dealings among nonkin are based on the assumption that every "stranger" will try to get the best of an exchange through cheating or stealing. As a result, trading expeditions are likely to be full of distrust and may bear a resemblance to war parties.

One interesting mechanism for facilitating trade between distant groups is known as **silent trade.** The objects to be exchanged are set out in a clearing, and the first group retreats out of sight. The other group comes out of hiding, inspects the wares, lays down what it regards as a fair exchange of its own products, and retreats again. The first group returns and, if satisfied, removes the traded objects. If not, it leaves the wares untouched as a signal that the balance is not yet even. In this fashion, the Mbuti of the Ituri Forest used to trade meat for bananas with Bantu agriculturalists, and the Vedda of Sri Lanka traded honey for iron tools with the Sinhalese.

Exchange relations become more personal when communities have more contact. Trade, for example, plays an important role in establishing alliances. Among the Yanomami, hostile villages may initiate alliances beginning with trade, then feasting, and eventually intermarriage, which solidifies relationships through kinship. Mutual exchange does not, however, guarantee mutually peaceful relationships. Groups such as the Yanomami can fall out of an alliance when personal hostilities intensify. One village may invite another to a "treacherous feast" in which the hosts attack their guests when they are least suspecting, and declare war (see Chapter 11).

More extensive trade relations occur between agricultural villages. Conditions for the development of trade markets are especially favorable in Melanesia, where villages in varied ecological niches produce different products for exchange. In New Guinea, for example, people regularly trade fish for pigs and vegetables. Among the Kapauku of western New Guinea (today, West Irian, Indonesia), full-fledged price markets involving shell and limited-purpose bead money may have existed before the arrival of European or Indonesian merchants. Generally speaking, however, trade based on marketing and all-purpose

money is associated with the evolution of the state (see Chapter 12) and with the use of soldiers and market police to enforce peaceful relations between buyers and sellers.

Perhaps the most common solution to the problem of trading with strangers in the absence of state-supervised markets is the establishment of special **trade partnerships.** In this arrangement, members of different communities regard one another as metaphorical or "fictive" kin. The members of trading expeditions deal exclusively with their trade partners, who greet them as "brothers" and give them food and shelter. Trade partners try to deal with one another in conformity with the principle of reciprocity. They deny an interest in getting the best of the bargain and offer wares as if they were gifts.

Trade in the Kula Ring

A classic example of trade partnerships is described in Bronislaw Malinowski's *Argonauts of the Western Pacific.* The Argonauts referred to here are the Trobriand Islanders, who trade with people on neighboring islands by means of daring canoe voyages across the open sea.

The **kula ring** is a system of exchange in the Trobriand Islands, where trading partners from different islands take risky voyages to exchange shell ornaments around the ring of islands; white cowrie shell armbands are traded in a counterclockwise direction, red shell necklaces are traded clockwise.

According to the men who take these risky voyages, the purpose of the kula trade is to exchange shell ornaments with their trade partners. The ornaments, known to the Trobrianders as *vaygu'a*, consist of white shell armbands and red shell necklaces. Armbands and necklaces are traded around the ring of islands in opposite directions, each eventually returning to point of origin. (See Figure 8.1.)

Participation in the kula trade is a major ambition of youth and a consuming passion of senior men. The vaygu'a have been compared with heirlooms or crown jewels. They vary in value, depending on their history. The older they are and the more admired their previous owners, the more valuable they become in the eyes of the Trobrianders. Like many other examples of special-purpose exchange media (see the discussion of money later in this chapter), kula valuables are seldom used to "buy" anything. They are, however, given as gifts in marriage and as rewards to canoe builders (Scoditti 1983). Most of the time, the ornaments are simply used for the purpose of obtaining other armbands and necklaces. To trade vaygu'a, men establish more or less permanent partnerships

New Guinea Market

Man at right is giving fish in exchange for yams at left.

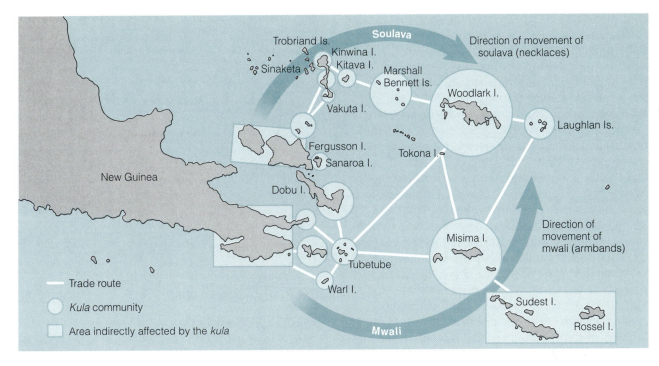

Figure 8.1

The ceremonial trading of necklaces and armshells in the kula ring encourages trade throughout Melanesia.

with each other on distant islands. These partnerships are usually handed down from one kinsman to another, and young men are given a start in the kula trade by inheriting or receiving an armband or a necklace from a relative.

When the expedition reaches shore, the trade partners greet one another and exchange preliminary gifts. Later the Trobrianders deliver the precious ornaments, accompanied by ritual speeches and formal acts concerned with establishing the honorable, giftlike

Kula Canoe

These large canoes are used by the Trobrianders for long-distance voyages.

character of the exchange. As in the case of reciprocal transactions within the family, the trade partner may not immediately be able to provide a shell whose value is equivalent to the one just received. He does not complain, because he expects his trade partner to work hard to make up for the delay by presenting him with even more valuable shells at their next meeting.

Why all this effort in order to obtain a few baubles of sentimental or aesthetic value? As is often the case, the etic aspects of the kula are different from the emic aspects. The kula ring entails more than a ceremonial exchange of valued shell ornaments. Utilitarian items are traded at the same time, so that people from different islands are able to exchange locally specialized food and craft products. The boats that take part in the kula expedition carry trade items of great practical value in the life of the island people who participate in the kula ring. While the trade partners fondle and admire their priceless heirlooms, members of the expedition trade for practical items: coconuts, sago palm flour, fish, yams, baskets, mats, wooden swords and clubs, green stone for tools, mussel shells for knives, creepers and lianas for lashings. These items can be bargained over with impunity. Although Trobrianders deny it, the vaygu'a are valuable not only for their qualities as heirlooms but also for their truly priceless gift of trade (Irwin 1983:71ff; Scoditti 1983:265).

More recent research among the Trobrianders has revealed a more complicated system of exchanges that goes beyond reciprocity. Kula is better understood as part of the Trobriand and the neighboring islands' system of achieving and validating political rank. There is a continued adjustment of political and social position. Trade and possession of highly valued shells create status and rank. Important men can enhance their status by acquiring particularly famous kula ornaments and by establishing a network of kula partnerships that extends throughout the islands. Those who come into possession of the most valuable shells are usually extremely able leaders who are accomplished navigators and, in former times, bold warriors (Campbell 1983:203). Thus in modern times, kula has persisted even though fewer practical items are traded.

Redistributive Exchange

As we shall see in Chapter 12, the evolution of economic and political systems is in large degree a consequence of the development of coercive forms of exchange that supplement or almost entirely replace reciprocal exchange. Coercive forms of exchange did not appear in sudden full-blown opposition to reciprocal forms. Rather, they probably first arose through what seemed to be merely an extension of familiar reciprocal forms.

Trobriander Yam House
Yams are collected by a centralized authority who retains a share for himself and redistributes the rest at feasts.

Redistribution involves the accumulation of large amounts of labor products produced by different individuals in a central place where they are sorted and counted and then given away to producers and nonproducers alike.

Considerable organizational effort is required if large quantities of goods are to be brought to the same place at the same time and given away in definite shares. This coordination is usually achieved by individuals who act as redistributors.

Typically, redistributors consciously attempt to increase and intensify production, for which they gain prestige in the eyes of their peers.

Nonstratified and stratified forms of redistribution must be distinguished from each other. As a nonstratified system of exchange, redistribution is carried out by a redistributor who (1) works harder than anyone else producing the items to be given away, (2) takes the smallest portion or none at all, and (3) is left with no greater material wealth than anyone else. In its nonstratified form, therefore, redistribution appears to be merely an extreme example of reciprocity; the generous provider gives everything away and for the moment gets nothing in return, except the admiration of those who benefit from the transaction. In the stratified form, however, the redistributor (1) lets others do most of the work, (2) retains the largest share, and (3) ends up with more material wealth than anyone else.

Table 8.1

Reciprocity versus Redistribution in Egalitarian and Stratified Societies

Egalitarian Societies	Stratified Societies
Members of egalitarian societies enjoy equal access to basic resources. No individual or group has appreciably more wealth, power, or prestige. There are as many positions of prestige as there are persons capable of filling them.[a]	In stratified societies there is differential access to basic resources, which are converted to private property. There is inequality in power, wealth, and prestige, and such inequality is permanent and formally recognized.[a]
Voluntary form of exchange based on reciprocity.	Coercive forms of exchange such as taxation.
Contributions given freely.	Members make obligatory payments to a central agency which later reallocated goods or services.
Redistributor works harder than anyone else, yet ends up with no more than everyone else.	Redistributor oversees but does not work harder; he or she retains the largest share and ends up with considerable wealth.
People get back all that they put into the pool or else they get back comparable value.	People may not get back everything they give to the redistributor.
Leaders have no power to coerce. They lead by example. Their prestige lasts as long as people agree with them.	The leader (chief or emperor) has considerable power over the labor force. He or she holds an inherited office and has regional control.
Ecological conditions: Intensification would rapidly lead to point of diminishing returns (see page 00).	*Ecological conditions:* If people work harder they can increase their standard of consumption without immediately depleting their habitat's resources.
	Production surplus makes regional distribution possible.
Reciprocity is maintained within and between communities.	Regional peace is maintained through a system of political ranking and through centralized administrative control.
Intercommunity reciprocity solidifies alliances and helps maintain temporary peace.	

[a]Based on Fried 1967.

Redistributive exchange, like reciprocal exchange, is usually embedded in a complex set of kinship relations and rituals that may obscure the etic significance of the exchange behavior. Redistribution often involves a ceremonial feast held to celebrate some important event such as a harvest, the end of a ritual taboo, the construction of a house, a death, a birth, or a marriage. A common feature of redistributive feasting is the boastful and competitive attitude of the redistributors and their kin with respect to other individuals or groups who have given feasts. This contrasts markedly with reciprocal exchange. Let us take a closer look at this contrast (see Table 8.1).

Reciprocity versus Redistribution

Boastfulness and acknowledgment of generosity are incompatible with the basic etiquette of reciprocal exchanges. Among the Semai of Central Malaya, no one even says "thank you" for the meat received from another hunter. Having struggled all day to lug the carcass of a pig home through the jungle heat, the hunter allows his prize to be cut up into exactly equal portions, which are then given away to the entire group. As Robert Dentan explains, to express gratitude for the portion received indicates that you are the kind of ungenerous person who calculates how much you give and take: "In this context saying thank you is very rude, for it suggests first that one has calculated the amount of a gift and second, that one did not expect the donor to be so generous. To call attention to one's generosity is to indicate that others are in debt to you and that you expect them to repay you. It is repugnant to many egalitarian peoples even to suggest that they have been treated generously" (1968:491).

Richard Lee (1969) tells how he learned about this aspect of reciprocity through a revealing incident. To please the !Kung, with whom he was staying, he decided to buy a large ox and have it slaughtered as a Christmas present. He spent days searching the neighboring Bantu agricultural villages looking for the largest and fattest ox in the region. Finally, he bought what appeared to be a perfect specimen. But one !Kung after another took him aside and assured him that he had been duped into buying an absolutely worthless animal. "Of course, we will eat it," they said, "but it won't fill us up—we will eat and go home to bed with stomachs rumbling." Yet when Lee's ox was slaughtered, it turned out to be covered with a thick layer of fat. Lee eventually succeeded in getting his informants to explain why they had claimed that his gift was valueless even though they certainly knew better than he did what lay under the animal's skin (Box 8.1).

In flagrant violation of these prescriptions for modesty in reciprocal exchanges, **redistribution** exchange systems involve public proclamations that the host is a generous person and a great provider. This boasting is one of the most conspicuous features of the **potlatches**, or redistributive feasts, that were once engaged in by the Native Americans who inhabit the northwest coast of the United States and Canada. In descriptions made famous by Ruth Benedict in *Patterns of Culture* (1934), the Kwakiutl redistributor seems like a virtual megalomaniac (see Box 8.2). In the potlatch, the guests behaved somewhat like Lee's !Kung. They grumbled and complained and never appeared satisfied or impressed. Nonetheless, in public they care-

fully counted all the gifts displayed and distributed. Both hosts and guests believed that the only way to throw off the obligations incurred in accepting these gifts was to hold a counter potlatch in which the tables were reversed (Jonaitas 1991).

The Infrastructural Basis of Redistribution and Reciprocity

Why do the !Kung esteem hunters who never draw attention to their own generosity, whereas the Kwakiutl and other redistributor societies esteem leaders who boast about how much they gave away? One theory is that reciprocity is a way of controlling intensification that would eventually lead to diminishing returns and environmental depletions.

Simple hunters and gatherers seldom have an opportunity to intensify production without rapidly reaching the point of diminishing returns. Intensification poses a grave threat in the form of faunal overkills.

To encourage the !Kung hunter to be boastful is to endanger the group's survival. In addition, reciprocity is advantageous for most hunter-gatherers because individuals and families experience a great deal of variation in their success from one day to the next. "The greater the degree of risk, the greater the extent of sharing" (Gould 1982:76). Sharing spreads the risk over many hunters, like commercial insurance policies spread the risk over many subscribers (Cashdan 1989:37). In contrast, the Kwakiutl (see Profile 5.2) had a seasonal abundance of natural resources which could be stored for lean winter months.

Kwakiutl of the Pacific Northwest

The signs over the doors read "Boston. He is the Head chief of Arweete. He is true Indian. Honest. He don't owe no trouble to white man" and "Cheap. He is one of the head chief of all tribes in this country. White man can get information." Photo was taken about 1901–1902.

The Kwakiutl mode of production is highly intensifiable and requires a coordinated effort in gathering and storing food for the winter months.

The Kwakiutl derive most of their food from the annual upriver runs of salmon and candlefish. Using aboriginal dip nets, the Kwakiutl and their neighbors could fish freely without affecting the overall rate of reproduction of these species because enough fish manage to make it upriver to spawn without depleting next year's supply. In March and April people from separate local groups gather for the great candlefish runs. They invest intense labor in harvesting candlefish and rendering its oil, which they store for home consumption and trade. Being storable, oil played an important part in the political economy. In August and September, they collect berries and the salmon runs begin. Both activities require a heavy labor investment both in collecting and storing of food. The greater the labor invested, the larger the harvest, with little or no decline in marginal productivity (Johnson and Earle 1987:163). Thus, it was ecologically feasible for the Kwakiutl to intensify production by using prestige and the privilege of boasting to reward those who worked harder or who got others to work harder (Isaac 1988; Mitchell and Donald 1988; Hayden 1992:534; Ames 1994).

Despite the overall abundance of resources, the Northwest Coast nevertheless experience alternating periods of abundance and shortage. A village enjoying

Redistribution in China

Meat is being divided into equal portions for the members of the group.

A.

B.

A. Spokesman for Kwakiutl chief making speech next to blankets about to be given away at a potlatch.   *B. The height of the pole and skill of the carvings and the animal ancestors shown validated the claim of chiefly rank.*

a good year would have a surplus of food that they could give away to a less fortunate village. The reward was increased prestige. When an impoverished and unprestigious group no longer had enough wealth to distribute and could not hold its own potlatches, the people abandoned their defeated redistributor-chief and took up residence among relatives in more productive villages. Thus the boasting and the giving away and displaying of wealth led to the recruitment of additional labor power for a particularly effective redistributor. This system also helps explain why Northwest Coast peoples lavished so much effort on the production of their world-famous totem poles. These poles bore the redistributor-chief's "crests" in the guise of carved mythic figures; title to the crests was claimed on the basis of outstanding potlatch achievements. The larger the pole, the greater the potlatch power and the more the members of poor villages would be tempted to change their residence and gather around another chief.

Before the coming of the Europeans, Kwakiutl potlatch feasts were probably less destructive (Box 8.3)

and more like Melanesian competitive feasts (see Chapter 12, discussion of big man feasts).

With the coming of the Europeans there was a shift toward more destructive forms of redistribution. Contact led to epidemics that decimated the population and intensified competition for manpower.

The impact of European diseases reduced the population of the Kwakiutl from about 10,000 in 1836 to about 2,000 by the end of the century. At the same time, the trading companies, canneries, lumber mills, and gold-mining camps pumped an unprecedented amount of wealth into the aboriginal economy. The percentage of people available to celebrate the glory of the potlatch dropped. Many villages were abandoned; rivalry intensified for the allegiance of the survivors.

A final and perhaps the most important factor in the development of destructive potlatches was the change in the technology and intensity of warfare. The earliest contacts in the late eighteenth century

Box 8.3   The Origin of Destructive Potlatches

Potlatching came under scientific scrutiny long after the people of the Pacific Northwest had entered into trade and wage labor relations with Russian, English, Canadian, and American nationals. Declining populations and a sudden influx of wealth had combined to make the potlatches increasingly competitive and destructive by the time Franz Boas began to study them in the 1880s (Rohner 1969). At this period, the entire tribe was in residence at the Fort Rupert trading station of the Hudson Bay Company, and the attempt on the part of one potlatch giver to outdo another had become an all-consuming passion. Blankets, boxes of fish oil, and other valuables were deliberately being destroyed by burning or by throwing them into the sea. On one occasion, a house almost burnt to the ground when the roof caught fire from too much fish oil poured on the fire (Benedict 1960:177). Potlatches that ended in this fashion were regarded as great victories for the potlatch givers.

between the Europeans and the Native Americans of the Northwest Pacific Coast centered on the fur trade. In return for sea otter skins, the Europeans gave guns to the Kwakiutl and to the Kwakiutl's traditional enemies. This trade had a double effect. On the one hand, warfare became more deadly; on the other hand, it forced local groups to fight one another for control of trade to get the ammunition on which success in warfare now depended. Small wonder, therefore, that as population declined, the potlatch chiefs were willing to destroy wealth that was militarily unimportant. They ordered the destruction of property in the vain hope that such spectacular demonstrations would enhance their prestige and bring people back to the empty villages so they would have the manpower for warfare and fur trade (Ferguson 1984).

Stratified Redistribution

A subtle line separates egalitarian from forms of **stratified redistribution.** In the egalitarian form, contributions to the central pool are voluntary, and the workers either get back all or most of what they put into it or they receive items of comparable value. In the stratified form, the workers must contribute to the central pool or suffer penalties, and they may not get back anything. Again, in the egalitarian form, the redistributor lacks the power to coerce followers to intensify production and must depend on their goodwill; in the stratified form, the redistributor has that power, and the workers must depend on that person's goodwill. The processes responsible for the evolution of one form of redistribution to another will be discussed in Chapter 12. Here, we will note only that fully developed forms of stratified redistribution imply the existence of a class of rulers who have the power to compel others to do their bidding. The expression of this power in the realm of production and exchange results in the political subordination of the labor force and in its partial or total loss of control over access to natural resources, technology, and the place, time, and hours of work.

Price Market Exchange: Buying and Selling

Marketplaces occur in rudimentary form wherever groups of strangers assemble and trade one item for another. Among hunter-gatherers and simple agriculturalists, marketplace trading usually involves the barter of one valuable consumable item for another: fish for yams, coconuts for axes, and so forth. In this type of market, before the development of all-purpose money (see the next section), only a limited range of goods or services is exchanged. The great bulk of exchange transactions takes place outside the marketplace and continues to involve various forms of reciprocity and redistribution. With the development of all-purpose money, however, **price market exchanges** came to dominate all other forms of exchange.

In a price market, the price of the goods and services exchanged is determined by buyers competing with buyers and sellers competing with sellers. Virtually everything that is produced or consumed soon comes to have a price, and buying and selling becomes a major cultural preoccupation or even an obsession.

One can engage in reciprocal exchange using money, as when a friend gives you a loan and does not specify when it must be repaid. Redistributive exchange can also be carried out with money, as in the collection of taxes and the disbursement of welfare payments. Or moneyless transactions, based on barter, can take place in the underground market economy, where people directly exchange goods and services as a way of avoiding paying taxes. But these types of exchanges differ from market exchanges in several important ways.

Buying and selling on a price market is a distinctive mode of exchange; the exchange involves specification of a precise time, quantity, and type of payment, and the participants' main concern is maximizing financial gain.

Price market exchanges are noteworthy for the anonymity and impersonality of the exchange process. Unlike either reciprocity or redistribution, once the money payment is concluded, no further obligation or responsibility need exist between buyer and seller.

Money

Money is a medium of exchange that has standard value. It is used as a means of payment for goods and services in a wide range of transactions where trade is well developed and economizing is a guiding principle.

The use of certain objects to symbolize and measure the social value of other objects occurs almost universally. Throughout much of East Africa, for example, cattle are a standard of value that can be used in exchange for a wife (see Chapter 9). In many parts of Melanesia, assorted shells, salt, and pigs are exchanged for stone implements, pottery, and other valuable artifacts.

These objects, however, do not possess all the characteristics of money associated with price market economies. Like modern coins and paper currency, money has the following characteristics:

- *Portability*—It comes in sizes and shapes convenient for being carried about from one transaction to the next.

- *Divisibility*—Its various forms and values are explicit multiples of each other.

- *Generality*—Virtually all goods and services can be measured by a single common monetary value.

- *Anonymity*—For most purchases, anyone with enough money to pay the market price can conclude a transaction.

- *Legality*—The money supply is controlled by a government and can't be duplicated or counterfeited.

By these criteria, cattle exchanged for wives are not money. Being neither very portable nor readily divisible, they would not be welcome at the supermarket checkout counter. As employed in bridewealth (see Chapter 9), cattle are frequently not convertible; that is, a large, beautiful, fat bull with a local reputation cannot readily be substituted for by two small and undistinguished animals. Furthermore, cattle lack generality because only wives can be "purchased" with them, and they lack anonymity because any stranger who shows up with the right amount of cattle will find he cannot simply leave the animals and take off with the bride. Cattle are exchanged for women only between kinship groups who have an interest in establishing or reinforcing preexisting social relationships. Finally, cattle are put into circulation by each individual household as a result of productive effort that is unregulated by any central authority.

Capitalism

The development of price markets accompanied the evolution of the first states. And they reach their

inequalities for services

Foraging for Food in Supermarkets
We try to maximize benefits in supermarkets and are seldom concerned with the social process.

highest development as part of the political economy known as **capitalism.** In capitalist societies, buying and selling by means of all-purpose money extends to land, resources, and housing. Labor has a price called *wages,* and money itself has a price called *interest.* In many cases, buyers and sellers don't even have face-to-face interaction.

Capitalism is associated with a change from production for use value to production for profit value.

Whereas production for use is aimed at satisfying specific material needs of individuals in households, capitalist production is aimed at accumulating wealth in order to purchase commodities for consumption. And because there is no end to the number of commodities one can purchase, efforts are invariably made to increase production.

By comparison with other forms of political economy, capitalism is aptly described as a system in which money can buy anything. This being so, everyone tries to acquire as much money as possible, and the object of production itself is not merely to provide valuable goods and services but to increase one's possession of money, that is, to make a profit, accumulate capital, and increase consumption for personal gain.

The rate of capitalist production depends on the rate at which profits can be made, and this in turn depends on the rate at which people purchase, use, wear out, and destroy goods and services. Hence, an enormous effort is expended on extolling the virtues and benefits of products in order to convince consumers that they should make additional purchases.

Prestige is awarded not to the person who works hardest or gives away the greatest amount of wealth but rather to the person who has the most possessions and who consumes at the highest rate. Capitalism inevitably leads to marked inequalities in wealth based on differential access to capital, technology, and resources.

As in all stratified political-economic systems, the rich use soldiers and police forces to safeguard their property and prevent the poor from confiscating their wealth and privileges. Without the protection of the army and police (which are paid for with the "surplus" collected by stratified redistributers), the accumulation of private wealth would not be possible.

A.

B.

*A. The distribution of traditional Trobriand skirts made by women is an important public event that was overlooked by Malinowski. **B.** Cowrie and rongo shells are used as money in the Solomon Islands.*

Profile 8.1   Primitive Capitalism? The Kapauku Case

In general, band and village societies lack the essential features of capitalism because, as we have seen, their exchange systems are based on reciprocal and redistributive exchanges rather than on price market exchanges. In some cases, however, nonstratified systems may have certain features strongly reminiscent of contemporary capitalism. The Kapauku Papuans of West Irian, Indonesia, are a case in point. According to Leopold Pospisil (1963), the Kapauku have an economy that is best described as "primitive capitalism." The economy is organized around individual accumulation of wealth and there are important wealth differences within the society. All Kapauku agricultural land is said to be owned individually; money in the form of shells and glass beads can be used to buy food, domesticated animals, crops, and land; money can also be used as payment for labor.

A closer look at the landownership, however, reveals fundamental differences. To begin with, access to land is controlled by kinship groups known as sublineages (see Chapter 11, in section titled "Unilineal Descent Groups"). No individual is without membership in such a group, and therefore no one is denied access to land. These sublineages control communal tracts of land, but the economic significance of land titles is minimal on several counts:

1. The price of land is so cheap that all the gardens under production have a market value in shell money less than the value of 10 female pigs.

2. Prohibition against trespass does not apply to sublineage kin.

3. Although even brothers will ask each other for land payments, credit is freely extended among all sublineage members, including giving land on loan.

4. Each sublineage is under the leadership of a headman (see Chapter 10) whose authority depends on his generosity, especially toward the members of his own sublineage. A rich headman does not refuse to lend his kinsmen whatever they need to gain access to the environment, because "a selfish individual who hoards money and fails to be generous never sees the time when his word is taken seriously and his advice and decisions followed, no matter how rich he may become" (Pospisil 1963:49).

Obviously, therefore, the wealth of the headman does not bestow the power associated with capitalist ownership. In Brazil or India, landlords can bar their tenants or sharecroppers from access to land and water regardless of the landlord's reputation. In the United States, under the rules of capitalist landownership, it is of no significance to the sheriff and the police officers when they evict farmers that the bank is being "selfish."

Pospisil states that although there are differences in wealth between sublineages, and sickness and misfortune of various sorts frequently lead to inequalities in physical well-being among kinship units, such misfortunes do not lead to the formation of a poverty class as they do under capitalism. Without central political controls, marked economic inequalities cannot be perpetuated for long because the rich cannot defend themselves against the demand of the poor that they be given credit, land, or whatever is necessary to end their poverty. Because wealth is displayed by generosity, a wealthy individual can retain his influence only if he distributes his wealth fairly among his fellow villagers. Thus, poverty, where it exists, does not result from a lack of access to land or credit. A stingy egalitarian redistributor is a contradiction in terms, for the simple reason that no police exist to protect such people from the murderous intentions of those whom they refuse to help. As Pospisil tells it, Selfish and greedy individuals, who have amassed huge personal properties, but who have failed to comply with the Kapauku requirement of "generosity" toward their less fortunate tribesmen, may be, and actually frequently are, put to death. Even in regions such as the Kamu Valley, where such an execution is not a penalty for greediness, a nongenerous wealthy man is ostracized, reprimanded, and thereby finally induced to change his ways (1963:49).

Property Ownership

Ownership of land and resources is one of the most important aspects of political control. It is as much political as economic because unequal access to the environment implies some form of coercion applied by political superiors against political inferiors.

Ownership of garden land in nonstratified societies is usually claimed by kin groups in village communities, but everybody belongs to such kin groups, and hence adults cannot be prevented from using the resources they need to make a living.

Landownership by landlords, rulers, or the government, however, means that individuals who lack title or tenure may be barred from using land even if it leads to death through starvation.

As we will see in Chapter 11, ownership of land and resources results from infrastructural processes that select for more dense and more productive populations. Landownership stimulates production because it forces food producers to work longer and harder than they would if they had free access to resources.

Landownership raises production because tenant food producers must work harder in order to pay the **rent** or tribute required for the opportunity to live or work on the owner's land.

This payment automatically compels tenants to increase their work input in order to produce for the landlord as well as for themselves. By raising or lowering rents, the landlord exercises a fairly direct measure of control over work input and production.

Because the extraction of rent is evolutionarily associated with an increase in food production, some anthropologists regard the payment of rent as indicative of the existence of **surplus** food—an amount greater than what is needed for immediate consumption by the producers.

The "surplus" food the landowner takes away as rent is not necessarily a superfluous quantity from the producers' standpoint.

The producers usually can very well use the full amount of their output to ease the costs of rearing children or to raise their own standard of living. If they surrender their produce, it is usually because they lack the power to withhold it. In this sense, all rent is an aspect of politics, because without the power to enforce property titles, rent would seldom be paid. Thus, there is a close resemblance between rent and taxation: Both depend on the existence of coercive power in the form of police and weapons that can be called into action if the taxpayer or tenant refuses to pay.

Two forms of property ownership existed in early agricultural states: one in which the governing elites claimed ownership over all landholdings, and appointed officials to oversee and collect tribute in the form of taxes, rent or labor services; and a second type in which land was owned privately by a class of landlords who inherited the land and maintained a class of peasants to produce surpluses. Agricultural states thus developed major inequalities between those who owned land and those who did not. As we

will see in Chapter 11, these coercive forms of extracting wealth from food producers probably arose from egalitarian forms of redistribution as a consequence of intensification and population pressure.

Patterns of Work

Among hunter-gatherer and simple agricultural societies, one finds very little specialization. Each man does the same kind of work as other men; each woman does the same kind of work as other women. But each adult performs many different tasks from day to day, in contrast to the standardized routines of contemporary factory or office employees. Moreover, the decision to switch from one task to another—from setting traps to making arrows or collecting honey, for example—is largely voluntary and arrived at either individually or by group consensus. Therefore, people in small-scale, nonstate societies probably do not experience work as a tedious aspect of life. Indeed, recent experimental reforms of factory work patterns are designed to let industrial workers work at varied jobs and to include them in "quality circles" that make decisions about how tasks are performed. These experiments represent attempts to recapture some of the enviable characteristics of work in small-scale, unspecialized economies.

In societies with hunter-gatherer and simple agricultural infrastructures, people do not spend as much time at work as they do in intensive agricultural or industrial societies. The !Kung San, for example, put in an average of only about 20 hours per week in hunting. The basic reason for this is that their mode of production is not intensifiable. Rather than run the risk of depleting the animal population below the point of recovery, the !Kung San move from one territory to another. They enjoy a good diet and don't have to work very hard to get it. In fact, the !Kung are able to secure all their basic food resources in less time than intensive agriculturalists or modern factory workers. When labor leaders and employers boast about how much progress has been made in obtaining leisure for today's working class, they have in mind a standard established in nineteenth-century Europe, when factory workers used to put in 12 hours a day or more. Before we enthusiastically endorse the progress that has been made through technological advances, we should keep in mind the work standards observed by foragers and horticulturalists.

Table 8.2 on page 120 summarizes the average time spent in total production and housework according to society type. Based on a sample of 102 studies of time allocation, Ross Sackett (1996) shows an overall

Table 8.2

Comparison of Average Daily Adult Labor in Hours Per Day*

Society Type	Men	Women
A. Production		
Foraging societies	4.2 h/d*	3.2 h/d
Horticultural societies	4.5	3.9
Agricultural societies	7.3	3.9
Industrial societies	7.5	3.6
B. Housework		
Foraging societies	1.9	3.7
Horticultural societies	1.6	3.6
Agricultural societies	1.1	5.7
Industrial societies	1.0	5.2
C. Total labor		
Foraging societies	5.7	6.1
Horticultural societies	6.1	7.6
Agricultural societies	8.4	9.9
Industrial societies	8.6	8.8

Source: Sackett 1996.

*(h/d: hours per day refer to a seven-day week)

increase in total labor expenditure (production and housework) as societies move from simple to more advanced technology. In less intensive systems, the average number of hours per day (h/d) spent at work ranges from 5.7 to 7.6 hours per day (h/d), whereas in agricultural societies the average work time is 8.4 for men and 9.9 h/d for women. The reason is that in agricultural societies, labor is intensified to produce food for both domestic consumption and to pay for taxes, rent, and other costs associated with a price market economy. Despite the many advantages of labor-saving devices and technological improvements, labor demands are similarly high in industrial society. Men average 8.6 and women 8.8 h/d, calculated on a seven-day work week so that weekends do not count as days of rest.

In terms of total labor (production and housework) men and women in industrial societies spend nearly 50 percent more time working than foragers and horticulturalists.

Work occupies an ever greater part of daily life among industrial wage earners. To the basic 8.6- and 8.8-hour day, add time for commuting and shopping and if there are children in the family, add time for chauffeuring children to and from after school activities, help with homework, and participation in school events.

Box 8.4 Production, Consumption and Free Time in Affluent Societies

Does modern affluence bring greater leisure and satisfy our basic needs better than previous less advanced economic systems? This question can be answered by comparing data on time allocation (based on production, consumption, and free time), among the horticultural Machiguenga of Peru and the industrial French middle class. Time use data shows that the French clearly spend more time in production and consumption activities than the Machiguenga; the Machiguenga have over 50 percent (14.8 versus 9.6 hours per day) more free time than the French. This situation reflects the increasing scarcity of time felt by most members of "more affluent" societies who produce more and consume more. In the context of perceived time scarcity, we convert free time into consumption time because we do not want to "waste time."

This brings up the question of whether consumer goods are needed in themselves or whether demand for them has been created by the producers. We cannot simply assume that goods are produced to meet people's real needs. The billions of dollars spent each year on advertising indicate that not all consumer wants arise from basic needs of the individual, but that some of these needs are created in consumers by the producers themselves. This turns things around. Instead of arguing, as economists usually do, that our economic system serves us well, we are forced to consider that it may be we who serve the system by somehow agreeing to want the things it seems bent on producing.

To most economists there is no justification for criticizing the purchasing habits of modern consumers. Purchases simply reflect personal preference, and it would be arrogant to judge the individual decisions of free men and women. Economists assume that if people had more satisfying pathways of consumption, people would choose them. But the role of advertising in creating wants leaves open the question whether consumption is aimed at the fulfillment of people's needs, or whether mass consumption is imposed from above to increase corporate profits. How else can we explain that in modern industrial society, no matter what the level of income, people's consumer spending is up to it. (Adapted from A. Johnson 1978)

A.   B.

Tokyo Stock Exchange

A. The public sale and purchase of shares in companies and corporations is a fundamental feature of capitalist economies. Buyers and sellers have no face-to-face interaction. Such markets function exclusively to maximize profits.   B. In some professions, people work long hours so that work becomes a surrogate home.

More recently a new and perhaps surpassing trend in work patterns has been described for corporate America. Arlie Russell Hochschild (1998) says people work long hours because they want to, not because they have to; people are escaping home by going to work. Although most people say that work is too demanding and the hours are too long, Hochschild found that male and female management-level workers in a Midwest Fortune 500 company regularly work 10- to 11-hour workdays (that's 8 A.M. to 6 or 7 P.M.) because they find work to be more satisfying and they have more support at work than they do at home. Work is a way of fleeing from the stresses of home life, where they encounter high labor costs in rearing "high quality" children, and parents and spouses feel less in control and less equipped to handle problems. It is not surprising that as the corporate workplace becomes more creative, and more interesting, it becomes more like a surrogate home, while the family home becomes an arena of stress, that offers less support or satisfaction.

Summary

1. All societies have an economy—a set of institutions that combines technology, labor, and natural resources to produce and distribute goods and services. The organizational aspects of economy are distinguished from its infrastructural aspects in order to explore the relationship between infrastructure and structure. Selection for different modes of exchange reflects differing degrees of intensifiability and population growth.

2. Exchange is an integral part of all economies, but the flow of goods and services from producers to consumers can be organized in several ways. Modern-day price markets and buying and selling are not universal. The idea that money can buy everything (or almost everything) has been alien to most of the human beings who have ever lived. Two other modes of exchange—reciprocity and redistribution—once played a more important economic role than price markets.

3. In reciprocal exchange, the time and quantity of the counterflow is not specified. This kind of exchange can be effective only when it is embedded in kinship or close personal relationships. Daily food distribution among the !Kung San is an example of reciprocal exchange. Control over the counterflow in reciprocal exchange is achieved by communal pressure against freeloaders and shirkers.

4. Reciprocity lingers on in price market societies within kinship groups and is familiar to many of

Michiguenga at Work

As in most slash-and-burn economies, Machiguenga men fell trees and clear the forest for new plantings. Here, a Machiguenga uses the felled trees to build a house.

Corporate Office Workers

Men in industrial society work 8.6 hours per day, compared to 5.7 hours for hunters and gatherers, and 6.1 hours for men in simple agricultural societies. Women work even longer hours.

us as gift giving to relatives and friends. In the absence of price markets and police or military supervision, trade poses a special problem to people accustomed to reciprocal exchange. Silent barter is one solution. Another is to create trading partners who treat each other as kin.

5. The kula is a classic example of how barter for necessities is carried out under the cloak of reciprocal exchanges. Redistributive exchange involves the collection of goods in a central place and its disbursement by a redistributor to the producers. In the transition from egalitarian to stratified forms of redistribution, production and exchange cross the line separating voluntary from coerced forms of economic behavior. In its egalitarian form, the redistributor depends on the goodwill of the producers; in the stratified form, the producers depend on the goodwill of the redistributor.

6. Redistribution is characterized by the counting of shares contributed and shares disbursed. Unlike reciprocity, redistribution leads to boasting and overt competition for the prestigious status of being a great provider.

7. The Kwakiutl potlatch is a classic example of the relationships between redistribution and bragging behavior. The predominance of redistribution over reciprocity is related to the intensifiability of various modes of production. Where production can be intensified without depletions, rivalrous re-

distributions may serve adaptive ecological functions, such as providing an extra margin of safety in lean years and equalizing regional production.

8. The development of destructive potlatches among the Kwakiutl may have been caused by factors stemming from contact with Europeans, such as the intensification of warfare, trade for guns and ammunition, and depopulation.

9. Price market exchange depends on the development of all-purpose money as defined by the criteria of portability, divisibility, generality, anonymity, and legality. Although some of these features are possessed by limited-purpose standards of value, all-purpose money and price markets imply the existence of state forms of control.

10. The greatest development of the price market mode of exchange is associated with the political economy of capitalism, in which virtually all goods and services can be bought and sold. Because capitalist production depends on consumerism, prestige is awarded to those who own or consume the greatest amount of goods and services. Price market exchanges are embedded in a political economy of control made necessary by the inequalities in access to resources and the conflict between the poor and the wealthy.

11. The Kapauku illustrate why price market institutions and capitalism cannot exist in the absence of a developed political form of control.

Labor-Saving Devices That Don't Save Work
The first assembly line. Ford's Highland Park, Michigan, magneto assembly line saved 15 minutes per unit and initiated the era of mass production in 1913—but the workers worked harder than ever.

12. Landownership becomes the focus of the mode of production and exchange in societies where there are political forms of control. Differential access to land leads to the exaction of rent and taxation, both compel tenants to increase their work input and production.

13. Paradoxically, advanced agriculturalists and factory and office workers labor longer hours than hunters and gatherers and simple agriculturalists. In the postindustrial corporate workplace, people choose to spend more time at work than at home, as home life has become more stressful.

AMERICA NOW

Emergent Varieties of Capitalism

Although Americans think of the United States as being a capitalist country, its political economy is actually best characterized as a mixture of capitalism and democratic state socialism—the same mixture that to varying degrees constitutes the political economies of Western Europe and Japan. Some 19.5 million people are directly employed by federal, state, and local governments. Approximately 1.4 million people are in the active military. Another 43 million depend largely on government social security payments of one form or another. Other forms of state, local, and federal pensions support at least 5.8 million people. The federal government disburses forms of financial assistance through many programs in a number of major categories. There are various types of medical aid disbursements, cash aid disbursements, food assistance programs, and types of housing allowances, as well as various jobs and job training programs. In fact the total number of individual disbursements is staggering. When added up, the total number of disbursements comes to over 190 million. This is not the end of the picture, as there are at least 1 million farm families that receive government agricultural subsidies. To a significant degree, U.S. citizens do depend on the redistribution of tax money rather than sharing in the profits made from capitalist free enterprise.

The United States has other political-economic features that depart from a pure capitalist model. The essence of capitalist enterprise is the freedom to buy and sell in competitive price-making markets. Price-making markets exist where there are enough buyers and sellers to enable buyers to compete with buyers, buyers to compete with sellers, and sellers to compete with sellers for the prices that best suit their

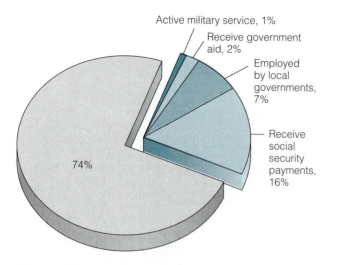

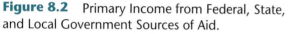

Active military service, 1%

Receive government aid, 2%

Employed by local governments, 7%

Receive social security payments, 16%

74%

Figure 8.2   Primary Income from Federal, State, and Local Government Sources of Aid.

The most important trend in capitalism in the 1990s is the emergence of *multinational, transnational,* and *supranational* corporations. Multinationals have their headquarters and do most of their business in one country but have markets and facilities around the globe. Transnationals also have headquarters in one country but depend on their international divisions for the bulk of their production and sales. When threatened by unions or government regulators, they move their operations from one country to another. Supranationals have multiple or mobile headquarters. Their managers are multiethnic and multilingual and feel no particular need to identify with a particular government or labor force. It seems likely that in the next decade, the power of the transnationals—some of which already have budgets equal to that of large countries—will expand at the expense of the power of national states.

respective interests. It has long been recognized that to preserve the free enterprise system, limitations must be placed on the ability of small groups of powerful buyers or sellers to gain control over a market to the extent that the prices they offer effectively determine the price that must be paid by anyone who wants a particular product or service.

Early in this century, the U.S. Congress passed laws against the formation of monopolies and actively pursued the breakup of companies that then dominated the railroad, meat-packing, and petroleum industries. The antimonopoly laws stopped short, however, of prohibiting the formation of semimonopolies or oligopolies—that is, companies that control not all but a major share of the market for a particular product. The trend toward oligopoly was already well advanced in the earlier part of this century. But after the end of World War II, the pace of acquisitions and expansions quickened. As a result, by 1980, the 50 largest U.S. manufacturing corporations owned 42 percent of all assets used in manufacturing, whereas the top 500 owned 72 percent of these assets (Silk 1985).

In 1988, 3,487 mergers worth $227 billion occurred among corporations worth more than $1 million (U.S. Bureau of the Census 1990:534). This trend has continued. In 1996 there were 10,324 mergers and acquisitions with a combined value of nearly 648 billion dollars. Worldwide there were 23,208 mergers and acquisitions topping the $1 trillion mark in total value.

KEY TERMS
capitalism
economizing
exchange
freeloader
kula ring
landownership
money
price market exchange
reciprocal exchange
reciprocity
redistribution
silent trade
stratified redistribution
surplus

QUESTIONS TO THINK ABOUT
1. What are the differences between redistribution in egalitarian versus stratified societies?
2. What is the difference between reciprocity and market exchange? What role does each play in our own society?
3. What infrastructural conditions help explain the Kwakiutl potlatch? What historical changes led to excess and destruction?
4. What effect does landownership (or lack of landownership) have on food production and distribution?

4. Objective of production: accumulate wealth

corbé

CHAPTER 9

Domestic Life

Japanese nuclear family at home.

The Household and the Domestic Sphere of Culture

Family Groups and the Mode of Production and Reproduction
The Nuclear Family
Polygamous Families
PROFILE: The Nyinba—A Polyandrous Society
The Extended Family
PROFILE: Chinese Extended Families—Costs and Benefits
One-Parent Domestic Groups

What Is Marriage?
Legitimacy

Economic Aspects of Marriage
Bridewealth
Bride Service

Dowry
Preferential Marriages

Domestic Groups and the Avoidance of Incest
Social and Cultural Advantages of Exogamy
Biological Risks of Inbreeding:
    The Observationalist Theory
Motivation for Incest Avoidance
Sim Pua Marriage: "Adopt a Daughter, Marry a Sister"
Westermark in the Kibbutz
Avoidance within the Family

Summary

America Now: Matrifocal Families

In this chapter we continue the comparative study of structural features, focusing on the variety of family groups and their relation to aspects of infrastructure. We catch our first glimpse of the astonishing variety of human family forms and of mating arrangements: monogamy, polygyny, and polyandry, secondary marriages, and preferred-cousin marriages, to mention only a few. Although this chapter is primarily descriptive, it takes up some perennially interesting questions. Is the nuclear family universal? What is marriage? Can marriage take place between partners of the same sex? Do husbands and wives have to live together for their relationship to qualify as marriage? Why do some types of marriages require a gift to the bride's family, whereas others require a gift to the groom's family? Why does every culture have a taboo against incest? Is the taboo based on instinctual sexual aversions, or is it a cultural adaptation? One important conclusion: There is no single, natural way to organize domestic life.

The Household and the Domestic Sphere of Culture

All societies have a domestic sphere of life. The focus of the domestic sphere is a dwelling space, shelter, residence, or household, in which certain universally recurrent activities take place. It is not possible to give a simple checklist of what these activities are because there is so much variety (Netting, Wilk, and Arnould 1984). In many cultures, domestic activities include preparation and consumption of food; cleaning, grooming, teaching, and disciplining the young; sleeping; and adult sexual intercourse. However, in no culture are these activities carried out exclusively within domestic household settings.

In the case of modern industrial cultures, this pattern is evident with respect to enculturation and education, which are increasingly carried out in special nondomestic buildings (schools or day care centers) under the auspices of specialists (teachers), who often spend more time with children than do the parents. Many village and band societies also separate their adolescent male children from the domestic scene to prepare them for adulthood, in the same way some parents send their children away to boarding school. In many parts of East Africa, adolescent boys are separated from the community to form a residential age set where they are trained to assume duties and responsibilities associated with cattle herding and raiding. Their mothers and sisters cook and keep house for them until they take wives. They remain together until they establish their own households and continue to be closely associated throughout their lives.

In many societies, married men spend a good deal of time in special men's houses. Food is handed in to them by wives and children, who are themselves forbidden to enter. One of the most interesting cases of the separation of cooking and eating occurs among the Ashanti of West Africa. Ashanti men eat their meals with their sisters, mothers, and maternal nephews and nieces, not with their wives and children. But it is the wives who do the cooking. Every evening in Ashanti land one sees a steady traffic of children taking their mothers' cooking to their father's sister's house (see Barnes 1960; Bender 1967).

Households change over time, as their members go through the stages of the cycle of birth, marriage, aging, and death. Among the Zumbagua peasants of the Ecuadorian Andes, households undergo a gradual transition, as young couples establish themselves, in stages, as separate households. During courtship, couples have sex in the fields, away from the houses where they eat and sleep. When they get married, they build a small hut that lacks a hearth for heating or cooking. This hut adjoins the house of the groom's or bride's parents. Now they sleep and have sex together under one roof, but they continue to cook and eat in their parents' kitchen. Their first children are brought up and cared for by the couple's parents. Only when a couple has several children will they finally build their own kitchen and begin to sleep, cook, eat, have sex, and nurture their offspring around their new hearth in their own household (Weismantel 1989).

The household is a domestic group whose members live together and cooperate on a daily basis in production and share the proceeds of labor and other resources held in common.

Household members organize and carry out a range of activities related to production, consumption, child rearing, inheritance and reproductive activities. Household inhabitants are usually kin, but may include nonkin as well. Similarly, households may contain nonresident members, who live and work elsewhere, but contribute to the household economy (Yanagisako 1979; Netting 1989; Blanton 1994). In this regard, the household is an etic behavioral unit that is defined in terms of the activities of the domestic economy. Members share food, labor, and material resources based on the requirements of the subsistence economy and the personnel available in the household. Resources are managed according to consensus and cooperation. The need to maintain enduring relationships over time results in explicit ideologies of family obligation and mutual support to sustain solidarity and cohesion between household members.

Family Groups and the Mode of Production and Reproduction

Family structure consists of the primary groups present in every society that satisfy basic human biopsychological needs and drives and sustain the health and well-being of its members. The focus of these groups is on kinship and family relations that provide food, shelter, and emotional, sexual, and reproductive needs. Anthropologists are concerned with understanding the functional roles of families and how they are transformed in relation to changes in infrastructure. These include traditional modes of production as well as global trends such as industrialization and urbanization that lead to patterns of employment, housing, demographics, and income distribution.

The Nuclear Family

Many anthropologists believe that at the center of all domestic organization is a group known as the **nuclear family,** which consists of husband, wife, and children. Anthropologist Ralph Linton held the view that the unit of father, mother, and child is the "bedrock underlying all other family structures," and he predicted that "the last man will spend his last hours searching for his wife and child" (1959:52). George Peter Murdock (1949, 1967) found the nuclear family

Zumbagua Peasants of the Peruvian Andes

> ### Box 9.1   Principal Forms of Human Marriage
>
> *Monogamy:* Marriage with one spouse exclusively and for life.
>
> *Serial monogamy:* Marriage with one spouse at a time but with remarriage after death or divorce.
>
> *Polygamy:* Marriage with more than one spouse at a time.
>
> *Polygyny:* Marriage with more than one wife at a time.
>
> *Polyandry:* Marriage with more than one husband at a time.

in every one of a sample of 250 societies. He concluded that it occurs universally because it fulfills vital functions that cannot be fulfilled as efficiently by other groups. These basic functions include

- The regulation of sexual activity
- Support in reproduction during pregnancy and nursing (education)
- Socialization of children by members of both sexes
- Cooperation in subsistence due to the sexual division of labor

Most anthropologists believe that the nuclear family is not the only group that can fulfill these functions. Other social units, including alternative institutions that may lie entirely outside the domestic sphere, can assume these functions as efficiently.

Nuclear families are prevalent in small-scale hunting-gathering societies, where a high degree of mobility is required due to seasonal variations in resource availability. These smaller nuclear families move on their own in search of food, but unite with several other family groups when resources are abundant. Flexibility enables nuclear family members to move in and out of camps and maintain ties across a wide regional network. Nuclear families are also adapted to the requirements of an industrial economy, particularly the middle class, where there is a high degree of geographic mobility, as people move to places where jobs and career opportunities are available. Unemployment insurance, savings, and health insurance sustain them when they are ill or in between jobs. Similarly, the social security system and the growth of retirement plans relieve nuclear family members of financial responsibility for their elderly parents and increase their independence and ability to move as needed.

African Polygyny
Co-wives live in separate dwellings and often are in competition with one another.

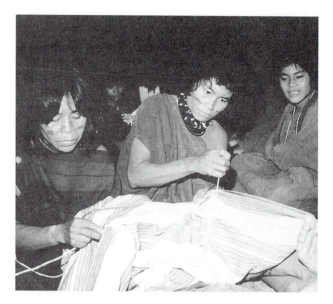

Machiguenga Co-wives
Co-wives are "sisters" and tend to form close bonds.

Polygamous Families

Historically, most cultures around the world have not followed the rule of **monogamy,** which restricts marriage to only one spouse at a time. In some societies that prescribe monogamy, it may be acceptable for a man or a woman to maintain a lover in a separate household as long as they are reasonably discreet. In other societies, including our own, serial monogamy (remarriage after death or divorce) is an acceptable alternative to lifelong marriage to one person. But in the overwhelming majority of world cultures, plural marriage or **polygamy** is permitted. In one form, called **polygyny,** several wives share a husband; in another, a much less common form called **polyandry,** several husbands share a wife.

Polygyny.   Polygyny occurs in over 80 percent of the societies in Murdock's (Murdock 1967) sample societies. We must, however, bear in mind that where it is practiced, polygyny is the preferred form of marriage, rather than the norm. Only 20–45 percent of the men actually have two or more wives. In some societies, only men of high rank can seek more than one wife and in stratified societies, only men of wealth can afford to do so.

Polygyny is common in horticultural societies where women are responsible for production. Under these conditions, women are valued for their labor as well as their role as childbearers. As long as land

is readily available, additional women in the household increase both the labor supply and the productive yield (White 1988). Among the Kapauku of New Guinea, women are responsible for growing yams and raising pigs. To achieve political prestige, a man depends on his wife's labor to maintain a large pig herd. It is common for Kapauku women to urge their husbands to pay bride price to take a second wife to help them with their work.

Conflict between co-wives is less likely in societies where women are the main food producers and polygyny increases domestic production.

Among the horticultural Machiguenga of lowland South America, co-wives share the same dwelling and a woman must give her permission before her husband can bring a co-wife into the household. Women in fact welcome the additional labor of a co-wife, as long as they are compatible. In **sororal polygyny,** a man marries two or more sisters. This is preferred among the Machiguenga because close kinship encourages cooperation and mutual trust. Sisters usually get along better and are more likely to create close bonds than women who are strangers. Machiguenga co-wives each maintain their own garden and have their own hearth but cooperate in a variety of tasks. Senior wives usually enjoy superior status and authority over younger wives and the rights and obligations among wives are clearly defined. This pattern is typical in cultures where land is still abundant and there is little rank or stratification among males.

Dissension and jealousy among co-wives is more likely in societies where women are economically dependent on men and are valued more as child bearers than as food producers.

Where men are responsible for most of the productive work, wealthy men will take secondary wives to demonstrate their status in society. In highly stratified societies, having many wives and concubines is one of the privileges of royalty. In other societies, polygyny is a symbol of prestige. Among the Gusii of Kenya, it is thought that having many wives shows that a man is important in the clan, he has control over people, and is equipped to solve disputes in the community (Hakansson and LeVine 1997). A polygynously married man also has more offspring, and more alliances through marriage. His co-wives, however, may not benefit equally from his status. They are likely to live in separate households and to see each other as competitors for their husband's wealth. Among the Gusii as well as in other parts of West Africa, land and livestock are inherited through males. Co-wives differ considerably in status and wealth. Although each woman has her allotted fields and livestock, the husband controls the property which is passed on to his sons. If a man marries more than one wife, his land is divided. The first wife gets the largest share, and subsequent wives are allocated land according to their rank (Ssennyonga 1997).

Polyandry.   Polyandry is a rare family form in which a woman marries two or more men at a time. It is found in less than 1 percent of societies and is most common in Nepal, Tibet, and India. The most common form is **fraternal polyandry.** All brothers in a family, including those who have not yet been born, are married to one woman. The wife and her husbands live together in a single household on the family estate. Sexual privileges rotate among the brothers. According to Nancy Levine, the Nyinba of Nepal place little value on sexual exclusivity and there is little overt sexual jealousy or competition. Given polyandry and the fact that women have extramarital affairs, there is always uncertainty about paternity. Yet Nyinba men do attempt to determine the paternity of children born in polyandrous marriages because real fathers and children have special relationships. Men place emphasis on having "sons of their own" so they will

have biological children to look after them in their old age (Levine 1988:168).

Polyandry is an alternative form of family in which a woman marries and resides with two or more husbands, either brothers or men who are unrelated. Polyandry avoids subdividing the family estate and reduces population growth.

The infrastructural basis of polyandry rests on the fact that it supports low population growth because each husband will have fewer offspring than if he was married to a wife he did not have to share. While polyandry prevents some women from marrying, single women do have children, but they have fewer children than married women. Second, it prevents the partition of family land by keeping the household with its resources undivided from one generation to the next. In Tibet and Nepal, agricultural and grazing lands are limited and scattered at various altitudes throughout the rugged terrain. Subdivision of family landholdings would leave the parcels too small to cultivate efficiently (Goldstein 1987). The principle of fraternal solidarity also permits economic specialization and increased income through multiple economic involvements such as farming, herding and long distance trade. Herding and trade often take the men away from their villages for long periods of time, leaving at least one brother at home to manage the estate. Thus, the more men a household includes, the greater its chances for economic success.

It is clear that polyandry is not the only way to organize and manage the domestic economy in harsh high-altitude environments. In fact, many nonpolyandrous groups live in the region, but what stands out is that polyandrous villagers such as the Nyinba are much wealthier and enjoy greater prosperity, undoubtedly because wealth is maintained intact over generations and population growth is inhibited.

Nancy Levine points out that ideologically the importance of polyandry extends beyond economics. The Nyinba have elaborate legends that portray the ancestors in harmonious polyandrous families and they idealize the solidarity of brothers as one of the core kinship ideals, equivalent to the obligation to support parents in their old age (Levine 1988:159). Nevertheless, there are disadvantages within the sibling group, particularly for younger men with much older wives, who have much lower chances of siring their own children. Men who have fathered few children are the most prone to initiate partition of the family estate (Levine and Silk 1997).

Profile 9.1   The Nyinba—A Polyandrous Society

The Nyinba are a Tibetan-speaking minority that lives in Nepal. They are devout Buddhists in an area surrounded by Hindus. Polyandry is a part of Buddhist Tibetan culture, which values reserved emotional attachments. Passion and sexual involvement are condoned, as long as they are not excessive. Young people are expected to have sex before marriage, and extramarital affairs are tolerated as long as they are not socially disruptive.

When a woman marries, she normally moves in with a group of brothers. She is expected to treat all her husbands with equal consideration and affection. Exclusive attachment is discouraged, as it risks alienating the others and threatens to break up the family. Occasionally more than one woman is involved in Nyinba marriages; for example, a group of sisters may marry a group of brothers. In fact, the Nyinba tolerate various marriage arrangements. Polyandry is preferred, but polygyny is permitted. There are also cases of *conjoint marriage,* where a man in a polyandrous marriage marries another woman and brings her into the household as his second wife. This tends to occur when there is a large sibling set and a man's needs are poorly met by his marriage. Mar-

riages with four or more brothers are the most difficult to sustain. It becomes problematic for wives to meet each man's expectation of having a son and to satisfy the domestic labor obligations for so many men. Another factor is the brother's parentage. The Nyinba say that the most successful polyandrous marriages involve brothers that have the same mother and father; those with different parents, especially different mothers, are more likely to experience failures in fraternal commitments that result in conjoint marriage. Yet there are inconveniences from conjoint marriage as well. Continual dissention threatens the risk of dividing the household estate. Unless a household lacks sufficient land to undergo partition, conjoint marriages are likely to split in terms of property and persons. Men form new households around the wife or wives with whom they are closest and the children they have fathered. The eldest brother and his family get the largest room, while the younger brother or brothers move into the storage quarters. The land is divided up among the brothers; the sons of brothers who lived in the joint family are entitled to shares from their fathers only. (Adapted from Levine 1988)

Nyinba Family

The Extended Family

In a majority of the societies studied by anthropologists, domestic life is dominated by groupings larger than simple nuclear or polygamous families. Some form of extended family is especially common. An **extended family** is a domestic group consisting of several related nuclear families and may include siblings, their spouses and their children, or parents and married children. Extended families may also be polygynous or polyandrous. Depending on the rules of residence, extended families may center around an older married couple, their sons, and their son's wives and children; their married daughters will have left to join the households of their husbands. Or extended families may center around a core of related women, with husbands marrying into the family to live with their wives' parents and sisters. Each household structure is different in its dynamics. Depending on the composition of household members, extended families provide different opportunities for family interaction, and patterns of authority.

The domestic life of the Bathonga of southern Mozambique, among whom one of the authors (MH) carried out fieldwork, was controlled by the senior men of the polygynous extended family's senior generation. These prestigious and powerful men in effect formed a board of directors of a family-style corporation. They made decisions about the domestic group's holdings in land, cattle, and buildings; they also or-

ganized the subsistence effort of the coresident labor force—especially of the women and children—by assigning fields, crops, and seasonal work tasks. They tried to increase the size of their cattle herds and supplies of food and beer, obtain more wives, and increase the size and strength of the entire unit. The younger brothers, sons, and grandsons in Bathonga extended families could not reach adulthood, marry, build a hut, carry out subsistence tasks, or have children unless they accepted the policies and priorities established by the senior males. Within the Bathonga polygynous extended-family households, nuclear families existed only in the interval during which a man had only one wife.

In traditional Chinese extended families, the senior couple manages the household. The family is a corporate enterprise characterized by a common budget, shared properties, and a strict pooling of income. The senior couple arranges marriages. Women brought into the household as wives for the senior couple's sons are placed under the direct control of their mother-in-law. Wives remain outsiders and are treated with suspicion and even hostility. A farm family goes to considerable trouble and expense to acquire a daughter-in-law, and the household members expect more from the bargain than the young girl can provide (A. Wolf 1995). She gradually learns to adjust to her status, but her only source of security comes from forming her own family, through

Extended Family, United States
The demand for labor was high on this Minnesota farm in 1895.

her own children and grandchildren (M. Wolf 1972). The father–son relationship is based on paternal dominance. The son continues to turn his income over to his father and to follow his father's wishes in all business dealings.

When a family has several daughters-in-law, cooking chores are often rotated so that on any given day a maximum contingent of the domestic labor force can be sent to work in the family's fields (Myron Cohen 1976). The degree to which the nuclear family is submerged and affaced by these arrangements is brought out by a *sim pua* marriage, a custom formerly found in certain Taiwanese households: "Adopt a daughter, marry a sister." To obtain control over their son's wife, the senior couple adopts a daughter, usually someone whose parents are very poor. They bring the girl into the household at a very early age and train her to be hardworking and obedient. Later they oblige their son to marry his stepsister. The couple remains economically dependent on the extended family within their midst, but is resistant to the marriage arrangement because of their intimate childhood association and socially imposed incest prohibitions (see p. 141).

Wenjiang, China
Guests bring wedding gifts in baskets.

Profile 9.2 Chinese Extended Families—Costs and Benefits

Throughout China, larger extended families tend to be wealthier and to have higher social standing (M. Cohen 1976). Large families are able to gain more wealth than small families for two reasons. One is that frugality is imposed on all members by strict parents in order to save as much as they can. The second advantage is that a large family allows for a division of labor. Additional sons can earn income outside the farm and the father can invest their income in additional parcels of land to increase the family's landholdings. Extended families thus provide a larger labor pool and can carry out a greater variety of simultaneous activities, with the proceeds contributing to the family's wealth. Large extended families make sacrifices to become wealthy, but not all families can hold up under the pressures and partition is often inevitable. It is said that families cannot stay wealthy for too long because sooner or later problems arise when some individuals refuse to contribute their labor or there is outright embezzlement of family funds (M. Cohen 1976:204; Pasternak et al. 1997:238).

In China today, the extended family still remains more functional than the nuclear family but young couples are increasingly demanding independence. According to Yunxiang Yan (1997) the decollectivization of farmland in the 1980s, led to an increase in both commercialism and family wealth. As a result, there is an accelerated trend toward the establishment of conjugal "husband–wife families," even before a couple has children. A number of factors contribute to the growing trend toward conjugal families. First, young couples want their privacy and want to manage on their own, without parental intervention. According to one young woman, in an extended family "You always feel as though you are being watched—there are eyes around the house all the time." Second, young couples are more prosperous and consume more now than in the past. Older parents, accustomed to saving, are uncomfortable with their adult children's spending patterns. The older parents prefer to have them leave if they can no longer control their purchases. Third, when couples get married, they now receive substantial gifts, including cash funds, which they are entitled to keep. These funds, which have become more substantial in recent years, make it possible for couples to leave the groom's parents' home and take advantage of new economic opportunities outside the old household (Yan 1996).

Box 9.2   The Causes of Matrifocality

Matrifocal families form under a variety of conditions. For example, early marriage of girls to men considerably older than themselves leads to high rates of widowhood while children are still young. Remarriage may be difficult or prohibited, as among upper caste Hindus in India. High rates of youthful widowhood and matrifocality may also be produced by warfare and political unrest (Mencher and Okongwu 1993). Dehavenon (1993:55) offers a more general account of the conditions that underlie most cases of matrifocality in the modern world as follows:

1. The mother has greater access to sources of income than the biological father.
2. Father's access to sources of wealth and income depends on migration or absence from home for extended periods.
3. Mother has greater access to housing.
4. Migration or higher mortality of males leads to a shortage of males available for marriage.

All these conditions underlie the high frequency of matrifocal households in the United States. (see "America Now" at the end of this chapter.)

One-Parent Domestic Groups

Millions of children throughout the world are reared in domestic groups in which only one parent is present. This arrangement may result from divorce or death of one of the parents. But it also may result from inability or unwillingness to marry. In the most common form of one-parent domestic arrangement, the mother is present and the father is absent. Such households are called *matrifocal*. The mother has a series of men as mates, usually one at a time, but sometimes several at a time. The man and woman usually reside together for brief periods, but over the years, the mother may spend long intervals without a resident mate (Box 9.2).

At one extreme, one-parent families are associated with well-paid employed single women (and, to a much lesser extent, men) who live alone with their children and manage to hire household help in lieu of kin and family. At the other extreme, a poor mother and her children may live together with her sisters and her mother and constitute a large extended family in which adult males play only temporary roles as visitors or lovers.

Matrifocal households are best known from studies carried out in the West Indies, Latin America, and U.S. inner cities (Stack 1974; Safa 1986; Smith 1990). But this form of household occurs throughout the world (Folbre 1991). Its incidence has been obscured by the tendency to regard such domestic units as aberrant or pathological (Moynihan 1965). In describing domestic groups, social scientists frequently concentrate on the emically preferred form and neglect etic behavioral actualities. Mother–child domestic groups often result from poverty, and hence are associated with many social ills and are regarded as undesirable. But we have no evidence that such domestic arrangements are inherently any more or less pathological, unstable, or contrary to "human nature" than the nuclear family.

What Is Marriage?

The concept of "**marriage**" is a basic part of the definition of nuclear, polygamous, and extended families and other forms of domestic organization. Although anthropologists are convinced that marriage occurs in every culture, we encounter great difficulty in coming up with a definition that can be applied universally. A famous definition proposed by Kathleen Gough (1968) can serve as a starting point for our discussion. It makes the following points:

- Marriage is a relationship established between a woman and one or more persons.
- This relationship assures that a child born to the woman is accorded full birth rights common to normal members of his or her society, provided that
- The child is conceived and born under certain approved circumstances.

According to Gough, for most if not all societies, this definition identifies a relationship "distinguished by the people themselves from all other kinds of relationships." Yet Gough's definition seems oddly at variance with English dictionary and native Western notions of marriage because it makes no reference to rights and duties of sexual access or to sexual performance.

Taiwan Marriage
Groom's extended family assemble for wedding ceremony.

In biological terms, sexuality and reproduction are not dependent on marriage; instead, marriage is a means of assigning social identity to children.

In omitting reference to sex as a necessary part of matrimonial relationships, Gough was influenced by historical research she used to supplement her fieldwork among the Nayar, a warrior caste of southern India that date back to before the British conquest.

The Nayar had an unusual marriage system, which can be best understood in the context of the traditional caste system, in which the Nayar were warriors and feudal landholders. Nayar households were matrilineal (see Chapter 10, "Unilineal Descent Groups" section) extended families in which the men specialized in military service and were away from their villages for many months at a time. Female sexuality was allowed free reign within certain rules. In order to bear children in a socially acceptable way, pubescent Nayar girls had to go through a four-day ceremony that linked them with a "ritual husband." Sexual relations were not a necessary component of this ceremony, and after it was over, the ritual husband and his wife did not live together nor have sex together. The ceremony merely legitimized her as a reproducer. The woman continued to live with her sisters, her mother, and her mother's brother and had sex with a series of visiting "husbands" of her own caste or of a higher one, who would spend the night with her at her home, and would leave early the next morning. If two men showed up on the same night, the visiting "husband" who arrived first would place his weapons outside the door to let others know they should come back another time. These arrangements do not reflect casual sex; there were strict rules governing who a woman could accept as a visiting "husband." Paternity was established by having one of the visiting "husbands" bestow gifts on the woman and bearing certain expenses associated with the birth of the child. A father had to be acknowledged in order for the child to have full birth rights. Otherwise the father incurred no further obligations, because the child belonged to the mother's kin group. Gough regarded the existence of the ritual husbands and approved visiting "husbands" as proof of the universality of marriage, because only ritually married Nayar women could have sexual relations and full birth rights were accorded only when fathers acknowledged their children.

Besides lacking any reference to sexual access, Gough's definition of marriage is also remarkable in another way. It does not necessarily involve a relationship between males and females, because it merely refers to a woman and "one or more" other persons of unspecified sex. What can be the reason for defining marriage as a relationship between a woman and "persons" rather than between "women and men"? Part of the answer is that in a number of African cultures women "marry" women. It works this way among the Dahomey: A woman, who herself is usually already married to a man, pays bridewealth (see p. 136) for a bride. The female bridewealth payer becomes a "female husband." She starts a family of her own by letting her "wife" become pregnant through relationship with designated males. The offspring of these unions fall under the control of the "female father", rather than the biological genitors. Note that this is another case of "marriage" that does not involve sexual relations.

Another example is the Nandi, a pastoral agricultural society in Kenya in which female–female marriage makes up about 3 percent of all marriages. This arrangement is related to patrilineal inheritance. Each married woman holds a separate fund of property (land and cattle), which is managed by her husband and inherited only by her sons and the sons of her co-wives. If the woman has no male heirs, her share of the property will be transmitted to other legal heirs (her co-wives' sons or to the sons of the husband's brother). But a barren Nandi woman can obtain a male heir by becoming the "female husband" of a younger woman. The female husband chooses the consort for her wife and becomes the legal "father" of her wife's children. According to Oboler (1988:77), "Except for the absence of the sex act, the relationship between the female husband and her wife is no different from that between a male husband and his wife." The "female husband" behaves in accordance with male role behavior; she discontinues sexual relations with men, including her male husband, she pays bridewealth (see later discussion) for her wife, she manages the family estate and has legitimate authority for her wife and children. In turn, she is able to pass on her share of the estate to her legal heirs, even if she herself is barren or without sons.

In contemporary European and American cultures, enduring mating relationships between coresident homosexual men or between coresident homosexual women are also often spoken of as marriage. It has thus been suggested that all reference to the gender of the people involved in the relationship should be omitted in the definition of marriage in order to accommodate such cases.

The task of understanding varieties of domestic organization is made more difficult when all these forms of mating are crammed into the single concept of marriage. Part of the problem is that when matings in Western culture are denied the designation "marriage," we tend to regard them as less honorable or less authentic relationships, and to impose legal penalties, as with gay couples who are denied access to a spouse's health insurance and sick leave benefits. And so anthropologists are reluctant to stigmatize woman–woman or man–man matings, or Nayar or matrifocal visiting-mate arrangements, by saying they are not marriages.

There is a simple way out of this dilemma. First, let us define marriage as the behavior, sentiments, and rules concerned with mating and reproduction in domestic contexts. This avoids offending people by using marriage exclusively for coresident heterosexual domestic mates. Let marital relationships be designated as heterosexual marriages, noncoresident marriages, man–man marriages, woman–woman marriages, or by any other appropriate specific nomenclature. Clearly, each form of mating has different ecological, demographic, economic, and ideological implications, so nothing is to be gained by arguing about whether they are or are not "real" marriages.

Legitimacy

The essence of the marital relationship, according to some anthropologists, is embodied in that portion of Gough's definition dealing with the assignment of "birth rights" over children. As Bronislaw Malinowski put it, "Marriage is the licensing of parenthood."

Legitimacy: (1) assigns birth status to the child, (2) legally entitles the child and/or the mother to the husband's property upon his death, and (3) determines who is responsible for the child and who controls the child's future.

It is true that women are universally discouraged from attempting to rear or dispose of their newborn infants according to their own whims, but most societies have several sets of rules defining permissible modes of conception and child rearing. For example, among the people who live in the small Brazilian towns that one of us (MH) has studied, four kinds of relationships occur between a man and a woman, all of which provide children with full birth rights: church marriage, civil marriage, simultaneous church and civil marriage, and consensual marriage. For a Brazilian woman, the most esteemed way to have children is through simultaneous church and civil marriage. This mode legally entitles her to a portion of her husband's property on his death. It also provides the added security of knowing that her husband cannot desert her and enter into a civil or religious marriage elsewhere. The least desirable mode is the consensual marriage because the woman can make no property claims against her consort, nor can she readily prevent him from deserting her. Yet as long as the father acknowledges paternity, the children of a consensual arrangement can make property claims against both father and mother while suffering no deprivation of birthrights in the form of legal disadvantages or social disapproval.

The point is not that a child is legitimate or illegitimate but rather that specific types of rights, obligations, and groupings emanate from different modes of sexual and reproductive relations. Few of the world's people are concerned with the question of whether a child is legitimate. Instead, the question concerns who will have the right of controlling the child's future. No society grants women complete "freedom of conception," but the restrictions placed on motherhood and the occasions for punishment and disapproval vary enormously.

Where the domestic scene is dominated by large extended families and where there are no strong restrictions on premarital sex, the pregnancy of a young unmarried woman is rarely the occasion for much concern. Under certain circumstances, an "unwed mother" may even be congratulated rather than condemned. Among the Kadar of northern Nigeria, as reported by M. G. Smith (1968), most marriages result from infant betrothals. These matches are arranged by the fathers of the bride and groom when the girl is 3 to 6 years old. Ten years or more may elapse before the bride goes to live with her betrothed. During this time, a Kadar girl may become pregnant. This will disturb no one, even if the biological father is a man other than her future husband: "Kadar set no value on premarital chastity. It is fairly common for unmarried girls to be impregnated or to give birth to children by youths other than their betrothed. Offspring of such premarital pregnancies are members of the patrilineage . . . of the girl's betrothed and are welcomed as proof of the bride's fertility" (p. 113).

The absence of concern about legitimacy in many non-Western cultures stands in stark contrast to the persecution of unwed mothers and their "bastard" children that dominated domestic life in Europe and the Americas as recently as the last century (Kertzer 1993). In industrial countries today, the legal and moral basis for discriminating against unwed mothers and their children is giving way to a growing acceptance of a woman's right to control her reproductive destiny with or without being married.

Every society has rules that define the conditions under which sexual relations, pregnancy, birth, and child rearing may take place, and that allocate privileges and duties in connection with these conditions. And every society has its own, sometimes unique, combination of rules and rules for breaking rules in this domain. It would be futile to define marriage by any one ingredient in these rules—such as legitimization of children—even if such an ingredient could be shown to be universal.

Economic Aspects of Marriage

Families collectively maintain an interest in the productive, reproductive, and sexual functions of their members. Individuals serve the interests of the group, and marriage must be seen primarily in the context of group interests. If a member of one extended family goes to live in the spouse's family, the spouse-givers expect something in return. The simplest form of such transactions is sister exchange, in which the groom's sister is given in marriage to her brother-in-law. Other forms of marital compensation are bridewealth, bride service and dowry.

Bridewealth

In a sample of 1,267 societies (Gaulin and Boster 1990:994), more than half participate in the institution known as **bridewealth.** Bridewealth (also known as **bride price**) is especially common where land is plentiful and the labor of additional women and children contributes to the wealth and well-being of the corporate group (Goody 1976). In bridewealth, the wife-receivers give valuable items to the wife-givers and thereby establish or reinforce alliances between the two families. As stated earlier in the chapter, bridewealth is not equivalent to the selling and buying of commodities in capitalist price market societies. The wife-receivers do not "own" their woman in any total sense; they must take good care of her, or her family will demand that she be returned to them.

Bridewealth compensates the bride's group for the loss of her labor and the children she bears, who become full members of the husband's group.

Bridewealth is found in societies where

- Women contribute a great deal to subsistence
- Women are valued as childbearers
- Land is readily available and there is sufficient work for all women

The amount of bridewealth is not fixed; it fluctuates within a certain range from one marriage to another. (In much of Africa, the traditional measure of bridewealth has been cattle although other valuables such as iron tools were also used. Nowadays, cash payments are the rule.) Among the Bathonga, a family that had many daughter-sisters was in a favorable position. The family would receive many cattle when the daughter-sisters got married. These cattle would then be used as bridewealth for the women's brothers: the more cattle, the more mother-wives; the more mother-wives, the larger the reproductive and productive labor force and the greater the material welfare and influence of the family.

Sometimes the transfer of wealth from one group to another is carried out in installments: so much on initial agreement, more when the woman goes to live

African Bridewealth

Cattle are commonly used as bridewealth in parts of Africa.

An Arranged Marriage in India

The personal interests of a married couple are subordinate to those of the couple's family kinship rules.

with her husband, and another, usually final, payment when she has her first child. Failure to have a child often voids the marriage; the woman goes home to her brothers and father, and the husband's family gets its bridewealth back.

When a man does not have the bridewealth requirement for marriage, he may be forced to postpone marriage well into his thirties. A man may also compete with his own father, who may prefer to marry another wife rather than give his livestock for his son's marriage. It is reported that among the Turkana of Kenya, if a man gets a woman pregnant without paying bridewealth, he must make a substantial payment but this lower "pregnancy" payment gives him no rights to either the woman or her children. The children remain with their mother and become members of her father's clan (Dyson-Hudson and Meekers 1996).

Bride Service

In **bride service,** a common alternative to bride price, the groom or husband compensates his in-laws by working for them for several months or years before taking his bride away to live and work with him and his extended family. Bride service is found in 14 percent of societies, mostly where there is little material wealth that can be transferred. In some cases, bride service substitutes for bridewealth or reduces the amount of bridewealth.

Bride service compensates the bride's family for the loss of a daughter. The groom moves in with the bride's family and works in exchange for his marital rights.

Dowry

Where women's productive and reproductive roles are less valued, wives may be regarded as an economic burden. Instead of paying bridewealth to the family of the bride, the groom's family may demand a reverse payment, called *dowry.*

Dowry is a transfer of goods or money from the bride's family to the bride. It represents compensation for the future support of the woman and her future children and is found in societies where women contribute relatively little to subsistence.

Dowry is found in societies where

- Land is in short supply
- Women's labor cannot be used to intensify production
- Families do not want too many children, because there is not enough land to pass on to heirs
- Females do not inherit land; instead, they are given a dowry as a share of her parent's estate

Dowry

Dowry is provided to the groom or the groom's family as compensation for support for the woman and her future children. Sometimes it is also given to the bride in lieu of a share of her parents estate.

Dowry is much rarer than bridewealth, occurring in only 3 percent of a sample of 1,267 societies (Gaulin and Boster 1990:994). The societies that have dowry are concentrated in the extremely populous states of Mediterranean Europe and southern Asia. Throughout this region, land is scarce and there is intensive agriculture involving animal-drawn plows guided by men, whereas women's work is largely confined to the domestic sphere. Whenever dowry payment consists of money or movable property instead of land, it tends to be associated with a low or oppressed status for women (Schlegel and Barry 1986:145; Bossen 1988; Schlegel and Eloul 1988).

An important feature of dowry is that it can be used to support social ranking. In some societies large dowry payments are used to attract a wealthy bridegroom from an upper-status family. This system, known as **hypergamy**, is used to improve a daughter's chance of "marrying up" and assure a better future for grandchildren. It is also presumed that a dowry will increase the likelihood that the woman and her children will be well treated. However, in

some cases hypergamy is associated with female infanticide. In northern India, for example, high dowry costs and a strong preference for males results in high rates of female infant mortality. It is financially more advantageous for families to raise sons whose brides will bring in large dowries than to have daughters whose marriages will require a large expenditure of wealth (Miller 1981).

The opposite of bridewealth is not dowry but *groom price,* in which the groom goes to live and work with the bride's family, and the bride's family compensates the groom's family for the loss of his productive and reproductive powers. This form of marriage compensation is extremely rare—only one well-documented case is known (the Nagovisi, see Nash 1974).

Preferential Marriages

The widespread occurrence of economic exchange during marriage implies that the corporate interests of domestic groups must be protected by rules that stipulate who is to marry whom. Having given a woman away in marriage, most groups expect either material wealth or women in exchange. Consider two domestic groups, A and B, each with a core of resident brothers. If A gives a woman to B, B may immediately reciprocate by giving a woman to A. This reciprocity is often achieved by a direct exchange of the groom's sister. But the reciprocity may take a more indirect form. B may return a daughter of the union between the B man and the A woman. The bride in such a marriage will be her husband's father's sister's daughter, and the groom will be his wife's mother's brother's son. Bride and groom are each other's cross-cousins (see Chapter 10, "Descent Rules" section). If A and B have a rule that such marriages are to occur whenever possible, then they are said to have preferential cross-cousin marriage.

Reciprocity in marriage is sometimes achieved by several intermarrying domestic groups that exchange women in cycles and are called **circulating connubia.** For example, A→B→C→A; or A→B and C→D in one generation and A→D and B→C in the next, and then back to A→B and C→D. These exchanges are enforced by preferential marriage with appropriate kinds of cousins, nephews, nieces, and other kin.

Another common expression of collective familial interest in marriage is the practice of supplying replacements for in-marrying women who die prematurely. To maintain reciprocity or to fulfill a marriage contract for which bridewealth has been paid, the brother of a deceased woman may permit the widower to marry one or more of the deceased wife's sisters. This custom is known as the **sororate** (a deceased woman is replaced in marriage by her sister). Closely related to this practice is the preferential marriage known as the **levirate**, in which the services of a man's widow are retained within the domestic unit by having her marry one of his brothers (a deceased husband is replaced in marriage by his brother). If the widows are old, the services rendered by the remarried widow may be minimal, and the levirate then functions to provide security for women who would otherwise not be able to remarry. Thus the organization of domestic life everywhere reflects the fact that husbands and wives usually originate in different domestic groups that continue to maintain a sentimental and practical interest in the marriage partners and their children.

Domestic Groups and the Avoidance of Incest

Marriage exchanges entail preference rules concerning whom one should or should not marry; some groups practice **exogamy**, in which members of the group must "marry out," whereas others practice **endogamy**, where members "marry in," within a defined group. Incest avoidance results in an almost universal rule of exogamy within the primary nuclear family. The term **incest taboo** refers to cultural beliefs prohibiting sexual relations with a close relative. Although universally unacceptable, not all cultures have explicit rules on nuclear family sexual relations—in some cultures it is considered simply unthinkable, whereas in others it is morally outrageous and punishable through supernatural retribution. The term **inbreeding avoidance**, in contrast, refers to behavioral patterns in which individuals avoid sexual contact with people who could be sexual partners were it not for their relatedness. It appears that in the vast majority of societies, sexual relations between members of the nuclear family are rare.

Many different explanations for incest avoidance have been given, yet there is a lack of coherence among the various theories and the taboo still presents a challenge to anthropological explanation. Two explanations are required: how the taboo originated and what motivates people to maintain the avoidance behavior over time.

The most universal prohibition is against sexual relations and marriage between parents and their children. In most cultures brother–sister sexual relations and marriage are also forbidden, but we know of several important exceptions, such as the ruling classes of the Incas, ancient Egypt, ancient China, and Hawaii (Bixler 1982). Most of these marriages were between half-siblings, but some were between full siblings.

Cleopatra

Eleven generations of brother–sister marriage preserved the purity of the royal lineage and kept the property of the royals intact.

The reasons for sister–brother marriage seem to have been religious and economic; a member of the royal family, who was partly a god, could not marry an "ordinary" human and, moreover, marriage within the family kept the royal wealth and property undivided.

In Egypt during Roman times (approximately from 30 B.C. to A.D. 600), not only elites, but also commoners practiced brother–sister marriage. Such marriages, according to historian Keith Hopkins (1980), were regarded as perfectly normal relationships, openly mentioned in documents concerning inheritance, business affairs, lawsuits, and petitions to officials. Census data from that era shows that between 15 and 20 percent of marriages were between full brothers and sisters and were not just within royal families, as it commonly believed (Scheidel 1996).

Social and Cultural Advantages of Exogamy

Incest avoidance among nuclear family members, and other forms of exogamy among domestic groups, can be effectively explained in terms of demographic, economic, and ecological advantages (Leavitt 1989). Exogamy is essential if small populations are to use their productive and reproductive potential effectively. Band societies rely on marriage exchanges to establish long-distance networks of kinspeople and to maintain peaceful relations with other groups. Bands that formed a completely closed breeding unit would be denied the mobility and territorial flexibility essential to their subsistence strategy. Once a band begins to obtain mates from other bands, reciprocal exchanges are built on a flow of mates and other valuables. Receivers must become givers. Therefore the taboo on mother–son, father–daughter, and brother–sister marriages can be interpreted as a defense of reciprocal exchange relationships against the ever-present temptation for parents to keep their children for themselves or for brothers and sisters to keep each other for themselves. If this happened, family groups would just incestuously "grow on their own" and would be totally self-sufficient (Stone: 1997:49).

Incest avoidance has positive social advantages. By forcing people to marry outside their immediate family, the incest taboo creates a wider network of interfamily alliances that enhances cooperation, social solidarity, and survival.

Biological Risks of Inbreeding: The Observationalist Theory

A number of investigators have argued that incest prohibitions defend against the biological costs of "marrying in." Close inbreeding increases the likelihood that offspring will suffer from congenital deformities. Relatives who carry defective genes and mate with each other will give birth to children who suffer from pathological conditions that lower their rate of reproduction. This **observationalist theory**, according to Daniel Fessler (1999), assumes that people in the past observed that repeated kinds of unions have

harmful effects. Societies that developed incest prohibitions had healthier populations and therefore were more successful than those that did not.

From a biological perspective, inbreeding avoidance prevents the most dangerous kinds of mating with close relatives.

Another argument asserts that inbreeding, simply by lowering the amount of genetic diversity in a population, might adversely affect the population's ability to adapt to new diseases or other novel environmental hazards (Leavitt 1990, 1992; cf. Uhlman 1992; Schields 1994).

This part of the argument has several weak spots. It is true that in large modern populations, incest leads to a high rate of stillbirths and congenitally diseased and impaired children (Bittles et al. 1991; Thornhill 1993). But the same results need not occur in small preagricultural societies where close inbreeding leads to the gradual purging of harmful recessive genes because such societies have little tolerance for infants and children who are congenitally handicapped and impaired. Repeated inbreeding over many generations has a purging effect and will lead to greater rarity of harmful recessive genes. Lack of support for impaired children eliminates the harmful genetic variations from future generations and results in populations that carry a much smaller "load" of harmful gene variants than modern populations (Livingstone 1969, 1982).

Motivations for Incest Avoidance

Many scholars believe that incest avoidance developed preculturally. This view has received support from field studies of monkey and ape mating behavior. As among humans, father–daughter, mother–son, and brother–sister matings are uncommon among our nearest animal relatives, although they do occur. In most nonhuman primates, males routinely leave their natal group at puberty to seek mating opportunities elsewhere (Boyd and Silk 1997:614; Pusey and Wolf 1996). Moreover, females will resist solicitations from related males more frequently than males resist approaches from related females, suggesting that females are more averse to inbreeding than males. Given the fact that females have a greater investment in reproduction (see discussion of female sexuality in Chapter 7), female disfavor of male relatives as sexual partners can be seen as evidence of female mate selectivity to avoid the risk of nonviable offspring (Fessler 1999).

Advocates of genetic theories of incest avoidance nevertheless recognized that genes are not likely to contain definite instructions for shutting down sex drives in the presence of siblings, children, and parents. Following the lead of Edward Westermark (1894), they proposed, instead, that members of the opposite sex have an innate tendency to experience a distinct feeling of aversion if they have been brought up in close physical proximity to each other during infancy and childhood (Shepher 1983). Westermark's principle is much in favor among evolutionary psychologists because it provides a way out of the dilemma posed by brother–sister incest among royalty. If different nurses and caretakers brought up brothers and sisters apart from each other in different houses, then, according to the Westermark principle, they might very well find each other sexually attractive enough to mate (Wilson 1978:38–39; Bixler 1982).

Westermark proposed that persons raised together or persons living closely together during early childhood, develop a natural aversion to having sexual relations with one another.

Westermak's conclusions do not explain how the aversion mechanism functions. Freud, in contrast, explains incest aversion as an intrapsychic process. As we discuss in Chapter 14, psychoanalytic theory assumes the desire for sexual relations within the family is strong, but such impulses are repressed into the unconscious, where they find expression in dreams and folklore. These feelings are therefore redirected away from the nuclear family by developing other erotic interests that eventually lead to marriage outside the family unit. The incest taboo thus guards against sexual competition that would disrupt the stability of the family.

Sim Pua *Marriage: "Adopt a Daughter, Marry a Sister"*

To test the Westermark theory, one cannot point to the mere occurrence of incest avoidance. Evidence must show that sexual ardor cools when people grow up together, independent of any existing norms that call for incest avoidance. Since this cannot be done experimentally without controlling the lives of human subjects, advocates of the theory lean heavily on two famous case studies that allegedly demonstrate the predicted loss of sexual ardor. The first of these concerns Taiwanese *sim pua* marriage, where husband and wife grow up together at close quarters. Studies show that such marriages lead to fewer children, greater adultery, and higher divorce rates than nor-

mal marriages, in which future wives and husbands grow up in separate households (Wolf and Huang 1980). But do these observations confirm Westermark's theory? In Taiwan, to seal a marriage bond, the families of a bride and groom normally exchange considerable wealth as a sign of their support for the newlyweds. But such exchanges are smaller or absent altogether in sim pua marriage. The Taiwanese explicitly recognize that "adopt a daughter, marry a sister" is an inferior, even humiliating, form of marriage. This difference makes it difficult to prove that sexual disinterest, rather than chagrin and disappointment over being treated like second-class citizens, is the source of the couple's relative infertility.

Wolf (1995) has countered such criticism by presenting data on the effect that age of adoption has on depressing fertility. He maintains the "Westermark effect" takes places during a critical period between birth and the age of 3. Girls who are adopted after age 3 do not have depressed fertility rates. He therefore argues that the negative social and economic stigma of this form of marriage does not account for the effects on lower fertility.

The problem with this rejoinder, however, is that a 2-year-old infant taken from her mother is likely to have different experiences than a child whose adoption takes place at a later phase of childhood. Clearly we need to know more about the experiences of infant and child adoptees and how they are treated while growing up in the home of their future husbands.

Westermark in the Kibbutz

The second case used to confirm Westermark's theory concerns an alleged lack of sexual interest displayed by boys and girls who were raised with each other from infancy through adolescence in the Israeli cooperative community known as a kibbutz. According to Joseph Shepher (1983), these boys and girls were so thoroughly "turned off" that, among marriages contracted by people who were reared in a kibbutz, not one involved men or women who had been reared together during infancy. He argues that such aversion is a "genetically determined predisposition to be imprinted against those with whom one has been cosocialized" (Shepher 1983:114). This evidence is impressive, but anthropologist John Hartung has discovered a flaw in the statistics. Out of a total of 2,516 marriages, Sheper found 200 in which both partners were reared in the same kibbutz although they were not all together in the same age group during the entire period from birth to age 6. One must now ask, of the 200 marriages from within the same kibbutz,

Children on Israeli Kibbutz Celebrating the Harvest
Until recently, kibbutz children were raised together in collective dormitories like brothers and sisters. None of them later became sexually interested in one another.

what was the chance that not a single one would be between a boy and a girl who were reared together during infancy? Because girls in the kibbutz were generally three years younger than the boys they married, only a very few marriages between people who were reared for the first six years in the same class could be expected. Actually, Hartung (1985) points out, that five marriages did occur between boys and girls who had been reared together for part of the first six years of their lives. Because Westermark's theory does not predict how long it takes for reared-together boys and girls to lose their interest in each other, Hartung believes these five marriages actually disconfirm the theory (Hartung 1985). Unfortunately, Joseph Shepher died before he had a chance to respond to Hartung and we shall have to wait for additional studies before reaching a decision on this issue.

Avoidance within the Family

The proposal that an instinctual sexual aversion occurs within the nuclear family is challenged by the growing evidence for the actual occurrence of incest within the family. Social workers estimate that tens of thousands of cases of incest occur in the United States annually, of which the great majority involve fathers imposing on young daughters (Glaser and Frosh 1988; Cicchetti and Carlson 1989). Two studies found that, compared with nonincestuous fathers, fathers who seduced their daughters generally did not engage in caretaking or spend time with their daughters while

they were young (Parker and Parker 1985; Williams and Finklehor 1995).

Another factor favoring nuclear family exogamy is the institution of marriage itself. Most marriages (despite the exceptions previously discussed such as the Nayar) limit the sexual freedom of the marriage partners. Thus the great majority of societies prohibit one or both spouses from having extramarital sex, that is, from committing adultery. Illicit sexual encounters between father and daughter and mother and son constitute a form of adultery. Mother–son incest is an especially threatening variety of adultery, particularly in societies that have strong male supremacist institutions (see Chapter 15). Not only is the wife "double-dealing" against her husband but the son is also "double-dealing" against his father. This may explain why the least common and emically most feared and abhorred form of incest is that between mother and son. It follows that father–daughter incest will be somewhat more common because husbands enjoy double standards of sexual behavior more often than wives do and are less vulnerable to punishment for adultery. Finally, the same consideration suggests an explanation for the relatively higher frequency of brother–sister matings and their legitimization as marriages in elite classes, as they do not conflict with the adultery rules for fathers and mothers.

After the evolution of the state, exogamous alliances between domestic groups continued to have important infrastructural consequences. Among peasants, exogamy increases the total productive and reproductive strength of the intermarried groups because it permits the exploitation of resources over a larger area than the nuclear or extended family could manage on an individual basis. Exogamy also facilitates trade, and raises the upper limit of the size of groups that can be formed to carry out seasonal activities requiring large labor inputs (communal game drives, harvests, and so on). Furthermore, in prestate societies, where intergroup warfare poses a threat to group survival, the ability to mobilize large numbers of warriors is decisive. Hence, in militaristic, highly male-centered village cultures, the exchange of sisters and daughters is frequently used to establish alliances. These alliances do not necessarily eliminate warfare between intermarrying groups, but they make it less common, as might be expected from the presence of sisters and daughters in the enemy's ranks (Tefft 1975; Kang 1979; Podolefsky 1984).

From a cultural perspective, incest rules are more significant for maintaining marriage alliances between families than for preventing sex within the confines of the family.

In cultures with classes and castes, endogamy often combines with extended family exogamy to maintain wealth and power within the ruling circles. But as already noted with royalty, even the nuclear family may become endogamous when there is an extreme concentration of political, economic, and military power. In addition, with the evolution of price market forms of exchange, the extended family tends to be replaced by nuclear family domestic units. Domestic group alliances lose some of their previous adaptive importance, and the traditional cultural functions of incest avoidance lose their force. Incest has been decriminalized in Sweden, for example, and some people advocate the same for the United States (Y. Cohen 1978; De Mott 1980). However, given the scientific knowledge that nuclear family incest is both genetically risky in populations carrying a heavy load of harmful recessive genes, the repeal of legislation against incest seems unlikely and unwise.

Main function of marriage: provide children w/ some status

Summary

1. The structural level of sociocultural systems is made up in part of interrelated domestic groups. Such groups can usually be identified by their attachment to a living space or domicile in which activities such as eating, sleeping, marital sex, and the nurturance and discipline of the young take place.

2. There is no single or minimal pattern of domestic activities. Similarly, the nuclear family cannot be regarded as the minimal building block of all domestic groups. Although nuclear families occur in almost every society, they are not always the dominant domestic group, and their sexual, reproductive, and productive functions can readily be satisfied by alternative domestic and nondomestic institutions.

3. In polygamous and extended families, the father–mother–child unit may not be separate from the other sets of other relatives and their multiple spouses. And there are many instances of domestic groups that lack a coresident husband-father. Although children need to be nurtured and protected, no one has defined the limits within which human domestic arrangements must be confined in order to satisfy human nature. One of the most important facts about human domestic arrangements is that no single pattern can be shown to be more "natural" than any other.

4. Family structure is closely related to the domestic mode of production. The nuclear family is associated with a high degree of mobility and economic autonomy; the extended family prevails where a large labor pool is advantageous in carrying out a variety of simultaneous economic activities. Polygyny is associated with female contribution to production and may serve as a means of enhancing a man's position in the community; polyandry avoids subdividing the family estate and occurs in only a few societies where farming and grazing land is limited.

5. Marriage practices also exhibit an enormous degree of variation. Although something similar to what is called *marriage* occurs all over the world, it is difficult to specify the mental and behavioral essence of the marital relationship. Man–man, woman–woman, female–father, and childless marriages make it difficult to give a minimal definition of marriage without offending someone. Even coresidence may not be essential, as the Nayar and other single-parent households demonstrate. And if we restrict the definition of marriage to coresident heterosexual matings that result in reproduction, we still find a staggering variety of rights and duties associated with the sexual and reproductive functions of the marriage partners and their offspring.

6. To understand coresident heterosexual reproductive marriage in extended families, marriage must be seen as a relationship between corporate family groups as much as between cohabiting mates. The divergent interests of these corporate groups are reconciled by means of reciprocal exchanges that take the form of sister exchange, bridewealth, suitor service, dowry, and groom price. Except for dowry, the common principle underlying these exchanges is that in giving a man or woman away to another extended family, the family of origin does not renounce its interest in the offspring, but expects compensation for the loss of a productively and reproductively valuable person.

7. A range of preferred and prohibited marriages reflect the pervasive corporate interests of domestic groups. Preferences for certain kinds of marriage exchanges create circulating connubia in which reciprocity between domestic groups may be direct or indirect. Such preferences may be expressed as a rule requiring marriage with a particular kind of cousin. Preferential marriage rules such as the levirate and sororate also exemplify the corporate nature of the marriage bond.

8. Most domestic groups are exogamous. This can be seen as a result of either instinctual programming or social and cultural adaptation. The discussion of exogamy necessarily centers on the incest prohibitions within the nuclear family. Father–daughter, sister–brother, and mother–son matings and marriages are almost universally forbidden. The chief

exception is brother–sister marriages, which occur in several highly stratified societies among the ruling elites among the Incas, Egyptians, and Hawaiians, and among Egyptian commoners in Roman times.

9. The instinct theory of incest avoidance, or Westermark effect, stresses evidence from Taiwan and Israel that suggests that children reared together develop a sexual aversion to each other. This aversion is seen as genetically determined because it reduces the risk of harmful genes. Other interpretations of the Taiwan and Israel studies can be made, however. A purely cultural theory of incest avoidance can be built out of the need for marriage exogamy to establish alliances through reciprocal marriage exchanges. In the future, the perpetuation of the incest taboos may be related exclusively to the increasing genetic dangers associated with close inbreeding in populations carrying a large load of harmful genes.

AMERICA NOW

Matrifocal Families

In 1965, with the release of a report by Daniel P. Moynihan, then U.S. Assistant Secretary of Labor, matrifocality received official recognition as the prime cause of the perpetuation of poverty among Blacks in the United States. According to Moynihan, because they lack a male father figure in their family Black male youths are not properly motivated to take jobs that are actually available. Adult men drift in and out of these households, and thus African-American male youths grow up without the aid and inspiration of a stable male figure who holds a steady job and who provides comfort and security for wife and children. Moynihan proposed that matrifocality was a cause not only of poverty but of crime and drug addiction as well. Explanations of poverty that appeal to enculturation experience within matrifocal households don't explain very much, because in most societies the phenomenon of matrifocality is itself a response to poverty. Setting aside the relatively small number of matrifocal families headed by middle- and upper-class professional women, the majority of matrifocal families in the United States are headed by low-income women who would prefer to marry if they could find an appropriate spouse. In many communities there are far fewer males than females and some may have poor economic prospects. Furthermore, poverty-class women in the United States do have greater access to sources of income than poverty-class men. Unemployment among poor minority males exceeds unemployment among poor minority women.

More important, poor women have access to welfare support for themselves and their children, whereas poor men are seldom favored with aid for dependent children. At the same time, it is women who have access to public housing and to housing subsidies. Poor women thus have little incentive to marry men who would be an economic burden to them. Lacking steady employment or job training, men gravitate toward making money in illegal enterprises. Many of them spend time in prison, a situation that is scarcely conducive to the formation of patrifocal or nuclear family households. Higher rates of mortality among marriage-age men further reduce the pool of potential mates for poor women (Dehavenon 1993).

In her study of the Flats, a Black ghetto in a midwestern U.S. city, anthropologist Carol Stack (1974) provides an account of the strategies that poverty-level families follow in attempting to maximize their security and well-being in the face of the inadequate wages of the unskilled male. Nuclear families do not exist in the Flats because the material conditions necessary for such families do not exist. Instead, the people of the Flats are organized into large female-centered networks of relatives and neighbors. The members of these networks engage in reciprocal economic exchanges, take care of one another's children, provide emergency shelter, and help one another in many ways not characteristic of middle-class domestic groups. In the Flats, the most important factors that affect interpersonal relationships between men and women are unemployment and the difficulty that men have in finding secure jobs. Losing a job, or being unemployed month after month, debilitates one's self-importance and independence and, for men,

Children of the Flats
Area of Carol Stack's study.

necessitates that they sacrifice their role in the economic support of their families. Then they become unable to assume the traditional father role as defined by American society. Ironically, as Stack points out, attempts by women on welfare to form nuclear families are efficiently discouraged by welfare policy. "Women come to realize that welfare benefits and ties with kin networks provide greater security for them and their children" (Stack 1974:113).

Fifty-four percent of African-American children and 27 percent of Hispanic children live with their mothers only. But the trend toward matrifocal households is also present among Whites: Seventeen percent of White children under the age of 18 live with mothers only, up from 8 percent in 1970. What's more, the great majority of matrifocal White households are headed by poor, nonprofessional women, not by high-income single mothers who choose motherhood because their biological clocks are ticking (U.S. Bureau of the Census 1994).

KEY TERMS
bride price
bride service
bridewealth
circulating connubia
dowry
endogamy
environment of evolutionary adaptedness
exogamy
extended family
hypergamy
inbreeding avoidance
incest taboo
legitimacy
levirate
marriage
monogamy
nuclear family
observationalist theory
polyandry
polygamy
polygyny
sororal polygyny
sororate

QUESTIONS TO THINK ABOUT

1. How does infrastructure influence the household composition? What are the social and economic ramifications of nuclear versus extended-family households?

2. What is meant by "Marriage is the licensing of parenthood?" Does this statement apply in U.S. society, today? What other rights are transmitted in marriage?

3. Evaluate the explanations offered for incest avoidance? Which do you prefer and why?

4. What is the difference between polygyny in Africa and polygyny in the Amazon basin?

5. What are the differences between polygyny and polyandry in terms of economics and household dynamics?

CHAPTER 10

Descent, Locality, and Kinship

Machiguenga Nuclear Family.

Couples reside matrilocally when they marry but after that residence is flexible; alternating residence, between the wife and husband's kin.

Kinship

Descent

Descent Rules: Cognatic and Unilineal Descent

Cognatic Bilateral Descent and Kindreds
Cognatic Ambilineal Descent and Cognatic Lineages
Unilineal Descent Groups

Postmarital Locality Patterns

Determinants of Bilateral Descent Groups
Determinants of Cognatic Lineages and Clans
Determinants of Unilineal Lineages and Clans
Causes of Patrilocality

Causes of Matrilocality
Causes of Avunculocality

Kinship Terminologies Systems

Eskimo Terminology
Hawaiian Terminology
Iroquois Terminology

Kin Terms Are Negotiated, Not Written in Stone

Summary

America Now: Changes in Family Structure

We continue with domestic organization. We examine the principal mental and emic components of domestic groups—namely, the concept of kinship through marriage and descent. Then we relate different varieties of kinship concepts to particular kinds of domestic groups and to the influence of infrastructural conditions. To top this off, we briefly explore different kinship terminologies—systems for classifying relatives. Like language, kinship studies demonstrate the power of culture to form systems of thought and behavior on the level of groups rather than on the level of individuals. We will see that how kinship, as a social construction, classifies members of a society into groups that structure marriage, residence, political obligations and property rights.

refers to a set of ideas and beliefs about an individual.

Kinship

The study of hundreds of cultures all over the world has led anthropologists to conclude that two principles are inherent in the organization of domestic life everywhere. The first is relatedness through **descent** or parentage from a common ancestor. The second is relatedness through marriage or **affinity.** People who are related to each other through descent or a combination of affinity and descent are relatives, or kin. And the domain of ideas constituted by the beliefs and expectations kin share about one another is called *kinship.*

Kinship refers to relationships that are based on parentage through descent, known as **consanguineal relations,** and to relatedness through marriage, known as **affinal relations.**

Kinship should not be confused with biological mating or biological descent. Kinship is an emic, culturally constructed concept; biologic matings and biological descent are etic concepts. As discussed previously, marriage may emically establish "parentage" with respect to children who are biologically unrelated to their culturally defined "father." Even where a culture insists that descent must be based on actual biological fatherhood, domestic arrangements may make it difficult to identify the biological father. For these reasons, anthropologists distinguish between the culturally defined "father" and the **genitor,** the actual biological father. A similar distinction is necessary in the case of "mother." Although the culturally defined mother is usually the **genetrix,** or biological mother, the widespread practice of adoption also creates many discrepancies between emic and etic motherhood.

Every society has a kinship system consisting of the following:

- Terms used to classify various categories of consanguineal and affinal kin
- Terms used to identify kin that are more socially significant than others
- Expected rights and obligations that different categories of kin have toward one another.

Descent

Descent is the belief that certain persons play an important role in the creation, birth, and nurturance of certain children. Theories of descent vary from culture to culture, but so far as we know, no human society is without such a theory (Scheffler 1973:749). Descent implies the preservation of some aspect of the substance or spirit of people in future generations and thus is a symbolic form of immortality (Craig 1979). Perhaps that is why every society believes in one form or another of descent.

In Western folk traditions, parents are linked to children by the belief that children have the same kind of "blood" as their parents. Each child's veins are thought of as being filled with blood obtained from mother and father in equal amounts. As a result of this imagery, "blood relatives" are distinguished from relatives who are linked only through marriage. This imagery led nineteenth-century anthropologists to use the ethnocentric term *consanguine* (of the same blood) to denote relations of descent. Westerners (including college professors) persist in talking about blood relatives even though we know that closely related individuals may have different blood types, distantly related or unrelated individuals may have the same blood type, and the closeness of a relationship is measured by the proportion of shared DNA and not by shared blood.

Descent need not depend on the idea of blood inheritance, nor need it involve equal contributions from both father and mother:

- The Ashanti of West Africa believe that blood is contributed only by the mother and that it determines only a child's physical characteristics, whereas a child's spiritual disposition and temperament are the product of the father's semen.
- The Trobrianders contend that semen does not play a procreative role. Here a woman becomes pregnant when a spirit of a deceased member of the matrilineage enters a woman's body and causes her to become pregnant. The fetus is formed by the

American Kindred

Thanksgiving is an occasion for both siblings and cousins to get together.

combination of the woman's blood and the ancestral spirit. The only procreative function of the Trobriand "father" is to help develop the fetus through frequent sexual intercourse. The mother's husband nourishes the fetus with his matrilineal essence and after the child is born, continues to nurture the child by working hard to provide it with food and wealth. (Although the Trobrianders practice premarital sex, girls usually are married by the time they are capable of becoming pregnant, so they have no evidence to refute the belief that conception is caused by the spirit of a matrilineal ancestor, and does not require a man's semen). (Weiner 1987).

A number of societies in lowland South America believe that it is possible to have several biological fathers:

■ The Bari of Venezuela believe that men who have intercourse with a woman during her pregnancy share the biological fatherhood of her child. The woman's cohabiting husband is considered the primary biological father; whereas the woman's lovers are secondary fathers. The husband is usually aware of the lovers. When a woman gives birth, she typically names all the men she had intercourse with during her pregnancy. These secondary fathers are obligated to provide gifts of fish and game to the child, which is likely to contribute to the child's increased chances of survival (Beckerman et al. 1998).

■ Among the Mehinacu of Brazil it is believed that the fetus is built up in the course of repeated acts of sex. A man's semen contains the seed, which is planted in the woman's body. Fathering a child does not occur in a single act, rather repeated acts of sexual relations are required during which the father and any other men who have intercourse with the mother gradually "make" the baby together. The woman's role is less active; she simply shelters the fetus in her womb (Gregor 1977:261).

Despite the many theories about the nature of procreative roles, all cultures affirm the existence of some special contribution made by both male and female to the reproductive process although they may contribute quite unevenly and with vastly different expectations concerning rights and obligations.

Descent Rules: Cognatic and Unilineal Descent

By reckoning their descent relationships, individuals are apportioned different duties, rights, and privileges in regard to many different aspects of social life. Descent may be used to determine a person's name, family, residence, rank, property, ethnicity, nationality, and many other statuses.

Anthropologists distinguish two major classes of descent rules: the cognatic and the unilineal.

△ Male

○ Female

= Is married to

| Is descended from

☐ Is the sibling of

◬ Ego whose genealogy is being shown

Figure 10.1 How to Read Kinship Diagrams

Anthropologists use "ego" to denote the "I" from whom kinship relations are being reckoned.

- **Cognatic descent** rules are those in which both male and female parentage are used to establish any of the above-mentioned duties, rights, and privileges.
- **Unilineal descent** rules restrict parental links exclusively to males or exclusively to females.

The most common form of cognatic rule is **bilateral descent**, the reckoning of kinship evenly and symmetrically along maternal and paternal links in ascending and descending generations through individuals of both sexes (Figures 10.1 and 10.2).

The second, less common variety of cognatic rule is called **ambilineal descent** (Fig. 10.3). Here **ego** (the individual of reference from whom the kinship terminological system is constructed) has a choice of either maternal or paternal links, depending on which kin group provides greater opportunities. As in bilateral descent, ego traces descent through males and females, but the links can go back and forth over time,

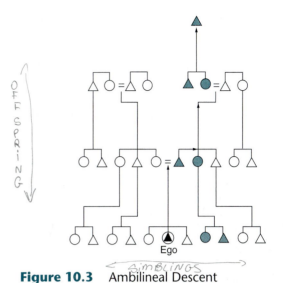

Figure 10.3 Ambilineal Descent

Ego traces descent through both males and females, but not equally and not simultaneously.

including some female ancestors or descendants but excluding others, and including some male ancestors or descendants and excluding others. In other words, with ambilineal descent, ego does not reckon descent simultaneously and equally through mothers and fathers, but chooses to affiliate with either the mother's or father's kin group.

Moving on now to unilineal descent, we find two main varieties: patrilineality and matrilineality. When **patrilineal descent** is reckoned, ego follows the ascending and descending genealogical links through males only (Figure 10.4). Note that this does not

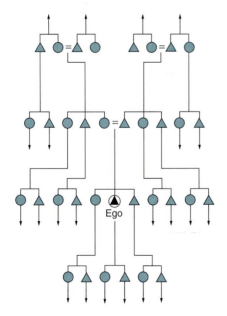

Figure 10.2 Bilateral Descent

Everyone on the diagram has a descent relationship with ego.

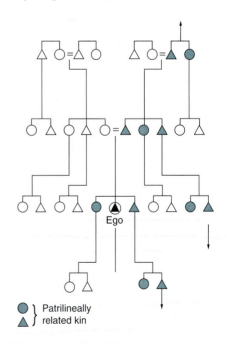

● ⎫ Patrilineally
▲ ⎭ related kin

Figure 10.4 Patrilineal Descent

Descent is traced exclusively through males.

mean that the descent-related individuals are only males; in each generation, ego has relatives of both genders. However, in the passage from one generation to another, only the male links are relevant; children of females are dropped from the descent reckoning.

When **matrilineal descent** is reckoned, ego follows the ascending and descending links through females only (Figure 10.5). Once again, note that males as well as females can be related matrilineally; only in the passage from one generation to another are the children of males dropped from the descent reckoning.

One of the most important logical consequences of unilineal descent is that it segregates the children of siblings of the opposite sex into distinct categories. This effect is especially important in the case of cousins. Note that with patrilineal descent, ego's father's sister's son and daughter do not share common descent with ego, whereas ego's father's brother's son and daughter do share common descent with ego. In the case of matrilineal descent, the same kind of distinction results with respect to ego's "cousins" on the mother's side. Children whose parents are related to each other as brother and sister are known as *cross cousins*; children whose parents are related to each other as brother and brother or sister and sister are known as *parallel cousins* (Figure 10.6).

Each of these descent rules provides the logical basis for mentally aligning people into emic kinship groups. These groups exert great influence on the way people think and behave in both domestic and extradomestic situations. An important point to bear in

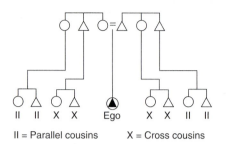

Figure 10.6   Cross-Cousins and Parallel Cousins

mind about kinship groups is that they need not consist of coresident relatives; members of the same lineages and clans, for example, may be found in different households and different villages. We proceed now to a description of the principal varieties of kinship groups.

Cognatic Bilateral Descent and Kindreds

In societies that practice bilateral descent, such as our own, a person is related equally to both the mother's and father's side of the family. Bilateral descent applied to a wide span of kin and across a number of generations may lead to the concept of groups known as **kindreds** (Figure 10.7). A kindred consists of ego's close bilateral relatives who form a group that comes together for such occasions as when ego is born, mar-

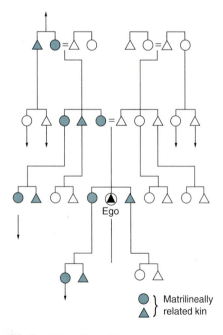

Figure 10.5   Matrilineal Descent
Descent is traced exclusively through females.

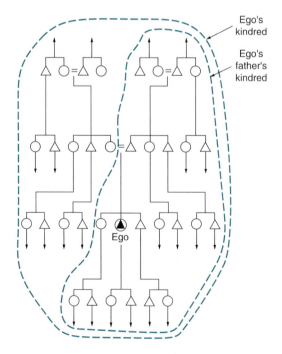

Figure 10.7   Kindreds
Children have kindreds that are different from those of either parent.

ries, gives a feast, etc. When modern-day Americans and Europeans use the word *relatives,* they are referring to their kindreds. The main characteristic of the kindred is that the span and depth of bilateral reckoning are open-ended. Relatives within a kindred can be judged as "near" or "far," depending on the number of genealogical links that separate them, but there is no definite or uniform principle for making such judgments or for terminating the extension of the kinship circle. An important consequence of this feature, as shown in Figure 10.7, is that kindreds are ego centered: egos and their siblings have a kindred whose membership is different from that of everyone else. As a result, everyone in a kindred-based society belongs to different overlapping kin groups. This means that it is impossible for coresident domestic groups to consist of kindreds and very difficult for kindreds to maintain corporate interests in land and people.

Cognatic Ambilineal Descent and Cognatic Lineages

The open-ended, ego-centered characteristics of the bilateral kindred can be overcome by specifying one or more apical (topmost) ancestors from whom descent is traced through the mother's or father's kinship group. In some societies, individuals must choose either the paternal or maternal line, in others, individuals can move back and forth from one descent group to another. Ambilineal descent thus provides for more flexibility and choice than a unilineal system. Individuals can choose in accordance with the relative advantages offered by affiliating with one or another set of relatives. For example, if a man has older brothers who are already farming the family land, he may choose to affiliate with his wife's kin group if she has no brothers laying claim to the land. The resultant ambilineal descent group logically has a membership that is the same regardless of which ego carries out the reckoning. This is called the **cognatic lineage** (Figure 10.8).

In cognatic lineages all the descendents of an apical ancestor or ancestress reckon descent through any combination of male or female links.

Members of cognatic lineages may not be able to demonstrate the precise genealogical links relating them to the apical lineage founder. Also, because of its flexibility and loose membership rules, a cognatic lineage is less cohesive and loyalties tend to be weaker than in a unilineal descent group. For example, people who share the same name as the apical ancestor

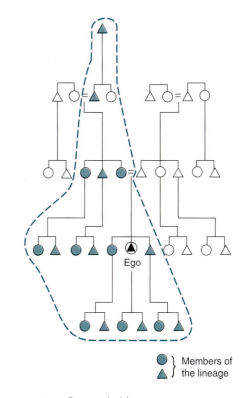

Figure 10.8   Cognatic Lineage

Descent is traced to an apical ancestor through males and/or females.

can claim membership in the cognatic lineages of Scotland (misnamed "clans;" see Neville 1979).

Unilineal Descent Groups

All the people who trace descent patrilineally from a particular male ancestor form a *patrilineage* (Figure 10.9), whereas all the people who trace descent matrilineally from a particular female ancestress form

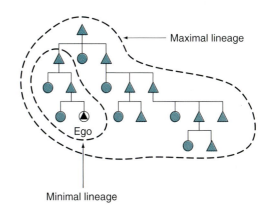

Figure 10.9   Patrilineages

Everyone on the diagram belongs to the same maximal lineage.

a *matrilineage*. Each of these unilineal kin groups contain the same set of people from any ego's viewpoint.

Unilineal descent groups have a clearly defined membership that delineates lineage members from nonmembers.

Membership in a unilineal descent group comes through a direct line from father or mother to child. As a result, the descent group is a discrete group with no overlapping membership. It is a permanent enduring unit that acts as a **corporate group**—it is a unified entity, it holds common property, and it lives on even though some of the members die out. These features make unilineal descent groups ideally suited for the following etic functions:

- Forming a coresident domestic group
- Regulating marriage (people must marry outside the unilineal descent group)
- Corporately owning land and allocating it to its members
- Settling disputes and joining forces for attacking enemies or for defense (Pasternack, Ember and Ember 1997:268)

In addition, unilineal descent groups provide a source of political unity through the belief in shared ancestry and the importance of kinship.

Lineage segmentation allows closely related lineages to unite to oppose a threat from more distantly related lineage segments.

Some societies go through a process of segmentation that enables lineages to integrate members in different localities. Some large lineages, known as *maximal lineages,* consist of smaller lineages known as sublineages. Sublineages that consist of only three generations are known as *minimal*. They consist of close matrilineal or patrilineal kinsmen who support each others against more distant minimal lineages; but will join forces with these same kinsmen in the event of a dispute with a more distant lineage segment (see Figure 10.9). Such a system provides an organizational advantage that enables groups to mobilize both larger raiding parties and larger defensive forces.

When unilineal descent from a specific ancestor is not based on demonstrated genealogical links, the group that results is known as either a *patriclan* or a *matriclan*. **Clan** members believe they are related to one another through links that go back to the beginning of time; sometimes they believe their common ancestor is a mythic animal. In many cases, however, it is difficult to decide whether a culture has unilineal lineages or unilineal clans.

Table 10.1

Principal Varieties of Postmarital Residence

Name of Pattern	Place Where Married Couple Resides
Neolocality	Apart from either husband's or wife's kin
Bilocality	Alternately shifting from husband's kin to wife's kin
Ambilocality	Some couples with husband's kin, others with wife's kin
Patrilocality	With husband's father
Matrilocality	With wife's mother
Avunculocality	With husband's mother's brother
Amitalocality	With wife's father's sister
Uxorilocality	With the wife's kin (several of the above may be combined with uxorilocality)
Virilocality	With the husband's kind (several of the above may be combined with virilocality)

Postmarital Locality Patterns

To understand the processes responsible for the evolution of different varieties of domestic groups and different ideologies of descent, we must discuss one additional aspect of domestic organization: *postmarital residence* (where a newly married couple goes to live). Table 10.1 describes the principal postmarital residence practices.

Postmarital residence rules govern with whom or near whom a couple will reside after marriage. It determines whether a couple will be surrounded by the husband's or wife's kin, and what kind of support each can expect to have.

Postmarital residence practices influence descent rules because they determine who will enter, leave, or stay in a domestic group (Murdock 1949; Naroll 1973). They thus provide domestic groups with distinctive cores of people related by descent and marriage.

But what determines a culture's residence rules? In many cases, residence rules reflect a society's basic patterns of production and reproduction because they are a means of organizing and justifying the structure of domestic groups in relation to particular infrastructural constraints and opportunities.

Determinants of Bilateral Descent Groups

Bilateral descent is associated with various combinations of neolocality, ambilocality, and bilocality (see

Table 10.2

Relationship between Residence and Descent in the *Ethnographic Atlas*

	Postmarital Residence				
Kin Groups	*Matrilocal*	*Avunculocal*	*Patrilocal*	*Other*	*Total*
Patrilineal	1	0	563	25	588
Matrilineal	53	62	30	19	164

Sources: Divale and Harris 1976; Murdock 1967.

Table 10.1 for definitions of locality patterns). These locality practices in turn usually reflect a high degree of mobility and flexibility among nuclear families. Mobility and flexibility, as we have seen (Profile 5.1), are useful for simple hunters and gatherers, and are an intrinsic feature of band organization. The !Kung San, for example, are primarily bilateral, and this reflects in turn a predominantly bilocal postmarital residence pattern. !Kung San camps contain a core of adult siblings of both sexes, plus their spouses and children and an assortment of more distant bilateral and affinal kin. Each year, in addition to much short-time visiting, about 13 percent of the population makes a more or less permanent residential shift from one camp to another, and about 35 percent divide their time equally among two or three different camps (Lee 1979:54). When a person wants to move, he or she has a wide range of kin at many different locations and can choose to activate any of several available kin ties. This mobility and flexibility is advantageous for people who must rely on hunting and gathering for their livelihood.

In industrial societies, bilaterality is associated with a similar flexibility and mobility of nuclear families. (In the United States, about 20 percent of domestic groups change their residence each year.) Bilaterality in this case reflects a neolocal pattern that is advantageous with respect to wage labor opportunities and the substitution of price market money exchanges for kinship-mediated forms of exchange. Whereas the !Kung San always live with relatives and depend on kindreds and extended families for their subsistence, industrial-age nuclear families often live far away from any relatives whatsoever and interact with their kindreds primarily at holidays, weddings, and funerals.

Determinants of Cognatic Lineages and Clans

Cognatic lineages and cognatic clans are associated with **ambilocality.** In this form of postmarital residence, the married couple elects to stay on a relatively

permanent basis with either the wife's or the husband's domestic group. **Bilocality** differs from ambilocality only in implying rather short intervals between shifts of residence between wife's kin and husband's kin. **Neolocality** differs from both bilocality and ambilocality in not establishing residence with kin groups at all.

Ambilocality differs from the bilocality of simple hunting-and-gathering societies in that the lower frequency of residence change. Because ambilocality implies a relatively more sedentary form of village life, there is somewhat greater potential for developing exclusive "corporate" interests in people and property. Yet all cognatic descent groups, whether bilateral or ambilineal, have less potential for corporate unity than unilineal descent groups, a point to which we return in a moment.

One example of how cognatic lineages work has already been discussed in Chapter 8 in the case of the Pacific Northwest Coast potlatchers. There, the Kwakiutl potlatch chiefs sought to attract and hold as large a labor force as they possibly could. (The more people a village put to work during a salmon run, the more fish they could catch.)

The core of each village consisted of a chieftain and his followers, usually demonstrably related to him through ambilineal descent and constituting a cognatic lineage known as a *numaym*. The chieftain claimed hereditary privileges and noble rank on the basis of ambilineal reckoning from his noble forebears. Validation of this status depended on his ability to recruit and hold an adequate following in the face of competition from like-minded neighbor chieftain competitors. The allowance for choosing one's descent group and the uncertainty surrounding the descent group's corporate estate are typical of cognatic lineages in other cultures as well.

Determinants of Unilineal Lineages and Clans

Although there is no basis for reviving nineteenth-century notions of universal stages in the evolution of kinship (see Appendix), certain well-substantiated general evolutionary trends do exist. For example, simple hunting-and-gathering societies tend to have cognatic descent groups and bilocal residence because their basic ecological adjustment demands that local groups remain open, flexible, and nonterritorial. With the development of horticulture and more settled village life, the identification between domestic groups or villages and definite territories increased and became more exclusive. Population density increased and warfare became more intense, for reasons to be discussed in Chapter 11, contributing to the need for group unity and solidarity (Ember et al. 1974). Under these conditions, unilineal descent groups with well-defined localized membership cores, a heightened sense of solidarity, and an ideology of exclusive rights over resources and people became the predominant form of kinship group.

Using a sample of 797 agricultural societies, Michael Harner (1970) found that a very close statistical association exists between an increased reliance on agriculture as opposed to hunting and gathering and the replacement of cognatic descent groups by unilineal descent groups. Horticultural village societies that are organized unilineally outnumber those that are organized cognatically 380 to 111 in Harner's sample. Moreover, almost all the unilineal societies display signs of increased population pressure, as indicated by the depletion of wild plant and food resources.

Unilineal descent groups are closely associated with one or the other variety of unilocal residence—that is, patrilineality with patrilocality and matrilineality with matrilocality. In addition, there is a close correlation between avunculocality and matrilineality.

With **patrilocality**, fathers, brothers, and sons form the core of the domestic group; whereas with **matrilocality**, mothers, sisters, and daughters form the core of the domestic group. But what about avunculocality? (Here things start to get a little rough, but hold on!)

With **avunculocality**, mother's brothers and sister's sons form the core of the domestic unit. Sister's son is born in her husband's mother's brother's household, but as a juvenile or adult, sister's son leaves this household and takes up residence with his own mother's brother. The way in which avunculocality works and the reason for its association with matrilineality will become clearer in a moment, as we examine the infrastructural causes of matrilocality and patrilocality.

Causes of Patrilocality

The overwhelming majority of known societies have male-centered residence and descent patterns. Seventy-one percent of 1179 societies classified by George Murdock (1967) are either patrilocal or virilocal; in

the same sample, societies that have patrilineal kin groups outnumber societies that have matrilineal kin groups 588 to 164. Patrilocality and patrilineality are thus the statistically "normal" mode of domestic organization. They predominate not only in societies that have plows and draft animals or that practice pastoral nomadism, as was once thought, but also in simple horticultural and slash-and-burn societies (Divale 1974).

It is difficult to escape the conclusion that patrilocality among village societies prevails because cooperation among males is more often crucial than cooperation among females. Specifically, men are more effective in hand-to-hand combat than women, and women are less mobile than men during pregnancy and when nursing infants. As a consequence, men generally monopolize the weapons of war and the hunt, leading to male control over trade and politics. The practice of intense small-scale warfare between neighboring villages may be a crucial factor in promoting a widespread complex of male-centered and male-dominated institutions (Divale and Harris 1976). We will return to the issue of sex and gender hierarchies in Chapter 15.

Causes of Matrilocality

Why matrilocality? One theory holds that when women's role in food production became more important, as in horticultural societies, domestic groups tended to be structured around a core of females. This theory, however, must be rejected because there is no greater association between horticulture and matrilocality than between horticulture and patrilocality (Divale 1974; Ember and Ember 1971). Moreover, why would field labor require a degree of cooperation so high that only women from the same domestic groups could carry it out efficiently? And why would it require all brothers and sons to be expelled from the natal domestic group (Burton and White 1987)?

The question we must ask concerning the origin of matrilocality is this: Under what conditions would the male specialties of warfare, hunting, and trade benefit from a shift to matrilocality (keeping in mind the clear advantage a shift from patrilocality to matrilocality offers to women)? The most likely answer is that when warfare, hunting, and trade change from quick, short-distance forays to long-distance expeditions lasting several months, matrilocality is more advantageous than patrilocality. When patrilocal males leave a village for extended periods, they leave behind their patrilineal kin group's corporate interests in property and people to be looked after solely by their wives. The allegiance of their wives, however, lies with another patrilineal kin group. A patrilocal group's women are drawn from different kin groups and have little incentive to cooperate among themselves in the absence of the male managers of the corporate domestic units into which they have married. No one is home "to mind the store," so to speak.

Matrilocality solves this problem because it structures the domestic unit around a permanent core of resident mothers, daughters, and sisters who have been trained to cooperate with each other from birth and who identify the "minding of the store" with their own material and personal interests. Thus, matrilocal domestic groups are less likely to be disrupted by the prolonged absence of their adult males. Furthermore, the ability to launch and successfully complete long-distance expeditions implies that neighboring villages will not attack each other when the men are away. Peace back home is best assured by forming the expeditions around a core of males drawn from several neighboring villages or different households within a given village.

Among patrilocal, patrilineal villages, the belligerent territorial teams consist of patrilineally related kin who constitute competitive "fraternal interest groups." These groups make shifting alliances with neighboring villages, exchange sisters, and raid each other. Most combat takes place between villages that are about a day's walk from each other. Matrilocal, matrilineal cultures, in contrast, are bonded not by the exchange of women but by the inmarrying of males from different domestic groups. Scattering fathers and brothers into several different households in different villages prevents the formation of competitive and disruptive fraternal interest groups.

Thus, matrilocal, matrilineal societies such as the Iroquois of New York, the Huron of Ontario, and the Iban of Borneo enjoy a high degree of internal peace. But most matrilineal societies, including Iroquois, Huron, and Iban, also have a history of intense warfare directed outward against powerful enemies (Gramby 1977; Trigger 1978). The matrilineal Nayar, to cite another example, were a soldier caste in the service of the kings of Malabar (see Chapter 9). Also among the matrilocal Mundurucu of the Amazon, conflict between villages was unheard of and interpersonal aggression was suppressed. But the Mundurucu launched raids against enemies hundreds of miles away, and unrelenting hostility and violence characterized their relations with the "outside world" (Murphy 1956). We will encounter other examples of bellicose matrilineal societies in Chapter 15.

Causes of Avunculocality *Ego lives w/ mother's brothers*

Matrilocal, matrilineal societies generally favor marriage between members of the same village (village

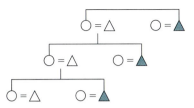

Figure 10.10   Avunculocality
All the males in the shaded area are related to each other as mother's brothers or sister's sons. (Tracing the lines across and up and down with your finger may help.)

endogomy), or at least the same neighborhood, so that male members of the matrilineage do not have to be dispersed. Otherwise, males must move into their wives' residential groups at marriage and must relinquish control over their sons to the members of their wives' kin groups. One way to solve this problem is to loosen the male's marital obligations (already weak in matrilocal societies) to the point where he need not live with his wife at all. This is the path followed by the Nayar. Nayar men, you may recall from Chapter 9, had no home other than their natal domestic unit; they were not responsible for their children—whom they were scarcely able to identify—but they had no difficulty keeping their sisters and their nephews and nieces under fraternal and avuncular control. But a more common solution to the tension between male interests and matrilineality is the development of avunculocal patterns of residence. It is a remarkable fact that more matrilineal groups are avunculocal than are matrilocal (see Table 10.2).

Under avunculocality, a male, at marriage, goes to live with his mother's brothers in their matrilineal domestic unit; his wife joins him there. At maturity, a male ego's son will in turn depart for ego's wife's brother's domestic unit. Thus, the male core of an avunculocal domestic unit consists of a group of brothers and their sister's sons. This arrangement maintains a male fraternal interest group in the residential core of the matrilineal descent group. Avunculocality thus provides the best of two worlds for males who aspire to military and political leadership. They can influence and receive support from their sisters' sons and daughters, and at the same time, they can influence their own unmarried sons and daughters. Avunculocality is thus suited to maintain the corporate interests of lineage and is correlated with the emergence of bellicose chiefdoms (Keegan and MacLachlan 1989).

After a society has adopted matrilocality and developed matrilineal descent groups, changes in the original conditions may lead to a restoration of the patrilocal, patrilineal pattern. At any given moment, many societies are probably in a transitional state between one form of residence and another and one form of kinship ideology and another. Because the changes in residence and descent may not proceed in perfect tandem at any particular moment—that is, descent changes may lag behind residence changes—one should expect to encounter combinations of residence with the "wrong" descent rule. For example, a few patrilocal societies have matrilineal descent, and one matrilocal society has patrilineal descent (see Table 10.2). But evidence indicates a very powerful strain toward consistency in the alignment among domestic groups; in their ecological, military, and economic adaptations; and in their ideologies of descent.

Kinship Terminologies

Another aspect of domestic ideology that participates in the same strain toward functional consistency is *kinship terminology*. Every culture has a special set of terms (such as *father, mother, cousin*) for designating types of kin. The terms plus the rules for using them constitute a culture's kin terminological system.

Lewis Henry Morgan was the first anthropologist to realize that despite the thousands of languages on earth, and despite the immense number of kinship terms in these languages, there are only a handful of basic types of kin terminological systems. These systems can best be defined by the way terms are applied to a small set of kin on ego's own and ego's parent generation. Here we will examine three well-known systems in order to illustrate the nature of the causal and functional relationships that link alternative kinship terminologies to the other aspects of domestic organizations. (These are basic terminological types: Actual instances often vary in details.)

Eskimo Terminology

The kin terminological system with which most North Americans are familiar is known as **Eskimo,** shown in Figure 10.11. This system has two impor-

tant features: First, none of the terms applied to ego's nuclear relatives—1, 2, 6, 5—is applied outside the nuclear family, and second, there is no distinction between maternal and paternal links. This means that the system makes no distinction between cross- and parallel cousins or between cross- and parallel aunts or uncles.

Societies that use Eskimo terminology generally lack corporate descent groups. The nuclear family stands out as a separate and functionally dominant productive and reproductive unit. Separate kin terms are used for nuclear family members that are not extended to any other kin type.

Nuclear family members are given a terminological identity separate from all other kin types (such as mother, father, sister, brother). Beyond the nuclear family, all cousins are lumped under a single term (7). This is also true for aunts and uncles from the mother's and the father's side and reflects the strength of bilateral as opposed to unilineal descent.

The theoretical predictions concerning Eskimo terminology are strongly confirmed by the tabulations of G. P. Murdock's *Ethnographic Atlas* (1967). Of the 71 societies having Eskimo terminology, only 4 have large extended families, and only 13 have unilineal descent groups. In 54 of the 71 Eskimo terminology societies, descent groups are entirely absent or are represented only by kindreds.

As the name implies, "Eskimo" is frequently found among simple hunters and gatherers. As we have seen, simple hunting-and-gathering groups must remain mobile to cope with the movements of game and the seasonal fluctuations in the availability of plant foods. In industrial societies, the same terminological pattern reflects the high level of wage-induced social and geographic mobility.

Hawaiian Terminology

Another common kin terminological system is known as **Hawaiian.** This system is easiest to portray since it has the fewest number of terms (Fig. 10.12). In some versions, even the distinction between the sexes is

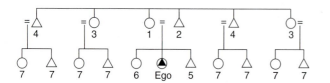

Figure 10.11   Eskimo Terminology

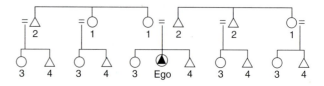

Figure 10.12   Hawaiian Terminology

dropped, leaving one term for the members of ego's generation and another for the members of ego's parents' generation.

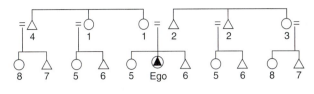

Figure 10.13   Iroquois Terminology

In Hawaiian terminology, the same term is applied to people inside and outside the nuclear family; a single term is used for all relatives of the same sex and generation.

For example, a person's mother, mother's sister, and father's sister are all referred to as "mother." Hawaiian terminology is thus compatible with situations where the nuclear family is submerged within a domestic context dominated by extended families and other corporate descent groups. In Murdock's *Ethnographic Atlas,* 21 percent of the Hawaiian terminology societies do indeed have large extended families. In addition, well over 50 percent of Hawaiian terminology societies have some form of corporate descent group other than extended families.

Theoretically, most of these descent groups should be cognatic rather than unilineal. The reason for this prediction is that the merging of relatives on the maternal side with those on the paternal side indicates an indifference toward unilineality, and an indifference toward unilineality is logically consistent with ambilineal or bilateral descent. However, data from Murdock's ethnographic sample only partially support this prediction. Indeed, many more Hawaiian terminology societies have cognatic as opposed to unilineal descent, but there are also many exceptions for which as yet no generally accepted explanation is available.

Iroquois Terminology

In the presence of unilineal kin groups, we find a worldwide tendency to distinguish parallel from cross-cousins, as previously noted. This pattern is widely associated with a similar distinction in the first ascending generation, whereby father's brothers are distinguished from mother's brothers, and father's sisters are distinguished from mother's sisters.

Iroquois terminology distinguishes between cross- and parallel cousins and cross- and parallel aunts and uncles. This pattern of merging occurs as a result of the shared membership of siblings in corporate unilineal descent groups and marriage alliances based on cross-cousin marriage between such groups.

Mother's sister is called by the same term as mother, father's brother is called by the same term as father.

Parallel cousins are given the same term as ego's brothers and sisters and cross-cousins are regarded either as potential spouses or in-laws (Figure 10.13). In Murdock's ethnographic sample, 166 societies have Iroquois terminology. Of these, 119 have some form of unilineal descent group (70 percent).

We have only skimmed the surface of a few of the many fascinating and important problems in the field of kinship terminology. But perhaps enough has been said to establish at least one point: Kin terminological systems possess a remarkable logical coherence. Yet like so many other aspects of culture, kin terminological systems are never the planned product of any inventive genius. Most people are unaware that such systems even exist. Clearly, the major features of these systems represent recurrent unconscious adjustments to the prevailing conditions of domestic life. Yet many details of kin terminologies, as well as of other kinship phenomena, still are not well understood.

Cross-Cousin Marriage
The Machingenga use Iroquois kin terminology. They marry classificatory cross-cousins who are "spouses" and "in-laws" whereas parallel cousins are "brothers" and "sisters".

Kin Terms Are Negotiated, Not Written in Stone

Anthropologists recognize that while kinship terminologies are internally logical, there are contradictions in the actual usage and application of kin terms. Kinship is one of the central organizing principles of human social life, but there is always room for negotiation of kinship status. As Richard Lee learned among the !Kung, "the principles of kinship do not constitute an invariant code of laws written in stone, but instead a whole series of codes, consistent enough to provide structure but open enough to be flexible" (1993:62). The flexibility of kinship systems makes it possible to transform relationships through reclassification in order to invoke a desired role relationship.

Biological descent and marriage ties are often inadequate to fulfil certain social requirements. If genealogical connections are lacking, people may have recourse to "fictive" kin ties, that is, relations that are socially constructed, rather than biologically based.

Fictive kin ties may be established through the negotiation of kinship when genealogical connections are lacking. People invoke relations that are defined by kinship role requirements and these ties can be extended to others who become kin according to kinship rules.

Many anthropologists have found themselves "incorporated" into a community by way of fictive kin ties. All it takes is one kin tie to become fully connected to an extended family group and be granted affective ties and social obligations modeled on those appropriate to blood relatives.

Negation of kin ties is another means of redefining relationships. Often there are overlapping kin ties and more than one way to reckon genealogy. This results in double relationships that can be manipulated to suit individual needs or to adjust to changing social circumstances. Among the Mehinacu of Brazil, double relationships arise when people extend kinship beyond their circle of true kin. A person's kinship term for more distant kin relatives is based on his parents' position within the network of relationships. Because the system is bilateral and kin ties are traced equally through both parents, people often have overlapping relationships. The ambiguity can become problematic when a person tries to invoke a specific relationship, such as sexual relationships with a distant cross-cousin. According to Thomas Gregor, Mehinacu girls will sometimes respond by saying, "No! I am like your true sister. When I get married my husband and you will be brothers-in-law" (1977:291). Sometimes a man will argue to show how

they can legitimately be considered cross-cousins, but if the girl is not interested she will base her rejection of the ambiguity of their kin ties. Kinship is continually redefined to make or break alliances and rationalized to fit the circumstances at hand. Careful genealogical accounts are kept when wealth or succession are at stake. Otherwise a certain amount of individual discretion is exercised in defining the outer limits of individual kin groups.

Summary

1. To study kinship is to study the ideologies that justify and normalize the corporate structure of domestic groups. The basis of kinship is the tracing of relationships through marriage and descent. Descent is the belief that certain persons play a special role in the conception, birth, or nurturance of certain children. Many folk theories of descent exist, none of which corresponds precisely to modern scientific understandings of procreation and reproduction.

2. The principal varieties of cognatic descent rules are the bilateral and the ambilineal; these are associated, respectively, with kindreds on the one hand, and with cognatic lineages and clans on the other. The principal varieties of unilineal descent are matrilineality and patrilineality. These are associated, respectively, with patri- and matrilineages or patri- and matriclans.

3. An important key to understanding alternative modes of descent and domestic organization is the pattern of postmarital residence. Bilateral descent and bilateral descent groups are associated with neolocality, bilocality, and ambilocality. More specifically, the flexible and mobile forms of band organization are facilitated by bilocality, whereas the greater isolation of nuclear families in price–market economies gives rise to neolocality. Cognatic lineages and clans, on the other hand, give functional expression to ambilocality, whereby a person can affiliate with either the mother's or the father's kinship group.

4. Unilineal domestic groups reflect unilocal patterns of residence. These patterns in turn imply well defined membership cores and an emphasis on exclusive rights over resources and people. A strong correlation exists between patrilocality and patrilineality on the one hand, and among matrilineality, matrilocality, and avunculocality on the other. Patrilocal and patrilineal groups are far more common than matrilocal, matrilineal, or avunculocal

groups. A reason for this is that warfare, hunting, and trading activities among village societies are monopolized by males. These activities, in turn, are facilitated by stressing the coresidence of fathers, brothers, and sons and the formation of fraternal interest groups.

5. Under conditions of increasing population density and pressure on resources, local groups may find it adaptive to engage in long-distance expeditions for war, trade, and hunting. Such expeditions are facilitated by breaking up the fraternal interest groups and structuring domestic life around a residential core of mothers, sisters, and daughters—or, in other words, by developing a matrilocal, matrilineal organization. Because males in matrilineal, matrilocal societies continue to dominate military and political institutions, they are inclined to keep their male relatives close to home after marriage. This tendency accounts for the fact that as many matrilineal societies are avunculocal as are matrilocal.

6. Thus, the principal function of alternative rules of descent and postmarital residence may be described as the establishment and maintenance of networks of cooperative and interdependent kinspeople aggregated into ecologically effective and militarily secure domestic production and reproduction units. For such units to act effectively and reliably, they must share an organizational ideology that interprets and validates the structure of the group and the behavior of its members. Kinship is that shared organizational ideology.

7. This interpretation of descent and postmarital residence rules can also be applied to the principal varieties of kin terminological systems. Such systems tend to classify relatives in conformity with the major features of domestic organization, locality practices, and descent rules. Eskimo terminology, for example, is functionally associated with domestic organizations in which nuclear families tend to be mobile and isolated. Hawaiian terminology is functionally associated with cognatic lineages and cognatic clans. And Iroquois terminology, with its emphasis on the distinction between cross- and parallel cousins, is functionally associated with unilinear descent groups.

8. Although kinship terminologies are consistently applied in every culture, kinship structures are open and flexible. Nonrelatives are incorporated by way of fictive kinship, whereby social obligations and affective content is modeled on those of appropriate blood relatives. Social relationships can also be manipulated, to suit individual needs or to adjust to changing circumstances, through the negotiation of kin ties.

AMERICA NOW

Changes in Family Structure

Because of rapidly changing economic and technological developments, nowhere can these flexible boundaries be better observed than by examining the changes in the American family over the past decades. At the beginning of the century, most marriages were entered into for life, and families were headed by male breadwinners. Each couple had an average of three or more children and the children were brought up by their natural parents unless the marriage was terminated by death. Today, single-parent domestic groups are the fastest-growing form of family, up by 80 percent since 1960. Largely as a result of divorce, separation and the growth of female-headed households, families have had to devise novel ways of coping with life under changing conditions. Carol Stack (1974) and Jagna Sharff (1998) have shown how urban poor use extended kinship ties as a strategy for sustaining life as people go through economy-driven changes.

Whether or not the "traditional" family with full-time domesticity was ever a reality, it certainly is not today. There has been a virtual explosion of new family forms in the last half century: surrogate motherhood, new reproductive technologies, a major increase in single mothers and matrifocal households, "blended families," open adoption, and gay and lesbian families.

Blended Family
Although the traditional nuclear family is still a cultural ideal, many people remarry and bring their children into newly formed households.

No longer is there a single, culturally dominant family pattern; instead, Americans have crafted a multiplicity of family and household arrangements. Another point seems to be clear, that poor families are not the only ones who seek new kinship arrangements as creative responses to changing economic and social conditions.

Other trends that can be seen as directly linked to these alternative family practices are an increase in the number of intergenerational households, and households composed of nonbiological "families." Now we can identify a new middle class with "crowded," rather than "empty nests," filled with "incompletely launched young adults," a pattern that has long been associated with less privileged families (Stacy 1991:254). Families are reorganizing and diversifying, adopting a kinship arrangement that has been "long familiar to the less privileged," similar to the innovative arrangements the urban poor described by Stack and Sharff.

Along with the shift in infrastructural conditions in the last half-century, from a heavily industrialized production-oriented economy to a highly technological service and information economy, have come many superstructural changes. What was perceived as odd, not "respectable" or even deviant is now commonplace and frequently accepted by the society at large. A willingness to experiment, and the formation of families by conscious choice can be seen as supporting factors in the emergence of new family forms. A Yale University study showed that by a ratio of 3 to 1 people defined the family as "a group of people who love and care for each other" rather than just those biologically or legally connected in marriage (Stacey 1990:270). A study of "counterculture" families who came of age in the 1960s, shows that many did not sustain their unconventional lifestyle over time. But their conscious desire to adopt new family forms set the foundation for the reorganization of middle-class family forms that later followed. Their family experiments were examples of many of the practices that later diffused into the wider society. Today, many Americans no longer recall a time when single parenthood by choice or an unmarried couple raising children was a rare or stigmatizing path to take (Weisner and Bernheimer 1998:252).

Another example of culturally evolved kinship ties are those which have been forged by gay and lesbian men and women. Kath Weston, who studied lesbian and gay families in the San Francisco area, found that in response to anticipated or actual exclusion by their "natural" families, gays and lesbians have forged a new ideological basis for kinship by proclaiming:

Lesbian Mothers
People are redefining kinship and family.

"Love makes a family." Many see a relationship's ability to weather conflict as itself a sign of kinship. They say family members are people who "are there for you;" people you can count on (1991:113). These "chosen families" have flexible boundaries and are often inclusive of former lovers who make the transition from lover to friend without disrupting the relationship. Most importantly, these chosen family members provide material and emotional support within and across households. They include people who not only share enduring solidarity but who also provide services for one another out of strong bonds of affection. Thus, the "chosen families" of lesbians and gays are both responses to the perceived or actual loss of traditional kin support, and products of conscious choice.

As we have learned, who is defined as "family" does not necessarily reflect biological connection, or even marriage relationships. Many different forms of family have always existed as cultural responses that enable people to adapt to their circumstances. In America now, families are once again adapting to the material, economic, and emotional requirements of our complex, ever changing times. The diversity of family forms seen in America today is evidence that the boundaries of kinship are flexible, and expand (or contract) to allow people to cope more effectively with their changing circumstances.

KEY TERMS

affinal relations
affinity
ambilineal descent
ambilocality
avunculocality
bilateral descent
bilocality
clan
cognatic descent
cognatic lineage
consanguineal relations
corporate group
descent
Eskimo terminology
fictive kinship
Hawaiian terminology
Iroquois terminology
kin
kindred
kinship

lineage segmentation
matrilineal descent
matrilocality
neolocality
patrilineal descent
patrilocality
unilineal descent

QUESTIONS TO THINK ABOUT

1. Describe the infrastructural conditions that help explain why foraging and industrial societies both have cognatic descent groups?

2. What role does consanguineal and affinal kinship have in arranging marriage and controlling competition between groups?

3. How does internal versus external warfare influence locality and descent?

4. Why is kinship so important to anthropologists? What does real and fictive kinship tell us about the beliefs and expectations people hold toward one another?

Handwritten notes:

Ego identifies male/female relatives in either or both sides

Maximize # relatives → Hunters & Gathers → Nomadic

bilateral → Both sides (mom & Dad)

cognatic {
ambilineal → ego is related to just one side
→ across throughout genera (synchronic & diachronic)

I) Descent
unilineal / unilateral

Trace descendents through only one of the parents

II) Post Marital Residence Patterns Pg. 152

new household

Neolocal
Ambilocal - you move in to both
bilocal

Patrilocal
Matrilocal
Avunculocal
amitalocal

III) Kinship Terminology Systems
Eskimo
Hawaiian
Iroquois
Sudanese

Clan: an anestor has to be identified, and other members have to find themselves related to him/her or it.

affine
consanguine
Fictive Kin
Metaphorical

· Ascriptive: privilege after the baby is born such as social status.
· Achievement Values: athletics
- austronauts
- T.V stars
- models

CHAPTER 11

Law, Order, and War in Nonstate Societies

Cheyenne warriors.

Law and Order in Band and Village Societies
Primitive Communism?
Mobilizing Public Opinion
Shamans and Public Opinion

Headmanship
PROFILE: The Mehinacu—Maintaining Peace
The Leopard Skin Chief

Nonkin Associations: Sodalities

Warfare among Hunters and Gatherers

Warfare among Sedentary Village Societies

Why War?
PROFILE: The Yanomami—Warfare and Game Animals
Yanomami Warfare
Yanomami Trekking
Warfare and Female Infanticide
Warfare and Trade Goods

Warfare, the Politics of Prestige, and the Big Man System
PROFILE: The Mae Enga—A Big Man Society

Summary

As we continue with the structural aspect of socio-cultural systems, the focus shifts to the maintenance of political cohesion and law and order within and between band and village societies. These societies enjoy a high degree of personal security without having written laws, police officers, jails, or any of the other parts of modern criminal justice systems. How do they do it? This is not to say that band and village societies have no violence. On the contrary, feuds and armed combat do occur even among hunter-gatherers and small-village societies that have very low population densities. Some anthropologists argue that the propensity to engage in armed combat is part of human nature. Others, however, point out that even low-density populations may have scarce resources worth fighting over. In one important case, at least, a scarce resource seems to be game animals. War, as we shall see, springs no more from human nature than does peace.

Law and Order in Band and Village Societies

In every society, people have conflicting interests. Even in band-level societies, old and young, sick and healthy, men and women do not want the same thing at the same time. Moreover, in every society people want something that others possess and are reluctant to give away. Every culture, therefore, must have structural provisions for resolving conflicts of interest in an orderly fashion and for preventing conflicts from escalating into disruptive confrontations. Band and village societies, however, have distinctive conflicting interests and distinctive methods for preventing disruptive confrontations.

Despite the presence of conflict, simple hunter-gatherer societies enjoy a high degree of personal security without having any rulers or law-and-order specialists.

They have no kings, queens, dictators, presidents, governors, or mayors; police forces, soldiers, sailors, or marines; CIA, FBI, treasury agents, or federal marshals. They have no written law codes and no formal law courts; no lawyers, bailiffs, judges, district attorneys, juries, or court clerks; and no patrol cars, paddy wagons, jails, or penitentiaries. This is also true of many village societies. How do people in band and village societies get along without law enforcement specialists and facilities, while modern societies are so dependent on them? The basic reasons for the differences are

- Small size of the bands and villages
- Central importance of domestic groups and kinship in their social organization
- Absence of marked inequalities in access to technology and resources

Small size means that everyone knows everyone else personally; therefore, the group can identify stingy, aggressive, and disruptive individuals and expose them to the pressure of public opinion. The centrality of domestic group and kinship relations means that reciprocity can be the chief mode of exchange and that members of the domestic group have personal incentives to uphold collective interests. Prestige is accorded to those who appear generous, whereas confrontations result in the loss of a person's good name. Finally, equality of access to technology and natural resources means that food and other forms of wealth cannot be withheld by a wealthy few whereas others endure shortages and hardships.

Primitive Communism?

Among small band and village societies, all adults usually have access to the rivers, lakes, beaches, and oceans; to all the plants and animals; and to the soil and the subsoil. Insofar as these are basic to the extraction of life-sustaining energy and materials, they are communal property (Lee 1990). Among the !Kung San, waterholes and hunting-and-gathering territories are said to be "owned" by the residential core of particular bands. But neighbors who ask for permission to visit and exploit the resources of a particular camp are seldom refused.

Neighboring bands contain many intermarried kin, and therefore commonly share access to resources as a result of mutual visiting.

Even people who come from distant bands and who lack close kin ties with the hosts are usually given permission to stay, especially for short periods, because all parties understand that the hosts may return the visit at some future date (Lee 1979:337). !Kung elderly are cared for by relatives and nonrelatives alike. No one, not even childless people are denied support in their old age (Lee 1990:175).

Everyone among the !Kung is recognized as entitled to the necessities of life, by right of being a member of society.

The prevalence of communal ownership of land, however, does not mean that simple hunter-gatherers lack private property altogether. There is little support for the theory that "primitive communism," is a universal stage in the development of culture marked by the complete absence of private property. Many material objects are effectively controlled ("owned") by specific individuals in band-level societies, especially items the user has produced. The members of even the most egalitarian societies usually believe that weapons, clothing, containers, ornaments, tools, and other "personal effects" ought not to be taken away or used without the consent of the "owner." However, the chance is remote that theft or misappropriation of such objects will lead to serious conflict (Woodburn 1982). Why not?

First, the accumulation of material possessions is rigidly limited by the recurrent need to break camp and travel long distances on foot. In addition, most utilitarian items may be borrowed without difficulty when the owner is not using them. If there are not enough such items to go around (arrows, projectile points, nets, bark or gourd containers), easy access to the raw materials and mastery of the requisite skills provide the have-nots with the chance of making their own. Moreover, among societies having no more than a few hundred people, thieves cannot be anonymous. If stealing becomes habitual, a coalition of the injured parties will eventually take action. If you want something, better to ask for it openly. Most such requests are readily obliged, because reciprocity is the prevailing mode of exchange. Finally, contrary to the experience of the successful modern bank robber, no one can make a living from stealing bows and arrows or feather headdresses, because band-level societies have no regular market at which such items can be exchanged for food (see Chapter 8).

The existence of private property does not lead to inequalities in wealth and power because, according to the rules of reciprocity, people can openly ask for possessions and such requests cannot be denied.

Mobilizing Public Opinion

When disputes occur in small egalitarian societies, disputants rely on the backing of their kin group for support.

In the absence of law-and-order institutions such as police and courts, people seek the support of kinfolk as they press their claims against other members of the community. As long as the disputants feel they have the backing of their kin groups, they will continue to press their claims and counterclaims. The

Yanomami Club Fight
Egalitarian societies are not without problems of law and order.

members of their kin groups, however, are not eager to be caught in a situation in which they are opposed by a majority of people. Public opinion influences the support disputants can expect from their kin. Often what matters is not so much who is morally right or wrong, or who is lying or telling the truth; the important thing is to mobilize public opinion on one side or the other decisively enough to prevent the outbreak of large-scale feuding.

The Inuit song duel is a classic example of how public opinion influences the support that disputants can expect from their respective kin groups.

Among the central and eastern Inuit, mobilization of public support can be achieved independently of abstract principles of justice or even reference to the events that led to the dispute. Here, it is common for a man involved in a dispute to claim that the other has stolen his wife. The counterclaim is that she was not stolen but left voluntarily because her husband "was not man enough" to take good care of her. The issue is settled at a large public meeting. Unlike a court, no testimony is taken in support of either of the two versions of why the wife has left her husband. Instead, the disputants take turns singing insulting songs at each other, accusing their opponent of sexual excess or impotence. The "court" of public opinion responds to each performance with different degrees of laughter. Eventually one of the singers gets flustered, and the hooting and hollering raised against him become total; even his relatives have a hard time not laughing (Box 11.1).

The Inuit have no police or military specialists to see to it that the "decision" is enforced. Yet chances are that the man who has lost the song duel will give in because he can no longer count on anyone to back

Box 11.1   Inuit Song

Something was whispered

Of a man and wife

Who could not agree

And what was it all about?

A wife who in rightful anger

Tore her husband's furs,

Took their boat

And rowed away with her son.

Ay-ay, all who listen,

What do you think of him

Who is great in his anger

But faint in strength,

Blubbering helplessly?

He got what he deserved

Though it was he who proudly

Started this quarrel with stupid words.

(Adapted from Rasmussen 1929:231–232)

may survive on the strength of his own vigilance and fighting skill. He will probably have to kill again, however, and with each transgression, the coalition against him becomes larger and more determined, until finally they may kill him in an ambush.

has sensitivity concerning beliefs of the group

Shamans and Public Opinion

In small, egalitarian societies, part-time magico-religious specialists known as **shamans** play an important role in mobilizing public opinion and in eliminating persistent sources of conflict.

Most cultures reject the idea that misfortune results from "natural" causes. If animals suddenly become scarce or if several people fall sick, they assume that somebody is practicing **witchcraft** by using their psychic powers to harm others through supernatural means. It is the shaman's job to identify the culprit. Normally this is done through the art of divination, or clairvoyance. Putting themselves into trances with the aid of drugs, tobacco smoke, or monotonous drumming (see Chapter 17, in the section titled "Shamanistic Cults"), shamans discover the name of the witch. The people demand vengeance, and the culprit is ambushed and murdered.

The chances are that the accused individual never attempted to carry out any witchcraft at all! In other words, the witches are probably wholly "innocent" of the crime with which they have been charged. Nonetheless, the shaman's witchcraft accusations usu-

him up if he chooses to escalate the dispute. Nonetheless, the defeated man may decide to go it alone, and wife stealing does occasionally lead to murder. When this happens, the man who has lost public support

Song Contest

Innuit "disputants" in "court" in eastern Greenland.

Kuikuru Shaman

The shaman is leaving the village with his assistants on the way to a nearby lake to recover the lost soul of a patient lying ill in the house seen in the background. The shaman intends to dive to the bottom of the lake and wrest the soul away from the evil spirit who stole it from the patient, and then implant it back into the patient's body.

ally conserve rather than destroy the group's feeling of unity because the person identified as the perpetrator is regarded as a troublemaker and lacks support from his or her kin (Box 11.2.) This system, however,

is not "fail-safe." Many cases are known of witchcraft systems that seem to have broken down because witchcraft accusations have led to a series of destructive retaliations and murders.

Headmanship

To the extent that political leadership can be said to exist at all among small societies, it is exercised by *headmen* or, less commonly, headwomen.

The headman, unlike such specialists as king, president, or dictator, is a relatively powerless figure incapable of compelling obedience.

When he gives a command, he is never certain of being able to punish physically those who disobey. (Hence, if he wants to stay in "office," he gives few direct commands.) Among the Inuit, leadership is especially diffuse, being closely related to success in hunting. A group will follow an outstanding hunter and defer to his opinion with respect to choice of hunting spots. But in all other matters, the "leader's" opinion carries no more weight than that of any other adult. In contrast, the political power of genuine rulers depends on their ability to expel or exterminate any readily foreseeable combination of nonconforming individuals and groups. Genuine rulers control access to basic resources and to the tools and weapons for hurting or killing people.

Among the !Kung San, each band has its recognized "leaders." Such leaders may speak out more than others and are listened to with a bit more deference than is usual, but they "have no formal authority" and "can only persuade, but never enforce

Box 11.2   How to Choose a Witch

Gertrude Dole (1966) reported the following events among the Kuikuru—an egalitarian Brazilian Indian society. Lightning had set fire to two houses. The shaman went into a trance and discovered that the lightning had been sent by a man who had left the village some years previously and had never returned. This man had only one male relative, who was also no longer living in the village. Before the accused witch had departed, he had tried unsuccessfully to court a girl whom the shaman's brother wanted to marry. During his trance, the shaman carried out a dialogue with various members of the village. When he finally disclosed the identity of the culprit,

he was readily believed. As the excitement grew, the shaman's brother and several companions left the village to kill the man suspected of witchcraft (1966:761). Among the Kuikuru, a change of residence from one village to another usually indicates that there is trouble brewing and that, in effect, the individual has been ostracized. Thus, the witch was not a randomly chosen figure but one who fulfilled several well-defined criteria: a history of disputes and quarrels within the village, a motivation for continuing to do harm (the unsuccessful courtship), and weak backing from kin.

Mehinacu Headmanship

In front of the men's house, the headman is redistributing presents given to him by the ethnographer.

their will on others" (Lee 1979:333–334; 1982). When Richard Lee asked the !Kung San whether they had "headmen" in the sense of powerful chiefs, he was told, "Of course we have headmen! In fact we are all headmen. Each one of us is headman over himself" (1979:348).

There are no mechanisms for forcing people in band and village societies to do what they do not want to do because they can simply move away to another location.

A similar pattern of leadership is reported for the Semai of Malaya. Despite recent attempts by the Malayan government to bolster the power of Semai leaders, the headman is merely the most prestigious figure among a group of peers. In the words of Robert Dentan, who carried out fieldwork among these egalitarian shifting horticulturalists, "[The headman] keeps the peace by conciliation rather than coercion. He must be personally respected. Otherwise people will drift away from him or gradually stop paying attention to him" (1968, p. 681).

The Semai recognize only a few occasions on which he can assert his authority:

- Dealing as a representative of his people with non-Semai
- Mediating a quarrel, if invited by the quarreling parties to do so
- Selecting and apportioning land for fields

Most of the time a good headman gauges the general feeling about an issue and bases his decision on that, so that he is more a spokesman for public opinion than a molder of it.

The headman among Brazilian Indian groups, such as the Mehinacu of Brazil's Xingu National Park, is a thankless and frustrating job. The first one up in the morning, the headman tries to rouse his companions by standing in the middle of the village plaza and shouting. If a task needs to be done, it is the headman who starts doing it, and it is the headman who works at it harder than anyone else (see Profile 11.1 on page 168).

The headman must set an example not only for hard work but also for generosity.

After a fishing or hunting expedition, he is expected to give away more of the catch than anyone else; if trade goods are obtained, he must be careful not to keep the best pieces for himself.

The headman motivates individuals to avoid conflict and restrain violence.

Without political authority to enforce rules against violence, the headman must rely on interpersonal skills to motivate people to avoid confrontations. When malicious gossip and accusations break out, he uses his oratory skills to diffuse the hostility by

Profile 11.1   The Mehinacu—Maintaining Peace

Location: Tropical forest along the headwaters of the Xingu River in Central Brazil.

Density: The Mehinacu, who number nearly 150 people, are one of nine separate villages in the Xingu National Park; the overall density is less than one person per square mile.

Production: Slash-and-burn horticulture with an extraordinarily abundant supply of fish.

Time of Study: 1967–1989.

The Mehinacu are part of a wider Xingu cultural system under government protection, beyond the reach of missionaries, ranchers, and farmers. The Mehinacu and their neighbors are refugees from larger more aggressive native groups that were decimated in the late 1800s through contact with Western disease. Present-day Xingu communities are autonomous villages representing four major language groups, that trade, intermarry, and participate in one another's rituals.

The Mehinacu recognize some members as being of chiefly descent. Although referred to as "chief," the leader is in fact a headman, who unlike a chief (see Chapter 12), does not have the power to coerce, nor does he live significantly better than anyone else. The most significant qualifications for Mehinacu leadership are learned skills and personal attributes. The chief, for example, is expected to excel at public speaking. Each evening he should stand in the center of the plaza and exhort his fellow tribesmen to be good citizens. He must call on them to work hard in their gardens, to take frequent baths, not to sleep during the day, not to be angry with each other, and honor sexual taboos. In addition to being a skilled orator, the chief is expected to be a generous man. This means that when he returns from a successful fishing trip, he will bring most of his catch out to the men's houses where it is cooked and shared by the men of the village. His wife must be generous, bringing manioc cakes and pepper to the men whenever they call for it. Further, the chief must be willing to part with possessions. When

one of the men catches a harpy eagle (whose feathers are used for headdresses), for example, the chief must buy it from him with a valuable shell belt in the name of the entire village. A chief should also be a man who never becomes angry in public. In his public speeches he should never criticize any of his fellow tribesmen, no matter how badly they may have affronted the chief or the village as a whole (Gregor 1969).

Within the village, allegations of witchcraft are common, as deaths from natural causes are usually attributed to witches. The fear of witches makes people conduct themselves with restraint and avoid confrontations. The same fear also applies to the headman, who continually worries that his leadership might provoke a disgruntled witch. Because no one can be sure who is a witch, a policy of appeasement and courtesy is generally followed. Villagers honor requests for food and possessions not only because of the rules of reciprocity and mutual cooperation, but because otherwise they might become the victims of sorcery. If conflict escalates, families leave the community for extended periods by moving off to a nearby campsite or staying with kinsmen in neighboring communities.

Peace between villages is sustained by bringing villagers together to exchange goods and partake in ceremonial events and ritual wrestling matches, but these are sporadic events and people need constant reminders of the need to maintain peace. Besides intertribal and local ceremonies, the Mehinacu readily talk about the dangers of not being peaceful, the horrors of warfare and the ugliness of violence. They despise and fear the conduct of non-Xingu communities who in the past raided their villages. No prestige is given to a warrior. Displays of anger and aggression are seen as vivid reminders of the failure to exercise restraint. Violent outsiders are cast as negative role models, and nonviolence is a symbolic ethnic boundary marker that sets the "civilized" Mehinacu apart from other "savage" animal-like people (Gregor 1994).

---

eloquently reminding people of the dangerous consequences of expressing anger.

The Leopard Skin Chief

As we have seen, the ever-present danger confronting societies that lack genuine rulers is that their kinship groups tend to react as units to real or alleged aggression against one of their members. In this way, disputes involving individuals may escalate. The worst danger arises from disputes that lead to homicide. The members of most simple band and village soci-

eties believe that the only proper reaction to a murder is to kill the murderer or any convenient member of the murderer's kin group. Yet the absence of centralized political authority does not mean that blood feuds cannot be brought under control.

Mechanisms for preventing homicide from flaring into a protracted feud include the transfer of substantial amounts of prized possessions from the slayer's kin group to the victim's kin group.

Leopard Skin Chief *lives among people who is not related to him. Et in Sudan.*

The **leopard skin chief** is an outside mediator, believed to have supernatural powers, who is called on to resolve disputes between kin groups and prevent the escalation of hostilities.

The leopard skin chief is the only one who can ritually cleanse a murderer. If a homicide takes place, the killer flees at once to the leopard skin chief's house, which is a sanctuary respected by all Nuer. Nonetheless, the leopard skin chief lacks even the rudiments of political power; the most he can do to the reluctant members of the slain man's relatives is to threaten them with various supernatural curses. Yet, the desire to prevent a feud is so great that the injured relatives eventually accept the cattle as compensation.

This practice is especially common and effective among pastoral peoples, whose animals are a concentrated form of material wealth and for whom bride price is a regular aspect of kin group exogamy. For example, the Nuer, a pastoral and farming people who live near the Upper Nile in the Sudan, have no centralized political leadership (Box 11.3). The Nuer settle their feuds (or at least deescalate them) by transferring 40 or more head of cattle to the victim's relatives. If a man has been killed, these animals will be used to "buy" a wife whose sons will fill the void left by the man's death. The dead man's closest kin are obliged to resist the offer of cattle, demanding instead a life for a life. However, more distant kin do their best to convince the others to accept the compensation. In this effort, they are aided by certain semisacred arbitration specialists. The latter, known as *leopard skin chiefs,* are usually men whose kin groups are not represented locally and who can hence act more readily as neutral intermediaries.

Nonkin Associations: Sodalities

Although relations of affinity and descent dominate the political life of headman-type societies, nonkin relations and groups also occur to a limited extent. Such groups, known as sodalities, are special-purpose groups.

Sodalities serve widely different functions—among them economic, military, religious, and recreational. These associations usually involve people drawn from different domestic groups who participate in various special-purpose activities.

A common form of sodality is the exclusive men's or women's association, or club. These usually involve men or women who partake in public or secret performances that reinforce solidarity through ritual displays of aggression. We will discuss these organizations as an aspect of gender antagonism in Chapter 15.

Age-grade associations, or age sets, are another common form of sodality, already mentioned with respect to the Masai warrior camps (see Chapter 9, "The Domestic Sphere of Culture" section). Among the Samburu, another group of East African pastoralists, all men initiated into manhood over a span of about 12 to 14 years composed an age-set whose members had a special feeling of solidarity that cut across domestic and lineage kin groups. The age-set members advance as a group from junior to senior status or grade. As juniors they were responsible for military combat, and as seniors they were responsible for initiating and training the upcoming age-sets (Bernardi 1985; Spencer 1965).

A classic case of sodality is the native North American military associations that developed on the Great Plains after the introduction of the horse. Among the Crow and the Cheyenne these associations tried to outdo one another in acts of daring during combat and in horse-stealing expeditions. Although the members of each club did not fight as a unit, they met in their teepees to reminisce and sing about their exploits, and they wore distinctive insignia and clothing.

Gretel and Pertti Pelto (1976:324) have aptly compared these organizations to the Veterans of Foreign Wars and the American Legion because their main function was to celebrate military exploits and to uphold the honor and prestige of the "tribe." However, in prestate societies, military sodalities would take turns supervising and policing the general population during large-scale group activities such as collective hunts, or long migrations to new territories. For example, sodalities prevented overeager hunters from stampeding the buffalo herds, and they suppressed rowdy behavior at ceremonials by fining or banishing disruptive individuals. But these were only seasonal functions, because only during the spring and summer, when food was abundant, could large numbers of unrelated people congregate (Moore 1987:201ff).

Warfare among Hunters and Gatherers

We turn now to the subject of warfare as an aspect of the maintenance of law and order between nonstate societies. War is armed combat between groups of people who constitute separate territorial teams or political communities (Otterbein 1994). By this definition, feuds, "grudge fights," and "raiding" constitute warfare. Some anthropologists hold that warfare is universally practiced, and that it occurred as far

back in time as the early Stone Age (Lizot 1979:151; Keeley 1996). By excluding feuds and raids from their definitions of warfare, however, others hold that warfare was absent or uncommon until the advent of chiefdoms and states (Ferguson 1989a:197; Reyna 1989). Several hunter-gatherer societies—the Andaman Islanders, the Shoshoni, the Yahgan, the Mission Indians of California (Lesser 1968; MacLeish 1972), and the Greenland Eskimo (Weyer 1932:109–110) have been offered as exceptions to the claim that warfare is a universal feature of human social life. Bonta (1993) lists some 50 societies that are classified as nonviolent. But the peacefulness of some of these groups may result from having been defeated and forced into more marginal territories when warfare was practiced in earlier times. William Divale (1972) lists 37 hunting-and-gathering societies in which warfare (feuds and raids included) is known to have been practiced. But some anthropologists attribute these cases to the shocks of contact with state societies (Ferguson and Whitehead 1992).

Archaeologists who have studied the pattern of dented, broken, and perforated bones suggest that warfare occurred among simple hunter-gatherers during periods of population increase and environmental stress. For example, in the Channel Islands off the coast of California, skull fractures attributable to clubs and projectiles increase in tandem with the growth of population during the prehistoric period. A similar increase on the mainland where populations could disperse over a larger territory was not observed (Walker 1988). Similarly, violence appears to be the cause of death among young and mature adult males during periods of resource deprivation as seen in the high rate of projectile injuries in skeletal remains exhibiting poor health (Lambert 1997).

There is a fine line between warfare and personal retribution among hunters and gatherers. This is well illustrated in the example of armed conflict among the Tiwi of Bathurst and Melville islands, northern Australia. As recounted by C. W. Hart and Arnold Pilling (1960), a number of men from the Tiklauila and Rangwila bands developed personal grievances against a number of men who were residing with the Mandiimbula band. The aggrieved individuals, together with their relatives, put on the white paint of war, armed themselves, and set off, some 30 strong, to do battle with the Mandiimbula at a predetermined clearing. Both sides then exchanged a few insults and agreed to meet formally in the morning.

During the night, individuals from both groups visited each other, renewing acquaintances. In the morning, the two armies lined up at the opposite sides of the battlefield. Hostilities were begun by elders shouting insults and accusations at particular individuals in the enemy ranks. Although some of the old men urged that a general attack be launched, their grievances turned out to be directed not at the Mandiimbula band but at specific individuals: "Hence when spears began to be thrown, they were thrown by individuals for reasons based on individual disputes" (Hart and Pilling 1960:84). Marksmanship was poor because it was the old men who did most of the spear-throwing. "Not infrequently the person hit was an old woman . . . whose reflexes for dodging spears were not as fast as those of the men. . . . As soon as somebody was wounded . . . fighting stopped immediately until the implications of this new incident could be assessed" (p. 84).

Hunters and gatherers seldom try to annihilate each other. They often retire from the field after one or two casualties have occurred, yet the cumulative effect may be quite considerable.

Overall, foragers have less warfare than nonforagers. Most foragers described in the ethnographic record have small populations, and many are surrounded by more powerful societies so that going to war would not be cost effective or feasible (Ember and Ember 1997). Remember that the average !Kung San band has only about 30 people. If such a band engages in war only twice in a generation, each time with the loss of only one adult male, casualties due to warfare would account for more than 10 percent of all adult male deaths. This is an extremely high figure when one realizes that less than 1 percent of all male deaths in Europe and the United States during the twentieth century have been battlefield casualties.

Warfare among Sedentary Village Societies

Although village peoples, including complex hunter-gatherers and small agricultural societies, were not the first to practice warfare, they did expand the scale and ferocity of military engagements. Village peoples have more possessions to defend, such as storehouses filled with food, garden lands with crops growing on them, or prime fishing locations.

The more people invest in improving their environment, the more likely they will defend their territory and take land or other resources from the defeated group.

They cannot resolve disputes with other villages by simply moving off to a more remote territory. Thus warfare among village societies is likely to be more costly in terms of battle casualties than among nonsedentary hunters and gatherers.

Among the Yanomami of Brazil and Venezuela, who are reputed to have had one of the world's most warlike cultures, sneak raids and ambushes account for about 33 percent of adult male deaths and about 7 percent of adult female deaths from all causes (Chagnon 1974:160–161). Although the Yanomami deny they go to war to seize territory, the etic outcome of violent confrontations is the displacement of the weaker group by the more dominant group. Following the aftermath of a club fight between two neighboring groups, the winner refused to reconcile, telling the defeated headman, "You must go away; you must leave . . . we must be the masters of this place" (Biocca [1971]1996:217–250). Hostilities escalated, the weaker headman was killed, others were massacred at a treacherous feast, and finally the remaining survivors left in search of new territory at a distant location (also Chagnon [1983]1997:217–250).

Why War?

Anthropologists have offered a number of explanations for warfare in nonstate societies: (1) war as instinct, (2) war as sport and entertainment, (3) war as revenge, (4) war as a struggle for reproductive success, and (5) war as a struggle for material benefits.

1. *War as instinct:* This explanation proposes that we humans have innate aggressive tendencies that make us hate other people and want to kill them. Warfare is just one of the ways by which this tendency expresses itself (Wrangham and Peterson 1996).

   Comment: As a species, we are certainly capable of aggression on an unparalleled scale. But the capacity for collective violence does not explain the occurrence of war, because even warlike societies fight only occasionally, and some societies have no war at all. Thus, this peacetime wartime cycle cannot be explained by the constants of human nature. Rather, the explanation for warfare must be sought in the variable conditions of society and culture that evoke violence instead of reciprocity and conciliation. Furthermore, aggressive tendencies can be expressed in ways other than by armed combat—they can be suppressed, controlled, or resolved through effective mechanisms of conflict resolution. War is a particular form of organized activity that has developed during cultural evolution just as have other structural features, such as trade, the division of labor, and reciprocity that involve the human capacity for cooperation and conflict management (Knauft 1987, 1994).

2. *War as sport and entertainment:* War is a big game. People enjoy the thrill of using martial arts, testing

their courage and risking their lives in combat. (It's better than the movies.)

Comment: Combat is seldom entered into light-heartedly; the warriors need to "psych themselves up" with ritual dancing and singing, and often set out only after they have subdued their fears by taking psychotropic drugs. Furthermore, warfare violently disrupts people's lives; it brings casualties and a general decline in the quality of life—health deteriorates, people are afraid to leave the village, they bicker, and are in constant fear of attack.

3. War as revenge: This is the most common explanation for going to war given by nonstate combatants. It is frequently accompanied by the belief that the spirits of the ancestors who have been killed in previous battles will not rest unless a relative of the culprit is killed in turn. The desire for revenge keeps wars going generation after generation whether the combatants win or lose.

Comment: Vengeance is undoubtedly a powerful motivation. But it does not have an unlimited power to keep wars going. As Brian Ferguson (1992:223) points out with respect to the Yanomami, combatants can declare that their ancestors have been avenged and stop fighting. Why do some societies manage isolated homicides without further vengeance, whereas others do not? Vengeance is thus an emic rationalization for continuing hostilities, but it does not explain why the hostilities got started, nor why old hostilities give way to new ones. As Ferguson explains,

In my view, the Yanomami control revenge; they are not controlled by it. For people other than the victim's very closest kin, revenge is a real but highly malleable motivating factor. There are frequently many dormant reasons for seeking revenge, and if none exists, some can be made up. They come to the fore in conflict situations because that is one way to frame materially self-interested actions in moral terms. Vengeance is "good to think" and good to persuade. But a focus on vengeance will not elucidate why wars happen. (1995:354)

4. War as a struggle for reproductive success: Sociobiologists explain nonstate warfare as a means of obtaining higher rates of reproductive success: Fierce warriors are more attractive as mates. They gain marital and reproductive benefits, and they have more wives, and a greater number of surviving children. Napoleon Chagnon (1989, 1990) has attempted to show how this theory applies to warfare among the Yanomami, where men who have killed have more wives and children, on the average, than men who have not killed. This may make revenge killing a successful social strategy for achieving reproductive success and a strong

contributing factor in perpetuating warfare in prestate societies.

Comment: But the predicted relationship between fierceness in war and reproductive success is in doubt among the Yanomami (Ferguson 1989a; compare with Chagnon 1989). One of the problems is that those who "live by the spear" are more likely to "die by the spear." In fact, the man with the greatest number of kills among the Yanomami (22) died without leaving any descendants. This theory has also been shown to be inapplicable to the Cheyenne, one of the most warlike of the Indian peoples who lived in the region of the Great Plains. The fiercest Cheyenne warriors were young men who were so indifferent to the risks of battle that combat for them was in effect a form of suicide. Not only did they die young but many also took vows of chastity in order to concentrate all their energies on war, and died without heirs (Moore 1990).

5. War in general is a struggle for material benefits: It is fought only to the extent that it provides material advantages for some of the combatants.

Comment: Among nonstate societies, warfare provides the winners with access to valuable resources such as game animals and garden lands. Of course, warfare has its costs, principally in the form of combat deaths. But much evidence suggests that nonstate warfare results in substantial immediate material gains related to the relief of population pressure. In his study of warfare among the Mae Enga of the western highlands of Papua, New Guinea (Profile 11.3), Mervyn Meggitt estimates that aggressor groups succeeded in gaining significant amounts of enemy land in 75 percent of their wars. "Given that the initiation of warfare usually pays off for the aggressors, it is not surprising that the Mae count warfare as well worth the cost in human casualties" (1977:14–15). More general confirmation of this point has been supplied by Melvin and Carol Ember (1992, 1997), who have found in a study of 186 societies that preindustrial people mostly go to war to cushion or moderate the impact of unpredictable (rather than chronic) food shortages and that the victorious side almost always takes land or other resources from the losers. This is the point of view held by cultural materialists and the one that we consider to be the most useful explanation (Balee 1984; Biolsi 1984; Ferguson 1984, 1989a, 1989b, 1995; Johnson and Earle 1987; Keeley 1996; Shankman 1991; but see Knaupft 1990 for a contrary view).

Band and village people go to war because they lack alternative solutions to problems of securing resources in response to population pressure and environmental depletion.

Profile 11.2   The Yanomami—Warfare and Game Animals

Location: Amazon rain forest of southern Venezuela and northern Brazil. Most of the population lives in the highlands, away from the major rivers, except for about 5 percent who live in Venezuela along the Orinoco River.

Production: Slash-and-burn horticulture, mostly bananas and plantains along with frequent trekking to hunt and collect wild foods away from the communal house.

Population density: Villages ranging in size from 30 to 100 persons; sometimes growing to 200 before fissioning; approximately one person per square mile.

Time of study: A number of researchers have worked with the Yanomami from 1964 to the present.

The Yanomami provide an important test of the theory that warfare has an infrastructural basis even among band and village groups that have very low population densities. The Yanomami, with a population density of less than one person per square mile, derive their main source of food calories, with little effort, from the plantains and banana trees that grow in their forest gardens.

The Yanomami burn the forest to get these gardens started, but bananas and plantains are perennials that provide high yields per unit of labor input for many consecutive years. Because the Yanomami live amid the world's greatest tropical forest, the little burning they do scarcely threatens to "eat up the trees." A typical Yanomami village has fewer than 100 people in it, a population that could easily grow enough bananas or plantains in nearby garden sites without ever having to move. Yet the Yanomami villages constantly break up into factions that move off into new territories.

Despite the apparent abundance of resources, the high level of warfare in some Yanomami territories is probably related to population pressure arising from resource depletion. The resource in question is meat. The Yanomami lack domesticated sources of meat and must obtain their animal foods from hunting and collecting. Moreover, unlike many other inhabitants of the Amazon basin, the Yanomami traditionally did not have access to big-river fish and other aquatic animals that elsewhere in the

Yanomami Warriors
Preparations for battle include body painting and "line-ups."

(continued)

Yanomami Grievances

Grievances between villages can be resolved with a chest-pounding duel like this one. This event is more like a sporting contest and results in no further animosity unless someone is severely injured. Then emotions flare and more serious fights can ensue.

Amazon region provided high-quality animal foods sufficient to supply villages inhabited by over 1,000 people. Of course, human beings can remain healthy on diets that lack animal foods; however, meat, fish, and other animal products contain compact packages of proteins, fats, minerals, and vitamins that have made them extremely appealing and efficient sources of nutrients throughout most of history and prehistory (Eaton et al. 1988).

According to Napoleon Chagnon (1997), the frequency and intensity of conflict in Yanomami villages increases in relation to village size. Chagnon attributes this to the failure of the political organization to effectively govern a large population; the political system—with its

"powerless" headman—cannot control the factions that occur in large villages. Chagnon attributes conflict to intense competition among men for wives; men attempt to acquire more than one wife to increase their status—some men succeed in obtaining several wives, whereas others have none (the shortage of women is compounded by female infanticide, described later). The Yanomami say they fight to capture women and to take revenge for past killings, but these "reasons for fighting" do not explain the ecological context in which warfare takes place—the Yanomami were an expanding population in a restricted environment with resources that are rapidly depleted.

Table 11.1

The Universal Pattern: Warfare among the Yanomami

Infrastructure	Structure	Superstructure
Increased population pressure and an imbalance in sex ratios due to infanticide	Weak leadership ("powerless headman") unable to contain factions in large communities	Male supremacist complex • Preference for male babies • Preference for fierce warriors
Competition over faunal resources	Polygyny (intensifying the shortage of women)	Rewarding warriors with mates and sex
Competition over access to steel tools	Marriage exchange and ceremonial feasting to cement alliances between groups	Endocannibalism (ingesting the ashes of the deceased) to revenge the dead

Yanomami Warfare

The theory relating meat to warfare among the Yano-mami is this: As Yanomami villages grow, intensive hunting diminishes the availability of game nearby. Meat from large animals grows scarce, and people eat more small animals, insects, and larvae. The point of diminishing returns draws near. Increased tensions within and between villages lead to the breaking apart of villages before they permanently deplete the animal resources. Tensions also lead to the escalation of raiding, which disperses the Yanomami villages over a wide territory, and also protects vital resources by creating no man's-lands, which function as game preserves (Harris 1984).

Opponents of this theory point to the fact that the Yanomami show no clinical signs of protein defi-ciency. Moreover, they have shown that Yanomami villages with low levels of protein intake (36 grams) seem to engage in warfare just as frequently as those with high protein intake (75 grams) per adult. Finally, they point out that the other groups in the Amazon enjoy as much as 107 grams of animal protein per capita and still go to war frequently (Chagnon and Hames 1979; Lizot 1977, 1979).

Kenneth Good (1987, 1989), however, maintains that obtaining adequate supplies of meat is a constant preoccupation among the Yanomami, and that meat is actually consumed only once or twice a week on the average. This accords with the observation made by Eric Ross (1979) that the average daily amount of animal food consumed is a misleading figure. Because of fluctuations in the number and size of animals cap-tured, many days actually pass during which the vil-lage has little or no available meat. On days when a large animal such as a tapir is caught, the consump-tion rate may rise to 250 or more grams per adult, but for weeks at a time the consumption rate may not rise above 30 grams per adult per day.

The absence of clinical signs of protein deficiency is not an argument against the theory that relates the quest for meat to warfare but rather supports the gen-eral point that band and village peoples can enjoy good health as long as they control population growth (see Chapter 6, section on Population Pressure).

The fact that villages with both high and low pro-tein intake have the same level of warfare does not test the theory either because warfare necessarily pits vil-lages at different stages of growth against each other (the big attack the little). Hence Yanomami groups with high levels of meat consumption, and thus little immediate material incentive to go to war, may have no choice but to engage in counterraids against large groups that are depleting their game reserves and raid-ing less populous neighbors in order to expand their hunting territory. Amazonian fauna are a fragile re-source, readily depleted with consequent decline in per capita meat consumption (Ferguson 1989a).

Is it possible for a tropical forest community to overexploit and deplete local resources in just a few years? Research among the Machiguenga (see Profile 5.3) by Michael Baksh (1985) shows that when 250 members from several previously dispersed commu-nities settle in a village, they soon experience a sig-nificant decline in faunal resources. In an attempt to maintain their previous standard of living, the vil-lagers had to travel to more distant hunting and fish-ing locations. Baksh's quantitative data show that during the 17 months he spent in the field, fishing ef-ficiency decreased sharply, as travel time quadrupled from 0.6 to 2.4 hours per trip (1984:128). Hunting was highly productive when the village first came into existence. Three years later, hunters had to travel several hours, or overnight and frequently returned empty-handed. Since then conflicts have increased dramatically and it is likely the community would have been abandoned if it were not for access to West-ern goods provided by missionaries and traders.

Yanomami Trekking

The desire to maintain or increase their level of meat consumption explains **trekking**, an important fea-ture of Yanomami life. Three or four times a year the Yanomami move out of their village as a group and go on a prolonged trek through the deep forest that lasts a month or more. Indeed, counting the time that the villagers also spend at distant campsites where they prepare new gardens, the Yanomami spend almost half the year away from their communal house. The desire for plant foods cannot provide the motive for going on a trek or planting new gardens, because the Yanomami could easily increase the size of their ex-isting gardens and have enough bananas and plan-tains to feed themselves by staying at home. Al-though they gather wild fruits while trekking, meat remains their main preoccupation. Good (1989, 1995) has shown that while on the trek, the efficiency of hunting improves considerably and the hunters find more meat. Were it not for these long sojourns away from the village, game near the village would soon be completely wiped out. While on their treks (or shorter hunting trips), the villagers are constantly on the lookout for places to plant their new gardens. Once these gardens begin to bear bananas and plan-tains, the old communal house is abandoned and a new one is built near the new gardens.

Kenneth Good makes two crucial points regarding this move. First, plenty of forested land suitable for expanding the old gardens remains available near the old communal house. Second, the new communal house and gardens are not located near the old house and gardens but several kilometers away. Clearly, then, the gardens are not moved in order to increase the efficiency of plant production, nor is the site of the house moved because it has become insect infested, decayed, or surrounded by human excrement (cf. Ferguson 1989b:250). (Why not simply build the new house on the other side of the old gardens?)

What moving accomplishes is that it improves the accessibility of game animals that have been hunted out or frightened away from the old sites. Warfare among the Yanomami and other tropical forest peoples therefore can be readily understood as a form of competition between autonomous villages for access to the best hunting territories.

After all, we have no difficulty in understanding why modern nations go to war to maintain access to oil. Why, then, should we find it unlikely that the Yanomami go to war to maintain or increase access to game?

Warfare and Female Infanticide

It is generally accepted that slightly more boys than girls are born on a worldwide basis and that the average sex ratio at birth is about 105 males to 100 females. This imbalance, however, is much smaller than that found among the Yanomami, whose sex ratios between boys and girls averages about 132:100. What accounts for this large imbalance? High junior-age sex ratios favoring males are characteristic of societies with high levels of warfare (Table 11.2) and it probably reflects direct and indirect infanticide practiced against females more often than against males. (See Chapter 6 for a discussion of indirect infanticide.) There is a strong correlation between societies that admit to practicing infanticide and those that were actively engaged in warfare when a census was first made of them. In these societies, at least, female

infanticide was more common than male infanticide (Divale and Harris 1976).

A plausible reason for the killing and neglect of female children is that success in nonindustrial warfare depends on the size of male combat teams; having more males is desirable because it increases the group's ability to protect its women and children from raids by neighboring villages.

Where weapons are muscle-powered clubs, spears, and bows and arrows, victory will belong to the group that has the largest number of aggressive males. Because infrastructure limits the number of people who can be reared by band and village societies, war-making band and village societies are compelled to rear more males than females. As we have seen, this culturally induced scarcity of women accounts for the frequency of fights over women—which the Yanomami identify as the prime cause of war. Unless the depletion of game animals is stabilized or reversed, warfare and female infanticide will continue to be practiced.

Warfare and Trade Goods

The Yanomami have long been misrepresented as a people whose culture remained virtually free of Western influences and who had remained outside the orbit of the capitalist world system until the 1960s. For some interior groups, this isolation was said to have lasted even into the 1980s. A study carried out by R. Brian Ferguson (1995) has demonstrated that in fact the Yanomami have a long history of contact with gold miners, missionaries, travelers, and traders. Ferguson accepts the general principle that nonstate warfare is a means of competing for scarce resources, but in his view what the Yanomami are competing for is not game but Western trade goods, specifically what is known as "steel": machetes, axes, pots, fishhooks.

The Yanomami villages strive to monopolize access to providers of Western goods; they use pleas, threats, and deceptions to control the flow of "steel." Western manufactures are passed along from village to village through networks of kinship. An incomplete listing of goods distributed by the Catholic mission at Iyewei-teri for 1960 to 1972 includes 3,850 machetes, 620 axes, 2,850 pots, 759,000 fishhooks, and large quantities of other items. Most of these goods were traded to more remote villages (Ferguson 1992:209).

An important point in the theory that relates warfare to trade goods is that when Yanomami villages split and move, it is generally in the direction that gets them closer to the sources of "steel."

Table 11.2

Sex Ratios and Warfare

Young Males per 100 Females	
Warfare present	128
Stopped 5–25 years before census	113
Stopped over 25 years before census	109

Sources: Divale and Harris 1976; Divale et al. 1978; cf. Hirschfeld et al. 1978.

Melanesian Pig Redistribution
Leaders, known as big men, show their generosity and thereby gain prestige by mobilizing resources for lavish feasts.

Ferguson accepts that game depletions are responsible for village fissioning but he believes that the desire for steel is also a driving force in warfare. A struggle for hunting territories and a struggle for Western trade goods may be going on at the same time.

It is quite possible that the level of warfare among the Yanomami was much lower before they had Western trade goods as well as hunting territories to fight over.

Warfare, the Politics of Prestige, and the Big Man System

Throughout Melanesia and the South Pacific, high population density gives rise to a new pattern of leadership known as the big man system. Most of the prime land is under continuous cultivation and people have to grow their crops on small, intensely utilized plots of land. The survival of each local descent group depends directly on its ability to keep neighboring groups from seizing its land at the first sign of weakness. To increase their defensive posture, local descent groups establish alliances through marriage exchanges, feasting and a system of debt and credit. A big man, who stands at the head of each local descent group, is in a ranked position of prestige relative to other powerful big men in the society. His position is based on his ability to extend his influence in advancing alliances with other descent groups and in settling disputes.

A **big man** is a local entrepreneur who successfully mobilizes and manipulates wealth on behalf of his group, in order to host large feasts that enhance his status and rank relative to other big men in the region. He is a man of prestige and renown, but has no formal authority or power, nor does he have more wealth.

Melanesian groups such as the Mae Enga of Papua New Guinea (Profile 11.3), who live in a densely populated environment with frequent warfare, attempt to

Profile 11.3   The Mae Enga—A Big Man Society

Location: The Western Highlands of New Guinea.

Production: Year-round sweet potato cultivation and pigs, with up to 49 percent of agriculture produce going to feed pigs.

Population Density: 85–250 persons per square mile.

Time of Research: The 1950s and 1960s

The Mae Enga are similar to the Tsembaga Maring, except that Enga population density is double that of the Tsembaga; land is more scarce and warfare is more frequent and oriented to seizing prime land from defeated groups (Meggitt 1977). Each household is responsible for its own subsistence but is part of a larger patrilineal subclan consisting of about 90 members, which has ceremonial and political functions. Households have heavy demands placed on them for contributions for bridewealth payments and mortuary payments to honor ancestors. These payments are used to host feasts that reflect back on the

subclan and its big man, who competes with other big men for recognition at the clan level. The clan, which averages 350 people (Meggitt 1965), is a corporate group with rights to land. It owns an ancestral dance ground where ceremonial exchanges are made with other clans.

According to Mervyn Meggitt, when the population density of a growing clan exceeds 250 persons per square mile, people become increasingly land hungry (1977:31). When disputes arise about garden boundaries, the big men from neighboring clans meet to work out the details to attack a third more vulnerable group and take over their land. A group's ability to defend its territory or seize new territory depends on how large a fighting force it can organize, based on the number of allies it can recruit. This in turn depends on the prestige and success of the clan's big man in amassing pigs to be given away at ceremonial exchanges, which puts him in a position to negotiate with neighboring clans on matters of war and peace.

neutralize the external threat from other Enga lineage groups by

- Maintaining a large unified group that shows strength in numbers, which makes others afraid to attack them

- Collaborating in accumulating food and wealth that is given away at ceremonies to increase their prestige and obligate other groups to reciprocate

- Being strong and wealthy so that they will be attractive as allies for defensive purposes, turning neighboring groups into either friends or outnumbered enemies who will be afraid to attack (A. Johnson 1989).

To achieve and maintain alliances to protect their boundaries, local descent groups must be willing to comply with their big man's requests for food and wealth so that he can gain prestige and advertise his group's attractiveness as an ally.

The Melanesian big man system is similar to that of the Kwakiutl (see Chapter 8) in that leaders compete to achieve a high rank by hosting elaborate feasts and giveaways. For the Kwakiutl, the big man manages stored goods and hosts feasts to gain prestige in order to secure resources during times of regional scarcity. In Melanesia, where there are no storageable resources and land is scarce, the big man hosts feasts to gain prestige, build alliances, and increase the groups' military strength.

Summary

1. Orderly relationships among the individuals and domestic groups in band and village societies are maintained without governments and law enforcement specialists. This is possible because of small size, predominance of kinship and reciprocity, and egalitarian access to vital resources. Public opinion is the chief source of law and order in these societies.

2. Individual or nuclear family ownership of land is absent among hunting-and-gathering bands and most village peoples. However, even in the most egalitarian societies people privately own some items. Still, the prevalence of the reciprocal mode of exchange and the absence of anonymous price markets render theft unnecessary and impractical.

3. The major threat to law and order among band and village societies stems from the tendency of domestic and kinship groups to escalate conflicts in support of real or imagined injuries to one of their members. Such support does not depend on abstract principles of right and wrong but on the probable outcome of a particular course of action in the face of public opinion. The Inuit song duel illustrates how public opinion can be tested and used to end conflicts between individuals who belong to different domestic and kinship groups.

4. Witchcraft accusations also give public opinion an opportunity to identify and punish persistent violators of the rules of reciprocity and other troublemakers. Shamans act as the mouthpiece of the community. Under stressful conditions, witchcraft accusations may build to epidemic proportions and become a threat to the maintenance of law and order.

5. Headmanship reflects the egalitarian nature of the institutions of law and order in band and village societies. Headmen can do little more than harangue and plead with people for support. They lack physical or material means of enforcing their decisions. Their success rests on their ability to intuit public opinion. As exemplified by the Nuer, avoidance of blood feud can be facilitated by the payment of compensation and by appeal to ritual chiefs who have even less political power than headmen.

6. Other instances of nonkin political organization take the form of voluntary associations or sodalities such as men's and women's clubs, secret societies, and age-grade sets. However, all these nonkin modes of political organization remain rather rudimentary and are overshadowed by the pervasive networks of kinship alliances based on marriage and descent, which constitute the "glue" of band and village societies.

7. Warfare concerns the maintenance of law and order between separate societies and cultures. Although simple hunter-gatherers engage in warfare, warfare is usually more intense among sedentary societies.

8. Warfare cannot be explained as a consequence of innate aggression, an enjoyable sport, a thirst for revenge, or a struggle for reproductive success. Warfare is a particular form of organized activity and only one of the many ways in which cultures handle aggression.

9. The causes of war in band and village societies are rooted in problems associated with production and reproduction, and almost always involve attempts to protect or improve standards of living.

10. Even where population densities are very low, as among the Yanomami, problems of depletion and

declining efficiency may exist. Thus warfare in nonstate contexts often limits populations and thus protects resources from depletion.

11. Among patrilocal band and village societies, warfare could have the effect of controlling population growth through the encouragement of direct and indirect female infanticide. Evidence for population pressure as a cause of nonstate warfare consists of cross-cultural studies that correlate unbalanced sex ratios with active warfare.

12. Warfare among the Yanomami appears to be primarily a struggle for access to game and hunting territories. The importance of game can be gauged by the fact that the Yanomami frequently split up their villages and move to new and distant garden sites even though they still have plenty of additional garden land nearby. The prominence of trekking by the Yanomami also indicates the importance of game in their lives.

13. New data, however, show that besides access to hunting territories, trade for Western manufactures may account for the special intensity and high frequency of Yanomami warfare, especially in recent decades.

14. The big man system found throughout Melanesia, is a political system based on rank, feasting, and alliance that regulates relations between local descent groups in an area of high population density and intense warfare.

Osteodonto Keratic culture:

KEY TERMS

age-grade associations

big man

ego

genitor

genitrix

headman

leopard skin chief

patrilineal descent

shaman

sodalities

trekking

witchcraft

QUESTIONS TO THINK ABOUT

1. What role does public opinion play in mediating disputes in prestate societies? How is this forum different from our own legal system?

2. What are the functions of a headman, and what are the limitations on his power?

3. What accounts for the relative peaceful nature of the Mehinacu?

4. What explanations do anthropologists give for Yanomami warfare?

5. What are the functions of a big man? What is his role in maintaining regional relations of war and peace?

CHAPTER 12

Origins and Anatomy of the State

The Evolution of Big Man Systems into Chiefdoms
PROFILE: The Suiai—Big Men and Warfare

Infrastructural and Structural Aspects of Political Control
PROFILE: The Trobriand Chiefdoms—Ranked Leadership

The Origins of States
PROFILE: Hawaii—On the Threshold of the State
PROFILE: Bunyoro—An African Kingdom
PROFILE: The Incas—A Native American Empire

Ideology as a Source of Power

The State and Physical Coercion

Summary

America Now: Law and Disorder

Liliuokalni, Queen of Hawaii (1891–93).

In this chapter, we contrast the forms of political life characteristic of band and village societies with those of chiefdoms and states. How did the relatively egalitarian societies that once prevailed throughout the world give way to class-structured societies that rank people high and low, and divide them into rulers and ruled? In seeking the answer to the origin of states, we shall take account of both structural and infrastructural factors such as risk management, technology, warfare and trade, that present political leaders with opportunities for control.

The Evolution of Big Man Systems into Chiefdoms

As noted in the last chapter, headmen often function as intensifiers of production and as redistributors. They get their relatives to work harder, and they collect and then give away the extra product. A village may have several headmen, each with his own group of kin-based followers. Big men emerge where technological and ecological conditions encourage intensification and leaders living in the same village become rivals. They vie with one another to hold the most lavish feasts and to redistribute the greatest amount of valuables. The most successful redistributors earn the reputation of being "big men" and gain prestige for themselves and their kin group (Hayden 1993a, 1995).

Where big man systems evolve into **chiefdoms**, changes take place in

Solomon Island Chiefs
They prefer to be called chiefs rather than mumis, as of old.

- *The size of the population*—chiefdoms are associated with larger communities
- *Leadership*—chiefdoms are based on stratification, with a hierarchy of offices at the regional and community level.

Chiefdoms are regional systems integrating several villages under an elite class of leaders. These leaders control and manage local resources from which they derive obligatory payments. These payments are used to establish the chief's rank and prestige.

Profile 12.1   The Suiai—Big Men and Warfare

Location: Bougainville in the Solomon Islands, Papua New Guinea

Production: Horticulture, primarily sweet potatoes and yams

Density: 34 persons per square mile

Time of Study: 1938–1939

Among the Siuai, a big man is called a *mumi*, and to achieve mumi status is every youth's highest ambition. A young man proves himself capable of becoming a mumi by working hard and by carefully restricting his consumption of meat and coconuts. Eventually, he impresses his wife, children, and near relatives with the seriousness of his intentions, and they vow to help him

prepare for his first feast. If the feast is a success, his circle of supporters widens and he sets to work readying an even greater display of generosity.

He aims next at the construction of a men's clubhouse in which his male followers can lounge about and in which guests can be entertained and fed. Another feast is held at the consecration of the clubhouse, and if this is also a success, the circle of people willing to work for him grows still larger, and he will begin to be spoken of as a mumi. Larger and larger feasts mean that the mumi's demands on his supporters become more irksome. Although they grumble about how hard they have to work, they remain loyal as long as their mumi maintains or increases his renown as a "great provider."

(continued)

Profile 12.1   The Suiai—Big Men and Warfare *(continued)*

Finally, the time comes for the new mumi to challenge the others who have risen before him. He does this at a *muminai* feast, where a tally is kept of all the pigs, coconut pies, and sago-almond puddings given away by the host mumi and his followers to the guest mumi and his followers. If the guest mumi cannot reciprocate in a year or so with a feast at least as lavish as that of his challengers, he suffers a great social humiliation, and his fall from mumihood is immediate. In deciding on whom to challenge, a mumi must be very careful. He tries to choose a guest whose downfall will increase his own reputation, but he must avoid one whose capacity to retaliate exceeds his own.

At the end of a successful feast, the greatest of mumis still faces a lifetime of personal toil and dependence on the moods and inclinations of his followers. Mumihood does not confer the power to coerce others into doing one's bidding, nor does it elevate one's standard of living above anyone else's. In fact, because giving things away is the essence of mumihood, great mumis may even consume less meat and other delicacies than an ordinary, undistinguished Siuai. The Kaoka, another Solomon Island group reported on by H. Ian Hogbin (1964:66), have this saying: "The giver of the feast takes the bones and the stale cakes; the meat and the fat go to the others."

At one great feast attended by 1,100 people, the host mumi, whose name was Soni, gave away 32 pigs plus a large quantity of sago-almond puddings. Soni and his closest followers, however, went hungry. "We shall eat Soni's reknown," his followers said.

Formerly, the mumis were as famous for their ability to get men to fight for them as they were for their ability to get men to work for them. Warfare had been suppressed by the colonial authorities long before Oliver carried out his study, but the memory of mumi war leaders was still vivid among the Siuai. As one old man put it, "In the olden times there were greater mumi than there are today. Then they were fierce and relentless war lead-

ers. They laid waste to the countryside and their clubhouses were lined with the skulls of people they had slain" (Oliver 1955:411).

In singing praises of their mumis, the generation of pacified Siuai call them "warriors" and "killers of men and pigs."

Oliver's informants told him that mumis had more authority in the days when warfare was still practiced. Some mumi war leaders even kept one or two prisoners who were treated like slaves and forced to work in the mumi's family gardens, and people could not talk "loud and slanderously against their mumis without fear of punishment." This fits theoretical expectations, because the ability to redistribute meat and other valuables goes hand in hand with the ability to attract a following of warriors, equip them for combat, and reward them with spoils of battle.

Rivalry among Bougainville's war-making mumis appeared to have been leading toward an islandwide political organization when the first European voyagers arrived. According to Oliver (1955:420), "For certain periods of time many neighboring villages fought together so consistently that there emerged a pattern of war-making regions, each more or less internally peaceful and each containing one outstanding mumi whose war activities provided internal social cohesion." These mumis enjoyed regional fame, but their prerogatives remained rudimentary. For example, the mumis had to provide their warriors with women brought into the clubhouses and with gifts of pork and other delicacies. Said one old warrior, "If the mumi didn't furnish us with women we were angry. All night long we would copulate and still want more. It was the same with eating. The clubhouse used to be filled with food, and we ate and ate and never had enough. Those were wonderful times" (Oliver 1955:415). Furthermore, the mumi who wanted to lead a war party had to be prepared personally to pay an indemnity for any of his men who were killed in battle and to furnish a pig for each man's funeral feast.

The size of chiefdoms can vary greatly. At the lower end, chiefdoms such as the Trobrianders are very similar to big man systems; at the upper end chiefdoms such as Hawaii approximate states. As the size increases, the distinctions between leaders and followers widen; big men have to build up power by attracting personal followers (see Box 12:1), whereas a chief comes to power that is vested in an inherited office. Big men who are successful redistributors are

hard to distinguish from the leaders of small chiefdoms. Whereas big men must achieve and constantly validate their status by recurrent feasts, chiefs inherit their offices and hold them even if they are temporarily unable to provide their followers with generous redistributions. Chiefs tend to live better than commoners; unlike headmen, they do not always keep only "the bones and the stale cakes" for themselves. Yet in the long run chiefs too must vali-

Box 12:1   Big Man versus Chief

Big Man

The big man's status is achieved through his ability to attract followers. His position is ranked among other big men according to prestige.

A big man's followers provide him with wealth that he in turn redistributes through feasts and a system of debt and credit. He must maintain the loyalty of his followers because he can be replaced if he is unable to continue to affirm his status through redistribution.

A big man does not have an improved standard of living. He may even end up with less, because of the importance of generosity. He wears shell ornaments during a feast but once it is over, he reverts to living like everyone else.

In the past, big men were fierce war leaders who rewarded their warriors with the spoils of battle and compensated the families of those who died in battle.

Chief

A chief holds an inherited office determined by virtue of his membership in a high-ranking lineage.

A chief's position is relatively permanent; he maintains his office even if he is unable to temporarily provide generously for his followers, but he can be deposed by a more powerful chief through defeat in war.

A chief lives better than commoners. He has more access to resources than anyone else. He is allowed to have many wives, he stores surplus yams, and owns prestige valuables that are used as political currency to compensate people for their services.

In the past, the chief used his storage facilities to support warriors on long-distance expeditions, expanding the territories under the chiefdom's control.

---

date their titles by waging successful war, obtaining trade goods, and giving away food and other valuables to their followers (Earle 1991, 1997; Hayden 1995).

Infrastructural and Structural Aspects of Political Control

The evolution of chiefdoms—and later states—depends on the leader's ability to control production and exchange and to mobilize resources to finance various institutions. These resources consist of food staples and wealth in the form of precious artifacts (Johnson and Earle 1987; Earle 1997).

A chief—and later an emperor—takes advantage of the opportunity to control resources by monopolizing the management of production and exchange and extracting a surplus that becomes the basis of his power. Four kinds of opportunities for control can be identified:

- *Risk management*—As we saw with the Kwakiutl, there is always a danger of regional food scarcity when there is high population density. Production of a food surplus provides a safeguard against starvation.

- *Ownership and management of technology that intensifies production*—As people produce more food,

technology helps offset the rising labor costs of increased agricultural output. Irrigation, as we saw in the case of Luts'un, permits intensified production through the management of water, which provides an opportunity to produce surpluses that support local chiefs.

- *Warfare*—For regional integration, warfare had to be brought under control. Although warfare alone does not necessarily lead to stratification, it enables chiefdoms to expand by incorporating and controlling populations that provide surplus production.

- *Large-scale trade*—Long-distance trade requires political coordination and management to construct roads or sea-going canoes. Trade provides access to valuable raw materials and storable food resources (to reduce the risk of food shortages), and it builds alliances that manage regional relations of war and peace.

Chiefdoms similar to the Trobrianders are found throughout the world. For example, the political organization of the Cherokee of Tennessee (and of other southeastern woodland Native Americans) bears a striking resemblance to the Trobrianders' redistribution–warfare–trade–chief complex. The Cherokee, like the Trobrianders, were matrilineal, and they waged external warfare over long distances. At the center of the principal settlements was a large, circular "council

Profile 12.2   The Trobriand Chiefdoms—Ranked Leadership

Location: A group of small coral islands about 120 miles north of the western tip of New Guinea.

Production: Intensive agriculture (yams and taro) and fishing, with regional specialization in fishing, agriculture and craft production.

Density: Ranging from 60 to 100 persons per square mile; mostly scattered along shallow coastal lagoons, and the interior.

Time of Study: Early 1900s and 1960s

The difference between big men and chiefs can be illustrated with the case of the Trobriand Islanders. Trobrianders have a pervasive concept of rank; the society is divided into elite and commoner matrilineal clans and subclans, through which collective title to garden land is inherited. The chiefs of high-ranking subclans compete among themselves to improve their regional position through the accumulation of wealth. The chief of the most powerful subclan assumes the position of "paramount chief." Unlike the Siuai mumis, the Trobriand chiefs occupy a hereditary office and can be deposed only through defeat in war. Malinowski describes a "paramount chief" who had control over more than a dozen villages, containing several thousand people. Only chiefs can wear certain shell ornaments as the insignia of high rank, and no commoner can stand or sit in a position that puts a chief's head at a lower elevation than anyone else's. Malinowski (1920) tells of seeing all the people present in the village of Bwoytalu drop from their verandas as if blown down by a hurricane at the sound of a drawn-out cry announcing the arrival of an important chief.

The Trobrianders attribute the distinctions of rank in their society to wars of conquest carried out long ago. Bronislaw Malinowski (1920) reports that the Trobrianders are keen on fighting and conduct systematic and relentless wars, venturing across the open ocean in their

canoes to trade—or, if need be, to fight—with the people of islands over 100 miles away. But the Trobriand chief's power rests ultimately on his ability to play the role of "great provider." Chiefs acquire up to a dozen or more wives, and are entitled to obligatory gifts of yams—which, along with kula valuables (see Chapter 8, "Trade in the Kula Ring" section), represent prestige and political currency—from each of his wives' brothers. These yams are delivered to the chief's village and displayed on special yam racks. Some of the yams are then distributed in elaborate feasts at which the chief validates his position as a "great provider"; the remainder are used to feed canoe-building specialists, artisans, magicians, and family servants who thereby become partially dependent on the chief's power. In former times, the yam stores also furnished the food for launching long-distance kula trading expeditions among friendly groups and raids against enemies (Brunton 1975; Malinowski 1935).

Even though the Trobrianders fear and respect their "great provider" war chiefs, they are still a long way from being a state society. Living on islands, the Trobrianders are not free to spread out; their population density has risen, but there are few opportunities for control. For example, the chiefs cannot monopolize enough of the production system to acquire great wealth and power. Perhaps one reason for this is that Trobriand agriculture lacks cereal grains. Because yams rot after four or five months (unlike rice or maize), the Trobriand "great provider" cannot manipulate people through dispensing food year-round, nor can he support a permanent police military garrison out of his stores. Another important factor is the open resources of the lagoons and ocean from which the Trobrianders derive their protein supply. The Trobriand chief cannot cut off access to these resources and hence can not exercise permanent coercive political control over subordinates.

house" where the council of chiefs discussed issues involving several villages and where redistributive feasts were held. The council of chiefs had a supreme chief who was the central figure in the Cherokee redistributive network. At harvest time, a large crib, identified as the "chief's granary," was erected in each field. "To this each family carries and deposits a certain quantity according to his ability or inclination, or none at all if he so chooses." The chief's granaries functioned as "a

public treasury to fly to for succor" in the case of crop failure, as a source of food "to accommodate strangers, or travellers," and as a military store "when they go forth on hostile expeditions." Although every citizen enjoyed "the right of free and public access," commoners had to acknowledge that the store really belonged to the supreme chief who had "an exclusive right and ability to distribute comfort and blessings to the necessitous" (Bartram 1958:326).

Trobriand Islanders Reenact War Dance

In the past, Trobriand armies conquered people from far away islands.

The Origins of States

Under certain conditions, large chiefdoms evolved into states. The state is a form of politically centralized society whose governing elites have the power to compel subordinates to pay taxes, render services, and obey the law (Carneiro 1981:69). The transformation of chiefdoms into states first occurred when dense populations came to subsist on intensifiable forms of agriculture, especially on the cultivation of staple grains such as rice, wheat, barley, or maize that could be stored for a year or more without becoming inedible. In addition, early state formation generally occurred when the dissatisfied factions of stratified chiefdoms who sought to flee from the growing power of paramount chiefs found themselves blocked by similarly stratified chiefdoms in adjacent territories or by features of the environment that required them to adopt a new and less efficient mode of production and to suffer a drastic decline in their standards of living. This condition is known as **circumscription.**

The significance of circumscription is that factions of discontented members of a chiefdom cannot escape from their elite overlords without suffering a sharp decline in their standard of living.

Many of the earliest states were circumscribed by their dependence on modes of production that required irrigation and were associated with fertile river valleys surrounded by arid or semiarid plains or mountains. But circumscription can also be caused by the transformation of low-yielding habitats into higher-yielding ones as a result of a long-term investment in the mounding, ditching, draining, and irrigating of a chiefdom's territory (Dickson 1987).

Three infrastructural conditions are instrumental in the transformation of chiefdoms to states:

- Population increase
- Intensive agriculture with storable staples
- Circumscription that restricts migration

Given these infrastructural conditions, certain changes in a chiefdom's political and economic structure become likely:

1. The larger and denser the population and the greater the surplus harvested, the greater the ability of the elites to support craft specialists, palace guards, and a standing professional army.

2. The more powerful the elite, the greater its ability to engage in long-distance warfare and trade, and to conquer, incorporate, and exploit new populations and territories.

3. The more powerful the elite, the more stratified its redistribution of trade wealth and harvest surplus.

4. The wider the territorial scope of political control and the larger the society's investment in the mode of production, the less opportunity a person has to flee and the less a person gains by fleeing.

Soon, contributions to the central store cease to be voluntary—they become taxes. Access to the farmlands and natural resources cease to be rights—they become dispensations. Food producers cease being the chief's followers—they become peasants who labor on their lands far from the ruler's palaces; redistributors cease being chiefs but become kings; and chiefdoms turn into states (Box 12.2 on page 186).

How do states mantain power

Box 12.2   Warning!

The transition from egalitarean village to chiefdom to state presented here is a "model" of how these political and economic systems might have evolved from each other. All transitions leading to the first states did not necessarily follow the same sequence. But it seems likely that some of them did. Thus the model should be regarded as hypothetical, awaiting the test of more empirical evidence.

Box 12.3   Two Kinds of Feedback

Negative: Changes are checked when certain limits are reached. Initial conditions tend to be restored.
Example: Household temperature stays slightly above or slightly below the level set on a thermostat.

Positive: Changes are not checked. Each successive change increases or amplifies the tendency to change.
Example: A microphone picks up the sound of its own loudspeaker and sends the signal back through its amplifier, which sends a stronger signal to the loudspeaker, resulting in a louder and louder squeal.

As the governing elites compel subordinates to pay taxes and tribute, provide military or labor services, and obey laws, the entire process of intensification, expansion, conquest, stratification, and centralization is amplified.

Control is continuously increased or "amplified" through a form of change known as *positive feedback* (Box 12.3). Where certain modes of production could sustain sufficient numbers of peasant farmers and warriors, this feedback process recurrently resulted in states conquering other states and in the emergence of preindustrial empires involving vast territories inhabited by millions of people (Carneiro 1981; R. Cohen 1984a; Feinman and Neitzel 1984; Fried 1978).

Once the first states came into existence, they themselves constituted barriers against the flight of people who sought to preserve egalitarian systems.

With states as neighbors, egalitarian peoples found themselves increasingly drawn into warfare and were compelled to increase production and to give their redistributor war chiefs more and more power in order to prevail against the expansionist tendencies of their neighbors.

Thus, most states of the world were produced by a great diversity of specific historical and ecological conditions (Fried 1967); once states come into existence, they tend to spread, engulf, and overwhelm nonstate peoples (Carneiro 1970; R. Cohen 1984a; Haas 1982; Hommon 1986; Kirch 1984; MacNeish 1981; Service 1975; Upham 1990).

Profile 12.3   Hawaii—On the Threshold of the State

Location: The north central part of the Pacific Ocean

Production: Irrigation and terracing, mainly yams, sweet potatoes, taro, and pigs.

Density: Approximately 39 persons per square mile in a landscape of steep terrain and varied rainfall. Populations are concentrated along the coast and in valleys with densities over 300 persons per square mile.

Time period: Before contact with Europeans, during the 1700s.

When visited by Captain James Cook in A.D. 1778, the Hawaiian Islands were divided into four markedly hierarchical polities, each containing between 10,000 and

100,000 persons and each on the threshold (if not past it) of becoming a full-fledged state. Each polity was divided into named districts containing populations that ranged from about 4,000 to 25,000 people. The districts were in turn divided into many elongated territorial units called *ahupua'a,* which extended inland from the coast to the higher elevations of the island's interior, and were each inhabited by an average of 200 persons. These inhabitants were of the commoner class, the *maka'ainana*—fishermen, farmers, and craftsworkers.

Each ahupua'a was administered by officials called *konohiki,* who were the local land managers who oversaw production for the powerful district chiefs, called *ali'i.* These ali'i based their claims to high chiefly status on genealogies that extended upward for ten generations. (Such genealogies, however, were constantly adjusted and negotiated.) District chiefs who provided the most political and military support were rewarded with grants of land. The chiefly class was topped off by a paramount figure called the *ali'i nui,* who was the owner of all lands and responsible for assigning privileges and administrative posts to the ali'i, in return for a portion of the local goods produced. In practice, the ali'i were in ceaseless turmoil over their relative rank, and the issue was decided by wars of conquest rather than genealogical reckoning. Competition for high office was intense. Following the death of a paramount chief, warfare followed as district chiefs competed for succession and control. Until the time of contact, no ali'i nui had managed to gain firm control over all the districts on an island.

Chiefs had legitimate managerial functions such as allocating land, organizing community rebuilding after periodic flooding, and most importantly, as managers of intensified agriculture. Hierarchical, taxlike forms of redistribution siphoned both food and craft items from the maka'ainana commoners to the ali'i. It was the konohiki's main responsibility to see to it that the commoners in his charge produced enough to satisfy the demands of the ali'i. The ali'i in turn used these "gifts" to pay the non–food-producing craft specialists; to reward his warriors, priests, allies, and konohiki; and of course, to make pay-ments to the paramount chief. Recent archaeological research demonstrates that the Hawaiian polities evolved out of more egalitarian chiefdoms as a result of the positive feedback among population increase, environmental depletions (deforestation and soil erosion), intensification of production (irrigation and pig husbandry), increased trade, escalating warfare, and competition for elite status. The process took place in three gradual stages (Earle 1989; Hommon 1986; Kirch 1984):

> **Phase I:** A.D. 500–1200. **Initial colonization and population growth.** Settlements are on best coastal sites. No irrigation is needed. Settlements are egalitarian and kinship-organized.
>
> **Phase II:** 1200–1500. **Expansion into less desirable interior island sites.** As population grows rapidly, production increases through the use of floodwater irrigation, mulching, and reduction of fallow periods.
>
> **Phase III:** 1500–1778. **Expansion of irrigation systems.** Intensification and expansion of agricultural production through terracing, and expanded irrigation; greater stratification as yields and "surplus" increase. Rivalry and warfare between chiefs, as they compete to gain access to land, taxes, and political power.

Hawaiian Chief Brings Gifts to Captain Cook
Hawaiian chiefs were able to amass large quantities of wealth and control a sizable labor force. They, however, lacked food resources that could be stored for long periods of time.

Would the Hawaiian polities have achieved a more stable and centralized state if their political history had not been interrupted by the landings of Europeans on their shores? According to the theory presented, the answer is no. It was only as a result of that contact that a unified Hawaiian kingdom was established in 1810.

All the conditions for state formation were present with one exception: The Hawaiian chiefs had no **storable staples** that could be used during times of drought or warfare. They did have storehouses for root crops such as taro and yams, which they used to sustain their followers during emergencies. But unlike grains, these root crops cannot be stored for a whole year or more.

David Malo, a nineteenth-century Hawaiian chief, noted that the storehouses of the Hawaiian kings were designed as a means of keeping people contented so that they would not desert them: "As the rat will not desert the pantry, so the people will not

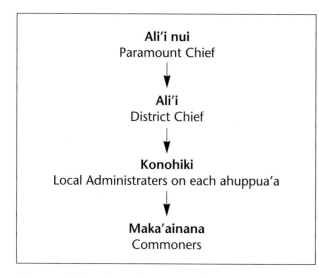

Figure 12.1   Hawaiian Political Hierarchy
(Adapted from Earle 1978)

Mukama of Bunyoro
This is a king, not a chief.

desert the king while they think there is food in his storehouse" (D'Altroy and Earle 1985:192). Lacking staple grains that provided the nutritional and energetic basis for the emergence of states elsewhere, the Hawaiian chiefs were unable to sustain large numbers of followers, especially during times of food shortage. Thus, no ali'i nui was able to achieve an enduring advantage over his rivals.

Profile 12.4   Bunyoro—An African Kingdom

Location: Uganda, East Africa

Production: Agriculture, with millet as the staple crop; cattle herding.

Density: Estimated 25 persons per square mile

Time Period: Early 1900s

The difference between a chiefdom and a state can be illustrated with the case of Bunyoro, a kingdom located in Uganda and studied by John Beattie (1960). At the time of Beattie's fieldwork, Bunyoro had a population of about 100,000 people and an area of 5,000 square miles. Supreme power over the Bunyoro territory and its inhabitants was vested in the Mukama, senior member of a royal lineage that reckoned its descent back to the beginning of time. The use of all natural resources, especially of farming land, was a dispensation specifically granted by the Mukama to a dozen or more "chiefs" or

to commoner peasants under their respective control. In return for these dispensations, quantities of food (especially the staple grain, millet), handicrafts, and labor services were funneled up through the power hierarchy into the Mukama's headquarters. The Mukama in turn directed the use of these goods and services on behalf of state enterprises. Thus, the basic redistributive pattern was still plainly in evidence.

Although the Mukama had a reputation for generosity, he clearly did not give away as much as he received. He certainly did not follow the Solomon Island mumis and keep only the stale cakes and bones for himself. Moreover, much of what he gave away did not flow back down to the peasant producers; instead, it remained in the hands of his genealogically close kin, who constituted a clearly demarcated aristocratic class. Part of what the Mukama took away from the peasants was bestowed on nonkin who performed extraordinary services on behalf of the state, especially in connection with military exploits. Another part was used to support a permanent palace guard and resident staff who attended to the Mukama's personal needs and performed religious rites deemed essential for the welfare of the Mukama and the nation, including custodian of spears, custodian of royal graves, custodian of the royal drums, custodian of royal crowns, placers of royal crowns on the king's head, custodians of royal thrones (stools) and other regalia, cooks, bath attendants, herdsmen, potters, barkcloth makers, and musicians. Many of these officials had several assistants.

In addition, the Mukama had a loosely defined category of advisers, diviners, and other retainers who hung around the court, attached to his household as dependents, in the hope of being appointed to a chieftainship. And then the Mukama had an extensive harem, many children, and the polygynous households of his brothers and of other royal personages who owed him allegience. To keep his power intact, the Mukama and portions of his court made frequent trips throughout Bunyoro land, staying at local palaces maintained at the expense of his chiefs and commoners.

Profile12.5   The Incas—A Native American Empire

Location: The Andean regions of present-day Ecuador, Peru, Bolivia, Chile, and Argentina.

Production: Hoe agriculture, with potatoes and quinoa as staples; alpaca, llama, and guinea pigs.

Density: 40 people per square mile (density is low because much of the terrain is arid and rocky).

Time period: The Inca empire reached its peak between 1476 and 1532.

In both the Old and New Worlds, state systems arose in which scores of former small chiefdoms were incorporated into highly centralized superstates or empires. In the New World, the largest and most powerful of these systems was the Inca Empire. At its prime, the Inca Empire stretched 1500 miles from northern Chile to southern Colombia and contained possibly as many as 6 million inhabitants. Because of government intervention in the basic mode of production, agriculture was organized in terms of villages, districts, and provinces. Each such unit was supervised by appointed government officials, known as *curacas,* responsible for planning public works and for delivering government-established quotas of laborers, food, and other material. The village, or *ayllu,* was a corporate kin group similar to the Hawaiian *ahupua'a.* The ayllu ranged in size from a few hundred people to perhaps a thousand. It operated a highly productive, intensive agricultural system that required terracing, irrigation, and management of crop rotation. Ayllu lands were divided into three parts, the largest of which was used to support the peasants. Harvests from the second and third parts were stored in granaries and turned over to support religious and state agents (D'Altroy and Earle 1985; D'Altroy

1992). The distribution of staples such as maize, potatoes, and quinoa, was entirely under the control of the curacas, who transported the food to administrative centers and to regional storehouses where food was kept for times of need—in case of food shortage. Likewise, when labor power was needed to build roads, bridges, canals, fortresses, or other public works, curacas recruited workers directly from the villages. Community lands remained under state ownership and the right to use them was granted in exchange for *mit'a,* or obligatory labor. Peasant communities were also obligated to produce craft goods for state use, particularly llama wool woven into cloth. Careful records of labor and storable wealth was kept by *khipu,* mnemonic devices made of rows of knotted string used to keep track of goods produced for the state.

Because of the size of the administrative network and the density of population, a large labor force could be placed at the disposal of the Inca engineers to construct a vast road system and monumental building projects. Thousands of miles of roads were built, along with bridges and stairways carved into hillsides, to connect the vast regions of the empire. In the construction of Cuzco's fortress of Sacsahuaman, probably the greatest masonry structure in the New World, 30,000 people were employed in cutting, quarrying, hauling, and erecting huge monoliths, some weighing as much as 200 tons. Labor contingents of this size were rare in medieval Europe but were common in ancient states such as Egypt, the Middle East, and China.

The Inca state expanded its power by conquering and integrating many of the warring ethnic chiefdoms into the empire. Instead of conquering land and expelling defeated populations, the Inca incorporated the

(continued)

Profile 12.5   The Incas—A Native American Empire *(continued)*

defeated populations into the empire. After conquering a new region, the state took ownership of the land, and appointed curacas to manage and expand local production, regulate the mit'a service and deliver the goods stockpiled in storehouses. The people, who were tired of the war, welcomed the opportunity for regional peace and the functional advantage of food storage to secure against shortages in food production due to climate fluctuations (Johnson and Earle 1987).

Control over the entire empire was concentrated in the hands of the Inca. He was the firstborn of the firstborn, a descendant of the god of the sun and a celestial being of unparalleled holiness. This god-on-earth enjoyed power and luxury undreamed of by the poor Mehinacu chief in his plaintive daily quest for respect and obedience. Ordinary people could not approach the Inca face to face. His private audiences were conducted from behind a screen, and all who approached him did so with a burden of wood or stone on their backs. When traveling, he reclined on an ornate palanquin carried by special crews of bearers. A small army of sweepers, water carriers,

woodcutters, cooks, wardrobe men, treasurers, gardeners, and hunters attended the domestic needs of the Inca in his palace in Cuzco, the capital of the empire.

The Inca ate his meals from gold and silver dishes in rooms whose walls were covered with precious metals. His clothing was made of the softest vicuna wool, and he gave away each change of clothing to members of the royal family, never wearing the same garment twice. The Inca enjoyed the services of a large number of concubines who were methodically culled from the empire's most beautiful young women. However, to conserve the holy line of descent from the god of the sun, his wife had to be his own full or half sister (see Chapter 9, "The Avoidance of Incest" section). When the Inca died, his wife, concubines, and many other retainers were strangled during a great drunken dance in order that he suffer no loss of comfort in the afterlife. Each Inca's body was eviscerated, wrapped in cloth, and mummified. Women with fans stood in constant attendance on these mummies, ready to drive away flies and to take care of the other things mummies need to stay happy.

Ideology as a Source of Power

Large populations, anonymity, and vast differences in wealth make the maintenance of law and order in state societies more difficult to achieve than in bands, villages, and chiefdoms. This accounts for the great elaboration of police and paramilitary forces and the other state-level institutions and specialists concerned with crime and punishment. Although every state ultimately stands prepared to crush criminals and political subversives by imprisoning, maiming, or killing them, most of the daily burdens of maintaining law and order against discontented individuals and groups are borne by institutions that seek to confuse, distract, and demoralize potential troublemakers before they have to be subdued by physical force.

Sacsahuaman

The principal fortress of the Inca Empire, near Cuzco, Peru.

Pomp and Ceremony

The crowning of Queen Elizabeth II in England was a mass spectacle viewed by millions.

Every state, ancient and modern, has specialists who perform ideological services in support of the status quo.

These services are often rendered in a manner and in contexts that seem unrelated to economic or political issues yet they serve to direct thoughts and actions. The main ideological apparatus of preindustrial states consists of magico-religious institutions (see Chapter 17, "Ecclesiastical Cults" section) that legitimize power relations within society. Religious ideology imparts an understanding of what is right, and what is natural. It is based on real experiences that people share in common, that lie outside the mind. These experiences are derived from material objects such as large public monuments, ceremonial facilities, and special regalia (such as fine clothes, a crown, or jewels), that represent the power of the dominant classes. Timothy Earle (1997) calls this the **process of materialization**, meaning that ideology becomes transformed from abstract ideas and values into material objects that become public symbols (DeMarrais et al. 1996). These public symbols create shared experiences that state rulers can manipulate and use to mold individuals' beliefs about the nature of power dynamics in the universe. Monuments—especially tombs of past rulers—and their adjoining ceremonial plazas, are part of the elaborate religions of the Inca, Aztecs, ancient Egyptians, and other nonindustrial civilizations that remind the populace of the greatness of the state. These symbols of power give perma-

nence to the powers and privileges of the ruling elite by providing a place where people can come together to witness the exalted status of their rulers.

Ceremonial events and imposing monuments transform the ruling ideology from abstract ideas into concrete shared experiences.

These powerful ideologies legitimize and uphold the doctrine of the divine descent of their rulers, by sanctifying the belief that the continuity of the universe requires the subordination of commoners to persons of noble and divine birth.

In many states, religion has been used to condition large masses of people to accept relative deprivation as necessity, to look forward to material rewards in the afterlife rather than in the present one, and to be grateful for small favors from superiors lest ingratitude call down a fiery retribution in this life or in a hell to come. (Religion, of course, has other functions, as we shall see in Chapter 17.) Yet it is important to remember that it is not ideology (emic perceptions in people's heads) that keeps subordinate segments of society where they are. Nor is their belief in the legitimacy of ruling class privilege responsible for their political and economic subordination. As we have seen, it is the monopolization of production and exchange and the extraction of surplus that become the basis of power for the ruling elites.

Ideology is a source of political power: it directs thoughts that legitimize the actions of the ruling elite and it motivates people to work for the interests of the ruling segment of society.

A considerable amount of conformity is achieved not by frightening or threatening people but by inviting them to identify with the governing elite and to enjoy vicariously the pomp of state occasions. Public spectacles such as religious processions, coronations, and victory parades work against the alienating effects of poverty and exploitation.

Today, the movies, television, and radio provide states with far more powerful means of thought control. Through modern media, the consciousness of millions of listeners, readers, and watchers is often manipulated along rather precisely determined paths by censors and propaganda specialists. However, thought control via the mass media need not take the form of government-directed propaganda and censorship. More subtle forms of control arise from the voluntary filtering of news by reporters and commentators whose career advancements depend on avoiding objective coverage (Chomsky 1989; Herman

Force Is Expensive
United Nations tanks in Kosovo try to keep the peace.

Thought Control in the United States
Saluting the flag instills loyalty in children.

and Chomsky 1988). "Entertainment" delivered through the air or by cable directly into the shanty-town house or tenement apartment is another form of thought control, perhaps the most effective "Roman circus" yet devised (Kottak 1990; Parenti 1986).

Compulsory universal education is another powerful modern means of thought control. Teachers and schools serve the instrumental needs of complex industrial civilizations by training each generation to provide the skills and services necessary for survival and well-being. But schools also teach civics, history, citizenship, and social studies. These subjects are loaded with implicit or explicit assumptions about culture, people, and nature that favor the status quo. All modern states use universal education to instill loyalty through mass rituals. These include saluting the flag; pronouncing oaths of allegiance; singing patriotic songs; and staging patriotic assemblies, plays, and pageants (Bowles and Gintis 1976; Ramirez and Meyer 1980).

In modern industrial states as in ancient ones, acceptance of extreme social and economic inequality depends on thought control more than on the exercise of naked repressive force. Children from economically deprived families are taught to believe that the main obstacle to achievement of wealth and power is their own intellectual merit, physical endurance, and will to compete. The poor are taught to blame themselves for being poor, and their resentment is directed primarily against themselves or against those with whom they must compete and who stand on the same rung of the ladder of upward mobility (DeMott 1990; Kleugel and Smith 1981).

The State and Physical Coercion

Although thought control can be an effective supplementary means of maintaining political control, there are limits to the lies and deceptions that governments can get away with. If people are experiencing stagnant or declining standards of living, no amount of propaganda and false promises can prevent them from becoming restless and dissatisfied. As discontent mounts, the ruling elites must either increase the use of direct force or make way for a restructuring of political economy. In China, popular dissatisfaction with the ruling class has been met in recent years by more direct physical repression. The great upheavals in the Soviet Union and Eastern Europe during the 1980s and 1990s also illustrate dramatically what can happen when ruling classes fail to deliver on their promises of a better life. No amount of thought control could hide the daily reality of long lines to buy food, the endless red tape, the shortages of housing and electricity, and the widespread industrial pollution characteristic of life behind the Iron Curtain.

Summary

1. Headmen, big men, chiefs, and kings are found in different forms of political organization: autonomous bands and villages, chiefdoms, and states, respectively.

2. The "big man" is a rivalrous form of leadership marked by competitive redistributions that expand and intensify production. As illustrated by the mumis of the Solomon Islands, being a big man is a temporary status requiring constant validation through displays of generosity that leave the big man poor in possessions but rich in prestige and authority. Because they are highly respected, big

men are well suited to act as leaders of war parties, long-distance trading expeditions, and other collective activities that require leadership among egalitarian peoples.

3. The evolution from big man society to chiefdom is marked by infrastructural and structural opportunities for control in four areas—risk management, control of technology that intensifies production, warfare and trade—that enable leaders to mobilize resources and increase their power.

4. Chiefdoms consist of several more or less permanently allied communities. Like big men, chiefs also play the role of great provider, expand and intensify production, give feasts, and organize long-distance warfare and trading expeditions. However, as illustrated by the Trobriand and Cherokee chiefdoms, chiefs enjoy hereditary status, tend to live somewhat better than the average commoner, and can be deposed only through defeat in warfare.

5. The power of chiefs is limited by their ability to support a permanent group of police military specialists and to deprive significant numbers of their followers of access to the means of making a living. In the transition from band and village organizations through chiefdoms to states, a continuous series of cumulative changes occurs in the balance of power between elites and commoners. The subtle gradations along this continuum make it difficult to say at exactly what point in the process we have chiefdoms rather than an alliance of villages, or states rather than a powerful chiefdom.

6. Dense populations, intensifiable modes of production, trade, storable grains, circumscription, and intense warfare provide the basic conditions for state formation. Hawaii is an example of a chiefdom whose lack of storable grains may have inhibited the transition to a state form of polity. The difference between chiefdoms and states is illustrated by the case of the Bunyoro (whose staple was the grain millet). The Mukama was a great provider for himself and his closest supporters but not for the majority of the Bunyoro peasants. Unlike the Trobriand chief, the Mukama maintained a permanent court of personal retainers and a palace guard.

7. The most developed and highly stratified form of statehood is that of empire. As illustrated by the Inca of Peru, the leaders of ancient empires possessed vast amounts of power and could not be approached by ordinary citizens. Production was supervised by a whole army of administrators and tax collectors. Although the Inca was concerned with the welfare of his people, they viewed him as a god to whom they owed everything rather than as a headman or chief who owed everything to them.

8. Because all state societies are based on marked inequalities between rich and poor, rulers and ruled, the maintenance of law and order presents a critical challenge. In the final analysis, it is the military with its control over the means of physical coercion that keep the poor and exploited in line. However, all states find it more expedient to maintain law and order by controlling people's thoughts. This is done in a variety of ways, ranging from universal education and state religions to public monuments and ceremonies that symbolically represent the power of the state

AMERICA NOW

Law and Disorder

The United States has one of the highest rates of violent crime found among industrial nations. In 1991, there were 24,700 murders; 106,000 rapes; 687,000 robberies; and 3 million burglaries. Someone is hit by gunfire in New York City every 88 minutes. In 1993, from January to November, 4,769 New Yorkers were hit by bullets. More people were murdered in New York in 1990 than died from colon cancer, breast cancer, or all accidents combined (Roberts 1993).

Actually, the violent crime rate declined in the mid-1990s. This was achieved through a massive prison-building spree and long mandatory sentences aimed

Law and Disorder

When discontent with the political economy mounts, people become restless and there is danger of a breakdown in law and order.

at locking up young offenders. In California more money has been spent on building jails than on building schools. Nationwide there are over 1 million prisoners in state and federal facilities (Butterfield 1996).

One reason for the high rate of violent crime in the United States is that U.S. citizens own far more pistols and rifles per capita than the citizens of other countries. (Switzerland is a notable exception: All men are part of the militia and *must* bear arms.) The right to bear arms is guaranteed by the U.S. Constitution. But the failure to pass stricter gun control laws itself reflects, in part at least, the pervasive, realistic fear of being robbed or attacked and the consequent desire to defend person and property. Hence, the cause of the high incidence of violent crimes must be sought at deeper levels of U.S. culture.

Much evidence links the unusually high rate of crime in the United States to the long-term, grinding poverty and economic hopelessness of America's inner-city minorities, especially of African Americans and Latinos. Although suburban crime has also risen, the principal locus of violent crime remains the inner cities. African Americans constitute 12 percent of the population but account for 61 percent of arrests for robbery and 55 percent of arrests for murder and manslaughter (Hacker 1992:181). One should note, however, that proportionately, African Americans themselves suffer more from violent crimes than do whites. A poor Black is 25 times more likely than a wealthy white to be a victim of a robbery resulting in injury and 8 times more likely to be a homicide victim. In fact, homicide is the ranking killer of African American males between 15 and 24 years of age. More black males die from homicide than from motor vehicle accidents, diabetes, emphysema, or pneumonia. (Two out of five Black male children born in an American city in 1980 will not reach age 25.) Over half of all Black teenagers are unemployed; further, in ghettos such as Harlem in New York City, the unemployment rate among Black youth may be as high as 86 percent (Brown 1978; National Urban League 1990).

The dominant classes of Western democracies rely more on thought control than on physical coercion to maintain law and order, but in the final analysis they too depend on guns and jails to protect their privileges. Disasters such as Hurricane Andrew in 1992 and the Los Angeles riots in 1994 quickly led to extensive looting and widespread disorder, proving that thought control is not enough, and that large numbers of ordinary citizens do not believe in the system and are held in check only by the threat of physical punishment (Curvin and Porter 1978; Weisman 1978).

KEY TERMS
big man
chief
circumscription
the process of materialization
storable staples

QUESTIONS TO THINK ABOUT

1. What are the characteristics of a big man? What are the limitations on his power?

2. What are the opportunities for control that enable leaders in chiefdoms (and later states) to increase the basis of their power? How does the opportunity to produce a surplus enable the chiefdom to expand?

3. What role do the following infrastructural conditions have on the transformation of chiefdoms to states: population growth, intensive agriculture, and circumscription?

4. What is the infrastructural and structural (administrative) basis of the Inca empire? How did the empire manage to incorporate such a vast territory into its control? What did the empire offer the people in return?

5. What is the role of ideology in reinforcing the power of state rulers? What importance do material objects have in transforming ideology into shared experience that support the status quo?

CHAPTER 13

Class and Caste

Down and out in Sao Paulo, Brazil.

Class and Power
Emics, Etics, and Class Consciousness
Class and Lifestyle

Peasant Classes

The Image of Limited Good

A "Culture of Poverty"?
Poverty in Naples

Castes in India
Caste from the Top Down and Bottom Up

Summary

America Now: Is There a Ruling Class in the United States?

Now we examine the principal varieties of stratified groups found in state societies. We begin with groups known as *classes*. We will see that people who live in state societies think and behave in ways that are determined to a great extent by their membership in stratified groups and by their position in a stratification hierarchy. The values and behavior of such groups are in turn often related to a struggle for access to the structural and infrastructural sources of wealth and power. In this regard, to what extent can subordinated classes be seen as the authors of their own fates? Do the poor have cultural traditions that keep them down? Shall we blame the unemployed for being unemployed? Next, we move on to the hierarchical groups known as *castes*, comparing them, especially castes in Hindu India, with classes and other hierarchical groups.

Class and Power

All state societies are organized into a hierarchy of groups known as classes. A **class** is a group whose members possess similar amounts of power within a stratified society. **Power** is the ability to force other people to obey requests or demands. In practice, power depends on the ability to provide or take away essential goods and services, and this ability in turn ultimately depends on who controls access to energy, resources, technology, and the means of physical and psychological coercion.

The beginnings of class hierarchies can be traced to big man and chiefdom societies. Chiefdoms often kept war captives as slaves and drew further distinctions of rank between commoners and a ruling elite. Even big man societies sometimes kept small numbers of slaves and recognized distinctions of rank for the members of the big man's family and his closest allies. But the fullest elaboration of class systems occurs in state societies.

All state societies necessarily have at least two classes arranged hierarchically: the rulers and the ruled.

Where more than two classes exist, they are not necessarily all arranged hierarchically with respect to each other. For example, fishermen and neighboring farmers are usually regarded as two separate classes because they relate to the ruling class in distinctive ways; have different patterns of ownership, rent, and taxation; and exploit entirely different sectors of the environment. Yet neither has a clear-cut power advantage or disadvantage with respect to the other. Similarly, anthropologists often speak of an urban as opposed to a rural lower class although the quantitative power differentials between the two may be minimal.

One other feature of classes should be noted: They come in relatively closed and open systems.

In **open-class systems,** people can move up or down the hierarchy as in modern Western democracies. In **closed-class systems,** there is little mobility up or down.

In medieval Europe, for example, serfs remained serfs for life. At their extreme, closed-class systems strongly resemble castes and ethnic groups.

Emics, Etics, and Class Consciousness

Class is an aspect of culture in which emic and etic points of view often differ sharply (Berreman 1981:18). Many social scientists accept class distinction as real and important only when the members of the class are aware of their class identity and act in unison. For a group to be considered a class, its members must be conscious of having common interests and a common identity. Other social scientists believe that classes exist only when people with similar forms and quantities of social power organize into interest groups such as political parties or labor unions. The position we favor is that classes exist if there are actual concentrations of power in certain groups, regardless of any shared awareness of class identity among the people concerned (such as the American corporate elite) and regardless of whether the groups are represented by political parties, unions, or other organizations.

From an etic and behavioral viewpoint, classes can exist even when the members of the class deny that they constitute a class.

Classes can exist even when, instead of collective organizations, they have organizations that compete, such as rival business corporations or rival unions (DeMott, 1990). Subordinate classes lacking class consciousness are obviously not exempt from the domination of ruling classes. Similarly, ruling classes containing antagonistic and competitive elements nonetheless dominate those who lack power. Of course, there is no disputing the importance of a people's belief about the shape and origin of their stratification hierarchy. Consciousness of a common plight among the members of a downtrodden and exploited class may very well lead to the outbreak of organized class warfare.

Consciousness is thus an element in the struggle between classes, but it is not essential for the existence of class differences.

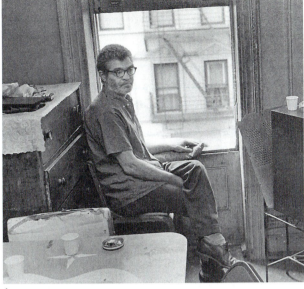

A.

B.

Poverty and Power

These people are both impoverished and disempowered. **A.** *An inner-city man;* **B.** *This tragic figure haunts the streets of Washington D.C., the capital of the richest country in the world.*

Class and Lifestyle

Classes differ from one another not only in amount of power per capita but also in broad areas of culture and lifestyle. Peasants, urban industrial wage workers, middle-class suburbanites, and upper-class chief executive officers of large corporations differ in their lifestyles. The contrast between them is as great as the contrast between life in an Inuit igloo and life in a Mbuti camp in the Ituri forest.

Classes have their own subcultures made up of distinctive work patterns, architecture, home furnishings, diet, dress, domestic routines, sex and mating practices, magico-religious rituals, art, and ideology. In many instances, different classes even have different dialects. Moreover, because their body parts may be exposed to sun, wind, and callus-producing friction, working-class people tend to look different from their "superiors." Further distinctions result from dietary specialties—the fat and the rich were once synonymous, as the expression "fat cats" reminds us. (Today, in advanced capitalist societies, fatness is a sign of a diet overloaded with fats and sugars, together with a lack of exercise, and is associated with poverty rather than with wealth.)

Throughout almost the entire evolutionary career of stratified societies, class identity has been at least as explicit as the distinction between male and female genders. The Chinese Han dynasty peasant, the Inca commoner, or the Russian serf could not expect to survive to maturity without knowing how to recognize members of the "superior" classes. Any lingering doubts were removed by state-enforced standards of dress: Only the Chinese nobility could wear silk clothing, only the European feudal overlords could carry daggers and swords, and only the Inca rulers could wear gold ornaments. Violators were put to death. In the presence of their "superiors," commoners still perform definite rituals of subordination, among which lowering the head, removing the hat, averting the eyes, kneeling, bowing, crawling, or maintaining silence unless spoken to occur almost universally.

Throughout much of the world, class identity continues to be sharp and unambiguous.

Among most contemporary nations, differences in class-linked lifestyles show little prospect of diminishing or disappearing. Indeed, given the convergence in former communist countries toward market economies, extremes of poverty and wealth may be on the rise. The contrast between the lifestyles of the rich and powerful and those of people living in peasant villages or urban shantytowns may be greater than ever before.

Class and Lifestyle
East Harlem

Class and Lifestyle
Hampton Beach, New Hampshire.

Caracas Shantytown
Squatters in Latin American cities often enjoy the best views since apartment houses were not built on hilltops because of lack of water. But the squatters have to carry their water up the hill in cans.

During the recent period of industrial advance, governing classes throughout the world have gone from horse-drawn carriages to Rolls Royces to private jets, whereas their subordinates find themselves without even a donkey or a pair of oxen. The elites now jet to the world's best medical centers to be treated with the most advanced medical technology, whereas vast numbers of less fortunate people have never heard of the germ theory of disease and can't even afford penicillin. Elites attend the best universities, whereas over 1.4 billion of the world's adults remain illiterate (Brown et al. 1993:122).

Peasant Classes

About 40 percent of the people in the world make a living from farming and are members of one kind of peasant class or another.

Peasants are people who use nonindustrial technologies to cultivate land in state societies and pay rent and/or taxes in the form of cash, crops, or services to elite groups for the use of the land.

All peasants produce a surplus that flows into the urban centers. In archaic states, the agricultural labor of peasants fed the craft workers, the merchants, the priesthood, the military and the political elite. The peasantry of medieval Europe, for example, paid half of their annual harvest to their lords. The productivity of intensive agriculture clearly benefited the ruling elite more than it benefited the peasants who produced the food.

Three major types of peasant class can be distinguished:

1. **Feudal peasants.** These peasants are subject to the control of a decentralized hereditary ruling class whose members provide military assistance to one another but do not interfere in one another's territorial domains.

Feudal peasants, or "serfs," inherit the opportunity to use a particular parcel of land; hence they are said to be "bound" to the land.

For the privilege of raising their own food, feudal peasants render unto the lord rent in kind or in money. Rent may also take the form of labor service in the lord's kitchens, stables, or fields (Bloch 1964).

Feudalism and feudal peasants are fast disappearing from the world, but a heritage of feudal class relations is an important component in the underdevelopment of many Third World countries. This heritage remains strong in several Central and South American countries, especially in Guatemala, El Salvador, Ecuador, and Peru. In these countries, landownership continues to be concentrated in huge estates owned by small numbers of politically powerful families. The peasants who live on or near these estates depend on the big landowners for access to land, water, loans, and emergency assistance. The extreme disparity in landholdings and the semifeudal relationships between the estate owners and the peasants lie behind the guerrilla movements that are found throughout this region (Stern 1988).

2. **Agromanagerial state peasantries.** Where the state is strongly centralized, as in ancient Peru, Egypt, Mesopotamia, and China, peasants may be directly subject to state control in addition to, or in the absence of, control by a local landlord class.Unlike the feudal peasants, agromanagerial peasants are subject to frequent conscription for labor brigades drawn from villages throughout the realm to build roads, dams, irrigation canals, palaces, temples, and monuments (Yates 1990).

Agromanagerial peasants provide **corvee labor** (forced labor) which is extracted by the state for the construction of public works. In return, the state makes an effort to feed its peasants in case of food shortages caused by droughts or other calamities.

The pervasive bureaucratic control over production and lifestyles in the ancient agromanagerial states has often been compared to the treatment of peasants who until recently were under communist rule in China, Albania, and Cambodia. The state in these countries was all powerful, setting production quotas, controlling prices, and extracting taxes in kind and in labor.

3. **Capitalist peasants.** In Africa, Latin America, India, and Southeast Asia, feudal and agromanagerial types of peasantries have been replaced by peasants who enjoy increased opportunities to buy and sell land, labor, and food in competitive price markets. Most of the world's remaining peasants belong to this category. The varieties of structured inferiority within this group defy any simple definition.

Capitalist peasants own land but most are in debt to large landowners; others are subordinate to banks that hold mortgages and promissory notes.

In more isolated or unproductive regions, holdings may be very small, giving rise to the phenomenon

Mexican Peasants
Plowing near Oaxaca.

known as "penny capitalism" (that is, frequent buying and selling of small quantities of food and handicrafts).

The Image of Limited Good

A recurrent question concerning the plight of contemporary peasant communities is the extent to which they are victims of their own values. It has often been noted, for example, that peasants distrust innovations and cling to their old ways of doing things. Based on his study of the village of Tzintzuntzan, in the state of Michoacan, Mexico, George Foster (1967) has developed a general theory of peasant life based on a concept called the **image of limited good**, the peasant worldview in which all desired things are considered finite so that if one person takes a lot, everyone else is deprived. According to Foster, the people of Tzintzuntzan, like many peasants throughout the world, believe that life is a dreary struggle, that very few people can achieve success.

According to the image of limited good, everything is perceived as finite: land, wealth, health, love, friendship, honor, respect, status, power, influence, safety, and security. Everything is scarce; successful individuals take more than their fair share from a common pool, thereby succeeding at the expense of other people.

Peasants can accept individuals who manage to increase their wealth if it comes from outside the village. However, if wealth comes from local activity, public opinion acts as a leveling mechanisms. For example, wealthy individuals may be forced to sponsor ceremonies, which reduce differential wealth. Successful peasants may also be the targets of gossip,

Box 13.1   A World of Limited Good

For the underlying, fundamental truth is that in an economy like Tzintzuntzan's, hard work and thrift are moral qualities of only the slightest functional value. Because of the limitations on land and technology, additional hard work does not produce a significant increment in income. It is pointless to talk of thrift in a subsistence economy because usually there is no surplus with which to be thrifty. Foresight, with careful planning for the future, is also a virtue of dubious value in a world in which the best-laid plans must rest on a foundation of chance and capriciousness.

Source: Foster 1967:150–151.

envy, physical violence, and hostility. Accordingly, peasants try to hide their good fortune and are reluctant to even attempt to change their way of life (see Box 13.1).

Because peasants are fearful that someone else might get the best of them, they are reluctant to cooperate or agree to leadership from within the community. This theory assumes that peasants also avoid economic progress and the accumulation of wealth because they want to avoid arousing envy and suspicion. Under these circumstances, peasant conservatism is seen as a rational attitude that provides the maximum of security.

Although an image of limited good exists in many peasant villages in Mexico and elsewhere, it is not clear that it prevents economic development.

In Tzintzuntzan, people were, if anything, overeager to accept community development projects sponsored by the United Nations. These projects ended in disasters that had more to do with inept aid policies than with the values held by the villagers. Further, most of the community's cash income came from jobs as migrant laborers in the United States. To get across the border, the migrants must bribe, scheme, and suffer great hardships. Yet 50 percent of them had succeeded in getting through, "many of them ten times or more" (Foster 1967:277).

Foster suggests, the image of limited good is not a crippling illusion but rather a realistic appraisal of the facts of life in a society where economic success or failure is capricious and hinged to forces wholly beyond one's control or comprehension.

James Acheson, who studied a community near Tzintzuntzan, has argued that without realistic economic opportunities, development would not occur.

If opportunities present themselves, some individuals will always take advantage of them, regardless of the image of limited good.

"It is one thing to say that Tarascans [the people of the region of Tzintzuntzan] are suspicious, distrustful, and uncooperative; it is another to assume that this lack of cooperation precludes all possibility for positive economic change" (Acheson 1972:1165; see also Acheson 1974; Foster 1974). The primary task in development is not only to change the peasants' view of their social and economic universe, but to provide expanding opportunities in an open system so peasants can feel safe in displaying initiative.

Ecuadorian Peasants

Note the "postage-stamp" farms on the steep hillsides.

A "Culture of Poverty"?

In studying the problems of people living in urban slums and shantytowns, Oscar Lewis thought he had found evidence for a distinct set of values and practices that he called the "**culture of poverty.**"

According to Oscar Lewis, some groups remain poor because they are crippled by certain cultural features that perpetuate poverty and that are passed down from one generation to the next.

Although not exactly comparable point by point, the concepts of the culture of poverty and the image of limited good resemble each other in many respects and represent similar attempts to explain the perpetuation of poverty by focusing on the traditions and values of subordinate classes.

Lewis (1966) pictured the poor in cities such as Mexico City, New York, and Lima as tending to be fearful, suspicious, and apathetic toward the major institutions of the larger society; as hating the police and being mistrustful of government; and as "inclined to be cynical of the church." They also have "a strong present-time orientation with relatively little disposition to defer gratification and plan for the future." This statement implies that poor people are less willing to save money and are more interested in "getting mine now" in the form of cellular phones, big-screen television, the latest-style clothing, and sporty automobiles. It also implies that the poor "blow" their earnings by getting drunk or going on buying sprees. Like George Foster, Lewis rec-ognized that in some measure the culture of poverty was partly a rational response to the objective conditions of powerlessness and poverty: "an adaptation and a reaction of the poor to their marginal position in a class-stratified society" (1966:21). But he also stated that once the culture of poverty comes into existence, it tends to perpetuate itself: "By the time slum children are six or seven they have usually absorbed the basic attitudes and values of their subculture. Thereafter they are psychologically unready to take full advantage of changing conditions or improving opportunities that may develop in their lifetime" (Lewis 1966:21). Lewis proposed that only 20 percent of the urban poor actually have the culture of poverty, implying that 80 percent fall into the category of those whose poverty results from infrastructural and structural conditions rather than from the traditions and values of a culture of poverty (Leeds 1970).

The concept of the culture of poverty has been criticized on the grounds that the poor have many values other than those stressed in the culture of poverty—values they share with other classes. Furthermore, values said to be distinctive of the urban poor are actually shared equally by the middle class. For example, being suspicious of government, politicians, and organized religion is not an exclusive poverty-class trait, nor is the tendency to spend above one's means. There is little evidence that the middle class as a whole lives within its income more effectively than poor people do. But when the poor mismanage their incomes, the consequences are much more serious. If the male head of a poor family yields to the temptation to buy

Image of Limited Good
Peasant women of Tzintzuntzan with their homemade pottery.

Squatters in Lima
Life on a garbage heap.

Box 13.2   The Causes of Poverty and Homelessness

The immediate cause of poverty and homelessness in advanced industrial countries such as Italy or the United States is the lack of jobs. But what determines the number of jobs available? Is it the amount of effort that the unemployed expend in trying to find employment? Many people seem to think that if only the poor and homeless would try harder, they would be able to find decent jobs. Government policies that seek to solve the problems of the poor and homeless by enrolling them in job training programs are based on the same premise—if the poor try harder, they will find employment. But this way of looking at poverty and homelessness involves a lot of misinformation and even hypocrisy, for it is the government (through the Federal Reserve System) that mandates what the rate of unemployment shall be. It does so by raising and lowering interest rates in order to prevent or lower inflation. (Raising interest rates slows down the rate of business expansion which in turn means fewer new jobs.) If the government were to create an abundance of jobs, working people would demand higher wages. In turn, the price of goods would go up and inflation would take over. The system as presently constructed demands that a certain percentage of people (at least 4 percent in the current estimates) must be losers in the competition for jobs that can raise people above the poverty line. Is it fair to blame the losers for their loss and to deny them the help they need?

Source: Adapted from Dehavenon 1995.

---

nonessential items, his children may go hungry or his wife may be deprived of medical attention.

The consequences of poverty result from being poor, not from an inability to defer gratification or live up to the norms of the dominant culture.

Poverty in Naples

Thomas Belmonte lived for a year in a slum neighborhood of Naples, Italy, a city that is known as the "Calcutta of Europe." Belmonte describes the neighborhood, Fontana del Re, as being inhabited by a subproletariat, or underclass, who lacked steady employment and who produced so little that they could not even be said to be exploited because they had nothing to be taken away from them. Gabriele, for example, collected metal junk and broke it into pieces with the help of his four children but also ran a little store during the day and drove a taxi for prostitutes at night. Others were part-time sailors, waiters, bartenders, dockworkers, and movers. Some groomed dogs, others were jacks-of-all-trades. Some were full-time smugglers, dope dealers, pickpockets, purse snatchers, and burglars. Still others were dressmakers, flower vendors, beggars, and old women who added to their small pensions "by selling contraband cigarettes and condoms, and greasy sandwiches and wine so bad it burned a hole through your gut." The children of Fontana del Re did odd jobs that earned them about 33 cents an hour. Pepe, the 11-year-old son of a cobbler, had a job in a TV repair shop; his face and chest were scarred from defective tubes that blew up when he tested them. Several neighborhood children made daily forays to pry open the trunks of parked cars. Other children carried trays of espresso to offices and shops.

The people of Naples have many of Oscar Lewis's culture of poverty traits. But most of these traits are attributed to being penniless and lacking steady employment, not to being a member of a particular subculture.

Poverty in Naples

The infamous one-room hovels of the Bassi, usually without ventilation, running water, separate toilets, or heating, are home for tens of thousands of Neapolitan families.

Box 13.3   The Broken Fountain: Culture or Poverty?

The poor hesitate to plan for the future because they are hard-put to stay afloat in the present, and not because of a "present-time orientation." They have no trouble re-calling the high and low points of their past. Their avoid-ance of banks relates to a realistic fear of inflation and a realistic mistrust of the literate officialdom. They do not patronize department stores because they prefer to culti-vate their own, more personalized networks of local credit, marketing, and exchange. In direct contradiction to Lewis's formulation, the poor of Naples purchase vital supplies wisely and in bulk. They place numerous cultural controls on consumption, wasting nothing. They are ha-bituated to delaying gratifications in terms of clothing, housing, plumbing, heating, travel, transportation, and entertainment. If in good times they allow themselves the one luxury of channeling surplus funds into good, abun-dant food, I think it ethnocentric to label them irrational or immature, since this is how they sublimate a histori-cally inherited and confirmed terror of hunger.

Confronted by a scarcity of opportunities, they be-come resigned, to preserve their sanity, and do not think to transcend their condition so long as they remain in underdeveloped Naples.... They have a culture that is simultaneously against poverty, adapted to the stresses of poverty, and mangled by poverty. But they have a culture which is also fashioned out of a great Mediter-ranean tradition, in the crucible of a great Mediter-ranean city. Their culture reflects their various and inge-nious strategies for survival and their low position in a hierarchy, in other words, it is a class culture as well as a regional one....

The Neapolitan urban poor are fashion-wise, street-wise, and urbane. They are not provincial. They live close to the gates of power in the wards of a great city, but un-like proletarians they are not integrated into the political and ideological currents of mass culture. They inhabit a world connected and apart from the main, a dense and crowded urban world, submerged; a crude, loud, pushy world where the moral order is exposed as a fraud which conceals the historical ascendancy of cunning and force. (Belmonte 1979:144)

Castes in India

Indian **castes** are closed, endogamous, and stratified descent groups.

Castes bear many resemblances to closed classes, eth-nic groups, and social races. No sharp line can be drawn between the castes of India and such groups as the Amish or African Americans in the United States or the Inca elite. However, some features of the In-dian caste hierarchy are unique and deserve special attention.

The unique features of Indian castes have to do with the fact that the caste hierarchy is an integral part of Hinduism, the religion of most people in In-dia. (This does not mean that one must be a Hindu in order to belong to a caste. Muslim and Christian castes also exist in India.)

It is a matter of religious conviction in India that all peo-ple are not spiritually equal and that the gods have estab-lished a hierarchy of groups.

This hierarchy consists of the four major **varnas**, or grades of being. According to the earliest traditions (for example, the Hymns of Rigveda), the four varnas correspond to the physical parts of Manu, who gave rise to the human race through dismemberment:

- his head became the Brahmans (priests)
- his arms the Kshatriyas (warriors)
- his thighs the Vaishyas (merchants and craftsmen)
- his feet the Shudras (menial workers)

According to Hindu scripture, an individual's varna is determined by a descent rule; that is, it corresponds to the varna of one's parents and is unalterable during one's lifetime.

The basis of all Hindu morality is the idea that each varna has its appropriate rules of behavior, or "path of duty" (**dharma**).

At the death of the body, the soul meets its fate in the form of a transmigration into a higher or lower being (**karma**). Those who follow their dharma will be re-warded with a higher point on Manu's body during their next life. Deviation from the dharma will result in reincarnation in the body of an outcaste or even a wild animal (Long 1987).

One of the most important aspects of the dharma is the practice of certain taboos regarding marriage, eating, and physical proximity.

Giati

Marriage below one's varna is generally regarded as a defilement and pollution. Acceptance of food cooked or handled by persons below one's varna is also a defilement and pollution, and any bodily contact between Brahman and Shudra is forbidden.

In parts of India, certain castes outside the varna structure were not only untouchable but also unseeable, and therefore these people could come out only at night. The worst of these restrictions became illegal after India gained its independence at mid-century.

Although the general outlines of this system are agreed on throughout Hindu India (Long 1987; Maloney 1987a; 1987b), enormous regional and local differences occur in the finer details of the ideology and practice of caste relationships. The principal source of these differences is the fact that it is not the varna but thousands of internally stratified subdivisions known as *jatis* (or subcastes) that constitute the real functional endogamous units. Moreover, even jatis of the same name ("washermen," "shoemakers," "herders," and so on) further divide into local endogamous subgroups and exogamous lineages (Klass 1979).

Today, India's legal system discourages discrimination based on caste identity. Yet caste still plays an important part in people's every day lives. Hindu religion continues to have powerful sanctions against those who violate caste prescriptions.

The people of India vary widely in skin color—in general people in the north tend to be lighter than those in the south. But unlike the racialized situation of America's blacks and whites (often also called castes), physical appearance does not indicate jati identity so that dark skin and high-caste status can occur together (Sanjek 1994a).

Caste from the Top Down and Bottom Up

There are two very different views of the Hindu caste system. The view that predominates among Westerners is top down. It conforms largely to the emics of the top-ranking Brahman caste.

Each caste and subcaste has a hereditary occupation that guarantees its members basic subsistence and job security.

The lower castes render vital services to the upper castes. Hence, the upper castes know they cannot get along without the lower castes and do not abuse them. In times of crisis, the upper castes will extend emergency assistance in the form of food or loans. Moreover, because the Hindu religion gives everyone a convincing explanation of why some are inferior

Untouchables
Caste in India must be seen from the bottom up to be understood.

and others superior, members of lower castes allegedly do not resent being regarded as a source of pollution and defilement, and have no interest in changing the status of their caste in the local or regional hierarchy (Dumont 1970).

The other view—the view from the bottom up—makes the Indian caste system hard to distinguish from other kinds of hierarchical groups such as classes and ethnic groups with which Westerners are familiar. Critics of the top-down view point out that whites in the United States once insisted that the Bible justified slavery and that the slaves were well treated, contented with their lot in life, and not interested in changing their status. According to Joan Mencher, who has worked and lived among the untouchable castes of southern India, the error in the top-down view is just as great in India as in the United States.

The lowest castes are not satisfied with their station in life and do not believe they are treated fairly by their caste superiors.

As for the security allegedly provided by the monopoly over such professions as smiths, washermen, barbers, and potters, such occupations taken together never engaged more than 10 to 15 percent of the total Hindu population. Thus caste professions never provided basic subsistence for the majority of the members of most castes. Among the Chamars, for example, who are known as leatherworkers, only a small portion of the caste engages in leatherwork. In the countryside, almost all Chamars provide a source of cheap agricultural labor. When questioned about their low station in life, many of Mencher's low-caste informants explained that they had to depend on the other castes because they had no land of their own. Did landowners in times of extreme need or crisis actually give free food and assistance to their low-caste dependents? "To my informants, both young and old, this sounds like a fairytale" (Mencher 1974, 1978).

Anthropological studies of actual village life in India have yielded a picture of caste relationships drastically opposed to the ideals posited in Hindu theology (Carroll 1977). One of the most important discoveries is that local jatis recurrently try to raise their ritual status. Such attempts usually take place as part of a general process by which local ritual status is adjusted to actual local economic and political power. Some low-ranking subcastes may passively accept their lot in life as a result of their karma assignment; such groups, however, tend to be wholly lacking in the potential for economic and political mobility. "But let opportunities for political and economic advance appear barely possible and such resignation is likely to vanish more quickly than one might imagine" (Orans 1968:878).

The propensity for jatis to redefine their spiritual level is seen in the widespread lack of agreement over the shape of local ritual hierarchies as seen by inhabitants of the same village, town, or region. Even the lowest "untouchables" may reject the position others assign to them (Khare 1984).

The study of caste "dissensus" has long been a central concern of village India researchers (Barber 1968). Kathleen Gough (1959) indicates that in villages of South India, the middle reaches of the caste hierarchy may have as many as 15 castes whose positions are ambiguous or in dispute.

Different individuals and families in the same caste give different versions of the rank order of their group in an attempt to redefine their status.

Elsewhere, even the claims of Brahman subcastes to ritual superiority are openly contested (Srinivas 1955). The conflict among jatis concerning their ritual position may involve prolonged litigation in the local courts and if not resolved may lead to violence and bloodshed (see Berreman 1981; Cohn 1955).

The stratification system of India is noteworthy not merely for the presence of endogamous descent groups possessing real or imagined racial and cultural differences. Every state-level society has such groups. It is, rather, that India has an extraordinary profusion of such groups. Nonetheless, the caste system of India is fundamentally similar to the systems of other countries that have closed classes and numerous ethnic and racial minorities.

Summary

1. Class differences involve both differential access to power and profound differences in lifestyles.

2. The understanding of class and all other forms of social stratification is made difficult by the failure to separate emic and etic versions of stratification hierarchies. From an etic and behavioral point of view, classes can exist even if the members show no emic recognition of their existence and even if segments of the same class compete.

3. In open hierarchies, ruling-class membership can change rapidly from one generation to the next. Similarly, subordinate classes need not be conscious of their identity and may exist only in an etic and behavioral sense.

4. About 40 percent of the people in the world today are members of peasant classes. Peasants are structured inferiors who farm with preindustrial technologies and pay rent or taxes.

5. Three major varieties of peasant can be distinguished: feudal, agromanagerial, and capitalist. Their structured inferiority depends in the first case on the inability to acquire land; in the second, on the existence of a powerful managerial elite that sets production and labor quotas; and in the third, on the operation of a price market in land and labor controlled by big landlords, corporations, and banks.

6. Among peasant classes, an image of limited good is widespread. However, contradictory values and attitudes encourage innovations and risk taking under appropriate structural and infrastructural conditions.

7. In Tzintzuntzan, despite the image of limited good, men struggled for a chance to work as migrant laborers, and both men and women participated in a series of ill-fated development experiments in the hope of bettering their lives.

8. The counterpart of the image of limited good for subordinate urban classes is the culture of poverty.

This concept focuses on the values and traditions of the urban poor as an explanation for poverty. However, many of the values in the culture of poverty, such as distrust of authority, consumerism, and improvidence, are also found in more affluent classes.

9. Much of the behavior of the underclass, as in the case of Naples, can be understood as a consequence of chronic unemployment.

10. Castes are closed endogamous groups that resemble classes and ethnic groups. They are epitomized by the varnas and jatis of India.

11. Traditional views of Indian castes have been dominated by top-down idealizations in which the lower castes are represented as voluntarily accepting their subordinate status.

12. Bottom-up studies show that Indian castes struggle for upward mobility and attempt to bring their caste's ranking in line with their economic status.

AMERICA NOW

Is There a Ruling Class in the United States?

Most Americans do not think of themselves as being members of a class, and class has always been downplayed as a factor in American history. Thus, according to former president George Bush, "Class is for European democracies or something else—it isn't for the United States of America. We are not going to be divided by class" (DeMott 1990:11). But like all state-organized societies, the United States is a stratified society and has a complex system of class, ethnicity, and race.

There is no doubt that the United States is a highly stratified society. This can be seen from the data on the distribution of wealth among U.S. families. According to the Federal Reserve research survey, in 1992 the richest ½ percent of U.S. families owned 22.8 percent of the total net wealth while the top 1 percent owned 30.4 percent and the top 10 percent owned 67.2 percent. That is, the top 10 percent owned more than twice the total of what the bottom 90 percent owned (Kennickell et al. 1996).

The most important question that can be asked about class in the United States is whether there is a ruling class. Paradoxically, this is a subject about which relatively little is known. The existence of a ruling class in the United States seems to be negated by the ability of the people as a whole to vote political officeholders in or out of office by secret ballot. Yet the fact that less than half of the voting-age population votes in presidential elections suggests that the majority of citizens distrust the candidates' promises or doubt that one candidate can do anything more than any other to make life significantly better. The actual selection of political candidates and the financing and conduct of election campaigns are controlled through special-interest groups and political action committees. Small coalitions of powerful individuals working through lobbyists, law firms, legislatures, the courts, executive and administrative agencies, and the mass media can decisively influence the course of elections and national affairs. The great bulk of the decision-making process consists of responses to pressures exerted by special-interest groups (Drew 1983; Sabato 1989). In the campaigns for Congress, the candidate who spends the most money usually wins.

Those who claim that the United States has no ruling class argue that power is dispersed among many different contending blocs, lobbies, associations, clubs, industries, regions, income groups, ethnic groups, states, cities, age groups, legislatures, courts, and unions, and that no coalition powerful enough to dominate all the others can form (Dahl 1981). But the crucial question is this: Is there a class of people who share a set of underlying interests in the perpetuation of the status quo and who by virtue of their extreme wealth are able to set limits to the kinds of laws and executive policies that are enacted and followed out?

The evidence for the existence of such a category of people consists largely of studies of the extent of interlocking memberships on corporate boards of directors and the concentration of ownership and wealth in giant corporations and well-to-do families. This kind of data alone cannot prove the existence of a ruling class, because the problem remains of how boards of directors and wealthy families actually influence decisions on crucial matters such as the rate of inflation, unemployment, national health service, energy policy, tax structure, resource depletion, pollution, military spending, and urban blight.

The concentration of wealth and economic power in the United States shows at least that there is a real potential for such influence to be exerted (Roberts and Brintnall 1982:259). According to the Federal Reserve Board (Kennickell et al. 1992), the richest 1 percent of U.S. families owned

45 percent of all nonresidential real estate

49 percent of all publicly held stock

78 percent of all trusts

62 percent of all business assets

About half of stocks and bonds are owned by institutional investors, who administer pension funds, trust funds, and insurance companies. It is the corporations, families, and people who control these institutional investors that have the greatest economic power. As a result of the wave of buyouts and mergers that took place in the United States during the 1980s and 1990s, the concentration of economic power has continued to increase. By the early 1990s, the share of wealth of the top 1 percent was approximately double what it had been in the 1970s (Thurow 1995).

A rough idea of the trend toward greater concentration of economic power can be derived from changes in family income. Between 1977 and 1989, the average pretax incomes of the top 1 percent of American families rose 77 percent, whereas the pretax incomes of the bottom 40 percent of families fell by between 1 and 9 percent. (Remember, these were the years when women were entering the labor force to supplement the male breadwinner's income.) The United States has greater extremes of rich and poor than any other industrial nation (Bradsher 1995).

Another revealing statistic is the growing disparity between the incomes of chief executive officers and ordinary employees. In the 1970s, CEOs made 35 times what employees made; in 1990, they were making 120 times more (Noah 1991), and by 1995 they were making close to 200 times what the average worker made (Weinstein 1995).

It is entirely possible, therefore, that a small group of individuals and families exerts a decisive influence over the policies of a small but immensely powerful group of corporations. Some of the individuals and families involved are well known. Besides the Mellons, they include Rockefellers, Du Ponts, Fords, Hunts, Pews, and Gettys. But it is a testament to the ability of the superrich to live in a world apart that the names of many other powerful families are unknown to the general public. Anthropologists have been remiss in not studying the patterns of thoughts and actions of the superrich (Nader 1972).

KEY TERMS

agromanagerial peasants
capitalist peasants
caste
class
closed-class systems
corvee labor
culture of poverty
feudal peasants
free agency
image of limited good
open-class systems
peasants
power
varnas

QUESTIONS TO THINK ABOUT

1. What is power, and under what conditions is it more likely to be enforced?

2. Why does Foster believe that the image of limited good hinders development in Mexico?

3. What is the culture of poverty, and why has the concept been criticized?

4. What are the features of caste stratification? How is caste hierarchy challanged?

CHAPTER 14

Ethnicity, Race, and Racism

German anti-racist protest march at Dachau.

Ethnicity
PROFILE: Diversity among Hispanic Americans
Ethnic Empowerment
Confronting Ethnocentrism

Biological Races versus Social Races versus Ethnic Groups
The One-Drop Rule
Biological Race and Culture

The Competitive Dynamics of Ethnic and Racial Groups
Assimilation or Pluralism?
The Dynamics of Pluralism in the United States
Racial and Ethnic Chauvinism versus
    Class Consciousness

PROFILE: Elmhurst–Corona—Joining Forces Across
    Ethnic and Racial Lines

Defining Racism
The Wages of Racism
Why Africa Lags
Social Race in the United States
Racism on Campus
The Tragedy of Urban Black Youth

Summary

America Now: Race, Poverty, Crime, Drugs, and Welfare

Two other hierarchical groups associated with the rise of the state—ethnic groups and social races—are the subject of this chapter. How ethnic groups and social races differ from classes and castes is one of the questions to be considered. We shall also address the worldwide confusion concerning the relationship of biological race to social races and ethnic groups. Then we explore the dynamic processes that lead to more or less successful outcomes of the competition among social races and ethnic groups. We will pay special attention to the alternatives of assimilation and pluralism in the United States, where White racism against African Americans and other "non-Whites" continues to flourish. This leads to a critique of the key evidence for White superiority. Ethnic and racial chauvinists of any ilk may have a hard time setting aside beliefs, often unconsciously held, about how Europeans came to dominate other cultures.

Ethnicity

One of the most important consequences of the rise of the state was the appearance of ethnic groups. States achieved prominence in political evolution precisely because of their ability to extend boundaries to include near and distant polities such as chiefdoms and other states. Ethnic groups first formed when conquered populations retained distinctive linguistic and cultural features associated with their preconquest status. In modern times, ethnic groups have formed as much through migration as through conquest.

An **ethnic group** is a group that has been incorporated into a state through conquest or migration, that maintains distinctive cultural and/or linguistic traditions, and has a sense of a separate, shared, and age-old identity.

Ethnic groups have always existed in state societies because people who live in separate regions develop separate cultural traditions and language dialects.

Members of ethnic groups often believe that they have a distinctive appearance, that they are descended from common ancestors, and that they share distinctive traditions and customs. Some ethnic groups, such as the "White ethnics" (Irish Americans, Italian Americans, Polish Americans, Jewish Americans, Greek Americans, and so forth) in the United States, see themselves as divisions or branches of a single racial group. But other ethnic groups (such as Cubans in Miami, Haitians in New York) may themselves recognize that they are not racially homogeneous.

Ethnicity is believed to be associated with distinctive cuisines, holidays, religious beliefs, dances, folklore, dress, and other traditions, but the single most powerful cultural source of ethnic identity is the possession of a common language or dialect. Use of a common language or dialect instills a sense of community that is powerful enough to override regional differences, differences of class, and the absence of other kinds of common cultural traditions.

The emergence of the ethnic category "Hispanic" in the United States illustrates this point. Hispanics include people who are recent immigrants from Spain, from the Spanish-speaking Caribbean islands, and from various parts of Mexico and Central and South America, plus descendents of the Spanish-speaking settlers in the West and Southwest. The cultures of Hispanic Americans, with the exception of their common language, differ at least as much as the cultures of Polish Americans and Italian Americans differ from each other (see Profile 14.1).

Profile 14.1   Diversity among Hispanic Americans

Hispanic groups in the United States (also called Latinos) are heterogeneous because of historical and local conditions, which have led to the creation of distinct cultural adaptations to American culture. According to the 1990 U.S. census, approximately 60% of Hispanic Americans are of Mexican origin, 12% are of Puerto Rican origin, 5% are of Cuban origin, and 23% are "other Hispanic," mostly from Central and South America and the Dominican Republic.

Differences in economic success and family structure distinguish Hispanic groups. For example, mainland Puerto Ricans, more than any other group, are economi-

cally disadvantaged. They have more families headed by single females and have the highest rate of welfare dependency. Despite the "advantage" of U.S. citizenship, Puerto Ricans are concentrated in urban areas of the northeast with declining manufacturing jobs. Between 1950-1970, population growth and a decline in subsistence agriculture in Puerto Rico resulted in high rates of labor expulsion and migration. In the U.S., Puerto Ricans faced discrimination in the highly unionized labor force. Because they were not subject to deportation, they would not work for low wages and were effectively excluded from the work force. Employers instead opted to hire

(continued)

Profile 14.1   Diversity among Hispanic Americans *(continued)*

other undocumented immigrant groups, such as East Indians and Dominicans, who were willing to work for less.

Cuban Americans, on the other hand, are exceptionally successful, especially the first wave of refugees that arrived in 1959 and received government assistance. Many are political refugees who are concentrated in Miami, where they have created an enclave economy with entrepreneurial activities and small businesses that create jobs for new arrivals and opportunities for economic mobility. Cuban Americans have also managed to preserve their culture. A section of Miami known as "Little Havana" has become a cultural center where artists, actors, and musicians preserve some Cuban traditions more than in Cuba itself.

Mexican Americans are by far the largest and oldest Hispanic group. Many have lived in the U.S. for several generations, as part of a Northern Mexican colonial population that dates back some 400 years. Two-thirds of Mexican Americans are concentrated in California, Texas and New Mexico; other states with more recent Mexican American populations include Illinois, Colorado, Arizona, and New Jersey. In the southwest, Mexicans have traditionally been a reliable source of agricultural wage labor. They have maintained close ties with relatives across the border and identify with Mexican culture. However, as the younger generation gains more education and economic power, the competitive individualistic norms of American culture are adopted. Other children of Mexican American immigrants may experience intense culture conflict due to what Diego Vigil (1988, 1997) terms "multiple marginalities"—confusion over identity, parents with limited education, a lack of well paying jobs. In most cases, the transition is achieved through identification with the mainstream but in others, these identity issues propel some Mexican American youths into gangs.

Hispanic populations are at different levels of integration into American society. Most American-born Hispanics speak better English than Spanish. Only a few call themselves Latino or Hispanic, and many want to be called "American." Many take on the attitudes and voting patterns of European Americans and believe there are too many immigrants in the U.S and that continued immigration depresses wages; up to 60 percent of second generation Hispanics favor legal sanctions against employers who hire undocumented workers.

Except for those who have very dark skin and are poor, most Hispanics are blending into the general population at least as fast as earlier white ethnic groups did. Many are moving into the suburbs, while immigrant newcomers find themselves working as undocumented workers in communities with segregated schools and with salaries that are 30 percent less than those of their legal counterparts. (Adapted from Weaver 1994a and Weaver 1994b)

Ethnic identity is amenable to change.

Throughout history, individuals and groups moved to new areas or changed their identities by acquiring membership in a different group. Many ethnic groups intermarried frequently and exchanged spouses to form political and economic alliances. There are also examples of individuals who changed their ethnic identities for personal reasons, or those who maintain multiple ethnicities and speak several languages (Smedley 1999).

As in the case of class identity, emic and etic versions of ethnicity may bear little resemblance to each other. Ethnics do not necessarily speak the language of their ancestors. Moreover, their ancestral customs are not necessarily the heritage of remote ancestors; some are actually the inventions of recent generations. Some

A Latino Extended Family in Texas
Some families date back several generations.

ethnic groups may neither speak the language of their ethnic ancestors nor preserve ancestral customs, old or new (Roosens 1989). Preservation of ethnic identity may merely result from marrying endogamously and using family names indicative of ethnic descent. Even high rates of intermarriage do not necessarily impede the continuity of an ethnic group: Various rules of descent can be used to retain the children of mixed marriages within the ethnic group of one of the parents.

Ethnic Empowerment

In a democracy, only those who speak up are heard; and outsiders never achieve a secure power base. Translated into the nitty gritty of ethnic politics, this means that for empowerment, nondominant ethnic groups need both to learn to speak loudly in their own voice and to rely primarily on their own material and ideological resources.

Wars and migration have been the major sources of the ethnic diversity we see around us. Captured and enslaved African peoples were transported against their will across the ocean, and Native Americans, defeated in their attempt to safeguard their homelands, were forced to move to distant reservations. Conquest also lies at the root of the Hispanic ethnic group in the Southwest and in California. Meanwhile, White ethnics, especially those from Ireland and from eastern and southern Europe, migrated under various degrees of compulsion in search of relief from religious or political persecution, military impressment, and the threat of outright starvation. Although each ethnic group has its distinctive history, they all share many experiences and have evolved along similar lines in response to similar pressures. Some groups, however, have been better prepared by their own cultural traditions to cope with the challenges of their new conditions of life.

Those ethnic groups with strong literate traditions and a history of individualized competition for upward mobility, are preadapted for competing in the rapidly changing world of an urban industrial society.

There is an ongoing effort to continue to promote ethnic pride and to revitalize old ethnic traditions, or to invent new ones. Young people, in unprecedented numbers, have taken up the study of languages spoken by their grandparents, promoted public festivals and parades to celebrate their cultural traditions, established various single-group ethnic social clubs, and vigorously campaigned to block or reverse affirmative action policies designed to help nonwhites.

Confronting Ethnocentrism

In the course of ethnic politics, each group tends to pay far more attention to its own origins, history, heroism, suffering, and achievements than to those of other ethnic groups. In this context, ethnicity turns out to mean an especially aggressive and virulent form of **ethnocentrism**, the sense that one's own ethnic group is superior to others.

The origins of ethnocentrism are linked to the concept of descent, the principle whereby individuals and groups establish their identities and relatedness.

Although theories of descent vary from culture to culture, the basic idea occurs universally, namely that individuals acknowledge a special relatedness to parents and to children that endures after death. Descent implies the preservation of some aspect of the substance or spirit of people in past and future generations and thus is a symbolic form of immortality. Descent lies at the heart of the formation of social races and ethnic groups. Various systems for identifying ethnic groups are in use throughout the world.

Whenever a large group interacts with another, a sense of unified opposition, whether it is based on religious, ethnic, national, or racial affiliation, can act as a dividing force. Individuals are not usually preoccupied with group identity until they are threatened. When a group is in conflict or at war with another group, members become acutely aware of their group identity—even to the point where it may outweigh concern for individual needs or survival. The preconditions for such conflicts usually consist of infrastructural deficiencies (resource shortages derived from population pressure) and differences in the distribution of wealth and quality of life. The more stressful the environment, the more likely neighboring groups will become preoccupied with one another.

The process of dehumanizing a perceived ethnic enemy may occur in stages—starting with intense prejudice toward an unwanted group and escalating to physical struggle through forced assimilation, resettlement, and genocide under the label of "ethnic cleansing." After the Holocaust, many believed that systematized atrocities could never occur again. But according to the Carter Center in Atlanta, ethnic terrorism is on the rise, with most conflicts taking place between ethnic groups within the boundaries of single countries; Protestants and Catholics in Ireland; Jews and Palestinians in Israel; Hutus and Tutsis in Burundi; and ethnic Albanians and Serbs in Kosovo, just to name a few (Volkan 1997).

Each ethnic group is the product of shared historical experiences that serve to unite and distinguish the group from others and give it a distinct identity.

The terms "**chosen trauma**" and "**chosen glory**" has been used to describe the collective memory of a past calamity or a heroic event that befell a group. These feelings about the past are brought into the present and that serves as a collective origin myth for defining a distinctive ethnic identity. Inclusion in the origin myth legitimates a people's status as members of a group. Adopting a chosen trauma enhances a sense of victimization that unifies the group and justifies ethnic aggression to reverse misfortune into triumph, whereas reactivating a chosen glory (such as a war of independence) is a legendary event that bolsters a group's self-esteem (Volkan 1997).

Biological Races versus Social Races versus Ethnic Groups

Biological races are etic populations in which several genes occur together with distinctive frequencies over many generations.

The popular conception of biological race is flawed because scientists do not agree on which genes should be used to establish racial boundaries. The problem is that as the number of genes that are used to distinguish one race from another increases, the less likely it is that they occur together over many generations (see Box 14.2). This lack of genetic continuity results from the fact that human populations exchange genes through mating, creating ever-changing patterns of genetic variations (Armelagos and Goodman 1994).

Racial classification schemes do not reflect any natural subdivision of the human species into biologically distinct groups.

Human populations have always engaged in so much interbreeding that it would be meaningless to speak of fixed boundaries between races. There is not enough genetic variation among humans to qualify any group as having distinct genetic traits. Genetically humans are far more similar to one another than they are different.

Despite the lack of genetic boundaries, undeniable physical differences between populations are used to classify people. These classifications are more appropriately called **social races**, or groups that are assumed to be biologically different from each other,

Box 14.2   Racial Classification Schemes Explain Very Little about Genetic Variation

The biological fact of human variation is that there are no traits that are inevitably associated with one another. Morphological features do vary from region to region, but they do so independently, not in packaged sets. For example, we could divide the world into two groups of blondes and brunettes, but if we start adding other traits like skin color, eye color, stature, blood type, etc., it wouldn't take long before we have a race with only one person in it. Despite the obvious physical differences between people from different regions, the vast majority of human genetic variation occurs within populations, not between them.

Only about 6 percent of human variation is accounted for by race, according to a classic study done in 1972 by geneticist Richard Lewontin of Harvard. While most anthropologists believe that race is no longer a useful concept for describing human variation, medical researchers find racial categories useful for organizing health related data; each year dozens of reports in health journals show purported differences between the races in susceptibility to disease, infant mortality rates, life expectancy, and other markers of public health. In the United States, African American infants are almost two

and a half times more likely to die within the first 11 months of life than non-African American infants. African Americans are almost twice as likely as Euro Americans to suffer from hypertension, or high blood pressure—a condition that carries with it an increased risk of heart failure and other cardiovascular diseases. And it's been shown that Native Americans are far more likely than other ethnic groups to carry an enzyme that makes it harder to metabolize alcohol; this would leave Native Americans genetically more vulnerable to alcoholism.

Are these studies pointing at genetic differences between the races, or are they using race as a convenient scapegoat for health deficiencies whose causes might better be explained by a person's socioeconomic status and environment? The higher incidence of hypertension in African Americans can be attributed to higher dietary sodium levels, increased exposure to psychological stress, and limited access to health care. The hope is for the medical community to treat hypertension in African Americans more aggressively, but whether the findings really say anything about the role of race in disease is another matter altogether. (Adapted from Shreve 1994)

Ethnic Festivals

A. An Irish Parade in New York;   *B. Fiesta day in Ybov City, Florida;*   *C. Italian Festival in Boston;*
D. Japanese Festival in Los Angeles.

but are in fact classified according to culturally defined categories such as common descent, skin tone, and facial features. Moreover, children of mixed marriages automatically get their racial identity from the minority parent, which is a culturally defined practice rather than one with any biological justification.

Social races are assumed to have a biological basis, but are in fact culturally constructed.

Human populations have always engaged in so much interbreeding that it would be meaningless to speak of fixed boundaries between races. Also, the distribu-

tion of hereditary physical traits does not follow clear boundaries; there is often greater variation within a "racial" groups than between them.

Social races differ from ethnic groups only as a matter of degree. Social races claim common ancestry based on the practice of endogamy and rules of descent. They or others believe that they can be picked out in a crowd simply on the basis of their looks. The resemblance between social races and ethnic groups is so close that many people use the terms **ethnic group** and **race** interchangeably. Others, however, claim that racial differences are more permanent and visible than the differences in dress or language found among ethnics (see Wolf 1994).

Social race is an emic construct that can be used politically to justify prejudice and stratification.

Some African Americans, for example, claim that racial markers become the focus for discrimination by dominant ethnic and racial groups because they are indelible. As a result, racially different individuals have no chance to escape from the persecution and discrimination of the dominant group. The argument is only valid, however, because of culturally constructed principles such as descent and physical characterizations that are employed to give individuals a racial identity. As a matter of fact, social race identity is no more indelible than ethnic identity based on linguistic or cultural differences: The continuity of social races depends on how much intermarriage takes place and on how the children of mixed marriages are classified.

The One-Drop Rule

Various systems for identifying social races are in use throughout the world today. In the United States, African Americans are not identified as a distinct social race solely on the basis of their skin color. Reliance on skin color alone would leave the identity of millions of people in doubt because skin color (and other "African" and "Caucasian" traits) varies across a broad spectrum of nuanced differences from very dark to brown to very light as a result of recent and remote interracial matings and marriages (Root 1992). In the context of slavery and its aftermath, when it was U.S. official policy to discriminate against Blacks, Whites needed some rule or principle to categorize people as either Black or White so that the discrimi-

natory measures could be applied to Blacks who looked like Whites, but not to Whites who looked like Blacks. To solve this quandary, Whites constructed a one-drop rule:

According to the **one-drop rule,** a Black person was anyone who had the slightest amount of Black "blood" as attested to by having even one ancestor who was known to have been identified as Black (whether or not this ancestor himself or herself was also a child of a mixed marriage or mating).

By the one-drop rule still in force today, children of a mixed marriage between one biologically White and one biologically Black parent are socially black (Root 1992; Spickard 1992:16). Louisiana law declares anyone with at least 1/32 "Negro blood" to be legally Black. But scientifically we know that all of us inherit half of our cell nucleus genes from mother and half from father, so it is clear that race is culturally constructed and the rule is arbitrary.

A very different construction of social race prevails in Latin America and the Caribbean Islands. In Brazil, for example, racial categorizations depend mainly on the perceptions that people have of each other's appearance, with equal emphasis on skin tone and hair form. But a person's "racial" identity may also be influenced by his or her wealth and profession. Brazilians use many more terms for identifying any individual's particular combination of traits. In one study (Marvin Harris 1970) 492 terms were encountered. Thus, two people of the same "color" can be classified in different categories depending on their profession and economic status. The one-drop rule doesn't exist in Brazil; ancestry or descent is not important for racial identity. This means that children can have a

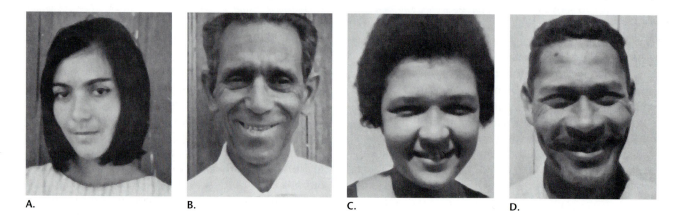

A.   B.   C.   D.

Brazilian Race-Color Variations

The great variety of facial features, skin color, and hair texture in modern Brazil suggests that it is futile to think about human beings in terms of a small number of fixed and sharply distinct races.

racial identity that is different from that of their parents, and further, that one child can be identified as the equivalent of "White" whereas his or her full brother or sister can be identified as the equivalent of "Black" (Harris et al. 1993). Although Brazil prides itself on its racial harmony, most darker-skinned Brazilians tend to be poorer and less educated. Brazilians of African descent, who are descendents of slaves, are poor because they have lacked access to land or commercial wealth, and upward social mobility is difficult. Poor darker-skinned Brazilians therefore face discrimination despite so much diversity (Kottak 1994).

Biological Race and Culture

The relationship between biological race and culture is a source of much confusion the world over. One of the most important tasks of anthropology is to clarify the difference between them.

Etically, a biological race is a population—an interbreeding group of people defined by a set of distinctive gene frequencies. A culture is a way of life.

A large-scale biological race does not have just one culture; it has hundreds of cultures. And these cultures cover the whole spectrum of cultural types, from bands and villages to states and empires. Thus people who belong to different biological races may possess very similar or even identical cultures, and people who possess very different cultures may belong to the same biological race.

In the United States, millions of racially diverse children and grandchildren of Asians and Africans have a way of life that is essentially similar to the way of life of the "Caucasian" majority. These biological and anthropological facts, however, are often ignored in the construction of social races. It is widely believed that certain traditions are inseparable from and exclusive to each social race, as implied, for example, in the concept "African culture." As we shall see momentarily, the sense of having a distinctive culture is important for the mobilization of resistance within disadvantaged social races and ethnic groups. However, the view that race and culture are rigidly linked is a form of racism that runs counter to all that is scientifically known about the transmissibility of cultures across racial and ethnic boundaries. It bears repeating that at birth, every healthy human infant, regardless of race, has the capacity to acquire the traditions, practices, values, and languages found in any of the world's five thousand or so different cultures.

The Competitive Dynamics of Ethnic and Racial Groups

The most important point to bear in mind about ethnic groups and social races is that they are invariably locked into a more or less open and conscious form of political, social, and economic struggle to protect or raise their positions in the stratification system. To a surprising degree, the class struggle predicted by Karl Marx has been overshadowed by race and ethnic struggles. Although class differences have rarely led to class consciousness and class solidarity, racial and ethnic groups the world over have been at the forefront of conscious and often violent struggles aimed at changing the stratification hierarchy.

Ethnic and racial groups rise or fall in the hierarchy depending on their numbers, their special cultural strengths and weaknesses, and their initial advantages or disadvantages during the formation of the stratification system. Thus, although many ethnic groups and social races are subject to severe forms of discrimination, segregation, and exploitation, others such as the Chinese living in Indonesia, may actually enjoy fairly high, though not dominant, status positions.

Assimilation or Pluralism?

Pluralism denotes the continuity of social races and ethnic groups within a regional or national population. The loss of a separate identity of an ethnic group or social race, through absorption by dominant groups, is called **assimilation.** The resurgence in recent times of an emphasis on ethnic and racial identity has made it clear that total assimilation is a rather rare outcome of the interaction of ethnic groups and social races with dominant groups. Some form of multiethnic and multiracial pluralism seems to be far more common. But the perpetuation of multiethnic and multiracial social groups differs in important ways from the preservation of their cultures.

Ethnic groups and social races may adopt the language of the majority, lose their old traditions, and become culturally similar to the dominant majority and yet remain unassimilated. (The change need not be one-sided—the dominant group may in turn adopt traditional ethnic foods and holidays, such as pizza and St. Patrick's Day.) Even extensive intermarriage need not lead to assimilation. This appears to be true of the European immigrant groups in the United States such as Scots, Germans, Jews, English, French, and Italians, whose rates of exogamy range as high as 30 or 40 percent (Alba 1990; Kivisto 1989). These groups maintain their identity through a principle of ambilineal descent (see Chapter 9, "Descent Rules" section), whereby children of mixed marriages shift from one ethnic identity to another as they see fit. The children of an Irish American–Italian American mixed marriage, for example, may invoke their Irish parent on Saint Patrick's Day and their Italian parent on the Feast of San Genaro.

Another important aspect of the dynamics of ethnic and racial groups is that these groups themselves consist of classes that do not necessarily have common interests.

Ethnic and racial elites may stand to gain more than the average person from intensifying group solidarity in the name of resisting assimilation.

Roger Sanjek (1972, 1977) studied the relationships among 23 "tribal" groups who live in the city of Accra, Ghana, and found that in terms of language, behavior, dress, residence, and facial markings, one group hardly differed from another. Nonetheless, politicians relied heavily on their "tribal" identities in competing for political office. Similarly, the tragic history of Lebanon cannot be understood apart from the private fortunes that both Christian and Muslim elites were able to amass as a result of drawn-out communal strife (Joseph 1978).

An emphasis on differences in language, religion, and other aspects of lifestyle increases a group's sense of solidarity, and this solidarity may help its members compete, especially in impersonalized, class-structured, capitalist societies.

Jewish, Chinese, Japanese, Greek, Syrian, Hindu, or Muslim merchants and businesspeople, for example, frequently enjoy important commercial advantages as a result of sharing information and obtaining loans and credit from their ethnic associates. Many Americans continue to use their ethnic networks actively when looking for jobs or a spouse. Many prefer to live in neighborhoods dominated by people with the same origins as themselves, and they continue to regard themselves as "Italians," "Poles," and so on, in addition to being Americans—two generations or more after their ancestors left the country of origin. Moreover, racial and ethnic consciousness, like class consciousness, is a necessary condition for mobilizing the mental and physical resources of vulnerable or downtrodden groups to defend or improve their position in the hierarchy. Thus, all ethnic and racial groups find themselves under pressure to cast their history and their achievements in the most favorable light.

The problem is that strong ethnic and racial solidarity carries with it the danger of backlash. In maintaining and increasing their own solidarity, social races and ethnic groups run the risk of increasing the dominant group's resentment and hence of becoming the scapegoats of discriminatory and even genocidal policies. The persecution of the Jews in Germany and Poland, the Hindu Indians in east and southern Africa, the Chinese in Indonesia, and the Muslims and Sikhs in India are some of the better-known examples of "successful" adaptations that were followed by mass slaughter or forced migrations.

The Dynamics of Pluralism in the United States

Although ethnic groups in the United States have moved toward assimilation, there is also a growing concern with preserving ethnicity identity. Glazer and Moynihan (1963) have stated that the most important point to be made about the "American melting-pot" is that it never occurred. They argue that, rather than eradicating ethnic differences, modern American society has actually created a new awareness in people, a concern about roots and origins. Plu-

Box 14.3   Ethnic Intolerance

After a massive earthquake in Soviet Armenia in 1988, the Soviets collected blood for Armenian victims from Armenia's neighbors, the Azerbaijanis. But the Armenians refused to accept it, even as the casualties rose to over twenty thousand. The long-standing hatred between the two groups had been suppressed during Soviet rule, but as Soviet republics gained independence, old ethnic conflicts over disputed territory reemerged. By the time of the earthquake, the Armenians would rather have died than accept Azerbaijani blood—a symbolic contamination of Armenian identity—into their veins (Volkan 1997). From a medical and biological point of view, there was, of course, no significant difference between Armenian and Azerbaijani blood.

ralism seems to be common. Even though ethnic groups may adopt the language of the majority, and become culturally similar to the dominant majority, they nevertheless maintain cultural traditions of their common ancestry. (The change need not be one-sided —the dominant group may adopt traditions such as St. Patrick's Day and foods such as pizza, sushi, and tacos.) As we will see, even extensive intermarriage need not lead to assimilation.

Racial and Ethnic Chauvinism versus Class Consciousness

The intensity of racial and ethnic struggles in the United States presents a counterpoint to the generally unconscious and confused nature of class relations. Racial and ethnic groups have a sense of their own identity and collective purpose, yet they exist within a larger, class-based system of stratification. The discrimination of minority enclaves by Euro-American majority groups and the prejudice that ethnic minorities feel toward one another are part of the political and economic struggle that preserves the overall pattern of class stratification. Instead of uniting to improve schools, neighborhoods, jobs, and health services, minority ethnic and racial groups often seek to achieve their own advancement at one another's expense. Ethnic chauvinism thus pits "have nots" against "have littles," and thereby allows the "haves" to maintain their wealth and power. Once again the emic–etic distinction is vital to the comprehension of this situation.

> Class-consciousness among minority ethnic groups has not developed in many cases because in the short run it has been disadvantageous for the White working class.

With the possibility for relatively high upward mobility, working-class Whites were disinclined to make an alliance with non-White members of the working class. African Americans and other non-White ethnic groups were abandoned (and actively persecuted) by working-class Euro-Americans—people of Italian, Polish, Irish, and Jewish descent. African Americans were left behind to suffer the worst effects of low wages, unemployment, and exploitation because large numbers of European ethnics thought that by abandoning other racial and ethnic groups, they increased their own chances of rising to middle-class status. Thus, European immigrants became middle class by heading toward suburbia, while segregation kept African Americans out of the suburbs, and redlining

made sure banks would not loan them money to buy homes in White neighborhoods (Brodkin 1994). However, it can be argued that working-class Whites have had to pay an enormous penalty for failing to unite with non-White poor and working classes. For example, in a 1970s study of a working-class neighborhood in Brooklyn, New York, Ida Susser (1982) found that racial divisions debilitated collective action and allowed elected officials and commercial developers a free hand that benefited middle- and upper-class Whites. "So long as racial issues kept white voters loyal, elected officials could ignore the needs of a poor white working-class constituency" (1982:208).

> One reason for the limited success of ethnically based political activism in the United States is that it provoked a reactive increase in the solidarity sentiments and activities of majority White ethnic groups.

In response to real or imagined threats to their schools, neighborhoods, and jobs, European ethnics resisted the attempts of non-Whites at gaining political power. They mounted antibusing campaigns and created new private and public school systems based on segregated suburban residence patterns. With time, however, both White and non-White minorities found they had to rethink the consequences of "ethnic chauvinism." As European ethnics left the cities for suburbia, cities became transformed from solidly white neighborhoods of the 1960s to some of the most ethnically mixed communities in the world.

The early stages of this transformation entailed a downgrading or disinvestment in local neighborhoods. As "poorer" people started moving in, deliberate downgrading took place; jobs were eliminated, landlords deferred maintenance, and government resources for neighborhoods declined. One such neighborhood is Elmhurst–Corona in New York.

> Assaults on the quality of life, brought on by the erosion of community resources in multiethnic neighborhoods, has finally prompted residents to cross the lines of race and ethnicity to bring about political change.

In Roger Sanjek's words, "Politics is more than attitudes. It is also about interpersonal connections and group action. . . . The struggles, defeats, and victories that constitute neighborhood politics occur, not because attitudes somehow change but because [people take action]" (1998:368–369).

Profile 14.2   Elmhurst–Corona—Joining Forces Across Ethnic and Racial Lines

At no one's request and by no one's design, Elmhurst–Corona, Queens, a New York City neighborhood, was transformed from a solidly White community to a heterogeneous ethnically mixed community. By 1990, Elmhurst–Corona was 45 percent Latin American, 26 percent Asian, and 10 percent African-American.

When African Americans and non-White immigrants first moved into the area, the shift to a multiethnic community produced racial and social tensions. As Whites noticed the changes, they voiced discontent. The new tenants were labeled as welfare recipients and were blamed for the overall deterioration of the community. Also, the growing immigrant newcomers of Elmhurst–Corona were misidentified as "illegal aliens." One local community board chairman referred to immigrant newcomers as "people pollution." In addition to the racial tensions a city fiscal crisis occurred in 1975. The city budget shrank 22 percent between 1975 and 1983, resulting in service cuts affecting every aspect of the "quality of life." The top five "quality of life" issues for all Elmhurst–Corona residents were school crowding, lack of youth recreation facilities, housing code violations, drug sales, and dissatisfaction with police response.

By the 1980s, a sense of estrangement from the city led to civic activism. People remembered the days when the government was on their side and wanted to restore the way it used to be. This mobilized key individuals to take action. As residents focused on solving problems, they turned to one another for support. Racial and class lines slowly began to blur. An Italian-American woman began petitioning to keep a police precinct house in the neighborhood by going door-to-door and setting up networks and block associations that included all ethnicities. Latin American and Asian groups became politically active for the first time. In 1980 an organization was formed to help members of the Hispanic community become part of the American political process by providing immigration assistance and registering voters. Korean merchants established ties with non-Koreans to enforce city sanitation collection for storeowners.

Bridging Ethnic and Racial Boundaries
Anthropologist Kyeyoung Park (front row second from left) led a group of African Americans and Latinos to Korea to promote better understanding of Korean history and culture.

In many cases, interethnic community activism is spearheaded by women.

As members of different ethnic groups began to work together, leadership shifted to females. This occurred in part because of women's concern for their children's safety. Also, many of Elmhurst–Corona's female leaders are accustomed to working in formal organizations where interpersonal skills and improvisation are more important than structured or titled positions. Women used their personal ties to lobby across racial and ethnic lines for various quality-of-life issues such as obtaining a security guard for the local library; petitioning for traffic signs, parking enforcement, and park cleanup; and organizing neighborhood safety patrols. As one resident commented, "We have to live with one another, or we won't survive."

Defining Racism

Racism is the belief that the cultural and intellectual characteristics of a population are linked to its biological racial character, with the notion that some races are inherently superior to others.

Racism as a cultural construct emerged out of historical circumstances. Many contemporary scholars believe that race is a relatively recent concept in human history and that its use coincides with colonial conquest and exploitation by Western European nations during the past five hundred years. Even though slavery existed prior to colonialism, they say, it never took the form of "racial" slavery. People of all physical and ethnic variations were subject to enslavement, but their bondage was never rationalized by denying that they were fully human (Smedley 1993).

Today, the term *racism* also refers to a social system in which certain groups are oppressed and exploited with the rationalization that they are racially (biologically) inferior. Racism implies a belief in a biologically determined hierarchy of human groups. Feelings about race are so sensitive in U.S. society that elaborate linguistic codes have developed to permit the indirect expression of racist views. Current codes of expressions for the exclusion of minorities from social equality include the need to "protect property values" (to keep minorities out of all-White neighborhoods) and "no busing of schoolchildren" (to keep school systems segregated).

Most White people do not see themselves as having a race and therefore are not cognizant of the privileges our society confers on people who have white skin. The privileges of being White entail advantages received simply by being born with features that are highly valued by society.

The Wages of Racism

Despite the evidence that the vast majority of sociocultural differences and similarities cannot be explained by biological variation, racial explanations continue to find favor on a popular level and in certain scientific circles. Many people remain convinced that some racial groups are naturally smarter, more musical, more athletic, or more spiritual than others.

These stereotypes arise from a common methodological problem: the failure to control for the effects of historical and cultural influences on the behavior of the groups in question.

In the nineteenth century, the failure of Blacks and other "races" to compete successfully against "White nations" in manufacturing, commerce, and war was taken as incontrovertible evidence that whites were a superior race. Had not whites from Europe and their descendants in North America gained political and economic control over almost the entire human species? Eager to justify their imperial expansion, Europeans and North Americans failed to see the hollowness of this argument. They conveniently forgot that history is full of tales of empires brought to their knees by peoples who were at one time considered to be unalterably backward, such as the "barbarians" who conquered Rome and China. It was not intellectual superiority that enabled Europeans to invent new technology and develop political complexity; their advantage was derived from differences in environment that contained animals and grains suitable for domestication and that enabled them to generate food surpluses to support large populations and political complexity. This advantage was largely accidental and unintended, yet gave European cultures a tremendous long-term advantage over other populations (Diamond 1997). (See Box 14.4.)

Why Africa Lags

Why do vast regions of Africa lag in terms of technological and political development? These deficits are

Box 14.4   African Ingenuity

Before European conquest, Africans had highly efficient social institutions and developed religious beliefs that were as complex, abstract, and meaningful as those found anywhere. It was in the realm of material culture that their achievements fell behind those of Europeans or Asians or even Native Americans. They did not build monumental cities like those of the Aztecs or Inca, they did not build ocean-going ships, and their tools and weapons were simple. Why African socities did not develop more complex technology is a subject for continuing debate but it is clear that this failure was not due to lack of ability. For example, all along the coast of West Africa, local blacksmiths quickly learned to repair the defective muskets that Europeans intentionally traded for slaves or gold. These blacksmiths became highly adept at mastering this foreign technology, including tempering locks and braz-

ing barrels. In fact, many blacksmiths were so skilled that the need to trade for guns fell dramatically. Some blacksmiths even manufactured muskets and made their own gunpowder, a development the French greeted with stark incredulity. In 1892 the French found convincing evidence of African inventiveness when they captured a workshop filled with gunpowder in hermetically sealed jars, cartridge cases, signal rockets, electric batteries, and the tools used to repair and make guns. A Portuguese visitor concluded that Africans were intelligent, and had learned to speak, read, and write many different languages. The ability of Africans to master not only European languages but multiple African languages as well, continues to impress foreign visitors today. (Adapted from Edgerton 2000)

well marked in the lands south of the Sahara where the highest concentration of people with dark skin occur. And this region is also the homeland of most of the slaves who were brought to the Americas. To understand why racial differences do not merit serious consideration as an explanation of black Africa's predicament, we must explore the historical reasons for Black Africa's lagging pace of development.

In A.D. 500, West Africa had feudal kingdoms—Ghana, Mali, Sanghay—which strongly resembled the feudal kingdoms of Europe except for the fact that the Africans were cut off by the Sahara from the heritage of technology and engineering that Rome had bequeathed to Europe. Subsequently, the great desert also inhibited the southward flow of Arabic influences that did so much to revitalize European science and commerce. The presence of the tsetse fly in the forested regions of Africa south of the Sahara meant that cattle could not be used as a source of traction power and milk products. Without traction animals, hoes rather than plows became the main agricultural implements. Horses, which became the chief engines of war in medieval Europe, were scarce or absent in tropical Africa.

Although the people who lived in the Mediterranean basin carried out their trade and warfare on ships and became maritime powers, their dark-skinned counterparts south of the Sahara lacked the means of naval defense. So when the first Portuguese ships arrived off the Guinea coast in the fifteenth century, the Europeans were able to seize control of the ports and seal the fate of Africa for the next 500 years.

After the Portuguese exhausted the gold mines, the Africans concentrated on hunting slaves to exchange for European cloth and firearms. The slave trade led to increased amounts of warfare, rebellion, and the breakup of the indigenous feudal states, cutting short the trajectory of Africa's political development and turning vast portions of the interior into a no-man's-land whose chief product was a human crop bred for export to the sugar, cotton, and tobacco plantations on the other side of the Atlantic.

When the slave trade ended, the Europeans tightened their control and forced the Africans to farm and mine for them. Meanwhile, colonial authorities tried to keep Africa subservient and backward by encouraging tribal wars, by limiting African education to the most rudimentary level possible, and above all, by preventing colonies from developing an industrial infrastructure that might have allowed them to compete on the world market after they achieved political independence.

Social Race in the United States

African Americans have been confronted with some of the same pressures and alternatives as White eth-nics, having lost most of their African cultural heritage and the knowledge of their ancestral languages. And like White ethnics, they have sought to increase their sense of unity and identity by revitalizing old and inventing new cultural traditions. Unlike White ethnics, however, they have never had the option of blending in with the rest of the population. In the United States, the category "White" has expanded over time to include Euro-Americans such as the Irish, Italians, and Jews who were once thought of as being different races (Sanjek 1994b). Also, in the absence of rigid rules of descent, the ethnic identity of children and grandchildren of ethnically mixed marriages tends to grow weaker and become more a matter of choice than of ascription (Leo 1993; Sanjek 1994b). Intermarriage has been an important social mechanism for reworking White ethnic distinctions, but relatively little intermarriage has occurred between Whites and African Americans. Moreover, intermarriage does not modify the social identities of African Americans. Today intermarriage remains subject to criticism from both Whites and African Americans. Rates of interracial marriage involving African Americans, although increasing, remain far lower than those of other racial minorities. Out of 54.7 million married couples, only 311 thousand are Black–White intermarriages (U.S. Bureau of the Census 1998). Under these circumstances, African Americans have understandably turned their attention away from assimilation and have redoubled their efforts to instill pride in being Black by emphasizing African American cultural achievements.

Racism on the Campus

One reason for the limited success of the black power movement in the United States is that it provoked a reactive increase in the solidarity sentiments and activities of the White ethnic groups. In response to real or perceived threats to their schools, neighborhoods, and jobs, "white ethnics"—people of Italian, Polish, Irish, and Jewish descent—fought back against Black power. During the 1980s and 1990s, tensions between Whites and Blacks and other minorities increased in regions and cities all across the United States. A wave of racially motivated verbal and physical abuse affected not only urban neighborhoods (such as New York's Howard Beach, Crown Heights, and Benson-hurst) but college campuses as well.

This resurgence of overt racism results in part from the fact that successive conservative governments have devalued civil rights, encouraged resentment against affirmative action, and fostered racial polarization by cutting back on critical social programs (Glasser 1989). But a deeper level of sociocultural causation needs to be considered. One must ask why

Box 14.5   Intermarriage

Fears of ethnic divide in the United States are being challenged by the rate at which couples of different races and ethnicities are marrying one another. Since 1960 the number of all categories of interracial couples in the United States has increased to 1.6 million, accounting for about 4 percent of U.S. marriages, a figure that is expected to continue to increase in the coming years.

Some demographers note that race could eventually lose much of its meaning in the United States, much as ethnicity has lost its meaning among many Anglo-Americans. Interracial tolerance is increasing as the nations' Hispanic and Asian populations continue to grow. Moreover, many new immigrants come from countries with mixed-race traditions, which may make them more open to interracial marriage.

Rates of interracial marriages involving African Americans, however, remain far lower than those for other racial minorities. This worries some observers who fear that while other racial groups gain pluralistic acceptance, African Americans could remain outside the mainstream. A *Washington Post* poll taken in 1997 found that nearly one in four Americans still finds marriage between African Americans and Caucasians "unacceptable," and other polls have found people more tolerant of White marriages to Latinos and Asian Americans.

Interracial marriage and the resulting mixed-race children are gradually blurring the racial boundaries that have long divided the nation. Not only are interracial unions complicating predictions about the future racial makeup of the nation, they are calling into question widely held concepts of race. The increasing rates of interracial marriage and evolving notions of race have forced the U.S. Census Bureau to rethink the types of

Interracial Marriage
People are calling into question widely held concepts of race and are now identifying themselves according to their own categories.

categories and classifications it will use in the 2000 census. The U.S. Census Bureau has changed its guidelines to allow people to identify themselves by using as many of the five official racial reporting categories as they see fit. But many mixed-marriage couples are worried that their non-white racial identity will be lost. (Adapted from Michael Fletcher, 1998)

---

such a political program became attractive during the 1980s. The answer may be that the electoral success of political leaders who were indifferent or even vindictive about the plight of the country's minorities was related to the marked deterioration in the economic prospects of the White majority. Polls reveal that many working- and middle-class Whites have grown apprehensive about being able to improve or even maintain their level of socioeconomic well-being. For the first time in U.S. history, many young people are convinced that they will not be able to live as comfortably as their parents. These fears are not groundless. The wave of racial and ethnic unrest coincided with a period during which the average real weekly earnings of production and nonsupervisory employees declined. Although unemployment remains

relatively low, there is a growing scarcity of secure white-collar jobs as a result of mergers and "downsizing" (Emspak 1996). It is understandable, therefore, why Whites should increasingly regard any form of affirmative action as "reverse discrimination" and have lost interest in extending a helping hand to the poor, especially to poor African Americans and Hispanics. Coming from segregated neighborhoods and segregated schools, African Americans and Whites seldom form friendships in their youth. They grow up as if they came from entirely different societies. It is no wonder, then, that when African Americans and Whites are thrown together in predominantly White high schools and colleges, African Americans may feel insecure and mass together for protection against insensitive or openly hateful treatment (Hacker 1992).

African American Student Union
Ethnic clubs are found on many American campuses.

The Tragedy of Urban Black Youth

Racism levels a psychological assault against African Americans who have been targeted because of their position at the bottom of the racial hierarchy. Audrey Smedley (1999) points out that individuals in the low-status minority races have accepted without question that there are drastic differences between Black and White culture, have become deliberately hostile to the dominant culture, and in some cases, have closed themselves off from opportunities that would enable them to compete more effectively in our present-day economy. The racial myth that holds that Blacks cannot achieve in intellectual endeavors has affected young Black children who have become inhibited from expressing intellectual curiosity. "It is not only slavery that robbed African Americans of their identity. Far more powerful and telling has been the cruelty of racism" (1999:698).

Summary

1. Ethnic groups are present in virtually all state societies. These groups differ from classes in having been formed through conquest or migration. They have internal class differences of their own and have a high level of group consciousness.

2. Ethnic groups differ from social races only in the degree to which ethnic groups stress cultural differences (actual or invented) over physical appearance.

3. Social race differs from biological race in that social race is unrelated to scientific understanding of heredity—as illustrated in the one-drop-of-blood rule and in the contrasting example of the Brazilian system for identifying the children of mixed matings.

4. Failure to understand the difference between biological race and culture is a common feature of the dynamics of social races and ethnic groups.

5. The term *race* denotes a population with a distinctive set of gene frequencies; *culture* denotes a way of life. A rigid linking of race and culture is a form of racism that runs counter to all that is scientifically known about the transmissibility of culture across racial and ethnic boundaries.

6. The most important point about the dynamics of racial and ethnic groups is that they almost always compete with other racial and ethnic groups, both dominant and subordinate, to defend and improve their standard of living.

7. Although class struggle has been consistently difficult to identify and raise to conscious levels, race and ethnic struggle, and race and ethnic consciousness are ubiquitous features of the contemporary world.

8. As part of the attempt to improve their position in the social and economic hierarchy, racial and ethnic groups attempt to mobilize their resources and instill a conscious pride in their identities. Thus, all racial and ethnic groups that seek to survive and improve their condition tend to recast their historical achievements in the most favorable light and to emphasize their cultural separateness. When they do so, the threat of backlash is ever present.

9. The United States provides a picture of how ethnic and racial dynamics operate in a complex multicultural society. Despite a high degree of homogenization of their cultures and much invention of tradition, White ethnic groups are maintaining their identities. By invoking ambilineal forms of descent, White European ethnics continue to identify with ancestral ethnic groups as a matter of choice.

10. The situation is less benign among African Americans, who are largely blocked by the one-drop rule from choosing their social race. Racism remains a salient feature of the relations between Whites of European origin and African Americans (and other "nonwhite" groups).

11. In the nineteenth century, the dominant political position of the European powers was interpreted as proof of the superiority of the White race. But efforts to rank human races as inferior or superior based on technological, commercial, or military

prowess are negated by the many historical examples of underdogs becoming top dogs, as in ancient Rome, China, and modern Japan. Racial explanations of Black Africa's underdevelopment must be rejected in favor of explanations that take into account the effects of sub-Saharan ecology, colonialism, and the slave trade.

12. From an anthropological point of view, racism must be rebutted whether espoused by the dominant or subordinate group. A dangerous backlash by White ethnics in the United States has developed in relation to declining wage levels and a heightened sense of competition for scarce resources. This has resulted in the further withdrawal of African Americans, including Black-imposed segregation on college campuses.

AMERICA NOW

Race, Poverty, Crime, Drugs, and Welfare

Unlike the European immigrants of previous generations, Blacks have with the passage of time become more, not less, concentrated inside their ghettos. To those who lack realistic chances to escape from the ghetto, the benefits of criminal behavior may seem to outweigh the risks of getting caught and being sent to jail. John Conyers, a member of the Black congressional caucus, writes, "When survival is at stake, it should not be surprising that criminal activity begins to resemble an opportunity rather than a cost, work rather than deviance, and a possibly profitable undertaking that is superior to a coerced existence directed by welfare bureaucrats" (1978:678).

The high odds against attaining economic success by going to school and acquiring the skills necessary to compete with Whites for the better jobs lies behind the decision of many African-American, Hispanic, and other minority youth to traffic in illicit drugs (Liebow 1967). A week spent selling crack can bring more wealth than a year of working as a dishwasher or fast-food server. Ironically, the most successful drug businesses are run by young men who refrain from taking drugs themselves and who display many of the characteristics associated with entrepreneurship in legitimate businesses. They break into the trade with a small investment, hire employees, keep careful accounts, strive to establish good relationships with their regular customers, encourage the consumption of their product, adjust prices to market conditions, and keep careful tabs on what their competitors are doing. Of course, the use of crack and other addictive substances has a devastating effect on the consumers, who use drugs to escape from a squalid reality. The people of the United States pay an enormous price for the drug trade in the form of increased crime rates, overburdened courts and jails, and drug-related health problems such as AIDS (Bourgois 1995; Massing 1989, 1996; T. Williams 1989).

A disproportionate share of violent urban crime in the United States is committed by Black and Hispanic juveniles brought up in matrifocal families that receive welfare allotments. This connection between juvenile delinquency and matrifocality reflects the fact that welfare benefits are set below poverty-level incomes. Almost all inner-city women on welfare, therefore, count on supplementary incomes from husbands-in-hiding, coresident male consorts, or former consort fathers of their children. Anthropologist Jagna Sharff (1980) found that all the mothers on welfare in a group of 24 Hispanic families living in New York City's Lower East Side had some kind of male consort. Few of the men in the house held regular full-time jobs, but even those who were unemployed chipped in something toward food and rent from selling stolen goods, dealing in marijuana or cocaine, and an occasional burglary or mugging. Some

Low-Cost Housing
Pruitt-Igoe public housing complex in St. Louis. Despite the shortage of low-cost housing, huge public housing projects were dynamited into rubble. They had become drug and crime infested and had been vandalized beyond repair.

women had only one consort, whereas others picked up money and gifts through more casual relationships.

In their early teens, young inner-city boys make substantial contributions to their household's economic balance through their involvement in street crime and dope peddling (Bourgois 1995). In addition, they confer an important benefit on their mothers in the form of protection against the risk of rape, mugging, and various kinds of ripoffs to which the ghetto families are perpetually exposed. Sharff found that mothers value sons for streetwise "macho" qualities, especially their ability to use knives or guns, which are needed to protect the family against unruly or predatory neighbors. Although the mothers did not actively encourage their sons to enter the drug trade, everyone recognized that a successful drug dealer could become a very rich man.

To get ahead in the drug business, one needs the same macho qualities that are useful in defending one's family. When a young man brings home his first drug profits, mothers have mixed feelings of pride and apprehension. In her sample of families on welfare, Sharff compiled a record of 10 male homicides in three years (see Table 14.1). (Because young ghetto males have a 40 percent chance of dying by age 25, a ghetto mother must have more than one son if she hopes to enjoy the protection of a streetwise male.)

Sharff (1995) has kept in touch with the people of the neighborhood for over 20 years. During that time, practically every male she knew eventually became involved with the criminal justice system. Indeed, recent studies show that about 1 of every 3 Black men in their twenties is in prison or on probation or parole in New York State (Butterfield 1996).

Lower East Side
The vicinity of Jagna Sharff's study.

Sharff presents data in support of the view that the prison population grows larger when economic conditions for the working and middle classes grow more adverse. Thus, the prisons are a mechanism not merely for controlling crime, but also for controlling the poor and for preventing them from trying to get a share of the nation's wealth.

Table 14.1

Male Homicides in 24 Welfare Families, 1976–1979

Victim's Age	Immediate Cause of Death
25	Shot in drug-related incident
19	Shot in dispute in grocery store
21	Shot in drug-related incident
28	Stabbed in drug-related incident
32	"Suicide" in a police precinct house
30	Stabbed in drug-related incident
28	Poisoned by adulterated heroin
30	Arson victim
24	Shot in drug-related incident
19	Tortured and stabbed in drug-related incident

Source: Sharff 1980.

KEY TERMS

assimilation
biological race
chosen glory
chosen trauma
ethnic group
one-drop rule
pluralism
racism
social race

QUESTIONS TO THINK ABOUT

1. What is the difference between biological race and social race?
2. Is race a useful concept in the social sciences?
3. What obstacles have kept ethnic groups from joining forces to improve their economic position in society?
4. What concessions made it possible for residents of Elmhurst–Corona to join forces to become politically active in their community?
5. In what ways have the experiences of African Americans been different from those of Euro-American immigrants?

CHAPTER 15

Gender Hierarchies

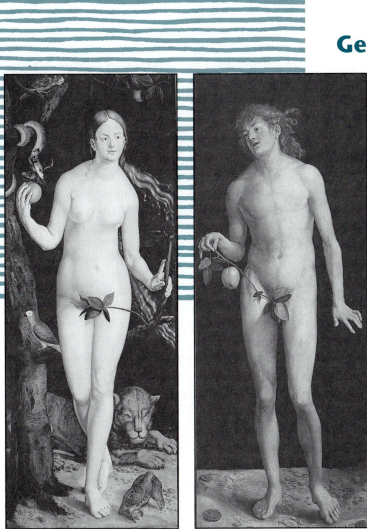

The story of Adam and Eve is thematically similar to myths that justify gender hierarchy.

Gender Differences

Gender Ideologies

The Relativity of Gender Ideologies

Are Women Equally Represented in Ethnographies?
PROFILE: The Trobrianders—Recognizing the Importance of Women

Gender Hierarchy

Variations in Gender Hierarchies
Women among Hunter-Gatherers
Women among the Matrilineal Iriquois
Women in West Africa
Women in India

Causes of Variation in Gender Hierarchies
Warfare and Gender Hierarchies
PROFILE: The Dahomey—Female Warriors

Hoes, Plows, and Gender Hierarchies

Gender and Exploitation

Gender and Hyperindustrialism

Summary

America Now: A Theory of Gender Hierarchy Change

Male and female and other genders are subject to the same kinds of hierarchical distinctions, advantages, and disabilities as classes, castes, ethnic groups, and social races. Here are some of the questions this chapter addresses: Do men and women interpret gender differences from the same perspective, or do they have different versions of which gender is dominant? What positions of authority can women achieve, and under what circumstances? How do the mode of production and the domestic and political economy affect the position of women? Are men and women separate but equal in band-organized societies? Why are gender relations more equal in some agricultural societies than in others? Is there a relationship between warfare and male domination? Why is low female status so closely associated with the use of the plow? And finally, what kinds of changes in gender roles can we expect as the industrial nations continue to develop high-tech infrastructures and service and information economies? In answering these questions, we will see that gender relations even in industrial societies have a long way to go before reaching equality.

Gender Differences

Anthropologists believe that gender is culturally constructed, as well as biologically determined. As we saw in Chapter 7, a person's sex is determined by chromosomes, hormones, and physical characteristics. Gender, in contrast, is culturally defined and constructed; each culture has its **"gender scripts"** (see Chapter 16, "Schemas and Cognition" section), which define what it means to be male and female and how men and women should interact in a variety of social settings. These scripts are learned through enculturation and are legitimized and sanctioned through gender-related ideologies contained in creation myths and by rituals that validate gender role authority and dominance (Sanday 1981).

Gender Ideologies

In many cultures, males believe that they are spiritually superior to females and that females are dangerous and polluting, weak, and untrustworthy.

One of the most widespread of all gender ideologies has as its explicit aim the retention of a male monopoly on knowledge of the myths and rituals of human origins and of the nature of supernatural beings.

The male knowledge monopoly embraces secret male initiation rites; male residence in a separate men's house, from which women and children are excluded; masked male dancers who impersonate the gods and other spiritual beings; the bull roarer, which is said to be the voice of the gods and which is whirled about in the bush or under cover of darkness to frighten the women and uninitiated boys. Any woman who admits to knowing the secrets of the cult is threatened with rape or execution (Gregor 1985:94ff; Hays 1988).

In contrast, in West African cultures, women are often portrayed as creative agents; their mythological charters describe women as progenitors of the people and agents for the fertility of the soil. Moreover, female deities are often found in societies where women are valued as food producers—where women are actively engaged in producing the crops and are farmers in their own right. However, myths of primordial matriarchy—a time when women held most positions of authority—are generally symbolic of defensive and insecure male status (see Box 15.1).

Rather than replicate a historical reality, myths of former rule by women provide ideological justification for male control.

The myth of matriarchy invariably highlights women's failure as rulers—because women did not know how to handle power—and reaffirms the inferiority of their present position (Bamberger 1974). In the case of the Mundurucu of the Brazilian Amazon (Box 15.1), the myth describes a reversal in the social order, when women controlled the sacred instruments. The women, however, did not know how to protect the trumpets and because of their incompetence, men took control of the instruments and became the dominant sex.

The Relativity of Gender Ideologies

How much of the male claim to spiritual superiority do women believe? To begin with, one must be skeptical that any subjugated group really accepts the reasons the subjugators give to justify their claims to superior status.

Much new evidence suggests that women have their own gender ideologies, which have not been properly recorded because earlier generations of ethnographers were primarily male and neglected or were unable to obtain the woman's point of view.

For example, male ethnographers have consistently interpreted the seclusion of menstruating women among the Yurok Indians of northern California as a demonstration of the need to protect men from the

Box 15.1   The Mundurucu Myth of the Sacred Instruments and Male Ascendancy

The sacred trumpets of the Mundurucu, called the *karoko,* are taboo to the sight of women, but the women once owned them. In fact, it was the women who first discovered the trumpets.

Three women named Yanyonbori, Tuembiru, and Parawaro would frequently hear music from some unknown source whenever they went to collect firewood. One day they became thirsty and went to search for water. Deep in the forest they found a shallow lake of which they had no previous knowledge. Another day they heard the music again, coming from the direction of the lake. At the lake, they found only fish in the water, which they were unable to catch.

Back in the village, one of the women had the idea of catching the fish with hand nets rubbed with a nut that made fish sleepy. Back at the lake, each woman caught one fish. These fish turned into hollow cylindrical trumpets. That is why each men's house now has a set of only three instruments. The women hid the trumpets in the forest and secretly played them every day.

The women, as possessors of the trumpets, gained ascendancy over men. The men had to carry firewood and fetch water, and also had to make the manioc cakes. The men were forced to enter the dwelling houses for a night, and the women marched around the village playing the trumpets. They then entered (what is now) the men's house and installed the instruments there. Then each woman went to the dwelling houses and forced the men into coitus. The men could not refuse, just as women today cannot refuse the desires of men. The next day the men took the trumpets from the women and forced them to go back to the dwelling house. The women wept at their loss. (Adapted from Murphy and Murphy 1985:114–115)

---

pollution of menstrual blood. Only in the 1980s did it become clear that Yurok women had a completely different sense of what they were doing (Buckley 1982; Child and Child 1985). Rather than feeling that they were being confined for the benefit of Yurok men, they felt that they were enjoying a privileged opportunity to get away from the chores of everyday life, to meditate on their life goals, and to gather spiritual strength (Box 15.2).

Although men may have one idea about which gender is more valuable, women may have quite a different idea.

Interior of Men's House, New Guinea
The men use masks to "terrify" the women and children.

Box 15.2   Yurok Woman's View of Menstrual Seclusion

A menstruating woman should isolate herself because this is the time when she is at the height of her powers. Thus, the time should not be wasted in mundane tasks and social distractions, nor should one's concentration be broken by concerns with the opposite sex. Rather, all of one's energies should be applied in concentrated meditation on the nature of one's life, "to find out the purpose of your life," and toward the "accumulation" of spiritual energy. The menstrual shelter, or room, is "like the men's sweathouse," a place where you "go into yourself and make yourself stronger." (Buckley 1982:48–49)

Box 15.3   !Kung Woman's Point of View

Women are strong; women are important. Zhun/twa [!Kung San] men say that women are the chiefs, the rich ones, the wise ones. Because women possess something very important, something that enables men to live: their genitals. A woman can bring a man life even if he is almost dead. She can give him sex and make him alive again. If she were to refuse, he would die! If there were no women around, their semen would kill men. Did you know that? If there were only men, they would all die. Women make it possible for them to live. (Shostak 1981:288, quoting Nisa)

Among the !Kung, who are generally regarded as having complementary and egalitarian gender roles, one woman at least felt that men were dependent on women far more than women were dependent on men. Men would die without women, she said (Box 15.3). Furthermore, women do not necessarily resent being excluded from male-centered rituals, because they do not attach much importance to what the men are doing with their bull roarers and masked dancing. Dorothy Counts tells how an old blind woman among the Kaliai of Papua New Guinea turned down the "honor" of being invited to remain in the village while the men performed their secret ceremonies. She left with the other women as she had always done, to feast and make lewd fun of the men's "secrets" (1985:61).

Why don't the women have myths and rituals of their own to validate their position and express their opposition to men? The following observation is made for the Mundurucu of the Brazilian Amazon, "Perhaps it is that the women have fewer anxieties, less of a feeling that they have a vested interest which can be lost. . . . They knew all about (the men's) ritual paraphernalia. . . and they were neither mystified or cowed. It is as if they investigated the secret sources of men's power—and found absolutely nothing" (Murphy and Murphy 1985:166–176).

Societies with explicit expressions of male dominance tend to assert male superiority as a defense against female dominance in the domestic domain.

Melford Spiro suggests that an ideology of male cultural dominance may be a defense mechanism in reaction to men's dependence on women. In Burma, for example, males are regarded as innately superior to females because of their sexual anatomy; the penis is regarded as a "noble" organ, and the vagina as "ignoble" and polluting. Men are also believed to possess *hpoun*—a psychospiritual essence that makes them intellectually, morally, and spiritually superior to females. Yet women enjoy a great degree of economic, legal, and social equality. Both men and women view the wife, not the husband, as the dominant partner in the marriage. Although the wife shows deference to her husband, she nevertheless dominates the domestic domain. She literally holds the purse strings by managing her husband's expenditures and controls many aspects of her husband's behavior such as the friends he brings home, and when and with whom he spends time away from home (Spiro 1993, 1997).

Are Women Equally Represented in Ethnographies?

Women ethnographers (Kaberry 1970 [1939]; Mathews 1985; Sacks 1971; Sanday 1981) have supplied much evidence that male anthropologists (who until recently were the main sources of cross-cultural data on gender roles) have often substantially underestimated or misconstrued the power of women. Even one of the greatest ethnographers, Bronislaw Malinowski, fell short of providing a balanced view of gender roles in his classic study of the Trobriand Islanders.

The distribution of power between the sexes is seldom simply a matter of men assuming dominance and women acquiescing (or vice versa). As the Trobriand study shows, male anthropologists in the past did not grasp the more subtle aspects of gender roles. Nor were women equally treated in ethnographies, in data collection, or as subjects of research.

Anthropologists responded by undertaking the challenge of rewriting anthropology "as if gender really mattered" (Di Leonardo 1991:8). They challenged the assumption of women's universal lower status by showing that women in many societies wield considerable amounts of power. Feminist anthropologists focused on the varying nature of women's power bases and the historical stages of gender equality or complementarity (Leacock 1978). Karen Brodkin [Sacks], for example, showed that women in African societies held dual statuses as sisters and wives; although dependent as "wives," as "sisters" women could attain economic autonomy through access to resources owned by their corporate kin group (1982).

Profile 15.1   The Trobrianders—Recognizing the Importance of Women

At harvest time in the Trobriands, brothers give their sisters' husbands gifts of yams. These yams provide much of the material basis for the political power of the Trobriand chiefs. Malinowski viewed the harvest gift as a kind of annual tribute from the wife's family to her husband, and therefore as a means of enhancing and consolidating male power. Annette Weiner has shown, however, that the harvest yams are given in the name of the wife and are actually as much a means of bolstering the value of being a woman as a means of conferring power on men.

Malinowski did not record the fact that the gift of yams had to be reciprocated and that the husband had to give the countergift not to his wife's brother but to his own wife. In return for the yams received in his wife's name, the Trobriand husband had to provide her with a distinct form of wealth consisting of women's skirts or bundles of pandanus and banana leaves, the materials used for making skirts. Moreover, much of a husband's economic activity is devoted to trading pigs and other valuables in order to supply his wife with large quantities of women's wealth. The skirts and bundles of leaves are publicly displayed and given away at huge funeral ceremonies known as *sagali* (which Malinowski knew about but did not describe in detail because he paid only limited attention to female culture). Weiner (1976:118) states that the sagali is one of the most important public events in Trobriand life:

> Nothing is so dramatic as women standing at a sagali surrounded by thousands of bundles. Nor can anything be more impressive than watching the deportment of women as they attend to the distribution. When women walk to the center [of the plaza] to throw down their wealth, they carry themselves with a pride as characteristic as that of any Melanesian bigman.

> Failure of a husband to equip his wife with sufficient women's wealth adversely affects his own prospects for becoming a big man. His brothers-in-law may reduce or eliminate their yam harvest gift if their sister cannot display and give away large quantities of bundles and skirts to relatives of the deceased.

Trobriand Island Yam House
Woman on left is wearing traditional skirt.

In Weiner's account, not only are men more dependent on women for their power than in Malinowski's account, but women also emerge as having far more influence in their own right. She concludes that all too often anthropologists "have allowed 'politics by men' to structure our thinking about other societies, leading us to believe erroneously that if women are not dominant in the political sphere of interaction, their power, at best, remains peripheral" (1976:228).

The term feminist anthropologist applies to anthropologists of any sex who are committed to achieving social, political, and economic equality of the sexes and giving equal voice to the woman's point of view. In an attempt to integrate feminism into anthropological research, attention shifted from studying the "invisible" world of women to the analysis of how gender is used to justify structured inequality of opportunity or access to public or private power (Rubin 1997).

The focus of feminist anthropology is understanding sexism as a system of inequality and producing useful knowledge for transforming oppressive relations.

The question posed is, What kinds of cultural conditions produce a system of domination by one sex over another? What would have to be changed in order to achieve a society without gender hierarchy?

Feminist ethnographers have given voice to "women's culture" by using the knowledge of women in other cultural settings to cast light on their own (Visweswaran 1997). But, although acknowledging women's resilience and their ability to manipulate the system in their favor, we must not forget that women are subjected to real power differences embodied in many gender hierarchies. It is well known that slaves can sometimes outwit masters, privates can frustrate generals, and children can get parents to wait on them like servants. The ability to buffer the effects of institutionalized inequality does not minimize the fact that women in many societies are deprived of the same rights and privileges as men.

Gender Hierarchy

The status of women is difficult to define because it contains multidimensional emic and etic viewpoints. Gender behavior is affected by public versus private setting, the life cycle, kin dynamics, and other systems of inequality related to rank, class, or race that produce other dimensions of power or oppression apart from gender. In other words, men and women have multiple identities and perceptions of relative gender status and power relations that are cross-cut by other hierarchies and ideologies.

The complexity of these features makes it difficult to determine whether women have "high" or "low" status. Westerners must be careful not to impose their cultural bias in evaluating gender behavior. Westerners, for example, might mistake public displays of politeness as displays of gender hierarchy. When a Machiguenga woman walks behind her husband in the forest, she is not kowtowing to a man but is being protected by her husband. In the United States the deference that men show to women by holding doors and walking curbside is an indication of good manners, and reflects more on the man than on the status of the women. To Westerners, giving bridewealth at marriage may appear as though women are treated as a commodity—bought and sold by male kinfolk—yet in the African context a woman would not be respected without it (see Box 15.4).

Box 15.4   Is Bridewealth Demeaning to Women?

In many African ethnic groups, bridewealth (See Chapter 9) is imperative for the legitimacy of the marriage. Westerners, however, have perceived and interpreted such exchanges as demeaning and a sign of women's oppression. The custom of bridewealth, however, is a deeply rooted cultural tradition that is not easily extirpated.

Recently, South African journalists have begun to question the practice of bridewealth on the grounds that it supports gender inequality. Some parents have also so commercialized the practice that bridewealth has become exorbitantly expensive, especially for educated daughters. The prospective husband may be expected to compensate the parents for most of the educational expenses they have incurred. This means paying the equivalent of over $5,000, an enormous sum by African standards.

To examine the extent to which bridewealth is supported by educated Africans, South African university students were given a questionnaire in which they were asked whether they approved of the practice. Eighty-eight percent of the students supported the practice of bridewealth payment. Of the men, 84 percent upheld the practice, as did 90 percent of the women. The students considered bridewealth an integral part of an African marriage because the custom heightened

- The husband's gratitude for a good wife
- His appreciation of the wife's dignity and worth

- The wife's assurance of her husband's continued recognition and respect

Noted also was that bridewealth helps control both the number of women available for marriage and the rate of divorce.

The findings of this study are of interest because one would expect that the majority of educated—and by extension Westernized—students would reject the practice of bridewealth. But this was not the case. The participants' views on bridewealth also coincide with those of other educated Africans. For example, President Nelson Mandela's daughter, Makaziwe, who holds a doctorate in cultural anthropology from the University of Massachusetts, was recently interviewed on the question of bridewealth, during an international conference on Women and Change. She responded as follows: "I have no problem with lobola (bridewealth). It is to solidify the relationship, to give respect to the woman and the child, so the man can in the future take care of the woman and children." After her remarks, there were reports that many equally high-powered African women confided they, too, supported bridewealth. Some seemed relieved Mandela had aired the issue publicly. (Adapted from T. S. Mwamwenda and L. A. Monyooe 1997)

Despite varying definitions of gender roles, males tend in the majority of societies to be assigned more aggressive and violent roles than females. From our previous discussions (in Chapters 11 and 12) of the evolution of political organization, it is clear that males often preempt the major centers of public power and control.

Headmen rather than headwomen dominate both egalitarian and stratified forms of trade and redistribution. The same male preeminence is evidenced by the Semai and Mehinacu headmen, the Solomon Island mumis, and the New Guinea big men (but see Counts 1985), the Nuer leopard skin chief, the Kwakiutl and Trobriand chiefs, the Bunyoro mukama, the Inca, the pharaohs, and the emperors of China and Japan. If queens reign, they generally do so as temporary holders of power that belongs to the males of the lineage.

Today, nothing more dramatically exposes the political subordination of women than the fact that in 1995 women comprised just over 11 percent of the members of the world's legislative bodies and 4 percent of national cabinets. In 1993, only six countries had women as heads of state (UNDP 1993:25).

Variations in Gender Hierarchies

Changes in gender roles are part of the broader evolutionary changes in the modes of production and reproduction that have led to population growth, competition for resources, political complexity, and increased stratification. As we will see, women in pre-state societies have in general fared better in peaceful, noncompetitive environments, suggesting that male dominance may be a response to stress associated with endemic warfare and competition over resources. In state societies, the intensification of male-controlled production has deprived women of access to productive means and has undermined their status by eroding the economic and political integrity of women's kin groups.

For those interested in directing social change and working for greater gender equality in the future, an awareness of past systems of gender stratification can help us understand what must be done to reduce gender inequalities.

Women among Hunter-Gatherers

In the words of Eleanor Leacock (1978:247), we cannot go from the proposition that "women are subordinate as regards political authority in most societies" to "women are subordinate in all respects in all societies." The very notions of "equality" and "inequality" may represent an ethnocentric misunderstanding of the kinds of gender roles that exist in many societies. Leacock (1978:225) does not dispute the fact that when "unequal control over resources and subjugation by class and by sex developed," it was women who in general became subjugated to men (recognizing, of course, that the degree of subjugation varied depending on local ecological, economic, and political conditions). In the absence of classes and the state, Leacock argues that gender roles were merely different, not unequal. Much evidence indicates that power of any sort, whether of men over men or men over women, was trivial or nonexistent in many (but not all) band and village societies, for reasons discussed in Chapter 11. Writing of her fieldwork among the Montagnais-Naskapi foragers of Labrador, Leacock (1983:116) recalls, "They gave me insight into a level of respect and consideration for the individuality of others, regardless of sex, that I had never before experienced."

In his study of the forest-dwelling Mbuti of Zaire, Colin Turnbull (1982) also found a high level of cooperation and mutual understanding between the men and women, with considerable authority and power vested in women. Despite his skills with bow and arrow, the Mbuti male does not see himself as superior to his wife. He "sees himself as the hunter, but then he could not hunt without a wife, and although hunting is more exciting than being a beater or a gatherer, he knows that the bulk of his diet comes from the foods prepared by the women" (p. 153).

Generally women hunt and collect only those animal species that do not require the use of spears, spear throwers, heavy clubs, or bows and arrows (Murdock 1967). The Agta of northeastern Luzon in the Philippines are an exception; there, women hunt deer and wild pigs with knives and bows and arrows. They traverse difficult terrain over considerable distances, using dogs to corner and hold their prey as they get ready for the kill. More recently Agta women have become entrepreneurial in other ways; they earn income from working for neighboring farmers, and purchase market goods for use and resale at a profit (Estioko-Griffin 1986; Estioko-Griffin, 1997).

Marjorie Shostak's (1981) biography of Nisa shows the !Kung to be another foraging society in which nearly egalitarian relationships between the sexes prevail. Shostak states that the !Kung do not show any preference for male children over female children. In matters relating to child rearing, both parents guide their offspring, and a mother's word carries about the same weight as a father's. Mothers play a major role in deciding whom their children will marry, and after marriage, !Kung couples live near the wife's family as often as the husband's. Women eat or distribute whatever food they have and bring back to camp whatever they choose.

African Elite
Women were able to command considerable wealth in regions of Africa with traditional low population density and female farming.

All in all, !Kung women have a striking degree of autonomy over their own and their children's lives. Brought up to respect their own importance in community life, !Kung women become multifaceted adults and are likely to be competent and assertive as well as nurturant and cooperative (Shostak 1981:246).

Women among the Matrilineal Iroquois

As we have seen, a high correlation exists between matrilineal matrilocal chiefdoms and intense external warfare (see Chapter 10, "Causes of Matrilocality" section). Although these societies should not be confused with matriarchies, women in matrilineal matrilocal societies often dominated domestic life and exercised important prerogatives in political affairs. The Iroquois can serve as an example.

The Iroquois were skillful warriors who subdued other Indian groups throughout the region. From their palisaded villages in upstate New York, they dispatched armies of up to 500 men to raid targets as far away as Quebec and Illinois. On returning to his native land, the Iroquois warrior joined his wife and children at their hearth in a village longhouse. The affairs of this communal dwelling were directed by a senior woman who was a close maternal relative of the warrior's wife. Because the women remained in their natal homes after marrying men from other villages, local kin groups revolved around mothers and sisters. Iroquois matrons—the elderly heads of house-

holds and work groups—organized the work that the women of the longhouse performed at home and in the fields. In turn, Iroquois agriculture yielded bountiful harvests that the matrons owned and distributed.

Because men engaged in external warfare against non-Iroquois villages, the women exercised control over the food supply.

When husbands returned from one of their expeditions—absences of a year or more were common—they slept and ate in the female-headed longhouses but had virtually no control over how their wives lived and worked. If a husband was bossy or uncooperative, the matron might at any time order him to pick up his blanket and get out, leaving his children behind to be taken care of by his wife and the other women of the longhouse.

Turning to public life, the formal apex of political power among the Iroquois was the Council of Elders, consisting of elected male chiefs from different villages. The longhouse matrons nominated the members of this council and could prevent the seating of the men they opposed. But they did not serve on the council itself.

Iroquois women influenced the council decisions by exercising control over the distribution of food.

If a proposed action was not to their liking, the longhouse matrons could withhold the stored foods, wampum belts, feather work, moccasins, skins, and furs under their control. Warriors could not embark on foreign ventures unless the women filled their bearskin pouches with the mixture of dried corn and honey for the men to eat while on the trail. Religious festivals could not take place, either, unless the women agreed to release the necessary stored food. Even the Council of Elders did not convene if the women decided to withhold food for the occasion (Brown 1975; Gramby 1977).

Women in West Africa

Women have relatively favorable gender statuses in the precolonial chiefdoms and kingdoms of the forested areas of West Africa. The region, which traditionally had low population densities and root crop agriculture, is known as an area of female farming, where men felled the trees and women performed the subsequent operations using a hand-held hoe. Among the Yoruba, Ibo (also called Igbo), and Dahomey, for example, women had their own fields and grew their own crops. They dominated the local markets and acquired considerable wealth from trade. To get married, West African men had to pay bride-wealth—iron hoes, goats, cloth, and in more recent times, cash. This transaction in itself indicated that the groom and his family and the bride and her family agreed that the bride was a very valuable person, and that her parents and relatives would not "give her away" without being compensated for her economic and reproductive capabilities (Bossen 1988; Schlegel and Eloul 1988). West African men and women believed that to have many daughters was to be rich.

Although men practiced polygyny, they could do so only if they consulted their senior wives and obtained their permission. Women, for their part, had considerable freedom of movement to travel to market towns, where they often had extramarital affairs. Furthermore, in many West African chiefdoms and states, women themselves could pay bride price and "marry" other women.

As we saw among the Nandi, marriage between women is a political and social relationship—not a sexual one (See Chapter 9, "What Is Marriage?" section). A female husband builds a house for her "wife" and arranges for a male consort to get her pregnant. By taking a wife, a woman assumes the status of head of household. By paying bridewealth for several such "wives," an ambitious West African woman could become the "father" of many children, establish control over a busy compound, and become rich and powerful. West African women also achieve high status outside the domestic sphere.

Like a big man, women in West Africa could command labor and wealth and were able to build a following by redistributing wealth and doing favors for others.

In West African kingdoms, women could mobilize other women through personal initiative and success in accumulating wealth.

West African women not only dominated the local markets but also belonged to female clubs and secret societies, participated in village councils, and mobilized en masse to seek redress against mistreatment by men.

Among the Ibo, women met in council to discuss matters that affected their interests as traders, farmers, or wives. A man who violated the women's market rules, let his goats eat a woman's crops, or persistently mistreated his wife runs the risk of mass retaliation. An offense against a woman was seen as one against all women. The miscreant male was awakened in the middle of the night by a crowd of women banging on his hut. They danced lewd dances, sang songs mocking his manhood, and used his back-yard as a latrine until he promised to mend his ways. They call it "sitting on a man" (Van Allen 1972).

The supreme rulers of these West African chiefdoms and states were almost always males. However, their mothers, sisters, and other female relatives occupied offices that gave them considerable power over both men and women. In some Yoruba kingdoms, the king's female relatives directed the principal religious cults and managed the royal compounds. Anyone wanting to arrange rituals, hold festivals, or call up communal labor brigades had to deal with these powerful women first, before gaining access to the king. Among the Yoruba, women occupied an office known as "mother of all women," a kind of queen over females, who coordinated the voice of women in government, held court, settled quarrels, and decided what positions women should take on the opening and maintenance of markets, levying of taxes and tolls, declarations of war, and other important public issues. And in at least two Yoruba kingdoms, Ijesa and Ondo, the office of queen-over-women may have been as powerful as the office of king-over-men. Every grade of male chief under the king-over-men had a corresponding grade of female chief under the queen-over-women. The king and the queen met separately with their respective councils of chiefs to discuss matters of state. They then conferred with each other. No action was taken unless both councils were in agreement (Awe 1977; Sudarkasa 1973).

Women in India

As we have seen (Chapter 2, "Emics, Etics, and Sacred Cows" section), Indian culture exhibits a distinct regional pattern with grain agriculture in the north and wet rice cultivation in the south. Unlike parents in West Africa, parents in northern India express a strong preference for sons over daughters. As Barbara Miller (1981, 1987, 1992) has shown, the women of India are an "endangered sex" as a result of the high rate of female infant and child death caused by parental neglect. A north Indian man who has many daughters regards them as an economic calamity rather than an economic bonanza. Instead of receiving bridewealth, the north Indian father pays each daughter's husband a dowry (see Chapter 9, "Economic Aspects of Marriage" section) consisting of jewelry, cloth, or cash. Unlike southern India—where daughters are seen as economically more valuable—a north Indian woman's dowry goes to the groom and his family and is used to finance a dowry for the groom's sister.

Discrimination against daughters affects women in a number of ways (Malhotra, Vanneman, and Kishor 1995):

- Women are denied access to education.
- Women marry earlier.
- Chastity is emphasized.
- Women start childbearing sooner and have higher rates of fertility.
- Child mortality rates are higher.
- Women marry exogomously—which deprives them of support from their natal kin.

In recent years, disgruntled or merely avaricious husbands have taken to demanding supplementary dowries. This has led to a spate of "bride burnings" in which wives who fail to supply additional compensation are doused with kerosene and set on fire by husbands who pretend the women killed themselves in cooking accidents (Crossette 1989; Sakar 1993; Sharma 1983). Moreover, wife beating seems to be widespread in India, again, especially in the northern states (Miller 1992).

North Indian culture has always been extremely unfriendly to widows. In the past, a widow was given the opportunity of joining her dead husband on his funeral pyre. Facing a life of seclusion with no hope of remarrying, subject to food taboos that brought them close to starvation, and urged on by the family priest and their husbands' relatives, many women chose fiery death rather than widowhood.

By contrast, in southern India—which has wet rice agriculture—there is much less discrimination against women. Women have a substantial productive role because labor-intensive wet rice cultivation involves more input from women than the cultivation of wheat or other crops. Women in southern India therefore have better access to such key resources as education and employment and other opportunities. Participation in agriculture and the paid labor force is the basis for greater autonomy. As a result,

- Women marry later.
- Fertility is lower.
- Child mortality rates are lower.
- Women's literacy rates are higher.

However, despite these important gains by women, men still have better access to job training and employment (Malhotra, Vabbenab, and Kishor 1995).

Causes of Variation in Gender Hierarchies

Many factors affect gender hierarchies, and none have thus far been shown to be primary determinants at all times and in all places.

> In general, women's material contributions and their ability to control distribution of resources enables them to achieve influence in both domestic and public affairs.

But no matter how much control women achieve, male dominance of some sort characterizes most human societies. In searching for key factors related to women's secondary status, we have argued that physical differences do not alone dictate or explain gender inequality. Physiological differences do not preclude women from participating in activities that require physical strength, but culture assigns tasks so that members of each sex do what they are physically able to do best. Males are trained to hunt and become warriors because hand-held weapons depend on muscle power, and most men have a small edge over women, particularly in life-and-death situations such as warfare.

Warfare and Gender Hierarchies

Warfare is a major factor influencing the status of women in band and village societies. Males on average have a physical advantage over females, especially in upper body strength. Because males constitute the main fighting force in band and village societies, they are trained to be fierce and aggressive, and to kill with a weapon far more often than women are. The training, combat experience, and monopoly that men possess over the weapons of war empower them to dominate women. Thus, the gender-equal !Kung and Machinguenga seldom if ever engage in

Male Supremacy
Aggressive sports such as football activate the male supremacist complex.

warfare, whereas the Yanomami, Sambia, and other bands and village socities with marked gender hierarchies do engage in frequent warfare.

Brian Hayden (Hayden et al. 1986) has tested the theory that wherever conditions favored the development of warfare among hunter-gatherers, the political and domestic subordination of women increased. Using a sample of 33 hunter-gatherer societies, he found that the correlation between low status for females and deaths due to armed combat was "unexpectedly high."

As discussed in Chapter 11, warfare is more likely to occur as the subsistence economy intensifies and competition increases for the best resources. The practice of warfare is responsible for a widespread complex of male supremacy among band and village societies (Harris 1977:57). The **male supremacist complex** is a by-product of male monopoly over weapons, training of males for combat and bravery, patrilineal bias in descent and residence, and other male-centered institutions. The reasons for such overwhelming male dominance in societies where warfare is pronounced seem relatively straightforward. The lives of group members depend to a greater degree on males and male assessment of social and political conditions. Male bravery during times of warfare is critical to the survival of local groups under lethal threat, where over one fourth of male deaths result from homicide and where defeat results in the capture of women and the displacement of whole groups from their ancestral land. The relationship between the intensity of warfare and male dominance is present among village peoples and simple patrilineal chiefdoms. Thus the Yanomami, with their high level of warfare, are well known for strong male biases and their practice of female infanticide. Eastern highland New Guinea is also noted for its male-centered communal cults, physical mistreatment of women and incessant warfare. As Daryl Feil (1987:69) puts it,

> (women) were whipped with cane if they spoke out of turn or presumed to offer their opinions at public gatherings; and were physically abused in marital arguments. Men could never be seen to be weak or soft in dealings with women. Men do not require specific incidents or reasons to abuse or mistreat women; it is part of the normal course of events. (p. 203)

Male supremacist behavior patterns are found in other male oriented communities. For example, the denigration of women and all things feminine is common in the military service and male-centered social groups, such as athletic teams and fraternities, where the male supremacist complex is activated. We must remember, however, that the correlation between intense warfare and female subordination does not hold in the case of matrilocal and matrilineal societies where warfare is practiced against distant foes, and therefore forestalls rather than encourages male control over production and domestic life (see Chapter 10, Causes of Matriliocality).

When the men are away from their villages for several months at a time, women are left in charge of the family economic holdings and exercise a great deal of control over decision making.

The correlation between frequency and intensity of warfare and male dominance also does not hold for advanced chiefdoms and states. Although stratified societies have bigger armies and wage war on a much grander scale than classless societies, the effect of warfare on women is less direct and generally less severe than in bands and villages (but not as favorable as in matrilineal societies).

In advanced chiefdoms and state societies, soldiering is reserved for professionals.

Most males no longer train from infancy to be killers of men, or even killers of animals (because few large animals are left to hunt, except in royal preserves). Instead, they themselves become unarmed peasants and are no less terrified of professional warriors than are their wives and children. Warfare does create a demand for suitably macho men to be trained as warriors, but in state societies most women do not have to deal with husbands whose capacity for violence has been honed in battle. Nor does women's survival depend on training their sons to be cruel and aggressive (except perhaps in preparation for the drug trade warfare described in Chapter 13). In advanced chiefdoms and states, therefore, female status depends less on the intensity, frequency, and scale of warfare than on whether the anatomical differences between men and women endow males or females with a decisive advantage in carrying out some crucial phase of production.

The fact that thousands of women served as combat troops in the Russian Revolution and in World War II on the Russian front as well as with the Viet Cong and other nineteenth- and twentieth-century guerrilla movements, and that they serve today as terrorists, police officers, and prison guards, does not alter the importance of warfare in shaping gender hierarchies among band and village peoples.

The weapons used by women in the modern context are firearms, not muscle-powered weapons.

This also holds true for the famous corps of female warriors who fought for the West African kingdom of

Profile 15.2   The Dahomey—Female Warriors

The Dahomey of West Africa provide an example of a society with full-time professional female warriors. Of a force of about 20,000 in the Dahomey army, 5,000 were women known as "Amazons." Because the king did not trust men to enter his palace after nightfall, he installed an all-female guard. Some of the women were unarmed and performed duties as scouts, porters, and drummers rather than as direct combatants. The elite of the female fighting force—numbering between 1,000 and 2,000— lived inside the royal compound and were known for their loyalty to the king. Before they were nearly all killed in combat by French troops in the early 1890s, the "Amazons" served their king for some 200 years.

To become a warrior, a woman had to be "reborn" in a ceremony in which she renounced all family ties and swore an oath of chastity from which they could only be released by the king. Celibacy was mandatory to avoid emotional ties to children or lovers that would pose a distraction from military duties. Those who became pregnant were accused of adultery and executed (Herskovits 1938). Many Dahomey female warriors were captured slaves from neighboring societies who were allowed to choose whether they wanted to remain slaves or become

warriors. As warriors, slaves could achieve high status and eventually gain their freedom. One female soldier who was taken prisoner and raised in Dahomey refused to allow her parents to free her, preferring to remain faithful to the Amazons, who eventually purchased her release.

During several recorded battles, Dahomey women fought as fiercely and as effectively as the men. But their principal arms were mainly muskets and blunderbusses, not spears or bows and arrows. The king supported the female battalions with impressive new uniforms and rewarded the most noteworthy warriors with honors, titles, and slaves. Their prowess, fierceness, and bravery are well documented. During the 1840s, female warriors led Dahomey's army to several victories, including one in which its male soldiers fled under fire, leaving the Amazons to win the battle.

European visitors often commented on their combat skills and physical appearance, describing them as "charming" and "graceful," even "ravishing." It was noted that the Dahomean women could complete the seven movements needed to reload a musket in thirty seconds compared to fifty seconds for men. (Adapted from Edgerton 2000)

Dahomey during the nineteenth century (see Profile 15.2). Clearly the circumstances that made it possible for the Dahomey to rely on female warriors did not exist in war-making bands and villages.

Hoes, Plows, and Gender Hierarchies

The contrasting gender hierarchies of West Africa and northern India are associated with two very different forms of agriculture. In West Africa, the main agricultural implement was not an ox-drawn plow, as in the plains of northern India, but a short-handled hoe (Goody 1976). The West Africans did not use plows because in their humid, shady habitat, the tsetse fly (see p. 220) made it difficult to rear plow animals. Besides, West African soils do not dry out and become hard-packed as in the arid plains of northern India, so that West African women using nothing but hoes were as capable as men of preparing fields and had no need for men to grow, harvest, or market their crops.

In northern India, on the other hand, men maintain a monopoly over the use of ox-drawn plows, which are indispensable for breaking the long dry season's hard-packed soils. Men achieved this monopoly for essentially the same reasons that they achieved a monopoly over the weapons of hunting and warfare:

Their greater bodily strength enabled them to be 15 to 20 percent more efficient than women. This advantage often means the difference between a family's survival and starvation, especially during prolonged dry spells when every fraction of an inch to which a plowshare penetrates beneath the surface and every minute less it takes a pair of oxen to complete a furrow are crucial

Man and Beast
An Indian farmer plowing with a pair of oxen.

for retaining moisture. As Morgan MacLachlan (1983) found in a study of the sexual division of labor in India, the question is not whether peasant women could be trained to manage a plow and a pair of oxen but whether, in most families, training men to do it leads to larger and more secure harvests.

Further support for this theory can be found in the more female-favorable gender roles that characterize southern India and much of Southeast Asia and Indonesia (Peletz 1987). In these regions, noted for their strong matrifocal and complementary gender relationships, rice rather than wheat is the principal crop. Rice cultivation involves the operation known as *transplanting,* during which the rice seedlings are pulled up and replanted in a more dispersed pattern. Women and children typically perform this crucial "stoop" labor.

Is a factor as simple as male control over plowing sufficient to explain female infanticide, dowry, and widows throwing themselves onto their husbands' funeral pyres? Not if one thinks only of the direct effects of animal-drawn implements on agriculture itself. However, in evolutionary perspective, this male specialty was linked to a chain of additional specializations that together can plausibly explain many features of the depressed status of women in northern India as well as in other agrarian state societies with similar forms of agriculture in Europe, southwestern Asia, and northern China.

Wherever men gained control over the plow, they became the master of large traction animals. Wherever they yoked these animals to the plow, they also yoked them to all sorts of carts and vehicles. Therefore, with the invention of the wheel and its diffusion across Eurasia, men yoked animals to the principal means of land transport.

> Control over the plow gave men control over the transportation of crops to market, and from there it was a short step to dominating long-distance trade and commerce and other professions.

Because men already dominated trade, they became the first merchants with the invention of money. As trade and commerce increased in importance, it was to men—already accustomed to keeping track of profits and losses—that the task fell of keeping records. Therefore, with the invention of writing and arithmetic, men came to the fore as the first scribes and accountants. By extension, men became the literate sex; they did reading, writing, and arithmetic. Therefore, men, not women, were the first historically known philosophers, theologians, and mathematicians in the early agrarian states of Europe, southwestern Asia, India, and China.

All these indirect effects of male control over traction animals acted in concert with the continuing gender role effects of warfare. By dominating the armed forces, men gained control over the highest administrative branches of government, including state religions. And the continuing need to recruit male warriors made the social construction of aggressive manhood a focus of national policy in every known state and empire. It is therefore no wonder that at the dawn of industrial times, men dominated politics, religion, art, science, law, industry, and commerce, as well as the armed forces, wherever animal-drawn plows had been the basic means of agricultural production.

Women and Children Transplanting Rice, Burma

Gender and Exploitation

As economic development proceeds, women tend to lose ground relative to men. Whenever modern technology is introduced, it benefits men more than women because women are relegated to sex-specific low-technology work at marginal wages. Also, as societies move from a subsistence economy to a monetary system, women's status suffers because their nonmonetary productive roles are not recognized, and the value of their unpaid work is much lower than that of men. When development projects are introduced, Western experts chose to deal with men, thereby depriving women of access to new sources of income. And, in an economic downturn, women are hit much harder then men because they were earning less to begin with. Thus, the ratio of women to men is greater in the poorest income groups. This trend, known as the **feminization of poverty**, in which women comprise a large portion of a nation's poor, has been growing since World War II. In addition to their lower wages and lack of access to sources of income, women are harder hit by poverty because men who father children may abandon them. The rearing of children then becomes the sole responsibility of women, especially when migration to urban centers provides men with new economic opportunities. In the United States the majority of female-headed households live below the poverty line because women earn less than men and many fathers fail to pay child support. In fact, the poverty rate of female-headed families is about three times that of male-headed house-

holds and six times that of married couples (Rodgers 1994; Susser 1996).

Often women are denied the same rights as men. In patriarchal societies, basic rights violations against women are treated as a women's issue rather than a human rights issue. From a legal standpoint, women in some cultures are denied the right to obtain a divorce and are more severely punished than men for adultery. They lack political rights such as the right to vote and hold political office and to make economic decisions, and they are often denied the right to an education. Moreover, violence and physical abuse against women by their partners is growing worldwide. We saw that in India, wife burnings have become more common, especially in lower-caste families because the husband can acquire another dowry when he remarries. Also, women more often than men are forced into prostitution or subjected to rape.

Gender and Hyperindustrialism

During the smokestack phase of industrialism, women had little opportunity to overthrow the patriarchal heritage of the classic Eurasian gender hierarchy. **Patriarchy**, or rule by father or a male authority, assumes that women are naturally subservient to their fathers and husbands. Although widespread, patriarchy exists in different forms and degrees, so that in principle, it can at some point in time be zero. **Matriarchy**, or political control by women, most likely never existed. It was formerly believed that matriarchy occured as a regular stage in the evolution of social organization, but such claims overestimated the political significance of matrilocal residence and matrilineal descent. The absence of matriarchies is an important fact, but its significance should not be exaggerated. Gender inequalities are not universal; women's status deteriorated with male monopoly over weapons and technology, and the emergence of political roles in which ruling class men acquire power over other men and women.

After an initial period of intense exploitation in factory employment in the early part of the century, American women were excluded from industrial work and confined to domestic tasks in order to assure the reproduction of the working class. Factory-employed male breadwinners collaborated in this effort in order to preserve their privileges and fend off the lowering of male wages. Indeed, most Americans during the 1950s didn't think that women should have equal wages, especially if they had a man to support them. A decisive break came in the 1960s, with the shift to the information and service infrastructure. This shift led to a call-up of literate women into low-paid, nonunionized information and service jobs, the feminization of the labor force, a fall in fertility rates to historic lows, and

Female Headed Household

Poor women with children have limited opportunities for productive employment.

Breaking the Gender Barrier

A. Neurosurgeon Francis Conley.   *B. Executive.*   *C. Construction Engineer.*   *D. Soldier.*
E. Pregnant worker.

Box 15.5   American Women Are Becoming a Formidable Force in Business

The rapidly growing numbers of women-run businesses are proof that women are not only successfully carving a niche in the corporate world, but creating an important economic force. Women-owned businesses employ one out of every four American workers. Between 1972 and 1992, the number of women-owned businesses increased twelve-fold, from 500,000 to 6 million—a rate of 300,000 per year (see Figure 15.1). Women's businesses generate $2.3 trillion in revenue, and the U.S. Department of Labor projects that by the year 2000, about half of America's businesses will have a female owner.

Because women are becoming a prominent business force, major corporations are rushing to meet the needs of women employers. Moreover, marketing divisions recognize that women represent a potentially lucrative market sector. Thus, they have created strategies to target women business owners, and are hiring women to lead them.

Studies have shown that women have different business styles from their male counterparts, and corpora-
tions are training their salespeople to understand these differences. For example, women tend to be consensus builders, and often take more time and require more information before making key purchasing decisions. Thus, when a woman business owner says she'll think about it, she literally means that; whereas for a man, this reply is a way of saying no. In addition, women place greater priority on establishing long-term relationships with suppliers, and once they contract with a supplier, they remain loyal. Third, because women value personal relationships, they tend to buy major items from a person rather than from a catalog. Also, when purchasing technology, women place greater value on service, such as a 24-hour toll-free hotline and a long-term warranty. One of America's largest financial institutions has identified three priorities for women in business: being taken seriously, establishing a relationship with a financial institution, and having information presented clearly. Men want these things also, but give them lower priority (Vrana 1997).

---

the destruction of the male breadwinner family (see America Now at the end of this chapter).

The anatomical and physiological differences between men and women (except to the extent that women still may wish to have children) have lost their relevance in today's **hyperindustrial** world. The term *hyperindustrial* refers to the fact that the world has now become more (not less) industrial, extending mass production into new areas. It is no accident that women's rights in hyperindustrial socities are rising as the strategic value of masculine brawn declines. Who needs extra muscle power when the decisive processes of production take place in automated factories or while people sit at desks in computerized offices? Men continue to fight for the retention of their old privileges, but they have been routed from one bastion after another, as women fill the need for service and information workers by offering competent performance at lower wage rates than males. Even more than the market women of West Africa, women in today's advanced industrial societies have moved toward gender parity based on their ability to earn a living without being dependent on husbands or other males.

A serious barrier to equality is the conflict between women's new roles in the workplace and the demands of the family and children. A sexual double standard still persists when it comes to housework. Many women have traded in their domestic roles for a double day in the paid workforce and the unpaid household. Although it is true that income disparities

between men and women have been closing, 80 percent of women who choose to have children are forced to choose occupations where job flexibility compensates for lower pay in order to accommodate child rearing. Yet, more women than ever before are taking advantage of new opportunities in the information and service economy. Women are also starting their own businesses; women-owned firms now number 8 million in the United States, and as one female business owner says, "Nothing levels a playing field like money" (Vrana 1997). (see Box 15.5).

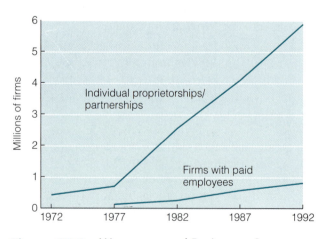

Figure 15.1   Women-owned Businesses Soar 1972–1992

Bureau of Labor Statistics

Summary

1. Gender groups are subject to the same kinds of hierarchical distinctions, advantages, and disabilities as classes, castes, ethnic groups, and social races.

2. In many cultures, males believe that they are spiritually superior to females and that women are a source of pollution. These beliefs are present in the male-centered cultures, which hold that women once dominated, but lost their power because of inappropriate conduct.

3. Women often do not accept these male versions of gender roles, as illustrated by the examples of the Yurok and Kaliai. Moreover, as demonstrated in the restudy of the Trobriand Islanders, male ethnographers have often underestimated the etic power of women.

4. Nonetheless, men have more frequently dominated women politically, and what would be the mirror image of patriarchy—matriarchy—is unknown.

5. Gender roles among hunter-gatherers are often egalitarian, as among the !Kung, Naskapi, Mbuti, and Agta.

6. Female-favorable gender roles are found in many matrilineal societies, such as the Iroquois, but perhaps the most powerful women in preindustrial societies lived in West Africa among the Yoruba, Ibo, and Dahomey.

7. In contrast, the male-dominant gender roles of northern India, endanger the survival and well-being of females, especially very young or very old females.

8. Variations in gender hierarchies among hunter-gatherers and village societies are closely correlated with the frequency and intensity of warfare carried out against nearby groups.

9. By contrast, long-distance warfare between village groups tends to promote matrilocality and a higher status for women.

10. At the advanced chiefdom and state levels, only specialist warriors receive training for armed combat; consequently, variations in gender hierarchies depend less on the frequency and intensity of warfare than on the significance of the anatomical differences of men and women for carrying out certain crucial agricultural tasks.

11. Underlying the contrast between West African gender relations and those of northern India are two contrasting modes of agricultural production: hoe agriculture and plow agriculture, respectively.

12. Women can use hoes as effectively as men, which leads to their controlling their own food supply, being involved in trade and markets, having an equal say in the management of household affairs, and wielding considerable political power.

13. In northern India, men outperform women in the critical task of preparing hard-packed soils for planting by means of ox-drawn plows, leading to the preference for sons, female infanticide, dowry, and the mistreatment of widows, in contrast to southern India and West Africa, where daughters are valued.

14. Further consequences of the Eurasian animal-drawn plow complex include male control over trade, accounting, mathematics, literacy, and church and state bureaucracies, as well as continued control over the army. Southern India, with its contrastive use of animals for puddling rather than plowing rice paddies and its more female-favorable gender roles, lends additional support to this theory.

15. In the early phase of the industrial revolution, married women were excluded from factory work and confined to the home as dependents in male breadwinner families.

16. After the 1950s, male aptitudes were no longer significant in the emerging information and service economy; women entered the labor force in unprecedented numbers, leading to increased independence from men and radical changes in gender roles, gender hierarchy, and family life.

17. Sex-based persecution remains a serious problem. Women are often denied basic human rights and are at a much greater disadvantage than men in poverty situations. Despite women's growing integration into the hyperindustrial economy, a major barrier to gender equality is women's greater burden at home. However, as women become more successful in the workplace, they are able to achieve greater parity with men.

AMERICA NOW

A Theory of Gender Hierarchy Change

All the recent trends toward parity in gender roles can be related to the hyperindustrial mode of production. The trend away from factory employment required and facilitated the call-up of female labor previously absorbed by child and home care; concurrently the premium placed on education for employment in nonmanufacturing jobs, together with the increase in the "opportunity costs" of pregnancy and parenting (that is, the amount of income forgone when women stop working to bear and raise children), inflated the costs of rearing children, weakened the marriage bond, depressed the fertility rate, and furthered the separation of the reproductive from the hedonistic components of sexuality.

The principal change that has occurred in the labor force is not merely an increase in the proportion of women who are employed but a growth in the proportion of employed women who are married and have children. Before World War II, only 15 percent of women living with husbands worked outside the home. By 1998, this proportion had risen to 65 percent (see Figures 15.2 and 15.3). What do these women do? Over 83 percent hold nonmanufacturing, service, and information-producing jobs—mostly low-level jobs that pay on the average only 75 percent of the wages earned by males (U.S. Bureau of the Census, 1997). In 1996 the median earnings figure for men was $557 per week, or an increase of 37 percent over eleven years. Women's median weekly earnings was $418, an increase of about 50 percent and about 75 percent of the median figure for men. The labor force participation rate for women continues to be on the rise. About 60 million women now participate in the labor force.

The link between feminization and the information and service economy is reciprocal: Women, especially married women, had formerly been barred from unionized, male-dominated manufacturing jobs

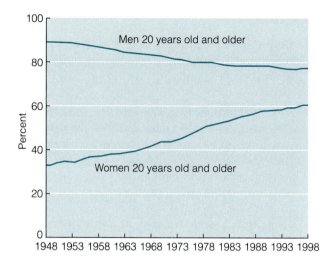

Figure 15.3   Labor Force Participation Rates for Adult Men and Women 1948–1998

Women have become a larger share of the labor force over time, and currently have a participation rate only 16 percentage points below that of men.

Bureau of Labor Statistics

in which they were seen by husbands and unions as a threat to the wage scale. The nonunionized and traditionally feminine information and service occupations—secretaries, schoolteachers, health workers, saleswomen, and so on—offered less resistance. Seen from the perspective of capital investment, the reserve army of housewives constituted a source of cheap, docile labor that made the processing of information and people a profitable alternative to investment in factories devoted to goods production. Thus the feminization of the labor force and the decline of goods manufacturing are closely related phenomena, although as we have seen, this relationship has nothing to do with the inherent capacities of the sexes for physical labor and factory work. Why did U.S. women respond in such large numbers to the service and information call-up? Ironically, their primary motivation was to strengthen the traditional multichild, male breadwinner family in the face of rising costs of food, housing, and education. Despite their lower rate of remuneration, married women's wages became critical for maintaining or achieving middle-class status.

As we have seen in Chapters 9 and 10, family structure is closely correlated with infrastructural conditions. It is impossible in the present case to mistake the direction of causality. Although multiple and complex feedbacks have operated at all stages of the process, the main thrust emanated from changes occurring at the infrastructural level—the shift from goods production to service and information produc-

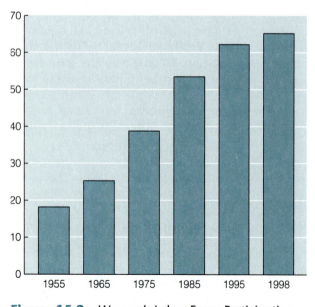

Figure 15.2   Women's Labor Force Participation 1955–1998

Percentage of women in the labor force with children under 6 years old.

Bureau of Labor Statistics

tion. Alterations at the structural level—marriage and the organization of the family—did not show up until a substantial commitment to the new mode of production had taken place. For example, the number of women who had husbands present and who were participating in the workforce had already risen from 15 to 30 percent by 1958. Yet not until 1970 did the feminist movement attain a level of national consciousness, when women shed their bras, held crockery-smashing parties, and marched down New York's Fifth Avenue shouting slogans like "Starve a rat tonight; don't feed your husband." These antics expressed the pent-up frustration of wives who were already in the labor force and experiencing the contradictions of the old and new gender roles. As noted by Maxine Margolis in her book *Mothers and Such:* "While the media devoted much space to bra-burning and other supposed atrocities of the women's movement, little attention was paid to the reality of women's work, which had set the stage for the revival of feminism" (1984:231). Writing from an economist's perspective, Valery Oppenheimer, in her book *Work and the Family,* makes the same point:

> There is no evidence that these substantial shifts in women's labor force participation were precipitated by prior changes in sex-role attitudes. On the contrary, changes in sex-role attitudes lagged behind behavioral changes, indicating that changes in behavior have gradually brought about changes in sex role norms rather than the reverse. Moreover, the evidence clearly indicates that the start of the rapid changes in women's labor force behavior greatly preceded the rebirth of the feminist movement. (1982:30)

As Oppenheimer explains further, this is not to say that "more equalitarian sex-role attitudes and a feminist ideological perspective are not major motivating forces," but "that these attitudes reinforce or provide an ideological rationale (or normative justification)" (1982:30).

To identify the infrastructural conditions of a social movement and to assign them a causal priority over values and ideas is not to diminish the role of values and ideas or of volition in the dynamism of history. Nonetheless, it is essential in this case, as well as in other controversial social movements, that both those who favor and those who oppose a particular change comprehend that some outcomes are more probable than others. In the present instance, for example, it seems highly improbable that women in the United States can be restored to their former situation as housewives. In order to resurrect the male breadwinner family and put women back behind the sink, the nation would have to revert to a more primitive phase of capitalism and industrialization, a course that even the most conservative antifeminists do not propose to take.

KEY TERMS
feminization of poverty
gender scripts
hyperindustrialism
male supremacist complex
matriarchy
patriarchy

QUESTIONS TO THINK ABOUT
1. In what ways are women believed to be spiritually inferior to men, and how can this phenomenon be explained?

2. What is the basis of women's dominant status in West African chiefdoms?

3. What accounts for the strong preference for males over females in northern India?

4. How does warfare affect the position of women in band and village societies as opposed to chiefdom and state societies?

5. What new challenges and opportunities for gender equality do women have in industrial and hyperindustrial societies?

CHAPTER 16

Psychological Anthropology

Father and son in Laos.

Culture and Personality
Freud's Influence
Is the Oedipus Complex Universal?

Cultural Patterns and Themes

Basic Personality Structure
Modal Personality
National Character
PROFILE: Japanese National Character

Childhood Training and Personality

The Influence of Subsistence Patterns
Child Training and Male Initiation Rites

The Six Cultures Study
The Effect of Social Environment on Children
Cultural Models of Child Care

Subsistence and Adult Personality

Schemas and Cognition

Culture and Mental Illness
Depression
Schizophrenia
PROFILE: Schizophrenia in Rural Ireland
Culture-Specific Psychoses

Summary

Earlier in this century, psychologically oriented anthropologists began to study the relationship between culture and personality. Did cultures shape people's personalities, or did their personalities shape their cultures? According to the followers of Sigmund Freud, some personality complexes occur universally and affect cultures everywhere. We shall see to what extent this is true. Others follow Freud in contending that culturally prescribed differences in childhood training greatly influence adult personality. But can it be said that all adults brought up in a particular culture, under a given mode of production, have the same personality? Do the Japanese, for example, have a distinctive national character? And what of the relationship between culture and mental health? Do certain forms of mental illness occur in only one culture?

Culture and Personality

The term **culture** refers to the patterned ways in which the members of a society think, feel, and behave. The term **personality** also refers to patterned ways of thinking, feeling, and behaving, but the focus is on the individual. Personality, as defined by Victor Barnouw (1985:8), "is a more or less enduring organization of forces within the individual associated with a complex of fairly consistent attitudes, values, and modes of perception which account, in part, for the individual's consistency of behavior." More simply, "Personality is the tendency to behave in certain ways regardless of the specific setting" (Whiting and Whiting 1978:57).

The concepts employed in describing the thinking, feeling, and behavior of personality types differ from those employed in describing infrastructure, structure, and superstructure, yet psychological processes are highly relevant for understanding social life. Psychologists talk about motives, values and emotions, whereas anthropologists see these concepts as derived from cultural traditions and ideologies that set forth standards and expectations for how people should feel and behave in given contexts.

Freud's Influence

Sigmund Freud, had a major influence on early culture and personality research. Freud's theory of **psychoanalysis** emphasized the importance of unconscious feelings, motives, and conflicts in determining personality and behavior. Today most psychological theories accept two important elements of Freudian theory:

- Adult personality is shaped by early experiences during infancy and childhood.

- Psychological development occurs in stages during which certain mental events regularly take place.

One of the most important stages in a child's development is the stage of sexual awareness, between the ages of 3 and 6, when the child, according to Freud, unconsciously wishes to possess the parent of the same sex and get rid of the parent of the opposite sex. Freud called this the **Oedipus complex**—Oedipus, according to ancient Greek legend, killed his father and married his mother.

According to Freud, boys and girls go through the Oedipal stage differently. The boy wishes for closeness and desires exclusive intimacy with his mother. He views his father as a rival and wishes to replace him. These feelings arouse fear in the young boy because in his fantasies, the boy will be punished by castration for wanting to be rid of his father. In learning to control and reject these unacceptable wishes, the growing boy acquires morality and learns to direct his aggression away from his father toward socially constructive activities.

Freud admitted that he did not quite know what to make of girls. He envisioned a parallel but fundamentally different trauma. A girl's sexuality is also initially directed toward her mother, but she soon makes a fateful discovery: She lacks a penis. She blames her mother for this and redirects her sexual desires away from her mother and toward her father. However, her love for the father and for other men is mixed with a feeling of envy, for they possess something she lacks. Freud believed that women would have a lingering sense of penis envy all of their lives.

Clearly, Freud's notions about gender roles were projections of his own experiences as a male in highly male-centered late–nineteenth-century Vienna where he lived and formulated his ideas. Sexual politics aimed at perpetuating the gender hierarchy, not science, provided the basis for his idea that women necessarily envied men and were destined always to be the second sex.

Some of Freud's followers later modified his theories. Karen Horney ([1939] 1967), one of the first analysts to challenge the notion of penis envy, said that if women feel inferior to men it is not because they are dissatisfied with their anatomy; they are dissatisfied because of the disadvantages of their second-class status. In fact, she said that if anyone has an envy problem, it is men. Men have womb envy—they envy women's ability to bear children. Horney argued that men glorify their genitals because they are unable to give birth and unconsciously fear women's sexual power.

Is the Oedipus Complex Universal?

Bronislaw Malinowski (1927) rejected Freud's contention that the oedipal complex is universal on the grounds that it does not exist in the same form in the matrilineal Trobriand family (see Chapter 10). He argued that the tension between father and son described by Freud resulted from the European system of patriarchy rather than from sexual competition for the mother. Trobriand males do not develop the same kind of complex because their mother's brother, not their father, exercises authority over them. Thus a Trobriand male grows up without the hate-love feelings toward his father that Freud postulated as being universal. Malinowski called this pattern of supportive relations between a father and son and an authoritarian mother's brother, the "matrilineal complex."

Later, however, Melford Spiro (1982) reexamined Trobriand ethnography and folklore to show there is evidence of oedipal conflict. The Trobriand male lives with his father and mother until he is an adolescent. This gives him plenty of opportunity to develop fantasies of possessing the mother and to develop feelings of sexual rivalry toward the father. Using folktales, Spiro establishes the existence of several oedipal correlates, including evidence of male siblings' competition for mother's love, unconscious castration anxiety, and a strong incestuous desire for sister and adolescent daughter. In some folktales, the attraction is deflected from the mother and father onto less threatening subjects, disguised as love for the sister and hostility toward the maternal uncle.

The oedipal theme takes on many forms in folktales around the world. Allen Johnson and Douglass Price-Williams (1996) surveyed 164 "family complex" folktales that describe incest and family violence. Where boys are concerned, such stories depict a struggle between a young man and a father figure, and an inappropriate close, often erotic, relationship between a young man and a mother figure. But stories about girls suggest that female oedipality differs from the Freudian version. A common theme is that the father is sexually attracted to the daughter, but the daughter does not reciprocate his feelings (see Box 16.1). Nor does the daughter view the mother as a competitor for the father; instead she joins in an alliance with the mother to resist the father's advances. Nancy Chodorow (1974, 1978) supports the view that the girl's attachment to her father is not exclusive, or as intense as that of the boy's for his mother. Unlike the boy who must turn away from the mother to achieve masculine independence, the daughter experiences continuity in her relationship with her

mother, which gives her a sense of interpersonal connection with the primary parent.

We can conclude that oedipal concerns appear to be universal to the extent that children grow up in families where there is emotional ambivalence and children have fantasies of an exclusive relationship with parents.

The content and severity of the Oedipus complex varies from one society to another in relation to the structure of the domestic group but most societies have stories about incest and violence.

Malinowski was not alone in regarding Freud's Oedipus complex as limited to patriarchal society. Horney ([1939] 1967) argues that the oedipal complex appears in class-structured, commercially competitive societies, where parents stimulate hostility in children through critical and domineering behavior. Similarly, tribal warfare, where the emphasis is on fierce competitive males, creates a "male supremacy complex." When the objective of child rearing is to produce aggressive, dominant males, young men will feel insecure about their manliness and there will be competition between males in adjacent generations.

Cultural Patterns and Themes

Many anthropologists have examined psychological concepts cross-culturally. Ruth Benedict, for example, showed that cultures mold personalities in distinctive ways, according to **cultural configurations**, which are unique social patterns that a culture has standardized. In her famous book *Patterns of Culture* (1934), Benedict described cultures as learned solutions to problems confronted by every society. Each culture is a uniquely integrated whole with a distinctive configuration of customs and values that influence individual psychology.

Benedict believed that each society develops a unique pattern, or cultural configuration, elaborating certain aspects of human experience and ignoring others.

For example, she described the Kwakiutl (see Profile 5.2) as "megalomaniac" because their potlatches are dominated by fantasies of wealth and power with an uninhibited will to be superior. Other cultures, such as that of the Pueblo Indians, she saw as Apollonian—given to moderation and the "middle of the road" in all things. She saw them as emphasizing cooperation

Box 16.1   Oedipal Myths

Father–Daughter Incest: Navaho, Native North American Myth

A man named Crow had many children. His oldest daughter was the prettiest, and Crow decided to make her his wife. He pretended he was ill and told his wife to make him a bed in a tree. He put a piece of liver under the bed and told his wife that if worms started falling out of it, she would know he was dead and must move away. Then she must give the oldest daughter in marriage to the first person she saw carrying four prairie dogs.

Crow did this so he could have intercourse with his daughter. But he had a big scar on the side of his head. After the worms fell out of the tree and his family moved away, he disguised himself and met his family with four prairie dogs in hand. No one recognized him, and his daughter was given to him as a wife.

One night he told his daughter to clean his head of lice. He knew she would recognize him by his scar, so he told her not to touch the other side of his head. The girl became curious and at night, while he was asleep, she looked to see if he had lice on the other side. She saw the big scar and knew it was her father.

She sneaked out and ran to her mother. She and her mother returned while her father was still asleep. When the mother saw it was her husband, she threw a rock at his head and that is how he was killed. (Adapted from Johnson and Price-Williams 1996:241–243)

Mother–Son Incest: Yamana, Native South American Myth

Although Little Woodpecker was very young, he had fallen in love with his mother. She carried him around in a bag and never took him out or left him alone. She often went to the forest to collect mushrooms, with her son in her bag. When she found a hidden spot, she set the bag down and her little son became a grown man. He climbed up the tree and picked many mushrooms, which he threw to the ground. He told his mother to lie down and part her legs so that he could see her vagina. He then threw the mushrooms at her vagina, which was a great pleasure for both of them. When the son came down from the tree, he lay down on his mother and she received him with great pleasure, for his penis was extremely large. When they got up, the son got back into the bag and became an infant again.

They continued to go to the forest to gather mushrooms and have intercourse. The other women wondered how she collected so many mushrooms in such a short time. They followed her unnoticed and watched as her son became a man, threw the mushrooms at her vagina, and lay down on her. The women were horrified and rushed back to tell her husband what they had seen.

When his wife returned, the husband waited until evening. When they were asleep, he took his knife and cut down the bag. The boy fell out and the father could see the boy's large penis. With horror he seized the knife and cut off his son's penis. The boy turned into a woodpecker, flew off into the forest and never returned to his parents' hut. (Adapted from Johnson and Price-Williams 1996: 293–295)

and communal activities, and avoidance of all strong emotions such as anger and jealousy.

Most anthropologists have rejected such attempts to use one or two psychological terms to describe whole cultures. Even the smallest hunter-gatherer societies have too many personalities to be summed up and depicted in terms of single labels.

Margaret Mead expanded on the idea that culture shapes human development. In her research on adolescent Samoan girls,

Margaret Mead set the stage for future research into the relationship between culture, childhood training, and adult personality by showing how children grow up under varied cultural conditions.

Her goal was to show that human nature was not "rigid and unyielding." In *Coming of Age in Samoa* (1928), she suggested that adolescence is not necessarily a turbulent emotional period for Samoan girls as it is in Western societies—the crisis of adolescence is relative to the demands a culture places on young people. Thus, the lesson proposed by Mead is similar to that of Ruth Benedict: The world's cultures do not adhere to the same cultural patterns. In *Sex and Temperament in Three Primitive Societies* (1935), Mead shows that in each of three New Guinea societies, men and women are expected to display different temperaments in terms of appropriate masculine and feminine characteristics. For example, Tchambuli men are preoccupied with art and their appearance. The men prepare elaborate costumes for ceremonial events,

Rather than attempt to sum up whole cultures under one or two psychological concepts, some anthropologists point to dominant themes or values that express the essential or main thought and feeling of a particular culture. The "image of limited good" is one such theme (see Chapter 13). Themes and values are readily translatable into personality traits. For example, the image of limited good reputedly produces personalities that are jealous, suspicious, secretive, and fearful. The culture of poverty (see Chapter 13) also has its psychological components—feelings of helplessness, and lack of future time orientation. An important theme in Hindu India is the "sacredness of life," and an important theme in the United States is "keeping up with the Joneses."

The problem with attempts to portray cultures in terms of a few dominant values and attitudes is that contradictory values and attitudes can usually be identified within the same cultures and even within the same individuals. Thus, although Hindu farmers believe in the sacredness of life (Opler 1968), they also believe in the necessity of using their cattle as beasts of burden; and although many people in the United States believe in trying to keep up with the Joneses, others believe that conspicuous consumption is foolish and wasteful. For this reason, assessments of personality must take into account intergroup differences to determine the extent to which characteristics are shared and whether emic values are carried out in behavior. It is not unusal for deliberate decisions to be overturned in response to larger social forces that determine the effectiveness (or ineffectiveness) of individual actions (Strauss and Quinn 1994:294).

whereas the women are the breadwinners—they do all the fishing and have real positions of power. The assignment of temperament in each society fits the cultural configuration but is one among several possibilities. Although there are patterns of gender difference (see Chapter 15), Mead urges that we recognize the diversity of human potentials and make room for those who cannot conform to conventional standards.

Care of Children
Cultures vary greatly in the amount of body contact between mother and infant. **A.** *Swazi mother and child.* **B.** *Arunta mother and child; mother has all-purpose carrying dish on her head and digging stick in her hand.*

The basic personality structure, in turn, has its own impact on culture by creating "**secondary**" **institutions** (ideology represented by folklore, religion, and art) that reflect the motives, conflicts and anxieties of members of society.

The shortcoming of the scheme is that it does not explain the relationship between secondary institutions and the adaptive requirements of society; ideology is a given, derived from basic personality. However, no attempt is made to demonstrate how subsistence, kinship and socialization influence secondary institutions.

Modal Personality

One problem with the basic personality structure concept is that it does not take individual differences into account. Even if all children had the same kinds of early experiences, there would still be diversity because of differences in innate temperament. The term **modal personality** refers to those traits or characteristics that occur with the highest frequency in a culture or subculture. Modal personality is a statistical concept; data are gathered by means of psychological tests administered to a sample of the population. The most commonly used is a projective test known as the Thematic Apperception Test (TAT). It consists of cards, showing pictures of people in various situations. Participants are asked to tell a story about each card. They tend to tell the story from the point of view of the character with whom they identify; in doing so they project their own personalities and reveal both conscious and unconscious wishes and motivations (Bock 1988:72). The cards are modified to make the figures and situations familiar to the people in the culture. Responses are recorded and scored to describe the pattern of psychological traits that distinguishes the population.

Cora DuBois (1944) was the first anthropologist to undertake a study of modal personality. Her research on the people of Alor, an island in Indonesia, involved collecting autobiographies, administering Rorschach

Javanese Girl and Brother
One way to free mother for work in the fields is to turn over the care of infants to a 7-year-old sister.

Basic Personality Structure

Abram Kardiner (1939) developed the concept of **basic personality structure**, which is the personality configuration displayed by most members of a society, as a result of shared early experiences and upbringing. This approach is a form of childhood determinism, and Kardiner used it to develop a causal model:

- Shared experiences are derived from "**primary**" **institutions** (economic factors, family and household organization, and customs of child rearing).

- These shared cultural experiences produce a basic personality structure.

Primary ⟶ Basic Personality ⟶ Secondary
Institutions   Structure   Institutions

(e.g., kinship, subsistence,   (e.g., religion, art,
      socialization)   folklore)

Figure 16.1 Kardiner's Model of Basic Personality Theory

Source: (Piker 1994: 9)

("ink blot") tests, and detailed accounts of socialization. The Rorschach tests were independently analyzed by DuBois and Kardiner, with a high degree of correspondence. The projective tests showed the Alorese to be suspicious, distrustful, fearful, and insecure—traits that can be explained by parental deprivation. This is supported by the ethnographic data: Alorese men engage in trade, and the women are the main food producers. Young children are left alone for hours and are prone to violent temper tantrums when mothers leave to work in their gardens.

National Character

When the populations involved are entire nations, the modal personality is often called **national character.** A common theme in national character studies, as elsewhere, is that child-rearing customs have a major impact on adult personality traits. Several studies of national character were made during World War II, to understand the psychology of the combatants. Because direct fieldwork was not possible, anthropologists did their research by studying "culture at a distance," through the analysis of books and newspapers, and through interviews with expatriates aimed at gathering material on memories of childhood and cultural attitudes. Japanese national character was the most puzzling to U.S. policymakers and the general public. In *The Chrysanthemum and the Sword* (1946), Ruth Benedict tried to explain the seemingly incomprehensible contradiction between (1) Japanese restrained aestheticism, expressed in Japanese flower arranging, and (2) fanatical militarism, expressed in the cult of the sword and samurai warrior. Benedict noted that these contradictions are grounded in socialization practices that induce

Box 16.3   The Japanese at Home

People are relaxed and do not worry about formalities. They can talk and joke about their innermost concerns. Even the most formal of women may be informal with close friends. They even tease each other about the formalities which they notice on other occasions. With close friends, one can argue, criticize, and be stubborn without endangering the relationship. There is inevitably a great deal of laughter mixed with mutual support and respect. It is partly the sharp contrast between seeing a close friend and a mere acquaintance that makes contacts with outsiders seem so stiff. The visitor to Japan who does not appreciate the difference in behavior toward friends and acquaintances is likely to consider the Japanese as more formal than they actually are. (Quoted in Sugimoto and Mouer 1983)

shame in children. Japanese children learn to subordinate personal desires to family and group demands. She explains that childhood shame is transformed into adult concern with saving face to avoid disgrace to themselves and family. Serious disgrace can be overcome only by honorable death in battle or by suicide.

These theories about Japanese national character changed after the war when the Japanese adapted to their defeat and took the lead in the peace movement in Asia, hardly confirming the portrait of wartime brutality. Moreover, it is now believed that subordi-

A.   B.   C.

Figure 16.2   National Character Steroetypes

Allen Funt's popular TV show "Candid Camera" frequently explored national character differences by means of informal cross-cultural experiments. The three scenes represented here show the same young woman in three different countries, standing at a curb with a suitcase filled with a 100 pounds of bricks. In each scene, she solicits a male passerby to help her get her suitcase across the street. In Country A, the man tugs and pulls at the suitcase with all of his might, finally managing to get it across the street. In Country B, the man tries to move the suitcase, but when he finds it unexpectedly heavy, he gives up and goes on his way. In Country C, on finding the bag too heavy for one person to pick up, the man enlists the aid of another male passerby, and the two of them carry it across with no difficulty. Can you guess which country each scene depicts? In view of the recent changes in gender roles, what other scenarios might be likely to occur today?

Answers: (A) England;   (B) France;   (C) United States

nation to the group does not necessarily entail the loss of individuality. The Japanese have different "faces" for different situations; group activities require public behavior appropriate in particular contexts (see Profile 16.1). Different "faces" are reflected in different speech forms used on different occasions (Hendry 1995:54). According to Takie Lebra (1992), the **public (interactional) self** is the surface layer of self that is exposed to appraisal by others. It varies according to its reference group—whether one stands with family, neighbors, or colleagues. The **private (inner) self** is more stable and authentic. It is immune to social relativity and provides a fixed core for self-identity. The private self is seen as morally superior and thus accounts for the ambivalence a Japanese person holds for the self-conscious, self-effacing self that is presented in public settings (1992: 106–112).

Japanese Men in a Public Setting

The public interactional self is exposed to appraisal by others.

Profile 16.1   Japanese National Character

Valid interpretations of personality configurations in alien cultures require great familiarity with the language and deep immersion in the context of everyday life. The experience of being a member of another society often cannot be adequately represented by simple contrasts and conventional categories. For example, the Japanese are stereotyped by Westerners as a people who are deferential, shy, self-effacing, conformist, and dependent on group approval. "Few Japanese," writes one anthropologist, "achieve a sense of self that is independent of the attitude of others" (cited in Kumagai and Kumagai 1986:314; cf. Plath 1983). Examples of exaggerated deference are found in the frequent bowing and elaborate courtesy of Japanese business conferences and the readiness with which Japanese identify themselves as a work team or a corporation rather than as individuals. Indeed, self-effacement has been linked by many observers to the secret of Japan's industrial success. Japanese management style plays down the difference between executives and workers. Everyone eats in the same company cafeteria, and groups of workers regularly join with management to solve problems of mutual interest in a cooperative rather than adversarial manner. However, another side of the Japanese personality is reserved for private and intimate occasions. If you are not a member of a Japanese family group and do not interact with family members when there are no guests or outside observers present, you would not see the strength of individual ego assertion that is also part of Japanese daily life.

Most Japanese are brought up to be adept at changing back and forth between the private assertive self and the deferential public self. The significance of these different modes of presenting one's self has little if anything to do with the inner psychological strength of the Japanese ego. Because Westerners have no real equivalent of a public formal mode of self-effacement, they have often incorrectly and unfavorably perceived Japanese personality. Lacking a Western equivalent, Westerners interpret the posture of self-effacement as indicative of hypocrisy and deviousness. On the other side, the Japanese are equally befuddled by the failure of Westerners to make a distinction between expressions of one's ego in public formal versus intimate private situations. As recounted by a Japanese social scientist, being a dinner guest in an American home can be especially perplexing: "Another thing that made me nervous was the custom whereby an American host will ask a guest, before the meal, whether he would prefer a strong or a soft drink [and after dinner] whether [he takes] coffee or tea, and—in even greater detail—whether one wants it with sugar, and milk, and so on." (Kumagai and Kumagai 1986:12). Although the visitor soon realized that the hosts were trying to be polite, he felt extremely uncomfortable with having to say what he would like, because in the self-effacing and deferential posture appropriate to being a guest in a Japanese home, one avoids expressions of personal preference with respect to what is being served. Guests are dependent on hosts and surrender all vestiges of personal preference. The hosts in turn must avoid embarrassing their guests by asking them to choose their own food. Unlike Americans, Japanese hosts do not discuss how they prepared the main dish. They say, "This may not suit your taste, but it is the best we could do." The guests are not supposed to be interested in knowing any of the details of this effort.

Learning Nurturance and Responsibility
Machiguenga infants and toddlers are constantly held by their mothers or older siblings.

The concept of basic personality structure, modal personality, and national character is hard to reconcile with the fact that every society includes a great range of personalities and that the more populous, complex, and stratified the society, the greater the variability. In every society, many individuals have personalities that deviate widely from the statistical mode (most frequent type), and the range of individual personalities produces wide overlaps between different cultures. So, how does the cultural context influence personality, and how do we explain intracultural variability? It has been suggested that differences in the types of experiences provided to individuals by different culture groups, including their structural position within the culture (occupational role, status, and other socially relevant groupings), produce behavioral regularities in a given setting (Bock 1988).

Anthony Wallace (1952) was the first to attend to the problem of interpersonal variability. In working with the Tuscarora Indians of North America, Wallace used Rorschach tests to show that even homogeneous societies accommodate a great deal of variability. By scrupulously attending to individual variability, he demonstrated a central personality tendency and then charted variability in relation to the modal type.

Childhood Training and Personality

Parents in a particular culture tend to follow similar childhood training practices involving the feeding, cleaning, and handling of infants and children. These practices vary widely from one society to another and are probably responsible for some cross-cultural differences in adult personalities. In some cultures, for example, nursing may be on demand at the first cry of hunger; in others feeding occurs at regular intervals at the convenience of the mother. Nursing at the mother's breast may last for a few months or several years or may not take place at all. Weaning may take place abruptly, as when the mother puts a bitter substance on her nipples or it may be gradual. In some cultures, infants are kept next to their mother's skin and carried wherever the mother goes; elsewhere, they may be left behind with relatives or other caretakers. In some cultures, infants are fondled, hugged, kissed, and fussed over by large groups of adoring children and adults; in others, they are kept relatively isolated and touched infrequently.

Treatment of infant sexuality also varies widely. In many cultures, mothers or fathers stroke their babies' genitals to soothe them and stop them from crying. Tibetan mothers go one step further, as reported by anthropologist Hildegard Diemberger (1993:89):

> Caili, an energetic and sensual woman, is playing with her youngest son, Migmar. I enter the house. Caili offers me a cup of barley beer and then continues to play with Migmar who really does not want to be disturbed. He drinks some milk from the breast and plays with his erect little penis. He offers it to his mother who sucks it tenderly and then continues to chat with me. Migmar is five years old.

Elsewhere, even the baby is prevented from touching its own genitals, and masturbation is severely punished. In the United States, Caili's behavior would be considered child sexual abuse and she would be hauled off to jail!

Another series of variables relevant to personality formation consists of later childhood and adolescent experiences: the importance of the mother versus other caretakers, responsibilities for sibling caretaking and other work children are expected to do, the composition of children's play groups and opportunities for formal schooling and literacy at home (Weisner and Gallimore 1977; Whiting and Edwards 1988). As we will see, children's experience with caretaking and sibling interaction impacts social skills such as nurturance and responsibility.

The Influence of Subsistence Patterns

Although early theories of basic personality structure asserted a relationship between child-rearing practices and adult behavior, they could not explain how child rearing is related to the culture as a whole. John Whiting and colleagues, in contrast, developed a model for psychocultural research that proposed a causal relationship between parts of culture designated as "antecedents" and parts seen as "consequences," with child rearing and the development of personality as a crucial connecting link.

As seen in the Whiting model for psychocultural research, the antecedent elements consist of infrastructural and structural aspects of culture that comprise the **maintenance system**, defined as the "basic customs surrounding the nourishment, sheltering, and protection of its members" (Whiting and Child 1953). It includes the mode of production and the organization of domestic and political life, as it affects how adults raise their children.

Different modes of production require different daily life routines, which impel parents to interact with their children in certain ways, to assign different tasks, and to reward or punish different types of behavior.

The maintenance system influences the child's learning environment, including task assignment, the people with whom the child interacts, the nature of those interactions, and the methods of teaching skills and emotional expression. These experiences, in turn, affect adult modal personality.

The psychocultural model states that economic, social, and political factors outside the control of parents and other caretakers have universal influence on how parents rear their children.

The model also suggests that modal personality influences culture. The assumption is that if people have similar experiences and similar personalities, they will be more likely to find the same beliefs more plausible than others. These cultural beliefs, called the *projective-expressive system,* are part of superstructure. For example, John Whiting and colleagues show that mother–child sleeping arrangements are correlated with harsh male initiation rites signifying the ritual transition from childhood to adulthood.

Child Training and Male Initiation Rites

According to Burton and Whiting (1961), boys who sleep exclusively with their mothers past early infancy identify with their mothers and develop a "cross-sex identity." Cross-cultural research shows that

- Exclusive mother–child sleeping arrangements are correlated with patrilocality and postpartum sex

taboos that forbid the father from having intercourse with the mother for a year or more after she has given birth,

- Long postpartum sex taboos are mostly found in tropical areas where infant diets are deficient in protein. Long-term nursing ensures the child's health, so men are forbidden from having sex with their wives to guard against early pregnancy.

Male initiation rites tend to occur in patrilocal societies where boys initially sleep exclusively with their mothers and develop a primary feminine identification.

A boy's primary identification with his mother creates a special problem in patrilineal and patrilocal societies, where adult males must make a strong identification with their fathers and other males. The conflicting roles are reconciled at the cultural level through **severe male initiation rites** involving circumcision or other forms of mutilation, and trials of courage and stamina that demonstrate a boy's manhood and strengthen his masculine identification (Burton and Whiting 1961; Harrington and Whiting 1972:491).

The Six Cultures Study

In the 1950s John Whiting and his associates organized a cross-cultural comparative study of child-rearing practices in six cultures. Six teams of researchers systematically collected information on the environments of childhood and children's daily behavior in East Africa, India, Okinawa, Mexico, the Philippines, and the New England region of the United States. A standard set of protocols was used in all the field studies; children were observed at specified times and places for five minutes, and their behavior was recorded in narrative form by trained observers. These behavioral records were later used to extract a category system of twelve social acts dealing with dominance, aggression, nurturance, and prosocial action (Munroe and Munroe 1994). It should be noted that all the behaviors described were found in all communities but there are differences in both the frequency of behaviors and their emphasis in expressed norms.

In analyzing the results of the study, John and Beatrice Whiting (1975) used two dimensions for comparing children's social behaviors:

- **Dimension A**, differentiating nurturance and responsibility from dependence and dominance.

- **Dimension B**, differentiating sociable and intimate from authoritarian and aggressive behavior

Dimension A was found to be related to differences in **technological complexity** (children stay home versus attend school):

Societies Emphasizing Nurturance and Responsibility	Societies Emphasizing Dependence and Dominance
Simpler, lacking superordinate authority	Complex, with class stratification
Require a high degree of cooperation within the family and community	Train children to be competitive and achievement oriented
Mothers have a heavy workload; children are required to do domestic chores and child caretaking	Children expected to do well in school; their domestic chores are more arbitrary

Dimension B was found to be related to differences in **social organization** (nuclear versus extended households):

Societies Emphasizing Sociable and Intimate Behavior	Societies Emphasizing Authoritarian and Aggressive Behavior
Organized around nuclear families	Organized around extended families
Husband and wife sleep together	Husband and wife sleep apart
Low overt husband–wife aggression; couple likely to have intimate relationship	High husband–wife aggression; a man's loyalties are divided between his parents, siblings, uncles and his wife
Father-child relations are closer	Father-child relations are more distant

According to Dimension A, children fall into two groups, those who perform a high rate of chores and those who do not. In technologically simple societies with subsistence agriculture, mothers have heavy workloads and train their children to be helpful and responsible at an early age by assigning them chores. In technologically complex societies, mothers expect their children to do schoolwork, which encourages a competitive orientation; the research shows that these children seek attention and dominance, instead of showing concern for others.

According to Dimension B (which does not overlap with Dimension A), children's behavior is correlated with household characteristics instead of complexity. In nuclear family households, relationships are more intimate, whereas in extended households, husbands are less likely to have a close relationship with their wives and children. The family lives with or near the husband's parents, and as is typical in patrilineal kinship systems, relationships are hierarchical with greater social control—resulting in increased display of authoritarian-aggressive behavior.

The Effect of Social Environment on Children

To understand what conditions influence the lives of families and children, psychological anthropologists look at the range of variation in children's behaviors in terms of the **social ecology of childhood**, the environment of children's experiences that is most likely to affect their development. Features that affect the behavior of parents and children include

- The community and physical space where behavior takes place

- The personnel (cast of characters) with whom people interact

- The activities (daily routines) that are customarily performed

Thomas Weisner (1979) describes the environmental effects of urban versus rural households on children's social behavior. He studied a group of Kenyan mothers and children who spend time in the countryside and in the city. Migration to wage labor in towns is common. Men work in the city and mothers come to visit with their preschool children. In the city, rooms are small, houses are close together, and neighbors are usually strangers. Urban mothers have more trouble with their children. Restricted to small rooms without older siblings present to care for younger children, the younger children engage in more socially disruptive behavior. Compared with their rural counterparts, urban children lack opportunities to engage in tasks and chores with older children present. In the city, younger children seek to dominate and act more aggressively toward each another. Traditional respect for elders is nevertheless maintained—the disruptiveness of urban children is directed toward younger siblings, more than toward mothers.

Cultural Models of Child Care

We have seen how economic and social conditions impact children's social behavior. But how do these conditions influence the cultural expectations parents have of their children? Even though in our own society, we notice that parents have different ideas about the "right" way to raise children, when we look at other societies, it becomes clear that despite this variation, American parents do share distinct goals that set them apart from parents in other cultures.

Robert LeVine and his colleagues (1994) use an ecological framework to compare parental behavior among the Gusii of Western Kenya (who were originally part of the Six Culture Study) and middle-class white Americans in the Boston region of the United States, to account for the contrasting ways infants in the two cultures are cared for by their mothers.

Among the Gusii (see Chapter 9, "Polygyny" section), childcare practices are geared to ensure the health and survival of infants. The fertility rate is high, with birth intervals of two to three years. Although the Gusii infant mortality rate has declined in recent years, the mode of reproduction and infant care represents a response to earlier demographic conditions when the demand for children exceeded their rate of survival. According to LeVine and others (1994), the Gusii follow a **pediatric model of child care**; the primary goal is protection of the baby from life-threatening illness and other hazards. Constant holding, soothing, and immediate response to infant distress are most frequent during the first two and a half years. Boston mothers, in contrast, follow a **pedalogical model of child care**, in which primary concern is directed at active engagement and social exchange to stimulate the behavioral and social development of the child.

Pedalogical Childcare
Western culture is primarily concerned with stimulating cognitive and social development.

The Gusii pediatric model emphasizes the modulation of infant excitement and training for respect and compliance, whereas the American pedagogic model is directed at optimizing verbal development and initiative. These models represent different cultural goals developed in response to the environment in which each group lives.

From an American middle-class perspective, Gusii child care may be viewed as failing to prepare the child for schooling through the early development of language skills and assertiveness. But the research shows that Gusii children do develop appropriate language and cognitive skills. LeVine and coworkers suggest that this raises problems for Western developmental theories, which assume a single "average expectable environment"—specific parental practices that promote cognitive, emotional, and language skills in Western contexts—is universally necessary for nor-

mal child development. They conclude, "The Gusii teach us that the absence, during the first 2 to 3 years, of specific parental practices that promote cognitive, emotional, and language skills in Western contexts, does not necessarily constitute failure to provide what every child needs" (1994:275). Similarly, the Gusii view many Western children as rude, uncontrolled, improperly selfish, and disrespectful to adults and older children. They feel Western children will be unprepared for cooperative work and will not show appropriate deferential behavior. But that certainly does not mean that Western children do not learn how to work effectively and function as successful well-adjusted adults.

Learning among the Gusii, as well as among children in most non-Western cultures, starts through participation in activities at home and in the larger community. Alan Fiske (1999) points out that children acquire most of their culture by observing and imitating practices, without formal instruction or verbal explanation. This does not mean that they learn at a slower rate, but that they assume a different cultural model for learning. In fact, when asked to explain practices they themselves learned through observation, informants are often unable to explain or describe how tasks are done, even though they are perfectly capable of performing them (see Box 16.4 on page 256).

Box 16.4   How Children Learn Their Culture

Anthropologists expect to find adults teaching children how to do things and explaining the reasons, but they find that very little of this takes place. Children learn their culture on their own initiative, without explanations. At first children perform tasks with supervision, perhaps working alongside an older sibling. Children are highly motivated to observe and imitate people they respect. As they observe the behavior being modeled, they spontaneously imitate the action, and receive corrective feedback if they do something wrong. They are never given an explanation of the nature of the deficiency but are expected to figure it out for themselves. Thus, if people acquire their culture in large part by observation, imitation, and incremental participation, then researchers must do the same—not by asking them to explain the rules or perceptual constructs—but by observing their behavior and learning about their culture the same way they acquire cultural skills and experiences. (Adapted from Fiske 1999)

Acquiring Cultural Skills
Children work along side older individuals and learn by imitating behavior.

TAT (Thematic Apperception Test)
This is one of many methods used by psychological anthropologists. These pictures, developed specifically for East Africa, present situations for expressing values about aggression. Respondents are asked to tell a story about "What is happening in the picture?" and "What ought to happen?" (From Edgerton, Robert B. 1971)

Subsistence and Adult Personality

Walter Goldschmidt (1965) designed a comparative study of four communities in East Africa, known as the Culture and Ecology Research Project, to study the relationship between the mode of production and personality attributes. This study bypassed child rearing and sought to show a direct relationship between subsistence activities and adult personality. Four tribal groups were selected, the Kamba, Hehe, Sebei, and Pokot. Within each of these cultures, there are groups that live primarily as pastoralists and others as

horticulturalists. Robert Edgerton (1971) used a battery of questionnaires and TAT tests (see drawings) to elicit cultural values and attitudes of adult members in eight communities (four tribal groups with two subsistence modes in each tribe) and to compare the effects of cultural membership versus mode of production on personality attributes.

The results show that both culture (tribal affiliation) and subsistence modes account for differences among the groups. For example, the researchers found uniformity within each tribal group so that a Pokot pastoralist is more like a Pokot farmer than he is like a pastoralist from another tribal group. At the same time, there are also clear differences between pastoralists and farmers that are consistent with the kinds of subsistence activities in which they engage.

The most significant differences are:

Farmers show more disrespect for authority.

Farmers favor conflict avoidance and show indirect aggression.

Farmers resort to secrecy, and emotional restraint.

Farmers mention witchcraft and magic more often, which is a sign of covert aggression.

Pastoralists show respect for authority, especially elders.

Pastoralists are more open about expressing feelings.

Pastoralists are more direct in their actions and believe people should be allowed to fight.

Pastoralists believe that sorcery occurs when anger is not dispelled.

Farmers are tied to the land and cannot easily move away. They resort to indirect aggression to avoid overt conflict with troublesome neighbors. Pastoralists maintain a high degree of mobility and can move if hostility surfaces. They act independently and aggress openly.

Farmers have higher population density due to a shortage of suitable farm land. Households are clustered together, and farmers need to maintain good relations with people who are their neighbors for life. Greater wealth differences among farmers create social tension. Also, farmers have to pay taxes or rents to landlords, which accounts for their resentment of authority.

Despite their independence, pastoralists have respect for authority, which is based on their reliance on elders for knowledge of herd and water management. Yet herding cattle requires pastoralists to be self-reliant and ready to protect their herd from theft and predatory animals. Whereas farmers are more restrained and fatalistic, pastoralists more freely express emotions, both positive and negative.

Schemas and Cognition

Psychological anthropologists have long been interested in the question of the relationship between culture and cognitive processes (how people think). The concept of *schema*, borrowed from cognitive psychology, reveals how thoughts about culture are organized in the minds of individuals. **Schemas** provide people with simplified models of what the world is like and how one ought to act, feel, and think (D'Andrade 1992, 1995). A classic example of a schema is what one can normally expect to happen if one goes to a restaurant:

Sit at a table.

Look at a menu.

Tell a waiter or waitress what we want.

Eat.

Wait for a check.

Pay it.

Go out.

(Adapted from Strauss 1992:198)

Such a sequence, sometimes called a *script,* is never exactly what happens in any particular instance, but the knowledge of such a schema organizes our perceptions of ongoing restaurant experiences or our understanding of stories of what happens when other people go to restaurants.

Schemas represent knowledge developed from prior experiences; they are abstract representations (not carbon copies) of perceived regularities that help us comprehend new events and experiences.

Cultures differ in their repertory of schemas. One that is found in Samoa, for example, is organized around the concept of *alofa,* loosely equivalent to our "love." It is associated with the following scenario: an old person is carrying a heavy burden, walking along the road on a hot day. Just as a New Yorker knows the script for a restaurant, so a Samoan knows what to do if such an encounter takes place:

Offer to carry the burden.

Bring the old person into the shade.

Serve a cooling drink.

(Strauss 1992: 198)

According to Roy D'Andrade (1992:30–31), cultural schemas help us understand people's motivations—what leads them to act as they do.

Schemas not only determine how we act and interpret the world but also serve as goals and models that motivate our behavior.

Schemas are culturally adaptive in that they organize motivation as well as knowledge. They set goals (both conscious and unconscious) for specific cultural contexts, define what certain events mean, and elicit culturally appropriate behavioral and affective responses.

According to Claudia Strauss (1992), schemas have different kinds of motivational force, based on a person's experience. In fact, goals embedded in a schema may be contradictory, and while people adhere to these goals, they cannot always follow them. For example, based on her research on career choices of five factory workers in Rhode Island, Strauss identifies two main schemas that have different motivational effects: *the success model* associated with initiative for "getting ahead," and the *breadwinner model,* which focuses on the interests of the family and the need for a steady paycheck.

Four of the five men she interviewed endorsed the success model, agreeing that hard work will bring success. But only one of the four made career moves that were strategically consistent with the goal for success. The other three shared the values but were not motivated to act accordingly. They did not view themselves as economically successful and felt that success values were less applicable to them. The role of breadwinner, in contrast, was seen as inevitable. All five felt they had to bring home the paycheck—the breadwinner role is not just an ideal but a way of life that is class and gender specific. They felt their obligation was to support their families and keep a steady paycheck coming. This forced them to subordinate their own goals for success. For these men, "it is not a question of striving for wealth above all, but of avoiding near-poverty" (1992:208).

The one man who rejected the success model turned out to be the one who worked harder than anyone else in the group. He had a large family to support and worked two jobs, including overtime. His rejection of the success model was based on his identification with the poor and his distaste for businesspeople, whom he saw as greedy and overly concerned with making money.

This research suggests that motivation is not automatically acquired through cultural messages. Culture is only partially successful in inculcating shared values in its members. Schemas organize alternative goals that may compete with one another. Therefore schema theory is useful for understanding how emic models are organized, but etic knowledge is needed to explain why some cultural messages are incorporated and others are ignored.

Culture and Mental Illness

Medical research has shown that such classic mental disorders as schizophrenia and manic-depressive disorder probably have important viral-genetic and chemical-neurological bases (Torrey 1980). This accords with the evidence that the rates of those diseases are similar among groups as diverse as Swedes, the Inuit, the Yoruba of West Africa, and modern Canadians (Murphy 1976; Warner 1985). However, there is no doubt that, though broad symptoms of the same mental diseases can be found cross-culturally, specific symptoms and the way they are perceived in different cultures vary considerably. In fact striking cultural and social class differences in both symptoms and outcome of mental disorders have been found (Jenkins et al.1991).

Depression

Feeling sad, "down" or "blue" at times is a normal emotion. Psychologists, however, consider **depression** to be a disorder when it goes beyond normal sadness, into a state of constant and excessive sadness, despair, and isolation.

The cultural conception of the problem of depression varies cross-culturally.

In Latin America, it is associated with a profound sense of tragedy that is part of a tradition of working through oppressive life circumstances, whereas among Anglo-Americans, suffering is not an expectable or acceptable state; it is something that must be overcome in order to pursue happiness. In some cultural contexts, people are willing to endure suffering associated with expressed sadness, whereas Americans more commonly voice anger and frustration.

A number of studies report a significantly higher rate of depression among women than men. For married women, depression is associated with the conflicts generated by the traditional female role. For women the predominant symptoms are more likely to be depressive episodes and phobias, whereas for men antisocial personality and alcohol abuse are more likely (Robins et al. 1984). Low socioeconomic status is also linked to vulnerability to depression. Thus, sociopolitical aspects of emotion clearly go beyond biological or psychological states of mind and must be viewed in terms of power relations and social inequalities.

Schizophrenia

Medical research has shown that classic mental disorders such as schizophrenia probably have important genetic and chemical-neurological bases. The same core signs of **schizophrenia** appear in cultures around the world: Hallucinations, delusions, inappropriate behavior and disturbance of thought. Despite biological vulnerability to the disease and similar broad symptoms, it appears that specific symptoms of schizophrenia vary cross-culturally and social environment may affect the course of the illness.

The World Health Organization (1968, 1979) conducted a nine-country study of schizophrenia that shows the incidence of core symptoms are similar worldwide, although the frequency and content of hallucinations appear to vary with reference to cultural and religious belief systems. Moreover, the study found that patients in the least developed countries had a better outcome than patients in the most developed countries.

In developing countries the extended family is an important resource for the treatment of schizophrenia and other disorders.

Patients in less developed countries with extended family involvement seek earlier treatment, are discharged sooner, and their recovery is more complete (Karno and Jenkins 1997).

Relatives in less developed countries continue to render emotional and physical support, while the community may blame the schizophrenic's bizarre behavior on some pesky spirit. In contrast, schizophrenics in industrial societies are often expelled from both family and community, deprived of emotional and physical support, isolated, and made to feel worthless and guilty. These culturally constructed conditions make the prospect for recovery much poorer in industrial societies despite the availability of modern medical therapies.

Families that respond with tolerance and acceptance toward schizophrenic family members contribute to improved outcome. Research in England, India, and the United States found that "expressed emotion" (EE)—a measure of criticism and hostility, on the part of family members—is associated with poor outcome. Among high-EE Anglo-American relatives, there is also doubt or disbelief in the legitimacy of the illness (Jenkins et al. 1986).

Culture influences people's response to schizophrenic family members.

A comparative study of Mexican-American and Anglo-American families with schizophrenic family members showed that Mexican-American families are typically lower in EE than Anglo-Americans. Janis Jenkins points out that the concept of **nervios** (nerves)—which describes a wide range of mental conditions—is used to account for schizophrenic illness. The term reduces the stigma associated with mental illness and reinforces tolerant inclusion. Many relatives report that they feel more affection for the patient and that they would never abandon their ill relative (Jenkins et al. 1986:45). This contrasts sharply with both Irish and Irish-American families, who adopt the heavily stigmatized term "mental," which virtually leads to complete family rejection and abandonment (see Profile 16.2).

Profile 16.2   Schizophrenia in Rural Ireland

According to the World Health Organization Statistics Report (1968), the psychiatric hospitalization rate for Ireland is 7.37 people per thousand, the highest recorded for any country in the world. Approximately half the Irish psychiatric hospital population is diagnosed as schizophrenic. The highest rates of the illness are among middle-aged bachelors from economically depressed areas in Ireland's conservative western counties. Male patients in the 35–45 age range outnumber female patients by two to one.

Nancy Scheper-Hughes (1979) proposes that the culture of western Ireland is schizophrenia-producing. Her research in the parish of Ballybran links the high rates of mental illness to the disintegration of rural Irish culture and the accompanying breakdown in traditional patterns of Irish familism.

Traditionally Irish countrymen managed the family farm by keeping landholdings intact. Children did not marry until late in life, when the father was ready to abdicate his control over the farm. The most capable son was chosen to inherit the farm and the parents moved into the "west room," where they lived out the remainder of their lives. One or more daughters might marry; otherwise the siblings either remained on the farm or took jobs in town (Arensberg 1968). Since the mid-nineteenth-century "Great Famine," celibacy and late marriage have tended to increase. These can be seen as adaptations to the high rural birthrates and land shortages.

The Irish family farmer cannot keep up with the forces of industrialization that have impacted the region.

Large-scale industrialized agriculture contradicts the basic values of the local small-scale farmer. Older villagers refuse to hire tractors or pay people to increase productivity. The dissatisfaction with life on small farms is greatest among girls and their mothers. Over 80 percent of the unmarried women reject the roles of wife and mother on the small farms. There is a steady migration of young women, as well as men, to England and other urban centers, at a younger age than ever before.

The result is a large male bachelor population with little hope of marriage. Only one in three adult males in Ballybran is married; there are sixty-four bachelors in the parish over age 35 but only twenty-seven unmarried women in their age group. The youngest son, who is usually the last one to escape, is apt to get stuck with the marginal farm and a life of celibacy and service to his elderly parents. The one "stuck" is often ridiculed by parents and friends. Even before the fact, he is labeled the "dummy," and in other ways made to feel inadequate.

Traditional patterns of child care have also been altered as a result of the breakdown of the extended farm family. Parents are ambivalent toward infants and children; children are seemingly greatly desired—the source of envy and jealousy among adult villagers who have none—and yet often resented by those who do have them. Small children are both overprotected and frequently ignored (Scheper-Hughes 1979:133). Child care is regarded as low-status work, suitable for old women, who were responsible for it in the past. Mothers say that

(continued)

Profile 16.2   Schizophrenia in Rural Ireland *(continued)*

the heavy workload is responsible for their not breast-feeding or singing lullabies to their children. Mothers do not cuddle infants, and there is low tolerance for crying. Passivity is rewarded; babies are left to "cry it out" or are tranquilized with brandy to keep them quiet. A child who questions an order or does not do what he or she is told, is subjected to a beating, so that fear becomes a strong sentiment among children toward their parents. Children learn to deal with disappointment and other emotional hurts with silent resentment. As adults, it is particularly bad for males to show signs of "weakness," such as tenderness or love. This early conditioning interferes with marital and sexual intimacy; it creates problems between men and women expressed in a lack of sexual vitality and reluctance for men to court and marry.

Marriages used to be arranged by parents. Today young people want to base marriage on romantic love, and women particularly expect sexual and emotional fulfillment. Sex, however, remains a conflict ridden area; husbands and wives are unable to communicate about such matters, and retreat into silent resentment. As one

man put it, "I missed a lot in never marrying. But if, by mistake, I'd taken the wrong woman, I would have got stuck for good" (Scheper-Hughes 1979:104).

Men express fears of impotence and have low self-esteem. They accept the burden of responsibility laid upon them and suffer most from trying to reconcile conflicting role demands. They are more passive and conforming to authority than women and show suppressed rage in anti-authoritarian fantasies. Women, on the other hand, show more open rebellious tendencies against parental control and a greater sense of autonomy, which prepares females for early emigration from the village and allows them to feel less guilt about leaving elderly family behind.

The connection between male celibacy and mental illness is associated with the economic changes that have led to the demise of the rural economy. The men who inherit the land experience emotional isolation, loss of self-esteem, and frustration by their inability to marry and continue the family farm. Scheper-Hughes concludes that the high rate of schizophrenia in rural Ireland results from the demise of the rural economy.

Culture-Specific Psychoses

Evidence for more powerful effects of culture on mental illness can be found in **culture-specific psychoses**—disorders that have a distinctive set of symptoms limited to only one or a few cultures (Simmons and Hughes 1985). There are several well-known examples of these culture-specific psychoses that are experienced and communicated in culturally specific forms in non-Western societies.

- *Pibloktoq* is a hysterical disorder characterized by agitated attempts to flee the presence of other people. It occurs among the Inuit and is also called Arctic hysteria. Unlike classic psychoses, pibloktoq strikes suddenly. Its victims leap up, tear off their clothes, move their limbs convulsively, and roll about naked in the snow and ice. One explanation for this behavior likens it to a severe case of "cabin fever." Cooped up in their small, crowded dwellings for long periods during which they are unable to vent their feelings of hostility, pibloktoq victims may become hysterical as a means of dealing with their pent-up frustrations. It seems more likely, however, that the underlying cause also lies in the highly carnivorous diet of the Inuits. Lacking plant foods and solar radiation, the Inuit are forced to rely on the consumption of sea mammal and polar

bear livers for their supply of vitamin A and vitamin D. Eating too much of these livers produces a poisonous excess of vitamin A, but eating too little can result in a deficit of vitamin D, which in turn leads to a deficit of calcium in the bloodstream. Both conditions—too much vitamin A and too little calcium in the blood—are known to be associated with convulsions and psychotic episodes (Landy 1985; Wallace 1972). Thus, pibloktoq is probably a consequence of the interaction between culturally determined living conditions and the chemistry of nutrition.

- *Amok* is a hysterical reaction in which young men attack other people and destroy their property. It is found primarily in New Guinea, only among men between ages 25–35. After a period of initial depression the victim emerges in a burst of energy and runs amok. He appears delirious. This is what the Gururumba of New Guinea describe as "being a wild pig," attacking people, bursting into houses and stealing things. Phillip Newman describes an event that lasted three days. "His actions had all the classic signs of anxiety hysteria: his speech and hearing were partially blocked . . . he behaved irrationally, and when he did speak it was either in the form of commands or blatant false statements. . . . When it was over, he claimed no mem-

Arctic Hysteria
The victim is an Innuit woman from Greenland.

ory of it" (1965:96). The victim left the village for several days, and while he was gone people talked about what had happened. They believed the young man was susceptible to the disorder because of his inability to deal with mounting economic pressures. On his return, people left him alone to function at a less intense level of community involvement, which allowed him to readjust to the demands of society.

■ ***Anorexia nervosa*** is an obsessive-compulsive disorder characterized by an unrealistic appraisal of one's body as overweight, resulting in self-starvation to achieve a more slender look. An estimated 5 to 10 percent of adolescent girls in the United States are currently affected. The disorder mostly afflicts Anglo-American, middle-class young women (Brumberg 1988). The cultural ideal of a slim body is associated with an expectation that perfection can be achieved through control and mastery of one's body. Victims of the disorder are "model children" who commonly feel inadequate in their social roles. They use their bodies as instruments of competition to gain mastery and fulfillment.

Summary

1. Culture and personality are closely related concepts concerned with the patterning of thoughts, feelings, and behavior. Personality is primarily a characteristic of individuals; culture is primarily a characteristic of groups. Yet it is possible to speak of the personality of a group—of a basic, modal, or typical personality.

2. Anthropologists who studied personality during the 1940s and 1950s generally accepted the Freudian premise that personality is molded by childhood experiences. This premise has led to an interest in both universal and culture-specific aspects of early childhood experiences and personality formation. Freud's theories, however, have been modified. Today most anthropologists acknowledge that oedipal conflicts may result from the emotional ambivalence of family relationships but emphasize that emotional content varies in relation to structural aspects of culture.

3. Early approaches to culture and personality attempted to characterize whole cultures in terms of central themes or patterns. Ruth Benedict believed each culture is organized around a distinctive configuration of customs and values that influence individual personality.

4. Margaret Mead emphasized that human nature is malleable. Knowledge of the range of variation of cultural patterns and the spectrum of enculturation practices should contribute to our understanding of alternatives to Euro-American culture.

5. An early causal model for explaining personality structure was developed by Abram Kardiner. He proposed that primary institutions (subsistence techniques) give rise to basic personality, which in turn creates or maintains secondary or projective institutions (religion, ideology, and so on.)

6. To understand cross-cultural variation in psychological characteristics, researchers have focused on child-rearing customs. The Whitings show that a culture's maintenance system (the means of production, settlement patterns, social structure and so forth) which influences task assignment and social structure, shapes children's social behavior.

7. The means of production also directly influences adult personality. Members of farming and pastoral communities show personality differences related to resource ownership, mobility, and defense.

8. The concept of schemas has been used to identify the cognitive organization of cultures. Schemas organize motivation and elicit culturally appropriate responses. Schemas, however, do not completely predict behavior; they provide a range of possibilities rather than a blueprint for behavior.

9. A wide range of personality types is found in any large population. This is not to deny that profound differences exist between personality patterns in different cultures. The Japanese, for example, have a distinctive disposition to separate ego-effacing from ego-asserting situations. This disposition, however, cannot be reduced to the stereotype that Japanese are hypocritical or devious; the Japanese have different presentations of self in public and private settings.

10. Classic mental disorders such as depression and schizophrenia are modified by cultural influences, yet they occur in many societies and probably result form interactions between cultural, biochemical, and genetic variables. Culture influences family response to mental illness and can affect the patients' prospects for recovery.

11. The high rate of mental illness in western Ireland suggests that family conditions may be pathogenic. The economic decline of the rural farm presents a burden for the youngest sons, who are left on the homestead to take care of their elderly parents—they are left with a worthless farm and no prospects of marrying.

12. Culture-specific psychoses such as *pibloktoq, amok,* and *anorexia* indicate that cultural factors may powerfully influence the state of mental health.

KEY TERMS

basic personality structure
cultural configurations
culture
culture-specific psychoses
depression
maintenance system
matrilineal complex
modal personality
national character
nervios
Oedipus complex
pedalogic model of child care
pediatric model of child care
personality
primary institutions
private (inner) self
psychoanalysis
public (interactional) self
schema
schizophrenia
secondary institutions
severe male initiation rites
social ecology of childhood
technological complexity

QUESTIONS TO THINK ABOUT

1. What modifications have anthropologists made to Freud's definition of the oedipal complex?
2. How do Ruth Benedict and Margaret Mead demonstrate that culture determines personality differences?
3. What role do "primary institutions" have in forming basic personality structure?
4. What are the strengths and weaknesses of national character studies?
5. How does social complexity and household structure influence children's behavior in the Six Cultures Study?
6. What ecological factors explain differences between the Gusii and Anglo-American childcare?
7. What are cultural schemas, and how do they influence behavior?
8. How does culture influence mental illness?

CHAPTER 17

Religion

Animism

Animatism and Mana

Natural and Supernatural

Magic and Religion

The Organization of Religious Beliefs and Practices
Individualistic Beliefs and Rituals
Shamanistic Cults
Communal Cults
PROFILE: Ndembu Communal Rites of Circumcision
Ecclesiastical Cults
PROFILE: The Religion of the Aztecs

Religion and Political Economy: High Gods

Revitalization Movements
Native American Revitalizations
Melanesian Cargo Cults

Taboo, Religion, and Ecology
Incest Taboo
Taboos against Pork
The Sacred Cow

Summary

America Now: The Electronic Church

Buddhist Monk, Rangoon, Myanmar.

Now we are entering the inner sanctum of superstructure, the domain of religion, myth, magic, ritual, and all the other aspects of cultures that are intended to mediate between ordinary beings and forces, on the one hand, and extraordinary beings and forces on the other. First some basic definitions will be needed. Then we shall try to classify the basic types of religious organizations and rituals. Finally, we shall range over the vast variety of religious behaviors, from puberty rites to messianic cults, from prayer to cannibal feasts, and from abominable pigs to sacred cows. Can aspects of religion be explained in terms of structure and infrastructure? To a considerable degree. Yet religion can frequently become a powerful force in its own right. Although infrastructural and structural conditions provide a means for understanding the origin of many specific beliefs and rituals, religion frequently plays a crucial role in strengthening the impulses leading toward major transformations in social life.

religion: idea of god/s
or no god

Animism

The earliest anthropological attempt to define religion was that of E. B. Tylor (1871). In his book *Primitive Culture,* he demonstrated that members of every society believe that inside the ordinary, visible, tangible bodies of humans and other life forms there is a normally invisible, normally intangible being: the soul. He named this belief **animism**.

Animism is the belief that humans share the world with a population of extraordinary, mostly invisible beings.

Why is animism universal? Tylor reasoned that if a belief recurred again and again in virtually all times and places, it could not be a product of mere fantasy. Rather, it must have grounding in evidence and in experiences that were equally recurrent and universal. What were these experiences? Tylor pointed to dreams, trances, visions, shadows, reflections, and death. During dreams, the body stays in bed; yet another part of us gets up, talks to people, and travels to distant lands. Trances and drug-induced visions also bring vivid evidence of another self, distinct and separate from one's body. Shadows and mirror images reflected in still water point to the same conclusion, even in the full light of normal wakefulness. The concept of an inner being—a soul—makes sense of all this. It is the soul that wanders off when we sleep, that lies in the shadows, and that peers back at us from the surface of the pond. Most of all, the soul explains the mystery of death: a lifeless body is a body permanently deprived of its soul.

Tylor has been criticized by twentieth-century anthropologists for his suggestion that animism arose merely as a result of the attempt to understand puzzling human and natural phenomena. Today, we know that religion is much more than an attempt to explain puzzling phenomena. Like other aspects of superstructure, religion serves a multitude of economic, political, and psychological functions.

Another important criticism of Tylor's stress on the puzzle-solving function of religion concerns the role of hallucinations in shaping religious beliefs. During drug-induced trances and other forms of hallucinatory experience, people "see" and "hear" extraordinary things that seem even more "real" than ordinary people and animals. One can argue, therefore, that animistic theories are not intellectual attempts to explain trances and dreams but direct expressions of extraordinary psychological experiences. Nonetheless, it cannot be denied that religion and the doctrine of souls also provides people with answers to fundamental questions about the meaning of life and death and the causes of events (Pandian 1992:88).

Although certain animistic beliefs are universal, each culture has its own distinctive animistic beings and its own specific elaboration of the soul concept. Even the number of a person's souls varies cross-culturally:

- The ancient Egyptians had two and so do many West African cultures: one from mother's ancestors and one from the father's.
- The J'varo of Ecuador (Harner 1984) have three souls. The first soul—the *mekas*—gives life to the body. The second soul—the *arutam*—has to be captured through a drug-induced visionary experience at a sacred waterfall. It confers bravery in battle to the possessor. The third soul—the *musiak*—forms inside the head of a dying warrior and attempts to avenge his death. It is to gain control over the musiak soul that the J'varo cut off the fallen warrior's head, "shrink" it, and bring it back to their village where it is the focus of rituals designed to transfer its powers to its captor.
- The Dahomey say that women have three souls and that men have four. Both sexes have an ancestor soul, a personal soul, and a *mawn* soul. The ancestor soul gives protection during life, the personal soul is accountable for what people do with their lives, and the mawn soul is a bit of the creator god, Mawn, who supplies divine guidance. The exclusively male fourth soul guides men to positions of leadership in their households and lineages.
- The Fang of Gabon have seven: a brain soul, a heart soul, a name soul, a life force soul, a body soul, a shadow soul, and a ghost soul (Riviere 1987).

Animatism and Mana

Robert Marett (1914) complained that Tylor's definition of religion as animism was too narrow. When people attribute lifelike properties to rocks, pots, storms, and volcanoes, they do not necessarily believe that souls cause the lifelike behavior of these objects. Hence, Marett introduced the term *animatism* to designate a supernatural force that does not derive its effect from souls.

Animatism is the belief in diffuse impersonal power that people can control under certain conditions.

Marett uses the Melanesian word *mana* to refer to a concentrated form of animatistic force.

Mana is the possession of concentrated animatistic force that gives certain objects, animals, and people extraordinary powers independent of power derived from souls and gods.

An adze that makes intricate carvings, a fishhook that catches large fish, a club that kills many enemies, or a horseshoe that brings "good luck" have large amounts of mana. People, too, may be spoken of as having more or less mana. A woodcarver whose work is especially intricate and beautiful possesses mana, whereas a warrior captured by the enemy has obviously lost his mana.

In its broadest range of meaning, mana simply indicates belief in a powerful force. In Western cultures, the concept of luck and charisma closely resemble the idea of mana. A horseshoe posesses a concentrated power that brings good luck. Vitamin pills are consumed by many millions of people in the expectation that they will exert a powerful effect on health and well-being. Soaps and detergents are said to clean because of "cleaning power," gasolines provide engines with "starting power" or "go-power," salespeople are prized for their "selling power," and politicians are said to have charisma or "vote-getting power." Many people fervently believe that they are "lucky" or "unlucky," which can be interpreted as a belief that they control varying quantities of mana.

Natural and Supernatural

Marett's idea that religion involves a belief in mana is problematical because the distinction between **natural** and **supernatural** is culturally defined. If a belief in a powerful supernatural force constitutes religion, then what prevents belief in the natural force of gravity, electricity, or other concepts of physics from being regarded as religious beliefs? Saying that mana is a supernatural force outside the realm of the observable world, whereas electricity is a natural force because it can be scientifically tested, does not solve this problem.

Most cultures do not distinguish between natural and supernatural realms.

In a society where people believe ghosts are always present, it is not necessarily either natural or supernatural to provide dead ancestors with food and drink. The culture may simply lack emic categories for "natural" and "supernatural." Similarly, when a shaman blows smoke over a patient and triumphantly removes a sliver of bone allegedly inserted by the patient's enemy, the question of whether the performance is natural or supernatural may have no emic meaning.

Writing of the Gururumba of the highlands of western New Guinea, Philip Newman notes that they "have a series of beliefs postulating the existence of entities and forces we would call supernatural." Yet the contrast between natural and supernatural is not emically relevant to the Gururumba themselves:

> It should be mentioned that our use of the notion "supernatural" does not correspond to any Gururumba concept: they do not divide the world into natural and supernatural parts. Certain entities, forces, and processes must be controlled partially through lusu, a term denoting rituals relating to growth, curing, or the stimulation of strength, while others need only rarely be controlled in this way. However, lusu does not contrast with

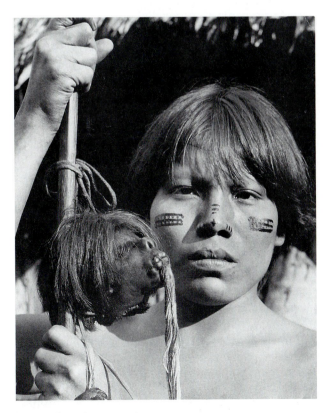

Jivaro Shrunken Head

any term denoting a realm of control where the nature of controls differ from lusu. Consequently lusu is simply part of all control techniques and what it controls is simply part of all things requiring human control. (1965:83)

Magic and Religion

In his famous book, *The Golden Bough* (1911–1915), Sir James Frazer attempted to define religion. For Frazer, the question of whether a belief was religious or not centered on the extent to which the participants felt they could make an entity or force do their bidding. If the participants felt insecure and humble and were inclined to supplicate and request favors and dispensations, their beliefs and actions were essentially **religious.** If they thought they were in control of the entities and forces governing events, felt no uncertainty about the outcome, and experienced no need for humble supplication, their beliefs and practices were examples of **magic** rather than of religion.

Frazer regarded prayer as the essence of religious ritual. But prayers are not always rendered in a mood of supplication. For example, prayers among the Navajo must be letter-perfect to be effective. Yet the Navajo do not expect that letter-perfect prayers will always get results. Thus, the line between prayers and "magical spells" is actually hard to draw.

Not all cultures approach their gods as supplicants. In many cultures, people try to intimidate, bribe, and lie to their gods. The Tsimshian of the Canadian Pacific Coast stamp their feet and shake their fists at the heavens and call their gods "slaves" as a term of reproach. The Manus of the Bismarck Archipelago keep the skulls of their ancestors in a corner of the house and try their best to please "Sir Ghost." However, if someone gets sick, the Manus may angrily

threaten to throw Sir Ghost out of the house. This is what they tell Sir Ghost: "This man dies and you rest in no house. You will but wander about the edges of the island [used for excretory functions]" (Fortune 1965:216).

Religion and magic are both symbolic systems that help people cope with the ambiguities, and anxieties, of everyday life. Religion, however, emphasizes explanation and is practiced regularly, whereas magic is a means of manipulation that targets specific, immediate problems. When people face danger or uncertainty, they turn to magic. According to Malinowski (1935), magic provides psychological safety, allowing people to perform tasks without being distracted by fears.

One can find an analogous use of magic in the little rituals and routines that baseball players engage in as they come up to bat, such as touching their caps, spitting or rubbing their hands. Other rituals include eating the same food at the same time of day, taking the same route to the ball park, wearing the same clothes, and carrying certain good luck charms in order to keep a winning streak going (Gmelch 1971). None of this has any real connection with getting a hit, but constant repetition reduces anxiety and can improve the players' performance.

The Organization of Religious Beliefs and Practices

Anthropologist Anthony Wallace (1966) distinguished four principal varieties of religious "cults"—that is, forms of organization of religious doctrines and activities—that have broad evolutionary implications. The passage of time has not brought forth a better classification. Wallace's four principal forms are (1) individualistic cults, (2) shamanistic cults, (3) communal cults, and (4) ecclesiastical cults, defined as follows:

Cult Type	Role Specialization	Political Complexity	Example
Individualistic	No role specialization Most basic form of religious life Each person enters into a relationship with animistic being when in need of control or protection	Egalitarian band and village societies	Inuit hunters, Crow warrior vision quest
Shamanistic	Part-time specialization Shamans work in direct communication with the supernatural, as diviners, curers, spirit mediums, and magicians They serve people in need, in exchange for gifts, fees, prestige, or power	Egalitarian band and village societies	!Kung, J'varo, and Tapirapé
Communal	Groups of nonspecialists perform rites for the community, deemed vital to the well-being of individuals and society	Lineage-based societies	Rites of solidarity; rites of passage among the Ndembu
Ecclesiastical	Full-time professional clergy who work as intermediaries between society and the supernatural in a hierarchical organization under the control of a centralized church	State societies	Aztec, Incas, (also Egyptians, Christianity, Judaism, Buddhism, and Islam)

Individualistic Beliefs and Rituals

Individualistic cults do not make distinctions between specialists and laypeople. One might call this "do it yourself" religion, where all people are their own specialists. As is common in native North and South America, individuals acquire a personal guardian spirit or supernatural protector—typically by means of a visionary experience induced by fasting, self-inflicted torture, or hallucinogenic drugs.

The Inuit.   The individualism of much of Inuit belief and ritual parallels the individualism of the Inuit mode of production. Hunters alone or in small groups constantly match their wits against the cunning and strength of animal prey and confront the dangers of travel over the ice and the threats of storms and month-long nights. The Inuit hunter is equipped with an ingenious array of technological devices that make life possible in the Arctic, but the outcome of the daily struggle remains in doubt. From the Inuit's point of view, it is imperative to be well equipped to handle both the danger of the harsh

physical elements and the danger of offending or not properly warding off unseen spirits and forces.

Vigilant individual effort is needed to deal with wandering human and animal souls, place spirits, Sedna (the Keeper of the Sea Animals), the Sun, the Moon, and the Spirit of the Air. Part of each hunter's equipment is his hunting song, a combination of chant, prayer, and magic formula that he inherits from his father or father's brothers or purchases from some famous hunter or shaman. In return for protection and hunting success given by his Spirit Helpers, the hunter has to observe certain taboos, refrain from hunting or eating certain species, or avoid trespassing in a particular locale. Moreover, a hunter should never sleep out on the ice edge. Note that some of these "superstitions" may alleviate psychological stress or have a practical value for hunting or some other aspect of Inuit life. Not sleeping out on the ice, for example, is a safety precaution.

The Crow.   For many native North Americans, a hallucinatory vision is the central experience of life. Young men need this hallucinatory experience to be

San Curing
Shaman in a trance.

Female Shaman
Piegan "medicine woman." Female shamans are as common as male shamans.

successful in love, warfare, horsestealing, trading, and all other important endeavors. In keeping with their code of personal bravery and endurance, they seek these visions primarily through self-inflicted torture.

Among the Crow a youth who craves the visionary experience of his elders, goes alone into the mountains, strips off his clothes, and abstains from food and drink. If this is not sufficient, he chops off part of the fourth finger of his left hand. Coached from childhood to expect that a vision would come, most Crow vision-seekers are successful. A buffalo, snake, chicken hawk, thunderbird, dwarf, or mysterious stranger appears; miraculous events unfold; and then these strange beings "adopt" the vision-seeker and disappear.

Scratches-face, who was one of Robert Lowie's informants, prayed to the morning star: "Old woman's grandson, I give you this (finger joint). Give me something good in exchange. . . . A good horse . . . a good-natured woman . . . a tent of my own to live in" (Lowie 1948 [1924]:6). Lowie reports that after cutting off his finger, Scratches-face saw six men riding horses. One of them said, "You have been poor, so I'll give you what you want." Suddenly the trees around them turned into enemy warriors who began to shoot at the six horsemen. The horsemen rode away but returned unscathed. The spokesman then said to Scratches-face, "If you want to fight all the people on the earth, do as I do, and you will be able to fight for three days or four days and yet not be shot." The enemy attacked again, but Scratches-face's benefactor knocked them down with a spear. According to Lowie (1948 [1924]:6), "In consequence of his blessing Scratches-face struck and killed an enemy without ever getting wounded. He also obtained horses and married a good-tempered and industrious woman."

Although each Crow's vision had some unique elements, they were usually similar in the following regards:

- Some revelation of future success in warfare, horse-raiding, or other acts of bravery was involved.
- The visions usually occurred at the end of the fourth day—four being the sacred number of the native North Americans.
- Practically every vision was accompanied by the acquisition of a sacred song.
- The friendly spirits in the vision adopted the youth.
- Trees or rocks often turned into enemies who vainly shot at the invulnerable spirit being.

Lowie concludes, "He sees and hears not merely what any faster, say in British Columbia or South Africa would see and hear under like conditions of physiological exhaustion and under the urge of generally human desires, but what the social tradition of the Crow tribe imperatively suggests" (1948 [1924]:14).

Shamanistic Cults

Shamans are women or men who are socially recognized as having special abilities for entering into contact with spirit beings and for controlling supernatural forces.

To become a shaman an individual must undergo a difficult apprenticeship to acquire the ability of entering into trance states. In trance the Shaman's powers increase. He or she can then heal the sick.

There are broad similarities in the techniques used by shamans to cure their patients. The shaman goes into a trance by smoking tobacco, taking drugs, beating on a drum, dancing monotonously, or simply by closing his or her eyes and concentrating. The trance begins with rigidity of the body, sweating, and heavy breathing. While in the trance, the shaman may act as a medium, transmitting messages from the ancestors. With the help of friendly spirits, shamans predict future events, locate lost objects, identify the cause of illness, battle with spirits on behalf of the patient, prescribe cures, and give advice on how clients can protect themselves against the evil intentions of enemies.

There is a close relationship between shamanistic cults and individualistic vision quests. Shamans are usually personalities who are psychologically predisposed toward hallucinatory experiences. In cultures that use hallucinogenic substances freely in order to penetrate the mysteries of the other world, many people may claim shamanistic status. Among the J'varo, one out of every four men is a shaman, because the use of hallucinogenic vines makes it possible for almost everyone to achieve the trance states essential for the practice of shamanism (Harner 1972:154). Elsewhere, becoming a shaman may be restricted to people who are prone to having auditory and visual hallucinations.

An important part of shamanistic performance in many regions of the world consists of simple tricks of ventriloquism, sleight of hand, and illusion. Siberian shamans, for example, signaled the arrival of the possessing spirit by secretly shaking the walls of a darkened tent. Throughout South America, the standard shamanistic curing ceremony involves the sleight-of-hand removal of slivers of bone, pebbles, bugs, and other foreign objects from the patient's body. The practice of these tricks should not be regarded as evidence that the shaman has a cynical or disbelieving attitude toward the rest of the performance. Michael Harner (1980), a modern proponent of shamanic rituals, insists there is nothing fraudulent about the **sucking cure.** It is not the object itself that is in the patient's body and causing the trouble; rather, it is the object's spiritual counterpart.

> Shamans put the material object in their mouth during the sucking cure because this helps withdraw its spiritual counterpart.

Although trance is part of the shamanistic repertory in hundreds of cultures, it is not universal. Many cultures have part-time specialists who do not make use of trance but who diagnose and cure disease, find lost objects, foretell the future, and confer immunity in war and success in love. Such persons may be referred to variously as magicians, seers, sorcerers, witch doctors, medicine men or medicine women, and curers. The full shamanistic complex embodies all these roles (Atkinson 1992; but see Winkelman 1990).

The !Kung. The !Kung use a method of healing based on the principle of **n/um**, which is the healing energy that originates from the gods. *N/um* is accessed during an all-night dance. As dancing intensifies, the n/um of the healers is activated in the healers through the *kia* (trance)—an enhanced state of consciousness that is both painful and feared. Healing is a routine cultural event among the !Kung, open to everyone. But to become a healer, a person must undergo intense training. By the time they reach adulthood, about half the men and 10 percent of the women have become healers.

The kia, or activated n/um, is said to boil fiercely within the healer (Katz 1982). Those who learn to heal are called the masters or owners of n/um. Healers are able to access the realm where the gods and spirits of dead ancestors live. These are the spirits that try to carry off the sick into their own realm by bringing misfortune and death. In the kia, healers express the wishes of the living by entering into a struggle with the spirits to rescue the souls of the sick. If the healer's n/um is strong, the spirits will retreat and the sick person will live.

The Tapirapé. Among the Tapirapé, a village people of central Brazil (Wagley 1977), shamans derive their powers from dreams in which they encounter spirits who become the shaman's helpers. Dreams are caused by souls leaving the body and going on journeys. Frequent dreaming is a sign of shamanistic talent. Mature shamans, with the help of the spirit familiars, can turn into birds or launch themselves through the air in gourd "canoes," visit with ghosts and demons, or travel to distant villages forward and backward through time.

Tapirapé shamans are frequently called on to cure illness. This they do with sleight of hand and the help of their spirit familiars while in a semitrance condition induced by gulping huge quantities of tobacco, which makes them vomit. It is interesting to note in conjunction with the widespread use of tobacco in

Native American rituals that tobacco contains hallucinogenic alkaloids and may induce visions when consumed in large quantities.

Charles Wagley provides us with the following description of a Tapirapé shaman. A shaman comes to his patient, and squats near the patient's hammock; his first act is always to light his pipe. When the patient has a fever or has fallen unconscious from the sight of a ghost, the principal method of treatment is by massage. The shaman blows smoke over the entire body of the patient; then he blows smoke over his own hands, spits into them, and massages the patient slowly and firmly, always toward the extremities of the body. He shows that he is removing a foreign substance by quick movement of his hands as he reaches the end of an arm or leg.

The more frequent method of curing, however, is by the extraction of a malignant object by sucking. The shaman squats alongside the hammock of his patient and begins to "eat smoke"—swallow large gulps of tobacco smoke from his pipe. He forces the smoke with great intakes of breath deep down into his stomach. Soon he becomes intoxicated and nauseated; he

Tapirapé Shaman
The shaman has fallen into a tobacco-induced trance and cannot walk unaided.

vomits violently and smoke spews from his stomach. He groans and clears his throat in the manner of a person gagging with nausea but unable to vomit. By sucking back what he vomits, he accumulates saliva in his mouth."

"In the midst of this process he stops several times to suck on the body of his patient and finally, with one awful heave, he spews all the accumulated material on the ground. He then searches in this mess for the intrusive object that has been causing the illness." Wagley reports that " Never once did I see a shaman show the intrusive object to observers. At one treatment a Tapirapé [shaman] usually repeats this process of "eating smoke," sucking, and vomiting several times. Sometimes, when a man of prestige is ill, two or even three shamans will cure side by side in this manner and the noise of violent vomiting resounds throughout the village" (Wagley 1943:73–74).

Communal Cults

No society is completely without communally organized religious beliefs and practices. Even the Inuit have group rites. Under the cross-examinations of shamans, frightened and sick individuals publicly confess violations of taboos that have made them ill and that have endangered the rest of the community. Through ritual, groups reinforce social integration.

Ritual leads to the reassertion of the status quo. As the group members come together in ritual celebration, they strengthen their sense of continuity that communicates a socially constructed meaning signifying the continuity of the group.

Communal rites fall into two major categories: (1) rites of solidarity and (2) rites of passage. In the **rites of solidarity**, participation in dramatic public rituals enhances the sense of group identity, coordinates the actions of the individual members of the group, and prepares the group for immediate or future cooperative action. **Rites of passage** celebrate the social movement of individuals into and out of groups or into or out of statuses of critical importance to the individual and to the community. Reproduction, the achievement of manhood and womanhood, marriage, and death are the principal worldwide occasions for rites of passage.

Communal Rites of Solidarity

Rites of solidarity are directed toward the welfare of the community rather than the individual. They reaffirm the power of the group, which transcends individuals.

Rites of solidarity are common among clans and other descent groups. Such groups usually have names and emblems that identify group members and set one group off from another. Animal names and emblems predominate, but insects, plants, and natural phenomena such as rain and clouds also occur. These group-identifying objects are known as **totems.**

Members of each totemic group believe they were descendents of their totem.

Members of each group customarily refrain from harming or eating their totem. The specific form of totemic belief, however, varies greatly, and no single totemic complex can be said to exist.

The Arunta of Australia provide one of the classic cases of totemic ritual. Here, an individual identifies with the totem of the sacred place near which one's mother passed shortly before becoming pregnant. These places contain the stone objects known as **churinga**, which are the visible manifestations of each person's spirit. The churinga are believed to have been left behind by the totemic ancestors as they traveled about the countryside at the beginning of the world. The ancestors later turned into animals, objects, and other entities. The sacred places of each totem are visited annually.

These totemic rituals have many meanings and functions. The participants are earnestly concerned with protecting their totems and ensuring their reproduction. But the exclusive membership of the ritual group also indicates that they are acting out the mythological dogma of their common ancestry.

The totem ceremonies reaffirm and intensify the sense of common identity of the members of a regional community.

The handling of the churinga confirms the fact that the totemic group has "stones" or, in a more familiar metaphor, "roots" in a particular land.

In contemporary American society, rites of solidarity are mostly secular events such as the Fourth of July parades and football games. Groups meet for traditional barbecues or watch college and professional games. These events become unifying cultural traditions that symbolize key features of American life. On Superbowl Sunday, for example, millions of Americans from diverse cultural backgrounds come together to watch televised football. Although the symbolism of football—teamwork and reward for consistency—are important, it is the common experience of participating in a national event that reinforces group solidarity.

Box 17.1   No Rites Hurt Too

Westerners are likely to be shocked and dismayed by examples of painful puberty rituals, but the system that has been substituted for such rituals may not have any clear advantage as far as eliminating pain and suffering. The passage from child to adult in advanced industrial societies is not marked by any rituals at all. No one is quite sure when adulthood begins. As a result, the young girl or boy must pass through a prolonged period of stress, known as adolescence, which is marked by high rates of accidents, suicides, and antisocial behavior. Which system is more cruel? (The Jewish bar mitzvah and bat mitzvah held at age 13 for boys and girls, respectively, creates boy-men and girl-women for whom adult status lies many years ahead. Catholic first communion is also only vaguely associated with the passage to adulthood.)

Communal Rituals: Rites of Passage

Rites of passage are ceremonies that mark changes in a person's social position that are of general public concern.

The most common occasions for rites of passage are birth, puberty, marriage, and death. The individual who is born, who reaches adulthood, who takes a spouse, or who dies is not the only one implicated in these events. Many other people must adjust to these momentous changes. Being born not only defines a new life but also brings into existence or modifies the position of parent, grandparent, sibling, heir, age-mate, and many other domestic and political relationships. Rites of passage are important public rituals that recognize a wider set of altered social relationships. Contemporary passage rites include confirmations, baptisms, bar and bat mitzvahs, and fraternity hazing. Rites of passage conform to a remarkably similar pattern among widely dispersed cultures (Eliade 1958; Schlegel and Barry 1979).

The three phases of rites of passage are separation, transition, and incorporation.

First the principal performers are separated from the routines associated with their earlier life and prepare to move from one place or status to another. Second, decisive physical and symbolic steps are taken to extinguish the old status. Often depersonalization accompanies separation; a person may leave his or her group and experience a symbolic "death." Army boot camp is a good example of liminality. Inductees are stripped of their former identity; they are issued a number, dressed in identical uniforms, and given short hair cuts, and all ties are severed during their confinement. Often these steps include the notion of killing the old personality. To promote "death and transfiguration," old clothing and ornaments are exchanged for new, and the body is painted or mutilated.

The second phase, known as the **liminal** phase, is a period of ambiguity during a person's transition between one status and another.

The liminal phase is a temporary ritual state during which the individual is cut off from normal social contacts to demarcate a contrast from regular social life.

According to Victor Turner (1967), **liminality** involves the suspension of social norms; a person's past and future positions in society are ignored and he or she is subjected to experiences that are different or even reversed from what they are in the ordinary world.

This is a limbo period where a person has left one place or state but has not yet joined another. Finally, the participants are ceremoniously returned to normal life.

Passing a Driver's Test
Getting a driver's license marks a much anticipated change in status.

Profile 17.1   Ndembu Communal Rites of Circumcision

Communitas can be seen in the male initiation ceremonies of the Ndembu of northern Zambia. Here, as in many African and Middle Eastern cultures, the transition from boyhood to manhood involves the rite of circumcision. Young boys are taken from their separate villages and placed in a special bush "school." They are circumcised by their own kinsmen or neighbors, and after their wounds heal, they are returned to normal life. Among the Ndembu the process of publicly transforming boys to men takes four months and is known as **mukanda.** Victor Turner (1967) has given a detailed account of a mukanda that he was permitted to witness in 1953. It began with the storage of food and beer. Then a clearing was made in the bush and a camp established. This camp included a hearth at which the mothers of the boys undergoing circumcision cooked for them. On the day preceding the circumcision the circumcisers danced and sang songs in which they expressed antagonism to the boys' mothers and made reference to the "killing" that was about to take place. The boys and their families assembled at the campsite, fires were lit, and a night of dancing and sexual license was begun.

"Suddenly the circumcisers entered in procession, carrying their apparatus. . . . All the rest of the gathering followed them as they danced crouching, holding up different items of apparatus, and chanting hoarsely. In the firelight and moonlight the dance got wilder and

wilder" (Turner 1967: 205). Meanwhile, "those who were about to die" sat in a line attended by their mothers and fathers. During the night they were repeatedly awakened and carried about by their male relatives. The next morning they were given a "Last Supper" (a last breakfast) by their mothers, "each mother feeding her son by hand as though he were an infant." The boys tried not to look terrified as, after breakfast, the circumcisers, their brows and foreheads daubed with red clay, danced about brandishing their knives.

The actual circumcision took place in another clearing some distance away from the cooking camp. The boys remained in seclusion at this site, which is known as the "place of dying." They slept in a brush lodge watched over and ordered about by a group of male "guardians." After their "last breakfast" the boys were marched down the trail toward the "place of dying." The guardians came rushing out, seized them, and tore off their clothes. The mothers were chased back to the cooking camp where they began to wail as at the announcement of a death. The boys were held by the guardians while circumcisers "stretch out the prepuce, make a slight nick on top and another underneath as guides, then cut through the dorsal section with a single movement and follow this by slitting the ventral section, then removing sufficient amount of the prepuce to leave the glans well exposed" (Turner 1967:216).

A.

B.

Ndembu Rites

A. Although the women are supposed to be terrified of the "monster," they are actually amused and skeptical.   B. The circumcision camp—the "place of dying."

Sometimes passage rites are collective. Collective liminality, called **communitas**, creates a community spirit and feeling of togetherness. People who experience *communitas* form a community of equals that is symbolically marked by reversals of ordinary behavior.

Ecclesiastical Cults

Ecclesiastical cults have a professional clergy or priesthood organized into a bureaucracy. This bureaucracy is usually associated with and under the control of a central temple. At secondary or provincial temple centers, the clergy may exercise a considerable amount of independence.

In general, the more highly centralized the political system, the more highly centralized the ecclesiastical bureaucracy.

The ecclesiastic specialists differ from both the Tapirapé shamans and the Ndembu circumcisers and guardians. They are formally designated persons who are elected or appointed to devote themselves to conducting rituals at regular intervals. These rituals usually include a wide variety of techniques for reinforcing support for the supremacy of the ruling class.

Throughout history the ecclesiastical specialists have generally lived much better than the population at large.

In many cases, it has been common for them to be part of the ruling class; material support for these full-time specialists is usually closely related to the power of taxation. As among the Inca (Profile 12.5), the state and the ecclesiastical specialists are both supported by the rent and tribute extracted from the peasants. Under feudalism (Chapter 13, "Peasant Classes" section), the ecclesiastical hierarchy derives its earnings from its own estates and from the gifts of powerful princes and kings. High officials in feudal ecclesiastical hierarchies are almost always kin or appointees of members of the ruling class. In modern ecclesiastical religions such as Christianity, Judaism, or Buddhism, a full time professional clergy is supported through dues, donations, and gifts.

There is a clear distinction between priests and laypersons.

The presence of ecclesiastical organizations produces a profound split among those who participate in ritual performances. On the one hand, there is an active segment, the priesthood; on the other, the passive "congregation," who are virtual spectators. The members of the priesthood must acquire intricate ritual, historical, calendrical, and astronomical knowledge. Often they are scribes and learned people who undergo special training to master the complex rituals needed to perform their role. This promotes spiritual dependence on the priesthood, which reinforces the stratification of state organizations.

It must be stressed, however, that the "congregation" does not altogether abandon individualistic shamanistic and communal beliefs and rituals. These

A.

B.

Ecclesiastical Cult
A. Celebration of Roman Catholic high mass.   *B. The celebration of Good Friday in Chichicastenango.*

practices are all continued, sometimes secretly, in neighborhoods, villages, or households, side by side with the "higher" rituals, despite more or less energetic efforts by the ecclesiastical hierarchy to stamp out what it often calls idolatrous, superstitious, pagan, heathen, or heretical beliefs and performances.

Although it is considered controversial, Michael Harner's (1977) explanation of the Aztec state's unique

Profile 17.2   The Religion of the Aztecs

The Aztecs of Mexico had an ecclesiastical religion whose priests were held responsible for the maintenance and renewal of the entire universe. By performing annual rituals, priests could obtain the blessing of the Aztec gods, ensure the well-being of the Aztec people, and guard the world against collapse into chaos and darkness. According to Aztec theology, the world had already passed through four ages, each of which ended in cataclysmic destruction. The fifth age is in progress, ruled over by the sun god and doomed to destruction sooner or later by earthquakes.

The principal function of the 5,000 priests living in the Aztec capital was to ensure that the gods governing the world were sufficiently pleased so that the end of the world would come later rather than sooner. The best way to please the gods was to give them gifts, the most precious being fresh human hearts, especially the hearts of war captives, because they were won only at great expense and risk.

Aztec ceremonial centers were dominated by large pyramidal platforms topped by temples. These structures were vast stages on which the drama of human sacrifice was enacted at least once a day throughout the year. First the victim would ascend to the top of the pyramid, where four priests would seize the victim and place him or her over the sacrificial stone. A fifth priest cut the victim's chest open with an obsidian knife and wrenched out the beating heart. The heart was smeared over the statue of the god and later burned. Finally, the lifeless body was flung over the edge of the pyramid where it was rolled back down the steps. During a four-day dedication ceremony of the main Aztec temple in Tenochtitlán, some 20,000 prisoners of war were sacrificed in this manner.

It is estimated that nearly 15,000 people were sent to death annually to placate the bloodthirsty gods. Most of these victims were prisoners of war, although local youths, maidens, and children were also sacrificed from time to time (Coe 1977; Berdan 1982; Vaillant 1966 [1941]). After being killed, the bodies of most of those who were sacrificed were rolled down the pyramid steps, dismembered, and probably cooked and eaten (Harner 1977; see Box 17.2 for evidence of Aztec cannibalism).

Prior to the emergence of states, many societies, especially chiefdoms, practiced human sacrifice and ritually consumed all or part of the bodies of prisoners of war (Harris 1985, 1989). Lacking the political-military means to tax and conscript large populations, chiefdoms had lit-

The Aztec Practice of Human Sacrifice Is Well Documented
Anthropologists still debate the reasons for such ritual sacrifice.

tle interest in preserving the lives of their defeated enemies. With the advent of the state, however, cannibalism and human sacrifice tended to disappear. As we have seen in Chapter 12, conquered territories were incorporated into the state, and the labor power of defeated populations was tapped through taxation, conscription, and tribute. Thus, preserving the lives of defeated peoples became an essential part of the process of state expansion.

The Aztecs, however, were an exception to this general trend. Instead of tabooing human sacrifice and cannibalism, the Aztec state made human sacrifice and cannibalism the main focus of ecclesiastical beliefs and rituals. As the Aztecs became more powerful, they sacrificed increasing numbers of prisoners of war and became more rather than less cannibalistic (see also Wolf 1998).

Box 17.2 The Evidence for Aztec Cannibalism

Bernadino de Sahagun, who started collecting data on the Aztecs in the 1540s, is generally considered to be the most honest and reliable historian and ethnographer of Aztec culture. In his *General History of the Things of New Spain,* he repeatedly describes the fate of the Aztec's sacrificial victims as follows: "After they had slain them and torn out their hearts, they took them away gently, rolling them down the steps. When they had reached the bottom, they cut off their heads and inserted a rod through them, and they carried the bodies to the houses which they called *calpulli,* where they divided them up in order to eat them" (Sahagun 1951:24).

Many other passages written by Sahagun and other historians of the conquest of Mexico tell the same story (Duran 1964).

Skull Rack

One of the smaller racks in the Aztec capital. The skulls in the photograph are sculpted in stone; during Aztec times, real skulls were exhibited on wooden structures as found in the ongoing excavations in Mexico City.

ecclesiastical cannibalism remains the best theory available. Harner starts from the fact that as a result of millennia of intensification and population growth, the central Mexican highlands had lost their best domesticable animal species. Unlike the Inca, who obtained animal foods from llama, alpaca, and guinea pigs—or the Old World states that had sheep, goats, pigs, and cattle—the Aztec had only semidomesticated ducks and turkeys and hairless dogs. Wild fauna, such as deer and migrating waterfowl, were not abundant enough to provide the Aztecs with more than 1 or 2 grams of animal protein per capita per day (compared with over 60 grams in the United States). The depleted condition of the natural fauna is shown by the prominence in the Aztec diet of bugs, worms, and "scum cakes," which were made out of algae skimmed off the surface of Lake Texcoco (see Harris 1979b; Sahlins 1978).

According to Harner, the severe depletion of animal resources made it uniquely difficult for the Aztec state to prohibit the consumption of human flesh while still pursuing its expansionist aims. Because of the severe depletion of animal resources, human flesh rather than animal flesh was redistributed as a means of rewarding loyalty to the throne and bravery in combat. Moreover, to have made serfs or slaves out of captives would only have worsened the animal food shortage. The Aztec state had much to lose by prohibiting cannibalism and little to gain.

It would have been far more puzzling if the Aztecs had not consumed the flesh of their prisoners of war after expending so much effort in capturing and killing them. In the history of humankind, it is not cannibalism that needs to be explained but the taboo against cannibalism (Villa et al. 1986). According to

Aztec Sacrificial Knife

Tim White, there is no doubt that cannibalism was a common practice. At archeological digs all over the globe, researchers have found evidence of cannibalism. Human bones were broken open for their marrow and smaller fragments were boiled to extract fatty residues. White (1997) concludes that it used to be thought that the Spanish made up—as propaganda, to justify their own cruelty—the stories of the Aztecs eating their prisoners. But now excavations in Mexico City are finding evidence—such as carefully splintered bones—that the Aztecs really were cannibals.

Religion and Political Economy: High Gods

Full-time specialists, monumental temples, dramatic processions, and elaborate rites performed for spectator congregations are incompatible with the infrastructure and political economy of hunters and gatherers. Similarly, the complex astronomical and mathematical basis of ecclesiastical beliefs and rituals is never found among band and village peoples.

The level of political economy also influences the way in which gods are thought to relate to each other and to human beings. For example, the idea of a single high god who creates the universe is found among cultures at all levels of economic and political development. These high gods, however, play different kinds of roles in running the universe after they have brought it into existence. Among hunter-gatherers and other nonstate peoples, the high gods tend to become inactive after their creation task is done (Sullivan 1987). To obtain assistance one must turn to a host of lesser gods, demons, and ancestor souls (see Hayden 1987). In stratified societies, the high god bosses the lesser gods and tends to be a more active figure, to whom priests and commoners address their prayers (Swanson 1960), although ordinary people may still revere the lesser gods more actively.

Societies whose rulers rely on religious indoctrination to secure and legitimize their position of power, have a different reward system than secular societies. In such societies, conformity is reinforced through the promise of spiritual rewards, especially promises of rewards in the afterlife or martyrdom in exchange for deprivation in this world or sacrifice in battle.

A plausible explanation for this difference is that nonstate cultures have no need for the idea of a central or supreme authority. Just as centralized control over people and strategic resources is absent in life, so in religious belief the inhabitants of the spirit world lack decisive control over each other. They form a more or less egalitarian group.

The belief that superordination and subordination characterize relationships among the gods helps obtain the cooperation and submission of the commoner classes in stratified societies.

One way to achieve conformity in complex stratified societies is to convince commoners that the gods demand obedience to the state. Myths and rituals express the commoners' dependence on the rulers' well-being—to challenge the ruler would be like challenging the very order of the universe. The priesthood dazzles, mystifies, and intimidates the commoners through the performance of highly intricate rituals and the construction of grandiose temples in order to discourage the commoners from opposing their rulers. Disobedience and nonconformity result not only in retribution administered through the state's police military apparatus but also in punishments in present or future life administered by the high gods themselves. In nonstate societies, for reasons discussed in Chapter 18, law and order are rooted in common interest. Consequently, there is little need for high gods to administer punishments to those who have been "bad" and rewards to those who have been "good."

Revitalization Movements

The relationship of religion to structure and infrastructure can also be seen in the process known as *revitalization*. Anthony Wallace (1970) defines a **revitalization movement** as "deliberate and organized attempts by some members of a society to construct a more satisfying culture through rapid acceptance of a pattern of multiple innovations." Most revitalization movements follow a fairly uniform process:

- A society is in the state of equilibrium.

- A society is pushed out of equilibrium by various forces such as climatic or biotic change, epidemic disease, war and conquest, and so forth.

- The society becomes disillusioned and disorganized.

- Social deterioration sets the stage for a revitalization movement to appear in an effort to bring about a more satisfying society.

- An individual or group constructs a new, idealistic image of culture that forms the basis for social action.

Under the severe stresses associated with colonial conquest and intense class or minority exploitation, religions tend to become movements concerned with achieving a drastic improvement in the immediate conditions of life or in the prospects for an afterlife. These movements are sometimes referred to as *nativistic, revivalistic, millennarian,* or *messianic.* The concept of revitalization is intended to embrace all the specific cognitive and ritual variants implied by these terms (Wallace 1966).

Revitalization occurs during times of cultural stress brought about by rapid change, foreign domination, and perceived deprivation.

Revitalization is a process of political and religious interaction among a depressed caste, class, ethnicity, or other subordinate social group and a superordinate group. Some revitalization movements emphasize passive attitudes, the adoption of old rather than new cultural practices, or salvation through rewards after death; others advocate more or less open resistance or aggressive political or military action. These differences largely reflect the extent to which the subordinate groups are prepared to cope with the challenge to their power and authority. Revitalizations that take place under conditions of massive suffering and exploitation sooner or later result in political and even military confrontations, even though both sides may overtly desire to avoid conflict (Worsley 1968).

Native American Revitalizations

Widespread revitalizations were provoked by the European invasion of the New World, the conquest and expulsion of the Native American peoples, and the destruction of their natural resources. The native peoples of the American West had been mostly confined to reservations by the 1870s; their economic base was ruined with the destruction of buffalo herds and occupation of their lands. The coercive authority imposed on them brought an atmosphere of total defeat and discouragement, which provides the conditions for numerous revitilization movements.

The most famous of the nineteenth-century revitalization movements was the Ghost Dance, also known (by whites) as the Messiah craze. The main phase of the Ghost Dance began in 1889 under the inspiration of a prophet named Wovoka. Wovoka and his followers envisioned a day when all their ancestors would return to life. Songs and dances revealed to Wovoka would make this happen. Ostensibly, Wovoka's teachings lacked political content, and as the Ghost Dance spread eastward across the Rockies, its political implications remained ambiguous.

Wovoka
Leader of the Ghost Dance.

For Native Americans of the Plains, the return of the dead meant that they would outnumber the whites and hence be more powerful.

The Sioux initiated a version of the Ghost Dance that included the return of all the bison and the extermination of the whites under a huge landslide. The Sioux led pure lives and believed that violence was no longer necessary because the world would change by itself. They put on Ghost Dance shirts, believing they would make them invulnerable to bullets. Nevertheless, the Ghost Dance frightened settlers who feared that the movement would spark a political uprising. After the Sioux leader, Sitting Bull was arrested and killed, the U.S. army ended the Ghost Dance movement by massacring 200 members of the Lakota Sioux—mainly women and children—at Wounded Knee, South Dakota, on December 29, 1890 (Mooney 1965).

A.

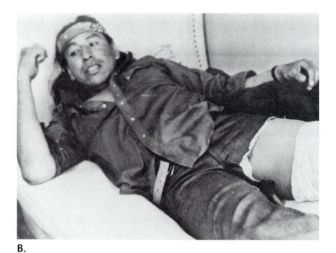

B.

Wounded Knee

A. In the first battle, in 1890, 200 Sioux Indians were killed by the U.S. Army.   *B. In the second battle, in 1973, militant Indians occupied the village of Wounded Knee, South Dakota, and exchanged gunfire with U.S. marshals.*

After all chance of military resistance was crushed, the Native American revitalization movement became more introverted and passive. Visions in which all the whites were wiped out ceased to be experienced, confirming once again the responsiveness of religion to political reality.

The development and spread of beliefs and rituals centering on peyote, mescal, and other hallucinogenic drugs is characteristic of many twentieth-century Native American revitalizations. Peyote ritual, as practiced in the Native American Church, involves a night of praying, singing, peyote eating, and ecstatic contemplation followed by a communal breakfast. Peyote, which is a small cactus that grows in northern Texas, produces vivid hallucinations. The peyote eaters are not interested in bringing back the buffalo or making themselves invulnerable to bullets; they seek self-knowledge, personal moral strength, and physical health (Stewart 1987).

Peyotism and allied cult movements do not, of course, signal the end of political action by the Native Americans. With the emergence of the "Red Power" movement, the Native Americans' attempt to hold onto and regain their stolen lands is being carried out through the work of lawyers, politicians, novelists, Washington lobbyists, sit-ins, and land-ins (Deloria 1969).

Melanesian Cargo Cults

In New Guinea and Melanesia, revitalization is associated with the concept of cargo. The typical vision of the leaders of Melanesian revitalization movements is that of a ship bringing back the ancestors and a cargo of European goods. In recent times, airplanes and spaceships have become the favorite means of delivering the cargo.

Inspired by the abundance of goods U.S. military forces displayed during the Pacific island campaigns of World War II, Melanesians developed the belief that they too would become wealthy. Some revitalizations stressed the return of the Americans. In 1944, a local leader named Tsek urged his people to destroy all trade goods and throw away their clothes in preparation for the return of the mysteriously departed Americans. Some of the American-oriented revitalizations have placed specific American soldiers in the role of cargo deliverers. On the island of Tana in the New Hebrides, the John Frumm cult cherished an old GI jacket as the relic of one John Frumm, whose identity is not otherwise known . The followers of "John Frumm" built landing strips, bamboo control towers, and grass-thatched cargo sheds. In some cases, beacons were kept ablaze at night and radio operators stand ready with tin-can microphones and earphones to guide the cargo planes to a safe landing. The natives were waiting for a total upgrading of their lives. They believed the phantom ships and planes would mark the beginning of a whole new era.

The Melanesians believed that the cargo planes and ships had been successfully loaded by their ancestors at U.S. ports and were on their way, but the local authorities had refused to permit the cargo to be landed.

In other versions, the cargo planes were tricked into landing at the wrong airport. In a metaphorical sense,

Superstructure: Symbols and Rituals

Symbolic Meaning of Color in China

Red is worn at weddings because it is the color of happiness. Here the woman is wearing a western style suit. The man wears a red tie and traditional red sashes.

White is the color of mourning. The closest kin wear white robes during funerals.

At the end of the mortuary ceremony, symbolic offerings are made to the deceased. Buns are spiritual food, paper money is the currency of the afterlife, and the cow is provided to serve the deceased.

Annual Dance Drama

The theme for this enactment in Northern Tibet is the triumph of good over evil.

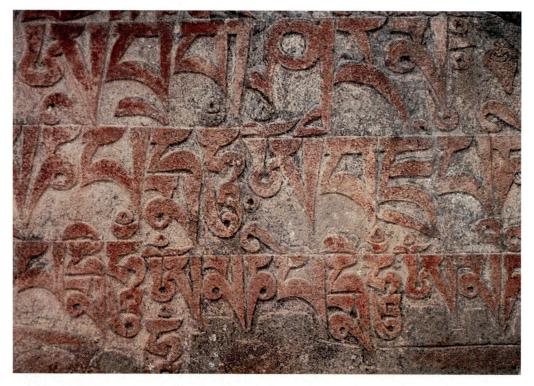

Tibetan Mani Stone

Mantras carved in stone turn people's thoughts to religion.

Mehinacu Spear Throwing Contest

During the Jawari festival, the Mehinacu invite neighboring villagers for a spear throwing contest. Insults are shouted as spears with wax tips are thrown at designated "cross cousins." The festival is an opportunity for venting frustrations and almost always ends amicably. But occasionally someone is injured, emotions get out of control, and the groups part in anger.

Ritual Feeding of the Spirits

The Kaiyapa ritual is performed repeatedly throughout the year. Teams of villagers dance to please the spirits, who are potentially dangerous. The Kaiyapa spirits are "fed" and food is redistributed in their name to all villagers.

Masai rite of passage marking the transition into adulthood in Kenya.

Masai bodypainting.

Decorated Samburu youth in Kenya.

Peyote Ceremony

Delaware Indians of Oklahoma spend the night in prayer and meditation. At right, they emerge to greet the dawn.

these sentiments apply to the actual conditions under colonialism. The peoples of the South Seas were indeed often tricked out of their lands and resources.

The confusion of the Melanesian revitalization prophets stems from naiveté about the workings of cultural systems.

The prophets did not understand how modern industrial wage labor societies are organized, nor comprehend how law and order are maintained among state-level peoples. Their leaders dismissed the standard European explanation of hard work equaling wealth as a calculated deception. Anyone could see that the European big men, unlike their native prototypes, scarcely worked at all. The natives insisted that the material wealth of the industrial age is really created in some distant place, not by humans, but by supernatural means.

To the Melanesians, the material abundance of the industrial nations and the penury of others constitute an irrational flaw, a massive contradiction in the structure of the world.

The belief system of the cargo cults vividly demonstrates why we can't assume that all people distinguish between natural and supernatural categories. Cargo leaders who have been taken to see modern Australian stores and factories in the hope that they would give up their beliefs return home more convinced than ever that they are following the best prescription for obtaining cargo. With their own eyes, they have observed the fantastic abundance the authorities refuse to let them have (Lawrence 1964).

Westerners are impressed by the natives' inability to understand European economic lifestyles. The implication is that the natives are too backward, or superstitious to grasp the principles of civilization. However, it is not that these natives cannot grasp the principles in question, it is that they find them unacceptable. When their leaders learned more about how Europeans produced wealth, they were less prepared to accept their explanation of why their people were unable to share in it. Without the cheapness of native labor and the expropriation of native lands, the colonial powers would never have gotten so rich. In one sense, the natives were entitled to the products of the industrialized nations even though they

A.

B.

John Frumm

A. Some members of the John Frumm cargo cult perform a ritual march. They await the day that John Frumm, their messiah, will return, bringing freedom and wealth. This movement has been in existence for more than forty years.   B. This cult is active on the Island of Tana in the new Hebrides.

couldn't pay for them. The cargo cult was their way of saying this.

Taboo, Religion, and Ecology

Human actions take on special meaning through the realm of the sacred. According to Durkheim, the power of the sacred, as opposed to the profane, is generated by society. Sacred objects may look like profane ones. The distinction between sacred and profane does not reside in the intrinsic properties of the object but in its symbolic representation and meaning. For example, sacramental wine symbolizing the blood of Christ, may not differ from ordinary table wine, yet it is defined as holy and treated in a reverential manner. Religious beliefs and social behavior are guided by what a culture deems sacred. Sacred propositions are taken to be unquestionably true because their sacred meaning elicits a sense of certainty in the validity of the proposition that is beyond question. A sanctified message is certified so there is no need to prove it.

Sanctity is the quality of unquestionable truthfulness credited by the faithful to unverifiable propositions.

Sanctity ensures that participants will fulfill their commitments and greatly increases the likelihood of conformity.

Roy Rappaport shows that sacred propositions provide a means of expression for ecological adaptation. With symbolic communication, it is possible to transmit a variety of messages because "to sanctify statements is to certify them" (1971:69). Because people are more likely to accept sanctified messages as true, their response will be more predictable. Sanctity, as we will see, takes behavior out of the hands of individual decision makers and increases the likelihood of compliance.

Incest Taboo

If religious sanctions evoke a sense of the sacred, it then follows that an appeal to the sacred nature of a rule governing interpersonal relations will resolve the uncertainties about what people ought to do or how they should behave. For example, the prohibition on incest is widely regarded as a sacred obligation. One plausible explanation is that people are strongly tempted to commit incest, but that the short-run satisfactions would have long-term negative consequences for them and for the community (see Chapter 9, "The Avoidance of Incest" section). By surrounding incest prohibitions with the aura of sacredness, the long-term individual and collective interest comes to prevail, and the ambiguities and doubts that the individual feels about renouncing the prohibited relationship are resolved more decisively than would otherwise be possible. This does not mean that incest does not occur or that all psychological doubts are removed, but that such doubts are brought under effective social control.

Taboos Against Eating Pork

Anthropologists have debated the issue of whether strongly held religious beliefs are ecologically adaptive. Do various religiously sanctioned taboos on the consumption of certain foods, for example, have negative nutritional consequences? Do such taboos sometimes actually contribute to a more efficient use of a society's infrastructural potential? In answering these questions, both the costs and benefits of not eating a particular food and the availability of more efficient alternatives must be considered.

A tension between short-run and long-run costs and benefits may also explain the origin of certain food taboos that are regarded as sacred obligations. Consider, for example, the ancient Israelite prohibition on the consumption of pork. Pigs require shade and moisture to regulate their body temperature. Moreover, unlike the domesticated ruminants such as cattle, sheep, and goats, pigs don't give milk. They also can't pull carts or plows, nor can they subsist on grass. With the progressive deforestation and desertification of the Middle East caused by the spread and intensification of agriculture and stock raising and by population growth, habitat zones suitable for pig rearing became scarce. Hence, an animal that was at one time reared and consumed as a relatively inexpensive source of fat and protein could no longer be reared and consumed by large numbers of people without reducing the efficiency of the main system of food production (Harris 1985). The temptation to continue the practice of pig raising persisted, however—hence, the invocation of sacred commandments in the ancient Hebrew religion. Note that the explanation of the ancient origins of this taboo does not account for its perpetuation into the present. Once in existence, the taboo against pork (and other foods) acquired the function of demarcating or bounding Jewish ethnic minorities from other groups and of increasing their sense of identity and solidarity. Outside the Middle East, the taboo no longer served an ecological function, but it continued to be useful on the level of structural relationships.

The Sacred Cow

The case of the sacred cattle of India conforms to the general theory that the flesh of certain animals is made taboo when it becomes very expensive as a result of ecological changes. Like pigs in the Middle East, cattle were sacrificed and eaten quite freely in India during the Neolithic period. With the rise of the state and of dense rural and urban populations, however, cattle could no longer be raised in sufficient numbers to be used both as a source of meat and as the principal source of traction power for pulling plows. But as the taboo on cattle use developed, it took a form quite different from the Israelite taboo on the pig. Whereas the pig was valued almost exclusively for its flesh, cattle were also valued for their milk and especially for their traction power. When pigs became too costly to be raised for meat, the whole animal became taboo and an abomination. But as cattle in India became too costly to be raised for meat, their value as a source of traction power increased. (The land had to be plowed more intensively as population grew.) Therefore, they had to be protected rather than abominated, and so the Hindu religion came to emphasize everyone's sacred duty to refrain from killing cattle or eating beef. The Hindu doctrine of *ahimsa* puts the full power of religion in support of the command not to kill cattle or eat beef, even in times of extreme food scarcity. Interestingly, the Brahmans (see Chapter 13, "Castes in India" section), who at one time were the caste responsible for ritually slaughtering cattle, later became the caste most concerned with their protection and most opposed to the development of a beef-slaughtering industry in India (Harris 1977, 1979a, 1985; cf. Simoons 1979).

What about sacred cattle today? Are the religious ban on the slaughter of cows (female cattle) and oxen (castrated male cattle) and the taboo against the consumption of beef functionally useful features of modern Hinduism? Everyone agrees that the human population of India needs more calories and proteins, yet the Hindu religion bans the slaughter of cattle and taboos the eating of beef. These taboos are often held responsible for allowing large numbers of aged, decrepit, barren, and useless cattle. Such animals are depicted as roaming aimlessly across the Indian countryside, clogging the roads, stopping the trains, stealing food from the marketplace, and blocking city streets . A closer look at some of the details of the ecology and economy of the Indian subcontinent, however, suggests that the taboo in question does not decrease the capacity of the present Indian system of food production to support human life.

As we saw in Chapter 2, the basis of traditional Indian agriculture is the ox-drawn plow. Each peasant farmer needs at least two oxen to plow the fields at the proper time of the year. Despite the impression of surplus cattle, the central fact of Indian rural life is that there is a shortage of oxen, because one-third of the peasant households own less than the minimum

A.

B.

Sacred Cows

The cows of Calcutta safely roam the streets and their owners can reclaim them when they are needed.

pair. It is true that many cows are too old, decrepit, and sick to have calves, and many oxen too weak to pull plows. At this point, the ban on slaughter and beef consumption is thought to exert its harmful effect, for the Hindu farmer is depicted as ritually obsessed with preserving the life of each sacred beast, rather than kill dry, barren, and weak cattle, no matter how useless it may become. From viewpoint of the poor farmer, however, these relatively undesirable creatures may be quite essential and useful. The farmer would prefer to have more vigorous cows, but is prevented from achieving this goal not by the taboos against slaughter but by the shortage of land and pasture (Chakravarti 1985a, 1985b; George 1990).

Even barren and weak cattle are by no means a total loss. Their dung makes an essential contribution to the energy system as fertilizer and as cooking fuel. Millions of tons of artificial fertilizer at prices beyond the reach of the small farmer would be required to make up for the loss of dung if substantial numbers of cattle were sent to slaughter. Because cattle dung is also a major source of cooking fuel, the slaughter of substantial numbers of animals would require the purchase of expensive dung substitutes, such as wood, coal, or kerosene. Cattle dung is relatively cheap because the cattle do not eat foods that can be eaten by people. Instead, they eat the stubble left in the fields and the marginal patches of grass on steep hillsides, roadside ditches, railroad embankments, and other nonarable lands. This constant scavenging gives the

impression that cows are roaming around aimlessly, devouring everything in sight. But most cattle have an owner, and in the cities, after poking about in the market refuse and nibbling on neighbors' lawns, each animal returns to its stall at the end of the day.

In a study of the bioenergetic balances involved in the cattle complex of villages in West Bengal, Stuart Odend'hal (1972) found that "basically, the cattle convert items of little direct human value into products of immediate human utility." Their gross energetic efficiency in supplying useful products was several times greater than that characteristic of agroindustrial beef production. He concludes that "judging the productive value of Indian cattle based on Western standards is inappropriate."

Although it might be possible to maintain or exceed the present level of production of oxen with substantially fewer cows of larger and better breeds, the question arises of how these animals would be distributed among the poor farmers. Are the farmers who have only one or two decrepit animals to be driven from the land?

Aside from the problem of whether present levels of population and productivity could be maintained with fewer cows, there is the theoretically more crucial question whether the taboo on slaughter accounts for the ratio of cows to oxen. Despite the ban on slaughter, Hindu farmers cull their herds and adjust sex ratios to crops, weather, and regional conditions. The cattle are killed by various indirect means of neglect. As discussed in Chapter 2, culling unwanted female calves results in having over 200 oxen for every 100 cows in the Gangetic plain in northern India where oxen are needed for traction, despite the fact that the region is one of the most religiously orthodox in India (Vaidyanathan et al. 1982).

There are additional reasons for concluding that the Hindu taboo has a positive effect on the carrying capacity of the ecosystem. Cows seldom go to waste because animals that die a natural death are consumed by the untouchables, who are not obligated by the beef-eating taboos, and their skin is preserved as leather. Moreover, the function of the ban on slaughter is critical during famines. When hunger strikes the Indian countryside, the slaughter taboo helps the peasants resist the temptation to eat their cattle. If this temptation were to win out over religious scruples, they would not be able to cultivate the land and plant new crops when the rains begin. Thus the intense resistance to the slaughter and consumption of beef takes on a new meaning in the context of the efficiency of the low-energy Indian infrastructure. In the words of Mohandas Gandhi: "Why the cow was selected for apotheosis is obvious to me. The cow was in India the best companion. She was the giver of plenty. Not only did she give milk but she also made agriculture possible" (Gandhi 1954:3).

Summary

1. E. B. Tylor defined religion as animism or the doctrine of souls. According to Tylor, from the idea of the soul arose the idea of all godlike beings, and the idea of the soul itself arose as an attempt to explain phenomena such as trances, dreams, shadows, and reflections.

2. Tylor's definition has been criticized for failing to consider the multifunctional nature of religion and for overlooking the compelling reality of direct hallucinatory contact with extraordinary beings. And as the J'varo belief in three souls demonstrates, each culture uses the basic concepts of animism in its own distinctive fashion.

3. Marett sought to supplement Tylor's definition of religion with the concepts of animatism and mana. Animatism is the belief in an impersonal life force in people, animals, and objects. The concentration of this force gives people, animals, and objects mana, or the capacity to be extraordinarily powerful and successful. This concept does not readily separate mana from such forces as electricity or gravity.

4. The Western distinction between natural and supernatural is of limited utility for defining religion. As the case of the Gururumba indicates, in many cultures there are no supernatural versus natural controls, only controls.

5. Frazer tried to cope with the enormous variety of religious experience by separating religion from magic. Humility, supplication, and doubt characterize religion; routine cause and effect characterize magic. This distinction is difficult to maintain in view of the routine and coercive fashion in which animistic beings are often manipulated.

6. The principal varieties of belief and ritual show broad correlations with levels of political economic organization. Four levels of religious organization or cult can be distinguished: individualistic, shamanistic, communal, and ecclesiastical.

7. Inuit and Crow religions illustrate the individualistic or do-it-yourself level. Each individual carries out a series of rituals and observes a series of taboos that are deemed essential for survival and well-being, without the help of any part-time or full-time specialist.

8. No culture is devoid of shamanistic cults, the next level, defined by the presence of part-time magico-religious experts, or shamans, who have special talents and knowledge, usually involving sleight of hand, trances, and possession. As the case of !Kung and Tapirapé shamanism indicates, shamans are frequently employed to cure sick people; often they identify and destroy evildoers as well. Communal cults, involving public rituals deemed essential for the welfare or survival of the entire social group, also occur to some extent at all political economic levels. Two principal types of communal ritual can be distinguished: rites of solidarity and rites of passage. As illustrated by the Arunta totemic rituals, rites of solidarity reaffirm and intensify a group's sense of common identity and express in symbolic form the group's claims to territory and resources. As illustrated in the Ndembu circumcision rituals, rites of passage symbolically and publicly denote the extinction or "death" of an individual's or group's socially significant status and the acquisition or "birth" of a new socially significant status.

9. Finally, ecclesiastical cults are those dominated by a hierarchy of full-time specialists or "priests" whose knowledge and skills are usually commanded by a state-level ruling class. To preserve and enhance the well-being of the state and of the universe, historical, astronomical, and ritual information must be acquired by the ecclesiastical specialists. Ecclesiastical cults are also characterized by huge investments in buildings, monuments, and personnel and by a thoroughgoing split between the specialist performers of ritual

and the great mass of more or less passive spectators who constitute the "congregation."

10. With the development of the state, the objective of warfare shifted from that of routing enemy populations to incorporating them within imperial systems.

11. This brought an end to the practice of sacrificing and eating prisoners of war. However, it was difficult for the Aztec state to refrain from rewarding its armies with the flesh of enemy soldiers in its effort to justify, expand, and consolidate ruling-class power. The Aztecs' consumption of human flesh was an expression of an adaptive strategy; it could not be suppressed because alternative sources of animal foods had been depleted.

12. Revitalization movements, such as those of Native Americans and Melanesians, constitute another category of religious phenomena that cannot be understood apart from political-economic conditions. Under political-economic stress, subordinate castes, classes, minorities, and ethnic groups develop beliefs and rituals concerned with achieving a drastic improvement in their immediate well-being or their well-being in a life after death. These movements have the latent capacity to attack the dominant group directly or indirectly through political or military action; in contrast, they may turn inward and accommodate by means of passive doctrines and rituals involving individual guilt, drugs, and contemplation.

13. Religious beliefs and rituals also exhibit adaptive relationships in the form of taboos. The ancient Israelite pig taboo, for example, can be understood as an adaptation to the changing costs and benefits of pig rearing brought about by population increase, deforestation, and desertification.

14. The sacred cow of India serves as a final example of the way in which taboos and whole religions adapt to changing political, economic, and ecological contexts.

AMERICA NOW

The Electronic Church

Protestant fundamentalism and the various born-again Christian revitalization movements have been able to use television to expand membership and raise funds. These televangelists recruit their following through a personal "gospel of wealth"—they promise material success and physical well-being to the true believer. Their message appeals especially to people who are sick, old, or isolated; impoverished by unemployment or underemployment; bewildered by the changes in sex mores and the family; and frightened by crime in the streets. According to televangelist Jim Bakker: "The scripture says, 'Delight yourself in the Lord and he'll give you the desire of your heart.' Give and it shall be given unto you." Bakker tells how one man prayed for a Winnebago mobile home, color brown, and got just that. Says Bakker: "Diamonds and gold aren't just for Satan—they're for Christians, too" (Bakker 1976). (Unfortunately, Bakker's appetite for diamonds and gold led him to sell lifetime vacations in nonexistent condos, and he was sentenced to jail for fraud and embezzlement.)

On his "Old Time Gospel Hour," Moral Majority leader Jerry Falwell asks the faithful to turn over one-tenth of their income: "Christ has not captured a man's heart until He has your pocketbook." Two million potential contributors whose names and addresses are kept in a computer databank receive frequent requests for money, one of which reads, "Maybe your financial situation seems impossible. Put Jesus first in your stewardship and allow him to bless you financially" (*Time,* 1 October 1979:68).

Finding himself $50 million short of the funds needed to complete his City of Faith hospital complex near Tulsa, Oklahoma, video evangelist Oral Roberts raised money with the aid of swatches from a "miracle cloth." "My hands feel as if there is a supernatural heat in them," he declared. "My right hand is especially hot right now." Following God's instructions, Roberts began to turn out millions of swatches imprinted with his right hand. In return, those who acquire the cloth are promised "special miracles" (*Newsweek,* 10 September 1979).

Another televangelist, Pat Robertson, recruits followers and raises funds through what he calls the Kingdom Principles: The Bible says the more you give to Jesus, the more you will get back in return. And the harder it is to give, the greater will be the increase. Thus, as described in Rifkind and Howard (1979:108), "A woman in California who was on a limited income and in poor health decided to trust God and to step out in faith on the Kingdom Principles. She was already giving half her disability money to the 700 Club to spread the gospel of Jesus Christ. But just last week, she decided to go all the way and give God the money she spends for cancer medicine—$120 a month. And three days later—get this!—from an entirely unexpected source, she got a check for $3,000!"

Televangelism became increasingly competitive as the number of programs and channels devoted to fundraising grew. At the beginning of the 1990s televangelism was rocked by a series of scandals and sev-

The Electronic Church

Jerry Falwell's "Old Time Gospel Hour" being televised live from Lynchburg, Virginia, to a network of 391 television stations. Cameras can be seen on the balcony and in the center of the audience.

eral of its greatest stars were sent to jail. Between 1986 and 1992 the number of families watching religious programming fell from 15.1 to 9.5 million (Hadden 1993; Schultze 1991). But it seems likely that televangelism has suffered only a temporary setback. The experience of other cultures and historical epochs demonstrates that stresses brought on by rapid cultural change usually find expression in spiritual yearning, questing, and experimenting that lead to an expansion and intensification of religious activity, broadly defined. All the major world religions were born during times of rapid cultural transformations. Buddhism and Hinduism arose in the Ganges Valley of northern India during an epoch of deforestation, population increase, and state formation. Judaism arose during the prolonged migrations of the ancient Israelites. Christianity arose in conjunction with attempts to break the yoke of Roman imperialism. Islam arose during the transition from a life of pastoral nomadism to that of trade and empires in Arabia and

North Africa. Protestants split from Catholicism as feudalism gave way to capitalism. As we have seen, messianic and millenarian cults swept across the Great Plains as the American Indians lost their lands and hunting grounds, while in the wake of the European colonization of New Guinea and Melanesia, hundreds of cargo cults, devoted to acquiring worldly wealth with the assistance of ancestors returned from the dead, spread from island to island. There is reason to believe, therefore, that the rising intensity of nontraditional religious activity in the United States constitutes an attempt to solve or to escape from the problems of malfunctioning consumerism, unemployment, the upending of gender roles, the breakup of the breadwinner family, alienation from work, oppressive government and corporate bureaucracies, feelings of isolation and loneliness, fear of crime, and bewilderment about the root cause of so many changes happening at once.

KEY TERMS

animatism

animism

communitas

ecclesiastical cults

individualistic cults

liminality

magic

mana

natural realm

n/um

religion

revitalization movements

rites of passage

rites of solidarity

sanctity

shaman

sucking cure

supernatural realm

totems

QUESTIONS TO THINK ABOUT

1. What are some of the psychological and social functions of religion?

2. How would you explain the efficacy of shamanic curing?

3. What are rites of passage, and what is their function for the individual and the group?

4. In what ways are revitalization movements both religious and political in nature? Give examples that show how the attempts of local prophets try to effect a more satisfying society?

5. How do taboos help resolve the conflict between short-term benefits and long term-costs?

6. How can sacred injunctions have economic and ecological consequences? Give examples.

CHAPTER 18

Art

Masked dancers, Dogon, Mali.

What Is Art?

Art as a Cultural Category
Art and Invention
Art and Cultural Patterning
Art and Religion
Art and Politics

The Evolution of Music and Dance

Verbal Arts
Myth and Binary Contrasts
The Complexity of Primitive Art: Campa Rhetoric

Summary

This chapter is concerned with additional aspects of superstructure—namely, the thought and behavior associated with painting, music, poetry, sculpture, dance, and other media of art. What is art? Is art as defined by Western art critics a valid definition of art in other cultures? How and why do the specific forms and styles of artistic expression vary from one culture to another? Is art ever created only for art's sake? We shall see that art is not an isolated sector of human experience. It is intimately connected with and embedded in religion, politics, technology, and many other components of human social life.

What Is Art?

Alexander Alland (1977: 39) defines *art* as "play with form producing some aesthetically successful transformation-representation." The key ingredients in this definition are play, form, aesthetic, and transformation:

- **Play** is an enjoyable, self-rewarding aspect of activity that cannot be accounted for simply by the utilitarian or survival functions of that activity.
- **Form** involves a set of restrictions on how the art play is to be organized in time and space—the rules of the game of art.
- **Aesthetic** refers to the existence of a universal human capacity for an emotionally charged response of appreciation and pleasure when art is successful.
- The term **transformation-representation** refers to the communicative aspect of art that conveys information through symbols or metaphors.

Art represents something that is not represented in its literal shape, sound, color, movement, or feeling. It communicates information, not in its literal form or shape, but in **metaphors** or **symbols** that convey ideas and emotions that carry greater meaning than the objects for which they stand (see Chapter 4, "Language and Symbolic Representation" section).

Art, expressed through music, painting, sculpture, and dance, is found in every known society, suggesting that it has important functions in human life. Art provides emotional gratification and contributes to social well-being. All people derive some level of aesthetic appreation and enjoyment from art. For the artist, artistic expression is an outlet for emotional energy. For nonartists, art can elicit powerful emotional responses that may or may not be shared.

Art also helps sustain, integrate, and organize social life. Through various symbols, art in all its forms reflects and shapes values, beliefs, and other ideological themes. As Alland points out, play, adherence to form, and an aesthetic sense are found in many nonhuman animals. Chimpanzees, for example, like to play with paints. Their adherence to form can be demonstrated by their placement of designs in the center of blank spaces or by their balancing of designs on different parts of a page. (They don't simply paint right off the page.) An aesthetic sense can be inferred by their repeated attempts to copy simple designs such as circles and triangles accurately. Just as grammatical language remains rudimentary among apes in nature, so too does their artistry. Although the rudiments of art can be found in our primate heritage, only *Homo sapiens* can justly be called the "artistic animal."

Art as a Cultural Category

Although it is possible to identify art as an etic category of thought and behavior in all human cultures, an emic distinction between art and non-art is not universal (just as the distinction between natural and supernatural is not universal). What most Westerners mean by art is a particular emic category of modern Euro-American civilization. Euro-American schoolchildren are enculturated to the idea that art is a category of activities and products that stands opposed to the category of nonart. They learn to believe, in other words, that some paintings, carvings, songs, dances, and stories are not art.

Chimpanzee Artist
A 2-year-old chimpanzee finger painting at the Baltimore Zoo. Note attempt to center painting.

In Western civilization, a particular performance is deemed artistic or not by a distinct group of authorities—an art establishment—who make or judge art and who control the museums, conservatories, critical journals, and other organizations and institutions devoted to art as a livelihood and style of life.

Most cultures lack any semblance of an art establishment. This does not mean they lack art or artistic standards (Anderson 1992). A painted design on a pot or a rock, a carved mask or club, or a song or chant in a puberty ordeal is subject to critical evaluation by both performers and spectators. All cultures distinguish between less satisfactory and more satisfactory aesthetic experiences in decorative, pictorial, and expressive matters.

Basic to the modern Western idea of art and nonart is the exclusion of designs, stories, and artifacts that have a definite use in day-to-day subsistence activities and that are produced primarily for practical purposes or for commercial sale. Carpenters are distinguished from people who make wooden sculptures, bricklayers from architects, house painters from those who apply paint to canvas, and so forth.

The opposition between art and practicality is seldom found in other cultures.

A.

B.

C.

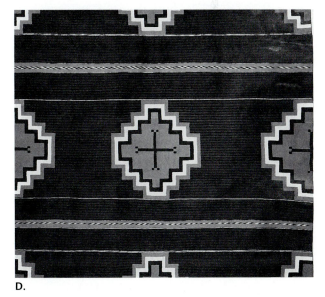

D.

Art Has Many Media

*Native American cultures produced these objects. **A.** Gold mummy mask with green stone eyes: Chimu, Peru. **B.** Feathers of blue and yellow form the design of a Tapirapé mask: Brazil. **C.** Ceramic jar: Nazca, Peru. **D.** Blanket, in blue, black, and white, with stripes and frets: Navajo.*

In most cultures works of art are produced and performed in harmony with utilitarian objectives. People everywhere, whether specialists or nonspecialists, derive pleasure from playfully embellishing and transforming the contours and surfaces of pots, fabrics, wood, and metal products. All cultures, however, recognize that certain individuals are more skilled than others in making utilitarian objects and in embellishing them with pleasing designs. Anthropologists generally regard skilled wood carvers, basketmakers, potters, weavers, or sandalmakers as artists.

Art and Invention

Play is a form of exploratory behavior that permits human beings to try out new and possibly useful responses in a controlled and protected context.

The playful, creative urge that lies behind art, therefore, is probably closely related to the creative urge that lies behind the development of science, technology, and new institutions.

Art and technology often interact, and it is difficult to say where technology ends and art begins, or where art ends and technology begins.

The beautiful symmetry of nets, baskets, and woven fabrics is essential for their proper functioning. Even

!Kung San Plays the Bow
Thumb plucks the string; mouth opens and closes, moving along string to control tone and resonance. Which came first: bow for hunting or bow for making music?

the development of musical expression may have technological benefits. For example, there was probably some kind of feedback between the invention of the bow as a hunting weapon and the twanging of taut strings for musical effect. No one can say which came first, but cultures with bows and arrows usually have musical strings. Wind instruments, blowguns, pistons, and bellows are all related. Similarly, metallurgy and chemistry relate to experimentation with the ornamental shape, texture, and color of ceramic and textile products. The first fired ceramics were figurines rather than utilitarian pots (Vandiver et al. 1989). Thus, it is practical to encourage craftworkers to experiment with new techniques and materials. Small wonder that many cultures regard technical virtuosity as mana (see Chapter 17, "Animation and Mana" section). Others regard it as the gift of the gods, as in the classical Greek idea of the Muses—goddesses of oratory, dance, and music—whose assistance was needed if worthy artistic performances were to occur.

Art and Cultural Patterning

Most artwork is deliberately fashioned in the image of pre-existing forms. It is the task of the artist to replicate these forms by original combinations of culturally standardized elements—familiar and pleasing sounds, colors, lines, shapes, movements, and so on. Of course, the artist must always add some playful and creative ingredient, or it will not be art. However, if the transformation-representation is to communicate something—and it must communicate something if it is to be a successful work of art—the rules of the game cannot be the artist's own private invention. Complete originality, therefore, is not what most cultures strive after in their art.

Each culture tends to repeat traditional and familiar elements, thus generating a characteristic sound, look, or feel.

For example, Northwest Coast Native American sculpture is well known for its consistent attention to animal and human motifs rendered in such a way as to indicate internal as well as external organs. These organs are symmetrically arranged within bounded geometrical forms. Maori sculpture, in contrast, requires that wooden surfaces be broken into bold but intricate filigrees and whorls. Among the Mochica of ancient Peru, the sculptural medium was pottery, and Mochica pots are famous for their representational realism in portraiture and in depictions of domestic and sexual behavior. Hundreds of other easily recognizable and distinctive art styles of different cultures can be identified. The continuity and integrity of these

Kwakiutl Mask
Mask within a mask within a mask. Whale conceals bird, which conceals human face, which conceals face of wearer; another Kwakiutl masterpiece.

styles provide the basic context for a people's understanding and liking of art.

Establishment art in modern Western culture is again unique in its emphasis on formal originality. Westerners take it as normal that art must be interpreted and explained by experts in order to be understood and appreciated. Since the end of the nineteenth century, the greatest artists of the Western art establishment are those who break with tradition, introduce new formal rules, and at least for a time render their work incomprehensible to a large number of people. Joined to this deemphasis of tradition is the peculiar and recent Western notion of artists as lonely people struggling in poverty against limitations set by the preexisting capability of their audience to appreciate and understand true genius.

Thus, the creative, playful, and transformational aspects of modern art have gotten the upper hand over the formal and representational aspects. Contemporary Euro-American artists consciously strive to be the originators of entirely new formal rules. They compete to invent new transformations to replace the traditional ones.

Modern aesthetic standards hold that originality is more important than intelligibility.

Indeed, a work of art that is too easily understood may be condemned. Many artists take it for granted that novelty must result in a certain amount of obscurity. What accounts for this obsession with being original?

One important influence is the reaction to mass production. Mass production leads to a downgrading of technical virtuosity. It also leads to a downgrading of all artwork that closely resembles the objects or performances others have produced. Another factor to be considered is the involvement of the modern artist in a commercial market in which supply perennially exceeds demand. Artists in band and village societies are not obsessed with being original except to the extent that it enhances the aesthetic enjoyment of their work. Their livelihood does not depend on obtaining an artistic identity and a personal following.

Another reason for the obsession with originality is the high rate of cultural change in modern societies. To some extent, the emphasis on artistic originality merely reflects and expresses this rate of change. Finally, the alienating and isolating tendencies of modern mass society may also play a role. Much modern art reflects the loneliness, puzzlement, and anxiety of the creative individual in a depersonalized and hostile urban, industrial milieu.

Art and Religion

The history and ethnography of art are inseparable from the history and ethnography of religion. The

Mochica Pot
A pre-Columbian portrait made by the Mochica of northern Peru.

earliest paintings found on the walls of caves are generally assumed to have been painted as part of ancient religious rituals.

Art is intimately associated with all four organizational levels of religion.

At the individualistic level, magical songs are often included among the revelations granted the vision seekers of the Great Plains. Even the preparation of trophy heads among the J'varo must meet aesthetic standards, and singing and chanting are widely used during shamanistic performances. On the communal level, puberty rituals, as among the Ndembu (Profile 17.1), provide occasions for dancing and myth and storytelling. Body painting is also widely practiced in communal ceremonies, as among the Arunta. Singing, dancing, and the wearing of masks are common at both puberty and funeral rituals. Furthermore, much artistic effort is expended in the preparation of religiously significant funeral equipment such as coffins and graveposts. Many cultures include ceremonial artifacts such as pottery and clubs, points, and other weapons among a deceased person's grave goods. Ancestors and gods are often depicted in statues and masks that are kept in men's houses or in shrines. Churingas, the Aranda's most sacred objects, are artfully incised with whorls and loops depicting the route followed by the ancestors during the dream time. Finally, on the ecclesiastical level, art and religion are fused in pyramids, monumental avenues, stone statuary, monolithic calendar carvings, temples, altars, priestly garments, and a nearly infinite variety of ritual ornaments and sacred paraphernalia.

Clearly, art, religion, and magic satisfy many overlapping psychological needs in human beings. They are media for expressing sentiments and emotions not easily expressed in ordinary life. They impart a sense of mastery over or communion with unpredictable events and mysterious, unseen powers. They impose human meanings and values on an indifferent world—a world that has no humanly intelligible meanings and values of its own. They seek to penetrate behind the facade of ordinary appearance into the true, cosmic significance of things. And they use illusions, dramatic tricks, and sleight of hand to get people to believe in them.

Art and Politics

Art is also intimately related to politics. The relationship is especially clear in the context of state-sponsored art. As we have seen, in stratified societies, religion is a means of social control. To strengthen this control, the skills of the artist are harnessed by the ruling class

Ba Kota Funerary Figures
The Ba Kota of the Gabon Republic place the skeletal remains of dead chiefs in bark boxes or baskets surmounted by Mbulu-ngulu guardian figures of wood, faced with brass or copper sheets or strips. Although the figure expresses the creative individuality of the artist, it also conforms to stylistic pattern.

to instill religious notions of obedience and to sanctify the status quo. State-sponsored monumental architecture was a visible representation of the power of the gods and the rulers. Contrary to the popular modern image of the artist as a free spirit disdainful of authority, most state-level art is politically conservative; artists preserved the status quo by creating magnificent works of art that represented the awesome power of the state (Paztory 1984:20).

Ecclesiastical art generally interprets the world in conformity with prevailing myths and ideologies, justifying inequities and exploitation.

Art makes the gods visible as idols. Gazing on massive stone blocks carved as if by superhuman hands, commoners comprehend the necessity for subservience. They are awed by the immense size of pyramids and by the processions, prayers, pomp, and sacrifices carried out by priests in dramatic settings—golden altars, colonnaded temples, great vaulted roofs, huge ramps and stairways, windows through which only the light from heaven passes.

The church and state have been the greatest patrons of the arts in all but the past few hundred years of history.

With the rise of capitalism, ecclesiastical and civil institutions in the West became more decentralized, and wealthy individuals largely replaced church and state as patrons of the arts. Accumulating valuable art objects by individuals served as another way to display one's power. At the same time, individualized sponsorship of artists promoted greater flexibility and freedom of expression. Politically neutral, secular, and even revolutionary and sacrilegious themes became common. The arts became established as individualistic, secular forms of expression and entertainment. To protect and preserve its newfound autonomy, the art establishment adopted the doctrine of "art for art's sake." But once they were free to express themselves as they saw fit, artists were no longer sure what they wanted to express. They devoted themselves more and

more to idiosyncratic and obscure symbols organized into novel and unintelligible patterns, as noted earlier in this chapter. And the patrons of art, concerned less and less with communication, increasingly looked toward the acquisition and sponsorship of art as a prestigious commercial venture that yielded substantial profits, tax deductions, and a hedge against inflation.

The Evolution of Music and Dance

Some anthropologists hold that structural and infrastructural components directly influence the formal characteristics and aesthetic standards of different cultural styles. According to Allan Lomax and his associates (Lomax 1968; Lomax and Arensberg 1977), for example, certain broad characteristics of song, music, and dance are closely correlated with a culture's level of subsistence.

Bands and villages in general tend to have a different complex of music, song, and dance than do chiefdoms and states.

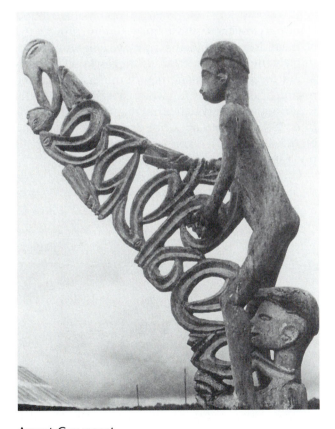

Asmat Gravepost
Around the world, much talent has been lavished on commemorating the dead, but styles and media vary enormously.

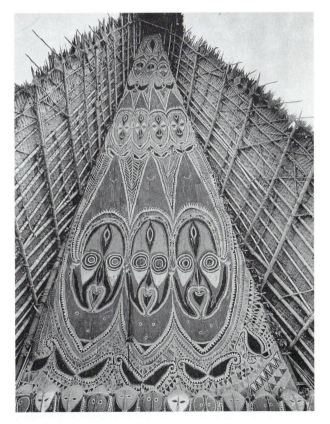

Art and Architecture
Brightly painted faces on a men's house in Sepik River basin, New Guinea.

Gold Death Mask of Tut
Another example of the interrelationship of art, religion, and politics.

Dividing cultures into those that are low and those that are high on the scale of subsistence technology leads to the following correlations:

- *Musical intervals:* The less advanced subsistence systems employ musical scales in which notes are widely separated—that is, have intervals of a third

or more. Advanced subsistence systems employ scales that are marked by more and smaller intervals.

- *Repetition in song text:* The less advanced subsistence cultures employ more repetition in their lyrics—fewer words, over and over again.

- *Complexity and type of orchestra:* Less advanced subsistence systems use only one or two kinds of instruments and small numbers of each. Advanced subsistence is correlated with musical performances involving more performers and a greater variety of instruments.

- *Dance styles:* The advanced subsistence systems are correlated with dance styles in which many body parts—fingers, wrists, arms, torso, legs, feet, toes—have distinctive movements to make or "parts to play."

The more advanced the subsistence system, the more the dance style tends to emphasize complex curving motions, as opposed to simple up-and-down or side-to-side steps like hopping or shuffling.

Lomax sees these correlations as resulting from direct and indirect influence of subsistence. Large, complex orchestration, for example, reflects the structural ability of a society to form large, coordinated groups. Dance styles, in contrast, may simply express the characteristic movements employed in using such implements of production as digging sticks versus plows or complex machines. Some dances can be regarded as training for work, warfare, or self-defense, but obviously dance has many other functions (Box 18.1). Modern rock, for example, has a strong erotic component, expressed through pelvic gyrations and thrusts.

Lomax's correlations have been criticized on technical grounds relating to sampling and coding pro-

---

Box 18.1   Some Social Functions of Music, Song, and Dance

1. *Emotes:* Lets people "blow off steam," makes them feel good.
2. *Socializes:* Teaches traditions.
3. *Educates:* Develops poise and confidence in performance.
4. *Bonds:* Creates a sense of togetherness among performers.
5. *Rallies:* Prepares for dangerous situations (for example, warfare and journeys).
6. *Aggresses:* Lets people "show their stuff" harmlessly.
7. *Worships:* Brings people closer to the gods.
8. *Seduces:* Arouses sexual passions, displays charms.
9. *Coordinates:* Gets people to work or move together, as in sea chanties or military marches.
10. *Entertains:* Prevents boredom.

cedures (see Kaeppler 1978). But, Lomax's attempt to measure and compare music and dance styles, and to relate them to social structure and subsistence, constitutes an important avenue of approach.

Verbal Arts

All societies use words as a form of creative expression. Verbal arts fall under the general heading of folklore, which includes jokes, proverbs, folksongs, limericks, prayers, myths, and folktales. Folktales serve as a charter for how a culture expects its members to think and behave; heroes and heroines are triumphant because they possess admirable traits, whereas antagonists are punished for character flaws.

Folktales are traditional narratives from the deep past that reflect social situations that play on ordinary human fears and desires.

Typically myths involve creations and the people who tell them and serve as the ultimate rationale for how events have unfolded. The main character is a god or culture hero who successfully brings a necessity such as fire or sun to humanity. Myths are believed to be true by the people who tell them and serve as the ultimate rational for how events have unfolded.

Myths are sacred tales in which deities appear to explain issues of human existence.

Myth and Binary Contrasts

Anthropologists have found considerable evidence suggesting that certain formal structures recur in widely different traditions of oral and written literature, including myths and folktales.

These structures are characterized by binary contrasts—that is, by two elements or themes that can be viewed as standing in diametric opposition to each other.

Many examples of recurrent binary contrasts can be found in Western religion, literature, and mythology: good versus bad, up versus down, male versus female, cultural versus natural, young versus old, and so forth. According to the French anthropologist Levi-Strauss, the founder of the research strategy known as **structuralism** (see Appendix), the reason these binary contrasts recur so often is that the human brain is "wired" in such a way as to make binary contrasts appealing, or "good to think."

From the structuralist point of view, the main task of the anthropological study of literature, mythology, and folklore is to identify the common, unconscious binary contrasts that lie beneath the surface of human thought and to show how these binary contrasts undergo unconscious transformation-representations.

Consider the familiar tale of Cinderella: A mother has two daughters and one stepdaughter. The two daughters are older, the stepdaughter is younger; the older ones are ugly and mean, whereas Cinderella is beautiful and kind. The older sisters are aggressive; Cinderella is passive. Through a kind fairy godmother, as opposed to her mean stepmother, Cinderella goes to the ball, dances with the prince, and loses her magical shoe. Her sisters have big feet, she has little feet. Cinderella wins the prince. The unconscious deep structure of this story might include the following binary oppositions:

passive	aggressive
younger	older
smaller	larger
good	evil
beautiful	ugly
culture	nature
fairy godmother	stepmother

Structuralists contend that the enjoyment people derive from tales and their durability across space and time derive from the unconscious oppositions and their familiar yet surprising representations.

Structural analyses of literature, art, myths, rituals, and religion abound in anthropology. However, they are surrounded by considerable controversy, primarily because it is not clear whether the binary oppositions discerned by the anthropologists really exist as unconscious realities in the minds of the people being studied. It is always possible to reduce complex and subtle symbols to less complex and gross symbols and then finally to emerge with such flat oppositions as culture versus nature or male versus female. But this does not mean that these categories are emically significant within the local cultural context.

The Complexity of Primitive Art: Campa Rhetoric

A common misconception about the arts of band and village societies is that they are necessarily more simple or naive than art in modern industrial societies (Titon et al. 1984). Although, as we have just seen, many stylistic aspects of art have undergone an evolution from simple to more complex forms, other aspects may have been as complex among Stone Age hunter-gatherers as they are today. The case of Campa rhetoric illustrates this point.

Rhetoric is the art of persuasive public speaking and is closely related to the theatrical arts.

As Gerald Weiss (1977) has discovered, the preliterate Campa, who live in eastern Peru near the headwaters of the Amazon river, use most of the important rhetorical devices cultivated by the great philosophers and orators of ancient Greece and Rome. Their object in public discourse is not merely to inform, but to persuade and convince. "Campa narration is 'a separate time,' where a spellbinding relationship between narrator and audience is developed, with powerful rhetorical devices employed to create and enhance the quality of that relationship" (1977:173).

Here are a few examples of these devices, as translated by Weiss from the Campa language, which belongs to the native American family of languages known as Arawak:

- *Rhetorical questions:* The speaker makes the point that the Campa are deficient in their worship of the sky god, the sun, by asking a question that he himself will then answer: "Do we supplicate him, he here, he who lives in the sky, the sun? We do not know how to supplicate him."

- *Iterations (effect by repetition):* The speaker imparts an emphatic, graphic, cinematic quality to the point by repeating some key words: "The enemy comes out of the lake: And so they emerged in great numbers—he saw them emerge, emerge, emerge, emerge, emerge, emerge, emerge, emerge, emerge, all, all."

- *Imagery and metaphor:* Death is alluded to in the phrase "the earth will eat him." The body is described as "the clothing of the soul."

- *Appeal to evidence:* To prove that the oilbird was formerly human in shape: "Yes, he was formerly human—doesn't he have whiskers?"

- *Appeal to authority:* "They told me long ago, the elders, they who heard these words, long ago, so it was."

- *Antithesis (effect by contrast):* A hummingbird is about to raise the sky rope, which the other larger creatures have failed to do: "They are all big whereas I am small and chubby."

In addition, the Campa orator uses a wide variety of gestures, exclamations, sudden calls for attention ("watch out, here it comes"), asides ("imagine it, then"; "careful that you don't believe, now"). Altogether, Weiss lists 19 formal rhetorical devices used by the Campa.

Summary

1. Creative play, formal structure, aesthetic feelings, and symbolic transformations are the essential ingredients in art. Although the capacity for art is foreshadowed in the behavior of nonhuman primates, only humans are capable of art involving "transformation-representations."

2. The distinctive human capacity for art is thus closely related to the distinctive human capacity for the symbolic transformations that underlie the semantic universality of human language.

3. Western emic definitions of art depend on the existence of art authorities and critics who place many examples of play, structured aesthetic, and symbolic transformation into the category of nonart. The distinction between crafts and art is part of this tradition. In contrast, anthropologists regard skilled craftspersons as artists.

4. Art has adaptive functions related to creative changes in other sectors of social life. Art and technology influence each other, as in the case of instruments of music and the hunt, or in the search for new shapes, colors, textures, and materials in ceramics and textiles.

5. Despite the emphasis on creative innovation, most cultures have art traditions or styles that maintain formal continuity through time. This makes it possible to identify the styles of cultures such as the Northwest Coast Native Americans, Maori, or Mochica. The continuity and integrity of such styles provide the basic context for a people's understanding of and liking for the artist's creative transformations.

6. Establishment art in modern Western culture is unique in emphasizing creativity as well as original transformations . This drive for originality results in the need to break with tradition and development of novel and obscure styles. Lack of communication between the Western artist and the rest of society may be caused by the artist's reaction to mass production, commercialization of art markets, rapid rate of cultural change, and the depersonalized milieu of urban industrial life.

7. Art and religion are closely related. This relationship can be seen in the songs of the vision quest;

preparation of shrunken heads; singing and chanting in shamanistic performances; shamanistic myths; storytelling; singing and dancing; Arunta churingas; and many other aspects of individual, shamanistic, communal, and ecclesiastical cults. Art and religion satisfy many similar psychological needs, and it is often difficult to tell them apart.

8. Art and politics are also closely related. This relationship is clear in state-sponsored ecclesiastical art, much of which functions to keep people in awe of their rulers. It is only in recent times, with the rise of decentralized capitalist states, that art has enjoyed any significant degree of freedom from direct political control.

9. To the extent that bands, villages, chiefdoms, and states represent evolutionary levels, and to the extent that art is functionally related to technology, economy, politics, religion, and other aspects of the universal cultural pattern, the content of art has clearly evolved. A more controversial finding is that styles of song, music, and dance—including musical intervals, repetition in song texts, complexity and type of orchestra, body part involvement, and amount of curvilinear motion—have also undergone evolutionary changes.

10. But as the example of Campa rhetoric shows, the art styles of band and village peoples can be highly sophisticated.

11. The structuralist approach to art attempts to interpret myths, rituals, and other expressive performances in terms of a series of unconscious universal binary oppositions. Common binary oppositions can be found in the Cinderella myth, but these may not be emically valid categories.

KEY TERMS
aesthetic
art
folktales
form
metaphoric or symbolic statement
myth
play
rhetoric
structuralism
transformation-representation

QUESTIONS TO THINK ABOUT
1. How is art distinct from other forms of communication?
2. How does art in traditional society compare with art in modern Western society?
3. What kinds of economic influences are found in artistic forms?
4. How is art a medium of both conservative and revolutionary political expression?
5. What is the relationship between art and religion? What psychological needs do both satisfy?

CHAPTER 19

Applied Anthropology

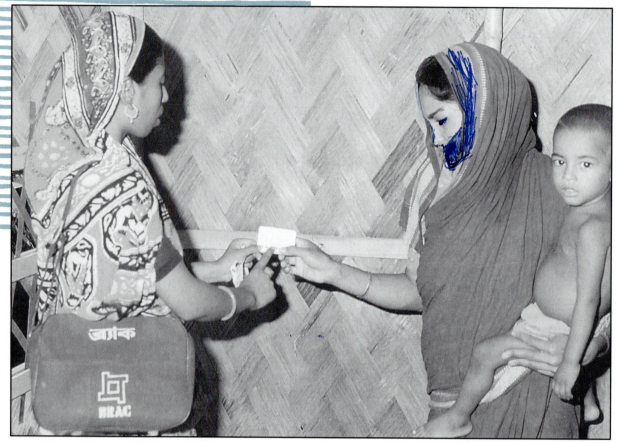

Family planning worker, Bangladesh.

What Is Applied Anthropology?

Research, Theory, and Action

What Do Applied Anthropologists Have to Offer?
Detecting and Controlling Ethnocentrism
A Holistic View
Emic and Etic Views of Organizations

Applied Anthropology and Development
Without Holism: An Andean Fiasco
The Haitian Agroforestry Project
Archaeology and Agricultural Development
Archaeology and Environmental Protection: Garbalogy
Economic Development: Seaweed Farming in Zanzibar
Preserving a Way of Life: Security for the Cree

Medical Anthropology
AIDS (Acquired Immune Deficiency Syndrome)
Alzheimer's Disease

Refugee Health Care

Demographics: The U.S. Census Undercount

Forensics

Business and Anthropology

Poverty and Health
Witnessing for the Hungry and Homeless

Anthropological Advocacy
To Advocate or Not To Advocate: Is That the Question?

Summary

Up to now, you have probably been thinking that at least some of this is pretty interesting stuff (I hope). But what good is it? Does it have any practical use? Well, a lot of people (and not only anthropologists) think it does. Herein we explore some of the relationships between anthropological research and the attempt to achieve practical goals by organizations that sponsor or use such research. The sample of cases presented in this brief survey does not fairly represent the great variety of applied projects being carried out by anthropologists. This rapidly growing field is hard to keep up with.

What Is Applied Anthropology?

Since World War II, an increasing number of anthropologists have become involved in research that has immediate practical applications. Such anthropologists are said to practice applied anthropology.

Applied anthropology is problem-oriented research in which anthropologists use their skills and knowledge to discover and explain factors that influence human behavior and solve practical problems.

The core of applied anthropology consists of research commissioned by public or private organizations in the hope of achieving practical goals of interest to those organizations. Such organizations include federal, state, local, and international government bureaus and agencies, such as the U.S. Department of Agriculture (USDA), U.S. Department of Defense, U.S. National Park Service, U.S. Bureau of Indian Affairs (BIA), U.S. Agency for International Development (USAID), World Bank, World Health Organization (WHO), Food and Agricultural Organization (FAO), various drug abuse agencies, education and urban planning departments of major cities, and municipal hospitals—to mention only a few. In addition, private organizations that have hired or contracted with anthropologists to carry out practical, goal-oriented research include major industrial corporations, research foundations such as Planned Parenthood and the Population Council, and various branches of the Rockefeller and Ford Foundations' International Crops Research Institutes (Chambers 1985; Willigen 1991).

Research, Theory, and Action

Although the hallmark of applied anthropology is involvement in research aimed at achieving a special practical result, the extent to which the applied anthropologist actually participates in bringing about the desired result varies from one assignment to another. At one extreme, the applied anthropologist may merely be charged with developing information the sponsoring organization needs in order to make decisions. In other instances, the applied anthropologist may be asked to evaluate the feasibility of a planned program or even to draw up a set of plans for achieving a desired goal (Husain 1976). More rarely, the anthropologist, alone or as a member of a team, may be responsible for planning, implementing, and evaluating a whole program from beginning to end. When anthropologists help implement a program, they are said to be practicing **action anthropology.**

It is often difficult to draw a line between applied and nonapplied research.

Abstract theorizing about the causes of sociocultural differences and similarities can itself be construed as applied anthropology if it provides a general set of principles to which any action program must conform if it is to achieve success. For example, general theories about the causes of underdevelopment or of urban poverty (see Chapter 13, "A Culture of Poverty" section) can have considerable practical consequences even though the research behind these theories may not have been sponsored by organizations with the expressed goal of eliminating underdevelopment and urban poverty. Similarly, a better understanding of the processes responsible for the evolution of advanced industrial societies may be of immediate relevance to organizations that advise firms and governments on investment policies. Applied anthropology premised on blatantly incorrect theory is "misapplied anthropology" (Cohen 1984b).

What Do Applied Anthropologists Have to Offer?

The effectiveness of applied anthropology is enhanced by three distinctive attributes of general anthropology discussed in Chapter 2:

Relative freedom from ethnocentrism and Western biases

Concern with holistic sociocultural systems

Concern with both ordinary etic behavioral events and the emics of mental life

Detecting and Controlling Ethnocentrism

The applied anthropologist can assist sponsoring organizations by exposing the ethnocentric, culture-bound assumptions that often characterize cross-cultural contacts and that prevent change-oriented programs from achieving their goals.

By adhering to the principle of cultural relativism, applied anthropologists seek to understand the cultural barriers that may affect change-oriented programs.

For example, Western-trained agricultural scientists tend to dismiss peasant forms of agriculture as backward and inefficient, thereby overlooking the cumulative wisdom embodied in age-old practices handed down from generation to generation (Netting 1993). The attitude of Western experts toward the use of cattle in India is a case in point (see Chapter 17, "The Sacred Cow" section). Anthropologists are more likely to reserve judgment about a traditional practice such as using cattle to plow fields, whereas a narrowly trained specialist might automatically wish to replace the animals with tractors.

Again, applied anthropologists could add a valuable perspective to the attempt to set up a health care delivery system. Simply modeling it after those with which Western-trained doctors are familiar may not be the answer. Providing expensive staffs, costly hospitals, and the latest electronic gadgetry, for example, is not necessarily the way to improve the quality of health services (Cattle 1977:38). For example, the American notion that milk is the "perfect food" has led to much grief and dismay throughout the world. Many populations in less developed countries have been sent tons of surplus milk in powdered form as nutritional supplements, yet the people lacked the enzyme needed to digest lactose, the predominant form of sugar in milk. Finally, Western notions of hygiene automatically suggest that mothers must be persuaded not to chew food and then put it in their babies' mouths. Yet it was found that in the case of the Pijoan Indians of the U.S. Southwest, premastication of infant foods effectively combated the iron-deficiency anemia that afflicts infants who are fed exclusively on mother's milk (Freedman 1977:8).

A Holistic View

As industrial society becomes increasingly specialized and technocratic (that is, dominated by narrowly trained experts who have mastered techniques and the use of machines others do not understand), the need for anthropology's holistic view of social life becomes more urgent. In diverse fields (for example, education, health, economic development), narrow sets of easily quantified variables, such as standardized tests for students, or rates of productivity are increasingly being used to simplify an organization's performance. All too often, however, the gain in verifiability is offset by a loss in "validity" (or "meaning-

fulness"). Easily quantified variables may represent only a small part of a much bigger system whose larger set of difficult-to-measure variables could cancel out the observed effects of the small set of variables (Bernard 1994:41).

Holism is the idea that the various components of a sociocultural system are linked; a change in one part of the system leads to changes in other parts of the system.

For example, after World War II, the U.S. auto industry found it could earn more money by building heavier and more powerful cars without paying too much attention to the question of how long the cars would function without need of repairs. Other sets of variables—namely, the ecological consequences of auto emission pollution, the political and military conditions that made it possible for the United States to enjoy low oil prices, and the perception by foreign auto producers that there was a market for small, fuel-efficient, reliable, and long-lasting vehicles—were considered irrelevant to the task of maximizing the U.S. auto industry's profits. Hence, what appeared in a narrow context to be a highly objective measure of success (large profits and domination of the U.S. auto market) turned out in a longer time frame to be devoid of validity.

Thus, in commonsense language, anthropological holism boils down to being aware of the long term as well as the short term, the distant as well as the near, parts other than the one being studied, and the whole as well as the parts. Without understanding the needs and attitudes of local communities, even a seemingly straightforward and simple project can end up as a disaster (Box 19.1).

Etic and Emic Views of Organizations

Technification and specialization are usually accompanied by the growth of bureaucracy. An essential component of bureaucracy is an emic plan by which the units within an organization are related to each other and according to which individuals are expected to perform their tasks.

In most sociocultural systems, the etic behavioral aspects of organizations and situations differ substantially from the mental emics of the bureaucratic plan.

Anthropologists who are trained to approach social life from the ground up, and who are concerned with everyday events as they actually unfold often can provide a view of organizations and situations that the bureaucracy lacks. Thus, anthropologists have studied schools, factories, corporations, and hospitals

Box 19.1   Kazanga

The Universal Bank, having decided to launch a big development program in a remote region, sent a team of development experts to visit the country and talk to the chiefs. The team arrived at a settlement of mud huts and cattle corrals. The team leader asked the chief to assemble the villagers so that he could explain all the good things that the Universal Bank was going to do for them. When the villagers were seated the development expert stood up and said, "You are very lucky that the Universal Bank has decided to bring progress to your land."

"Kazanga!" The people shouted.

"You are going to get roads, schools and hospitals."

"Kazanga!" They shouted again.

"You are going to have electric lights and running water."

"Kazanga!" They roared back.

"TVs, VCRs, Big Macs, and a landing strip for jumbo jets."

"Kazanga!"

With everybody in a jovial mood, smiling and laughing, the chief asked the development experts if they would like to see the rest of the village. They agreed and he led them down the path that went to the cattle corrals, with the whole village following. As they neared the first corral, the chief pointed downward and said,

"Oh, by the way, be careful. Don't step in the Kazanga."

Box 19.2   A Partial List of the Domains of Applied Anthropology

Agricultural development

Alcohol and drug behavior

Alternative energy

Appropriate and affordable housing

Combating and exposing racism, sexism, and ageism

Community action (helping to complete community projects)

Criminal justice and law enforcement

Cultural resource management (archaeology)

Depletions and sustainable production

Design and architecture

Disaster research

Economic development

Education and schools

Employment and labor

Environmental protection

Gender and development

Gerontology (alternative treatment of the elderly)

Government and private bureaucracies

Health and medicine

Industrial productivity

Land claims (Native American)

Military forces

Multinational corporations (adaptation to multicultural globalization)

Nutrition and diet

Population regulation

Poverty

Refugees and resettlement

in a manner that provides both emic and etic viewpoints—to look at what is meaningful and relevant to the students, workers, and managers in the organizations as well as what is happening in terms of everyday events as they unfold.

Applied Anthropology and Development

The number of applications for applied anthropology is constantly growing, making it difficult to provide a complete list of these activities, nor will it be practical to provide examples of each category listed in Box 19.2. The examples that follow are intended merely to provide a sense of the broad scope of applied anthropological projects that have been carried out during the last decade.

One of the most important subfields of applied anthropology focuses on the problem of agricultural development in peasant and small-farmer communities.

As mentioned previously (Chapter 13, "Peasant Classes" section), anthropologists have studied peasants more often than they have studied other kinds of groups. Their knowledge of the conditions and aspirations of peasant life makes anthropologists useful as consultants to or members of interdisciplinary projects aimed at raising Third World standards of living (Barlett and Brown 1985).

Without Holism: An Andean Fiasco

International experts tried without success to get the peasant Indians of Chimborazo Province in Ecuador to substitute high-yield Australian merino sheep for the scrawny sheep the Indians owned. If the Indians would use them to breed new flocks, they could have them free of charge. Finally, one "progressive" Indian accepted the offer and raised a flock of cross-bred merinos that were far woollier and heavier than the traditional Indian sheep.

Unfortunately, the Indians of Chimborazo compete with other ethnic and racial groups for scarce resources. Non-Indian, Spanish-speaking farmers who live in the lower valleys resented the attention being paid to the Indians; they began to fear that the Indians would be emboldened to press for additional economic and social gains, which would undermine their own positions. The merinos attracted someone's attention, and the whole flock was herded into a truck and stolen. The rustlers were well protected by public opinion, which regarded the animals as "too good for the Indians anyway."

The "progressive" innovator was left as the only one in the village without sheep. Variables such as ethnic and class antagonisms, opportunities for theft, and the political subservience of peasants are not part of the expertise of sheep breeders, but awareness of these factors nonetheless proved essential to the achievement of their goals.

The Haitian Agroforestry Project

The Haitian Agroforestry Project is a good example of how anthropology can contribute to agricultural development. Planned and directed in its initial phase by anthropologist Gerald Murray, the project has successfully induced Haitian peasants to plant millions of fast-growing trees in steep hillside farmlands threatened by erosion. Depletion of soil as a result of rapid runoff from treeless hillsides has long been recognized as one of Haiti's greatest problems. In addition, trees are needed as a source of charcoal—the principal cooking fuel in poor households—and as a source of building materials. Many other reforestation programs have been tried in Haiti, but they have met with little or no success, either because the funds for planting were squandered or diverted by government bureaucrats or because peasants refused to cooperate and protect the seedlings from hungry goats.

Haitian Agroforestry Project
These trees are of the species Leucaena leucophala and are about two-and-one-half years old. Several other species are also being planted.

The Haitian Agroforestry Project was designed to avoid both pitfalls. In accepting a $4 million grant from the U.S. Agency for International Development (USAID), Murray insisted on an unusual stipulation: No funds were to be transferred to the Haitian government or through the Haitian government. Instead, the funds were to be given to local community groups—private voluntary organizations—interested in peasant welfare. In practice, the majority of these groups were grassroots religious associations formed by Catholic or Protestant priests, pastors, or missionaries. The project provided these groups with seedlings of fast-growing species matched to local ecological conditions and with expert advisors. The private voluntary organizations, in turn, undertook to assemble and instruct the local farmers and to distribute the seedlings to them free of charge, provided each farmer agreed to plant a minimum of 500 (G. Murray 1984).

Unless the peasants themselves were motivated to plant the seedlings and to protect them, the project could not succeed.

Box 19.3   The Theory behind the Haitian Reforestation Project

Gerald Murray predicts that cash-oriented agroforestry will become a major feature of peasant agriculture throughout the Third World. He interprets cash-oriented agroforestry as a response to a set of infrastructural conditions that are similar to the conditions associated with the rise of agricultural modes of production out of hunting and gathering: widespread depletion of a natural resource and population pressure. Peasants, having depleted the trees on which they depend for soil regenera-

tion, fuel, and building material, will now find it to their advantage to plant trees as one of their basic crops. In Murray's words (personal communication), "The anthropologically most important element of the model is the diachronic (evolutionary) component in which I am positing a scarcity-and-stress-generated readiness for a repeat in the domain of fuel and wood of the transition from foraging to planting which began some 15 millennia ago in the domain of food."

Murray's analysis of why previous projects had been unable to obtain the peasants' cooperation was based on his firsthand knowledge of Haitian peasant life and on certain principles of anthropological theory. Haitian peasants are market oriented: They produce crops for cash sale. Yet previous attempts to get them to plant trees stipulated that the trees should not be sold. Instead, the peasants were told that they were an unmarketable national treasure. Thus, trees were presented as exactly the opposite of the cash crops that the peasants planted on their own behalf. Putting himself in the peasants' shoes, Murray realized that previous reforestation projects had created an adverse balance of costs over benefits for the peasants. It was perfectly rational for the peasants to let their goats eat the seedlings instead of donating their labor and land to trees that they would be forbidden to harvest (or could only harvest 30 or 40 years in the future). Accordingly, Murray decided to distribute the trees as a cash crop over which the peasants would

have complete control. The project merely informed the peasants how to plant the trees and take care of them. They were also shown how to set the seedlings in rows between which other crops could be planted until the trees matured. They were told, too, how fast the trees would grow and how much lumber or charcoal they could expect to get at various stages of growth. Then the peasants were left on their own to decide when it would be in their best interest to cut some or all of them (Murray 1991).

The project's goal was to assist 5,000 peasant families to plant 3 million trees in 4 years. After 10 years (1981–1991), it had in fact assisted 200,000 families to plant 50 million trees (Murray 1995:180). Considerable numbers of trees have already been used for charcoal and for building purposes. Although it remains to be seen how much extra income will eventually be generated and how much erosion has been curtailed, Murray's basic analysis appears to have been correct (Box 19.3 and Box 19.4).

Box 19.4   Co-opting the Demon behind Deforestation

I propose that we look carefully at the "demon" which is currently blamed for putting the final touches on the environment of Haiti—the market which currently exists for charcoal and construction materials. It is this market, many would argue, which sabotages forever any hopes of preserving the few remaining trees in Haiti.

I would like to argue that it is precisely this market which can restore tree growth to the hills of Haiti. The demon can be "baptized" and joined in wedlock to the ecological imperatives whose major adversary he has been

up till now. With creative programming we can turn the tables on history and utilize the awe-inspiring cash-generating energy present throughout Haitian society in a manner which plants trees in the ground faster than they are being cut down. If this is to be done, it must be the peasant who does it. But he will not do it voluntarily or spontaneously unless tree planting contributes to the flow of desperately needed cash into his home. I propose that the mechanism for achieving this is the introduction of cash-oriented agroforestry. (G. Murray 1984:147)

Archaeology and Agricultural Development

Agricultural development is not exclusively the concern of cultural anthropologists.

Archaeological knowledge of the past can contribute directly to improvements in the present.

In Bolivia, on the marshy and barren shores of Lake Titicaca, for example, archaeological studies have revealed the presence of an intricate system of canals, terraces, and raised fields constructed between 1,000 and 1,500 years ago. During this period, archaeological evidence shows, potatoes and the Native American grain called quinoa were grown successfully despite the freezing conditions that prevail in the high Andes. Further research demonstrated that the ancients were able to grow their crops because the water in the crisscrossing canals absorbed enough heat during the day to prevent killing frosts at night.

American and Bolivian archaeologists then proceeded to test their theory by establishing experimental fields that conformed to the ancient design. These fields had crop yields that were at least double those of the other fields. Moreover, severe frosts that decimated the crops grown in the standard modern manner had little effect on the those grown in the ancient manner (Ferraro et al. 1994:211–212).

Archaeology and Environmental Protection: Garbalogy

Most of the garbage and waste produced by modern industrial societies ends up in landfills.

Garbalogy—the study of waste disposal—uses archaeological techniques to examine and classify the garbage-disposal habits of suburban householders.

Matching the etic data obtained from direct observation with the data recorded on questionnaires, William Rathje and his associates (Rathje and Murphy 1992) discovered a wide discrepancy between what people said and what they did. For example, people consistently underestimated the amount of alcohol, pastries, and fatty foods they consumed compared with the evidence of their consumption seen in their discarded garbage. These findings are important for health workers and nutritionists because they indicate that simple questionnaires about what people eat cannot be relied on to provide an accurate picture of etic behavioral practices. Rathje also found a considerable discrepancy between the amount of refuse that people said they recycled and the actual amount observed.

In more recent phases of this garbalogy project by Rathje and Murphy, attention has shifted to excavations of landfills, with three issues of public concern in mind: first, the actual content of landfills; second, determining the rate of refuse decomposition; and third, the movements of heavy metals and other hazardous substances inside and outside the landfill. Contrary to popular beliefs about what goes into municipal landfills, plastics constitute only 5 percent by weight and 12 percent by volume of the fill. Paper is the chief ingredient in the modern landfill, making up between 40 and 50 percent by volume and weight. Discarded telephone books alone account for an enormous portion of the landfill.

The garbalogists have also discovered that the decomposition of organic substances in landfills occurs more slowly than was previously believed. Heads of lettuce, kaiser rolls, hot dogs, guacamole, and corncobs with their kernals intact defy decomposition for decades. Paper again is the chief culprit, with tons of newspapers fit to read surviving intact for over a decade, despite high moisture levels within the fill.

The study of the movement of heavy metals such as lead and mercury provides the latest focus of garbalogist research (Rathje and Murphy 1992). Although the amount of toxic metals introduced into landfills is well known, their movement and concentration within landfills have not previously been established. As with the other aspects of landfill processes, the study of heavy metal movement is of

William Rathje
Leader of the Garbage Project, Tempe, Arizona.

considerable practical importance for the design and maintenance of municipal landfill facilities.

Economic Development: Seaweed Farming in Zanzibar

Applied cultural anthropologists working as members of research teams often are asked to help evaluate the effects of innovations on the standard of living of rural populations. Anthropologists Staffen Eklund and Per Pettersson (1992), under the auspices of the Institute for Marine Sciences in Zanzibar and the Swedish Agency for Research Collaboration with Developing Countries, undertook the task of evaluating the effects of a program designed to augment the role of seaweed farming in the Zanzibar economy. Commercial seaweed farming was introduced there in 1988–1989 by two companies that buy the seaweed from local farmers and sell it to multinational corporations.

Currently, seaweed farming provides more income for the average farm family than can be earned from traditional sources.

Eklund and Pettersson discovered that women had become the principal producers and beneficiaries of seaweed farming. In contrast to their role in traditional agriculture, these women maintained control over the income from seaweed cultivation and used it to purchase items that belong to women's traditional sphere of interest such as clothing and kitchen utensils. Women were able to play this role because seaweed cultivation requires intensive work for only a few days per month and does not interfere with their pursuit of traditional agricultural practices. Although seaweed farming seems to be a successful means of economic development, the anthropologists see some dark clouds on the horizon. Because the beaches and tidal flats suitable for seaweed cultivation are limited in extent, little additional expansion of seaweed production seems possible. Moreover, the seaweed cultivators find themselves increasingly under pressure from people who covet the very same beaches and tidal flats for the purpose of developing a tourist industry. Although the anthropologists make no specific suggestions for the resolution of this problem, their analysis could be used as the basis for remedial action in the future.

Preserving a Way of Life: Security for the Cree

In 1976 the government of Quebec initiated an Income Security Program for the Cree who traditionally

Cree

Cree Indian carrying recently caught beaver.

earned their living by hunting, fishing, trapping, and gathering in the region of James Bay. This program was part of the settlement reached concerning development of the hydroelectric resources of northern Quebec on lands traditionally used by the Cree. Anthropologists Colin Scott and Harvey Feit (1992) undertook the task of evaluating the impact of the hydroelectric project on the traditional economy of the Cree. They gathered data on the time the Cree spent hunting, fishing, and engaging in other income-producing activities. They interviewed and held informal conversations with local administrators and Cree leaders. And they directly observed daily life in the hunting camps and villages. They reached the following conclusions: The Income Security Program had led to increased participation in intensive hunting, fishing, and trapping; the organization of these subsistence practices remained "traditional" in form, although more people were involved and more advanced technologies were being used; substantial increases in the purchase of modern manufactured items had increased the efficiency of the subsistence base; improved access to transportation was changing the relationship between the Cree and their resources; and hunters were producing more food than was needed for family consumption, but this surplus was being distributed through networks of unrelated Cree.

Anthropologists find that it is possible to provide substantial improvements in the standard of living of native people without destroying the basic fabric of their culture.

Medical Anthropology

A central focus of applied anthropology is the interaction among culture, disease, and health care.

Anthropologists have, for example, studied the ethnography of everyday life in hospitals, organizations that offer a rich source of jarring discrepancies between the emics of various staff specialists and the etics of patient care. From the perspective of the hospital bureaucracy, its various rules and regulations are designed to promote the health and well-being of patients. In fact, numerous studies have shown that the main effect of many rules and regulations is to shock and depersonalize the patients and to create in them a level of apprehension comparable to that observed in a Ndembu boy awaiting the rite of circumcision in the "place of death." Unfortunately, discovering what is wrong with hospitals and health care delivery is easier than discovering how to change them for the better. As Melvin Konner, who is an M.D. and an anthropologist, has pointed out, medical anthropologists may be lessening their effectiveness as agents of change by adopting an adversarial and negative tone. "Modern medicine," writes Konner (1991:81), is "not a conspiracy against humanitarianism, cost efficiency, comprehensible language, patient compliance, patient autonomy, cultural differences, folk beliefs about health, or any of the other nonmedical dimensions it handles less than perfectly." Konner does not deny that physicians tend to ignore cultural factors in disease, practice "defensive medicine" aimed more at protecting themselves against lawsuits than at curing their patients, and rely excessively on technology. But these defects arise from systemic forces rather than the venality of physicians as a group: "If insurance companies prefer to pay for expensive hospital care of the dying rather than dignified hospices or home care, that is not the fault of physicians. If society lacks compassion for the ill poor, making the doctor–patient encounter intolerably brief, stressful and inadequate for both, it is neither fair or analytically satisfying to blame the doctor or to rail against 'bourgeois' medicine" (Konner 1991:81). Medical anthropology has an important role to play in helping physical anthropologists and medical researchers understand the interaction between cultural and natural factors that cause people to become ill.

AIDS (Acquired Immune Deficiency Syndrome)

As of 1999, over 30.6 million people worldwide were infected with HIV (human immunodeficiency virus), which is the cause of AIDS. AIDS is mainly a sexually transmitted disease that has a complex epidemiology. The risk for getting AIDS seems to be related to patterns of sexual and related behaviors as exhibited by different populations. One way to stop or slow the spread of the virus and the disease it causes is to identify and modify risk-increasing and risk-decreasing patterns of behavior.

Anthropologists are making a contribution to efforts to prevent AIDS by providing detailed ethnographic studies of the behavior of high- and low-risk populations (Mac-Queen 1994; Merson 1993).

The case of AIDS among the Baganda of Uganda illustrates the need for detailed ethnographic knowledge. Uganda has one of the highest HIV infection rates in the world. And the rate is highest not among men, but among women ages 20 to 30. AIDS prevention programs advise women to protect themselves by sticking to one partner. In theory, this advice corresponds to traditional mating patterns and should be readily accepted. Why, then, are the infection rates so high? One problem is that the Baganda have rules for breaking the rule of monogamy. Thus, Baganda women recognize the need to seek an additional partner if they find themselves under severe economic distress. Women who affirm this rule-breaking rule were actually found to have significantly higher rates of infection. Clearly, therefore, a woman can follow the advice to stick with one man only if she has alternative means of supplementing her income. Moreover, though women may practice monogamy, the men traditionally expect to have more than one wife plus additional sexual partners. Finally, most men and women know that condoms reduce the risk of contracting AIDS, but men are adamant in their refusal to use them, and Baganda women cannot refuse to have sex with their husbands (adapted from McGrath et al. 1992).

A particularly tragic aspect of the AIDS epidemic is that mothers can transmit the virus to newborns during birth. This outcome is not automatic, however; not all children of infected mothers become infected. But if they do, they have a short life expectancy. Of all HIV-positive women, intravenous drug users are the least likely to opt for terminating their pregnancies. The reason for this seems obvious: As intravenous drug users, these women have lost their sense of responsibility and are unable to think of the consequences of their behavior for their children. The full extent of their depravity is seemingly revealed by the fact that many of these women already have children whom they are unable to take care of and who are being raised by relatives or adoptive parents. But this reasoning can be stood on its head. An anthropological study carried out in the Bronx, New York, suggests a wholly different interpretation: Women who find themselves isolated by disease, poverty, and drug addiction desperately want to have children of their own to reaffirm their status as women and as human beings. It is the very fact that their children have been taken away from them that motivates them to get pregnant and have another child despite the terrible risk that they may not be able to see the child grow to adulthood (adapted from Pivnik et al. 1991).

Alzheimer's Disease

Cultural anthropologist Neil Henderson (1993) of the Suncoast Gerontology Center in Tampa, Florida, used his knowledge of ethnic cultural differences to develop support groups for the victims of Alzheimer's disease and their families. One of the main goals of the project was to develop a clear understanding of how ethnic and cultural factors interact with the disease syndrome. The steps taken were

- A survey that provided information on attitudes about Alzheimer's
- Recruiting and training of ethnic group leaders
- Announcing the existence of ethnic minority support groups in ethnic media
- Selection of a "culturally neutral" meeting site
- Meetings of the support groups conducted in an informal manner, promoting a sense of family among the group members

This project was regarded as highly effective by participants.

Refugee Health Care

Diverse populations have migrated to industrial countries due to difficult economic or political conditions in their homelands. Because they come from very different medical systems and health cultures, refugees pose a challenge to the health care system in their host countries (McElroy and Townsend 1996). For example, a majority of Vietnamese refugees entering the United States test positive for inactive tuberculosis. As a matter of prevention, infected but inactive patients are treated with the antibiotic isoniazid (INH). The unpleasant side effects of this treatment, however, prompt patients to either stop taking medication, or to take it sporadically

According to Karen L. Ito (1999), barriers to Vietnamese-American compliance include cultural influences of family and peers along with traditional concepts of illness and medicine. Advice from family and peers transmits and reinforces beliefs about illness that may contradict Western medical advice. For example, a widespread belief in China and Southeast Asia is that certain foods and physical states are yang ("hot") whereas others are yin ("cold"). Health requires that the yin and yang be in balance. Treatments based on the yin/yang, hot/cold theory often conflict with Western notions of the causes of health and disease.

Patients taking the INH antibiotic report that the medication makes them feel "hot," referring to symptoms of irritability or a rash, which are common side effects. Those who complied by taking the medicine did so because of encouragement and support from family members, some of whom prepared or purchased "cooling" foods to offset the "hot" symptoms. Noncompliant patients were discouraged by family and peers who told them not to take the pills, because they were not sick. They further argued that the medicine is bad for their health, as evidenced by the "hot" symptoms. To increase compliance, medical providers need to understand a community's varying cultural

Asian Refugees
Refugees have culturally constructed notions of health and illness that may conflict with standard bio-medical practice.

interpretations of illness and drug therapy. With the increasing cases of active tuberculosis and rising numbers of drug-resistant strains, it is important to improve community health education programs that increase compliance to prevent the development and spread of disease.

Demographics: The U.S. Census Undercount

After the 1990 U.S. Census was completed, it became evident that many members of minority groups, especially Latinos and African Americans, had not been counted. The Bureau of the Census funded 29 ethnographic study teams to find out why the undercount had occurred. The team that worked in the Bronx, New York, concentrated on two apartment houses located in a predominantly Latino neighborhood. The study team gained the confidence of the residents through affiliation with a local social service agency and introductions from a locally respected building superintendent.

Anthropologists found that the dangerous environment of Latino and African-American neighborhoods, problems with mail delivery, unknown addresses, and the mobility of the population led to the omission of entire households in the 1990 census.

In addition, undercounts made within households were caused by concealment to avoid affecting social service aid and by the complexity of household structures—kin and nonkin members and high mobility. The principal investigator estimates an omission rate of 25 percent in the census for the study population. Unexpectedly, status as an undocumented immigrant, competence in English, and literacy seemed to have little effect on the omission rate. The principal investigator makes these recommendations: Women should be used as enumerators because they are less threatening than men when knocking on unfamiliar doors. Also, enumerators should have racial and ethnic origins similar to those of the people they are visiting. And housing records should be verified with census records to avoid discrepancies (Dominguez and Mahler 1993).

Forensics

Physical anthropologists are highly trained in human anatomy and human biology. Hence, they are often called upon to serve in a **forensic** capacity—that is, to assist the courts and law enforcement agencies in identifying corpses and in determining the circumstances surrounding the death of suspected victims of foul play.

Careful examination of the skeletal and dental remains enables forensic specialists to identify the sex and age of a corpse and to estimate the date of death and burial and the nature of the implements used against the victim.

An example of anthropological forensics at work has been described by Douglas Ubelaker (1994). Ubelaker assisted in the identification of a murder victim whose skeleton was found near Rapid City, South Dakota. The police believed that the victim was a Native American man who had been missing for several months. They had a suspect but they needed a positive identification of the victim in order to go to trial. Ubelaker determined that the victim was between 30 and 46 years old, that he had died from blows to the face and head from a blunt instrument, and that he was probably of Native American descent. X-rays from the missing man's health record showed healed fractures that matched healed fractures of the victim's leg and elbow. They also showed a small notch on his right shoulder blade that was present on the skeleton. The possibility remained, however, that this notch was not peculiar to the victim, but was a feature that occurred quite frequently among Native American populations. To rule out this possibility, Ubelaker examined 200 skeletons in the Smithsonian Institution's collection of Native American skeletons. None of them possessed the notch. The identity of the deceased was confirmed, and the accused murderer was then brought to trial (Ferraro et al. 1994).

Business and Anthropology

Anthropologists have used their knowledge of foreign cultures to help business function more successfully in multicultural settings. With the globalization of trade and increase in international joint ventures, corporations have had to open foreign facilities and employ multinational labor forces. At home, U.S. companies have similarly had to hire an ever growing multiethnic workforce. U.S. companies have not been very adept at handling the wide range of cultural customs, assumptions, and language use that is necessary to function successfully in a multicultural and international business arenas. Cultural ignorance often leads to misunderstandings that are costly in terms of lost contracts, ineffective marketing strategies and such labor problems as low morale and lack of dedication.

Anthropologists have used participant observation and interview techniques to study organizational culture. Ferraro (1994) has observed that business organizations have cultures not unlike those studied by traditional anthropologists. Business organizations, like people in small-scale societies, have corporate myths and rituals, adhere to corporate norms and behavior, and have socially stratified roles and statuses with conflicting interests and loyalties.

Ethnographic techniques have been used to diagnose management problems afflicting U.S. companies that must train and oversee an ethnically diverse workforce. To retain workers, managers find that they must welcome multiple perspectives. Managers must tap the talents of all employees—by involving employees in the organizational process, companies can more effectively meet their organization's business goals (Kogod 1998).

Businesses are turning to anthropologists to make recommendations on how to improve relations with their employees. For example, anthropologists were called into a midwestern meat-packing plant to explain the causes for high worker turnover. The company studied by Don Stull, Ken Erickson, and Miguel Giner (1996) was an industry leader in benefits and wages, yet workers complained about poor working conditions and low morale. The research team concluded that the problems were the result of ineffective communication between the white Anglo supervisors and the predominately Hispanic and Asian work crew. By spending time alongside the workers on the meat cutting floor and hanging out with workers after hours, the researchers made the following recommendations:

- *Improve the quality of translated material*—employee handbooks, signs, and postings translated from English into Spanish reflect inadequate literacy in Spanish; some Spanish versions are both insulting and misleading.

- *Show recognition of worker knowledge*—skilled Hispanic employees possessed valuable skills not taught in training but were treated as unskilled labor.

- *Acknowledge employee innovations*—management did not recognize workers for their improving production.

- *Solicit safety suggestions from employees*—employees felt management did not pay sufficient attention to safety until someone got hurt.

These suggestions helped management bridge the gap between the goals of the company and the interests of the workers in order to improve worker loyalty, safety, and productivity.

Poverty and Health

Although the study of poverty might seem to be more appropriate for cultural anthropologists, physical anthropologists actually occupy a key position in the attempt to understand the relationship between poverty and numerous disabilities suffered by the poor, especially children who are poor. Physical anthropologist Deborah Crooks (1995) has attempted to provide an overview of the intricate feedbacks that link poor health and performance to disabling cultural and biological conditions under poverty. For example, the ability of children to succeed at school is related to their diets—to the experience of hunger, overconsumption of starchy foods, and the breathing and ingestion of toxic substances such as lead. Poor children are disabled by allergens emitted by cockroaches and mites. They tend to have lower birth weights as a result of their mothers' poor health and addiction to tobacco and other drugs. For reasons not completely understood, poor children also grow more slowly and have shorter stature than more affluent children.

Children who are born in poverty and who grow up in poverty may be at extreme disadvantage for cognitive functions and literacy, which again impairs scholastic achievement.

Their attention spans, dropout rates, school absences, grade repetition, and overall academic performance are all affected adversely.

Crooks concludes with the following comments about the role of biological applied anthropology:

Biological anthropologists bring a unique perspective and set of skills that enables the linking of biological data to social outcome. . . . Complex multivariate analysis linked to ethnographic data provides a more thorough picture of the lives of children in [the] context of their environments. Collaboration with our cultural colleagues may further enhance our ability to unravel the complex linkages outlined in this model. . . . Continued research of this sort will provide a clearer understanding of the consequences of poverty, enhancing the success of policy implementation resulting from our research. (1995:81)

Understanding the Plight of the Homeless

Anthropologists study the homeless to understand how agencies can better serve their needs.

Witnessing for the Hungry and Homeless

Applied anthropologists may serve as expert witnesses concerning the violation of a group's rights.

Sociocultural anthropologist Anna Lou Dehavenon (1989–1990) has studied the causes of urban hunger and homelessness in New York City and has served as an expert witness in court cases designed to help the poor. Her work has focused on two problems: the plight of individuals and families who need food and shelter on an emergency basis, and the plight of individuals and families whose welfare entitlements have lapsed as a result of bureaucratic apathy and ineptitude.

By doing fieldwork in the city's emergency assistance units, Dehavenon was able to document the failure of these units to find temporary shelter for homeless families until the early hours of the morning. A lawsuit brought against the city used her data to compel the city's Human Resource Administration to find suitable shelter during regular working hours if possible but in no case later than midnight.

Dehavenon discovered that the appearance of families seeking emergency food help was also closely connected with the administrative phenomenon known as "churning."

Churning results when people on welfare lose their entitlements as a result of a real or inaccurately recorded failure on their part to comply with bureaucratic requirements.

The requirements most often at issue have to do with failure to keep appointments with a caseworker as indicated in a mailed notification or failure to supply requested information or fill out a questionnaire. The most common reasons for not complying with these administrative rules stem from problems of communication. Mailboxes are frequently broken into; postal employees give up trying to find the persons being contacted and mark the envelope "whereabouts unknown." And, of course, a considerable amount of correspondence sent by people in compliance to welfare offices is not routed to the proper desk. Moreover, many welfare recipients are ill and cannot keep their appointments. Regardless of the reason, the welfare recipients lose their entitlement until the case can be reopened pending completion of proper forms and other procedures that may take as long as two or three months. While this administrative churning is going on, an estimated 18,000 people a month who are legally entitled to assistance find themselves in a food emergency, which often means that an individual or family has been without solid food for two days or has incurred considerable weight loss over the previous month. Others find themselves without money for rent—hence, the connection between churning and the people showing up at the emergency assistance units (see Box 19.5).

Box 19.5   Apathy or Hostility?

Profound indifference to the plight of the poor may explain their ever-worsening condition of the past several years. Churning, however, is difficult to explain as a product of indifference alone. Rather, it is the direct and logical consequence of a government policy that places a high premium on preventing the erroneous issuance of benefits, but often seems to care much less if eligible recipients are denied the assistance they desperately need to survive. Unless our society is one consumed by hostility to the poor, it must put a stop to this perverse policy and secure for poor people the benefits to which they are entitled. (Dehavenon 1989–1990:254)

By documenting and measuring these problems, by bringing them to the attention of high-ranking administrators in the city government, by proposing administrative reforms, and by releasing information to the news media, Dehavenon's research has helped bring about a substantial reduction in the amount of churning. For example, welfare recipients are now alerted to look for mail setting up appointments. The Human Resources Administration has also made a start toward abandoning the policy of dropping people whose mail comes back "whereabouts unknown" or who fail to return questionnaires. But much remains to be done. Some of Dehavenon's additional recommendations and goals:

- People who have medical problems or lack a fixed address should receive important notices by messenger.

- All missed appointments should be automatically rescheduled once.

- Recipients should have 60 days to comply with an administrative requirement.

- Their cases should not be closed but suspended so that as soon as they are in compliance, their payments can resume retroactively.

Anthropological Advocacy

The fact that the implementation phase of a project is often controlled by administrators or politicians who will not accept the anthropologist's analysis or suggestions has led a number of applied anthropologists to adopt the role of advocate.

The **advocacy** role requires the anthropologist to actively support a group of people and often involves political action.

Advocacy anthropologists have fought to improve conditions in women's jails, lobbied in state legislatures for raising welfare allotments, submitted testimony before congressional committees in support of child health care programs, lobbied against the construction of dams and highways that would have an adverse effect on local communities, and engaged in many other consciousness-raising and political activities.

To Advocate or Not To Advocate: Is That the Question?

Despite her involvement with poverty problems, Dehavenon regards herself as an expert witness rather than as an advocate for the poor.

Many applied anthropologists collect relevant knowledge and construct alternative plans but prefer not to be categorized as professional advocates.

Some hold the view that the only legitimate professional function of the applied anthropologist is to provide administrators, politicians, or lawyers with an objective analysis of a situation or organization and that, at most, action should be limited to suggesting but not implementing a plan. In this way, applied anthropologists hope to preserve the scientific standing of anthropology, because an all-out attempt to achieve a practical goal frequently involves rhetorical skills and cajolery, and may increase the risk of biased presentations (D'Andrade 1995). Against this view, advocacy anthropologists insist that the objectivity of anthropology and the other social sciences is illusory and that failure to push for the implementation of a goal represents a form of advocacy in itself. The objectivity is illusory, they argue, because political and personal biases control the commitment to study one situation rather than another (to study the poor rather than the wealthy, for example; see Chapter 13, America Now). And refraining from action is itself a form of action and therefore a form of advocacy because one's inaction assures that someone else's actions will weigh more heavily in the final outcome. Anthropologists who do not actively use their skills and knowledge to bring about what they believe to be a solution simply make it easier for others with opposite beliefs to prevail. Such anthropologists are themselves part of the problem (Scheper-Hughes 1995).

No consensus exists among anthropologists about how to resolve these views of the proper relationship between knowledge and the achievement of controversial practical goals. Perhaps the only resolution of this dilemma is the one that now exists: We must search our individual consciences and act accordingly. In conclusion, it should be emphasized that we have looked at only a few of the many faces of applied anthropology; many other equally important and interesting cases could have been presented.

Summary

1. Applied anthropology is concerned with research that has practical applications. Its core consists of research sponsored by public and private organizations with an interest in achieving practical goals.

2. The role of the applied cultural anthropologist may consist merely in researching the possible means of attaining such goals; sometimes it includes drawing up plans and helping implement them, as well as evaluating the results of implementation.

3. Applied anthropologists involved in implementation are known as practitioners of action anthropology. Beyond that core, other forms of research may also be considered part of applied anthropology. For example, abstract theorizing often has important practical implications, as in the case of alternative theories about the causes of underdevelopment or urban poverty.

4. Applied anthropology has three major and distinctive contributions to make to the analysis and solution of urgent practical problems: (a) exposure of ethnocentric biases; (b) a holistic viewpoint stressing the long as well as the short term, the interconnectedness of the parts of a sociocultural system, and the whole of the system as well as its parts; and (c) a commitment to distinguishing etic behavioral events from emic plans and ideologies.

5. All too often, the intended effects of an organization's plans and policies differ sharply from their actual everyday etic consequences.

6. One important focus of applied cultural anthropology is the problem of underdevelopment. The Haitian Agroforestry Project is an example of anthropological research, planning, implementation, and evaluation—in this case, applied to the goal of getting peasants to plant and protect trees. Another development project sketched in this chapter involved the protection of Cree culture while fostering increased reliance on modern technology. The case of seaweed farming in Zanzibar shows how advantages in one sector of a changing culture may lead to conflicting development objectives.

7. Not all development projects are based on sociocultural research. As the garbalogy research project shows, applied archaeology has much to contribute to understanding consumption and the management of natural as well as cultural resources.

8. Another focus of applied anthropology is medical anthropology. Studies of health care delivery systems and of everyday life in hospitals have attracted considerable interest among anthropologists. Many anthropologists have recently become involved in the attempt to slow the spread of HIV. The epidemiology of AIDS presents puzzles that can be solved only by a detailed ethnographic knowledge of the sexual behavior of people who have and have not contracted the disease. Applied medical anthropologists are also contributing to programs to better integrate victims of Alzheimer's disease into support groups that benefit both the patients and those who care for them.

9. Another interesting domain is applied demographics. Few people realize that sociocultural anthropologists have been called on to study why minority groups are underenumerated in the U.S. Census by as much as 25 percent.

10. Applied physical anthropology also makes many contributions that the public is not aware of. Forensic anthropology provides important services to the criminal justice system. And as the study relating poverty to health and school achievement demonstrates, the combination of biological and sociocultural perspectives presents the best way to approach many important social issues.

11. Finally, as brought out in the case of the "churning" of welfare recipients in a merciless bureaucratic machine, anthropologists have a legitimate role in helping people who cannot help themselves.

12. Applied anthropologists work through direct advocacy or through research that is primarily fact-finding and objective. Which route to follow is a matter of individual values.

KEY TERMS   ethnocentric / bias

advocacy

action anthropology

applied anthropology

churning

forensics

garbalogy

holism

medical anthropology

QUESTIONS TO THINK ABOUT

1. Why must applied anthropology assume a holistic view? How can long-term effects be different from short-term effects?

2. Why must change-oriented programs avoid ethnocentrism in achieving their goals? What might happen if they do not?

3. Why are both emic and etic approaches important for understanding how organizations work?

4. Why might a target population resist economic change? Under what circumstances is economic change more likely to be accepted?

5. How can anthropologists help corporations at home and abroad?

6. How can applied anthropologists help improve medical care and treatment of disease?

7. How can applied anthropology bring administrative reforms to problems of the poor and homeless?

A History of Theories of Culture

The Enlightenment

Nineteenth-Century Evolutionism

Social Darwinism

Marxist Evolutionism

The Reaction to Nineteenth-Century Evolutionism

Diffusionism

British Functionalism and Structural Functionalism

Culture and Personality

The New Evolutionism

Dialectical Materialism

Cultural Materialism

Sociobiology

Structuralism

Particularizing Approaches

This appendix serves as a brief outline of the history of the development of anthropological theories. It also presents the main research strategies employed by contemporary anthropologists.

The impulse lying behind the development of cultural anthropology is probably as old as our species. Members of different human groups have always been curious about the customs and traditions of strangers. The fact that people who live in different societies build different kinds of shelters, wear different kinds of clothing, practice different kinds of marriages, worship different spirits and gods, and speak different languages has always been a source of puzzlement. The most ancient and still most common approach to these differences is to assume that one's own beliefs and practices are normal expressions of the true or right way of life, as justified by the teachings of one's ancestors and the commandments or instructions of supernatural beings. Most cultures have origin myths that set forth the sequence of events leading to the beginning of the world and of humanity, and to the adoption of the group's way of life. The failure of other groups to share the same way of life can then be attributed to their failure to be true, real, or normal human beings.

The Enlightenment

As Europe entered the age of exploration and mercantile expansion, interest in describing and explaining cultural diversity increased. The discovery and exploration of a whole "New World"—the Americas—opened the eyes of philosophers, political leaders, theologians, and scientists to astonishing contrasts in the human condition.

Toward the middle of the eighteenth century, during the period known as the Enlightenment, the first systematic attempts to offer scientific theories of cultural differences began to emerge. The common theme of these theories held by scholars such as Adam Smith, Adam Ferguson, Jean Turgot, and Denis Diderot, was the idea of progress.

Cultures were seen as different not because they expressed innate differences in human capacities or preferences, but because they expressed different levels of rational knowledge and achievement.

It was believed that humankind, including Europe's ancestors, had at one time lived in an "uncivilized" condition, lacking a knowledge of farming and animal husbandry, laws, and governments. Gradually, however, guided by the ever-expanding role of reason in human affairs, humankind progressed from a "state of nature" to a state of enlightened civilization. Cultural differences thus largely resulted from the different degrees of intellectual and moral progress achieved by different peoples.

Nineteenth-Century Evolutionism

The idea of cultural progress was the forerunner of the concept of cultural evolution that dominated theories of culture during the nineteenth century.

According to evolutionism, cultures were usually regarded as moving through various stages of development, ending up with something resembling Euro-American lifestyles.

Auguste Comte postulated a progression from theological to metaphysical to positivistic (scientific) modes of thought. Georg Wilhelm Friedrich Hegel saw a movement from a time when only one man was free (the Asiatic tyrant) to a time when some were free (Greek city-states) to a time when all would be free (European constitutional monarchies). Others wrote of an evolution from status (such as slave, noble, or commoner) to contract (employee and employer, buyer and seller); from small communities of people who knew each other's faces to large, impersonal societies; from slave to military to industrial societies; from animism to polytheism to monotheism; from magic to science; from female-dominated horticultural societies to male-dominated agricultural societies; and from many other hypothetical earlier and simpler stages to later and more complex ones.

One of the most influential schemes was that proposed by the American anthropologist Lewis Henry Morgan in his book *Ancient Society*.

Morgan divided the evolution of culture into three main stages: savagery, barbarism, and civilization. These stages had figured in evolutionary schemes as early as the sixteenth century, but Morgan subdivided them and filled them out in greater detail and with greater reference to ethnographic evidence than had anyone else.

(Morgan himself carried out a lifelong study of the Iroquois, who lived near his hometown of Rochester, New York.) Morgan held that during "lower savagery," subsistence was based exclusively on gathering wild foods. People mated promiscuously, and the basic unit of society was the small nomadic "horde," which owned its resources communally. By the period of "upper savagery," the bow and arrow had been invented, brother–sister marriage was prohibited, and descent was reckoned primarily through women. With the invention of pottery and the beginning of farming came the transition to barbarism. Incest prohibitions were extended to include all descendants in the female line, and clan and village became the basic structural units.

The development of metallurgy marked the upper phase of barbarism; descent shifted from the female to the male line, men married several women at one time (polygyny), and private property appeared. Finally, the invention of writing, the development of civil government, and the emergence of the monogamous family marked the beginning of "civilization."

Social Darwinism

Europe and America were seen as the pinnacles of cultural progress, and the white race (especially its male half) was seen as the epitome of biological progress. This fusion of biological evolutionism with cultural evolutionism is often but incorrectly attributed to the influence of Charles Darwin. In fact, the development of biological interpretations of cultural evolution preceded the appearance of Darwin's *On the Origin of Species* (1859), and Darwin was himself greatly influenced by social philosophers such as Thomas Malthus and Herbert Spencer. Malthus's notion that population growth led to an inevitable "struggle for existence" had been elaborated by Spencer into the idea of the "survival of the fittest" in social life before Darwin published his theories of biological evolution.

The success of Darwin's biological theory of the survival of the fittest (he called it "natural selection") greatly enhanced the popularity of the view that social and cultural evolution also depended on biological evolution.

After the publication of Darwin's *On the Origin of Species,* a movement known as Social Darwinism appeared, which was based on the belief that cultural and biological progress depended on the free play of competitive forces in the struggle of individual against individual, nation against nation, and race against race.

The most influential Social Darwinist was Herbert Spencer, who went so far as to advocate the end of all attempts to provide charity and relief for the unemployed and impoverished classes and the so-called backward races on the grounds that such assistance interfered with the operation of the "law of the survival of the fittest" and merely prolonged the agony and deepened the misery of those who were "unfit."

Spencer used Social Darwinism to justify the capitalist free enterprise system, and his influence continues to be felt among advocates of unrestrained capitalism as well as among advocates of white supremacy.

Marxist Evolutionism

Although the writings and thoughts of Karl Marx were diametrically opposed to Social Darwinism, Marxism was also heavily influenced by the prevailing nineteenth-century notions of cultural evolution and progress. Marx saw cultures passing through the stages of primitive communism, slave society, feudalism, capitalism, and communism. Moreover, like many of his contemporaries, Marx stressed the importance of the role of struggle in achieving cultural evolution and progress.

All history, according to Marx, was the outcome of the struggle between social classes for control over the means of production.

The proletarian class, brought into existence by capitalism, was destined to abolish private property and bring about the final stage of history: communism.

On reading Morgan's *Ancient Society,* Marx and his associate Friedrich Engels thought they had found a confirmation of their idea that during the first stage of cultural evolution there was no private property and that the successive stages of cultural progress had been brought about by changes in the "mode of production."

For example, the development of agriculture coincided with the transition from savagery to barbarism in Morgan's scheme. Morgan's *Ancient Society* provided the basis for Engels's *The Origin of the Family, Private Property and the State,* which until the middle of the twentieth century served as a cornerstone of Marxist anthropology.

The Reaction to Nineteenth-Century Evolutionism

Early in the twentieth century, anthropologists took the lead in challenging the evolutionary schemes and doctrines of both the Social Darwinists and the Marxist Communists. In the United States, Franz Boas and his students developed the dominant theoretical position, which was known as historical particularism.

According to Boas, nineteenth-century attempts to discover the laws of cultural evolution and to schematize the stages of cultural progress were founded on insufficient empirical evidence. Boas argued that each culture has its own long and unique history.

> To understand or explain a particular culture, the best one can do is to reconstruct the unique path it had followed.

The emphasis on the uniqueness of each culture amounted to a denial of the prospects for a generalizing science of culture. Another important feature of historical particularism is the notion of cultural relativism, which holds that there are no higher or lower forms of culture. Such terms as *savagery, barbarism,* and *civilization* merely express the ethnocentrism of people who think that their way of life is more normal than those of other peoples.

To counter the speculative "armchair" theories and ethnocentrism of the evolutionists, Boas and his students also stressed the importance of carrying out ethnographic fieldwork among non-Western peoples. As the ethnographic reports and monographs produced by the historical particularists multiplied, it became clear that the evolutionists had indeed misrepresented or overlooked the complexities of so-called primitive cultures and that they had grossly underestimated the intelligence and ingenuity of the non-Caucasoid, non-European peoples of the world.

> Boas's most important achievement was his demonstration that race, language, and culture were independent aspects of the human condition.

Since both similar and dissimilar cultures and languages are found among people of the same race, the Social Darwinist notion that biological and cultural evolution were part of a single process had no merit.

Diffusionism

Another early twentieth-century reaction to nineteenth-century evolutionism is known as *diffusionism.* According to its advocates, the principal source of cultural differences and similarities is not the inventiveness of the human mind but the tendency of humans to imitate one another.

> Diffusionists see cultures as a patchwork of elements derived from a haphazard series of borrowings from near and distant peoples.

In the critical case of the origin of Native American civilizations, for example, diffusionists argued that the technology and architecture of the Inca of Peru and the Aztecs of Mexico were diffused from Egypt or from Southeast Asia rather than invented independently (see Chapter 2 for a critique of diffusionism).

British Functionalism and Structural Functionalism

In Great Britain, the dominant early twentieth-century research strategies are known as *functionalism* and *structural functionalism.* According to the functionalists, the main task of cultural anthropology is to describe the recurrent functions of customs and institutions rather than to explain the origins of cultural differences and similarities.

> According to one of the leading functionalists, Bronislaw Malinowski, the attempt to discover the origins of cultural elements was doomed to be speculative and unscientific because of the absence of written records.

Once we have understood the function of an institution, argued Malinowski, then we have understood all we will ever understand about its origins.

A. R. Radcliffe-Brown was the principal advocate of structural functionalism. According to Radcliffe-Brown, the main task of cultural anthropology was even narrower than that proposed by Malinowski. Whereas Malinowski emphasized the contribution of cultural elements to the biological and psychological welfare of individuals, Radcliffe-Brown and the structural functionalists stressed the contribution of the biological and psychological welfare of individuals to the maintenance of the social system.

> For the structural functionalists, the function of maintaining the system took precedence over all other functions.

But like Malinowski, the structural functionalists labeled all attempts to find origins as speculative history.

> Thus, the functionalists and structural functionalists evaded the question of the general, recurrent causes of cultural differences, while emphasizing the general, recurrent functional reasons for similarities.

This set the functionalists and structural functionalists apart from the diffusionists as much as from the nineteenth-century evolutionists. Nor were the functionalists and structural functionalists sympathetic to Boas's historical particularism. But like Boas and his students, the British functionalists and structural functionalists stressed the importance of carrying out fieldwork, insisting that only after two or more years of immersion in the language, thoughts, and events of another culture could anthropologists provide valid and reliable ethnographic descriptions.

Culture and Personality

In turning away from the nineteenth-century notions of causality and evolution, many anthropologists, influenced by the writings of Sigmund Freud, attempted to interpret cultures in psychological terms. The writings of Freud and the antievolutionism of Boas set the stage for the development of the approach known as culture and personality. Two of Boas's most famous students, Ruth Benedict and Margaret Mead, pioneered in the development of culture and personality theories. As we saw in Chapter 16, many advocates of the culture and personality approach stress the importance of early childhood experiences in the formation of a basic or modal type of adult personality or national character.

Some culture and personality theories attempt to explain how shared experiences produce a common basic personality that creates and sustains cultural differences and similarities.

In general, however, culture and personality advocates do not deal with the problem of why the beliefs and practices that mold particular personality types or national characters occur in some cultures but not in others. They have also been faulted for overgeneralizing about cultural patterns based on stereotypes and ignoring the variations among the people they study.

The New Evolutionism

After World War II, increasing numbers of anthropologists became dissatisfied with the antievolutionism and lack of broad generalizations and causal explanations characteristic of the first half of the century. Under the influence of Leslie White, an effort was launched to reexamine the works of the nineteenth-century evolutionists such as Lewis Henry Morgan, to correct their ethnographic errors, and to identify their positive contribution to the development of a science of culture.

White pioneered in postulating that the overall direction of cultural evolution was largely determined by the quantities of energy that could be captured and put to work per capita per year (see Chapter 5, "Energy and the Evolution of Culture" section).

At the same time (about 1940 to 1950), Julian Steward laid the basis for the development of the approach known as *cultural ecology,* which stressed the interaction of natural conditions such as soils, rainfall, and temperature with cultural factors such as technology and economy as the cause of both cultural differences and similarities.

The return to broad evolutionary points of view in the second half of the twentieth century among American cultural anthropologists was stimulated by archaeological evidence that diffusion could not account for the remarkable similarities between the development of states and empires in the New and Old Worlds (see Box 2.1). The step-by-step process by which Native American peoples in the Andean and Meso American regions independently developed their own elaborate civilizations is now fairly well known, thanks to modern archaeological research.

Julian Steward was especially impressed with the parallels in the evolution of the ancient civilizations of Peru, Mexico, Egypt, Mesopotamia, and China, and called for a renewed effort by anthropologists to examine and explain these remarkable uniformities.

Yet Steward was careful to distinguish his scheme of cultural evolution from the more extreme versions of nineteenth-century evolutionism. According to Steward, the problem with these earlier evolutionists was that they postulated a single, or unilinear, set of stages for all cultures, whereas he postulated many, or multilinear, paths of development depending on initial environmental, technological, and other conditions.

Dialectical Materialism

Both White and Steward were influenced by Marx and Engels's emphasis on changes in the material aspects of modes of production as the mainspring of cultural evolution. However, neither accepted the full set of Marxist propositions embodied in the point of view known as *dialectical materialism,* which gained considerable popularity among Western anthropologists for the first time in the 1960s and 1970s.

Dialectical materialists hold that history has a determined direction—namely, that of the emergence of communism and classless society. The sources of this movement are the class conflicts caused by the internal contradictions of sociocultural systems.

To understand the causes of sociocultural differences and similarities, social scientists must not only study these contradictions but also take part in the "dialectical" struggles that lead to progress toward communism. The most important contradiction in all societies is that between the means of production (roughly, the technology) and the relations of production (who owns the means of production).

In the words of Karl Marx: "The mode of production in material life determines the general character of the social, political, and spiritual process of life. It is not the consciousness of men that determines their existence, but on the contrary, their social existence determines their consciousness" (1970 [1859]: 21).

Cultural Materialism

Further elaboration of the theoretical perspectives of Marx, White, and Steward has led to the appearance of the point of view known as *cultural materialism.*

Cultural materialism is a research strategy that holds that the primary task of anthropology is to give material causal explanations for the differences and similarities in thought and behavior found among human groups.

Like dialectical materialists, cultural materialists hold that this task can best be carried out by studying the material constraints to which human existence is subjected. These constraints arise from the need to produce food, shelter, tools, and machines, and to reproduce human populations within limits set by biology and the environment. These are called *material constraints* or *conditions* in order to distinguish them from constraints or conditions imposed by ideas and other mental or spiritual aspects of human life such as values, religion, and art. For cultural materialists, the most likely causes of variation in the mental or spiritual aspects of human life are the differences in the material costs and benefits of satisfying basic needs in a particular habitat.

Cultural materialists differ from dialectical materialists mainly in rejecting the notion that anthropology must become part of a political movement aimed at destroying capitalism and furthering the interests of the proletariat.

Cultural materialists allow for a diversity of political motivations among anthropologists united by a common commitment to the development of a science of culture. In addition, cultural materialists reject the notion that all important cultural changes result from the playing out of dialectical contradictions, holding that much of cultural evolution has resulted from the gradual accumulation of useful traits through a process of trial and error.

Sociobiology

Sociobiology is a research strategy that attempts to explain some sociocultural differences and similarities in terms of natural selection. It is based on a refinement of natural selection known as the *principle of inclusive fitness.* This principle states that natural selection favors traits that spread an individual's genes by increasing not only the number of an individual's offspring, but the number of offspring of close relatives, such as brothers and sisters, who carry many of the same genes.

What controls biological evolution is whether a trait increases the inclusive total of an individual's genes in succeeding generations and not merely the number of one's own progeny. Applied to cultural evolution, human sociobiology states that cultural traits are selected if they maximize an individual's reproductive success.

Selection does not necessarily bring about a one-to-one correlation between genes and behavior but between genes and tendencies to behave in certain ways rather than others. For example, sociobiologists hold that the tendency for humans to forage in a manner that optimizes energy produced per unit of time invested is selected because it maximizes reproductive success (Wilson 1975, 1978; Lewontin et. al 1984).

In contrast, the cultural materialist perspective does not posit that useful traits are always selected because they maximize reproductive success. In the case of optimal foraging theory, for example (see Chapter 5), the favorable balance of energetic benefits over costs in satisfying an individual's nutritional needs is sufficient to understand why individuals capture certain animals and not others, without reference to its effects on reproductive success. Moreover, contrary to sociobiological principle, humans do not always seek to maximize reproductive success. The most glaring discrepancy is the low rate of reproductive success characteristic of the affluent classes in industrial society. The behavior of one-child American families scarcely seems to be dominated by the urge to have as many children as possible.

Structuralism

Not all post–World War II approaches to cultural theory are aimed at explaining the origin of cultural differences and similarities. In France, under the leadership of Claude Levi-Strauss, the point of view known as *structuralism* has been widely accepted.

Structuralism is concerned only with the psychological uniformities that underlie apparent differences in thought and behavior.

According to Levi-Strauss, these uniformities arise from the structure of the human brain and unconscious thought processes. The most important structural feature of the human mind is the tendency to dichotomize, or to think in terms of binary oppositions, and then to attempt to mediate this opposition by a third concept, which may serve as the basis for yet another opposition.

A recurrent opposition present in many myths, for example, is culture versus nature. From the structuralist point of view, the more cultures change, the more they remain the same, since they are all merely variations on the theme of recurrent oppositions and their resolutions. Structuralism, therefore, is concerned with explaining the similarities among cultures, but not with explaining the differences. See the section "Myth and Binary Contrasts" in Chapter 18 for an example of a structuralist analysis.

Particularizing Approaches

Mention must also be made of the fact that many anthropologists known as *postmodernists* challenge the discipline and reject all general causal viewpoints, holding that the chief aim of ethnography ought to be the study and interpretation of the emics of different cultures—their worldviews, symbols, values, religions, philosophies, and systems of meanings. During the 1980s, these approaches grew in popularity and were characterized by rejection of the distinction between observer and observed, etics and emics, and science and nonscience.

Postmodernists question whether anthropology is or should be a science. They believe that knowledge is shaped by culture and therefore anthropologists cannot be objective in their research.

Extreme relativism and antievolutionism reminiscent of Franz Boas's historical particularism also characterize recent approaches. For many contemporary cultural anthropologists, the main task of ethnography is to become familiar with a culture in the way one becomes familiar with a book or a poem, and then to "read" or interpret it as if one were a literary critic. The goal of these anthropologists is not to discover the scientific truth about a culture but to compose interpretations about the "other"—the other culture—that are elegant and convincing.

One recent manifestation of this line of development is called *deconstruction*. It focuses on the hidden intentions and unexpressed biases of the author of an ethnography rather than on the question of what the culture being described is really like.

Because deconstructionists feel that anthropologists cannot be objective in their research, they write about how their own culture influences their perspective on the people they are studying.

Although deconstructionists make valid points about the need to expose biases and prejudices in scientific descriptions (remember Malinowski and his neglect of the woman's point of view), their flat rejection of scientific truth as a goal of ethnography results in fragmented, contradictory, and essentially nihilistic notions about the human condition.

References

In the citation system used in this text, the names in parentheses are the authors of the publication mentioned or of publications that support the description or interpretations of matters being discussed. The year following the name is the year of the publication and should be used to identify specific sources when more than one publication of an author is included. Letters following a date (e.g., 1990a) distinguish different publications of the same author for the year. Specific page numbers following the date are provided only for direct quotes or for controversial points. All items in the bibliography have been cited in the text.

Acheson, James M. 1972. "Limited Good or Limited Goods: Response to Economic Opportunity in a Tarascan Pueblo." *American Anthropologist,* 74:1152–1169.

———. 1974. "Reply to George Foster." *American Anthropologist,* 76:57–62.

Adair, Linda, and Barry Popkin. 1992. "Prolonged Lactation Contributes to Depletion of Maternal Energy Reserves in Filipino Women." *Journal of Nutrition,* 122:1643–1655.

Adams, H. 1990. African and African American Contributions in Science. Base Line Essay. Portland: Multnomah School District.

Agar, Michael. 1994. *Language Shock: Understanding the Culture of Conversation.* New York: William Morrow.

Akmajian, Adrian, et al. 1992. *Linguistics: An Introduction to Language and Communication,* 3rd ed. Cambridge: MIT Press.

Alba, Richard. 1990. *Ethnic Identity: The Transformation of White America.* New Haven: Yale University Press.

Albers, Patricia. 1989. "From Illusion to Illumination: Anthropological Studies of American Indian Women." In *Gender and Anthropology,* Sandra Morgan, ed., pp. 132–170. Washington DC: American Anthropological Association.

Aldous, Peter. 1992. "French Venture Where US Fears to Tread." *Science,* 257(5066):25.

Algaze, Guillermo. 1993. "Expansionary Dynamics of Some Early Pristine States." *American Anthropologist,* 95:304–333.

Alland, Alexander, Jr. 1977. *The Artistic Animal: An Inquiry into the Biological Roots of Art.* Garden City, NY: Doubleday/Anchor Books.

Ames, Kenneth. 1994. "The Northwest Coast: Complex Hunter-Gatherers, Ecology and Social Evolution." *Annual Review of Anthropology,* 23:209–229.

Anderson, Richard. 1992. "Do Other Cultures Have Art?" *American Anthropologist,* 94:926–929.

Arensberg, Conrad. 1968. *The Irish Countryman.* New York: The Natural History Press. Originally published 1937.

Armelagos, George. 1990. "Health and Disease in Prehistoric Populations in Transition." In *Disease in Populations in Transition: Anthropological and Epidemiological Perspectives,* A. Swedlund and G. Armelagos, eds., pp. 127–144. New York: Bergin and Garvey.

Armelagos, George, A. Goodman, and K. Jacobs. 1991. "The Origins of Agriculture: Population Growth During a Period of Declining Health." *Population and Environment,* 13:9ff.

Armelagos, George, and Allan Goodman. 1994. "The Case Against Race." Paper read at the Southern Anthropological Society Meeting, Atlanta, April 28.

Asfaw, Berhane et al. 1999. "*Australopithecus garhi:* A New Species of Early Hominid from Ethiopia." *Science* 284:629–635.

Atkinson, Jane. 1992. "Shaminisms Today." *Annual Review of Anthropology,* 21:307–330.

Awe, Bolanlie. 1977. "The Iyalod in Traditional Yoruba Political Systems." In *Sexual Stratification: A Cross Cultural View,* Alice Schlegel, ed., pp. 270–291. New York: Columbia University Press.

Bakker, Jim. 1976. *Move That Mountain.* Plainfield, NJ: Logos International.

Baksh, Michael. 1984. *Cultural Ecology and Change of the Machiguenga Indians of the Peruvian Amazon.* Unpublished doctoral dissertation. Ann Arbor, MI: University Microfilms International.

———. 1985. "Faunal Food as a 'Limiting Factor' on Amazonian Cultural Behavior: A Machiguenga Example." *Research in Economic Anthropology,* 7:145–175.

Balee, William. 1984. "The Ecology of Ancient Tupi Warfare." In *Warfare, Culture and Environment,* Brian Ferguson, ed., pp. 241–265. Orlando, FL: Academic Press.

Bamberger, Joan. 1974. "The Myth of Matriarchy: Why Men Rule in Primitive Society." In *Woman, Culture and Society,* Michelle Zimbalist Rosaldo and Louise Lamphere, eds., pp. 263–280. Stanford, CA: Stanford University Press.

Barber, Bernard. 1968. "Social Mobility in Hindu India." In *Social Mobility in the Caste System,* J. Silverberg, ed., pp. 18–35. The Hague: Mouton.

Barfield, Thomas. 1993. *The Nomadic Alternative.* Englewood Cliffs, NJ: Prentice Hall.

Barlett, Peggy. 1989. "Industrial Agriculture." In *Economic Anthropology,* Stuart Plattner, ed. Stanford, CA: Stanford University Press.

Barlett, Peggy, and Peter Brown. 1985. "Agricultural Development and the Quality of Life: An Anthropological View." *Agriculture and Human Values,* 2:28–35.

Barnes, J. A. 1960. "Marriage and Residential Continuity." *American Anthropologist,* 62:850–866.

Barnouw, Victor. 1985. *Culture and Personality,* 4th ed. Homewood, IL: Dorsey Press.

Barth, Frederick. 1961. *Nomads of South Persia.* Boston: Little, Brown.

Bartram, William. 1958. *The Travels of William Bartram,* Francis Harper, ed. New Haven: Yale University Press.

Bar-Yosef, Ofer, and B. Vandermeersch. 1993. "Modern Humans in the Levant." *Scientific American* (April), pp. 94–100.

Bates, Daniel. 1996. *Human Adaptive Stategies: Ecology, Culture, and Politics.* Boston: Allyn and Bacon.

Bayliss-Smith, Timothy. 1977. "Human Ecology and Island Populations: The Problems of Change." In *Subsistence and Survival: Rural Ecology in the Pacific,* T. Bayliss-Smith and R. Feachem, eds., pp. 11–20. New York: Academic Press.

Beattie, John. 1960. *Bunyoro: An African Kingdom.* New York: Holt, Rinehart and Winston.

Beckerman, Stephen, Roberto Lisarralde, Carol Ballew, Sissel Schroeder, Christina Fingleton, Angela Garrison and Helen Smith. 1998. "The Bari Partible Paternity Project: Preliminary Results." *Current Anthropology,* 39:164–167.

Bell, Daniel. 1973. *The Coming of Post-Industrial Society: A Venture in Social Forecasting.* New York: Basic Books.

Belmonte, Thomas. 1979. *The Broken Fountain.* New York: Columbia University Press.

Belsham, Martha. 1988. "The Clerical Worker's Boss: An Agent of Job Stress." *Human Organization,* 47: 361–367.

Ben-Ari, E., B. Moeran, and J. Valentine 1990. *Unwrapping Japan: Society and Culture in Anthropological Perspective.* Manchester: University of Manchester.

Bender, Donald. 1967. "A Refinement of the Concept of Household: Families, Co-Residence, Domestic Functions." *American Anthropologist,* 69:493–503.

Benedict, Ruth. 1934. *Patterns of Culture.* Boston: Houghton Mifflin.

———. 1960. *Patterns of Culture.* New York: Mentor.

———. 1946. *The Chrysanthemum and the Sword.* Boston: Houghton Mifflin.

Bentley, G., T. Goldberg, and G. Jasienka. 1993. "The Fertility of Agricultural and Non–Agricultural Traditional Societies." *Population Studies,* 47:269–281.

Berdan, Frances. 1982. *Aztecs of Central Mexico.* New York: Holt, Rinehart and Winston.

Berlin, Brent, and Paul Kay. 1991. *Basic Color Terms: Their Universality and Evolution.* Berkeley: University of California Press.

Bermejo, M., G. Illera, and J. Sabater-PI. 1989. "New Observations on the Tool-Behavior of Chimpanzees from Mt. Assirik (Senegal, West Africa)." *Primates,* 30(1):65–73.

Bernard, H. Russell. 1981. "Issues in Training in Applied Anthropology." *Practicing Anthropology,* 3(Winter):

———. 1994. *Research Methods in Anthropology,* 2nd ed. Thousand Oaks, CA: Sage.

Bernard, H. Russel, ed. 1998. *Handbook of Methods in Cultural Anthropology.* London: Alta Press.

Bernardi, Bernardo. 1985. *Age Class Systems: Social Institutions and Politics Based on Age.* New York: Cambridge University Press.

Berra, Tim M. 1990. *Evolutionism and the Myth of Creationism: A Basic Guide to the Facts in the Evolution Debate.* Stanford, CA: Stanford University Press.

———. 1975. "Bazaar Behavior: Social Identity and Social Interaction in Urban India." In *Ethnic Identity: Cultural Continuity and Change,* L. Romanucci-Ross and G. de Vos, eds., pp. 71–105. Palo Alto, CA: Mayfield.

———. 1981. *Social Inequality.* New York: Academic Press.

Besharov, Douglas J. 1989. "Targeting Long-Term Welfare Recipients." In *Welfare Policy for the 1990's,* Phoebe H. Cottingham and David T. Ellwood, eds., pp. 146–164. Cambridge: Harvard University Press.

Bickerton, Derek. 1990. *Language and Species.* Chicago: University of Chicago Press.

Biocca, Ettore. 1996. *Yanoama The Story of Helena Valero, a Girl Kidnapped by Amazon Indians.* New York: Kodansha International. Originally published 1996.

Biolsi, Thomas. 1984. "Ecological and Cultural Factors in Plains Indians Warfare." In *Warfare, Culture and Environment,* Brian Ferguson, ed., pp. 141–168. Orlando, FL: Academic Press.

Bittles, Alan, et al. 1991. "Reproductive Behavior and Health in Consanguineous Marriages." *Science,* 2(52):789–794.

Bixler, Ray. 1982. "Comment on the Incidence and Purpose of Royal Sibling Incest." *American Ethnologist,* 9:580–582.

Blackwood, Evelyn. 1984. "Sexuality and Gender in Certain North American Indian Tribes: The Case of Cross-Gender Females." *Signs,* 10:27–42.

———. 1986. "Breaking the Mirror: The Construction of Lesbianism and the Anthropological Discourse on Homosexuality." In *Anthropology and Homosexual Behavior,* Evelyn Blackwood, ed., pp. 1–18. New York: Haworth Press.

Blanton, R. E., 1994. *Houses and Households: A Comparative Study.* New York: Plenum Press.

Bloch, Marc. 1964. "Feudalism as a Type of Society." In *Sociology and History: Theory and Research,*

W. J. Cahnman and A. Bokskoff, eds., pp. 163–170. New York: Free Press.

Bock, Philip. 1988. *Rethinking Psychological Anthropology: Continuity and Change in the Study of Human Action.* New York: W. H. Freeman.

Bock, Phillip, ed. 1994. *Handbook of Psychological Anthropology.* Westport, CT: Praeger.

Boesch, Christophe, and Hedwige Boesch. 1984. "Mental Map in Wild Chimpanzees: An Analysis of Hammer Transports for Nut Cracking." *Primates,* 25(2):169–170.

———. 1991. "Dim Forest, Bright Chimps." *Natural History* (September), pp. 50–56.

Bongaarts, John. 1980. "Does Malnutrition Affect Fertility? A Summary of the Evidence." *Science,* 208: 564–569.

———. 1994a. "Can the Growing Human Population Feed Itself?" *Scientific American* (March), pp. 36–42.

———. 1994b. "Population Policy Options in the Developing World." *Science,* 263:771–776.

Bongaarts, John, and F. Odile. 1984. "The Proximate Determinants of Fertility in Sub-Saharan Africa." *Population and Development Review,* 10:511–537.

Bonta, Bruce. 1993. *Peaceful Societies: An Annotated Bibliography.* Belmont, CA: Wadsworth.

Bonvillian, Nancy. 1997. *Language, Culture and Communication: The Meaning of the Message.* Englewood Cliffs, NJ: Prentice Hall.

Boserup, Ester. 1965. *The Condition of Agricultural Growth: The Economics of Agrarian Change under Population Pressure.* Chicago: Aldine.

Bossen, Laurel. 1988. "Toward a Theory of Marriage: The Economic Anthropology of Marriage Transactions." *Ethnology,* 27:127–144.

Bourgois, Phillipe. 1995. *In Search of Respect: Selling Crack in the Barrio.* Cambridge, England: Cambridge University Press.

Bowles, S., and H. Gintis. 1976. *Schooling in Capitalist America.* New York: Basic Books.

Boyd, Robert, and Joan Silk. 1997. *How Humans Evolved.* New York: Norton.

Brace, C. Loring. 1996. "Review of the Bell Curve." *Current Anthropology,* 37 (Supplement):S156–161.

Bradley, Candice. 1997. "Why Fertility Is Going Down in Margoli." In *African Families and the Crisis of Social Change,* Thomas Weisner et al., eds. Westport, CT: Bergin and Garvey.

Bradsher, Keith. 1995. "Gap in Wealth in U.S. Called Widest in West." *The New York Times,* April 17, pp. A1ff.

Brecher, Jeremy, and Tim Costello. 1994. *Global Village or Global Pillage.* Boston: South End Press.

Brodkin (Sacks), Karen. 1994. "How Did Jews Become White Folks?" In *Race,* Steven Gregory and Roger Sanjek, eds., pp. 78–102. New Brunswick, NJ: Rutgers University Press.

Brown, Judith K. 1975. "Iroquois Women: An Ethnohistoric Note." In *Toward an Anthropology of Women,* Rayna Reiter, ed., pp. 235–251. New York: Monthly Review Press.

Brown, Lester, H. Kane, and E. Ayres. 1993. *Vital Signs.* New York: W. W. Norton.

Brown, Lester, et al. 1991. *State of the World 1991: A Worldwatch Institute Report on Progress Toward a Sustainable Society.* New York/London: Norton.

———. 1994. "Facing Food Insecurity." In *State of the World 1994,* Lester Brown, ed., pp. 177–197. New York: W. W. Norton.

Brown, Ronald. 1978. Testimony: Hearings Before the Subcommittee on Crime, House of Representatives, 95th Congress, Serial No. 47. Washington, DC: U.S. Government Printing Office.

Brozan, Nadine. 1985. "U.S. Leads Industrialized Nations in Teen Age Births and Abortions." *The New York Times,* March 13, pp. 1, 22.

Brumberg, Joan Jacobs. 1988. *Fasting Girls: The Emergence of Anorexia Nervosa as a Modern Disease.* Cambridge, MA: Harvard University Press.

Brunton, Ron. 1975. "Why Do the Trobriands Have Chiefs?" *Man,* 10(4):545–550.

Buchbinder, Geogeda. 1977. "Nutritional Stress and Population Decline Among the Maring of New Guinea." In *Malnutrition, Behavior and Social Organization,* Lawrence S. Greene, ed., pp. 109–142. New York: Academic Press.

Buckley, Thomas. 1982. "Menstruation and the Power of Yurok Women." *American Ethnologist,* 9:47–90.

Burton, Michael, and D. White. 1987. "Sexual Division of Labor in Agriculture." In *Household Economies,* M. MacLachlan, ed. Lanham, MD: University Press of America.

Burton, Robert V., and J. Whiting. 1961. "The Absent Father and Cross-Sex Identity." *Merrill-Palmer Quarterly of Behavior and Development,* 7(2):85–95.

Butterfield, Fox. 1996. "Study Finds Disparity in Justice for Blacks." *The New York Times,* February 13, p. 8A.

Buvinic, Mayra. 1984. "Women's Issues in Third World Poverty: A Policy Analysis." In *Women and Poverty in The Third World,* Eva Mueller, ed., pp. 14–31. Baltimore: Johns Hopkins University Press.

Cain, Meade. 1977. "The Economic Activities of Children in a Village in Bangladesh." *Population and Development,* Review 3:201–227.

Caldwell, John C. 1982. *Theory of Fertility Decline.* New York: Academic Press.

Caldwell, J., et al. 1983. "The Causes of Demographic Change in Rural South India: A Micro Approach." *Population and Demographic Review,* 8:689–727.

Caldwell, John, and Pat Caldwell. 1993. Cultural Factors Tending to Sustain High Fertility. In *Population Growth and Reproduction in Sub-Saharan Africa.* G. T. Acsadi, G. Johnson-Acsadi, and R. A. Bulatao, eds. Washington, DC: The World Bank.

Callender, Charles, and Lee Kochems. 1983. "The North American Berdache." *Current Anthropology,* 24:443–470.

Campbell, Shirley. 1983. "Kula in Vakuta: The Mechanics of Keda." In *The Kula: New Perspectives on Massim Exchange,* J. Leach and E. Leach, eds., pp. 201–227. Cambridge, England: Cambridge University Press.

Carneiro, Robert. 1970. "A Theory of the Origin of the State." *Science,* 169:733–738.

———. 1981. "Chiefdom: Precursor of the State." In *The Transition to Statehood in the New World,* Grant Jones and Robert Kautz, eds., pp. 37–75. New York: Cambridge University Press.

Carroll, Lucy. 1977." 'Sanskritization,' 'Westernization,' and 'Social Mobility': A Reappraisal of the Relevence of Anthropological Concepts to the Social Historian of Modern India." *Journal of Anthropological Research,* 33(4):355–371.

Carstairs, G. M. 1967. *The Twice Born.* Bloomington: Indiana University Press.

Cashdan, Elizabeth. 1989. "Hunters and Gatherers: Economic Behavior in Bands." In *Economic Anthropology,* Stuart Plattner, ed., pp. 21–48. Stanford, CA: Stanford University Press.

Cattle, Dorothy. 1977. "An Alternative to Nutritional Particularism." In *Nutrition and Anthropology in Action,* Thomas Fitzgerald, ed., pp. 35–45. Amsterdam: Van Gorcum.

Chagnon, Napoleon. 1974. *Studying the Yanomamo.* New York: Holt, Rinehart and Winston.

———. 1989. "Response to Ferguson." *American Ethnologist,* 1989:565–569.

———. 1997. *Yanomamo,* 5th ed. New York: Harcourt Brace Jovanovich.

Chagnon, Napoleon. 1997. *Yanomamo,* 5th ed. Fort Worth, TX: Harcourt, Brace.

Chagnon, Napoleon. 1990. "Reproductive and Somatic Conflicts of Interests in the Genesis of Violence and Warfare Among Tribesmen. In *The Anthropology of War,* J. Haas, ed., pp.77–104. Cambridge: Cambridge University Press.

Chagnon, Napoleon, and Raymond Hames. 1979. "Protein Deficiency and Tribal Warfare in Amazonia: New Data." *Science,* 203:910–913.

Chakravarti, A. K. 1985a. "Cattle Development Problems and Programs In India: A Regional Analysis." *Geo Journal,* 10:21–45.

———. 1985b. "The Question of Surplus Cattle in India: A Spatial View. *Geografska Annala,* 67B:121–130.

Chambers, Erve. 1985. *Applied Anthropology: A Professional Guide.* Englewood Cliffs, NJ: Prentice Hall.

Child, Alice, and J. Child. 1985. "Biology, Ethnocentrism, and Sex Differences." *American Anthropologist,* 87:125–128.

Chodorow, Nancy. 1974. "Family Structure and Feminine Personality." In *Woman, Culture, and Society,* M. Rosaldo and L. Lamphere, eds., Stanford, CA: Stanford University Press, pp. 43–66.

Chodorow, Nancy. 1978. *The Reproduction of Mothering.* Berkeley: University of California Press.

Chomsky, Noam. 1973. "The General Properties of Language." In *Explorations in Anthropology: Readings in Culture, Man, and Nature,* Morton Fried, ed., pp. 115–123. New York: Crowell.

———. 1989. *Necessary Illusions: Thought Control in Democratic Societies.* Boston: South End Press.

Cicchetti, Dante, and Vicki Carlson, eds. 1989. *Child Maltreatment: Theory and Research on the Causes and Consequences of Child Abuse and Neglect.* New York: Cambridge University Press.

Coe, Michael. 1977. *Mexico,* 2nd ed. New York: Praeger.

Cohen, Joel. 1995. "Population Growth and the Earth's Human Carrying Capacity." *Science,* 269:341–346.

Cohen, Mark N. 1977. *The Food Crisis in Prehistory.* New Haven, CT: Yale University Press.

———. 1987. "The Significance of Long-Term Changes in Human Diet and Food Economy." In *Food and Evolution: Toward a Theory of Human Food Habits,* M. Harris and E. Ross, eds., pp. 261–283. Philadelphia: Temple University Press.

Cohen, Mark, and G. Armelagos, eds. 1984. *Paleopathology and the Origin of Agriculture.* New York: Academic Press.

Cohen, Myron. 1976. *House United, House Divided.* New York: Columbia University Press.

Cohen, Ronald. 1984a. "Warfare and State Foundation: Wars Make States and States Make Wars." In *Warfare, Culture and Environment,* Brian Ferguson, ed., pp. 329–355. Orlando, FL: Academic Press.

———. 1984b. "Approaches to Applied Anthropology." *Communication and Cognition,* 17:135–162.

Cohen, Yehudi. 1978. "The Disappearance of the Incest Taboo." *Human Nature,* 1(7):72–78.

Cohn, Bernard. 1955. "Changing Status of a Depressed Caste." In *Village India: Studies in the Little Community,* M. Marriott, ed. *American Anthropological Association Memoirs,* 83:55–77.

Collinvaux, Paul, and Mark Bush. 1991. "The Rain-Forest Ecosystem As a Resource for Hunting and Gathering." *American Anthropologist,* 93:153–162.

Condominas, George. 1977. *We Have Eaten the Forest.* New York: Hill and Wang.

Conyers, John. 1978. "Unemployment Is Cruel and Unusual Punishment." Hearings before the House Subcommittee on Crime, House of Representatives. Ninety-fifth Congress, Serial No. 47, pp. 647–679. Washington, DC: U.S. Government Printing Office.

Constanza, R. 1991. *The Science and Management of Sustainability.* New York: Columbia University Press.

Counts, Dorothy. 1985. "Tamparonga: The Big Women of Kaliai (Papua New Guinea)." In *In Her Prime: A New View of Middle-Aged Women,* J. Brown and V. Kerns, eds., pp. 49–64. South Hadley, MA: Bergin and Garvey.

Craig, Daniel. 1979. "Immortality Through Kinship: The Vertical Transmission of Substance and Symbolic Estate." *American Anthropologist,* 81:94–96.

Crooks, Deborah. 1995. "American Children at Risk: Poverty and Its Consequences for Children's Health, Growth, and School Achievement." *Yearbook of Physical Anthropology,* 38:57–86.

Crossette, Barbara. 1989. "India Studying the 'Accidental' Deaths of Hindu Wives." *The New York Times,* January 15, p. 4.

Curvin, Robert, and Bruce Porter. 1978. "The Myth of Blackout Looters." *The New York Times,* July 13, p. 21.

Dahl, Robert. 1981. *Democracy in the United States,* 4th ed. Boston: Houghton Mifflin.

Dalton, George. 1969. "Theoretical Issues in Economic Anthropology." *Current Anthropology,* 10:63–102.

D'Altroy, T., and T. K. Earle. 1985. "Staple Finance, Wealth Finance, and Storage in the Inca Political Economy." *Current Anthropology,* 26:187–206.

D'Altroy, Terrence. 1992. *Provincial Power in the Inca Empire.* Washington, DC: Smithsonian Institution Press.

D'Andrade, Roy. 1992. "Cognitive Anthropology". In *New Directions in Psychological Anthropology,* T. Schwartz, G. White, and C. Lutz, eds., pp. 47–67. New York: Cambridge University Press.

D'Andrade, Roy. 1995. *The Development of Cognitive Anthropology.* Melbourne, Australia: Cambridge University Press.

Darwin, Charles. 1998. *On the Origin of Species.* New York: Random House. Originally published 1859.

Das Gupta, Monica. 1978. "Production Relations and Population: Rampur." *Journal of Development Studies,* 14(4):177–185.

Dasgupta, Partha. 1995. "Population, Poverty, and the Local Environment." *Scientific American,* February, pp. 40–44.

Deacon, Terrence. 1997. *The Symbolic Species: The Co–evolution of Language and the Brain.* New York: Norton.

Dehavenon, Anna Lou. 1989–1990. "Charles Dickens Meets Franz Kafka: The Maladministration of New York City's Public Assistance Programs." *New York University Review of Law and Social Change,* 17:231–254.

———. 1993. "An Etic Model for the Scientific Study of the Causes of Matrifocality." In *Where Did All the Men Go?* Joan Mencher and Anne Okongwu, eds., pp. 53–69. Boulder, CO: Westview.

Dehavenon, Anna Lou. 1995. "A Cultural Materialist Approach to the Causes of Hunger and Homelessness in New York City." In *Science, Materialism, and the Study of Culture,* Martin Murphy and Maxine Margolis, eds., pp. 111–131. Gainseville: University of Florida Press.

DeLameter, John. 1995. "The NORC Sex Survey." *Science,* 270:501–503.

Deloria, Vine. 1969. *Custer Died for Your Sins.* London: Collier-Macmillan.

DeMarrais, Elizabeth, L. J. Castillo, and T. Earle. 1996. Ideology, Materialization and Power Strategies. *Current Anthropology,* 37:15–31.

De Mott, Benjamin. 1980. "The Pro-Incest Lobby." *Psychology Today* (March), pp. 11–16.

———. 1990. *The Imperial Middle: Why Americans Can't Think Straight About Class.* New York: Morrow.

Denevan, William. 1992. "The Pristine Myth: The Landscape of the Americas in 1492." *Annals of the Association of American Geographers,* 82:369–385.

Dentan, Robert. 1968. *The Semai: A Non-Violent People of Malaya.* New York: Holt, Rinehart and Winston.

Devereaux, George. 1967. "A Typological Study of Abortion in 350 Primitive, Ancient, and Pre-Industrial Societies." In *Abortion in America,* H. Rosen, ed., pp. 95–152. Boston: Beacon Press.

De Waal, Frans. 1996. "The Biological Basis of Peaceful Coexistence: A Review of Reconciliation Research on Monkeys and Apes." In *A Natural History of Peace,* Thomas Gregor, ed. Nashville, TN: Vanderbilt University.

De Waal, Frans. 1999. "Cultural Primatology Comes of Age." *Nature,* 399:635–636.

Dewalt, Kathleen M., B. R. Dewalt, with C. B. Wayland. 1998. Participant Observation. In *Handbook of Methods in Cultural Anthropology,* H. Russell Bernard, ed. London: Alta Press.

Diamond, Jared. 1997. *Guns, Germs and Steele: The Fates of Human Societies.* New York: Norton.

Dickman, Mildred. 1984. "Concepts and Classification in the Study of Human Infanticide: Sectional Introduction and Some Cautionary Notes." In *Infanticide: Comparative and Evolutionary Perspectives,* Glen Hausfater and Sarah Blaffer Hrdy, eds. New York: Aldine.

Dickson, D. Bruce. 1987. "Circumscription by Anthropogenic Environmental Destruction: An Expansion of Carneiro's (1970) Theory of the Origin of the State." *American Antiquity,* 52(4):709–716.

Diemberger, Hildegard. 1993. "Blood, Sperm, Soul and the Mountain." In *Gendered Anthropology,* Teresa del Valle, ed., pp. 88–127. New York: Routledge.

Di Leonardo, Micaela. 1991. "Introduction: Gender, Culture, and Political Economy Feminist Anthropology in Historical Perspective." In *Gender at the Crossroads of Knowledge: Feminist Anthropology in the Postmodern Era,* Micaela di Leonardo, ed. Berkeley: University of California Press.

Diop, Cheik Anta. 1991. *Civilization or Barbarism: An Authentic Anthropology.* Brooklyn, NY: Lawrence Hill Books.

Divale, William. 1972. "Systematic Population Control in the Middle and Upper Paleolithic: Inferences Based on Contemporary Hunters and Gatherers." *World Archaeology,* 4:221–243.

———. 1974. "Migration, External Warfare, and Matrilocal Residence." *Behavior Science Research,* 9:75–133.

Divale, William, and Marvin Harris. 1976. "Population, Warfare and the Male Supremacist Complex." *American Anthropologist,* 78:521–538.

Divale, William, M. Harris, and D. Williams. 1978. "On the Misuse of Statistics: A Reply to Hirschfeld et al." *American Anthropologist,* 80:379–386.

Dole, Gertrude. 1966. "Anarchy Without Chaos: Alternatives to Political Authority Among the Kui-Kuru." In *Political Authority,* M. J. Swartz, V. W.

Turner, and A. Tuden, eds., pp. 73–88. Chicago: Aldine.

Dominguez, Boanerges, and Sarah Mahler. 1993. *Alternative Enumeration of Undocumented Mexicans in the South Bronx*. Ethnographic Evaluation of the 1990 Decennial Census Report Series. Washington, DC: Center for Survey Methods Research, U.S. Bureau of the Census.

Donald, Leland. 1997. *Aboriginal Slavery on the Northwest Coast of North America*. Berkeley: University of California Press.

Drew, Elizabeth. 1983. *Politics and Money: The New Road to Corruption*. New York: Macmillan.

DuBois, Cora. 1944. *The People of Alor*. New York: Harper.

Dumond, Don. 1975. "The Limitation of Human Population: A Natural History." *Science,* 1987: 713–721.

Dumont, Louis. 1970. *Homo Hierarchicus: The Caste System and Its Implications,* Mark Sainsbury, trans. Chicago: University of Chicago Press.

Duncan, Greg, Jeanne Brooks-Gunn, and Pamela Klebanov. 1993. "Economic Deprivation and Early Childhood Development." Ann Arbor: University of Michigan (photocopy).

Duran, Diego. 1964. *The Aztecs: The History of the Indies of New Spain,* New York: Orion Press.

Duranti, Alessandro. 1997. *Linguistic Anthropology.* Cambridge, England: Cambridge University Press.

Dyson–Hudson, Rada, and J. Terrence McCabe. 1985. *South Turkana Nomadism: Coping with an Unpredictably Varying Environment*. New Haven, CT: HRAF (Human Relations Area Files) Press.

Dyson-Hudson, Rada, and Dominique Meekers. 1996. "The Universality of African Marriage Reconsidered: Evidence from the Turkana." *Ethnology,* 35:301–320.

Earle, Timothy. 1978. *Economic and Social Organization of a Complex Chiefdom: The Halelea District, Kauai, Hawaii*. Anthropological Papers, no. 63. Ann Arbor: Museum of Anthropology, University of Michigan.

———. 1989. "The Evolution of Chiefdoms." *Current Anthropology,* 30:84–88.

———, ed. 1991. *Chiefdoms: Power, Economy, and Ideology*. Cambridge, England: Cambridge University Press.

———. 1997. *How Chiefs Come to Power: The Political Power in Prehistory*. Stanford, CA: Stanford University Press.

Eaton, S. Boyd, Marjorie Shostak, and Melvin Konner. 1988. *The Paleolithic Prescription: A Program for Diet and Exercise and a Design for Living*. New York: Harper & Row.

Edgerton, Robert B. 1971. *The Individual in Cultural Adaptation: A Study of Four East African Peoples*. Berkeley: University of California Press.

Edgerton, Robert. 2000. *War Is Our Pastime: The Women Warriors of Dahomey*. Boulder, CO: Westview Press.

Ehrenberg, Margaret. 1989. *Women in Prehistory*. Norman: University of Oklahoma Press.

Eklund, Staffen, and Per Pettersson. 1992. "Mwani Is Money: The Development of Seaweed Farming on Zanzibar and Its Socioeconomic and Sociocultural Effects in the Village of Paje." Stockholm: Department of Social Anthropology, Stockholm University.

Eliade, M. 1958. *Birth and Rebirth: The Religious Meaning of Initiation in Human Culture*. New York: Harper & Row.

Ember, Carol, and Melvin Ember. 1992. "Resource Unpredictability, Mistrust, and War." *Journal of Conflict Resolution,* 36:242–262.

———. 1997. "Violence in the Ethnographic Record: Results of Cross-Cultural Research on War and Aggression." In *Troubled Times, Violence and Warfare in the Past,* D. L. Martin and D. W. Frayer, eds., pp. 1–20. The Netherlands: Gordon and Breach.

Ember, Carol, Melvin Ember, and B. Pasternack. 1974. "On the Development of Unilineal Descent." *Journal of Anthropological Research,* 30:69–94.

Ember, Melvin. 1982. "Statistical Evidence for an Ecological Explanation of Warfare." *American Anthropologist,* 84:645–649.

Ember, Melvin, and Carol Ember. 1971. "The Conditions Favoring Matrifocal Versus Patrifocal Residence." *American Anthropologist,* 73:571–594.

Emspak, Frank. 1996. "Where Have All the Jobs Gone?" *Chronicle of Higher Education,* April 5, pp. B1–B2.

Engels, Friedrich. 1990. *Origin of the Family, Private Property, and the State*. New York: International Publishers. Originally published 1884.

Erickson, Paul. 1998. *A History of Anthropological Theory.* Peterboro, Canada: Broadview Press.

Errington, Fredrick, and Deborah Gewertz. 1987. *Cultural Alternatives and a Feminist Anthropology*. New York: Cambridge University Press.

Estioko-Griffin, Agnes. 1986. Daughters of the Forest. *Natural History,* 95(5):36–43.

Estioko–Griffin, Agnes, and P. Bion Griffin. 1997. "Woman the Hunter: The Agta." In *Gender in Cross–Cultural Perspective,* Caroline B. Brettell and Carolyn F. Sargent, eds., pp. 219–227. Upper Saddle River, NJ: Prentice Hall.

Evans-Pritchard, E. E. 1940. *The Nuer, A Description of the Modes of Livelihood and Political Institutions of a Nilotic People*. Oxford: Clarendon Press.

———. 1970. "Sexual Inversion Among the Azande." *American Anthropologist,* 72:1428–1433.

Exter, Thomas. 1991. "The Cost of Growing Up." *American Demographics,* 13(8):59ff.

Fausto-Sterling, Ann. 1993. *The Sciences,* March–April, pp. 20–24.

Fei, Hsiao-T'ung, and Chang Chih-I. 1947. *Earthbound China: A Study of Rural Economy in Yunnan*. Chicago: University of Chicago Press.

Feil, Daryl. 1987. *The Evolution of Highland Papua New Guinea Societies*. New York: Cambridge University Press.

Feinman, G., and J. Neitzel. 1984. "Too Many Types: An Overview of Sedentary Prestate Societies in the

Americas." In *Advances in Archaeological Method and Theory*, M. B. Schiffer, ed., pp. 39–102. New York: Academic Press.

Ferguson, Brian R. 1984. "Introduction: Studying War." In *Warfare, Culture and Environment*, Brian Ferguson, ed., pp. 1–61. Orlando, FL: Academic Press.

———. 1989a. "Game Wars? Ecology and Conflict in Amazonia." *Journal of Anthropological Research*, 45:179–206.

———. 1989b. "Ecological Consequences of Amazonian Warfare." *Ethnology*, 27:249–264.

———. 1992. "A Savage Encounter: Western Contact and the Yanomami War Complex." In *War in the Tribal Zone: Expanding States and Indigenous Warfare*, R. Brian Ferguson and Neil Whitehead, eds., pp. 199–227. Santa Fe, NM: School of American Research Press.

———. 1995. *Yanomami Warfare: A Political History*. Santa Fe, NM: School of American Research.

———. 1997. "Violence and War in Prehistory." In *Troubled Times, Violence and Warfare in the Past*, Ferguson and Whitehead, eds., pp. 321–356. The Hague, The Netherlands: Gordon and Breach.

Ferguson, R. Brian, and N. Whitehead, eds. 1992. *War in the Tribal Zone: Expanding States and Indigenous Warfare*. Santa Fe, NM: School of American Research Press.

Ferraro, Gary P. 1994. *The Cultural Dimension of International Business*. Englewood Cliffs, NJ: Prentice Hall.

Ferraro, Gary, Wendy Travathan, and Janet Levy. 1994. *Anthropology: An Applied Perspective*. St. Paul, MN: West.

Fessler, Daniel. 1999. "Toward an Evolutionary Psychology of Inbreeding Avoidance." Unpublished manuscript, University of California at Los Angeles.

Fessler, Daniel. 1999. *Toxic Sex, an Essay on Incest and Other Things*. Manuscript, Department of Anthropology, University of California at Los Angeles.

Feuchtwang, Stephan. 1993. "The Chinese Race Nation." *Anthropology Today*, 9:14–15.

Fiske, Alan Page. 1999. "Learning a Culture the Way Informants Do: Observing, Imitating, and Participating." Unpublished manuscript. Department of Anthropology. University of California at Los Angeles.

Fittkau, E. J., and H. Klinge. 1973. "On Biomass and Trophic Structure of the Central Amazon Rain Forest Ecosystem." *Biotropica*, 5:1–14.

Fletcher, Michael. 1998. "Interacial Marriage Eroding Barriers." *Washington Post*, December 29, 1998.

Folbre, Nancy. 1991. *Women on Their Own: Global Patterns of Female Headship*. Washington, DC: International Center for Research on Women.

Fortune, Reo. 1965. *Manus Religion*. Lincoln, NE: University of Nebraska Press.

Foster, George, M. 1967. *Tzintzuntzan: Mexican Peasants in a Changing World*. Boston: Little, Brown.

———. 1974. "Limited Good or Limited Goods: Observations on Acheson." *American Anthropologist*, 76:53–57.

Foster, George, and Barbara Anderson. 1978. *Medical Anthropology*. New York: Wiley.

Fouts, Roger S., and Deborah H. Fouts. 1985. "Signs of Conversation in Chimpanzees." Paper given at meeting of AAAS, Los Angeles, May 28–31.

———. 1989. "Loulis in Conversation with the Cross-Fostered Chimpanzees." In *Teaching Sign Language to Chimpanzees*, R. Allen Gardner, Beatrix T. Gardner, and Thomas E. Van Cantfort, eds., pp. 293–307. Albany, NY: State University of New York Press.

Frayer, David, et al. 1993. "Theories of Modern Human Origins: The Paleontological Test." *American Anthropologist*, 95:14–50.

Frayser, Suzanne. 1985. *Varieties of Sexual Experience: An Anthropological Perspective on Human Sexuality*. New Haven, CT: HRAF (Human Relations Area Files) Press.

Frazer, James. 1911–1915. *The Golden Bough*, 3rd ed. London: Macmillan.

Freedman, Robert. 1977. "Nutritional Anthropology: An Overview." In *Nutrition and Anthropology in Action*, Thomas Fitzgerald, ed., pp. 1–23. Amsterdam: Van Gorcum.

Fried, Morton H. 1967. *The Evolution of Political Society: An Essay in Political Anthropology*. New York: Random House.

Fried, Morton H. 1978. "The State, the Chicken, and the Egg; or What Came First?" In *Origins of the State*, Ronald Cohen and Elman Service, eds., pp. 35–47. Philadelphia: Institute for the Study of Human Issues.

Frisancho, A. R., J. Matos, and P. Flegel. 1983. "Maternal Nutritional Status and Adolescent Pregnancy Outcome." *American Journal of Clinical Nutrition*, 38:739–746.

Frisch, R. 1984. "Body Fat, Puberty and Fertility." *Science*, 199:22–30.

Fritz, Gayle. 1994. "Are the First American Farmers Getting Younger?" *Current Anthropology*, 35:305–309.

Fulton, Robert, and Steven Anderson. 1992. "The Amerindian 'Man–Woman': Gender, Liminality, and Cultural Continuity." *Current Anthropology*, 33:603–609.

Gailey, Christine Ward. 1997 "Feminist Ethnography." In *Handbook of Methods in Cultural Anthropology*, H. Russell Bernard, ed. Walnut Creek, CA: Alta Mira Press.

Gajdusek, D. C. 1977. "Unconventional Viruses and the Origin and Disappearance of Kuru." *Science*, 197:943–960.

Gal, S. 1989. "Language and Political Economy." *Annual Review of Anthropology*, 18:345–367.

Galaty, John G., and Douglas L. Johnson. 1990. *The World of Pastoralism: Herding Systems in Comparative Perspective*. London: Belhaven Press.

Galef, B. G. 1992. "The Question of Animal Culture." *Human Nature*, 3:157–178.

Gandhi, Mohandas K. 1954. *How to Serve the Cow.* Ahmedabad, India: Navajivan Publishing.

Gardner, B. T., and R. A. Gardner. 1971. "Two-Way Communication with a Chimpanzee." In *Behavior of Non-Human Primates*, A. Schrier and F. Stollnitz, eds., vol. 4, pp. 117–184. New York: Academic Press.

———. 1975. "Early Signs of Language in Child and Chimpanzee." *Science*, 187:752–753.

Garon, Sheldon M. 1987. *The State and Labor in Modern Japan.* Berkeley: University of California Press.

Garson, Barbara. 1988. *The Electronic Sweatshop: How Computers Are Transforming the Office of the Future into the Sweatshop of the Past.* New York: Simon & Schuster.

Gaulin, Stephen, and James S. Boster. 1990. "Dowry as Female Competition." *American Anthropologist*, 92:994–1005.

Gay, Judith. 1986. " 'Mummies and Babies' and Friends and Lovers in Lesotho." In *Anthropology and Homosexual Behavior*, Evelyn Blackwood, ed., pp. 97–116. New York: Haworth Press.

Geertz, Clifford. 1973. *The Interpretation of Cultures.* New York: Basic Books.

Gelbard, Alene. 1997. Population 101. *Population Today.* Washington DC: Population Research Bureau.

George, Sabu, R. Abel, and B. Miller. 1992. "Female Infanticide in Rural South India." *Economic and Political Weekly*, 30:1153–1156.

George, Shanti. 1990. "Agropastoral Equations in India: Intensification and Change of Mixed Farming Systems." "Dimorphism and Stature Among Human Societies." *American Journal of Physical Anthropology*, 53:441–456.

Gibbons, Ann. 1991. "Deja Vu All Over Again: Chimp Language Wars." *Science*, 251:1561–1562.

Gilmore, David. 1990. *Manhood in the Making: Cultural Concepts of Masculinity.* New Haven, CT: Yale University Press.

Givens, David, and Susan Skomal. 1993. "The Four Fields: Myth and Reality." *Anthropology Newsletter*, 34, May, p. 1ff.

Glaser, Danya, and S. Frosh. 1988. *Child and Sexual Abuse.* Chicago: Dorsey Press.

Glasser, Ira. 1989. "How Long America?" *Civil Liberties*, Summer, pp. 12ff.

Glazer, Nathan and Daniel P. Moynihan. 1963. *Beyond the Melting Pot.* Cambridge, MA: Harvard University Press.

Gmelch, George. 1971. "Baseball Magic." *Transaction* 8(8):39–54.

Goddard, Victoria. 1996. *Gender, Family and Work in Naples.* England: Berg Publishers Ltd.

Goldschmidt, W. 1965. "Variation and Adaptability of Culture." *American Anthropologist*, 67:400–447.

Goldstein, Melvyn. 1987. "When Brothers Share a Wife." *Natural History*, 96:39–49.

Goliber, Thomas J. 1997. "Population and Reproductive Health in Sub–Saharan Africa." *Population Bulletin*, 52(4). Washington, DC: Population Reference Bureau.

Good, Kenneth. 1987. "Limiting Factors in Amazonian Ecology." In *Food and Evolution: Toward a Theory of Human Food Habits*, M. Harris and E. Ross, eds., pp. 407–426. Philadelphia: Temple University Press.

———. 1989. Yanomami Hunting Patterns: Trekking and Garden Relocation as an Adaptation to Game Availability in Amazonia, Venuzuela. Unpublished doctoral dissertation, University of Florida.

Good, Kenneth. 1995. "Hunting Patterns and Village Fissioning Among the Yanomami." In *Science, Materialism, and the Study of Culture*, Martin Murphy and Maxine Margolis, eds., pp.81–95. Gainsville: University Press of Florida.

Goodall, Jane. See Van Lawick-Goodall, Jane.

Goodwin, Marjorie Harness. 1990. *He-Said-She-Said: Talk as Social Organization among Black Children.* Bloomington: Indiana University Press.

Goody, Jack. 1976. *Production and Reproduction.* New York: Cambridge University Press.

Goody, Jack. 1986. *The Logic of Writing and the Organization of Society.* Cambridge, England: Cambridge University Press.

Goudsblom, Johan. 1992. *Fire and Civilization.* New York: Penguin.

Gough, E. Kathleen. 1959. "Criterion of Castle Ranking in South India." *Man in India*, 39:115–126.

———. 1968. "The Nayars and the Definition of Marriage." In *Marriage Family and Residence*, Paul Bohannon and J. Middleton, eds., pp. 49–71. Garden City, NY: Natural History Press.

Gould, Richard. 1982. "To Have and Not to Have: The Ecology of Sharing Among Hunter-Gatherers." In *Resource Managers: North American and Australian Hunter-Gatherers*, Nancy Williams and Eugene Hunn, eds., pp. 69–91. Boulder, CO: Westview Press.

Graber, Robert. 1992. "Population Pressure, Agricultural Origins, and Global Theory: Comment on McCorriston and Hole." *American Anthropologist*, 94:443–445.

———. 1991. "Population Pressure, Agricultural Origins, And Cultural Evolution: Constrained Mobility or Inhibited Expansion?" *American Anthropologist*, 93:692–697.

Gramby, Richard. 1977. "Deerskins and Hunting Territories: Competition for a Scarce Resource of the Northeastern Woodlands." *American Antiquity*, 42:601–605.

Gray, Patrick, and Linda Wolfe. 1980. "Height and Sexual Dimorphism and Stature Among Human Societies." *American Journal of Physical Anthropology*, 53:441–456.

Greenberg, Joseph. 1968. *Anthropological Linguistics: An Introduction.* New York: Random House.

Gregersen, Edgar. 1982. *Sexual Practices: The Story of Human Sexuality*. London: Mitchell Beazley.

———. 1986. "Human Sexuality in Cross Cultural Perspective". In *Alternative Approaches to the Study of Sexual Behavior*, Donn Byrne and Kathryn Kelley, eds., pp. 87–102. Hillsdale, NJ: Erlbaum.

Gregersen, Edgar. 1994. *The World of Human Sexuality*. New York: Irvington.

Gregor, Thomas. 1973. "Privacy and Extra-Marital Affairs in a Tropical Forest Community". In *Peoples and Cultures of Native South America*, Daniel R. Gross, ed., pp. 242–262. New York: Doubleday/ The Natural History Press.

———. 1977. *Mehinacu*. Chicago: University of Chicago Press.

Gregor, Thomas. 1985. *Anxious Pleasure: The Sexual Lives of an Amazonian Peoples*. Chicago: University of Chicago Press.

Gregor, Thomas, ed. 1996. *A Natural History of Peace*. Nashville, TN: Vanderbilt University Press.

Gregor, Thomas. 1994. Symbols and Rituals of Peace in Brazil's Upper Xingu. In *The Anthropology of Peace and Nonviolence*, Leslie Sponsel and Thomas Gregor, eds, pp. 241–258. Boulder, CO: Lynne Rienneer.

Gross, Daniel R. 1975. "Protein Capture and Cultural Development in the Amazon Basin." *American Anthropologist*, 77:526–549.

Gross, Daniel R. 1981. "Reply to Beckerman." Mss.

———. 1984. "Time Allocation: A Tool for the Study of Cultural Behavior." *Annual Review of Anthropology*, 13:519–558.

Gulliver, P. 1955. *The Family Herds*. London: Routledge & Kegan Paul.

Haas, Jonathan. 1982. *The Evolution of the Prehistoric State*. New York: Columbia University Press.

———. 1992. *Two Nations: Black and White, Separate, Hostile, Unequal*. New York: Scribner's.

Hadden, Jeffrey. 1993. "The Rise and Fall of American Televangelism." *Annals*, 527:113–130.

Hakansson, N. Thomas, and Robert LeVine. 1997. "Gender and Life Course Strategies among the Gusii." In *African Families and the Crisis of Social Change*, T. Weisner, C. Bradley, and P. Kilbride, eds., pp. 253–267. Westport, CT: Bergin and Garvey.

Hamer, Dean. 1993. "Linkage Between DNA Markers on the X Chromosome and Male Sexual Orientation." *Science* 261:321–327.

Hamilton, Sahni, B. Popkin, and D. Spice. 1984. *Women and Nutrition in Third World Countries*. South Hadley, MA: Bergin and Garvey.

Handwerker, W. P. 1983. "The First Demographic Transition: An Analysis of Subsistence Choices and Reproductive Consequences." *American Anthropologist*, 85:5–27.

Hannerz, Ulf. 1998. "Transnational Research." In *Handbook of Methods in Cultural Anthropology*, H. Russell Bernard, ed. London: Alta Mira Press.

Haraway, Donna. 1989. *Primate Visions: Gender, Race, and Nature in the World of Modern Science*. New York: Routledge.

Harner, Michael J. 1970. "Population Pressure and the Social Evolution of Agriculturalists." *Southwestern Journal of Anthropology*, 26:67–86.

———. 1972. *The Jivaro: People of the Sacred Waterfalls*. Garden City, NY: Natural History Press.

———. 1977. "The Ecological Basis for Aztec Sacrifice." *American Ethnologist*, 4:117–135.

———. 1980. *The Way of the Shaman: A Guide to Power and Healing*. New York: Bantam.

———. 1984. *The Jivaro: People of the Sacred Waterfall*. Berkeley: University of California Press.

Harrington, Charles, and J. Whiting. 1972. "Socialization Process and Personality." In *Psychological Anthropology*, Francis Hsu, ed., pp. 469–507. Cambridge, MA: Schenkman.

Harris, David. 1987. "Aboriginal Subsistence in a Tropical Rain Forest Environment: Food Procurement, Cannibalism and Population Regulation in Northeastern Australia." In *Food and Evolution: Toward a Theory of Human Food Habits*, Marvin Harris and Eric Ross, eds., pp. 357–385. Philadelphia: Temple University Press.

Harris, Helen. 1995. "Rethinking Polynesian Heterosexual Relationships: A Case Study on Mangaia, Cook Islands." In *Romantic Passion*, William Jankowiak, ed., pp. 96–127. New York: Columbia University Press.

Harris, Marvin. 1977. *Cannibals and Kings: The Origins of Cultures*. New York: Random House.

———. 1979a. "Comments on Simoons' Questions in the Sacred Cow Controversy." *Current Anthropology*, 20:479–482.

———. 1979b. *Cultural Materialism*. New York: Random House.

———. 1979c. "Reply to Sahlins." *The New York Review of Books*, June 28, pp. 52–53.

———. 1984. "Animal Capture and Yanomamo Warfare: Retrospective and New Evidence." *Journal of Anthropological Research*, 40:183–201.

———. 1985. *Good to Eat: Riddles of Food and Culture*. New York: Simon & Schuster.

———. 1989. *Our Kind: Who We Are, Where We Came From, Where We Are Going*. New York: Harper & Row.

Harris, Marvin. 1995. "Anthropology and Postmodernism." In *Science, Materialism, and the Study of Culture*, Martin Murphy and Maxine Margolis, eds., pp. 62–77. Gainesville: University of Florida Press.

Harris, Marvin, and Eric Ross, eds. 1987. *Death, Sex, and Fertility*. New York: Columbia University Press.

Harris, M., J. Gomes Consorte, J. Lang, and B. Byrne. 1993. "Who Are the Whites? Imposed Census Categories and the Racial Demography of Brazil." *Social Forces*, 72:451–462.

Hart, C. W. M., and A. R. Pilling. 1960. *The Tiwi of North Australia*. New York: Holt, Rinehart and Winston.

Hart, Keith. 1985. "The Social Anthropology of West Africa." *Annual Review of Anthropology*, 14:243–272.

Hartung, John. 1985. "Review of Incest: A Bisocial View, by J. Sheper." *American Journal of Physical Anthropology,* 67:169–171.

Hassan, Fekri. 1978. "Demographic Archaeology." In *Advances in Archaeological Method and Theory,* Michael Schiffer, ed., pp. 49–103. New York: Academic Press.

Hassan, Fekri. 1981. *Demographic Archaeology.* New York: Academic Press.

Hawkes, Kristen. 1993. "Why Hunter-Gatherers Work: An Ancient Version of the Problem of Public Goods." *Current Anthropology,* 34:341–361.

Hawkes, Kristen, Kim Hill, and J. O'Connell. 1982. "Why Hunters Gather: Optimal Foraging and the Ache of Eastern Paraguay." *American Ethnologist,* 9:379–398.

Hawkes, K., J. F. O'Connell, and N. G. Blurton-Jones. 1995. "Hadza's Children's Foraging: Juvenile Dependancy, Social Arrangments, and Mobility Among Hunter-Gatherers." *Current Anthropology,* 36:688–700.

Hayden, Brian. 1987. "Alliances and Ritual Ecstasy: Human Responses to Resource Stress." *Journal for the Scientific Study of Religion,* 26:81–91.

———. 1992. "Conclusions: Ecology and Complex Hunter/Gatherers." In *A Complex Culture of the British Columbia Plateau,* Brian Hayden, ed., pp. 525–559. Vancouver: University of British Columbia Press.

———. 1993a. *Archaeology: The Science of Once and Future Things.* New York: W.H. Freeman

———. 1993b. "The Dynamics of Emerging Inequality." Paper Read at the Annual Meetings of the Society for American Archaeology, St. Louis.

Hayden, Brian. 1995. "Pathways to Power." In *Foundations of Social Inequality,* T. Douglas Price and Gary Feinman, eds., pp. 15–86. New York: Plenum.

Hayden, Brian, M. Deal, A. Cannon, and J. Casey. 1986. "Ecological Determinants of Women's Status Among Hunter/Gatherers." *Human Evolution,* 1(5):449–474.

Hays, Terence E. 1988. " 'Myths of Matriarchy' and the Sacred Flute Complex of the Papua New Guinea Highlands." In *Myths of Matriarchy Reconsidered,* Deborah Gewertz, ed., pp. 98–120. Sydney, Australia: University of Sydney.

Headland, Thomas, and R. Bailey. 1991. "Introduction: Have Hunter-Gatherers Ever Lived In Tropical Rainforest Independantly of Agriculture?" *Human Ecology,* 19:115–122.

Headland, Thomas N., Kenneth L. Pike, and Marvin Harris. 1990. *Emics and Etics: The Insider/Outsider Debate.* Newbury Park, CA: Sage.

Heider, Karl G. 1972. *The Dani of West Irian.* Reading, MA: Addison-Wesley.

Henderson, Neil. 1993. *Ethnic and Cultural Issues in Long Term Care of Minority Elderly.* Tampa: National Eldercare Institute on Long Term Care and Alzheimer's Disease at the Suncoast Gerontology Center, University of South Florida.

Hendry, Joy. 1987. *Understanding Japanese Society.* London: Routledge.

Herbers, J. 1985. "Non-Relatives and Solitary People Make Up Half of New Households." *The New York Times,* November 20, p. 1.

Herdt, Gilbert. 1984a. "Semen Transactions in Sambia Cultures." In *Ritualized Homosexuality in Melanesia,* Gilbert Herdt, ed., pp. 167–210. Berkeley: University of California Press.

———. 1984b. "Ritualized Homosexuality Behavior in the Male Cults of Melanesia 1862–1983: An Intro- duction." In *Ritualized Homosexuality in Melanesia,* Gilbert Herdt, ed., pp. 1–81. Berkeley: University of California Press.

———. 1987. *The Sambia: Ritual and Custom in New Guinea.* New York: Holt, Rinehart and Winston.

Herdt, Gilbert. 1997. *Same Sex, Different Cultures.* Boul- der, CO: Westview Press.

Herman, Edward S. and Noam Chomsky. 1988. *Manu- facturing Consent: The Political Economy of the Mass Media.* New York: Pantheon Books.

Herman, Ellen. 1996. "All in the Family: Lesbian Moth- erhood Meets Popular Psychology in a Dysfunc- tional Era". In *Inventing Lesbian Cultures in America,* Ellen Lewin, ed., pp. 83–104. Boston: Beacon Press.

Hern, Warren. 1992. "Shipibo Polygyny and Patrilo- cality." *American Ethnologist,* 19:501–522.

Herskovitz, M. 1938. *The Dahomey.* New York: J.J. Augustin.

Hewes, Gordon. 1992. "Comment on McCauly." *Current Anthropology,* 33:162.

Hewlett, Barry S. 1991. "Demography and Child Care in Preindustrial Societies." *Journal of Anthropological Research,* 47(1):1–37.

Hill, Jane. 1978. "Apes and Language." *Annual Review of Anthropology,* 7:89–112.

Hill, Jane, and Bruce Mannheim. 1992. "Language and World View." *Annual Review of Anthropology* 21: 381–406.

Hirschfeld, Lawrence, J. Howe, and B. Levin. 1978. "Warfare, Infanticide and Statistical Inference: A Comment on Divale and Harris." *American Anthropologist,* 80:110–115.

Hochschild, Arlie Russell. 1998. *Time Bind: When Work Becomes Home and Home Becomes Work.* New York: Henry Holt.

Hockett, Charles, and R. Ascher. 1964. "The Human Revolution." *Current Anthropology,* 5:135–147.

Hogbin, H. Ian. 1964. *Guadacanal Society: The Koaka Speakers.* New York: Holt, Rinehart and Winston.

Holland, Dorothy. 1992. "The Woman Who Climbed Up the House." In *New Directions in Psychological Anthropology,* pp. 68–79. New York: Cambridge University Press.

Holmes, Bob. 1994. "Biologists Sort the Lessons of Fish- eries Collapse." *Science,* 264:1252–1253.

Holton, Gerald. 1994. *Science and Anti–Science.* Cam- bridge: Harvard University Press.

Hommon, Robert. 1986. "Social Evolution in Ancient Hawaii." In *Island Societies: Archaeological Ap-*

proaches to Evolution and Transformation, Patrick Kirch, ed., pp. 55–69. New York: Cambridge University Press.

Hopkins, Keith. 1980. "Brother–Sister Marriage in Ancient Egypt." *Comparative Studies in Society and History,* 22:303–354.

Horney, Karen. 1967. *Feminine Psychology.* New York: Norton. Originally Published 1939.

Horowitz, Tony. 1994. "Mr. Edens Profits from Watching His Workers' Every Move." *Wall Street Journal,* December 1, p. A9.

Hunt, Robert. 1988. "Size and Structure of Authority in Canal Irrigation Systems." *Journal of Anthropological Research,* 44:335–355.

Husain, Tariq. 1976. "The Use of Anthropologists in Project Appraisal by the World Bank." In *Development from Below: Anthropologists and Development Situations,* David Pitt, ed., pp. 71–81. The Hague: Mouton.

Irwin, Geoffrey. 1983. "Chieftainship, Kula and Trade in Massim Prehistory." In *The Kula: New Perspectives on Massim Exchange,* J. Leach and E. Leach, eds., pp. 29–72. Cambridge, England: Cambridge University Press.

Isaac, Barry. 1988. "Introduction." In *Prehistoric Economies of the Pacific Northwest Coast,* Barry Isaac, ed., pp. 1–16. Greenwich, CT: JAI Press.

———. 1992. "Discussion." *Research in Economic Anthropology, Supplement,* 6:441–442.

Itani, Jun'ichiro. 1961. "The Society of Japanese Monkeys." *Japan Quarterly,* 8:421–430.

Itani, Jun'ichiro and A. Nishimura. 1973. "The Study of Infra-Human Culture in Japan." In *Precultural Primate Behavior,* E. W. Menzell, ed., pp. 26–50. Basel: S. Karger.

Ito. Karen. 1999. "Health Culture and the Clinical Encounter: Vietnamese Refugees' Responses to Preventive Drug Treatment of Inactive Tuberculosis." *Medical Anthropology Quarterly,* 13(3):1-27.

Jacobs, Sue. 1978. "Top-down Planning: Analysis of Obstacles to Community Development in an Economically Poor Region of the Southwestern United States." *Human Organization,* 37(3): 246–256.

Jacobs, Sue, and C. Roberts. 1989. "Sex, Sexuality, Gender, and Gender Variance." In *Gender and Anthropology,* Sandra Morgan, ed., pp. 438–462. Washington, DC: American Anthropological Association.

Jenkins, J. H. 1988. "Ethnopsychiatric Interpretations of Schizophrenic Illness: The Problem of *Nervios* Within Mexican-American Families." *Culture, Medicine and Psychiatry,* 12:301–329.

Jenkins, J. H., M. Karno, A. de la Selva, and F. Santana. 1986. "Expressed Emotion in Cross–Cultural Context: Familial Responses to Schizophrenic Illness Among Mexican Americans." In *Treatment of Schizophrenia,* M. J. Goldstein, I. Hand, and K. Hahlweg, eds., pp. 35–49. Berlin: Springer.

Jenkins, Janis H., A. Kleinman, and B. Good. 1991. "Cross-Cultural Studies of Depression." In *Psychological Aspects of Depression,* J. Becker and A. Kleinman, eds., pp. 67–99. Hillsdale, NJ: Erlbaum.

Jensen, Neal. 1978. "Limits to Growth in World Food Production." *Science,* 201:317–320.

Jermain, Robert, Harry Nelson, Lynn Kilgore, Wenda Trevanthan. 1997. *Introduction to Physical Anthropology.* Belmont, CA: Wadsworth.

Jitsukawa, Mariko, and Carl Djerassi. 1994. "Birth Control in Japan: Realities and Prognosis." *Science,* 265:1048–1051.

Joans, Barbara. 1984. "Problems in Pocatello in Linguistic Misunderstanding." *Practicing Anthropology,* 6(3,4):6ff.

Johnson, Allen, and Timothy Earle. 1987. *The Evolution of Human Societies from Foraging Groups to Agrarian States.* Stanford, CA: Stanford University Press.

Johnson, Allen, and Orna Johnson. 1987. *Time Allocation Among the Machiguenga of Shimaa.* New Haven, CT: HREF (Human Relations Area Files) Press.

Johnson, Allen, and Douglass Price–Williams. 1996. *Oedipus Ubiquitous: The Family Complex in World Folk Literature.* Stanford, CA: Stanford University Press.

Johnson, Allen, and R. Sackett. 1998. "Direct Systematic Observation of Behavior." *In Handbook of Methods in Cultural Anthropology,* H. Russell Bernard, ed. London: Alta Mira Press.

Johnson, Allen. 1978. "In Search of the Affluent Society." *Human Nature,* 1(9):50–59.

Johnson, Allen. 1989. "Horticulturalists: Economic Behavior in Tribes." In *Economic Anthropology,* Stuart Plattner, ed. Stanford, CA: Stanford University Press.

Johnson, Allen. 2000. *The Matsigenka.* Manuscript. University of California at Los Angeles.

Johnson, Donald. 1993. "A Skull to Chew On." *Natural History,* May:52–53.

Johnson, Donald, and James Shreeve. 1989. *Lucy's Child: The Discovery of a Human Ancestor.* New York: Morrow.

Johnson, Orna. 1978. *Domestic Organization among the Machiguenga Indians of Southeastern Peru.* Unpublished doctoral dissertation, Columbia University.

Johnson, Orna. 1980. The Social Context of Intimacy and Avoidance: A Videotape Study of Machiguenga Meals. *Ethnology.* XIX. (3): 353–366.

Jonaitis, Aldona. 1991. *Chiefly Feasts: The Enduring Kwakiutl Potlatch.* Seattle: University of Washington Press.

Jones, Delmos. 1976. "Applied Anthropology and the Application of Anthropological Knowledge." *Human Organization,* 35:221–229.

Joseph, Suad. 1978. "Muslim–Christian Conflicts in Lebanon: A Perspective on the Evolution of Sectarianism." In *Muslim–Christian Conflicts: Eco-*

nomic, Political and Social Origins, S. Joseph and B. Pillsbury, eds., pp. 63–98. Boulder, CO: Westview Press.

Josephy, Alvin. 1982. *Now That the Buffalo's Gone: A Study of Today's American Indians.* New York: Knopf.

Jurmain, Robert, Harry Nelson, Lynn Kilgore, and Wanda Trevathan. 1997. *Introduction to Physical Anthropology.* Belmont, CA: Wadsworth.

Kaberry, Phyllis. 1970. *Aboriginal Woman, Sacred and Profane.* London: Routledge. Originally Published 1939.

Kaeppler, Adrienne. 1978. "Dance in Anthropological Perspective." *Annual Review of Anthropology,* 7:31–49.

Kang, Elizabeth. 1979. "Exogamy and Peace Relations of Social Units: A Cross-Cultural Test." *Ethnology,* 18:85–99.

Kardiner, Abram (with Ralph Linton). 1939. *The Individual and His Society.* New York: Columbia University Press.

Karno, Marvin, and J. Jenkins. 1997. "Cultural Considerations in the Diagnosis of Schizophrenia and Related Disorders and Psychotic Disorders Not Otherwise Classified." In *DSM-IV Sourcebook,* T. Widiger, A. Frances, H. Pincus, R. Ross, M. First, and W. Davis, eds., vol. 3, pp. 901–908. Washington, DC: American Psychiatric Association.

Katz, Phyllis, and S. A. Taylor. 1988. *Eliminating Racism: Profiles in a Controversy.* New York: Plenum.

Katz, Richard. 1982. *Boiling Energy: Community Healing among the Kalahari Kung.* Cambridge: Harvard University Press.

Kay, Paul, and W. Kempton. 1984. "What Is the Sapir—Whorf Hypothesis?" *American Anthropologist,* 86:65–79.

Keegan, William F., and Morgan D. MacLachlan. 1989. "The Evolution of Avunculocal Chiefdoms: A Reconstruction of Taino Kinship and Politics." *American Anthropologist,* 91:613–630.

Keeley, Lawrence. 1988. "Hunter-Gatherer Economic Complexity and 'Population Pressure': A Cross-Cultural Analysis." *Journal of Anthropological Archaeology,* 7:373–411.

———. 1996. *War Before Civilization.* New York: Oxford University Press.

Keller, Janet. 1992. "Schemes for Schemata." In *New Directions in Psychological Anthropology,* Tim Schwartz, G. White, and C. Lutz, eds., pp. 59–67. New York: Cambridge University Press.

Kelly, Raymond. 1976. "Witchcraft and Sexual Relations." In *Man and Woman in the New Guinea Highlands,* P. Brown and G. Buchbinder, eds., pp. 36–53. Washington, DC: Special Publication No. 8, American Anthropological Association.

Kelly, Robert L. 1995. *The Foraging Spectrum, Diversity in Hunter Gatherer Lifeways.* Washington, DC: Smithsonian Institution Press.

Kendall, Carl. 1984. "Ethnomedicine and Oral Rehydration Therapy: A Case Study of Ethnomedical Inves-

tigation and Program Planning." *Social Science and Medicine,* 19(3):253–260.

Kennickell, Arthur, et al. 1992. "Technical Working Paper." Washington, DC: Federal Reserve.

———. 1996. "Weighting Design for the 1992 Survey of Consumer Finances." Washington, DC: Federal Reserve.

Kertzer, David. 1978. "Theoretical Developments in the Study of Age Group Systems." *American Ethnologist,* 5(2):368–374.

———. 1993. *Sacrificed for Honor: Italian Infant Abandonment and the Politics of Reproductive Control.* Boston: Beacon.

Khare, Ravindra. 1984. *The Untouchable as Himself: Identity and Pragmatism Among the Lucknow Chamars.* New York: Cambridge University Press.

Khazanov, K. M. 1994. *Nomads and the Outside World.* Madison: University of Wisconsin Press.

Kirch, Patrick. 1984. *The Evolution of Polynesian Chiefdoms.* New York: Cambridge University Press.

Kivisto, Peter, ed. 1989. *The Ethnic Enigma: The Salience of Ethnicity for European-Origin Groups.* Philadelphia: Balch Institute Press.

Klass, Morton. 1979. *Caste: The Emergence of the South Asian Social System.* Philadelphia: ISHI.

Kleugel, James and E. R. Smith. 1981. "Beliefs About Stratification." *Annual Review of Sociology,* 7:29–56.

Knauft, Bruce M. 1987. "Reconsidering Violence in Simple Human Societies: Homicide Among the Gebusi of New Guines." *Current Anthropology,* 28:457–500.

———. 1990. "Melanesian Warfare: A Theoretical History." *Oceania,* 60:250–311.

Knauft, Bruce. 1994. The Human Evolution of Cooperative Interest. In *The Anthropology of Peace and Nonviolence,* Leslie Sponsel and Thomas Gregor, eds., pp. 71–94. Boulder, CO: Lynne Rienneer.

Koertge, Noretta, ed. 1998. *A House Built on Sand: Exposing Postmodernist Myths About Science.* New York: Oxford University Press.

Kogod, Kanu S. 1998. "The Bridges Process: Enhancing Organizational Cultures to Support Diversity." In *Applying Cultural Anthropology,* Gary P. Ferarro, pp. 74–83. Belmont CA: Wadsworth.

Konner, Melvin. 1991. "The Promise of Medical Anthropology: An Invited Commentary." *Medical Anthropology Quarterly,* 5:78–82.

Korbin, Jill. 1981. "Conclusions". In *Child Abuse and Neglect: Cross-Cultural Perspectives,* Jill Korbin, ed. Berkeley: University of California Press.

Korbin, Jill. 1987. "Child Maltreatment in Cross-Cultural Perspective: Vulnerable Children and Circumstances." In *Child Abuse and Neglect: Biosocial Dimensions,* Richard Gelles and Jane Lancaster, eds. New York: Aldine.

Kottak, Conrad. 1990. *Prime-Time Society: An Anthropological Analysis of Television and Culture.* Ann Arbor: University of Michigan Press.

Kottak, Conrad. 1994. *Cultural Anthropology.* New York: McGraw-Hill.

Kroeber, Alfred L. 1948. *Anthropology.* New York: Harcourt Brace.

Kumagai, Hisa, and Arno Kumagai. 1986. "The Hidden 'I' in Amae: Passive Love and Japanese Social Perception." *Ethos,* 14:305–320.

Kusin, Jane, S. Kardjati, and H. Renqvist. 1993. "Chronic Undernutrition in Pregnancy and Lactation." *Proceedings of the Nutrition Society,* 52:19–28.

Kuznar, Lawrence. 1997. *Reclaiming a Scientific Anthropology.* Walnut Creek, CA: Alta Mira Press.

Labov, William. 1972. *Language in the Inner City.* Philadelphia: University of Pennsylvania Press.

Labov, William. 1973. Some Features of the English of Black Americans. In *Variations of Present Day English,* R. W. Bailey and J. L. Robinson, eds. New York: Macmillan.

Lakoff, R.T. 1990. *The Politics of Language in Our Lives.* New York: Basic Books.

Lambert, Patricia. 1997. Patterns of Violence in Prehistoric Hunter Gatherer Societies of Coastal Southern California. In *Troubled Times Violence and Warfare in the Past,* D. L. Martin and D. W. Frayer, eds., pp. 77–110. The Netherlands: Gordon and Breach.

Landy, David. 1985. "Pibloktok and in Nutrition: Possible Implications of Hypervitaminosis A." *Social Science and Medicine,* 21:173–185.

Lang, H., and R. Gohlen. 1985. "Completed Fetility of the Hutterites: A Revision." *Current Anthropology,* 26(3):395.

Langdon, Steve. 1979. "Comparative Tlingit and Haida Adaptation to the West Coast of the Prince of Wales Archipelago." *Ethnology,* 18:101–119.

Lauman, Edward. 1994. *The Social Organization of Sexuality.* Chicago: University of Chicago Press.

Lawrence, Peter. 1964. *Road Belong Cargo: A Study of the Cargo Movement in the Southern Madang District, New Guinea.* Manchester, England: University of Manchester Press.

Leacock, Eleanor Burke. 1978. "Women's Status in Egalitarian Society: Implication for Social Evolution." *Current Anthropology,* 19:247–275.

———. 1983. "Ideologies of Male Dominance as Divide and Rule Politics: An Anthropologist's View." In *Women's Nature,* Marian Lowe and Ruth Hubbard, eds., pp. 111–121. New York: Pergamon Press.

Leakey, Richard and Roger Lewin. 1993. *Origins Reconsidered: In Search of What Makes Us Human.* New York: Doubleday.

Leavitt, Gregory. 1989. "Disappearance of the Incest Taboo." *American Anthropologist,* 91:116–131.

———. 1990. "Sociobiological Explanations of Incest Avoidance: A Critical Review of Evidential Claims." *American Anthropologist,* 91:971–993.

———. 1992. "Inbreeding Fitness: A Reply to Uhlman." *American Anthropologist,* 94:448–449.

Lee, Richard. 1969. "Eating Christmas in the Kalahari." *Natural History,* 78(December):14ff.

Lee, Richard. 1968. "What Do Hunters Do for a Living, or How to Make Out on Scarce Resources." In *Man the Hunter,* R. B. Lee and I. DeVore, eds., pp. 30–43. Chicago: Aldine.

———. 1979. *The !Kung San: Men and Women in a Foraging Society.* Cambridge, England: Cambridge University Press.

———. 1990. "Primitive Communism and the Origin of Social Inequality." In *The Evolution of Political Systems: Sociopolitics of Small-Scale Sedentary Societies,* Steadman Upham, ed., pp. 225–246. New York: Cambridge University Press.

———. 1993. The Dobe Jo/'hoansi. Fort Worth, TX: Harcourt Brace.

Lee, Richard, and Mathias Guenther. 1991. "Oxen or Onions? The Search for Trade and the Truth in the Kalahari." *Current Anthropology,* 32:593–601.

Lee, Richard, and Mathais Guenther. 1995. "Errors Corrected or Compounded: A Reply to Wilmsen." *Current Anthropology,* 36:298–305.

Leeds, Anthony. 1970. "The Concept of the Culture of Poverty: Conceptual, Logical, and Empirical Problems, with Perspectives from Brazil and Peru." In *The Culture of Poverty: A Critique,* E. Leacock, ed., pp. 226–284. New York: Simon & Schuster.

Leo, John. 1993. "The Melting Pot Is Cooking." *U.S. News & World Report,* July 5, p. 15.

Lesser, Alexander. 1968. "War and the State." In *War: The Anthropology of Armed Conflict and Aggression,* M. Fried, M. Harris, and R. Murphy, eds., pp. 92–96. Garden City, NY: Natural History Press.

Lett, James. 1991. "Interpretive Anthropology, Metaphysics, and the Paranormal." *Journal of Anthropological Research,* 47:305–329.

Levine, Nancy. 1988. *The Dynamics of Polyandry: Kinship Domesticity, and Population of the Tibetan Border.* Chicago: University of Chicago Press.

Levine, Nancy, and Joan Silk. 1997. "Why Polyandry Fails: Sources of Instability in Polyandrous Marriages." *Current Anthropology,* 38:375–398.

LeVine R. and LeVine S. 1979. *Nyansongo: A Gusii Community in Kenya.* Six Cultures Series, vol 2. New York: Wiley.

LeVine, Robert, S. Levine, P. Leiderman, T. Brazelton, S. Dixon, A. Richman, and C. Keefer. 1994. *Child Care and Culture: Lessons from Africa.* New York: Cambridge University Press.

Lewin, Ellen. 1996. "'Why in the World Would You Want to Do That?': Claiming Community in Lesbian Commitment Ceremonies." In *Inventing Lesbian Cultures in America,* p. 105. Ellen Lewin, ed. Boston: Beacon Press.

Lewis, Oscar. 1966. *La Vida: A Puerto Rican Family in the Culture of Poverty—San Juan and New York.* New York: Random House.

Lewontin, R., S. Rose, and L. Kamin. 1984. *Not in Our Genes: Biology, Ideology, and Human Nature.* New York: Pantheon.

Libra, Takie Sugiyama. 1992. "Self in Japanese Culture." In *Japanese Sense of Self,* Nancy Rosenberger, ed. Cambridge, England: Cambridge University Press.

Lieberman, Philip. 1991. *The Evolution of Speech, Thought, and Selfless Behavior.* Cambridge, MA: Harvard University Press.

Liebow, Elliot. 1967. *Tally's Corner: A Study of Negro Street Corner Men.* Boston: Little, Brown.

Lindsey, Robert. 1985. "Official Challenges Outlets That Offer Explicit Videotapes." *The New York Times,* June 3, pp. 1, 9.

Lindzey, Gardner. 1967. Some remarks concerning incest, the incest taboo, and psychoanalytic thoery. *American Psychologist,* 22:1051–1059.

Linton, Ralph. 1959. "The Natural History of the Family." In *The Family: Its Function and Destiny,* R. Anshen, ed., pp. 30–52. New York: Harper & Row.

Livingstone, Frank B. 1969. "Genetics, Ecology, and the Origins of Incest and Exogamy." *Current Anthropology,* 10:45–62.

———. 1982. "Comment on Littlefield, Lieberman, and Reynolds." *Current Anthropology,* 23:651.

Lizot, Jacques. 1977. "Population, Resources and Warfare Among the Yanomano." *Man,* 12:497–517.

———. 1979. "On Food Taboos and Amazon Cultural Ecology." *Current Anthropology,* 20:150–151.

Lockard, Denyse. 1986. "The Lesbian Community: An Anthropological Approach." In *Anthropology and Homosexual Behavior,* Evelyn Blackwood, ed., pp. 83–96. New York: Haworth Press.

Lomax, Alan, ed. 1968. *Folksong Style and Culture.* AAAS Pub. No. 88. Washington, DC: American Association for the Advancement of Science.

Lomax, Alan, and Conrad Arensberg. 1977. "A Worldwide Evolutionary Classification of Cultures by Subsistence Systems." *Current Anthropology,* 18:659–708.

Long, Bruce. 1987. "Reincarnation." In *Encyclopedia of Religion,* vol. 12, pp. 265–269. New York: Macmillan.

Lostson, Preter. 1995. *Theories of Human Nature.* Peterboro, Canada: Broadview Press.

Lowie, Robert. 1948. *Primitive Religion.* New York: Liveright. Originally published 1924.

Ludwig, Hilborn, et al. 1993. "Uncertainty, Resource Exploitation, and Conservation: Lessons from History." *Science,* 260(5104):17–21.

Lunn, P. G. 1988. "Malnutrition and Fertility." In *Natural Human Fertility: Social And Biological Mechanisms,* P. Diggory et al., eds. pp. 135–152. New York: Macmillan.

MacCormack, Carol P. 1982. "Adaptation in Human Fertility and Birth." *Ethnography of Fertility and Birth,* Carol P. MacCormack, ed., pp. 1–23. New York: Academic Press.

MacLachlan, Morgan. 1983. *Why They Did Not Starve: Biocultural Adaptation in a South Indian Village.* Philadelphia: Institute for the Study of Human Issues.

MacLaury, Robert E. 1992. "From Brightness to Hue: An Explanatory Model of Color-Category Evolution." *Current Anthropology,* 33:137–186.

MacLeish, Kenneth. 1972. "The Tasadays: The Stone Age Cavemen of Mindanao." *National Geographic,* 142:219–248.

MacNeish, Richard. 1981. "The Transition to Statehood as Seen from the Mouth of a Cave." In *The Transition to Statehood in the New World,* Grant Jones and Paul Kautz, eds., pp. 123–154. New York: Cambridge University Press.

MacQueen, Kathleen. 1994. "The Epidemiology of HIV Transmission: Trends, Structure, and Dynamics." *Reviews in Anthropology,* 23:509–526.

Magmarella, Paul. 1993. *Human Materialism.* Gainsville, FL: University of Florida Press.

Mair, Lucy. 1969. *Witchcraft.* New York: McGraw-Hill.

Malhotra, Anju, Reeve Vanneman, and Sunita Kishnor. 1995. "Fertility, Dimentions of Patriarchy, and Development in India." *Population and Development Review,* 21(2):281–307.

Malinowski, Bronislaw. 1920. "War and Weapons Among the Natives of the Trobriand Islands." *Man,* 20:10–12.

———. 1927. *Sex and Repression in Savage Society.* London: Routledge & Kegan Paul.

———. 1929. *The Sexual Life of Savages in North-Western Melanesia.* New York: Harcourt, Brace & World.

———. 1935. *Coral Gardens and Their Magic.* 2 vols. London: Allen and Unwin.

Maloney, William. 1987a. "Dharma." *Encyclopedia of Religion,* vol. 4, pp. 239–332. New York: Macmillan.

———. 1987b. "Karma." *Encyclopedia of Religion,* vol. 8, pp. 261–266. New York: Macmillan.

Maltz, Daniel, and Ruth Borker, 1982. "A Cultural Approach to Male Female Miscommunication." In *Language and Social Identity,* Johns Gomperz, ed. Cambridge, England: Cambridge University Press.

Mamdani, Mahmood. 1973. *The Myth of Population Control: Family, Caste, and Class in an Indian Village.* New York: Monthly Review Press.

Manson, Joseph, and Richard Wrangham. 1991. "Intergroup Aggression in Chimpanzees and Humans." *Current Anthropology,* 32(4):369–390.

Marett, Robert. 1914. *The Threshold of Religion.* London: Methuen.

Margolis, Maxine. 1984. *Mothers and Such.* Berkeley: University of California Press.

———. 1994. *Little Brazil: An Ethnography of Brazilian Immigrants in New York City.* Princeton, NJ: Princeton University Press.

Marshall, Donald. 1971. "Sexual Behavior on Mangaia." In *Human Sexual Behavior,* D. Marshall and R. Suggs, eds., pp. 103–162. Englewood Cliffs, NJ: Prentice Hall.

Martin, John F. 1994. "Changing Sex Ratios: The History of Havasupai Fertility and Its Implications for Human Sex Ratio Variation." *Current Anthropology,* 35:255–280.

Marx, Karl. 1970. *A Contribution to the Critique of Political Economy.* New York: International Publishers. Originally published 1859.

Mason, J. Alden. 1957. *The Ancient Civilizations of Peru.* Harmondsworth, England: Penguin.

Massing, Michael. 1989. "Crack's Destructive Sprint Across America." *The New York Times Magazine,* October 1, pp. 38ff.

———. 1996. "Crime and Drugs: The New Myths." *New York Review of Books,* January, pp. 16–20.

Mathews, Holly. 1985. "We Are Mayordomo: A Reinterpretation of Women's Roles in the Mexican Cargo System." *American Ethnologist,* 12:285–301.

McCorkle, Constance. 1994. "The Cattle Battle in Cross-Cultural Context." *Culture and Agriculture,* 50:2–4.

McElroy, Ann and Patricia Townsend. 1996. *Medical Anthropology in Ecological Perspective.* Boulder, CO: Westview Press.

Mc Falls, Joseph. 1998. *Population: A Lively Introduction.* Washington, DC: Population Reference Bureau.

McGrath, Janet, et al. 1992. "Cultural Determinants of Sexual Risk Behavior for AIDS among Baganda Women." *Medical Anthropology Quarterly,* 6:153–161.

McGrew, W[illiam] C. 1977. "Socialization and Object Manipulation of Wild Chimpanzees." In *Primate Bio Social Development,* Susan Chevalier-Skolinkoff and Frank Poirier, eds., pp. 261–288. New York: Garland.

———. 1992. *Chimpanzee Material Culture: Implications for Human Evolution.* Cambridge, England: Cambridge University Press.

———. 1998. "Culture in Nonhuman Primates?" *Annual Reviews in Anthropology,* 27:301–328.

McGrew, W.C., C. Tutin, and P. Baldwin. 1979. "New Data on Meat Eating by Wild Chimpanzees." *Current Anthropology,* 20:238–239.

McGurk, F. C. J. 1975. "Race Differences Twenty Years Later." *Homo,* 26:219–239.

Mead, Margaret. 1970. *Culture and Commitment.* Garden City, NY: Natural History Press.

Meggitt, Mervyn. 1965. *The Lineage System of the Mae Enga of New Guinea.* New York: Barnes and Noble.

Meggitt, Mervyn. 1977. *Blood Is Their Argument: Warfare Among the Mae Enga Tribesmen of the New Guinea Highlands.* Palo Alto, CA: Mayfield.

Mencher, Joan. 1974. "The Caste System Upside Down: Or, the Not So Mysterious East." *Current Anthropology,* 15:469–478.

Merson, Michael. 1993. "Slowing the Spread of HIV: Agenda for the 1990's." *Science,* 260:1266–1268.

Messenger, J. C. 1971. "Sex and Repression in an Irish Folk Community." In *Human Sexual Behavior: Variations in the Ethnographic Spectrum,* D. S. Marshall and R. C. Suggs, eds. New York: Basic Books.

Miller, Barbara. 1981. *The Endangered Sex: Neglect of Female Children in Rural North India.* Ithaca, NY: Cornell University Press.

———. 1987a. "Wife-Beating in India: Variations on a Theme." Paper read at the Annual Meetings of the American Anthropological Association, November.

———. 1987b. "Female Infanticide and Child Neglect in Rural North India." In *Child Survival,* Nancy Scheper-Hughes, ed., pp. 95–112. Boston: D. Reidel.

———. 1992. "Wife Beating in India: Variations on a Theme." In *Sanctions and Sanctuary: Cultural Perspectives on the Beating of Wives,* Dorothy Counts, Judith Brown, and J. C. Campbell, eds., pp. 173–184. Boulder, CO: Westview.

Miller, Barbara D[iane]. 1997. "Female Infanticide and Child Neglect in Rural North India." In *Gender in Cross–Cultural Perspective,* Caroline B. Brettell and Carolyn F. Sargent, eds., pp. 453–465. Upper Saddle River, NJ: Prentice Hall.

Miller, Barbara Diane. 1993. "The Anthropology of Sex and Gender." In *Sex and Gender Hierarchies,* Barbara H. Miller, ed., pp. 3–31. Cambridge, England: Cambridge University Press.

Millett, Kate. 1970. *Sexual Politics.* Garden City, New York: Doubleday.

Minturn, Leigh, and John T. Hitchcock. 1963. "The Rajputs of Khalapur, India." In *Six Cultures, Studies of Child Rearing.* B. B. Whiting, ed., pp. 203–361. New York: Wiley.

Minturn, L., and J. Stashak. 1982. "Infanticide as a Terminal Abortion Procedure." *Behavior Science Research* 17:70–90.

Mishel, Lawrence, and David Frankel. 1990. "The State of Working America." Report by the Economic Policy Institute, Washington, DC.

Mitchell, D., and L. Donald. 1988. "Archaeology and the Study of Northwest Coast Economies." In *Prehistoric Economies of the Pacific Northwest Coast,* Barry Isaac, ed., pp. 293–351. Greenwich, CT: JAI Press.

Miyadi, D. 1967. "Differences in Social Behavior Among Japanese Macaque Troops." In *Progress in Primatology,* D. Starck, R. Schneider, and H. Kuhn, eds., pp. 228–231. Stuttgart, Germany: Gustav Fischer.

Mooney, James. 1965. *The Ghost Dance Religion.* Chicago: University of Chicago Press. Originally published 1896.

Moore, Jerry, ed. 1997. *Visions of Culture: Anthropological Theories and Theorists.* Walnut Creek: Alta Mira Press.

Moore, John. 1990. "The Reproductive Success of Cheyenne War Chiefs: A Contrary Case to Chagnon's Yanomamo." *Current Anthropology,* 31:322–330.

Moore, John. 1987. *The Cheyenne Nation.* Lincoln: University of Nebraska Press.

Moran, Emilio. 1999. *Human Adaptability, An Introduction to Ecological Anthropology.* Boulder, CO: Westview Press.

Morgan, Lewis Henry. 1994. *Ancient Society.* Tucson: University of Arizona Press. Originally published 1877.

Morgan, Marcyliena. 1995. "Theories and Politics in African American English." *Annual Reviews of Anthropology* 23:325–35.

Morren, George. 1984. "Warfare in the Highland Fringe of New Guinea: The Case of the Mountain Ok." In *Warfare, Culture and Environment,* Brian Ferguson, ed., pp. 169–208. Orlando, FL: Academic Press.

Morris, C. 1976. "The Master Design of the Inca." *Natural History,* 85(10):58–87.

Moynihan, Daniel P. 1965. *The Negro Family, the Case for National Action.* Washington, DC: U.S. Department of Labor.

Mueller, Eva. 1984. "Measuring Women's Poverty in Developing Countries." In *Women and Poverty in the Third World,* Eva Mueller, ed. Baltimore: Johns Hopkins University Press.

Munroe, Ruth, and Robert Munroe. 1994. "Field Observations of Behavior as a Cross Cultural Method." In *Handbook of Psychological Anthropology,* Phillip Bock, ed. Westport, CT: Praeger.

Murdock, George P. 1949. *Social Structure.* New York: Macmillan.

———. 1967. *Ethnographic Atlas.* Pittsburgh: University of Pittsburgh Press.

Murdock, George, and C. Provost. 1973. "Factors in the Division of Labor by Sex." *Ethnology,* 12:203–225.

Murphy, Martin F., and M. Margolis, 1995. "An Introduction to Cultural Materialism." In *Science, Materialism, and the Study of Culture,* Martin F. Murphy and M. Margolis, eds. Gainesville: University Press of Florida.

Murphy, Robert. 1956. "Matrilocality and Patrilineality in Mundurucu Society." *American Anthropologist,* 58:414–434.

———. 1976. "Man's Culture and Women's Nature." *Annals of the New York Academy of Sciences,* 293: 15–24.

Murphy, Yolanda, and Robert F. Murphy. 1985. *Women of the Forest.* New York: Columbia University Press.

Murray, Gerald. 1984. "The Wood Tree as a Peasant Cash Crop: An Anthropological Strategy for the Domestication of Energy." In *Haiti—Today and Tomorrow: An Interdisciplinary Study,* Charles Fost and A. Valdman, eds., pp. 141–160. Lanham, MD: University Press of America.

———. 1991. "The Tree Gardens of Haiti: From Extraction to Domestication." In *Social Forestry: Communal and Private Management Compared,* D. Challinor and M. Frondorf, eds., pp. 35–44. Washington, DC: Johns Hopkins School of Advanced International Studies.

———. 1995. "Peasants, Projects and Anthropological Models." In *Science, Materialism and the Study of Culture,* Martin Murphy and Maxine Margolis, eds., pp. 159–184. Gainsville: University Press of Florida.

Mwamwenda, T. S., and L. A. Monyooe. 1997. "Status of Bridewealth in an African Culture." *Journal of Social Psychology,* 137:269–272.

Nadel, S. F. 1952. "Witchcraft in Four African Societies." *American Anthropologist,* 54(1):18–29.

Nader, Laura. 1972. "Up the Anthropologist—Perspectives Gained from Studying Up." In *Reinventing Anthropology,* Dell Hymes, ed., pp. 284–311. New York: Random House.

———. 1980. *No Access to Law.* New York: Academic Press.

Nag, Moni. 1972. "Sex, Culture, and Human Fertility: India and the United States." *Current Anthropology,* 13:231–238.

———. 1983. "The Impact of Sociocultural Factors on Breastfeeding and Social Behavior." In *Determinants of Fertility in Developing Countries,* Rodolfo A. Bulatao, Ronald D. Lee, with Paula E. Hollerbach and John Bongaarts, eds., pp. 163–198. New York: Academic Press.

Nag, Moni, and N. Kak. 1984. "Demographic Transition in the Punjab Village." *Population and Development Review,* 10:661–678.

Nag, Moni, Benjamin White, and Robert Peet. 1978. "An Anthropological Approach to the Study of the Economic Value of Children in Java and Nepal." *Current Anthropology,* pp. 239–306.

Nardi, Bonnie. 1983. "Reply to Harbison's Comments on Nardi's Modes of Explanation in Anthropological Population Theory." *American Anthropologist,* 85:662–664.

Naroll, Raul. 1973. "Introduction." In *Main Currents in Anthropology,* R. Naroll and F. Naroll, eds., pp. 1–23. Englewood Cliffs, NJ: Prentice Hall.

Nash, Jill. 1974. "Matriliny and Modernization: The Nagovisi of South Bougainville." *New Guinea Research Bulletin,* no. 55. Canberra, Australia.

National Research Council. 1992. *Sustainable Agriculture and the Environment in the Humid Tropics.* Washington, DC: National Academy Press.

National Urban League. 1990. State of Black America.

Nelson, Sarah. 1993. "Gender Hierarchy and the Queens of Silla." In *Sex and Gender Hierarchies,* Barbara Miller, ed., pp. 297–315. New York: Cambridge University Press.

Nelson, Kristen. 1986. "Labor Demand, Labor Supply, and the Suburbanization of Low-Wage Office Work." In *Production, Work, Territory: The Geographical Anatomy of Industrial Capitalism,* A. Scott and M. Storper, eds., pp. 149–171. Boston: Allen and Unwin.

Netting, Robert. 1986. *Cultural Ecology.* Waveland Press.

———. 1989. "Small holders, Householders, Freeholders: Why the Family Farm Work Well Worldwide." In *The Household Economy: Reconsidering the Domestic Mode of Production,* Richard Wilk, ed., pp. 221–244. Boulder, CO: Westview Press.

Netting, Robert M. C. C. 1993. *Smallholders, Householders: Farm Families and the Ecology of Intensive, Sustainable Agriculture.* Stanford, CA: Stanford University Press.

Netting, Robert M. C. C., Richard R. Wilk, and Eric J. Arnould. 1984. *Households: Comparative and Historical Studies of the Domestic Group.* Berkeley: University of California Press.

Neville, Gwen. 1979. "Community Form and Ceremonial Life in Three Regions of Scotland." *American Ethnologist,* 6:93–109.

Newitt, Jane. 1985. "How to Forecast Births." *American Demographics,* January, pp. 30–33, 51.

Newman, Philip L. 1965. *Knowing the Gururumba.* New York: Holt, Rinehart and Winston.

Nishida, T. 1987. "Learning and Cultural Transmission in Nonhuman Primates." In *Primate Societies,* B. B. Smuts et al., eds., pp. 462–474. Chicago: University of Chicago Press.

Noah, Timothy. 1991. "Number of Poor Americans Is Up." *Wall Street Journal,* September 27, p. A2.

Numbers, Ronald. 1992. *The Creationists.* New York: Knopf.

Oakley, A. 1985. *Sex, Gender, and Society.* London: Gower/Maurice Temple Smith.

Oboler, Regina Smith. 1988. "Is the Female Husband a Man? Woman/Woman Marriage Among the Nandi of Kenya." *Ethnology,* 19:69–88.

Odend'hal, Stuart. 1972. "Energetics of Indian Cattle in Their Environment." *Journal of Human Ecology,* 1:3–22.

Odum, H.T. 1971. *Environment, Power, and Society.* New York: Wiley-Interscience.

Oliver, Douglas. 1955. *A Solomon Island Society: Kinship and Leadership Among the Siuai of Bougainville.* Cambridge, MA: Harvard University Press.

Opler, Morris. 1968. "The Themal Approach in Cultural Anthropology and Its Application to North Indian Data." *Southwestern Journal of Anthropology,* 24:215–227.

Oppenheimer, Vallery. 1982. *Work and the Family: A Study in Social Demography.* New York: Academic Press.

Orans, Martin. 1968. "Maximizing in Jajmaniland: A Model of Caste Relations." *American Anthropologist,* 70:875–897.

Ortiz de Montellano, B. R. 1978. "Aztec Cannibalism: An Economic Necessity?" *Science,* 200:611–617.

———. 1983. "Counting Skulls: Comments on the Aztec Cannibalism Theory of Harner-Harris." *American Anthropologist,* 85:403–406.

Ortner, Sherry, and H. Whiteheads, eds. 1981. *The Cultural Construction of Gender and Sexuality.* Cambridge, England: Cambridge University Press.

Ottenheimer, Martin. 1984. "Some Problems and Prospects in Residence and Marriage." *American Anthropologist,* 86:351–358.

Otterbein, Keith. 1994. *Feuding and Warfare.* Amsterdam: Gordon and Breach.

Pandian, Jacob. 1992. *Culture, Religion and the Sacred Self: A Critical Introduction to the Anthropological Study of Religion.* Englewood Cliffs, NJ: Prentice Hall.

Paredes, J. Anthony, and Mary Pohl. 1995. "Anthropology and Multiculturalism in a University Curriculum: A Case Study." *Critique of Anthropology,* 15: 193–202.

Parenti, Michael. 1986. *Inventing Reality: The Politics of Mass Media.* New York: St. Martin's Press.

Parker, Hilda, and Parker, Seymour. 1986. "Father–Daughter Sexual Abuse: An Emerging Perspective." *American Journal of Orthopsychiatry,* 56: 531–549.

Parker, Sue. 1985. "A Social-Technological Model for the Evolution of Languages." *Current Anthropology,* 26:617–639.

Pasternak, Burton, Carol Ember, and Melvin Ember. 1976. "On the Conditions Favoring Extended Family Households." *Journal of Anthropological Research,* 32(2):109–123.

Pasternak, Burton, Carol Ember, and Melvin Ember. 1997. *Sex, Gender, and Kinship: A Cross-Cultural Perspective.* Englewood Cliffs, NJ: Prentice Hall.

Paztory, Esther. 1984. "The Function of Art in Mesoamerica." *Archeology,* January–February, pp. 18–25.

Peletz, Michael G. 1987. "Female Heirship and the Autonomy of Women in Negeri Sembilan, West Malaysia." In *Research in Economic Anthropology: A Research Annual,* Barry L. Isaac, ed., vol. 8, pp. 61–101. Greenwich, CT: JAI Press.

Pelto, Pertti and Gretel Pelto. 1976. *The Human Adventure: An Introduction to Anthropology.* New York: Macmillan.

Percival, L., and K. Quinkert. 1987. "Anthropometric Factors." In *Sex Differences in Human Performance,* Mary Baker, ed., pp. 121–139. New York: Wiley.

Perrons, Diane. 1995. "Gender Inequalities in Regional Development." *Regional Studies,* 29:5: 465–478.

Peterson, J. T. 1978. *The Ecology of Social Boundaries: Agta Foragers of the Philippines.* Urbana: University of Illinois Press.

Peterson, Nicholas. 1993. "Demand Sharing and the Pressure for Generosity Among Foragers." *American Anthropologist,* 95:860–874.

Pfaffenberger, Bryan. 1992. "Social Anthropology of Technology." *Annual Review of Anthropology,* 21:491–516.

Piker, Steven. 1994. "Classical Culture and Personality. In Handbook of Psychological Anthropology, Philip Bock, ed., Westport, CT: Greenwood Press.

Pimentel, David, L. E. Hurd, A. C. Bellotti, et al. 1973. "Food Production and Energy Crisis." *Science,* 182:443–449.

Pimentel, D[avid], and M. Pimentel. 1985. "Energy Use for Food Processing for Nutrition and Development." *Food and Nutrition Bulletin,* 7(2):36–45.

Pimentel, David, et al. 1975. "Energy and Land Constraints in Food Protein Production." *Science,* 190:754–761.

Pinker, Steven. 1994. *The Language Instinct: How the Mind Creates Language.* New York: Morrow.

Pivnik, Anitra, et al. 1991. "Reproductive Decisions Among HIV-Infected, Drug-Using Women: The Importance of Mother–Child Co-Residence." *Medical Anthropology Quarterly,* 5:153–169.

Plath, David, ed. 1983. *Work and Life Course in Japan.* Albany, NY: State University of New York Press.

Plattner, Stuart. 1989. "Introduction." In *Economic Anthropology,* Stuart Plattner, ed., pp. 1–20. Stanford, CA: Stanford University Press.

Podolefsky, Aaron. 1984. "Contemporary Warfare in the New Guinea Highlands." *Ethnology,* 23: 73–87.

Pospisil, Leopold, 1963. *The Kapauku Papuans of West New Guinea.* New York: Holt, Rinehart and Winston.

Post, John. 1985. *Food Shortage, Climatic Variability, and Epidemic Disease in Pre-Industrial Europe.* Ithaca, NY: Cornell University Press.

Price, D. 1995. "Energy and Human Evolution." *Population and Environment,* 16:301–319.

Price, David. 1993. *The Evolution of Irrigation in Egypt's Fayoum Oasis: State, Village and Conveyance Loss.* Unpublished doctoral dissertation, University of Florida.

Price, John. 1980. "On Silent Trade." *Research in Economic Anthropology,* 3:75–96.

Pusey, Ann, and A. Wolf. 1996. "Inbreeding Avoidance in Animals." *Trends in Ecology and Evolution,* 11(5): 201–206.

Ragone, Helena. 1994. *Surrogate Motherhood.* Boulder, CO: Westview Press.

Ramirez, F., and J. Meyer. 1980. "Comparative Education: The Social Construction of the Modern World System." *Annual Review of Sociology,* 6:369–399.

Rappaport, Roy. 1971. "Ritual, Sanctity, and Cybernetics" *American Anthropologist,* 73(1):59–76.

Rappaport, Roy A. 1967. "Ritual Regulation of Environmental Relations among a New Guinea People." *Ethnology,* 6:17–30.

———. 1968. *Pigs for the Ancestors: Ritual in the Ecology of a New Guinea People.* New Haven, CT: Yale University Press.

———. 1984. *Pigs for the Ancestors: Ritual in the Ecology of a Papuan New Guinea People,* 2nd ed. New Haven, CT: Yale University Press. Originally published 1968.

———. 1994. "Humanity's Evolution and Anthropology's Future. In *Assesing Cultural Anthropology,* Robert Borofsky, ed. New York: McGraw-Hill.

Rathje, William, and Cullen Murphy. 1992. *Rubbish! The Archaeology of Garbage.* New York: HarperCollins.

Reed, C. M. 1984. "Maritime Traders in the Archaic Greek World." *The Ancient World,* 10:31–43.

Renfrew, Colin. 1994. "World Linguistic Diversity." *Scientific American,* January, pp. 116–123.

Reyna, S. P. 1989. "Grudge Matching and War: Considerations of the Nature and Universality of War." Paper presented at the American Anthropological Association annual meeting, Washington, DC, November 15.

Rickford, John. 1997. "Suite for Ebony and Phonics." *Discover,* 18(12):82–87.

Riddle, J., and J. W. Estes. 1992. "Oral Contraceptives in Ancient and Medieval Times." *American Scientist,* 80:226–233.

Rifkind, Jeremy, and Ted Howard. 1979. *The Emerging Order: God in the Age of Scarcity.* New York: Putnam.

Riviere, C. 1987. "Soul: Concepts in Primitive Religions." In *The Encyclopedia of Religion,* pp. 426–430. New York: Macmillan and Free Press.

Roberts, Ron, and D. Brintnall. 1982. *Reinventing Inequality.* Boston: Schenkman.

Roberts, Sam. 1993. "Fighting the Tide of Bloodshed on Streets Resembling a War Zone." *The New York Times,* November 15, p. B12.

Robins, L., J. Helzer, M. Weissman, D. Gruenberg, Burke and D. Regier. 1984. "Lifetime Prevalence of Specific Psychiatric Disorder in Three Sites." *Archives of General Psychiatry,* 41:949–958.

Rodgers, Joan R. 1994. "Female–headed Families: Why Are They So Poor?" *Review of Social Economy,* 52(2): 22–49.

Roosens, Eugene. 1989. *Creating Ethnicity: The Process of Ethnogeneis.* Newbury Park, CA: Sage.

Root, Marla, ed. 1992. *Racially Mixed People in America.* Newbury Park, CA: Sage.

Rosaldo, Michelle Zimbalist. 1974. "Woman, Culture, and Society: A Theoretical Overview." In Michelle Zimbalist Rosaldo and Louise Lamphere, eds., *Woman, Culture and Society,* pp. 17–42. Stanford, CA: Stanford University Press.

Ross, Phillip. 1991. "Hard Words." *Scientific American,* April, pp. 137–147.

Roth, Eric. 1985. "A Note on the Demographic Concommitants of Sedentism." *American Anthropologist,* 87:380–381.

Royce, W. F. 1987. *Fishery Development.* New York: Academic Press.

Rubin, Deborah S. 1997. "What Adding Women Has Stirred Up: Feminist Issues in Teaching Cultural Anthropology." In *The Teaching of Anthropology: Problems, Issues, and Decisions,* Conrad Phillip Kottak, Jane J. White, Richard H. Furlow, and Patricia C. Rice, eds., pp. 133–143. London: Mayfield.

Sabato, Larry. 1989. *Paying for Elections: The Campaign Finance Thicket.* New York: Priority Press.

Sackett, Ross. 1996. *Time, Energy, and the Indolent Savage: A Quantitative Cross–Cultural Test of the Primitive Affluence Hypothesis.* Unpublished doctoral dissertation. University of California at Los Angeles.

Sacks, Karen B. 1971. Economic *Bases of Sexual Equality: A Comparative Study of Four African Societies.* Unpublished doctoral dissertation. University of Michigan.

Sacks, Karen Brodkin. 1994. "How Did Jews Become White Folks?" In *Race,* Steven Gregory and Roger Sanjek, eds., pp. 78–102. New Brunswick, NJ: Rutgers University Press.

[Sacks] Brodkin, Karen. 1982. *Sisters and Wives: The Past and Future of Sexual Equality.* Chicago: University of Illinois Press.

Safa, Helen I. 1986. "Economic Autonomy and Sexual Equality in Caribbean Society." *Social and Economic Studies,* 35(3):1–20.

Sahagun, Bernardino de. 1951. "Book 2—The Ceremonies." In *General History of the Things of New Spain,* Florentine Codex, A. J. O. Anderson and C. E. Dibble, trans. (from Aztec). In 13 parts, Part III. Santa Fe, NM: School of American Research, and Salt Lake City: University of Utah.

Sahlins, Marshall. 1978. "Culture as Protein and Profit." *The New York Review of Books,* November 23, pp. 45–53.

Sakar, Jayanta. 1993. "Till Death Do Us Part: Dowries Contribute to a Rise in Violence Against Indian Women." *Far Eastern Economic Review,* October 28, pp. 40–41.

Sanday, Peggy Reeves. 1973. "Toward a Theory of the Status of Women." *American Anthropologist,* 75:1682–1699.

———. 1981. *Female Power and Male Dominance: On the Origins of Sexual Inequality.* Cambridge, England: Cambridge University Press.

Sanderson, Stephen. 1988. *Macrosociology: An Introduction to Human Societies.* New York: Harper & Row.

Sanderson, Stephen. 1991. *Macrosociology: An Inroduction to Human Societies* (2nd ed.). New York: HarperCollins.

Sanjek, Roger. 1972. Ghanian Networks: An Analysis of Interethnic Relations in Urban Situations. Unpublished doctoral dissertation, Columbia University.

———. 1977. "Cognitive Maps of the Ethnic Domain in Urban Ghana: Reflections on Variability and Change." *American Ethnologist,* 4:603–622.

———. ed. 1990. *Fieldnotes: The Making of Anthropology.* Ithaca, NY: Cornell University Press.

———. 1994a. Introduction: The Enduring Inequalities of Race. In *Race,* Steven Gregory and Roger Sanjek, eds., pp. 1–17. New Brunswick, NJ: Rutgers University Press.

———. 1994b. "Intermarriage and the Future of Races in the United States." In *Race,* Steven Gregory and Roger Sanjek, eds., pp. 103–130. New Brunswick, NJ: Rutgers University Press.

———. 1998. *The Future of Us All.* Ithaca, NY: Cornell University Press, 1998.

Sankar, Andrea. 1986. "Sisters and Brothers, Lovers and Enemies: Marriage Resistance in Southern Kuangtung." In *Anthropology and Homosexual Behavior,* Evelyn Blackwood, ed., pp. 69–81. New York: Haworth Press.

Sakar, Jayanta. 1993. "Till Death Do Us Part: Dowries Contribute to a Rise in Violence Against Indian Women." *Far Eastern Economic Review,* October 28, pp. 40–41.

Sapir, Edward. 1921. *Language: An Introduction to the Study of Speech.* New York: Harcourt, Brace.

Savage-Rumbaugh, S., and R. Levin. 1994. *Kanzi: The Ape at the Brink of the Human Mind.* New York: Wiley.

Savage-Rumbaugh, Sue. 1987. "Communication, Symbolic Communication, and Language: Reply to Seidenberg and Petitto." *Journal of Experimental Psychology: General,* 116:288–292.

Savage-Rumbaugh, Sue, et al. 1990. "Symbols: Their Communicative Use, Comprehension, and Combination by Bonobos (*Pan paniscus*)." In *Advances in Infancy Research,* vol. 6, Carolyn Rovee-Collier and Lewis P. Lipsitt, eds., pp. 222–254. Norwood, NJ: ABLEX.

———. 1993. *Language Comprehension in Ape and Child.* Chicago: University of Chicago Press.

Scheffler, Harold. 1973. "Kinship, Descent, and Alliance." In *Handbook of Social and Cultural Anthropology,* J. Honigman, ed., pp. 747–793. Chicago: Rand McNally.

Scheidel, Walter. 1996. Brother–Sister and Parent–Child Marriage Outside Royal Families in Ancient Egypt and Iran: A Challenge to the Sociobiological View of Incest Avoidance? *Ethology and Sociobiology,* 17: 319–340.

Scheper-Hughes, Nancy. 1979. *Saints, Scholars, and Schizophrenics: Mental Illness in Rural Ireland.* Berkeley: University of California Press.

———. 1984. "Infant Mortality and Infant Care: Cultural and Economic Constraints on Nurturing in Northeast Brazil." *Social Science and Medicine,* 19(5):535–546.

———. 1992. *Death Without Weeping: The Violence of Every Day Life in Brazil.* Berkeley: University of California Press.

———. 1995. "The Primacy of the Ethical: Propositions for a Militant Anthropology." *Current Anthropology,* 36:409–440.

Schields, N. M. 1993. "The Natural and Unnatural History of Inbreeding and Outbreeding." In *The Natural History of Inbreeding and Outbreeding,* N. W. Thornhill, ed., pp. 143–169. Chicago: University of Chicago Press.

Schlegel, Alice, ed. 1972. *Male Dominance and Female Autonomy.* New Haven, CT: HRAF (Human Relations Area Files) Press.

Schlegel, Alice. 1991. "Status, Property, and the Value of Virginity." *American Ethnologist,* 18:719–734.

Schlegel, Alice, and H. Barry. 1979. "Adolescent Initiation Ceremonies: A Cross-Cultural Code." *Ethnology,* 18:199–210.

———. 1986. "The Cultural Consequences of Female Contributions to Subsistence." *American Anthropologist,* 88:142–150.

Schlegel, Alice, and R. Eloul. 1988. "Marriage Transactions: Labor, Property and Status." *American Anthropologist,* 90:291–309.

Scoditti, G. 1983. "Kula on Kitava." In *The Kula: New Perspectives in Massim Exchange,* J. Leach and E. Leach, eds., pp. 249–273. New York: Cambridge University Press.

Scott, Colin, and Harvey Feit. 1992. *Income Security for Cree Hunters: Ecological, Social and Economic Effects.* Montreal: McGill Programme in the Anthropology of Development.

Scrimshaw, Susan. 1983. "Infanticide as Deliberate Fertility Regulation." In *Determinants of Fertility in Developing Nations: Supply and Demand for Children,*

R. Bulatao and R. Lee, eds. New York: Academic Press.

———. 1984. "Infanticide in Human Populations: Societal and Individual Concerns." In *Infanticide: Comparative and Evolutionary Perspectives,* Glen Hausfater and Sarah Blaffer Hrdy, eds. New York: Aldine.

Serrin, William. 1984. "Experts Say Job Bias Against Women Persists." *The New York Times,* November 25, pp. 1, 18.

Service, Elman R. 1975. *Origins of the State and Civilization: The Processes of Cultural Evolution.* New York: Norton.

Shankman, Paul. 1991. "Culture Contact, Cultural Ecology, and Dani Warfare." *Man,* 26:299–321.

Sharff, Janga [Wojcicka]. 1980. *Life on Dolittle Street: How Poor People Purchase Immortality.* Final Report, Hispanic Study Project No. 9, Department of Anthropology, Columbia University.

———. 1981. "Free Enterprise and the Ghetto Family." *Psychology Today,* March.

———. 1995. "We Are All Chickens for the Colonel: A Cultural Materialist View of Prisons." In *Science, Materialism, and the Study of Culture,* Martin Murphy and Maxine Margolis, eds., pp. 132–158. Gainsville: University Press of Florida.

———. 1998. *King Kong on E Street: Families and the Violence of Poverty on the Lower East Side.* Boulder, CO: Westview Press.

Sharma, Ursula. 1983. "Dowry in North India: Its Consequences for Women." In *Women and Property,* Renee Hirschon, ed., pp. 62–74. London: Croom Helm.

Shepher, Joseph. 1983. *Incest: A Biosocial Point of View.* New York: Academic Press.

Short, Richard. 1984. "On Placing the Child Before Marriage, Reply to Birdsell." *Population and Development Review,* 9:124–135.

Shostak, Marjorie. 1981. *Nisa, The Life and Words of a !Kung Woman.* Cambridge, MA: Harvard University Press.

Shreve, James 1994. "Terms of Estrangement." *Discover.* pp. 57–63.

Silk, Leonard. 1985. "The Peril Behind the Takeover Boom." *The New York Times,* December 29, Sec. 3, p. 1.

Sillén-Tullberg, Birgitta, and Anders P. Møller, 1993. The relationship between concealed ovulation and mating systems in anthropoid primates: A phylogenetic analysis. *American Naturalist,* 141(1):1–25.

Simmons, R. C., and C. C. Hughes, eds. 1985. *The Culture-Bound Syndromes.* Dordrecht: D. Reidl.

Simoons, Frederick. 1979. "Questions in the Sacred Cow Controversy." *Current Anthropology,* 20: 467–493.

Skinner, G. William. 1993. "Conjugal Power in Tokugawa Japanese Families: A Matter of Life or Death." In *Sex and Gender Hierarchies,* Barbara Miller, ed., pp. 236–270. New York: Cambridge University Press.

Small, Meredith. 1992. "The Evolution of Female Sexuality and Mate Selection in Humans." *Human Nature,* 3(2):133–156.

———. 1993. *Race in North America: Origin and Evolution of a Worldview.* Boulder, CO: Westview Press.

———. 1999. "Race" and the Construction of Human Identity. *American Anthropologist,* 100(3):690–702.

Smith, Eric Alden, and S. Abigail Smith. 1994. "Inuit Sex-Ratio Variation." *Current Anthropology,* 35: 595–624.

Smith, Eric, and Bruce Winterhalder. 1992. *Evolutionary Ecology and Human Behavior.* Hawthorne, NY: Aldine de Gruyter.

Smith, M. G. 1968. "Secondary Marriage Among Kadera and Kagoro." In *Marriage, Family, and Residence,* P. Bohannan and J. Middleton, eds., pp. 109–130. Garden City, NY: Natural History Press.

Smith, Raymond T. 1988. "Kinship and Class in the West Indies: Genealogical Study of Jamaica and Guyana." *Cambridge Studies in Social and Cultural Anthropology,* 65. New York: Cambridge University Press.

Snowden, Charles T. 1990. "Language Capacities of Nonhuman Animals." *Yearbook of Physical Anthropology,* 33:215–243.

Soloway, Jaqueline S., and Richard B. Lee. 1990. "Foragers, Genuine or Spurious?" *Current Anthropology,* 31(2):109–146.

Sorenson, Richard. 1972. "Socio-Ecological Change Among the Foré of New Guinea." *Current Anthropology,* 13:349–383.

Sorenson, Richard, and P. E. Kenmore. 1974. "Proto-Agricultural Movement in the Eastern Highlands of New Guinea." *Current Anthropology,* 15:67–72.

Soustelle, Jacques. 1970. *Daily Life of the Aztecs.* Stanford, CA: Stanford University Press.

Spencer, P. 1965. *The Samburu: A Study of Gerontocracy in a Nomadic Tribe.* Berkeley: University of California Press.

Spengler, Joseph. 1974. *Population Change, Modernization, and Welfare.* Englewood Cliffs, NJ: Prentice-Hall.

Spickard, Paul. 1992. "The Illogic of American Racial Categories". In *Racially Mixed People in America,* Marla Root, ed., pp. 12–23. Newbury Park, CA: Sage

Spira, Alfred, et al. 1992. "AIDS and Sexual Behavior in France." *Nature,* 360:407–409.

Spiro, Melford. 1954. "Is the Family Universal?" *American Anthropologist,* 56:839–846.

———. 1982. *Oedipus in the Trobriands.* Chicago: University of Chicago Press.

———. 1993. "Gender Hierarchy in Burma: Cultural, Social and Psychological Dimensions." In *Sex and Gender Hierarchies,* Barbara H. Miller, ed., pp. 316–333. Cambridge, England: Cambridge University Press.

———. 1997. *Gender Ideology and Psychological Reality: An Essay on Cultural Reproduction.* New Haven, CT: Yale University Press.

Spuhler, James. 1985. "Anthropology, Evolution, and Scientific Creationism." *Annual Review of Anthropology,* 14:103–133.

Srinivas, M. N. 1955. "The Social System of a Mysore Village." In *Village India: Studies in the Little Community,* M. Marriot, ed., pp. 1–35. Memoir 83. Washington, DC: American Anthropological Association.

Ssennyonga, Joseph. 1997. "Polygyny and Resource Allocation in the Lake Victoria Basin." In *African Families and the Crisis of Social Change,* T. Weisner, C. Bradley, and P. Kilbride, eds., pp 268–282. Westport, CT: Bergin and Garvey.

Stacey, Judith. 1990. *Brave New Families: Stories of Domestic Upheaval in Late Twentieth Century America.* New York: Basic Books.

Stack, Carol. 1974. *All Our Kin: Strategies for Survival in a Black Community.* New York: Harper & Row.

Steinhart, John, and Carol Steinhart. 1974. "Energy Use in the U.S. Food System." *Science,* 184:307–317.

Stern, Steve J. 1988. "Feudalism, Capitalism, and the World System in the Perspective of Latin America and the Caribbean." *American Historical Review,* 93:829–897.

Stewart, Omer. 1987. *Peyote Religion: A History.* Norman, OK: University of Oklahoma Press.

Stone, Linda, and Caroline James. 1997. "Dowry, Bride–Burning, and Female Power in India." In *Gender in Cross–Cultural Perspective,* Caroline B. Brettell and Carolyn F. Sargent, eds., pp. 270–279. Upper Saddle River, NJ: Prentice Hall.

Strauss, Claudia. 1992. "What Makes Tony Run: Schemas As Motives Reconsidered." In *Human Motives and Cultural Models,* Roy D'Andrade and Claudia Strauss, eds., pp. 197–224. New York: Cambridge University Press.

Strauss, Claudia and Naomi Quinn. 1994. "A Cognitive/Cultural Anthropology." In *Assessing Cultural Anthropology,* Robert Borofsky, ed. New York: McGraw-Hill.

Stringer, C. B. 1992. "Replacement, Continuity, and the Origin of Modern *Homo Sapiens.*" In *Continuity or Replacement? Controversies in Homo Sapiens Evolution,* G. Brauer and F. H. Smith, eds., pp. 9–24. Rotterdam: Balkema.

Stull, Donald D., Ken C. Erickson, and Miguel Giner. 1996. "Management and Multiculturalism." *Meat & Poultry,* 42(4):44–50.

Sudarkasa, N. 1973. *Where Women Work: A Study of Yoruba Women in the Marketplace and in the Home.* Ann Arbor, MI: University of Michigan Museum.

Suggs, David, and A. Miracle, eds. 1993. *Culture and Human Sexuality.* Pacific Grove, CA: Brooks/Cole.

Sugimoto, Y., and R. Mouer. 1983. *Japanese Society: A Study in Social Reconstruction.* London: Kegan Paul.

Sullivan, Lawrence. 1987. "Supreme Beings." In *The Encyclopedia of Religion,* M. Eliade, ed. New York: Macmillan.

Susman, Randal. 1994. "Fossil Evidence for Early Hominid Tool Use." *Science,* 265:1570–1572.

Susser, Ida. 1982. *Norman Street.* New York: Oxford University Press.

———. 1996. "The Construction of Poverty and Homelessness in U.S. Cities." *Annual Review of Anthropology,* 25:411–435.

Swanson, Guy E. 1960. *The Birth of the Gods: The Origin of Primitive Beliefs.* Ann Arbor, MI: University of Michigan Press.

Swasy, Alecia, and C. Hymowitz. 1990. "The Workplace Revolution." *The Wall Street Journal Reports,* February 9:R6–R8.

Swisher, C. C., et al. 1994. "Age of the Earliest Known Hominids in Java, Indonesia." *Science,* 263:1118–1121.

Tannen, Deborah. 1990. You Just Don't Understand: *Women and Men in Conversation.* New York: Ballantine Books.

Tefft, Stanton. 1975. "Warfare Regulation: A Cross-Cultural Test of Hypotheses." In *War: Its Causes and Correlates,* Martin Nettleship et al., eds., pp. 693–712. Chicago: Aldine.

Testart, Alain. 1982. "The Significance of Food-Storage Among Hunter-Gatherers: Residence Patterns, Population Densities and Social Inequalities." *Current Anthropology,* 23(3):523–537.

Thomas, Lewis. 1986. "Peddling Influence." *Time,* March 3, pp. 26–36.

Thornhill, Nancy (ed.). 1993. *The Natural History of Inbreeding and Outbreeding.* Chicago: University of Chicago Press.

Thurow, Lester. 1995. "Why Their World Might Crumble." *The New York Times Magazine,* November 19, pp. 78–79.

Thurston, Robert. 1939. *A History of the Growth of the Steam Engine.* Ithaca, NY: Cornell University Press.

Titon, J. T., et al. 1984. *Worlds of Music: An Introduction to the Musics of the World's Peoples.* New York: Schirmer Books.

Tomasello, Michael. 1994. "The Question of Chimpanzee Culture." In *Chimpanzee Cultures,* R. Wrangham, W. C. McGrew, F. B. de Waal, and P. G. Heltne, eds. Cambridge, MA: Harvard University Press.

Torrey, E. F. 1980. *Schizophrenia and Civilization.* New York: Jason Aronson.

Trevor-Roper, H. 1983. "The Invention of Tradition: The Highland Tradition of Scotland". In *The Invention of Tradition,* Eric Hobsbawm and Terrance Ranger, eds., pp. 15–41. New York: Cambridge University Press.

Trigger, Bruce. 1978. "Iroquois Matriliny." *Pennsylvania Archaeologist,* 48:55–65.

———. 1982. "The Ritualization of Potential Conflict Between the Sexes Among the Mbuti." In *Politics and History in Band Societies,* Eleanor Leacock and Richard Lee, eds., pp. 133–155. Cambridge, England: Cambridge University Press.

Turner, Victor. 1967. *The Forest of Symbols: Aspects of Ndembu Ritual.* Ithaca, NY: Cornell University Press.

Tylor, Edward B. 1871. *Primitive Culture.* London: J. Murray.

Ubelaker, Douglas. 1994. "Positive Identification of American Indian Skeletal Remains from Radiographic Comaridon." *Journal of Forensic Sciences,* 35:466–472.

Uhlman, Allon. 1992. "A Critique of Leavitt's Review of Sociobiological Explanations of Incest Avoidance." *American Anthropologist,* 94:446–448.

UNDP (United Nations Development Programme). 1993. *Human Development Report.* New York: Oxford University Press.

U.S. Bureau of the Census. 1990. *Statistical Abstract of the United States.* Washington, DC: U.S. Government Printing Office.

———. 1994. *Statistical Abstract of the United States.* Washington, DC: U.S. Government Printing Office.

U.S. Bureau of the Census. 1997. *Statistical Abstract of the United States.* Washington, DC: U.S. Government Printing Office.

Upham, Steadman. 1990. *The Evolution of Political Systems: Sociopolitics in Small-Scale Sedentary Societies.* New York: Cambridge University Press.

Vaidyanathan, A., N. Nair, and M. Harris. 1982. "Bovine Sex and Age Ratios in India." *Current Anthropology,* 23:365–383.

Vaillant, George C. 1966. *The Aztecs of Mexico.* Baltimore: Penguin. Originally Published 1941.

Van Allen, J. 1972. "Sitting on a Man: Colonialism and the Lost Political Institutions of Igbo Women." *Canadian Journal of African Studies,* 6(2):165–182.

Vandiver, Pamela B., et al. 1989. "The Origins of Ceramic Technology at Dolni Vestonice, Czechoslovakia." *Science,* 246:1002–1008.

Van Lawick-Goodall, Jane. 1986. *The Chimpanzees of Gombe.* Cambridge, MA: Harvard University Press.

Vigil, James Diego. 1988. *Barrio Gangs: Street Life and Identity in Southern California.* Austin, TX: University of Texas Press.

———. 1997. *Personas Mexicanas: Chicano Highschoolers in a Changing Los Angeles.* Fort Worth, TX: Harcourt Brace College Publishers.

Villa, Paola, et al. 1986. "Cannibalism in the Neolithic." *Science,* 233:431–437.

Visweswaran, Kamala. 1997. "Histories of Feminist Ethnography." *Annual Review of Anthropology,* 26:591–621.

Volkan, Vamik. 1997. *Blood Lines: From Ethnic Pride to Ethnic Terrorism.* New York: Farrar, Straus & Giroux.

Vrana, Debora. 1997. "Women in Business Flex Their Muscles." *The Los Angeles Times,* September 3, 1997.

Wagley, Charles. 1943. "Tapirap Shamanism." *Boletim Do Museu Nacional (Rio de Janeiro) Anthropologia,* 3:1–94.

———. 1977. *Welcome of Tears.* New York: Oxford University Press.

Walker, Deward. 1972. *The Emergent Native Americans.* Boston: Little, Brown.

Walker, Phillip L. 1988. "Cranial Injuries as Evidence of Violence in Prehistoric California." *American Journal of Physical Anthropology,* 80:313–323.

Wallace, Anthony F. C. 1952. *The Modal Personality Structure of the Tuscarora Indians as Revealed by the Rorschach Test.* Bureau of American Ethnology Bulletin No. 150. Washington, DC: Smithsonian Institution.

———. 1966. *Religion: An Anthropological View.* New York: Random House.

———. 1970. *Culture and Personality,* 2nd edition. New York: Random House.

———. 1972. "Mental Illness, Biology and Culture." In *Psychological Anthropology,* Francis Hsu, ed., pp. 363–402. Cambridge, MA: Schenkman.

Warner, Richard. 1985. *Recovery from Schizophrenia: Psychiatry and Political Economy.* London: Routledge and Kegan Paul.

Watson, James. 1977. "Pigs, Fodder, and the Jones Effect in Postipomean New Guinea." *Ethnology,* 16:57–70.

Watson, Richard. 1990. "Ozymandius, King of Kings: Postprocessual Radical Archaeology as Critique." *American Antiquity,* 55:673–689.

Weatherford, Jack. 1988. *Indian Givers: How the Indians of the Americas Transformed the World.* New York: Crown.

Weaver, Thomas. 1994. "Latino Legacies: Crossing National and Creating Cultural Boundaries." In *Handbook of Hispanic Cultures in the United States: Anthropology,* Thomas Weaver, ed., pp. 15–38. Houston, TX: Arte Publico Press.

———. 1994. "The Culture of Latinos in the United States." In *Handbook of Hispanic Cultures in the United States: Anthropology,* Thomas Weaver, ed., pp. 38–58. Houston, TX: Arte Publico Press.

Weber, Peter. 1994. "Safeguarding Oceans." In *State of the World,* Lester Brown, ed., pp. 41–59. New York: W. W. Norton.

Weil, Peter. 1986. "Agricultural Intensification and Fertility in the Gambia (West Africa)." In *Culture and Reproduction: An Anthropological Critique of Demographic Transition Theory,* W. P. Handwerker, ed., pp. 294–320. Boulder, CO: Westview Press.

Weiner, Annette. 1976. *Women of Value, Men of Renown.* Austin: University of Texas Press.

———. 1987. *The Trobrianders of Papua New Guinea.* New York: Holt, Rinehart and Winston.

Weinstein, Michael. 1995. "Why They Deserve It." *The New York Times Magazine,* November 19, pp. 102–103.

Weisman, Steven. 1978. "City Constructs Statistical Profile in Looting Cases." *The New York Times,* August 14, p. 1.

Weismantel, Mary. 1989. "Making Breakfast and Raising Babies." In *The Household Economy: Reconsidering the Domestic Mode of Production,* Richard Wilk, ed., pp. 55–72. Boulder, CO: Westview.

Weisner, Thomas S. 1979. "Urban–Rural Differences in Sociable and Disruptive Behavior of Kenya Children." *Ethnology,* 18(2): 153–172.

Weisner, Thomas, and Lucinda Bernheimer. 1998. "Children of the 1960s at Midlife: Generational Identity and the Family Adaptive Project." In *Welcome to Middle Age! and Other Cultural Fictions*, Richard Shweder, ed., pp. 211–255. Chicago: University of Chicago Press.

Weisner, Thomas, and Ronald Gallimore. 1977. "My Brother's Keeper: Child and Sibling Caretaking." *Current Anthropology*, 18:169–190.

Weiss, Gerald. 1977. "Rhetoric in Campa Narrative." *Journal of Latin American Lore*, 3:169–182.

Weitzman, Lenore. 1985. *The Divorce Revolution: Consequences for Women and Children in America.* New York: Free Press.

Weller, Susan C. 1998. "Structured Interviewing and Questionnaire Construction." In *Handbook of Methods in Cultural Anthropology*, H. Russell Bernard, ed. London: Alta Mira Press.

Werge, R. 1979. "Potato Processing in the Central Highlands of Peru." *Ecology of Food and Nutrition*, 7:229–234.

Werner, Dennis. 1979. "A Cross-Cultural Perspective on Theory and Research on Male Homosexuality." *Journal of Homosexuality*, 4:345–362.

Westermark, E. 1894. *The History of Human Marriage.* New York: Macmillan.

Westoff, Charles. 1986. "Fertility in the United States." *Science*, 234:544–559.

Weston, Kath. 1991. *Families We Choose: Lesbians, Gays, Kinship.* New York: Columbia University Press.

———. 1993. "Lesbian/Gay Studies in the House of Anthropology." *Annual Review of Anthropology*, 22:339–367.

Weyer, E. 1932. *The Eskimos.* New Haven, CT: Yale University Press.

White, Benjamin. 1982. "Child Labour and Population Growth in Rural Asia." *Development and Change*, 13:587–610.

White, Douglas. 1988. "Rethinking Polyandry Co-Wives, Codes and Cultural Systems." *Current Anthropology*, 29:529–572.

White, Tim. 1997. Quoted in ABCNEWS.com HYPERLINK http://www.abcnews.com/sections/scitech/cannibals www.abcnews.com/sections/scitech/cannibals 827/index.html.

White, Leslie. 1949. *The Science of Culture.* New York: Grove Press.

Whiten, A. J. Goodall, W. C. McGrew, T. Nishida, V. Reynolds, Y. Sugiyama, C. E. G. Tutin, R. W. Wrangham, R., and C. Besch. 1999. "Cultures in Chimpanzees." *Nature*, 399:682–685.

Whitesides, George. 1985. "Nut Cracking by Wild Chimpanzees in Sierra Leone, West Africa." *Primates*, 26:91–94.

Whiting, Beatrice, and C. Edwards. 1988. *Children of Different Worlds: The Formation of Social Behavior.* Cambridge, MA: Harvard University Press.

Whiting, Beatrice, and John Whiting. 1975. *Children of Six Cultures.* Boston: Harvard University Press.

Whiting, John, ed. 1969. "Effects of Climate on Certain Cultural Practices." In *Environmental and Cultural Behavior: Ecological Studies in Cultural Anthropology*, A. P. Vayda, ed., pp. 416–455. Garden City, NY: Natural History Press.

Whiting, John. 1993. "The Effect of Polygyny on Sex Ratio at Birth." *American Anthropologist*, 95:435–442.

Whiting, John, and Beatrice Whiting. 1978. "A Strategy for Psychocultural Research." In *The Making of Psychological Anthropology*, George Spindler, ed., pp. 41–61. Berkeley: University of California Press.

Whiting, John, and I. Child. 1953. *Child Training and Personality: A Cross–Cultural Study.* New Haven, CT: Yale University Press.

Whorf, Benjamin. 1956. *Language, Thought, and Reality.* New York: Wiley.

Whyte, Martin K. 1978. *The Status of Women in Preindustrial Societies.* Princeton, NJ: Princeton University Press.

Williams, Linda M., and David Finkelhor. 1995. "Paternal Caregiving and Incest: Test of a Biosocial Model." *American Journal of Orthopsychiatry*, 65:101–113.

Williams, Terry. 1989. *The Cocaine Kids: The Inside Story of a Teenage Drug Ring.* Reading, MA: Addison-Wesley.

Williams, Walter. 1986. *The Spirit and the Flesh: Sexual Diversity in American Indian Culture.* Boston: Beacon Press.

Willigen, John Van. 1986. *Applied Anthropology: An Introduction.* South Hadley, MA: Bergin and Garvey.

———. 1991. *Anthropology in Use: A Source Book on Anthropological Practice.* Boulder, CO: Westview Press.

Wilmsen, Edwin N. 1982. "Biological Variables in Forager Fertility Performance: A Critique of Bongaart's Model." Working Paper No. 60, African Studies Center, Boston University.

Wilmsen, Edwin, and James Denbow. 1990. "Paradigmatic History of San-speaking Peoples and Current Attempts at Revision." *Current Anthropology*, 31:489–524.

Wilson, David. 1998. *Indiginous South Americans of the Past and Present: An Ecological Perspective.* Boulder, CO: Westview Press.

Wilson, E. O. 1975. *Sociobiology: The New Synthesis.* Cambridge, MA: Harvard University Press.

———. 1978. *Human Nature.* Cambridge: Harvard University Press.

Wilson, Monica. 1963. *Good Company: A Study of Nyakyusa Age-Villages.* Boston: Little, Brown.

Winkelman, Michael. 1990. "Shamans and Other 'Magico-Religious' Healers." *Ethos*, 18:308–351.

Witowski, Stanley, and Cecil A. Brown. 1978. "Lexical Universals." *Annual Review of Anthropology*, 7:427–451.

———. 1985. "Climate, Clothing, and Body-Part Nomenclature." *Ethnology*, 24:197–214.

Wolf, Arthur P. 1995. *Sexual Attraction and Childhood Association.* Stanford, CA: Stanford University Press.

Wolf, A. P., and C. S. Huang. 1980. *Marriage and Adoption in China, 1845–1945.* Stanford, CA: Stanford University Press.

Wolf, Eric. 1994. "Perilous Ideas: Race, Culture, People." *Current Anthropology,* 35:1–12.

———. 1998. *Envisioning Power: Ideologies of Domination and Crisis.* Berkeley: University of California Press.

Wolf, Marjorie. 1972. *Women and the Family in Rural Taiwan.* Stanford, CA: Stanford University Press.

———. 1975. "Women and Suicide in China." In *Women in Chinese Society,* Marjorie Wolf and Roxane Witke, eds. Stanford, CA: Stanford University Press.

Wolpoff, Milford, and Rachel Caspari. 1997. *Race and Human Evolution: A Fatal Attraction.* New York: Simon and Schuster.

Wood, James. 1990. "Fertility in Anthropological Populations." *Annual Review of Anthropology,* 19:211–242.

Woodburn, James. 1982. "Egalitarian Societies." *Man,* 17:431–451.

World Health Organization. 1968. *Statistics Reports,* 21:529–551. Geneva: World Health Organization.

———. 1979. *Schizophrenia: An International Follow Up Study.* New York: Wiley.

Worsley, Peter. 1968. *The Trumpet Shall Sound: A Study of "Cargo" Cults in Melanesia.* New York: Schocken.

Wrangham, Richard, and Dale Peterson. 1996. *Demonic Males, Apes and the Origins of Human Violence.* New York: Mariner Books.

Yan, Yunxiang. 1996. *The Flow of Gifts: Reciprocity and Social Networks in a Chinese Village.* Stanford, CA: Stanford University Press.

———. 1997. "The Triumph of Conjugality: Structural Transformation of Family Relations in a Chinese Village." *Ethnology,* 36:191–212.

Yanagisako, Sylvia Junko. 1979. "Family and Household: The Analysis of Domestic Groups." *Annual Reviews in Anthropology,* 8:161–205.

Yates, Robin D. S. 1990. "War, Food Shortages, and Relief Measures in Early China." In *Hunger in History: Food Shortage, Poverty, and Deprivation,* Lucile F. Newman et al., eds., pp. 147–176. Cambridge, MA: Basil Blackwell.

Zentella, A. C. 1990. "Returned Migration, Language and Identity: Puerto Rican Bilinguals in *Dos Worlds/ Two Mundos.*" *International Journal of the Sociology of Language,* 84:81–100.

A

action anthropology—Oriented to applying and helping implement a planned program in a given organization or cultural setting.

adaptation—The process by which organisms, or cultural elements, undergo change in form or function in response to threats to their existence and their ability to reproduce.

adaptive capacity—Previously established ability of a minority to compete—to hold territory and successfully reproduce—in a given sociocultural context.

aesthetic—Refers to a universal human capacity for emotionally charged response when art is successful.

affinal—Relatedness through marriage. Compare with CONSANGUINEAL.

affinity—Relatedness through marriage. Compare with DESCENT.

affixes—Bound MORPHEMES that occur at the initial position in a word.

African American Vernacular English (AAVE)—The dialect of English used by many African Americans in the United States in familiar and informal settings.

age grades—In some societies, formally institutionalized segmentation of the population, by sex and chronological age, with RITES OF PASSAGE announcing the transition from one status to the next.

agriculture—The cultivation of domesticated crops.

agromanagerial peasants—Peasants in centralized states who are subject to CORVÉE labor.

agropastoralism—Also known as mixed farming, maintains soil fertility by raising animals as well as crops by using the animal's manure as fertilizer.

alleles—Variants of GENES that occupy the same location on corresponding CHROMOSOMES.

allophone—A variant of a PHONEME; all the contrastive sounds with the class of sounds designated by a particular phoneme.

amibilineal descent—A form of COGNATIC DESCENT in which individuals have a choice of reckoning kinship along either maternal or paternal links. Compare with BILATERAL DESCENT.

ambilocality—Residence of a couple after marriage alternatively with either the husband's or wife's kin.

animal culture—The behavioral repertoire of nonhuman animals that is learned rather than inherited through genetics.

animatism—The attribution of humanlike consciousness and powers to inanimate objects, natural phenomena, plants, and animals.

animism—Belief in personalized yet disembodied beings such as souls, ghosts, spirits, and gods. Compare ANIMATISM.

anthropological linguistics—The study of how people use language in particular cultures or subcultures.

applied anthropology—Research that has immediate practical applications aimed at helping cultural groups, organizations, businesses, and governments solve a wide range of problems.

arbitrariness—Refers to the fact that the meanings of words and other kinds of symbols have no inherent or necessary relationship to the physical properties of the symbols themselves.

archaeology—The study of past, rather than living, human societies. Archaeologists study cultural remains such as tools, pottery, and buildings as well as human fossils.

art—Play with form producing some aesthetically successful transformation-representation.

artifacts—Material objects made by human hands, having specifiable uses and functions.

ascribed atatus—The attributes of an individual's position in SOCIETY that are involuntary and often inevitable, based on sex or descent.

ascription—See ASCRIBED STATUS.

assimilation—The loss of separate identity of an ethnic group or social race through absorption by a dominant group. Compare with PLURALISM.

australopithecines—Apes that lived in southern Africa about 2.4–3 million years ago, believed to be the ancestors of modern humans. They had small brains and canine teeth but had upright posture and were able to walk on two legs.

avunculocality—Residence of a couple after marriage with or near the groom's mother's brother.

B

band, local—A small, loosely organized group of hunter-gatherer families, occupying a specifiable territory and tending toward self-sufficiency.

basic personality—Culturally defined psychological traits exhibited by members of a social group.

basic personality structure—The personality configuration displayed by most members of a society as a result of common early childhood experiences.

berdache—A male transvestite who assumes a sanctioned female role among Native American peoples.

bigman—Political leader who does not occupy a formal office and whose leadership is based on prestige, not authority.

bilateral descent—A form of COGNATIC DESCENT in which kinship is reckoned evenly and symmetrically along maternal and paternal links. Compare with AMBILINEAL DESCENT.

biological anthropology—See PHYSICAL ANTHROPOLOGY.

biological race—An etic population in which several genes occur together with distinctive frequencies over many generations.

bipedalism—Locomotion in which an animal walks on its two hind legs.

blood feud—Vengeful confrontation between opposing groups of kin, set off by real or alleged homicide or other crimes, and involving continuing alternative retaliation in kind.

Boserup's theory—Holds that food production rises to the level demanded by population growth.

bride-price—See BRIDEWEALTH.

bride service—Work performed by the groom for his bride's family for a variable length of time, either before or after marriage.

bridewealth—A substantial gift of goods or money given to the bride's kin by the groom or his kin at or before the marriage.

C

capitalism—A socioeconomic system characterized by a class division between the owners of the means of production who are motivated by profit and the workers who lack direct access to the productive resources and must sell their labor.

capitalist peasants—Peasants who buy and sell land and labor but most are in debt to banks and mortgage holders.

cargo cult—A revitalization movement native to Melanesia based on the expectation of the imminent return of ancestors in ships, planes, and trains bringing treasures of European-manufactured goods.

carrying capacity—The population of a species that a particular area or ecosystem can support without suffering irreversible deterioration.

caste—Widely applied as a term to a self-enclosed CLASS or Ethnic group; a stratified, endogamous descent group.

chiefdom—A centralized political system with authority vested in formal, often hereditary office, integrating more than one community but not necessarily the whole society or language group.

chosen glory—A historical event that induces feelings of success and triumph, which can bring members of a large group together.

chosen trauma—The collective memory of a calamity that once befell a group's ancestors.

chromosomes—Threadlike structures within the cell nucleus, containing DNA, that transmit information that determines heredity.

churning—This administrative phenomenon occurs when people on welfare lose their entitlements as a result of a real or inaccurately recorded failure on their part to comply with bureaucratic requirements.

circulating connubia—Several intermarrying domestic groups that exchange spouses in cycles.

circumcision—The ritual removal of the foreskin of a male's penis or of the tip of a woman's clitoris.

clan—A set of kin whose members believe (but cannot necessarily prove) that they are descended from a common ancestor or ancestress.

class, social—One of the stratified groupings within a society, characterized by specific attitudes and behavior and by differential access to power and to basic resources. Less endogamous and more open than castes or minorities.

clitoridectomy—The ritual removal of a portion of a female's clitoris.

code switching—Alternating between languages or dialects within a single conversational segment.

cognatic descent—Form of DESCENT in which relationships are traced through both males and females.

cognatic lineage—All the descendants of an apical ancestor or ancestress reckon descent through any combination of male or female links.

collaterals—Persons who are consanguineal kin, possessing a common ancestor, but in different lines of descent, such as cousins.

communal rites—Ceremonies, largely religious, carried out by the social group—usually by nonprofessional specialists and celebrants.

communitas—Collective LIMINALITY that creates a community spirit and feeling of togetherness.

complementary opposition—The process by which groups unite into more and more inclusive units as they are confronted with more and more inclusive coalitions of antagonistic groups.

consanguine—"Blood" relative, or people related by birth. Compare with AFFINAL.

corvée—A forced labor draft imposed by a government for public road and building construction, often in lieu of monetary taxes.

couvade—Customary restrictions on the activities of a man often associated with his wife's lying-in and birth of their child.

cross cousins—Persons of either sex whose parents are siblings of the opposite sex; offspring of a father's sister and mother's brother. Compare PARALLEL COUSINS.

cultural anthropology—The study of people living in past and present-day societies; how they make a living, how they interact with each other, the institutions that organize them into society, and the beliefs they hold.

cultural configurations—The distinctive standardized ways in which cultures mold personalities.

cultural evolution—Technological or material innovations that improve opportunities for a population to achieve reproductive success.

cultural materialism—The research strategy that attempts to explain the differences and similarities in thought and behavior found among human groups by studying the material constraints to which humans are subjected. These material constraints include the need to produce food, shelter, tools, and machines, and to reproduce human populations within limits set by biology and the environment.

cultural relativism—The principle that all cultural systems are inherently equal in value and that the traits characteristic of each system need to be assessed and explained within the context in which they occur.

cultural takeoff—Crucial for understanding the origins of modern humans. Once the capacity for language and language-assisted thought processes developed, a vast number of cultural differences and similarities could arise and disappear independently of changes in genotypes.

culture—The learned patterns of behavior and thought characteristic of a societal group.

culture of poverty—A depiction of the poor as fearful, suspicious, apathetic toward major institutions and present time oriented. This concept has been criticized for blaming poor people for their poverty.

culture-specific psychosis—Mental disorder that has a distinctive set of symptoms limited to a specific culture.

D

deliberate teaching—The performance by older individuals that increases the probability that younger individuals will directly observe and copy behavior in order to perform on their own.

depression—A constant state of excessive sadness, despair, and isolation.

descent—Relatedness through parentage from a common ancestor. Compare with AFFINITY.

diffusion—The process by which cultural traits, ways, complexes, and institutions are transferred from one cultural group to another.

diglossia—Two languages or dialects used interchangeably according to social circumstances.

direct observation of behavior—Systematic observations aimed at obtaining accurate data on what people are doing and how much time they spend in various activities.

displacement—The ability to communicate about items or events with which the communicators are not in direct contact.

divination—Arrival at an expectation or judgment of future events through the interpretation of omens construed as evidence.

DNA (Deoxyribonucleic Acid)—The long-stranded molecules that are the principal component of chromosomes. Varied arrangements of DNA determine the genetic code and the genotype.

dowry—A substantial gift of goods or money given at marriage to a husband or his group by his wife's group; in some instances, it is the wife who controls the compensation, in which case the transfer of wealth resembles a form of inheritance for the bride.

E

ecological anthropology—The study of cultural and biological responses related to the survival, reproduction and health, and spatial distribution of human populations.

ecology—The study of the total system of relationships among all the organisms and environmental conditions characteristic of a given area or region.

economizing—Choices people make that they believe provide the greatest benefit to them; also lowering costs while maximizing return on effort.

economy—The management of the production, distribution, and consumption of the natural resources, labor, and other forms of wealth available to a cultural system.

egalitarian—A type of societal group that lacks formalized differentiation in access to, and power over, basic resources among its members.

ego—The focal person or reference point when reckoning kinship.

emics—Descriptions or judgments concerning behavior, customs, beliefs, values, and so on, held by members of a societal group as culturally appropriate and valid. See also ETICS.

enculturation—The process by which individuals—usually as children—acquire behavioral patterns and other aspects of their culture from others, through observation, instruction, and reinforcement.

endogamy—The principle that requires ego to take a spouse from a group or status of which ego is a member.

Eskimo terminology—Separate kin terms are used for nuclear family members that are not extended to any other kin type. Americans use Eskimo kin terminology.

estrus—A period of sexual receptivity, which usually corresponds with ovulation.

ethnic group—This term refers to any group of people within a larger cultural unit who identify themselves as a distinct entity, separate from the rest of that culture.

ethnocentrism—The tendency to view the traits, ways, ideas, and values observed in other cultural groups as invariably inferior and less natural or logical than those of one's own group.

ethnographic present—The description of a traditional culture at the time it was studied. Readers are cautioned that most cultures described in the ethnographic present have undergone culture change or may no longer exist.

ethnography—The systematic description of contemporary cultures.

etics—The techniques and results of making generalizations about cultural events, behavior patterns, artifacts, thought, and ideology that are independent of the distinctions and beliefs that are significant and appropriate from the native actors' point of view. See also EMICS.

exchange—The practice of giving and receiving valued objects and services.

exogamy—The rule that forbids an individual from taking a spouse from within a prescribed local, kin, status, or other group in which they are both members.

extended family—A domestic unit consisting of two or more related nuclear families.

extensive agriculture—A low energy ecological adaptation, such as slash and burn, that relies on extensive land use. See INTENSIVE AGRICULTURE.

F

family—A domiciliary and/or kin grouping, variously constituted of married and related persons and their offspring, residing together for economic and reproductive purposes. See also NUCLEAR FAMILY; EXTENDED FAMILY.

feasting—A form of redistribution in which wealthy individuals host periodic feasts in exchange for prestige.

fecundity—The physiological capacity to produce live children.

feminization of poverty—The fact that women comprise a disproportionately large percentage of a nation's poor because they generally earn lower wages and lack access to the same sources of income as men.

feudal peasants—PEASANTS who are allowed to farm land owned by the ruling class in return for a portion of the harvest or rent in kind or money.

feudal system—A type of historical socioeconomic organization involving a network of obligations, in which the PEASANTS are structured inferiors to their lord and are bound to provide certain payments and services in exchange for apparent privileges.

fictive kinship—Kin ties established through negotiation of kinship rather than genealogical connections.

folktales—Traditional narratives from the distant past that reflect social situations that play on ordinary human fears and desires.

form—The rules of how art is organized.

fossils—Remains or traces of plants or animals preserved—usually by mineralization—from the geological past.

freeloader—A person who receives without reciprocating in return.

functionalism—Theoretical perspective that considers social practices and beliefs in terms of their contribution to social stability.

functions—The systemic needs served by artifacts, patterns of behavior, and ideas; the ways in which cultural traits contribute toward maintenance, efficiency, and adaptation of the cultural system.

G

gender—Acquired cultural and psychological attributes that relate to EMIC meaning associated with culturally defined sex-based identities.

gender scripts—Define what it means to be male and female in a given cultural context.

gene flow—The movement of genetic material from one GENE POOL to another as a consequence of interbreeding.

gene pool—The sum and range of variety of genes present within a given breeding population.

genes—The basic chemical units of heredity, found at particular loci on the chromosomes.

genitor—The ETIC male source of the sperm responsible for the birth of a particular child.

genotype—The total gene complement received by an individual organism from its parents; as distinguished from the external appearance manifest in the phenotype.

geographic race—A breeding population, usually of considerable spatial extent, that can be described in terms of the frequencies of specifiable, characterizing genetic traits.

ghost dance—A REVITALIZATION movement that appeared on the North American Plains during the nineteenth century, awaiting the departure of the whites and the restoration of Indian traditional ways.

groom price—Compensation given to a man's matrilineal group when he resides with his wife's matrilineal group. Very rare.

H

Hawaiian terminology—The same kin terms are applied to people inside and outside the nuclear family. A single term is used for relatives of the same sex and generation.

headman—In an egalitarian group, the head who may lead those who will follow, but is usually unable to impose sanctions to enforce his decisions or requests or deprive others of equal access to basic resources.

heteroglossia—The use of multiple dialects or languages based on social context and social setting.

homeostasis—The resistance of some systems to change; the tendency to remain in equilibrium.

hominids (hominidae)—The taxonomic family, including all living and extinct types and races of humans and protohumans.

hominids—Any member of the family Hominidae, including all species of AUSTRALOPITHECUS and HOMO.

homo erectus—Emerged in Africa and migrated to Europe and Asia. *H. erectus* is succeeded by the oldest members of our species, *H. sapiens*.

homo habilis—The earliest species in the genus of hominids, known for manufacturing tools. *Homo habilis* was discovered at many sites in East Africa and dates back to about 2 million years ago.

homo sapiens—Considered an ancestor to modern humans. *Homo sapiens* extended from Africa, to Europe and into Asia and appear in the fossil record about from 1.6 million years ago to 400,000 years ago.

horticulture—Cultivation of crops using simple hand tools such as a hoe or digging stick, without fertilization or irrigation. See SLASH AND BURN.

hypergamy—The use of DOWRY payments to achieve upward mobility by attracting a bridegroom from an upper-status family.

hyperindustrial—Refers to the fact that the world has become more (not less) industrial, extending mass-production into new areas and greater reliance on machines.

I

ideology—Cognitive and emotional aspects of the EMIC superstructure.

image of limited good—PEASANT'S view the universe as one in which all desired things exist in finite quantity; hence gains in one area are assumed to involve losses in another. This notion results in resistance to economic development.

inbreeding avoidance—A behavioral pattern in which individuals avoid sexual contact with people who could be sexual partners, were it not for their relatedness.

incest—Socially prohibited mating and or marriage, as within certain specified limits of real or putative KINSHIP.

incest taboo—Cultural beliefs prohibiting marriage and sexual relations with a close relative. The limits of the taboo vary and depend directly on the society's kinship system and forms of social organization.

individualistic cults—Religious practices based on personal relations between specific individuals and specific supernatural powers.

industrialization—An advanced stage of techno-economic development observed particularly in modern states and colonizing powers, characterized by advanced technologies, mass production, and consumerism.

infanticide—Underinvestment and neglect (inadequate feeding, withholding physical and emotional support), and deliberate killing (smothering, excessive physical punishment, and starvation) of infants.

innate capacity for grammar—The premise that at the deepest level all human languages share an inborn species-specific structure.

intensive agriculture—A high energy ecological adaptation, such as plow agriculture, that involves substantial environmental modification through intensive labor. See EXTENSIVE AGRICULTURE.

Iroquois terminology—Distinguishes between cross and parallel relatives. Marriage is based on cross-cousin marriage.

irrigation civilization—An advanced type of preindustrial society associated with the control of extensive facilities for crop irrigation and land drainage. Usually characterized by highly centralized political institutions.

K

kin—A set of relatives who are related by either CONSANGUINEAL or AFFINAL ties (ties of descent or marriage).

kindred—Consists of ego's close bilateral relatives. A kindred is not a bounded group because everyone in a kindred belongs to different overlapping groups.

kin group—A social aggregate of individuals related by either consanguineal ties of descent or affinal ties of marriage.

kinship—A culturally recognized system for classifying relatives by ties of descent or marriage.

kinship terminology—The system of terms by which members of a KIN GROUP customarily address or refer to one another, denoting their relationship.

the Kula ring—A trade route established among the island groups immediately to the east and north of New Guinea. The reciprocal exchange of soulava (necklaces) for mwali (cowrie armbands) operates in a circle comprising all the islands.

L

lactation amenorrhea—Disruption of the menstrual cycle associated with the production of the hormone prolactin during breastfeeding.

landownership—Title to land that restricts access to land use unless rent or tribute is paid.

language family—A group of related languages historically derived from a common antecedent language.

law of energy and the evolution of culture—Proposed by Leslie White, it states that (1) culture evolves as the amount of energy harnessed increases; (2) culture evolves as the efficiency of energy utilization increases. The first part of the law is supported, whereas the second part is in question.

law of the minimum—States that growth is limited by the minimum availability of any one necessary resource rather than by the abundance of all necessary resources.

legitimacy—Assigns birth status to a child and determines the economic rights and responsibilities of the parents.

leopard skin chief—An outside mediator among the Nuer, believed to have supernatural powers, who is called on to resolve disputes between kin groups.

levirate—Custom favoring the remarriage of a widow to her deceased husband's brother.

libido—Sexual desire

liminality—The suspension of social norms (a limbo period) when a person is cut off from normal social life and ceremonially transformed from one status to another.

lineage—A kin group whose members can actually trace their relationship through specific, known genealogical links along the recognized line of DESCENT, as either matrilineal or patrilineal.

M

magic—The practice of certain rituals that are presumed to coerce desired practical outcomes.

maintenance system—The basic customs surrounding the nourishment, sheltering, and protection of the members of a culture.

majority—The superordinate group in a hierarchy of racial, cultural, or religious minorities. The majority is usually, but not necessarily, not only politically and economically dominant but more numerous as well.

male inseminating rituals—Same-sex rituals that enable boys to advance to a higher status. They do not preclude marriage, which offers a different form of social achievement and sexual desire.

male supremacist complex—A by-product of male monopoly over weapons, training for combat, female infanticide, and patrilineal descent and residence. It is characterized by an emphasis on male bravery and denigration of women.

Malthusian theory—Predicted that population would always increase more rapidly than the food supply, thereby dooming a large portion of humanity to poverty and hunger.

mana—A term for the impersonal pervasive power expected in certain objects and roles. See also animatism.

marriage—A socially sanctioned form of heterosexual mating and coresidence establishing duties and obligations with respect to sex and reproduction; variant forms are homosexual matings and childless marriages.

matriarchy—Political control by women. Although some societies are more gender equal than others, it is widely believed that matriarchy did not occur in human evolution. Compare with PATRIARCHY.

matrifocal family—A domestic group comprising one or more adult women, and their offspring, within which husbands-fathers are not permanent residents.

matrilineal complex—Malinowski's characterization of supportive father-son relations among the Trobrianders, compared with the rivalry found in patrilineal societies. Compare with OEDIPUS COMPLEX.

matrilineality—Descent reckoning through females exclusively.

matrilocality—A pattern of residence in which a married couple lives with or near the wife's parents.

maximization—Behavior directed toward producing as much as possible of a given good.

maximum sustainable yield—The level of production immediately prior to the point of diminishing returns. No one has yet demonstrated that this is a realistic goal for resource management; in fact, throughout history and prehistory, resources have often been overexploited.

messianic movement—A movement offering REVITALIZATION or salvation through following the spiritual or activist leadership of a prophetic individual or messiah; often against vested authority.

metaphor.—See symbol.

minority—Subordinate endogamous descent groups based on racial, cultural, or religious criteria found in all state societies.

mixed farming.—See agropastoralism.

modal personality—Those traits or characteristics that occur with the highest frequency in a culture or subculture.

money as a medium of exchange—An item which symbolizes command over goods or services which serves as a common measure of value, medium of exchange, and as a standard of deferred payment.

money—A medium of exchange that has standard value.

monogamy—Marriage between one man and one woman for their lifetimes.

morphemes—The smallest sequence of sounds to which a definite meaning is attached.

morphology—The study and description of the systematic ways that words are formed from lesser units.

myths—Sacred tales that explain issues of human existence.

N

national character—An approach to describing the distinctive psychological characteristics of other cultural groups.

natural selection—The process by which differential reproductive success changes the frequency of genes in populations. One of the major forces of evolution.

negative feedback—A self correcting mechanism that returns system variables to a determined range.

neolocal residence—Residence of a couple after marriage apart from the parental domicile of either spouse.

nervios (nerves)—A cultural description of a wide range of mental conditions, including those responsible for schizophrenic behavior.

nomadic pastoralism—An adaptation associated with herding animals over vast distances in search of pasture. Compare with TRANSHUMANCE.

nonrenewable resources—Irreplaceable resources such as fossil fuels.

nuclear family—A basic social grouping consisting of married male and female parents and their offspring.

n/um—!Kung concept of a healing energy that originates from the gods.

O

Oedipus complex—A boy's unconscious wishes for closeness and exclusive intimacy with his mother and feelings of rivalry toward his father.

one-drop rule—Defines a Black person as anyone who has the slightest amount of Black "blood," or one ancestor who was known to have been identified as Black.

optimal foraging theory—The principle that foragers utilize wild food resources in direct proportion to the caloric effort to obtain them.

organic evolution (biological evolution)—The change of old forms of structures into new structures as the frequency of new or old genes in a population is altered.

P

parallel cousins—Persons whose parents are siblings of the same sex; the sons and daughters of two sisters or of two brothers.

parallel cultural evolution—Evolution represented by instances in which significant aspects, patternings, or institutions in two or more cultural systems undergo similar adaptations and transformations; presumably in response to the operations of similar causal and dynamic factors.

participant observation—A research method that involves spending a considerable amount of time among the people being studied—observing, questioning, and when possible taking part in the important events of the group.

pastoral nomads—Peoples who raise domesticated animals and do not depend on hunting, gathering, or the planting of their own crops for a significant portion of their diets.

pastoralism—An ecological adaptation to marginal areas of Asia and Africa where natural resources cannot support agriculture; hence the needs of domestic animals for pasture and water greatly influence settlement and migration.

patriarchy—Rule by father or male authority. Although widespread, patriarchy exists in different forms and degrees. Contrast with MATRIARCHY.

patrilineality—Descent reckoning through males exclusively.

patrilocality—A pattern of residence in which a married couple lives with or near the husband's parents.

peasants—Food-producing farm workers who form the lower economic stratum in preindustrial and underdeveloped societies, subject to exploitative obligations in the form of rent, taxes, tribute, and forced labor service.

pedagogical model of child care—Child care in which the primary concern is stimulation of behavioral, cognitive, and social development.

pediatric model of child care—Child care in which the primary goal is the protection of the child from life-threatening illness and other hazards.

personality—The structuring of the inherent constitutional, emotional, and intellectual factors that determine how a person feels, thinks, and behaves in relation to the patterning of a particular cultural context.

phenotype—The characteristics of an individual organism that are the external, apparent manifestations of its hereditary genetic composition, resulting from the interaction of its genotype with its environment. See also genotype.

phonemes—A sound (PHONE), or the several variants of such a sound (ALLOPHONES), that native speakers perceive as contrastive with each other and as significant for the meaning of an utterance.

phones—The emic units of sounds that contrast with one another and that are the building blocks of PHONEMES.

phonetics—A branch of linguistics that records actual sounds produced by humans.

physical anthropology (biological anthropology)—The study of the animal origins and biologically determined nature of humankind. Also the study of evolution and physical variation of humans and nonhuman primates.

play—An enjoyable aspect of activity characteristic of art.

pluralism—The continuity of social races and ethnic groups within a regional or national population. Compare with ASSIMILATION.

political economy—The role of political authority and power in production, distribution, and consumption of goods and services.

polyandry—Marriage of one woman with two or more males simultaneously.

polygamy—Marriage involving more than one spouse of either sex.

polygyny—Marriage of one male with two or more females simultaneously.

population growth—Birth rate minus mortality, not counting migration.

population pressure—The pressure on resources that forces people to intensify production to obtain the same amount of food from the environment.

positive feedback—A mechanism that drives a system beyond a given range, causing instability and ultimately a changed system.

potlatch—Ceremonial redistributive feast accompanied by the giving of food and gifts to guests, practiced by the Indians of the Northwest coast. See FEASTING and REDISTRIBUTION.

power—The ability to control the behavior of others.

price market exchange—The price of goods and services is determined by buyers and sellers.

primary institutions—Economic institutions, domestic organization and child care that affects basic personality structure. Compare with SECONDARY INSTITUTIONS.

private inner self—The more authentic self that, in Japanese culture, provides a fixed core for self-identity. Compare with PUBLIC INTERACTIONAL SELF.

productivity—A property of language that allows the speaker to send an infinite number of novel messages.

psychoanalysis—Emphasizes the importance of unconscious feelings, motives, and conflicts in determining personality and behavior.

public interactional self—The surface layer of self that is exposed in Japanese culture to appraisal by others. Compare with private inner self.

R

race—Large populations characterized by a bundle of distinctive gene frequencies and associated with continents or extensive regions.

raciology—The scientific study of the relationship between race and culture.

racism—The belief that the cultural and intellectual characteristics of a population are linked to its biological racial heritage, with the notion that some races are inherently superior to others.

rainfall agriculture—Uses naturally occurring rainfall as a source of moisture.

reciprocal exchange—Involves mutual giving and receiving among people of equal status without overt calculation or stipulation of immediate return.

reciprocity—A mode of transfering goods and/or valuables without overt reckoning of economic worth or overt reckoning that a balance need be reached, to establish or reinforce ties between persons. See RECIPROCAL EXCHANGE.

redistribution—A collection of goods or valuables from a group, followed by reallocation by a centralized authority who does not retain a greater share. Compare with STRATIFIED REDISTRIBUTION.

rent—A payment in kind or in money for the opportunity to live or work on the owner's land.

reproductive success—A measure of an individual's genetic contribution to subsequent generations.

revitalization movement—Reaction by a minority group to coercion and disruption, often under messianic leadership, aiming to reclaim lost status, identity, and well-being.

rhetoric—The art of persuasion in public speaking, closely related to theatrical arts.

rites of passage—Communally celebrated rituals that mark the transition of an individual from one institutionalized STATUS to another.

rites of solidarity—Rites that confirm the unity of a group.

ritual—Organized and stereotyped behavior intended to influence supernatural powers.

roles—Patterns of behavior associated with specific statuses.

S

sanctity—The quality of unquestionable truthfulness surrounding unverifiable propositions that increases the likelihood of conformity to sacred propositions.

schema—EMIC characterization that reveals how thoughts about culture are organized. It provides a model of what the world is like and how one ought to think and act.

schizophrenia—Mental illness with core universal symptoms that include hallucinations, delusions, and disturbances of thought and behavior.

secondary institutions—Ideology, religion, and art that is impacted by a culture's basic personality structure. Compare with PRIMARY INSTITUTIONS.

segmentary lineages—A hierarchy of inclusive lineages which function to lend support in conflict situations.

semantic universality—A communication system that can convey information about the past, present, or future, whether real or imaginary.

severe male initiation rites—Rites of passage that involve circumcision or other forms of mutilation and trials of courage and stamina to demonstrate manhood.

sex—Anatomical and physiological attributes of the sexes. Compare with GENDER.

shaman—A part-time practitioner of magico-religious rites of divination and curing, skilled in sleight of hand and the techniques of trance and possession.

shamanistic cults—Cults in which special individuals (SHAMANS) have relationships with supernatural powers that ordinary people lack.

silent trade—Trade without face-to-face interaction, in which items are set out in a clearing and exchange is silently negotiated.

sister exchange—A form of marriage in which two males marry each other's sister (or sisters).

slash and burn—Refers to shifting cultivation with recurrent clearing and burning of vegetation and planting in the burnt fields. Fallow periods for each plot last longer than periods of cultivation.

social ecology of childhood—The environment of children's experiences that is most likely to affect their development (community, physical space, cast of characters and daily routines).

social race—Groups that are assumed to be biologically different from one another but are in fact classified according to culturally defined categories.

society—A group within which all aspects of the UNIVERSAL PATTERN occur with a high density of interaction among its members and having a geographical locus.

sociolinguistics—A field of linguistics concerned with language use—with how speakers make their utterances in social situations and for social purposes.

sodalities—Associations of people drawn from different domestic groups that participate in special-purpose activities, such as a club or professional association.

sororate—Custom by which a deceased wife is replaced by a sister.

status—Position or standing, socially recognized, ascribed to or achieved by an individual or group. Compare role.

storable staples—Food such as grain that can be stored for a whole year or more and used as food reserves during periods of drought or warfare.

stratification—An arrangement of statuses or subgroups within a society according to socially superior and inferior ranks that produce inequality.

stratified redistribution—Obligatory payments of goods and valuables collected by a centralized authority. Only a portion of the goods is given back. The redistributor retains the largest share and ends up with considerable wealth. Compare with redistribution.

structuralism—Concerned with uniformities that arise from unconscious thought and the structure of the brain.

subculture—A culture associated with a minority, majority, class, caste, or other group within a larger sociocultural system.

subsistence—How people obtain the necessities of life, particularly food and shelter, from the environment.

sucking cure—Part of the curing performance in which objects (representing spirit producing illness) are removed from the patient's body.

suitor service—BRIDEWEALTH rendered in the form of labor.

surface structure—The directly observed form of an utterance.

surplus—Refers to production over and above the immediate subsistence needs of food producers and their dependents. Surplus, however, is not superfluous from the producers' standpoint.

symbol—An object or behavior that has culturally defined meaning, without necessarily relating to its inherent physical quality. A symbol conveys greater meaning than the object for which it stands.

symbolic thought—Thought representative or suggestive of an idea or emotion other than that carried by an object itself.

syntax—The sequential patterning of MORPHEMES permitted in a language.

T

taboo—A culturally determined prohibition on an activity, plant, animal, person, or place.

TAT (Thematic Apperception Test)—A method used by psychological anthropologists to study cultural values. Subjects are asked to describe what is happening in a picture and what they think ought to happen.

the Sapir-Whorf hypothesis—The theory of linguistic relativity which states that the perception of reality varies in accordance with the language of the speaker.

Thomas Malthus—British economic and demographic theorist known for his prediction that increasing population, if not checked, will result in massive food shortages.

tool—An object, not part of the user's body, that the user holds or carries during or just prior to use and that is used to alter the form or location of a second object with which it was previously unconnected.

totemism—A form of communal cult in which all members of a kin group have mystical relations with one or more natural objects from which they believe the are descended.

totems—Plants, animals, phenomena, or objects symbolically associated with particular descent groups as identifying insignia.

transformation-representation—The communicative aspect of art that conveys information through symbols.

transhumance—A pastoralist strategy that moves camps and animals to higher and cooler maintain pastures in the heat of the summer and to lower elevations in the winter. Compare with NOMADIC PASTORALISM.

trekking—A prolonged hunting and gathering trip common among the Yanomami, during which villagers break up into small groups and stay at distant campsites.

tribute—The rendering of goods, either food or wealth, to an authority such as a chief, emperor, or king.

U

unilineal descent—The reckoning of descent either exclusively through males or exclusively through females.

universal pattern—A set of categories comprehensive enough to afford logical and classificatory organization for the range of artifacts, traits, ways, and institutions to be observed in all cultural systems.

uxorilocal residence—When the husband lives in the wife's home.

V

values—Shared ideas or standards about the worthiness or appropriateness of goals and lifestyles.

virilocal residence—When the wife lives in the husband's home.

W

warfare—Formalized armed combat by teams of people who represent rival territories or political communities.

witchcraft—The practice of harming people by supernatural means; through psychic powers, not through the use of tangible objects.

Name Index

Acheson, James, 200
Adair, Linda, 78
Agar, Michael, 45
Alba, Richard, 215
Albers, Patricia, 101
Aldous, Peter, 96
Alland, Alexander, Jr., 288
Ames, Kenneth, 113
Anderson, Richard, 99, 289
Arensberg, Conrad, 259, 293
Armelagos, George, 80, 212
Arnould, Eric J., 126
Ascher, R., 39
Asfaw, Berhane, 31
Atkinson, Jane, 269
Awe, Bolanlie, 233

Bailey, R., 61
Bakker, Jim, 284
Baksh, Michael, 63, 175
Balee, William, 172
Bamberger, Joan, 226
Barber, Bernard, 205
Barfield, Thomas, 69
Barlett, Peggy, 70
Barnes, J. A., 126
Barnouw, Victor, 245
Barry, H., 138, 271
Barth, Frederick, 67
Bartlett, Peggy, 302
Bartram, William, 184
Bar-Yosef, Ofer, 33
Bates, Daniel, 66, 68
Bayliss-Smith, Timothy, 69
Beattie, John, 189
Beckerman, Stephen, 148
Bell, Daniel, 72
Belmonte, Thomas, 202, 203
Belsham, Martha, 73
Bender, Donald, 126
Benedict, Ruth, 112, 115, 246, 247, 250, 317
Bentley, G., 82
Berdan, Frances, 274
Berlin, Brent, 45
Bernard, H. Russel, 16, 300
Bernardi, Bernardo, 170
Bernheimer, Lucinda, 160
Berreman, Gerald, 196, 205

Bickerton, Derek, 33
Biocca, Ettore, 171
Biolsi, Thomas, 172
Bittles, Alan, 140
Bixler, Ray, 139, 141,
Blackwood, Evelyn, 101, 102
Blanton, R. E., 126
Bloch, Marc, 198
Boas, Franz, 315, 316, 317, 319
Bock, Philip, 249, 252
Boesch, Christophe, 29
Boesch, Hedwige, 29
Bongaarts, John, 76, 78, 80
Bonta, Bruce, 170
Bonvillian, Nancy, 46
Borker, Ruth, 46
Boserup, Ester, 58, 62, 77
Bossen, Laurel, 138, 233
Boster, James, 136, 138
Bourgois, Phillipe, 223, 224
Bowles, S., 192
Boyd, Robert, 42, 140
Bradley, Candice, 88
Bradsher, Keith, 207
Brintnall, D., 206
Brodkin [Sacks], Karen, 228
Brown, Cecil A., 44
Brown, Judith, 232
Brown, Lester, 56, 59, 67
Brown, Peter, 302
Brown, Ronald, 194, 198
Brozan, Nadine, 103
Brumberg, Joan Jacobs, 261
Brunton, Ron, 184
Buckley, Thomas, 227
Bureau of Labor Statistics, 242
Burton, Robert V., 154, 253
Bush, Mark, 65
Butterfield, Fox, 194, 224

Cain, Meade, 82
Caldwell, John, 81, 83, 84, 87, 88
Caldwell, Pat, 87
Callender, Charles, 99
Campbell, Shirley, 110
Carlos, John, 43
Carlson, Vicki, 142

Carneiro, Robert, 185, 186
Carroll, Lucy, 205
Carstairs, G. M., 96
Cashdan, Elizabeth, 112
Caspari, Rachel, 32
Cattle, Dorothy, 300
Chagnon, Napoleon, 171, 172, 174, 175
Chakravarti, A. K., 282
Chambers, Erve, 299
Chang Chih-I, 67
Child, Alice, 227
Child, I., 253
Child, J., 227
Chodorow, Nancy, 246
Chomsky, Noam, 43, 191, 192
Cicchetti, Dante, 142
Cleaver, Eldridge, 48
Coe, Michael, 274
Cohen, Joel, 55
Cohen, Mark N., 80, 82
Cohen, Myron, 132
Cohen, Ronald, 186, 299
Cohen, Y., 143
Cohn, Bernard, 205
Collins, Randall, 13
Collinvaux, Paul, 65
Condominas, George, 65
Conley, Francis, 239
Constanza, R., 56
Conyers, John, 223
Cook, James, 186
Counts, Dorothy, 228, 231
Crooks, Deborah, 309
Crossette, Barbara, 234
Curvin, Robert, 194

Dahl, Robert, 206
D'Altroy, Terrence, 194
D'Andrade, Roy, 13, 257, 311
Darwin, Charles, 26, 315
Dasgupta, Partha, 83, 84
de Waal, Frans, 36
Deacon, Terrence, 44
Dehavenon, Anna Lou, 133, 144, 202, 310
DeLamater, John, 96
Deloria, Vine, 278
DeMarrais, Elizabeth, 191

DeMott, Benjamin, 143, 192, 196, 206
Denbow, James, 57
Denevan, William, 57
Dentan, Robert, 111, 167
Devereux, George, 78
Dewalt, B. R., 4
DeWalt, Kathleen, 4
Di Leonardo, Micaela, 228
Diamond, Jared, 219
Dickman, Mildred, 84
Dickson, D. Bruce, 185
Diderot, Denis, 314
Diemberger, Hildegard, 252
Divale, William, 153, 154, 170
Djerassi, Carl, 78
Dole, Gertrude, 166
Dominguez, Boanerges, 308
Donald, Leland, 60, 113
Drew, Elizabeth, 206
DuBois, Cora, 249, 250
Dumond, Don, 82
Dumont, Louis, 204
Duran, Diego, 275
Duranti, Alessandro, 46
Durkheim, Emile, 280
Dyson-Hudson, Rada, 68, 137

Earle, Timothy, 60, 113, 172, 182, 187, 188, 189, 190
Eaton, S. Boyd, 174
Edgerton, Robert B., 219, 236, 256
Edwards, C., 252
Eklun, Staffen, 305
Eliade, Mircea, 271
Eloul, R., 138, 233
Ember, Carol, 154, 171
Ember, Melvin, 101, 154, 171
Emspak, Frank, 221
Engels, Friedrich, 315, 317
Erickson, Ken, 309
Errington, Fredrick, 93
Estes, J. W., 77, 78
Estioko-Griffin, Agnes, 231
Evans-Pritchard, E. E., 169

Falwell, Jerry, 284
Family Economics Research Group (USDA), 90
Fausto-Sterling, Anne, 93
Fei Hsiao-t'ung, 67
Feil, Daryl, 235
Feinman, G., 186
Feit, Harvey, 305
Ferguson, Adam, 314
Ferguson, R. Brian, 115, 170, 172, 175, 176
Ferraro, Gary, 304, 308, 309
Fessler, Daniel, 140
Finkelhor, David, 142
Fiske, Alan Page, 255, 256
Fittkau, E. J., 65
Fletcher, Michael, 221
Folbre, Nancy, 133,
Fortune, Reo, 266
Foster, George, 199, 200
Fouts, Deborah H., 34
Fouts, Roger S., 34
Frayer, David, 32
Frayser, Suzanne, 95
Frazer, James, 266
Freedman, Robert, 300
Freud, Sigmund, 141, 245, 246, 317
Fried, Morton H., 111, 186
Frisancho, A. R., 78
Frisch, Rose, 78
Frosh, S., 142
Frumm, John, 278
Fulton, Robert, 99
Funt, Allen, 250

Gal, S., 47
Galaty, John G., 69
Galef, B. G., 29
Galilei, Galileo, 16
Gallimore, Ronald, 252
Gandhi, Mohandas, 283
Gardner, B. T., 34
Gardner, R. A., 34
Garson, Barbara, 73
Gaulin, Stephen, 136, 138
Gay, Judith, 102
Geertz, Clifford, 3, 9
George, Shanti, 86, 282
Gewertz, Deborah, 93
Gibbons, Ann, 29
Gilmore, David, 93
Giner, Miguel, 309
Gintis, H., 192
Glaser, Danya, 142
Glasser, Ira, 220
Glazer, Nathan, 216
Gmelch, George, 266
Gohlen, R. G., 76

Goldschmidt, Walter, 256
Goldstein, Melvyn, 129
Goliber, Thomas J., 87
Good, B., 65
Good, Kenneth, 175
Goodall, Jane, 28, 30, 31
Goodman, M., 212
Goodwin, Marjorie Harness, 46
Goody, Jack, 42, 136, 236
Goudsblom, Johan, 54
Gough, Kathleen, 133, 205
Gould, Richard, 112
Graber, Robert, 77
Gramby, Richard, 155, 232
Greenberg, Joseph, 33
Gregersen, Edgar, 95, 97, 99
Gregor, Thomas, 98, 148, 168, 226
Griffin, P. Bion 231
Gross, Daniel R., 65
Guenther, Mathias, 57
Gulliver, P., 68

Haas, Jonathan, 186
Hacker, Andrew, 103, 194, 221
Hadden, Jeffrey, 285
Hakansson, N. Thomas, 129
Hamer, Dean, 99
Hames, Raymond, 175
Hamilton, Sahni, 78
Handwerker, W. P., 80
Hannerz, Ulf, 4
Haraway, Donna, 13
Harner, Michael, 154, 264, 268, 274
Harrington, Charles, 253
Harris, D., 72
Harris, Helen, 95
Harris, Marvin, 13, 19, 65, 81, 87, 153, 154, 175, 214, 215, 235, 274, 275, 281
Hart, C. W., 170, 171
Hartung, John, 141, 142
Hassan, Fekri, 82
Hawkes, Kristen, 61
Hayden, Brian, 59, 113, 182, 235, 276
Hays, Terence E., 226
Headland, Thomas N., 18, 61
Henderson, Neil, 307
Hendry, Joy, 251
Herbers, J., 103
Herdt, Gilbert, 99, 100, 101, 103

Herman, Edward S., 191, 192
Hern, Warren, 80
Herskovits, M. 236
Hewes, Gordon, 45
Hill, Jane, 34, 49
Hochshild, Arlie Russell, 120
Hockett, Charles, 39
Hogbin, H. Ian, 182
Holton, Gerlad, 13
Hommon, Robert, 186, 187
Hopkins, Keith, 139
Horney, Karen, 245, 246
Horowitz, Tony, 73
Howard, Ted, 284
Huang, C. S., 141
Hughes, C. C., 260
Hunt, Robert, 62
Husain, Tariq, 299
Hymowitz, C., 72

Irwin, Geoffrey, 110
Isaac, Barry, 113
Itani, Jun'ichiro, 29
Ito, Karen L., 307

Jacobs, Sue, 93
James, Caroline, 140
Jenkins, J. H., 258, 259
Jitsukawa, Mariko, 78
Johanson, Donald, photo, 3
Johnson, Allen, 60, 63, 77, 112, 113, 121, 172, 182, 190, 246, 247
Johnson, Douglas, 69
Johnson, Orna, 63
Jonaitas, Aldona, 112
Joseph, Suad, 216

Kaberry, Phyllis, 228
Kaeppler, Adrienne, 295
Kak, Moni, 83
Kang, Elizabeth, 142
Kardiner, Abram, 249, 250
Karno, Marvin, 258
Katz, Richard, 269
Kay, Paul, 44, 45
Keegan, William F., 155
Keeley, Lawrence, 59, 77, 170, 172
Kelly, Raymond, 100
Kelly, Robert L., 60, 61
Kempton, W., 44
Kenmore, P. E., 65
Kennickell, Arthur, 206
Kertzer, David, 86, 136
Khare, Ravindra, 205
Khazanov, K. M., 69

Kirch, Patrick, 186, 187
Kishor, Sunita, 234
Kivisto, Peter, 215
Klass, Morton, 204
Klinge, H., 65
Knauft, Bruce M., 171, 172
Kochems, Lee, 99
Kogod, Kanu S., 309
Konner, Melvin, 306
Korbin, Jill, 84
Koskrity, Paul, 46
Kottak, Conrad, 192, 215
Kroeber, Alfred, 46
Kumagai, Arno, 251
Kumagai, Hisa, 251
Kusin, Jane, 78

Labov, William, 47, 48
Lakoff, Robin T., 49
Lambert, Patricia, 170
Landy, David, 260
Lang, H., 76
Lauman, Edward, 96, 103
Lawrence, Peter, 279
Leacock, Eleanor, 228, 231
Leavitt, Gregory, 140
Lebra, Takie Sugiyama, 251
Lee, Richard, 57, 58, 59, 61, 81, 107, 111, 112, 153, 158, 163, 167
Leeds, Anthony, 201
Leo, John, 220
Lesser, Alexander, 170
Lett, James, 13
Levin, R., 29, 34
LeVine, Robert, 129, 255
Levine, S., 129, 130
Levi-Strauss, Claude, 295, 318, 319
Lewin, Ellen, 103
Lewis, Oscar, 201
Lewontin, Richard, 212, 318
Liebow, Elliot, 223
Liliuokalani, Queen, 180
Lindsey, Robert, 103
Linton, Ralph, 127
Lizot, Jacques, 170, 175
Lockard, Denyse, 102
Lomax, Alan, 293, 295
Long, Bruce, 203, 204
Lowie, Robert, 268
Ludwig, Hilborn, 56
Lunn, P. G., 78

MacCormack, Carol P., 78
MacLachlan, Morgan D., 155, 237
MacLaury, Robert E., 45

MacLeish, Kenneth, 170
MacNeish, Richard, 186
MacQueen, Kathleen, 306
Mahler, Sarah, 308
Malhotra, Anju, 234
Malinowski, Bronislaw, 96, 97, 108, 184, 228, 229, 246, 266, 316, 319
Malo, David, 187
Maloney, William, 204
Malthus, Thomas, 315
Maltz, Daniel, 46
Mamdani, Mahmood, 83
Mandela, Makaziwe, 230
Mandela, Nelson, 230
Manheim, Bruce, 49
Manson, Joseph, 34
Marett, Robert, 264
Margolis, Maxine, 3, 245
Marshall, Donald, 95
Martin, John F., 80
Marx, Karl, 215, 315, 317
Massing, Michael, 223
Mathews, Holly, 228
Mc Falls, Joseph, 88, 89
McCabe, J. Terrence, 68
McCorkle, Constance, 65
McElroy, Ann, 307
McGrew, William C., 30, 306
Mead, Margaret, photo, 3, 13, 247, 248, 317
Meekers, Dominique, 137
Meggitt, Mervyn, 172, 177
Mencher, Joan, 133, 204, 205
Mercator, Gerardus, 251
Merson, Michael, 306
Messinger, J. C., 96
Meyer, J., 192
Miller, Barbara Diane, 138, 233, 234
Minturn, Leigh, 78
Miracle, A., 95
Mitchell, D., 113
Miyadi, D., 29
Møller, Anders P., 94
Monyooe, L. A., 230
Mooney, James, 277
Moore, John, 170, 172
Moran, Emilio, 54, 55,
Morgan, Lewis Henry, 156, 314, 315, 317
Morgan, Marcyliena, 47
Morren, George, 64
Mouer, R., 250
Moynihan, Daniel P., 144, 216
Munroe, Robert, 253
Munroe, Ruth, 253,

Murdock, George Peter, 97, 127, 128, 152, 154, 156, 157
Murphy, Cullen, 304
Murphy, Martin F., 3
Murphy, Robert, 227, 228, 258
Murphy, Robert F., 155
Murphy, Yolanda, 227, 228
Murray, Gerald, 302, 303
Mwamwenda, T. S., 230

Nader, Laura, 207
Nag, Moni, 79, 82, 83, 96
Nardi, Bonnie, 81
Naroll, Raul, 152
Nash, Jill, 138
National Research Council, 54
National Urban League, 194
Neitzel, J., 186
Nelson, Harry, 73
Netting, Robert, 54, 126, 300
Neville, Gwen, 151
Newitt, Jane, 90
Newman, Philip, 265
Nisa of the !Kung, 97–98, 228
Nishida, T., 30
Nishimura, A., 29
Noah, Timothy, 207

Oboler, Regina Smith, 135
Odend'hal, Stuart, 282
Odile, F., 80
Odum, H. T., 55,
Okongwu, Anne, 133
Oliver, Douglas, 182
Opler, Morris, 248
Oppenheimer, Valery, 245
Orans, Martin, 205
Ortner, Sherry, 93
Otterbein, Keith, 170

Pandian, Jacob, 264
Paredes, J. Anthony, 6
Parenti, Michael, 192
Parker, Hilda, 142
Parker, Seymour, 142
Pasternak, Burton, 132
Patterson, Francine, 34
Paztory, Esther, 292
Peletz, Michael G., 237
Pelto, Gretel, 170
Pelto, Pertti, 170
Peterson, Dale, 36
Pettersson, Per, 305
Piao, James, 12

Piker, Steven, 249
Pilling, Arnold, 170, 171
Pimentel, David, 70
Pimentel, M., 70
Pinker, Steven, 33, 42
Pivnik, Anitra, 307
Plath, David, 251
Podolefsky, Aaron, 142
Pohl, Mary, 6
Polanyi, Karl, 106
Popkin, Barry, 78
Population Research Bureau, 89
Porter, Bruce, 194
Posposil, Leonard, 118
Post, John, 80
Price, D., 54, 62
Price-Williams, Douglas, 246, 247
Priestley, Joseph, 16
Pusey, Ann, 140

Radcliffe-Brown, A. R., 316
Raddock, David M., 12
Ragone, Helena, 90
Ramirez, F., 192
Rappaport, Roy A., 63, 64, 280
Rasmussen, Knud, 165
Rathje, William, 304
Renfrew, Colin, 50
Reyna, S. P., 170
Rickford, John, 47, 52
Riddle, J., 77, 78
Rifkind, Jeremy, 284
Riviere, C., 264
Roberts, C., 93
Roberts, Oral, 284
Roberts, Ron, 193, 206
Robertson, Pat, 284
Robins, L., 258
Rodgers, Joan R., 238
Rohner, Ronald, 115
Roosens, Eugene, 211
Root, Marla, 214
Ross, Eric, 81, 87, 175
Ross, Phillip, 51
Roth, Eric, 82
Royce, W. F., 56
Rubin, Deborah S., 228

Sabato, Larry, 206
Sackett, Ross, 119, 120
Sacks, Karen Brodkin, 228
Safa, Helen I., 133
Sahagun, Bernadino de, 275
Sahlins, Marshall, 275
Sakar, Jayanta, 234

Sanday, Peggy Reeves, 226, 228
Sanderson, Stephen, 72
Sanjek, Roger, 4, 16, 204, 216, 217, 220
Sankar, Andrea, 102
Sapir, Edward, 44
Savage-Rumbaugh, S., 29, 34
Scheffler, Harold, 147
Scheidel, Walter, 140
Schepper-Hughes, Nancy, 85, 86, 259, 260, 311
Schick, Kathy, 29
Schields, N. M., 140
Schlegel, Alice, 138, 271, 233
Schultze, Quentin, 285
Scoditti, G., 108, 110
Scott, Colin, 305
Scratches-face, 268
Scrimshaw, Susan, 78, 84
Service, Elman R., 186
Shankman, Paul, 172
Sharff, Jagna Wojcicka, 223, 224
Sharma, Ursula, 234,
Shepher, Joseph, 141
Shostak, Marjorie, 98, 102, 228, 231, 232
Shreve, James, 212
Silk, Joan, 42, 124, 129, 140
Sillén-Tullberg, Birgitta, 94
Simmons, R. C., 260
Simoons, Frederick, 281
Sitting Bull, 277
Skinner, G. William, 86
Small, Meredith, 94
Smedley, Audrey, 210, 222
Smith, Adam, 314
Smith, E. R., 195
Smith, Eric, 61
Smith, M. G., 136
Smith, Raymond, 133
Smith, Tommie, 43
Snowden, Charles T., 35
Soloway, Jacqueline S., 57
Sorenson, Richard, 65
Spencer, Herbert, 315
Spencer, P., 170
Spengler, Joseph, 82
Spickard, Paul, 214
Spira, Alfred, 96
Spiro, Melford E., 228, 246
Ssennyonga, Joseph, 129
Stack, Carol, 133, 144, 145
Stacy, Judith, 160

Stashak, J., 78
Stern, Steve J., 199
Steward, Julian, 317
Stewart, Omer, 278
Stone, Linda, 140
Strauss and Quinn, 248
Strauss, Claudia, 257, 258
Stringer, C. B., 32
Stull, Donald D., 309
Sudarkasa, N., 233
Suggs, David, 95
Sugimoto, Y., 250
Sullivan, Lawrence, 276
Susser, Ida, 217, 238
Swanson, Guy E., 276
Swasy, Alecia, 72

Tannen, Deborah, 46
Tefft, Stanton, 142
Testart, Alain, 59
Thornhill, Nancy, 140
Thurow, Lester, 207
Titon, J. T., 296
Torrey, E. F., 258
Toth, Nicholas, 29
Townsend, Patricia, 307
Trevor-Roper, H., 210
Trigger, Bruce, 155
Turgot, Jean, 314
Turnbull, Colin, 231
Turner, Victor, 271, 272
Tylor, Edward Burnett, 9, 264

U.N. Development
    Programme, 231
U.S. Bureau of Labor
    Statistics,
U.S. Bureau of the Census,
    90, 124, 145, 220, 221,
    242
U.S. Department of
    Agriculture, 90
Ubelaker, Douglas, 308
Uhlman, Allon, 140
United Nations, 89
Upham, Steadman, 186

Vaidyanathan, A., 283
Vaillant, George C., 274
Van Allen, J., 233
Vandermeersch, B., 33
Vandiver, Pamela B., 290
Vanneman, Reeve, 234
Vigil, Diego, 210
Villa, Paola, 275
Visweswaran, Kamala, 230
Volkan, Vamik, 211, 212, 216
Vrana, Debora, 240

Wagley, Charles, 269, 270
Walker, Deward, 170
Wallace, Alfred, 26
Wallace, Anthony F. C.,
    252, 260, 266, 276, 277
Warner, Richard, 258

Washington Post, 221
Watson, Richard, 13
Wayland, C. B., 4
Weaver, Thomas, 210
Weber, Peter, 56
Weil, Peter, 83
Weiner, Annette, 148, 229
Weinstein, Michael, 207
Weisman, Steven, 194
Weismantel, Mary, 126
Weisner, Thomas, 160, 252, 254
Weiss, Gerald, 296
Weller, Susan C., 4
Werner, Dennis, 100
Westermark, Edward, 141, 142
Westoff, Charles, 90
Weston, Kath, 99, 160
Weyer, E., 170
White, Benjamin, 82
White, Douglas, 128
White, J., 154
White, Leslie, 16, 69, 317
White, Timothy, 276
Whitehead, H., 93
Whitehead, Neil, 170
Whitesides, George, 29
Whiting, Beatrice, 245, 253
Whiting, John, 80, 245, 252, 253
Whitten, Andrew, 31

Whorf, Benjamin, 44, 45, 49
Whyte, Martin K., 94
Wilk, Richard R., 126
Williams, Linda M., 142
Williams, T., 223
Williams, Walter, 99
Willigen, John Van, 299
Wilmsen, Edwin, 57
Wilson, E. O., 141
Wilson, Monica, 318
Winkelman, Michael, 269
Winterhalder, Bruce, 61
Witkowski, Stanley, 44, 45
Wolf, A. P., 141
Wolf, A., 131
Wolf, Eric, 213, 274
Wolf, Marjorie, 132
Wolpoff, Milford, 32
Wood, James, 78
Woodburn, James, 59, 164
Worsley, Peter, 277
Wovoka, 277
Wrangham, Richard, 34, 36

Yan, Yunxiang, 132
Yanagisako, Sylvia Junko, 126
Yates, Robin D. S., 199

Zentella, A. C., 49

A

AAVE (African-American Vernacular English), 47–48, 49
abortion, 20, 84. *See also* birth control, infanticide.
Accra, Ghana, ethnicity in, 216
Aché hunters, Paraguay, 60
acid rain and population growth, 88
action anthropology, 299
adaptation, 27
adaptive strategy, 27
adopt-a-daughter, marry-a-sister (*sim pua*) marriage, 132
advertising in capitalism, 20, 117, 121
advocacy and anthropology, 311
aesthetics, 288
Afar desert of Ethiopia, 31
Afar language, 31
affinal relations, 147
affinity, 147
affirmative action, 221
Africa
    click languages in, 40
    economic lag of, 219–220
    fertility rates in, 88
    gender roles, 228–229, 230
    ingenuity, 219
    Ituri forest hunters of, 14
    mortality rates in, 88
    See also individual nations and groups.
African-American language, 47–48, 49
African Americans, 215, 217
    and arrest rate, 194
    discrimination against, 213
    hypertension among, 212
    matrifocality among, 144–145
    youth among, 221, 223–224
African Brazilians, 215
African-American Vernacular English (AAVE), 47–48
age at marriage, 79
age-grade associations, 99, 170
age roles, 20
age sets, 170
aggression, 254
    among apes, 35
    and survival of species, 26
agricultural development and archaeology, 304
agricultural societies, work patterns in, 119, 120

agriculture, 59, 61–67
    and gender hierarchy, 236
    and health, 80
    industrialism and, 70
    intensification of, 185
    irrigation and, 57, 62, 66, 67, 304
    male dominance of, 237
    plows and, 236–237
    slash-and-burn, 62
    See also horticultural societies, slash-and-burn agriculture.
agroforestry, in Haiti, 302–303
agromanagerial state peasantries, 199
agropastoralism, 65. *See also* pastoralism.
Agta of the Philippines, 44, 231
ahimsa, 281
AIDS (acquired immune deficiency syndrome), 103, 306–307
Albanian ethnic conflict, 211
allergens and poverty, 309
alliances
    and children, 81
    and exogamy, 142
    and matrilocality, 155
Alorese of Indonesia, 249–250
Alta do Cruzeiro village, Brazil, 85–86
Alzheimer's disease, 307
Amazon river region, 63, 95, 296
    hunting in, 65, 173–175
    Mundurucu of, 155, 226–227, 228
    Tapirapé of, 269–270
    Yanomami of, 108, 171, 172, 173–175, 176, 235
ambilineal descent, 150
ambilocality, 152, 153
amenorrhea, 79
American Legion, 170
Ameslan (American Sign Language), 34
amitalocality, 152
amok hysteria, 260
anal sex, 97, 101
anarchy among Nuer, 169
Ancient Society (Lewis Henry Morgan), 314, 315
Andaman Islanders, 170
Andes region, 126, 302, 317. *See also* Incas, Peru.
animal biomass in rain forest, 65

animal husbandry and pastoralism, 65, 67, 68. *See also* cattle, pastoralism, pigs.
animal traction power, 54, 236–237
animatism, 264–265
animism, 264
anorexia nervosa, 261
anthropological advocacy, 311
anthropological linguistics, 2. *See also* language analysis, language, linguistics.
anthropological research and action, 299
anthropology, 2
    action, 299
    advocacy and, 311
    and feminism, 229
    and gender, 229
    applied, 2, 6, 299, 301–305
    biological, 2, 6, 309–310
    business and, 308–309
    corporations and, 124, 308–309
    cultural, 2, 6, 16–17
    demographics and, 308
    development and, 6, 301–305
    ecological, 4, 55
    economic, 4
    forensic, 6, 308
    linguistic, 46
    medical, 5, 6, 306
    physical, 2, 6
    political, 5
    psychological, 5
    urban, 6
    why study, 5–6
antimonopoly laws, 124
antithesis (effect by contrast), 296
Apaches, 14
apes
    and aggression, 35
    and language, 33–35
    and tools, 28
    See also chimpanzees, primates.
applied anthropology, 2, 6, 299, 301–305
aquaculture, 57
Arab pastoralists, 68
Aranda people, 292
Arawak language, 296
archaeology, 2, 6, 304–305
architecture, 15
Arctic Circle, 59
Arctic hysteria, 260
Arctic life, 268

Argonauts of the Western Pacific
    (Bronislaw Malinowski), 108
Armenian ethnicity, 216
armor, 15
art, 20
    and invention, 290
    and religion, 291–293
    as a cultural category, 288–290
    cultural patterning of, 290–291
    male dominance in, 237
    See also aesthetics.
Arunta of Australia, 270, 292
Ashanti of West Africa, 126, 147–148
Asia, 237, 250. *See also individual*
    nations and groups.
Asian Americans, 215, 218. *See also*
    individual nations and groups.
Asmat gravepost, 292
assimilationism, 215–216, 220. *See*
    also ethnicity, race.
Australia, 59. *See also individual ethnic*
    groups.
Australia, Arunta of, 270
Australian lifestyle and cargo cults,
    279–280
Australian merino sheep, 302
Australopithecus afarensis, 31
Australopithecus garhi, 31
authoritarian behavior, 254. *See also*
    leadership.
authority, appeal to, 296. *See also*
    ideology.
automation and gender roles, 240.
    See also hyperindustrialism.
avunculocality, 152, 154, 155
Azande of the Sudan, 99, 100, 102
Azerbaijani ethnicity, 216
Aztecs, 266, 274–276, 316

B

Ba Kota of Gabon Republic, 292
Baganda of Uganda, 306–307
Bali, 11
Ballybran parish, Ireland, 259
band formation, 59
band size, 81
band societies, 163–166. *See also*
    foraging societies, hunter-
    gatherer societies.
Bangladesh, 82
Bantu agriculturists, 14, 108, 111
bar mitzvah, 271
Bari of Venezuela, 148
basic personality structure, 249, 252
Basseri of Iran, 67
bat mitzvah, 271
Bathonga of Mozambique, 18, 131
Bathurst Island, Australia, 170
behavior, stereotyped, 27
beliefs, 20
    about health, 307
    about the supernatural, 265–266
    and ethnocentrism, 211

semen, 96, 100, 101, 147–148
    See also religion, values.
bias and objectivity, 12
bicultural identity, 49, 209–212
big man systems, 177–178, 181–182.
    See also Hawaii, Mae Enga,
    Trobriand Islands.
bilateral descent, 150, 152–153
bilocality, 152, 153
binary contrasts, 295
biological anthropology, 2, 6,
    309–310
biological race, 212–215
bipedalism, 32
birth control, 79, 89–90. *See also*
    abortion.
birth rate, 79
birth spacing, 79
birth status, 135. *See also* caste, class,
    descent.
Blackness, defining, 214–215
Blacks. *See* Africa, African Americans,
    African Brazilians.
blended families, 160
blood relations, 147. *See also* kinship.
blood type, 212. *See also* race.
boasting and redistribution, 112. *See*
    also big man systems,
    potlatches.
Bolivia, 304
bonobo chimpanzees, 36
born-again Christians, 284–285
Boserup's population theory, 77
Botswana, 57, 59
bound morphemes, 40
bovicide in India, 19. *See also* cattle.
boy-inseminating rituals, 101
Brahman caste, 203, 204
Brazil
    anal sex in, 99
    art, 289
    infanticide in, 85–86
    landowner rights in, 118
    marriage in, 135
    Mehinacu of, 98, 167–168
    Mundurucu of, 155, 226–227, 228
    social race in, 214–215
    Tapirapé of, 269–270
    Yanomami of, 108, 171, 172,
    173–175, 176, 235.
breadwinner model schema, 257
breastfeeding, 78, 79, 300
bride burnings, 234
bride price, 136
bride service, 137
bridewealth, 116, 136, 230, 233. *See*
    also dowry.
British Columbia, Canada, 60
British functionalism, 316
Bronx, New York, 307, 308
Buddhism, 22, 130, 266, 273, 285.
    See also Tibet.
Bunyoro of Uganda, 188–189, 231

Burundi, ethnic conflict in, 211
business organizations, studying, 309
business and anthropology, 308–309
business, U.S. women in, 240

C

calcium deficiency, 260
caloric intake of !Kung San, 57
caloric yield of irrigation agriculture,
    67
calorie cost of industrial agriculture,
    70
Campa of Peru, 296
Canada, hunter-gatherers in, 60
candlefish, 60, 113
cannibalism, 274–276. *See also* Aztecs.
canoes, 54
Cantonese language, 52
capitalism, 20, 116–119, 121, 123
    and art, 292
    in the United States, 123, 124
    peasants in, 199
    See also corporations,
    hyperindustrialism,
    industrialism, price market
    economy.
cargo cults, 278–279, 280.
Caribbean Islands, social race, 214
Carriacou Island, Caribbean, 102
carrying capacity, 55, 56, 76. *See also*
    population pressure.
Carter Center, Atlanta, 211
cash aid, 123
caste in India, 203–205, 281. *See also*
    class, ethnicity, race.
casting metal, 54
Catholic church, 49, 176
Catholic ethnic conflict, 211
Catholic first communion, 271
cattle
    and culture, 248
    as currency, 116
    as gift redistribution, 111
    in India, 18–19, 281–283, 300
    See also East Africa, Kenya,
    pastoralism.
causality and language, 44
Central American Hispanics, 209
ceramics, 15, 54, 290–291
Chamars of India, 205
change by positive feedback, 186
Channel Islands, California, 170
charcoal, 54, 302
chastity, among the Kadar, 136
chemical fertilizers, 70
Cherokee of Tennessee, 183–184
Cheyenne of the Great Plains, 170,
    172
chiefdoms,
    among the Kwakiutl, 153
    and rise of state, 185
    evolution of, 181–183
    versus big man systems, 182

chiefly class in Hawaii, 186–188
child care and incest, 142, 248
child labor, 82, 84
child rearing,
    by gays/lesbians, 160
    cost of U.S., 89–90
    costs/benefits of, 80–84
childhood training and personality,
    252, 253
children,
    and school nutrition, 309
    effects of social environment on,
        254–255
    maltreatment of, 78
Chimborazo Province, Ecuador,
    302
chimpanzees,
    aggression among, 35
    art among, 288
    cooperation among, 36
    culture among, 29
    tool using among, 30, 31
    See also apes, hominids.
Chimu, Peru art, 289
China, 10, 231
    eating dog meat in, 12
    extended families in, 131–132
    health beliefs in, 307
    incest in, 139
    infanticide in, 86
    irrigation in, 66
    lesbianism in, 102
    redistribution in, 113
    repression in, 192
    tonal languages of, 40
    See also rice culture.
Chinese in Indonesia, 215
Chinese in Taiwan, 131, 140
chosen glory, 212
chosen trauma, 212
Christian ethnics, 216
Christianity, 49, 266, 273, 285
Chrysanthemum and the Sword, The
    (Ruth Benedict), 250
churingas, 292
churning in welfare bureaucracy, 310
circulating connubia, 138
circumcision, 272. See also male
    initiation rituals.
circumscription of societies, 185
clans, 152
class, 20
    and lifestyle, 197–198
    and power, 191, 196–198
    chauvinism, 217
    chiefly, 186–188
    closed/open, 196
    in the United States, 206–207
    language and, 46–48
    lifestyle and, 197–198
    working, 238
    See also caste, ethnicity, poverty,
        race, stratification.

class consciousness and racial/ethnic
    chauvinism, 217
climate change and population
    growth, 88
closed-class systems, 196
code switching in language, 48–49
coercion
    and ideology, 190–192
    and landownership, 119
    and rent, 119
    and the state, 192, 193–194
    See also power.
cognatic ambilineal descent, 151
cognatic bilateral descent, 150–151
cognatic clans, 153
cognatic descent, 148–152
cognatic lineages, 151, 153
cognition and schemas, 257
coital scheduling, 79–80
coitus interruptus, 79
colonization and potlatches, 114
Coming of Age in Samoa (Margaret
    Mead), 247
commerce, male dominance in, 237.
    See also price market exchange,
    trade.
commodities, in capitalism, 117,
    121. See also capitalism.
communal cults, 266, 270
communal land ownership, 164
communal rituals, 271
communism, "primitive," 163–164
communitas, 273
competition, 26–27, 106
    among racial/ethnic groups,
        215–218
    over hunting territory, 173–175
completed fertility rate, 79
computers and gender roles, 240
condoms, 103, 306
conjoint marriage, 130
consanguineal relations, 147
consensus and work patterns, 119
consumer goods and demand, 121
    See also advertising, capitalism.
consumption
    and capitalism, 117
    in affluent societies, 120
    in United States, 248
contraception, 20, 103, 306
    and abortion, 84
    and infanticide, 84
    for U.S. teens, 103
contract archeology, 6
contrast and myth, 295
cooperation, 106
    among apes, 35
    among Machiguenga, 63
    See also reciprocity.
corporate group family, 152
corveé labor, 199
Council of Elders, Iroquois, 232
crafts and art, 289

Cree of Quebec, 305
crime
    and guns in United States, 194
    in U.S. inner cities, 223–224
    See also violence.
cross cousins, 150
cross-cousin marriage, 157
Crow of the Great Plains, 100, 170,
    266, 267–268
crude birth rate, 79
crude death rate, 79
Cuban Americans, 209–210
cult types, 266
cultural anthropology, 2, 6, 16–17
cultural configurations, 246
cultural differences in childhood
    training, 252
cultural diversity, 6
cultural evolution, 33, 69–70
cultural innovation, 13
cultural maintenance system, 253
cultural materialism, 22–23. See also
    materialism.
cultural patterning of art, 290–291
cultural patterns, 246–247
cultural personality, 249–252
cultural relativism, 11
cultural rules, 16–17
cultural scripts, 257
cultural takeoff, 26, 32–33, 54
cultural themes, variations in, 248
culture, 9
    and art, 288–290
    and biological race, 215
    and chimpanzee termiting, 29
    and domestic sphere, 126
    and language, 42–43
    and mental illness, 258
    and personality, 245–246, 317
    of poverty, 202, 203, 248
    of sun, 14
Culture and Ecology Research
    Project, 256
culture shock, 4
culture-specific psychoses, 260
cunnilingus, 97
currency, 116
Czechoslovakia, ceramics in, 54

D

Dahomey of West Africa, 102
    animism among, 264
    female initiation among, 101
    woman-woman marriage among,
        134
    women warriors among, 235–236
    women's roles among, 232
dance, 20
    evolution of, 293–295
    social function of, 294
death rate, 79. See also disease,
    mortality, warfare.
deconstructionism, 319

dehumanization of minorities, 211
Delaware Indians of Oklahoma, 279
deliberate teaching, 30
demand creation, 121
demographic patterns, medical control of, 20
demographic transition, 87
demographics and anthropology, 308
dependence, defined, 254
depletion of resources, 57, 59, 88
depression and culture, 258
descent, 147–152, 211
descent rules, 148–152
descriptive linguistics, 6
designer babies, 90
developing countries and child labor, 84
development and applied anthropology, 6, 301–305
dharma, 203
dialect formation, 50–51
dialectical materialism, 317–318
diffusion, 13, 14, 16
diffusionism, 316
diglossia, 49
diminishing returns and carrying capacity, 55, 56, 76
DINKS, 90
dioxin pollution, 71
direct observation of behavior, 4
discipline, domestic, 20
discrimination,
    against women in India, 234
    racial/ethnic, 213, 217, 218
    "reverse," 221
disease, 80, 307
    and Kwakiutl, 114
    and Machiguenga, 63
    See also health.
displacement in language, 39
dispute resolution, 164
dissension and polyandry, 130
division of labor, 20, 67, 72
DNA kinship, 147
domestic culture, 126
domestic economy, 20
domestic groups and incest avoidance, 139
domesticated animals, 65
dominance, 254
Dominican Republic, 209
dowry, 137, 233, 238
draft power, 54, 65, 236–237
drug use, 223–224, 306–307
dual residence, among Machiguenga, 63

E

East Africa, 126, 254
    Bunyoro of Uganda, 188–189
    personality in, 256

thorn forest biomass in, 65
    See also individual nations and groups.
Ebonics, 47–48, 52
ecclesiastical cults, 266, 273–274
ecological anthropology, 4, 55
ecology,
    and environment, 55
    and religion, 280
    social, 255
economic anthropology, 4
economic development in Zanzibar, 305
economics of discrimination, 217
economy, 20, 106
ecosystems, 20, 283
Ecuador,
    animism in, 264
    Zumbagua of, 126
education, 20
    and fertility, 87–88
    and racism, 221
    compulsory universal, 192
egalitarian redistribution, 118. See also reciprocity.
egalitarian societies,
    and gender, 234
    and reciprocity, 111
    leadership in, 163–169
    redistribution in, 118
ego, in descent rules, 149
Egyptians, ancient, 139, 264, 266
electronic church in America, 284–285
electronic sweatshops, 73
Elmhurst-Corona, ethnic racial struggle in, 218
embryo technology, 90
emic view of organizations, 300–301
emics, 17, 18, 19
    and class consciousness, 196
enculturation, 10, 13, 20
endogamy, 139. See also exogamy.
energy and cultural evolution, 69
energy production, evolution of, 54
energy-capturing technology, 54
England, attitudes toward schizophrenia in, 259
English language, 40, 50, 51
Enlightenment period, 314
environment, 54, 55
environmental protection and garbalogy, 304–305
epidemic disease, 80
Eskimo kinship terminology, 156
estrous, 94
ethnic and racial chauvinism, 217
ethnic empowerment, 211
ethnic groups, 209–212, 212–215, 213, 217
ethnic identity, 215–216
ethnicity, 209–212
    and language, 46–48

ethnic pluralism, 215
ethnocentrism, 10–11, 316
    and development, 302
    confronting, 211–212
    controlling, 299–301
Ethnographic Atlas (George P. Murdock), 153, 156, 157
ethnographic present, 4, 57
ethnography, 4
    and business, 309
    and census, 308
    female representation in, 228–229
ethnology, 5
etics, 17 18, 19
    and class consciousness, 196
etic view of organizations, 300–301
Etoro of Papua New Guinea, 100
Euro-American art, 288, 291
Euro-American power groups, 217
Eurocentrism, 44, 219
Europe,
    big men in, 279
    immigration to United States from, 215–216
    infanticide in, 86
    sex in, 96
    uprisings in, 192
    See also individual nations and groups.
evidence, appeal to, 296
evolution of brain and language, 44
evolution of human species, 31–33
evolutionism, 315, 317
exchange, defined, 106
exogamy, 139
    advantages of, 140
    and trade, 142
exploitation and gender, 238
extended family, 131–132, 160
extramarital sex
    among Mehinacu, 98
    in United States, 103
    taboos against, 79

F

factory work, 119
fallow periods, 65
family,
    complex and incest, 142
    diversity in United States, 160
    economy, reciprocity in, 107
    extended, 131–132, 160
    functions of, 127
    incest avoidance in, 142–143, 246
    nuclear, 127
    organization of, 127–133
    structure of, 20, 242–243
    violence in, 246
Fang of Gabon, 264
farmer personality, 257
fatherhood, defined, 147. See also gender roles, semen beliefs.

feasting, 108, 181–182. *See also* big
    man systems, potlatches.
Feast of San Genaro, 216
fecundity, 78, 79
fellatio, 97
female-headed households, 238
female homosexuality, 101–102
female infanticide, 86, 176
female inferiority, belief in, 226. *See
    also* gender roles, women.
female sexuality, 93, 94, 96
female status and war, 235
feminism, 49, 229, 243
feminist anthropologists, 229
feminist ethnographers, 230
feminization of poverty, 238. *See also*
    poverty.
fertility, 20, 76
    and agriculturalists, 82
    and education, 87–88
    and nutrition, 78
    and production, 70
    and sedentary peoples, 82
    and U.S. child rearing, 89–90
    of soil, 65
fertility rates, 79, 88
fertilizer, 57, 67, 70
fetuses, treatment of, 78. *See also*
    abortion.
feudal peasants, 198
fictive kin, 108, 158
fieldwork, 3–4, 16–17
fire, 54
fisheries, 56, 57
floodplain irrigation, 62
folktales, 295
Fontana del Re, 202
food and population, 76, 88
food assistance programs, 123
food production
    among Kwakiutl, 113–115
    and population growth, 76–77
    in industrialism, 70
food storage, 60, 184, 185, 187, 190
foraging societies, 120, 171, 231. *See
    also* hunter-gatherer societies.
foraging strategies, 61
force and property, 117. *See also*
    coercion, power.
forced labor, 63
forensic anthropology, 6, 308
formal linguistics, 39
formal rules of conduct, 17
form in art, 288
Fort Rupert, Hudson Bay Company,
    115
fossil fuels, 54
France, 96
fraternal polyandry, 129
free enterprise, 124
freeloading and reciprocity, 107
free morphemes, 40
free time in affluent societies, 120

French language, 50
functionalism, 316

G

Gaelic language, 50
game animals and warfare, 173–175
games, 20
Ganges plain, 282
Ganges Valley deforestation, 285
Garbage Project, 304
garbalogy, 304
garden landownership, *119*
gasoline and production, 70
gay people in United States, 103,
    160. *See also* homosexuality.
gender
    and hyperindustrialism, 238–240
    and language, 46, 49
    and strength, 234
    versus sex, 93
gender differences, 226
    and depression, 258
    in literacy/numeracy, 237. *See also*
        gender roles.
gender discrimination in India, 234
gender exploitation, 238
gender hierarchy,
    change in, 241–243
    variations in, 234, 331–236
gender ideologies, 226–227
gender preferences and infanticide,
    86
gender roles, 20, 154, 155
    among !Kung, 228
    among U.S. Blacks, 144–145
    and female homosexuality,
        101–102
    and Oedipus complex theory,
        245
    and politics, 231
    and reproduction, 78
    and same-sex sex, 99
    in rice growing, 67
gender scripts, 226
*General History of the Things of New
    Spain* (Bernard de Sahagun),
    276
generation gap, 13
generosity and exchange, 118
genes, 26
genetic variation, 26, 212
genetics and homosexuality, 99
genetics, discoveries in, 16
genetrix, 147
genitor, 147
genotypes, 26
German language, 50
Ghana, 220
Ghost Dance, 277
gifts and trade, 108–110. *See also*
    alliances, kula ring trade.
God language, 49
gods, high. *See also* religion.

Golden Bough, The (Sir James Frazer),
    266
Gombe chimpanzees, 29
Gombe National Park, 28, 30, 35
Goodall, Jane, 28
gospel of wealth, 284
grammar, 40, 43
Great Famine in Ireland, 259
Great Plain, 170, 285
Greek language, 50
Greenland Eskimos, 170. *See also*
    Inuit song duels.
groom price, Nagovisi, 138
growth rate through prehistory, 82
Gururumba of New Guinea, 260,
    265–266
Gusii of West Africa, 129, 255

H

Haitian agroforestry, 302–303
Haitian Americans, 209
harems, 102
Harlem, 194
Hausa of West Africa, 102
Hawaii,
    big man warfare in, 182
    chiefdom in, 187–188
    incest in, 139
    language of, 40
    state formation in, 186–188
Hawaiian kinship terminology, 156
hazardous waste, 71. *See also*
    pollution.
headmanship, 166–168. *See also*
    leadership.
health
    and agriculture, 80
    and poverty, studying, 309
    and disease, 307–308
health services and ethnocentrism,
    300
Hebrew religion, 281. *See also*
    Judaism.
Hehe of East Africa, 256
hermaphrodites, 93
heteroglossia, 49
heterosexuality, 96–97. *See also*
    sexuality.
hierarchies, domestic, 20
high gods, 276
Hindi, 50
Hindu ahimsa doctrine, 281–283
Hindu farmers, 247
Hindu India, sexuality in, 95–96
Hindu remarriage, 133
Hispanic Americans,
    community activism among, 218
    diversity among, 209–210
    historical archeology, 6
    historical linguistics, 6
    historical particularism, 316
    in inner cities, 223–224
    matrifocal families of, 145

HIV infection, 306–307. *See also* AIDS.
hobbies, 20
hoes and gender, 236–237
holism, 2, 300, 302
Holocaust, 211. *See also* ethnocentrism, Jewish people.
homelessness, 202, 310
hominids, 27, 28, 31
Homo erectus, 31
Homo habilis, 31, 33
Homo sapiens, 2, 32, 54, 81, 93, 288
    female, 101–102
    genetic basis for, 99
homosexuality, 79
    in United States, 103
    male, 98–99
    ritualized, 100, 101, 102
Hopi language, 45
horticultural societies, 63
    polygyny in, 128
    work hours among, 120
    See also slash-and-burn agriculture.
horticulture. *See also* agriculture, slash-and-burn agriculture.
household functions, 126
housework
    and gender roles, 240
    as part of production, 120
housing allowances, 123
Hudson Bay Company, 115
human culture, capacity for, 26
human evolution, 33,
human fossil remains, 31
human paleontology, 6
Human Resources Administration, 311
human sacrifice, 274–276
human sexuality, 93–96
hunger, 310
hunger and food distribution, 88
hunger and poverty, 309
Huns, 68
hunter-gatherer societies, 59, 81, 235
    and foraging theory, 61
    and freeloading, 107
    and nuclear family, 127
    and reciprocity, 107
    and work patterns, 119
    !Kung San, 57–58
    types of, 59
    women among, 231
    See also foraging societies.
Huron of Ontario, 155
Hurricane Andrew, 194
Hutterite fertility, 76
Hutu ethnic conflict, 211
hypergamy, 138
hyperindustrialism, 72, 238–240
hypothesis, 5
hysteria, 260–261

I
Iban of Borneo, 155
Ibo (Igbo) of Yoruba, 232, 233
ideologies of gender, 226–227
ideology and power, 190–192
illegal alien label, 218
image of limited good, 199–201, 248
imagery in rhetoric, 296
immigrants, 218
immortality beliefs and ethnocentrism, 211
imprisonment in United States, 193–194
in vitro fertilization, 90
inbreeding avoidance, 139, 140
Incas, 139, 189–190, 231, 266, 273, 275, 316
incest, 139, 246
    forms of, 142
    in Sweden, 143
incest avoidance, 139–143
incest taboo, 139
income and U.S. taxation, 207
income gap in United States, 206–207
independent inventions in Old and New Worlds, 14
India, 11, 254
    and irrigation, 62
    and schizophrenia, 259
    castes in, 18–19, 203–205, 281–283
    cattle in, 300
    child labor in, 83
    dowry in, 138
    gender hierarchy in, 236
    gender roles in, 236, 237
    infanticide in, 86
    landowner rights, 118
    polyandry in, 129
Indians of Ecuador, 302
indirect infanticide, 85–86
individualistic cults, 266, 267
Indo-European language tense system, 45
Indonesia,
    Alorese of, 249
    Chinese in, 215
    gender roles in, 237
    Kapauku of, 118
    trade in, 108
    See also New Guinea, Papua New Guinea.
industrial archeology, 6
Industrial Revolution, 54
industrial societies,
    and nuclear family, 127
    food energy systems in, 70–71
    male dominance in, 237
    manufacturing in, 72
    production costs in, 71
    reproduction modes in, 87

work hours among, 120
    See also hyperindustrialism.
infant betrothals, 136
infanticide, 20, 77
    and contraception, 84
    and warfare, 176
    in Brazil, 85–86
    indirect, 78
    See also abortion, birth control.
informants, 4
information economy and women, 242
infrastructure, 20
    and political control, 183–184
    and population growth, 88
    of Japan, 21
INH (isoniazid), 307
inheritance and legitimacy, 135
Inis Beag, Ireland, 95, 96
initiation rituals, 272
innate capacity for grammar, 43
inner-city minorities and crime, 194
inner self, 251
innovation, 13, 22–23, 58–59
insecticides, 70
instinct as cause of war, 171
Institute for Marine Sciences in Zanzibar, 305
intensification, 56
    and fertility, 82
    of agriculture, 185
    of work, 119–120
interactional self, 251
interbreeding and race, 213
interest on loans, 117
intermarriage in United States, 220–221
intimate behavior, 254
Inuit song duels, 164–165, 260, 266, 267
invention and art, 290
invention, simultaneous, 16. *See also* innovation.
IPA (International Phonetic Alphabet), 40
Ireland
    and schizophrenia, 259–260
    ethnic conflict in, 211
Irish of Inis Beag, 95
Iron Curtain, 192
iron/steel use, 54
iron-deficiency anemia, 300
Iroquois kinship terminology, 157
Iroquois, 155, 157, 232, 314
irrigation, 57, 62, 66
    and Native American agriculture, 304
    and rise of states, 185
    in China, 66
    in Inca Empire, 189
irrigation agriculture, 62, 66
Islam, 266, 285
Israel, ethnic conflict in, 211

Italian language, 50
Italian-American activism, 218
iterations in rhetoric, 296
Ituri Forest, 108
Iwo Jima, 43

J
Japan, 231
    economy of, 123
    infanticide in, 86
    infrastructure of, 21
    national character of, 250–251
    structure of, 22
    superstructure of, 22
Japanese macaque culture, 29, 32
jatis (subcastes), 204, 205
Java, child labor in, 82
Jewish people, 211, 271, 281. *See also*
    Judaism.
job training programs, 123
John Frumm cult, 278, 280
Judaism, 49, 266, 273, 281, 285
juvenile delinquency in United
    States, 223–224
J'varo of Ecuador, 264, 266, 268, 292

K
Kadar of Nigeria, 136
Kalahari desert, 57
Kalahari !Kung, 102
Kaliai of Papua New Guinea, 228
Kamba of East Africa, 256
Kamu Valley, Kapauku, 118
Kanzi chimpanzee, 29, 34
Kapauku of New Guinea, 108, 118,
    128
karma, 203
Kenya, 68
    Gusii of, 255
    Nandi of, 135
    population growth, 88
    Turkana of, 137
kibbutz, incest avoidance in, 141–142
kilts, 210
kindreds, 151
kingship in Bunyoro, 188–189
kinship, 147
    and "blood," 147
    and landownership, 118
    and reciprocity, 107, 111
    and redistributive feasting, 111
    and single-parent families, 159
    flexibility of, 158
kinship terminologies, 156–158
Koko gorilla, 34
Korean-American activism, 218
Kosovo, ethnic conflict in, 211
Kshatriya caste, 203
Kuikuru of Brazil, 166
kula rings, 108–110, 184
!Kung San, 57, 59, 61, 64, 65, 102,
    231, 266, 269
    and warfare, 171

and work patterns, 119
bilaterality among, 153
birth spacing among, 81
communal life of, 163
energy production among, 69
feasting among, 111
gender egalitarianism among, 234
kinship among, 158
leadership among, 166, 167
modesty among, 112
music of, 290
reciprocity among, 107
reproduction among, 76
sexuality of, 97
women among, 228
Kwakiutl, 18, 49, 59, 60, 183, 246
    and food production, 113–115
    and redistribution, 112–114
    art of, 291
    big man systems of, 178
    cognatic lineages among, 153
Kyoto University, 29

L
labor,
    children and, 82–84
    corvee, 199
    daily, 119–120
    division of, 20
    in slash-and-burn societies, 62
    women and, 207
Labrador, 231
lactation amenorrhea, 79
lactation and nutrition, 78, 79
lactose intolerance, 300
Lake Texcoco, 275
Lakota Sioux, 277
land inheritance, 88
land ownership and access to
    production, 118, 119
land scarcity and animal husbandry,
    65, 68
language analysis, elements of,
    40–42
language
    and apes, 33–35
    and brain evolution, 44
    and consciousness, 46
    and ethnicity, 209, 210, 211
    and gender, 46
    and social class, 46–48
    and symbolic representation, 42
    and thought, 44–45
    and writing, 42
    complexity of, 44
    universal features of, 39–40
    classification of, 44
    evolution of, 44
language displacement, 39
language productivity, 39
Latin America
    and depression, 258
    matrifocality in, 133

social race in, 214–215
    *See also individual nations and
    groups.*
Latin language, 44, 50
Latinos, 209–210. *See also* Hispanic
    Americans.
law and order
    in band societies, 163–166
    in United States, 193–194
law of diminishing returns, 55
law of the minimum, 57
law, male dominance in, 237
leaching of topsoils, 62
lead poisoning and poverty, 309
leadership and kula rings, 110
learning, 27, 309
Lebanon, 216
legitimacy, 135
leopard skin chiefs, 168–169
lesbianism, 102, 103, 160. *See also*
    homosexuality.
levirate marriage, 139
libido, 78
Liebig's law of the minimum, 57
lifestyle and class, 197–198
lifestyle preservation, 305
Lima, Peru, 201
liminal phase in status, 271
limited good, image of, 199–201
lineage segmentation, 152
lineages, 152
linguistic anthropology, 46
linguistic change, 50–51
linguistic naming categories, 45–46
linguistics, 6
linguistics, structural, 40
literacy and gender politics, 237
literature, 20
lobola (bridewealth), 230
Los Angeles riots, 194
Losuia, Trobriand Islands, 92
Loulis chimpanzee, 34
Lucy, *Australopithecus afarensis*, 31
Luts'un village, South China, 66, 67,
    69, 183

M
Machiguenga, South America, 62, 63,
    128
    and hunting, 175
    gender hierarchies in, 234
    kinship in, 157
machinery for mining, 54, 70
Mae Enga of Papua New Guinea,
    172, 177–178
magic, 266
Mahale mountains, Africa, 30
maintenance system of culture, 253
Malabar, 155
Malaya, Semai of, 111, 167
male dominance, 226–227, 231, 235
    in West Africa, 233
    of agriculture, 237

male homosexuality, 98–99
male initiation rituals, 272, 253
male reproductive strategy, 226
male sex, 93
male superiority, belief in, 226
male supremacist complex, 235
Mali, 220
malnutrition and poverty, 309
Malthusian theory, 76–77
mana, 264–265, 290
management-worker relations, 309
Mandarin language, 52
Mandiimbula Tiwi band, 170, 171
Mangaia of Polynesia, sexuality in, 95
Manipur village in Punjab, 83
Manu, 203
Manus of Bismarck Archipelago, 3, 266
Maori sculpture, 290
marketplaces, 116. *See also* price market exchange, trade.
marriage,
    age at, 79
    and incest, 142
    and legitimacy, 135, 136
    between siblings, 139
    concept of, 133
    forms of, 127
    in Ireland, 259–260
    sim pua, 132
marriage type and fertility, 80
Marxist evolutionism, 315
Masai, 170
mass media and conformity, 192
mass production and art, 291
masturbation, 79, 93, 97
material benefits, and war, 172
material possessions, in band societies, 164
materialism, cultural, 22–23
materialism, dialectical, 317
materialization of ideology, 191
maternal nutrition and low birth weight, 309
mathematics, parallel development in, 15
matriclans, 152
matrifocality, 133
    in United States, 144, 223–224
    among U.S. Blacks, 144–145
matrilineal descent, 150, 232
matrilocality, 152, 154–155, 232
Matsigenka. *See* Machiguenga.
maximal lineages, 152
maximum sustainable yield, 56
Mbuti of Ituri Forest, Zaire, 108, 231
meaning, 20
meat, 65, 173–175. *See also* hunter-gatherer societies, protein.
medical aid, 123
medical anthropology, 5, 6, 306

Mehinacu of Brazil, 97, 98, 231
    headmanship among, 167–168
    kinship among, 158
    semen beliefs among, 148
Melanesia,
    big man systems in, 177–178
    cargo cults in, 278, 285
    competitive feasts in, 114
    male homosexuality in, 100
    melting-pot theory, 216
    semen beliefs in, 101
    trade in, 108
Melville Island, Australia, 170
menarche and nutrition, 78
menstrual seclusion, 227
mental and behavioral aspects of culture, 16
mental illness and culture, 258
mergers, 124
Mesoamerica, 13, 317. *See also* individual nations and groups.
Mesolithic growth rate, 82
Messiah craze, 277
messianic cults, 277
metallurgy, 15, 54
metaphors, 288, 296
Mexican Americans, 209–210. *See also* Hispanic Americans.
Mexico, 254
    Aztecs of, 266, 274–276, 316
    ceramics in, 54
    peasants in, 199–201
    slash-and-burn agriculture in, 62
Michoacan, Mexico, 199–201
Middle Eastern harems, 102
migrant agricultural labor, 210
migration and resource depletion, 57
migration and ethnicity, 211
military control, 20. *See also* warfare.
military, male dominance in, 237
milk, culture and, 300
millenarian movements, 277
minimal lineages, 152
minimum, law of the, 57
Mission Indians of California, 170
Mission Viejo, California, 11
missionary position sex, 97
mixed farming. *See* Agropastoralism.
mobility of families, 127
Mochica of Peru, 290–291
modal personality, 249–250
mode of production, 20
mode of reproduction, 20
money and gender, 237
money as medium of exchange, 116
Mongol pastoralists, 68
mongongo nuts, 57
monkey learning, 32
monogamy, 127, 128, 306–307
monopolies, 124
monopolization of U.S. power, 207
Montagnais-Naskapi of Labrador, 231

morphemes, 40
morphology, 40
mortality, 20, 79
mortality rates in Africa, 88
mother-child sleeping arrangements, 253
motherhood, 79, 90, 147
Mothers and Such (Maxine Margolis), 243
mounding, 62
Mukama of Bunyoro, 188–189
mukanda initiation ritual, 272
multiculturalism, 6
multinational corporations and anthropology careers, 124, 308–309
multiple-origins theory, 32
Mundurucu of Brazil, 155, 226–227, 228
music, 20, 290
    evolution of, 293–295
    social function of, 294
Muslim ethnics, 216. *See also* Islam.
mutations, 27
myths, 20, 295

N

n/um (trance state), 269
Nagovisi groom price, 138
Namibia, 57
Nandi of Kenya, 135, 233
Naples, Italy, 97, 202–203
natality, 20
national character, 250–252. *See also* personality structure.
Native American Church, 278
Native Americans, 285, 317
    and alcoholism, 212
    and gender, 101–102
    in the Amazon, 77
    landscape of, 57
    language of, 49
    oedipal myths of, 247
    of Arizona, 46
    of Great Plains, 99
    potlatches of, 112
    revitalization movements of, 277
natural disasters and population control, 80
natural selection, 26, 27, 315
natural, defined, 265–266
Navajo art, 289
Navajo religion, 266
Nayar warrior caste of India, 134, 135, 155
Nazca, Peru, 289
Ndembu of Zambia, 266, 272, 292
negative feedback change, 186
Neolithic growth rate, 82
neolocality, 152, 153
Nepal, polyandry in, 129
nervios, in Mexican culture, 259
New Delhi, 83

New England of United States, 254
New Guinea, 63, 64, 65, 184, 285
    amok state in, 260
    art, 292
    big men in, 231
    cargo cults in, 278
    gender roles in, 247
    Kapauku of, 128
    Mae Enga of, 172, 177–178
    male homosexuality in, 247
    Sambia of, 101
    supernatural in, 265–266
    trade in, 108
    See also Papua New Guinea.
New World, 60
New York City, crime in, 193
New York, Iroquois, 232
Nile River in the Sudan, 169
nomadic pastoralism, 67
nomadism in Kenya, 68
nonhuman culture, 26, 27–28
nonhuman reproductive strategies,
    27
nonrenewable resources, 55
nonviolence, 36, 170
Northwest Coast Native Americans,
    59, 60, 114, 153, 266, 290. *See
    also individual groups.*
Norwegian language, 52
nuclear family, 127
nuclear waste and population
    growth, 88
Nuer of the Sudan, 169, 231
numeracy and gender politics, 237
Nupe of West Africa, 102
nursing and male initiation rites, 253
nurturance of infants, 20, 254
nutrition, 57, 63, 65, 67, 78, 79,
    274–276
    and menarche, 78
    maternal, 309
Nuyorican, 49
Nyakyusa of East Africa, 102
Nyinba of Nepal, 129–130

O

Oakland, California, 46
objectivity and bias, 12
observationalist theory of incest
    avoidance, 140
oedipal myths, Native American, 247
Oedipus complex, 245, 246
Okinawa, 254
Oklahoma, Delaware Indians, 279
Old English, 51
Olduvai Gorge, 3
Old World, 60, 68
oligopolies, 124
On the Origin of Species (Charles
    Darwin), 315
one-drop rule of race, 214–215
one-parent domestic groups, 133
open adoption, 160

open-class systems, 196
optimal foraging theory, 61
orchestra, complexity of, 294
organic evolution, 26
organizational culture, studying, 309
orgasm, 79, 96
Origin of the Family, The (Friedrich
    Engels), 315
ownership of technology, 183
oxygen, 16

P

Pacific Northwest Coast peoples, 59,
    153, 266
packaging food, 70
Paleolithic growth rate, 82
Palestinian ethnic conflict, 211
paper, 15
Papua New Guinea, Suiai in,
    181–182, 228. *See also* New
    Guinea.
paradigms, 22,
Paraguay, 60
parallax of star, 16
parallel cousins, 150
parallel cultural developments, 14
parental love, economy of, 81
participant observation, 4, 16
participants, 4
particularism, 319
passage, rites of, 270
pastoral empires, 68
pastoralism, 67, 68
pastoralist personality, 257
patriarchy, 238
patriclans, 152
patrilineage, 151
patrilineality,
    and incest, 142
    and reproduction, 88
    and sexual restrictiveness, 97
    descent in, 149–150
patrilocality, 152, 154, 253
Patterns of Culture (Ruth Benedict),
    112, 246
Pax chimpanzee, 28
Pearl River delta, Kwantung, 102
peasant classes, 198–199
peasant ideology, 199–201
peasantry, Haitian, 302–303
pedagogic model of child care, 255
pediatric model of child care, 255
penis envy, 245
pensions, 123
Persian language, 50
personality,
    and childhood training, 252
    and cultural maintenance system,
        253
    and culture, 245, 317
    basic structure of, 249, 252
Peru, Machiguenga of, 63
Peru, pottery in, 290–291

pesticides, 70
peyote ritual, 278
Philippines, 254
Philippines, Agta of the, 44, 231
phone, in language, 40
phonemes, 40–41
phonemics, 40–41
phonetics, 40
physical anthropology 2, 6
pibloktoq (Arctic hysteria), 260
pig husbandry, 64, 128
Pijoan Indians of U.S. Southwest,
    300
Planned Parenthood, 103
play and art, 288, 290
plow farming, 65
plows and gender, 236–237
pluralism, 215–216
point of diminishing returns, 56
Pokot, 257
police, 20
political anthropology, 5
political control, 190–192
    and economy, 106
    and intensification, 185
    and U.S. class, 206–207
    infrastructure of, 183–184
political economy, 20
    and religion, 276
    of United States, 123
political organizations, 20
political repression, 192
political socialization, 20
political systems and trade, 110
politics and gender roles, 231, 237
pollution, 71, 88
polyandry, 127, 128, 130
polygamy, 127, 128
polygyny, 79, 80, 127, 128
    and lesbianism, 102
    in West Africa, 233
Polynesia, sexuality in, 96
population density, 57, 65
population genetics, 6
population growth, 77, 82
    and disease, 80
    and resource limitations, 63
    and production, 76–77
    and state formation, 185
    of world, 88
    rate, 82
population momentum, 89
population pressure, 173–175
    and ethnocentrism, 211
    and growth, 77
    and homosexuality, 100–101
pork, taboos against, 281
pornography in United States, 103
Portuguese language, 50
positive feedback change, 186
postindustrial society, 72
postmarital residence, types of, 152
postmodernism, 319

postpartum sex taboos, 253
potatoes and frost control, 304
potlatches, 112–115
poverty
    among Black youth, 221
    and child labor, 84
    and crime in United States, 194
    and depression, 258
    and health, 309
    and matrifocality, 144–145
    and race, 215, 218, 219
    and reproduction, 307
    causes of, 202
    feminization of, 238
    in Brazil, 85–86
    in Naples, 202–203
    in U.S. inner cities, 223–224
power,
    and gender, 230
    and storable food, 60, 119, 184, 187
    and surplus, 191
    and thought control, 192
    and Whites, 217
    in the United States, 206–207
    state, 190–192
preferential marriages, 138
pregnancy and nutrition, 78. *See also* reproduction.
preindustrial reproductive practices, 77–80
premarital sex, 97, 103
prestige and consumption, 117
price market exchange, 116–119, 124
primary institutions, 249
Primate Research Institute of Kyoto University, 29
primates, 6, 28, 29, 31, 33–35, 36
    evolution of, 32
    learning by, 30, 288
    masturbation among, 93
primatology, 6
"primitive" communism, 163–164
Primitive Culture (E. B. Tylor), 264
private (inner) self, 251
private property, 117, 118–119, 164
Private Property and the State (Friedrich Engels), 315
probabilistic determinism, 22
probabilities, 5
processing industrial food, 70
process of materialization, 191
production,
    among Kwakiutl, 113–115
    and birth spacing, 81
    and consumption, 120
    and depletion of resources, 57
    and economic structure, 106
    and housework, 119–120
    and infanticide, 84
    and population growth, 76–77, 88
    in capitalism, 117
    in industrialism, 70

    in slash-and-burn agriculture, 62
    intensification of, 56
    monopolization of, 191
    new modes of, 57
production mode, in United States, 72–73
productivity in language, 39
productivity of irrigation agriculture, 66
Prof chimpanzee, 28
profit and agroforestry, 303
projective-expressive system, 253
prolactin, 79
property, 118–119, 164, 183
property and force, 117
property rights and legitimacy, 135
protein needs, 65, 274–276
Protestant ethnic conflict, 211
Protestant fundamentalism, 284–285
Proto-Indo-European language, 50
Proto-West Germanic language, 50
pseudohermaphrodites, 93
psychoanalysis, 245
psychological anthropology, 5
psychoses, culture-specific, 260
public (interactional) self, 251
public opinion, 164, 206
public self, 251
Pueblo Indians, 246
Pueblos, 14
Puerto Rican language, 49
Puerto Ricans, 209
Punjab, child labor in, 83

Q

quality circles, 119
Quebec Iroquois, 232
quinoa and irrigation, 304

R

race, 212–213, 215, 216, 223–224
racial and ethnic chauvinism, 217
racial classification schemes, 212
racial/ethnic groups, 215–218
racial pluralism, 215–216
racism, 218–219, 220–221
raiding among apes, 35
rainfall agriculture, 62
rain forest,
    animals in, 65
    depletion of, 88
    soils of, 62
Rampur village near New Delhi, 83
Rangoon, Myanmar, 10
Rangwila Tiwi band, 170
rear entry sex, 97
reciprocal exchange, 106–107
reciprocity, 106–107
    among !Kung, 107
    and law and order, 164
    and private property, 164
    in marriage, 138
    versus redistribution, 111

redistribution
    and barter, 116
    and money, 116
    and stratification, 110
    exchange systems, 112
    versus reciprocity, 111
    stratified, 115–116
redistributive exchange, 110
Red Power movement, 278
refugee health care, 307–308
relatives, Euro-American, 151
relativity of truth, 12
religion, 266
    and art, 291–293
    and cattle, 281–283
    and ecology, 280
    and experience, 191
    and infanticide, 86
    and political economy, 276
    and pork, 281
    and sex, 97
    parallel development in, 15
    rituals in, 20
rent, 119
    and coercion, 119
    and surplus, 119
    and taxes, 119
replication of cultural patterns, 13
repression, 192
reproduction,
    and child labor, 84
    and production, 76–77, 84
    modes of, 20, 87
    preindustrial, 77–80
reproductive strategy, 94
reproductive success, 26, 172
reproductive technologies, 90
research and action, 299
research strategies, 22
residence after marriage, types of, 152
resources, 60, 65
    and population growth, 88
    depletion of, 57, 59
    nonrenewable, 55
    seasonal, 60, 112–115
    territory and, 63
respiration, 16
respondents, 4
responsibility, 254
retirement plans, 127
revenge as cause of war, 170–171, 172
reverse discrimination, 221
revitalization movements, 276–277
revivalism, 277
rhetoric, 296
rhetorical questions, 296
rice culture, 66, 67, 234, 237
risk management, and political control, 183
rites of passage, 270
rites of solidarity, 270

rituals,
    initiation, 270, 272
    lack of in United States, 271
    parallel development in, 15
Rohrschach test, 249–250
Romance languages, 50
Roman imperialism, 285
root crops, 65
rubber plantations, 63
rules for breaking rules, 17, 21
Rumanian language, 50
Russian language, 50
Russian Revolution, 235

S

sacredness of life, 248
sacrifice complex, parallel
    development in, 15
sacrifice, human, 274–276
sagali (women's wealth), 229
Sahara, history of, 220
salmon, 60
Sambia of New Guinea, 101
Samburu of Kenya, 18, 170
same-sex sexuality, 98–99, 101. See
    also homosexuality.
Samoa, alofa schema in, 257
sanctions, domestic, 20
Sanghay, 220
Sapir-Whorf hypothesis, 44–45
schemas and cognition, 257–258
schizophrenia and culture,
    258–260
school nutrition and learning, 309
science, 5, 12, 20, 22
    and relativity of truth, 12–13
    male dominance in, 237
scientific research, 22
scientific theory, 5
Scottish ethnicity, 210
scripts, 257
seasonal resource fluctuation, 60,
    112–115
seaweed farming in Zanzibar, 305
Sebei of East Africa, 256
secondary institutions, 249
self, 251
self-interest in economic decisions,
    106
Semai of Central Malaya, 111, 166,
    231
semantic universality, 33, 35, 39
semen beliefs, 96, 100, 101,
    147–148
Sepik River basin, New Guinea, 292
Serb ethnic conflict, 211
serfs, 198
serial monogamy, 127
service industry, 72–73, 242
sex,
    and gender, 93, 226
    and strength, 234
    positions for, 97

Sex and Temperament in Three
    Primitive Societies (Margaret
    Mead), 247
sexism and language, 49
sex ratio
    among Yanomami, 176
    and warfare, 176
    and polygyny, 80
sex taboos, 100, 253
sexuality and culture, 94–98, 136
shamanism
    among Machiguenga, 63
    and public opinion, 164–166
    and gender liminality, 102
shamanistic cults, 266, 268–270
shifting horticulture. See slash-and-
    burn agriculture, horticulture.
Shinto religion, 22
ships, 54
Shoshoni, 170
Shudra caste, 203, 204
Siberian shamans, 268
signing by apes, 34
sign languages, 334–35,
Sikhs, 11
silent trade, 107–108
silkworm workers, 102
sim pua marriage, 132, 141
simultaneous invention, 16
single-parent families, 133
Sinhalese of Sri Lanka, 108
Sioux Ghost Dance, 277
Six Cultures study, 253–255
slash-and-burn agriculture, 62, 65
    and depletion, 57
    among Tsembaga, 64
    See also horticulture.
slavery in United States, 204
smelting, 54
sociable behavior, 254
social class and language, 46–48
Social Darwinism, 315
social ecology of childhood, 255
social environment and children,
    254
social organization and descent,
    148–152
social organization, parallel
    development in, 15
social races, 212–215, 220
social security system, 123, 127
socialism in United States, 123
society, 9
sociobiology, 318
sociolinguistics, 6, 46
sodalities, 169–170
soil degradation, 62, 88
soil fertility, 65. See also fertilizer.
solidarity, rites of, 270
Solomon Islands, Papua New
    Guinea, 181–182, 231
song, social function of, 294
sororal polygyny, 128

sororate marriage, 138
South African bridewealth, 230
South American oedipal myths, 247
South China, irrigation agriculture
    in, 67. See also China.
Southeast Asian health beliefs, 307
South Pacific, big man systems in,
    177–178. See also Melanesia.
Soviet Armenia, 216
Soviet Union, repression in, 192
space and language, 45
Spanish language, 40, 50
speech community, 49
sports, 20
Sri Lanka, 108
St. Patrick's Day, 215, 217
Standard English, 47–48, 49
state and physical coercion, 192
state organization of Bunyoro,
    188–189
state organization of Incas, 189–190
state power and ideology, 190–192
state socialism, 123
states, origins of, 185
status at birth, 135. See also caste,
    class, gender, race,
    stratification.
steel trade goods, and warfare, 176
Stone Age, health in, 80
stoop labor and gender, 237
storable food and chiefdom power,
    60, 119, 184
storable staples and state formation,
    185, 187
stratification
    and endogamy, 143
    and exogamy, 143
    and force, 117
    and potlatches, 115
    and redistribution, 110–111,
        115–116
    and sex, 97
    in the United States, 206–207
structural analysis of myth, 295
structural functionalism, 316
structural linguistics, 39, 40
structuralism, 318–319
structure, 20, 21–22
struggle for survival, 26
subculture, 10
subsistence and personality,
    252–253, 256–257
subsistence cycle among Kwakiutl,
    60
subsistence level and music, 293–295
subsistence plow farming, 65
success model, 257
sucking cure, 268
Sudan, Azande of, 99
Suiai big men systems, 181–182
sunbathing, 14
Suncoast Gerontology Center, 307
supernatural beliefs, 265–266

superstructure, 20, 22
supranational corporations, 124
surplus collection in capitalism, 117
surplus extraction and power, 191
surplus food, 60, 119
surrogate motherhood, 90
sustainability, 56–57
sweatshops, 73
Swedish Agency for Research
        Collaboration with Developing
        Countries, 305
Swedish language, 52
Swiss Alps transhumance, 67
symbolic language, 42
symbolic thought, 43
symbols, 20, 288
syntax, 40, 41–42

T
taboos
        against pork, 281
        and ecology, 280
        on sex, 100
Taiwan, marriage in, 134, 141
takeoff, cultural, 26
Tampa, Florida, 307
Tana, New Hebrides, 278
Tanzania, 28, 30
Tapirapé of Brazil, 266, 269–270, 289
Tarascans of Mexico, 200
TAT (Thematic Apperception Test),
        249, 256
taxation, 20
        and coercion, 119
        and U.S. income, 207
tax collection, 116
Tchambuli gender roles, 247
technoenvironmental relationships,
        20
technology
        and depletion, 59
        and development, 54
        and intensification, 183
        and world hunger, 88
        of subsistence, 20
teen pregnancy, 103
telephone, 16
telescope, 16
televangelism, 284–285
tenant farming, 119
terracing, 189. See also rice culture.
territory and resources, 63
territory and warfare, 173–175
Tewa of Arizona, 46
textiles, 14
Thematic Apperception Test (TAT),
        249
thermometer, 16
thought and language, 44
thought control and power, 192
thorn forest, animals in, 65
Tibet
        Child rearing in, 252

language of, 130
polyandry in, 129
Tiklauila Tiwi band, 170
time and language, 45
time orientation, 248
time spent working, 57, 119–120
Times Beach, Missouri, 71
Tiwi of Bathurst and Melville Islands,
        170
tobacco smoking, 16
tools and learning, 28
totemic ritual, 270
totem poles and potlatches, 114
trade
        and exogamy, 142
        and money, 237
        and political control, 183
        and potlatches, 114
        and prices, 116
        and reciprocity, 107–108
        in kula rings, 108–110
trade goods and warfare, 176–177
trade partnerships, 108
tradition, inventing, 210
transformation-representation, 288
transhumance, 67
transnational corporations, 124
transplanting, 237
trekking among Yanomami, 175–176
tribute, 20
Trivandrum district of Kerala, India,
        18–19
Trobriand Islands,
        chiefdoms in, 183–184
        family roles in, 246
        gender roles in, 228–229
        semen beliefs in, 147–148
        sex in, 96–97
        trade in, 108–110
Tsembaga Maring of New Guinea,
        63, 64, 65, 69
Tsimshian of Canada, 266
tuberculosis, 307–308
tube wells, 62
Turkana of Kenya, 68, 137
Tutsi ethnic conflict, 211
Tzintzuntzan, Mexico, 199–201

U
U.S. Agency for International
        Development (USAID), 302
U.S. Census racial categories, 221. See
        also race.
U.S. Census undercount, 308
Uganda, AIDS in, 306–307
Uganda, Bunyoro of, 188–189
unconscious rules, 16–17
unemployment among Black U.S.
        youth, 194
unilineal descent, 149–152
United Kingdom, sex in, 96
United States,
        and child-rearing costs, 89–90

and schizophrenia, 259
anorexia in, 261
capitalism in, 123
electronic church in, 284–285
family changes in, 159–160
food energy systems of, 70
gender hierarchy change in,
        241–243
incest in, 142, 143
income gap in, 206–207
inner cities of, 133
landowner rights in, 118
matrifocal families in, 144
neolocality in, 153
population growth, 88
production mode, 72–73
race in, 214–215, 217, 223
rites of solidarity in, 270
ruling class in, 206–207
sexuality in, 96, 103
state sources of income in,
        123–124
universal pattern of culture, 19–20
untouchable castes, 204
unwed mothers, 136, 160
urban anthropology, 6
urban/rural hierarchies, 20
USAID (U.S. Agency for International
        Development), 302
uxorilocality, 152

V
Vaishya caste, 203
values, 12, 20
variation among organisms, 26
varnas (grade of being), 203
vaygu'a, 108
Vedda of Sri Lanka, 108
vegetarians, 65
Venezuela, Yanomami of, 171
verbal arts, 295–296
Veterans of Foreign Wars, 170
Viet Cong, 235
Vietnamese-American medical
        beliefs, 307
Vietnamese refugees, 307
village societies, law and order in,
        163–166
Villerville, France, 14
violence,
        and aggression, 26, 35, 254
        and gender roles, 231
        in family, 246
        in the United States, 93
        See also crime.
virginity, 97
virilocality, 152
vitamin needs, 260

W
wages, 117, 207
warfare, 20
        among foragers, 170, 171

warfare *(continued)*
   among sedentary village societies, 171
   and big man systems, 181–182
   and ethnicity, 211
   and exogamy, 142
   and female infanticide, 176
   and gender hierarchies, 234–235
   and gender roles, 237
   and matrilineal Iroquois, 232
   and patrilocality, 235
   and technology, 114–115
   and trade, 108, 176–177, 184
   and women, 235–236
   causes of, 171–172
   control of, 183
Washoe chimpanzee, 34
water degradation, 88. *See also* pollution.
water power, 54
wealth,
   and U.S. stratification, 206–207
   and women, 229
   gospel of, 284
   See also class, poverty.
weapons, 15
welfare in U.S. inner cities, 223–224
welfare programs, 116, 218, 310
West Africa,
   animism in, 264
   gender hierarchy in, 235–236
   gender roles in, 226
   Gusii of, 129
   households in, 126
   market women in, 240
   women warriors in, 235–236
   See also individual nations and groups.
West Bengal, 282
Western European economy, 123

Western manufactures and warfare, 176
West Indies, 133
West Irian, Indonesia, 108, 118
West Senegal, 29
wet dreams, 93
wheel, use of, 54
white-collar work and women, 242
White ethnics, 209
White matrifocal families, 145
White neighborhood racism, 219
Whiteness, defining, 214–215
White repression of Native Americans, 277–278
Whites, power of, 217
widows in India, 234
wife burnings, 238
wind power, 54
witchcraft and misfortunes, 165–166
within-species killing, 27
womb envy, 245
women
   among Iroquois, 232
   among !Kung, 228
   and education, 87–88
   and plow agriculture, 236–237
   and status, 87–88, 233–233
   and wealth, 229
   as census takers, 308
   denigration of, 235
   in India, 233
   in the labor force, 89–90, 207, 238, 241–243
   in West Africa, 232–233
   leading community, 218
   treatment of, 78–79, 230, 235
women-owned business, 240
women's culture, 229–230
Work and the Family (Valery Oppenheimer), 243

work and U.S. home life, 120
workforce,
   and African Americans, 144–145, 223–224
   children in, 82, 84
   women in, 238, 241–243
work hours, 119–120
working class, reproduction of, 238
work patterns, 20, 119–121
work standards, among foragers, 119
world population growth graphed, 89
World War II and cargo cults, 278
World War II and gender roles, 242
Wounded Knee, South Dakota, 278
writing,
   and gender politics, 237
   and language, 42
   parallel development in, 15

X

Xingu National Park, Brazil, 167–168
Xingu River, Brazil, 168

Y

Yahgan, 170
Yanomami of Amazon region,
   and trade goods, 176
   gender hierarchies, 235
   trade among, 108
   warfare among, 171, 172, 173–175
Yoruba of West Africa, 232, 233
Yunnan Province, 67
Yurok of California, 226–227

Z

Zambia, Ndembu of, 272
Zanzibar, seaweed farming in, 305
Zumbagua of Ecuadorian Andes, 126

p. 1, Keith Olson/Tony Stone Images; p. 3, (top left) Courtesy of Nancy Scheper-Hughes, (top right) Antonio Mari/ Gamma Liaison Network, (bottom left) Courtesy of Florida Museum of Natural History, (bottom middle) Irven DeVore/Anthro-Photo, (bottom right) © Joan Silk; p. 8, Ira Kirschenbaum/Stock Boston; p. 10, (top) Mini Forsyth/Monkmeyer Press Photo Service, (middle) Alan Carey/The Image Works; p. 11, (top left) UPI/ Bettmann, (bottom left) Spencer Grant/Stock Boston, (right) Michael Grecco/Stock Boston; p. 14, (left) Barbara Alper/Stock Boston, (right) Rapho/Photo Researchers; p. 17, (top left) © Elizabeth Crews, (top right) Spencer Grant/PhotoEdit, (bottom) AP/Wide World Photos; p. 18, (left) Sally Weiner Grota/Stock Market, (middle) UPI/Bettmann, (right) Cartier-Bresson/ Magnum Photos; p. 20, (left) Andy Sacks/Tony Stone Images, (right) L. Mangino/The Image Works; p. 21, (top left) David Wells/The Image Works, (top right) John Patrick/Black Star, (bottom left) Patricia Hollander Gross/Stock Boston, (bottom right) Jeff Albertson/ Stock Boston; p. 25, Courtesy of Institute of Human Origins; p. 28, Michael K. Nicholas/Magnum Photos; p. 29, Masao Kawai; p. 30 , Baron Hugo van Lawick; p. 31, Sevcik, GSU, Yerkes Language Research Center; p. 32, National Museum of Kenya; p. 33, (top left and right) Masao Kawai; p. 34, (top) Georgia State University Language Research Center, (bottom) The Gorilla Foundation; p. 35, © Joseph Manson and Susan Perry; p. 38, Judy Gelles/Stock Boston; p. 43, © UPI/Corbis-Bettmann; p. 47, Richard Lord/PhotoEdit; p. 49, Skjold/ The Image Works; p. 53, Wolfgang Kaeler; p. 58, Anthro-Photo; p. 59, Richard B. Lee/Anthro-Photo; p. 60, (left) Kevin T. Jones, University of Utah, Ache Project, (right) © Allen and Orna Johnson; p. 62, © Allen and Orna Johnson; p. 64, Cherry Lowman; p. 66, (left) Eastfoto, (right) Courtesy of The United Nations; p. 68, R. & S. Michaud; p. 69, Peter Menzel/Stock Boston; p. 71, (left) Paul Fortin/Stock Boston, (right) Owen Franken/Sygma; p. 73, Mark Lyons/New York Times Pictures; p. 75, Melvin Konner/Anthro-Photo; p. 76, Sean Sprague/ Stock Boston; p. 79, Mel Konner/Anthro-Photo; p. 81, J. P. Laffont/Sygma; p. 82, © Nancy Levine; p. 83, Courtesy of Moni Nag; p. 85, (left and right) Jennifer Scheper-Hughes; p. 92, Mark Sadan; p. 94, Alex Webb/ Magnum Photos; p. 95, Bruno Barbey/Magnum Photos; p. 99, James O. Wilson/ Liaison Agency; p. 100, (left) Courtesy of National Museum of the American Indian, Smithsonian Institution, (right) Anthro-Photo; p. 102, Bob Daemmrich/The Image Works; p. 103, Everett C. Johnson/Leo de Wys; p. 104, R. Lord/The Image Works; p. 105, Victor Englebert/Photo Researchers; p. 107, Irven deVore/Anthro-Photo; p. 108, Courtesy of The

United Nations; p. 109, AP/Wide World Photos; p. 110, Corbis/Caroline Penn; p. 113, (top) Neg. No. 42298/ Courtesy of the Department of Library Services, American Museum of Natural History, Photo by Edward Dossettler, (bottom) Montauk/Eastcott/Woodfin Camp & Assoc.; p. 114 (left) Neg. No. 336116, Courtesy of Department of Library Services, American Museum of Natural History, Photo by Dr. Frang, (right) S. J. Krasemann/Peter Arnold, Inc.; p.116, Mark Segal/Tony Stone Images; p. 117, (left) Corbis/Caroline Penn, (right) Irven DeVore/Anthro-Photo; p. 121 (left) Robin Moyer/ Gamma Liaison, (right) Fujifotos/The Image Works; p. 122 (right) Bill Lai/Liaison International; p. 125 (Charles Gupton/Stock Boston; p. 127, Mary Weismantel, Occidental College; p. 128, (left) © Emil Muench/ Photo Researchers, (right) © Allen and Orna Johnson; p. 130, © Nancy Levine; p. 131, The Bettmann Archive; p. 132, Gary Wolinsky/Stock Boston; p. 134, Myron L. Cohen; p. 137, (left) © Renee Lynn/Photo Researchers; p. 138, Steve Raymer/National Geographic Image Collection; p. 139, The Granger Collection, New York; p. 142, © Esti Musman, Kibbutz Galon; p. 144, Carol Stack; p. 148, Mark Antman/The Image Works; p. 157, © Allen and Orna Johnson; p. 159, M. Bridwell/ PhotoEdit; p. 160, Dana White/PhotoEdit; p. 162, University of Oklahoma Library, Western History Collections; p. 164, Peter Good; p. 165, Courtesy of Royal Danish Ministry of Foreign Affairs; p. 166, Robert L. Corneiri; p. 167, Thomas Gregor; p. 169, Pitt Rivers Museum, University of Oxford; p. 173, Kenneth R. Good; p. 177, © Kal Muller/Woodfin Camp & Assoc.; p. 180, Culver Pictures; p. 181, Eugene Gordon; p. 185, Wolfgang Kaehler/Corbis; p. 187, Corbis/Bettmann ; p. 190, George Hulton/Photo Researchers; p. 191, UPI/Bettmann; p. 192, (left) Georges Merillon/Liaison Agency, (right) AP/Wide World Photos; p. 193, Jerry Mennega/Liaison Agency; p. 195, Paulo Friedman/ Sygma; p. 197, (left) Charles Gatewood/The Image Works, (right) Fredrik Bodin/Stock Boston; p. 198, (top) Martha Cooper/Peter Arnold, Inc., (middle) Ira Kirschenbaum/Stock Boston, (bottom) UPI/Bettmann; p. 199, Robert Frerck/Odyssey; p. 200, Courtesy of The United Nations; p. 201, (left) Courtesy of The United Nations, (right) Paul Conklin/Monkmeyer Press; p. 202, Topham, The Image Works; p. 204, UPI/Bettmann; p. 208, Reuters/Bettmann; p. 210, © Bob Daemmrich/ Stock Boston; p. 213, (top left) Charles Gatewood/The Image Works, (top right) Sarah Putnam/The Picture Cube, (bottom left) Jeff Greenberg/Peter Arnold, Inc., (bottom right) Gary A. Conner/PhotoEdit; p. 218, © Allen and Orna Johnson; p. 221, Gale Zucker/Stock Boston; p. 222, David Young-Wolff/PhotoEdit; p. 223,

UPI/Bettmann; p. 224, Hispanic Study Project, J. W. Sharff, Director. Photo: Jennifer Benepe; p. 225, (left panel) A. Durer, *Eva.* Firenze, Uffizi; (right panel) A. Durer, *Adamo.* Prado, Madrid. Both panels courtesy of Art Resource, New York/SCALA; p. 227, Neg. 12583, Courtesy of Department of Library Services/American Museum of Natural History; p. 229, Wolfgang Kaeler; p. 232, Volkmar Wentzel/National Geographic Image Collection; p. 234, UPI/Bettmann; p. 236, McLaren/ Photo Researchers; p. 237, Kal Muller/Woodfin Camp & Assoc., p. 238, A. Ramey/PhotoEdit; p. 239, (top left) AP/Wide World Photos, (bottom left) © Bruce Laurance/Liaison International, (top right) Bruce Roberts/ Photo Researchers, (middle right) Betty Lane/Photo Researchers, (bottom right) Rob Chandall/Stock Boston; p. 244, Anthro-Photo; p. 248, (left and right) Courtesy of Department of Library Services/American Museum of Natural History; p. 249, Courtesy of The United Nations; p. 251, © Nichael Newman/PhotoEdit; p. 252, © Allen and Orna Johnson; p. 255, © ASAP/Israel Talby/ Woodfin Camp & Assoc.; p. 256, (left) © M. & E. Bernheim/Woodfin Camp & Assoc., (right top and bottom) Robert B. Edgerton, *"The Individual in Cultural Adaptation, A Study of Four East African Peoples,"* published by University of California Press, 1971. Copyright 1971 by The Regents of the University of California; p. 261, (left) Neg. 232188, (right) Neg. 232202, both courtesy of Library Services, American Museum of Natural History; p. 263, George Holton/Photo Researchers; p. 265, Hector R. Acebes/Photo Researchers; p. 267, Anthro-Photo; p. 269, Charles Wagley; p. 271, Spencer Grant/ PhotoEdit; p. 272, (both) Victor Turner, *"The Forest of Symbols: Aspects of Ndembu Ritual"* © 1967 by Cornell University. Used by permission of the publisher, Cornell University Press; p. 273, (left) Laima Druskis/Photo Researchers, (right) Robert Frerck, Odyssey Productions, Chicago; p. 274, Scala/Art Resource, NY; p. 277, Nevada Historical Society; p. 278, (left) Courtesy of the National Museum of the American Indian/Smithsonian Institu-

tion, (right) AP/Wide World Photos; p. 279, Courtesy of the National Museum of the American Indian/ Smithsonian Institution; p. 280, (left and right) Kal Muller/Woodfin Camp & Assoc.; p. 282, (left) Reuters/ Bettmann, (right) UPI/Bettmann; p. 285, AP/Wide World Photos; p. 287, Wolfgang Kaehler; p. 288, AP/Wide World Photos; p. 289, (all photos) courtesy of National Museum of the American Indian/Smithsonian Institution; p. 290, Richard Lee/Anthro-Photo; p. 291, (top) Neg. 31198, Courtesy of Department of Library Services, American Museum of Natural History. Photo: R. Weber, (bottom) Neg. 33264, courtesy of Department of Library Services, American Museum of Natural History. Photo: Rota; p. 292, de Havenon Collection; p. 293, (left) Eugene Gordon, (right) UPI/Bettmann; p. 294, The Metropolitan Museum of Art, New York. Photo: Harry Burton, Egyptian Exposition; p. 298, John Paul Kay/Peter Arnold, Inc.; p. 302, Michael Bannister, Department of Forestry, University of Florida; p. 304, Jean-Marc Giboux/Gamma Liaison; p. 305, Kevin Fleming/Woodfin Camp & Assoc.; p. 307, Darren McCollester/ Gamma Liaison; p. 310, Rick Browne/Stock Boston.

Photo Credits (color inserts): *Infrastructure: Producion:* p. 1, (all photos) © Nancy Levine; p. 2, (top) Kenneth R. Good, (middle left) © Allen and Orna Johnson, (middle right) Kenneth R. Good, (bottom left) © Allen and Orna Johnson, (bottom right) Kenneth R. Good; p. 3, (top) Yann Layma/Tony Stone Images; (middle) Bonnie Kamin, PhotoEdit; (bottom) Sean Sprague, Stock Boston; p. 4, (top left and right) © Nancy Levine, (bottom left and right) © Raquel Ackerman. *Superstructure: Symbols and Rituals:* p. 1, (all photos) © Xunxiang Yan; p. 2, (all photos) © Nancy Levine; p. 3, (both photos) © Thomas Gregor; p. 4, (top) © Y. Arthur-Bertrand/Peter Arnold, Inc, (bottom left) © Arthus/ Peter Arnold, Inc., (bottom right) © 1989 Champlong/ The Image Bank.